UNIX System Laboratories, Inc.
A Subsidiary of AT&T

UNIX® SYSTEM V/386 RELEASE 4
Programmer's Reference Manual

Copyright 1991 UNIX System Laboratories, Inc.
Copyright 1990, 1989, 1988, 1987, 1986, 1985, 1984 AT&T
Copyright 1989, 1988, 1987, 1986 Sun Microsystems, Inc.
Copyright 1985 Regents of the University of California
All Rights Reserved
Printed in USA

Published by Prentice-Hall, Inc.
A Division of Simon & Schuster
Englewood Cliffs, New Jersey 07632

No part of this publication may be reproduced or transmitted in any form or by any means—graphic, electronic, electrical, mechanical, or chemical, including photocopying, recording in any medium, taping, by any computer or information storage and retrieval systems, etc., without prior permissions in writing from UNIX System Laboratories, Inc. (USL).

ACKNOWLEDGEMENT

USL gratefully acknowledges the X/Open Company Limited for permission to reproduce portions of its copyrighted *X/Open Portability Guide, Issue 3*.

IMPORTANT NOTE TO USERS

While every effort has been made to ensure the accuracy of all information in this document, USL assumes no liability to any party for any loss or damage caused by errors or omissions or by statements of any kind in this document, its updates, supplements, or special editions, whether such errors are omissions or statements resulting from negligence, accident, or any other cause. USL further assumes no liability arising out of the application or use of any product or system described herein; nor any liability for incidental or consequential damages arising from the use of this document. USL disclaims all warranties regarding the information contained herein, whether expressed, implied or statutory, *including implied warranties of merchantability or fitness for a particular purpose*. USL makes no representation that the interconnection of products in the manner described herein will not infringe on existing or future patent rights, nor do the descriptions contained herein imply the granting or license to make, use or sell equipment constructed in accordance with this description.

USL reserves the right to make changes without further notice to any products herein to improve reliability, function, or design.

TRADEMARKS

UNIX is a registered trademark of UNIX System Laboratories, Inc. in the USA and other countries.
WE is a registered trademark of AT&T.
XENIX is a registered trademark of Microsoft Corporation.

10 9 8 7 6 5 4 3

ISBN 0-13-957549-9

**UNIX
PRESS**
A Prentice Hall Title

PRENTICE HALL

ORDERING INFORMATION

UNIX® SYSTEM V, RELEASE 4 DOCUMENTATION

To order single copies of UNIX® SYSTEM V, Release 4 documentation, please call (201) 767-5937.

ATTENTION DOCUMENTATION MANAGERS AND TRAINING DIRECTORS:
For bulk purchases in excess of 30 copies please write to:
Corporate Sales
Prentice Hall
Englewood Cliffs, N.J. 07632
Or call: (201) 592-2498

ATTENTION GOVERNMENT CUSTOMERS: For GSA and other pricing information please call (201) 767-5994.

Prentice-Hall International (UK) Limited, *London*
Prentice-Hall of Australia Pty. Limited, *Sydney*
Prentice-Hall Canada Inc., *Toronto*
Prentice-Hall Hispanoamericana, S.A., *Mexico*
Prentice-Hall of India Private Limited, *New Delhi*
Prentice-Hall of Japan, Inc., *Tokyo*
Simon & Schuster Asia Pte. Ltd., *Singapore*
Editora Prentice-Hall do Brasil, Ltda., *Rio de Janeiro*

AT&T UNIX® System V Release 4

General Use and System Administration

*UNIX® System V/386 Release 4 PC-Interface Administrator's Guide
*UNIX® System V/386 Release 4 Network User's and Administrator's Guide
*UNIX® System V/386 Release 4 Product Overview and Master Index
*UNIX® System V/386 Release 4 System Administrator's Reference Manual
*UNIX® System V/386 Release 4 User's Reference Manual
*UNIX® System V/386 Release 4 MULTIBUS® Reference Manual
*UNIX® System V/386 Release 4 MULTIBUS® Installation and Configuration Guide
*UNIX® System V/386 Release 4 Mouse Driver Administrator's Guide
*UNIX® System V/386 Release 4 Transport Application Interface Guide
 UNIX® System V Release 4 User's Guide
 UNIX® System V Release 4 System Administrator's Guide

General Programmer's Series

*UNIX® System V/386 Release 4 Programmer's Reference Manual
*UNIX® System V/386 Release 4 Programmer's Guide: SCSI Driver Interface
 UNIX® System V Release 4 Programmer's Guide: ANSI C and Programming Support Tools
 UNIX® System V Release 4 Programmer's Guide: Character User Interface (FMLI and ETI)
 UNIX® System V Release 4 Programmer's Guide: Networking Interfaces
 UNIX® System V Release 4 Programmer's Guide: POSIX Conformance
 UNIX® System V Release 4 Programmer's Guide: Support Services and Application Packaging Tools

System Programmer's Series

*UNIX® System V/386 Release 4 Device Driver Interface/Driver-Kernel Interface (DDI/DKI) Reference Manual
*UNIX® System V/386 Release 4 Integrated Software Development Guide
 UNIX® System V Release 4 Programmer's Guide: STREAMS

Migration Series

 UNIX® System V Release 4 ANSI C Transition Guide
 UNIX® System V Release 4 BSD/XENIX® Compatibility Guide
*UNIX® System V/386 Release 4 Migration Guide

Graphics Series

 UNIX® System V Release 4 OPEN LOOK™ Graphical User Interface Programmer's Reference Manual
 UNIX® System V Release 4 OPEN LOOK™ Graphical User Interface User's Guide
 UNIX® System V Release 4 Programmer's Guide: XWIN™ Graphical Windowing System Xlib— C Language Interface
 UNIX® System V Release 4 Programmer's Guide: OPEN LOOK™ Graphical User Interface
 UNIX® System V Release 4 Programmer's Guide: X11/NeWS® Graphical Windowing System NeWS
 UNIX® System V Release 4 Programmer's Guide: X11/NeWS® Graphical Windowing System Server Guide
 UNIX® System V Release 4 Programmer's Guide: X11/NeWS® Graphical Windowing System tNt Technical Reference Manual
 UNIX® System V Release 4 Programmer's Guide: X11/NeWS® Graphical Windowing System XVIEW™
 UNIX® System V Release 4 Programmer's Guide: XWIN™ Graphical Windowing System Addenda: Technical Papers
 UNIX® System V Release 4 Programmer's Guide: XWIN™ Graphical Windowing System The X Toolkit

*386 specific titles
Available from Prentice Hall

INTRODUCTION

INTRODUCTION

Introduction

This manual describes the programming features of the UNIX system. It contains individual manual pages that describe commands, system calls, subroutines, file formats, and other useful topics, such as the ASCII table shown on ascii(5). It provides neither a general overview of the UNIX system nor details of the implementation of the system.

Not all commands, features, and facilities described in this manual are available in every UNIX system. Some of the features require additional utilities that may not exist on your system.

The manual is divided into five sections:

1. Commands
2. System Calls
3. Subroutines:
    3C. C Programming Language Library Routines
    3S. Standard I/O Library Routines
    3E. Executable and Linking Format Library Routines
    3G. General Purpose Library Routines
    3M. Math Library Routines
    3X. Specialized Library Routines
4. File Formats
5. Miscellaneous Facilities

Section 1 (*Commands*) describes commands that support C and other programming languages.

Section 2 (*System Calls*) describes the access to the services provided by the UNIX system kernel, including the C language interface.

Section 3 (*Subroutines*) describes the available general subroutines. In many cases, several related subroutines are described on the same manual page. Their binary versions reside in various system libraries. See intro(3) for descriptions of these libraries and the files in which they are stored.

Section 4 (*File Formats*) documents the structure of particular kinds of files; for example, the format of the output of the link editor is given in a.out(4). Excluded are files used by only one command (for example, the assembler's intermediate files, if any). In general, the C language structures corresponding to these formats can be found in the directories /usr/include and /usr/include/sys.

Introduction

Section 5 (*Miscellaneous Facilities*) contains a variety of things. Included are descriptions of character sets, macro packages, etc.

References with numbers other than those above mean that the utility is contained in the appropriate section of another manual. References with (1) following the command mean that the utility is contained in this manual or the *User's Reference Manual*. In these cases, the SEE ALSO section of the entry in which the reference appears will point you to the correct book.

Each section consists of a number of independent entries of a page or so each. Entries within each section are alphabetized, with the exception of the introductory entry that begins each section. Some entries may describe several routines, commands, etc. In such cases, the entry appears only once, alphabetized under its "primary" name, the name that appears at the upper corners of each manual page. Subsections 3C and 3S are grouped together because their functions constitute the standard C library.

All entries are based on a common format, not all of whose parts always appear:

- The NAME part gives the name(s) of the entry and briefly states its purpose.
- The SYNOPSIS part summarizes the use of the program or function being described. A few conventions are used, particularly in Section 2 (*System Calls*):
  - `Constant width typeface` strings are literals and are to be typed just as they appear.
  - *Italic* strings usually represent substitutable argument prototypes and program names found elsewhere in the manual.
  - Square brackets [ ] around an argument prototype indicate that the argument is optional. When an argument prototype is given as *name* or *file*, it always refers to a file name.
  - Ellipses ... are used to show that the previous argument prototype may be repeated.
  - A final convention is used by the commands themselves. An argument beginning with a minus − or plus + sign is often taken to be some sort of flag argument, even if it appears in a position where a file name could appear. Therefore, it is unwise to have files whose names begin with − or +.

Introduction

- The **DESCRIPTION** part describes the utility.
- The **EXAMPLE(S)** part gives example(s) of usage, where appropriate.
- The **FILES** part gives the file names that are built into the program.
- The **SEE ALSO** part gives pointers to related information.
- The **DIAGNOSTICS** part discusses the diagnostic indications that may be produced. Messages that are intended to be self-explanatory are not listed.
- The **NOTES** part gives generally helpful hints about the use of the utility.

A "Table of Contents" and a "Permuted Index" derived from that table precede Section 1. The "Permuted Index" is a list of keywords, given in the second of three columns, together with the context in which each keyword is found. Keywords are either topical keywords or the names of manual entries. Entries are identified with their section numbers shown in parentheses. This is important because there is considerable duplication of names among the sections, arising principally from commands and functions that exist only to exercise a particular system call. The right column lists the name of the manual page on which each keyword may be found. The left column contains useful information about the keyword.

TABLE OF CONTENTS

TABLE OF CONTENTS

Table of Contents

1. Commands

intro(1)	introduction to programming commands
admin(1)	create and administer SCCS files
ar(1)	maintain portable archive or library
as(1)	assembler
cb(1)	C program beautifier
cc(1)	C compiler
cdc(1)	change the delta comment of an SCCS delta
cflow(1)	generate C flowgraph
cof2elf(1)	COFF to ELF object file translation
comb(1)	combine SCCS deltas
convert(1)	convert archive files to common formats
cscope(1)	interactively examine a C program
ctrace(1)	C program debugger
cxref(1)	generate C program cross-reference
delta(1)	make a delta (change) to an SCCS file
dis(1)	object code disassembler
dump(1)	dump selected parts of an object file
get(1)	get a version of an SCCS file
help(1)	ask for help with message numbers or SCCS commands
install(1M)	install commands
ld(1)	link editor for object files
ldd(1)	list dynamic dependencies
lex(1)	generate programs for simple lexical tasks
lint(1)	a C program checker
lorder(1)	find ordering relation for an object library
lprof(1)	display line-by-line execution count profile data
m4(1)	macro processor
make(1)	maintain, update, and regenerate groups of programs
mcs(1)	manipulate the comment section of an object file
nm(1)	print name list of an object file
prof(1)	display profile data
prs(1)	print an SCCS file
regcmp(1)	regular expression compile
rmdel(1)	remove a delta from an SCCS file
sact(1)	print current SCCS file editing activity
sccsdiff(1)	compare two versions of an SCCS file
sdb(1)	symbolic debugger
size(1)	print section sizes in bytes of object files

Table of Contents

strip(1) .... strip symbol table, debugging and line number information from an object file
tsort(1) .... topological sort
unget(1) .... undo a previous get of an SCCS file
val(1) .... validate an SCCS file
vc(1) .... version control
what(1) .... print identification strings
x286emul(1) .... emulate XENIX 80286
yacc(1) .... yet another compiler-compiler

2. System Calls

intro(2) .... introduction to system calls and error numbers
access(2) .... determine accessibility of a file
acct(2) .... enable or disable process accounting
adjtime(2) .... correct the time to allow synchronization of the system clock
alarm(2) .... set a process alarm clock
brk, sbrk(2) .... change data segment space allocation
chdir, fchdir(2) .... change working directory
chmod, fchmod(2) .... change mode of file
chown, lchown, fchown(2) .... change owner and group of a file
chroot(2) .... change root directory
close(2) .... close a file descriptor
creat(2) .... create a new file or rewrite an existing one
dup(2) .... duplicate an open file descriptor
exec: execl, execv, execle, execve, execlp, execvp(2) .... execute a file
exit, _exit(2) .... terminate process
fcntl(2) .... file control
fork(2) .... create a new process
fpathconf, pathconf(2) .... get configurable pathname variables
fsync(2) .... synchronize a file's in-memory state with that on the physical medium
getcontext, setcontext(2) .... get and set current user context
getdents(2) .... read directory entries and put in a file system independent format
getgroups, setgroups(2) .... get or set supplementary group access list IDs
getmsg(2) .... get next message off a stream
getpid, getpgrp, getppid, getpgid(2) .... get process, process group, and parent process IDs
getrlimit, setrlimit(2) .... control maximum system resource consumption
getsid(2) .... get session ID
getuid, geteuid, getgid, getegid(2)
.... get real user, effective user, real group, and effective group IDs
ioctl(2) .... control device

Table of Contents

kill(2)	send a signal to a process or a group of processes
link(2)	link to a file
lseek(2)	move read/write file pointer
memcntl(2)	memory management control
mincore(2)	determine residency of memory pages
mkdir(2)	make a directory
mknod(2)	make a directory, or a special or ordinary file
mmap(2)	map pages of memory
mount(2)	mount a file system
mprotect(2)	set protection of memory mapping
msgctl(2)	message control operations
msgget(2)	get message queue
msgop: msgsnd, msgrcv(2)	message operations
munmap(2)	unmap pages of memory
nice(2)	change priority of a time-sharing process
open(2)	open for reading or writing
pause(2)	suspend process until signal
pipe(2)	create an interprocess channel
plock(2)	lock into memory or unlock process, text, or data
poll(2)	input/output multiplexing
priocntl(2)	process scheduler control
priocntlset(2)	generalized process scheduler control
profil(2)	execution time profile
ptrace(2)	process trace
putmsg(2)	send a message on a stream
read(2)	read from file
readlink(2)	read the value of a symbolic link
rename(2)	change the name of a file
rmdir(2)	remove a directory
semctl(2)	semaphore control operations
semget(2)	get set of semaphores
semop(2)	semaphore operations
setpgid(2)	set process group ID
setpgrp(2)	set process group ID
setsid(2)	set session ID
setuid, setgid(2)	set user and group IDs
shmctl(2)	shared memory control operations
shmget(2)	get shared memory segment identifier
shmop: shmat, shmdt(2)	shared memory operations
sigaction(2)	detailed signal management

Table of Contents

sigaltstack(2) .... set or get signal alternate stack context
signal, sigset, sighold, sigrelse, sigignore, sigpause(2) .... simplified signal management
sigpending(2) .... examine signals that are blocked and pending
sigprocmask(2) .... change or examine signal mask
sigsend, sigsendset(2) .... send a signal to a process or a group of processes
sigsuspend(2) .... install a signal mask and suspend process until signal
stat, lstat, fstat(2) .... get file status
statvfs, fstatvfs(2) .... get file system information
stime(2) .... set time
swapctl(2) .... manage swap space
symlink(2) .... make a symbolic link to a file
sync(2) .... update super block
sysi86(2) .... machine specific functions
sysfs(2) .... get file system type information
sysinfo(2) .... get and set system information strings
termios: tcgetattr, tcsetattr, tcsendbreak, tcdrain, tcflush, tcflow, cfgetospeed,
    cfgetispeed, cfsetispeed, cfsetospeed, tcgetpgrp, tcsetpgrp, tcgetsid(2)
    .... general terminal interface
time(2) .... get time
times(2) .... get process and child process times
uadmin(2) .... administrative control
ulimit(2) .... get and set user limits
umask(2) .... set and get file creation mask
umount(2) .... unmount a file system
uname(2) .... get name of current UNIX system
unlink(2) .... remove directory entry
ustat(2) .... get file system statistics
utime(2) .... set file access and modification times
vfork(2) .... spawn new process in a virtual memory efficient way
wait(2) .... wait for child process to stop or terminate
waitid(2) .... wait for child process to change state
waitpid(2) .... wait for child process to change state
write, writev(2) .... write on a file

3. Functions

intro(3) .... introduction to functions and libraries
a64l, l64a(3C) .... convert between long integer and base-64 ASCII string
abort(3C) .... generate an abnormal termination signal
abs, labs(3C) .... return integer absolute value
addseverity(3C) .... build a list of severity levels for an application for use with fmtmsg
atexit(3C) .... add program termination routine
bsearch(3C) .... binary search a sorted table
catgets(3C) .... read a program message
catopen, catclose(3C) .... open/close a message catalogue
clock(3C) .... report CPU time used
conv: toupper, tolower, _toupper, _tolower, toascii(3C) .... translate characters
crypt, setkey, encrypt(3C) .... generate encryption
ctermid(3S) .... generate file name for terminal
ctime, localtime, gmtime, asctime, tzset(3C) .... convert date and time to string
ctype: isdigit, isxdigit, islower, isupper, isalpha, isalnum, isspace, iscntrl, ispunct,
    isprint, isgraph, isascii(3C) .... character handling
cuserid(3S) .... get character login name of the user
difftime(3C) .... computes the difference between two calendar times
directory: opendir, readdir, telldir, seekdir, rewinddir, closedir(3C) .... directory operations
div, ldiv(3C) .... compute the quotient and remainder
drand48, erand48, lrand48, nrand48, mrand48, jrand48, srand48, seed48,
    lcong48(3C) .... generate uniformly distributed pseudo-random numbers
dup2(3C) .... duplicate an open file descriptor
ecvt, fcvt, gcvt(3C) .... convert floating-point number to string
end, etext, edata(3C) .... last locations in program
fclose, fflush(3S) .... close or flush a stream
ferror, feof, clearerr, fileno(3S) .... stream status inquiries
ffs(3C) .... find first set bit
fmtmsg(3C) .... display a message on stderr or system console
fopen, freopen, fdopen(3S) .... open a stream
fpgetround, fpsetround, fpgetmask, fpsetmask, fpgetsticky, fpsetsticky(3C)
    .... IEEE floating-point environment control
fread, fwrite(3S) .... binary input/output
frexp, ldexp, logb, modf, modff, nextafter, scalb(3C)
    .... manipulate parts of floating-point numbers
fseek, rewind, ftell(3S) .... reposition a file pointer in a stream
fsetpos, fgetpos(3C) .... reposition a file pointer in a stream
ftw, nftw(3C) .... walk a file tree

Table of Contents

getc, getchar, fgetc, getw (3S) .... get character or word from a stream
getcwd (3C) .... get pathname of current working directory
getdate (3C) .... convert user format date and time
getenv (3C) .... return value for environment name
getgrent, getgrgid, getgrnam, setgrent, endgrent, fgetgrent (3C) .... get group file entry
getitimer, setitimer (3C) .... get/set value of interval timer
getlogin (3C) .... get login name
getmntent, getmntany (3C) .... get mnttab file entry
getopt (3C) .... get option letter from argument vector
getpass (3C) .... read a password
getpw (3C) .... get name from UID
getpwent, getpwuid, getpwnam, setpwent, endpwent, fgetpwent (3C)
  .... manipulate password file entry
gets, fgets (3S) .... get a string from a stream
getspent, getspnam, setspent, endspent, fgetspent, lckpwdf, ulckpwdf (3C)
  .... manipulate shadow password file entry
getsubopt (3C) .... parse suboptions from a string
gettimeofday, settimeofday (3C) .... get or set the date and time
gettxt (3C) .... retrieve a text string
getut: getutent, getutid, getutline, pututline, setutent, endutent, utmpname (3C)
  .... access utmp file entry
getutx: getutxent, getutxid, getutxline, pututxline, setutxent, endutxent,
  utmpxname, getutmp, getutmpx, updwtmp, updwtmpx (3C) .... access utmpx file entry
getvfsent, getvfsfile, getvfsspec, getvfsany (3C) .... get vfstab file entry
hsearch, hcreate, hdestroy (3C) .... manage hash search tables
initgroups (3C) .... initialize the supplementary group access list
insque, remque (3C) .... insert/remove element from a queue
isnan, isnand, isnanf, finite, fpclass, unordered (3C)
  .... determine type of floating-point number
l3tol, ltol3 (3C) .... convert between 3-byte integers and long integers
localeconv (3C) .... get numeric formatting information
lockf (3C) .... record locking on files
lsearch, lfind (3C) .... linear search and update
makecontext, swapcontext (3C) .... manipulate user contexts
makedev, major, minor (3C) .... manage a device number
malloc, free, realloc, calloc, memalign, valloc, (3C) .... memory allocator
mbchar: mbtowc, mblen, wctomb (3C) .... multibyte character handling
mbstring: mbstowcs, wcstombs (3C) .... multibyte string functions

memory: memccpy, memchr, memcmp, memcpy, memmove, memset(3C)
.... memory operations
mkfifo(3C) .... create a new FIFO
mktemp(3C) .... make a unique file name
mktime(3C) .... converts a tm structure to a calendar time
mlock, munlock(3C) .... lock (or unlock) pages in memory
mlockall, munlockall(3C) .... lock or unlock address space
monitor(3C) .... prepare execution profile
msync(3C) .... synchronize memory with physical storage
nl_langinfo(3C) .... language information
offsetof(3C) .... offset of structure member
perror(3C) .... print system error messages
popen, pclose(3S) .... initiate pipe to/from a process
printf, fprintf, sprintf(3S) .... print formatted output
psignal, psiginfo(3C) .... system signal messages
putc, putchar, fputc, putw(3S) .... put character or word on a stream
puts, fputs(3S) .... put a string on a stream
putenv(3C) .... change or add value to environment
putpwent(3C) .... write password file entry
putspent(3C) .... write shadow password file entry
qsort(3C) .... quicker sort
raise(3C) .... send signal to program
rand, srand(3C) .... simple random-number generator
realpath(3C) .... returns the real file name
remove(3C) .... remove file
scanf, fscanf, sscanf(3S) .... convert formatted input
setbuf, setvbuf(3S) .... assign buffering to a stream
setjmp, longjmp(3C) .... non-local goto
setlocale(3C) .... modify and query a program's locale
sigsetjmp, siglongjmp(3C) .... a non-local goto with signal state
sigemptyset, sigfillset, sigaddset, sigdelset, sigismember(3C) .... manipulate sets of signals
sleep(3C) .... suspend execution for interval
ssignal, gsignal(3C) .... software signals
stdipc: ftok(3C) .... standard interprocess communication package
stdio(3S) .... standard buffered input/output package
strcoll(3C) .... string collation
strerror(3C) .... get error message string
strftime, cftime, ascftime(3C) .... convert date and time to string

Table of Contents

string: strcat, strdup, strncat, strcmp, strncmp, strcpy, strncpy, strlen, strchr,
    strrchr, strpbrk, strspn, strcspn, strtok, strstr (3C) .... string operations
strtod, atof, (3C) .... convert string to double-precision number
strtol, strtoul, atol, atoi (3C) .... convert string to integer
strxfrm (3C) .... string transformation
swab (3C) .... swap bytes
sysconf (3C) .... get configurable system variables
system (3S) .... issue a shell command
tcsetpgrp (3C) .... set terminal foreground process group id
tmpfile (3S) .... create a temporary file
tmpnam, tempnam (3S) .... create a name for a temporary file
truncate, ftruncate (3C) .... set a file to a specified length
tsearch, tfind, tdelete, twalk (3C) .... manage binary search trees
ttyname, isatty (3C) .... find name of a terminal
ttyslot (3C) .... find the slot in the utmp file of the current user
ungetc (3S) .... push character back onto input stream
vprintf, vfprintf, vsprintf (3S) .... print formatted output of a variable argument list
elf (3E) .... object file access library
elf_begin (3E) .... make a file descriptor
elf_cntl (3E) .... control a file descriptor
elf_end (3E) .... finish using an object file
elf_errmsg, elf_errno (3E) .... error handling
elf_fill (3E) .... set fill byte
elf_flagdata, elf_flagehdr, elf_flagelf, elf_flagphdr, elf_flagscn, elf_flagshdr (3E)
    .... manipulate flags
elf_fsize: elf32_fsize (3E) .... return the size of an object file type
elf_getarhdr (3E) .... retrieve archive member header
elf_getarsym (3E) .... retrieve archive symbol table
elf_getbase (3E) .... get the base offset for an object file
elf_getdata, elf_newdata, elf_rawdata (3E) .... get section data
elf_getehdr: elf32_getehdr, elf32_newehdr (3E) .... retrieve class-dependent object file header
elf_getident (3E) .... retrieve file identification data
elf_getphdr: elf32_getphdr, elf32_newphdr (3E)
    .... retrieve class-dependent program header table
elf_getscn, elf_ndxscn, elf_newscn, elf_nextscn (3E) .... get section information
elf_getshdr: elf32_getshdr (3E) .... retrieve class-dependent section header
elf_hash (3E) .... compute hash value
elf_kind (3E) .... determine file type
elf_next (3E) .... sequential archive member access
elf_rand (3E) .... random archive member access

elf_rawfile(3E)	retrieve uninterpreted file contents
elf_strptr(3E)	make a string pointer
elf_update(3E)	update an descriptor
elf_version(3E)	coordinate library and application versions
elf_xlate: elf32_xlatetof, elf32_xlatetom(3E)	class-dependent data translation
nlist(3E)	get entries from name list
basename(3G)	return the last element of a path name
bgets(3G)	read stream up to next delimiter
bufsplit(3G)	split buffer into fields
copylist(3G)	copy a file into memory
dirname(3G)	report the parent directory name of a file path name
gmatch(3G)	shell global pattern matching
isencrypt(3G)	determine whether a character buffer is encrypted
mkdirp, rmdirp(3G)	create, remove directories in a path
p2open, p2close(3G)	open, close pipes to and from a command
pathfind(3G)	search for named file in named directories
regcmp, regex(3G)	compile and execute regular expression
regexpr: compile, step, advance(3G)	regular expression compile and match routines
str: strfind, strrspn, strtrns(3G)	string manipulations
strccpy: streadd, strcadd, strecpy(3G)	copy strings, compressing or expanding escape codes
intro(3M)	introduction to math libraries
bessel: j0, j1, jn, y0, y1, yn(3M)	Bessel functions
erf, erfc(3M)	error function and complementary error function
exp, expf, cbrt, log, logf, log10, log10f, pow, powf, sqrt, sqrtf(3M)	exponential, logarithm, power, square root functions
floor, floorf, ceil, ceilf, copysign, fmod, fmodf, fabs, fabsf, rint, remainder(3M)	floor, ceiling, remainder, absolute value functions
gamma, lgamma(3M)	log gamma function
hypot(3M)	Euclidean distance function
matherr(3M)	error-handling function
sinh, sinhf, cosh, coshf, tanh, tanhf, asinh, acosh, atanh(3M)	hyperbolic functions
trig: sin, sinf, cos, cosf, tan, tanf, asin, asinf, acos, acosf, atan, atanf, atan2, atan2f(3M)	trigonometric functions
assert(3X)	verify program assertion
crypt(3X)	password and file encryption functions
dlclose(3X)	close a shared object
dlerror(3X)	get diagnostic information
dlopen(3X)	open a shared object
dlsym(3X)	get the address of a symbol in shared object
libwindows(3X)	windowing terminal function library

Table of Contents

maillock(3X) .... manage lockfile for user's mailbox
malloc, free, realloc, calloc, mallopt, mallinfo(3X) .... memory allocator
sputl, sgetl(3X) .... access long integer data in a machine-independent fashion

4. File Formats

intro(4) .... introduction to file formats
a.out(4) .... ELF (Executable and Linking Format) files
ar(4) .... archive file format
core(4) .... core image file
limits(4) .... header file for implementation-specific constants
sccsfile(4) .... format of SCCS file
strftime(4) .... language specific strings
timezone(4) .... set default system time zone
utmp, wtmp(4) .... utmp and wtmp entry formats
utmpx, wtmpx(4) .... utmpx and wtmpx entry formats

5. Miscellaneous Facilities

intro(5) .... introduction to miscellany
ascii(5) .... map of ASCII character set
environ(5) .... user environment
fcntl(5) .... file control options
jagent(5) .... host control of windowing terminal
langinfo(5) .... language information constants
layers(5) .... protocol used between host and windowing terminal under layers(1)
math(5) .... math functions and constants
nl_types(5) .... native language data types
prof(5) .... profile within a function
regexp: compile, step, advance(5) .... regular expression compile and match routines
siginfo(5) .... signal generation information
signal(5) .... base signals
stat(5) .... data returned by stat system call
stdarg(5) .... handle variable argument list
types(5) .... primitive system data types
ucontext(5) .... user context
values(5) .... machine-dependent values
varargs(5) .... handle variable argument list
wstat(5) .... wait status
xtproto(5) .... multiplexed channels protocol used by xt driver

PERMUTED INDEX

PERMUTED INDEX

Permuted Index

l3tol, ltol3 convert between	3-byte integers and long integers .... l3tol(3C)
x286emul emulate XENIX	80286 .... x286emul(1)
integer and base-64 ASCII string	a64l, l64a convert between long .... a64l(3C)
abort generate an	abnormal termination signal .... abort(3C)
termination signal	abort generate an abnormal .... abort(3C)
value	abs, labs return integer absolute .... abs(3C)
abs, labs return integer	absolute value .... abs(3C)
floor, ceiling, remainder,	absolute value functions /remainder .... floor(3M)
utime set file	access and modification times .... utime(2)
file	access determine accessibility of a .... access(2)
elf_next sequential archive member	access .... elf_next(3E)
elf_rand random archive member	access .... elf_rand(3E)
elf object file	access library .... elf(3E)
get or set supplementary group	access list IDs /setgroups .... getgroups(2)
initialize the supplementary group	access list initgroups .... initgroups(3C)
machine-independent/ sputl, sgetl	access long integer data in a .... sputl(3X)
setutent, endutent, utmpname	access utmp file entry /pututline, ... getut(3C)
getutmpx, updwtmp, updwtmpx	access utmpx file entry /getutmp, ... getutx(3C)
access determine	accessibility of a file .... access(2)
acct enable or disable process	accounting .... acct(2)
accounting	acct enable or disable process .... acct(2)
/cos, cosf, tan, tanf, asin, asinf,	acos, acosf, atan, atanf, atan2,/ .... trig(3M)
/cosf, tan, tanf, asin, asinf, acos,	acosf, atan, atanf, atan2, atan2f/ .... trig(3M)
/coshf, tanh, tanhf, asinh,	acosh, atanh hyperbolic functions .... sinh(3M)
print current SCCS file editing	activity sact .... sact(1)
atexit	add program termination routine .... atexit(3C)
putenv change or	add value to environment .... putenv(3C)
object dlsym get the	address of a symbol in shared .... dlsym(3X)
mlockall, munlockall lock or unlock	address space .... mlockall(3C)
severity levels for an application/	addseverity build a list of .... addseverity(3C)
synchronization of the system/	adjtime correct the time to allow .... adjtime(2)
files	admin create and administer SCCS .... admin(1)
admin create and	administer SCCS files .... admin(1)
uadmin	administrative control .... uadmin(2)
and match/ regexp: compile, step,	advance regular expression compile .... regexp(5)
and match/ regexpr: compile, step,	advance regular expression compile .... regexpr(3G)
alarm set a process	alarm clock .... alarm(2)
	alarm set a process alarm clock .... alarm(2)
brk, sbrk change data segment space	allocation .... brk(2)
calloc, memalign, valloc, memory	allocator malloc, free, realloc, ... malloc(3C)
calloc, mallopt, mallinfo memory	allocator malloc, free, realloc, ... malloc(3X)
clock adjtime correct the time to	allow synchronization of the system .... adjtime(2)
sigaltstack set or get signal	alternate stack context .... sigaltstack(2)
Format) files	a.out ELF (Executable and Linking .... a.out(4)
/a list of severity levels for an	application for use with fmtmsg .... addseverity(3C)
elf_version coordinate library and	application versions .... elf_version(3E)
	ar archive file format .... ar(4)

Permuted Index   1

Permuted Index

library	ar maintain portable archive or	ar(1)
ar	archive file format	ar(4)
convert convert	archive files to common formats	convert(1)
elf_next sequential	archive member access	elf_next(3E)
elf_rand random	archive member access	elf_rand(3E)
elf_getarhdr retrieve	archive member header	elf_getarhdr(3E)
ar maintain portable	archive or library	ar(1)
elf_getarsym retrieve	archive symbol table	elf_getarsym(3E)
stdarg handle variable	argument list	stdarg(5)
varargs handle variable	argument list	varargs(5)
formatted output of a variable	argument list /vsprintf print	vprintf(3S)
getopt get option letter from	argument vector	getopt(3C)
string strftime, cftime,	ascftime convert date and time to	strftime(3C)
ascii map of	ASCII character set	ascii(5)
	ascii map of ASCII character set	ascii(5)
between long integer and base-64	ASCII string a64l, l64a convert	a64l(3C)
time to/ ctime, localtime, gmtime,	asctime, tzset convert date and	ctime(3C)
/sin, sinf, cos, cosf, tan, tanf,	asin, asinf, acos, acosf, atan,/	trig(3M)
/sinf, cos, cosf, tan, tanf, asin,	asinf, acos, acosf, atan, atanf,/	trig(3M)
/cosh, coshf, tanh, tanhf,	asinh, acosh, atanh hyperbolic/	sinh(3M)
or SCCS commands help	ask for help with message numbers	help(1)
as	assembler	as(1)
assert verify program	assert verify program assertion	assert(3X)
assert verify program	assertion	assert(3X)
setbuf, setvbuf	assign buffering to a stream	setbuf(3S)
tanf, asin, asinf, acos, acosf,	atan, atanf, atan2, atan2f/ /tan,	trig(3M)
asinf, acos, acosf, atan, atanf,	atan2, atan2f trigonometric/ /asin,	trig(3M)
/acos, acosf, atan, atanf, atan2,	atan2f trigonometric functions	trig(3M)
/asin, asinf, acos, acosf, atan,	atanf, atan2, atan2f trigonometric/	trig(3M)
tanh, tanhf, asinh, acosh,	atanh hyperbolic functions /coshf,	sinh(3M)
routine	atexit add program termination	atexit(3C)
double-precision number strtod,	atof, convert string to	strtod(3C)
strtol, strtoul, atol,	atoi convert string to integer	strtol(3C)
integer strtol, strtoul,	atol, atoi convert string to	strtol(3C)
elf_getbase get the	base offset for an object file	elf_getbase(3E)
signal	base signals	signal(5)
convert between long integer and	base-64 ASCII string a64l, l64a	a64l(3C)
a path name	basename return the last element of	basename(3G)
cb C program	beautifier	cb(1)
bessel: j0, j1, jn, y0, y1, yn	Bessel functions	bessel(3M)
Bessel functions	bessel: j0, j1, jn, y0, y1, yn	bessel(3M)
delimiter	bgets read stream up to next	bgets(3G)
fread, fwrite	binary input/output	fread(3S)
bsearch	binary search a sorted table	bsearch(3C)
tfind, tdelete, twalk manage	binary search trees tsearch,	tsearch(3C)
ffs find first set	bit	ffs(3C)
sync update super	block	sync(2)

2 Programmer's Reference Manual

Permuted Index

sigpending examine signals that are	blocked and pending	sigpending(2)
allocation	brk, sbrk change data segment space	brk(2)
table	bsearch binary search a sorted	bsearch(3C)
bufsplit split	buffer into fields	bufsplit(3G)
determine whether a character	buffer is encrypted isencrypt	isencrypt(3G)
stdio standard	buffered input/output package	stdio(3S)
setbuf, setvbuf assign	buffering to a stream	setbuf(3S)
	bufsplit split buffer into fields	bufsplit(3G)
an application for use/ addseverity	build a list of severity levels for	addseverity(3C)
elf_fill set fill	byte	elf_fill(3E)
size print section sizes in	bytes of object files	size(1)
swab swap	bytes	swab(3C)
cc	C compiler	cc(1)
cflow generate	C flowgraph	cflow(1)
cb	C program beautifier	cb(1)
lint a	C program checker	lint(1)
cxref generate	C program cross-reference	cxref(1)
cscope interactively examine a	C program	cscope(1)
ctrace	C program debugger	ctrace(1)
mktime converts a tm structure to a	calendar time	mktime(3C)
computes the difference between two	calendar times difftime	difftime(3C)
stat data returned by stat system	call	stat(5)
allocator malloc, free, realloc,	calloc, mallopt, mallinfo memory	malloc(3X)
allocator malloc, free, realloc,	calloc, memalign, valloc, memory	malloc(3C)
intro introduction to system	calls and error numbers	intro(2)
catclose open/close a message	catalogue catopen,	catopen(3C)
catalogue catopen,	catclose open/close a message	catopen(3C)
	catgets read a program message	catgets(3C)
message catalogue	catopen, catclose open/close a	catopen(3C)
	cb C program beautifier	cb(1)
pow, powf, sqrt, sqrtf/ exp, expf,	cbrt, log, logf, log10, log10f,	exp(3M)
SCCS delta	cc C compiler	cc(1)
	cdc change the delta comment of an	cdc(1)
fabs, fabsf, rint,/ floor, floorf,	ceil, ceilf, copysign, fmod, fmodf,	floor(3M)
fabsf, rint,/ floor, floorf, ceil,	ceilf, copysign, fmod, fmodf, fabs,	floor(3M)
/fabs, fabsf, rint, remainder floor,	ceiling, remainder, absolute value/	floor(3M)
tcflush, tcflow, cfgetospeed,	cfgetispeed, cfsetispeed,/ /tcdrain,	termios(2)
/tcdrain, tcflush, tcflow,	cfgetospeed, cfgetispeed,/	termios(2)
	cflow generate C flowgraph	cflow(1)
tcflow, cfgetospeed, cfgetispeed,	cfsetispeed, cfsetospeed,/ /tcflush,	termios(2)
tcgetsid/ /cfgetispeed, cfsetispeed,	cfsetospeed, tcgetpgrp, tcsetpgrp,	termios(2)
time to string strftime,	cftime, ascftime convert date and	strftime(3C)
allocation brk, sbrk	change data segment space	brk(2)
chmod, fchmod	change mode of file	chmod(2)
putenv	change or add value to environment	putenv(3C)
sigprocmask	change or examine signal mask	sigprocmask(2)
chown, lchown, fchown	change owner and group of a file	chown(2)

Permuted Index

process nice	change priority of a time-sharing .... nice(2)
chroot	change root directory .... chroot(2)
waitid wait for child process to	change state .... waitid(2)
waitpid wait for child process to	change state .... waitpid(2)
delta cdc	change the delta comment of an SCCS .... cdc(1)
rename	change the name of a file .... rename(2)
delta make a delta	(change) to an SCCS file .... delta(1)
chdir, fchdir	change working directory .... chdir(2)
pipe create an interprocess	channel .... pipe(2)
xtproto multiplexed	channels protocol used by xt driver .... xtproto(5)
ungetc push	character back onto input stream .... ungetc(3S)
isencrypt determine whether a	character buffer is encrypted .... isencrypt(3G)
ispunct, isprint, isgraph, isascii	character handling /iscntrl, ... ctype(3C)
mbtowc, mblen, wctomb multibyte	character handling mbchar: .... mbchar(3C)
cuserid get	character login name of the user .... cuserid(3S)
getc, getchar, fgetc, getw get	character or word from a stream .... getc(3S)
putc, putchar, fputc, putw put	character or word on a stream .... putc(3S)
ascii map of ASCII	character set .... ascii(5)
_tolower, toascii translate	characters /tolower, _toupper, ... conv(3C)
directory	chdir, fchdir change working .... chdir(2)
lint a C program	checker .... lint(1)
times get process and	child process times .... times(2)
waitid wait for	child process to change state .... waitid(2)
waitpid wait for	child process to change state .... waitpid(2)
wait wait for	child process to stop or terminate .... wait(2)
	chmod, fchmod change mode of file .... chmod(2)
and group of a file	chown, lchown, fchown change owner .... chown(2)
	chroot change root directory .... chroot(2)
/elf32_xlatetof, elf32_xlatetom	class-dependent data translation .... elf_xlate(3E)
/elf32_newehdr retrieve	class-dependent object file header .... elf_getehdr(3E)
table /elf32_newphdr retrieve	class-dependent program header .... elf_getphdr(3E)
elf_getshdr: elf32_getshdr retrieve	class-dependent section header .... elf_getshdr(3E)
inquiries ferror, feof,	clearerr, fileno stream status .... ferror(3S)
allow synchronization of the system	clock adjtime correct the time to .... adjtime(2)
alarm set a process alarm	clock .... alarm(2)
	clock report CPU time used .... clock(3C)
close	close a file descriptor .... close(2)
dlclose	close a shared object .... dlclose(3X)
	close close a file descriptor .... close(2)
fclose, fflush	close or flush a stream .... fclose(3S)
p2open, p2close open,	close pipes to and from a command .... p2open(3G)
/telldir, seekdir, rewinddir,	closedir directory operations .... directory(3C)
compressing or expanding escape	codes /strecpy copy strings, ... strccpy(3G)
translation	cof2elf COFF to ELF object file .... cof2elf(1)
cof2elf	COFF to ELF object file translation .... cof2elf(1)
strcoll string	collation .... strcoll(3C)
	comb combine SCCS deltas .... comb(1)

```
                         comb    combine SCCS deltas ............................................................. comb(1)
  open, close pipes to and from a    command  p2open, p2close .......................................... p2open(3G)
              system issue a shell    command ........................................................................ system(3S)
  help with message numbers or SCCS   commands  help ask for ...................................................... help(1)
                     install install    commands ....................................................................... install(1M)
   intro introduction to programming   commands ............................................................................ intro(1)
            cdc change the delta      comment of an SCCS delta ..................................................... cdc(1)
              mcs manipulate the      comment section of an object file ........................................ mcs(1)
  convert convert archive files to    common formats ............................................................ convert(1)
 stdipc: ftok standard interprocess    communication package ................................................. stdipc(3C)
                    file sccsdiff     compare two versions of an SCCS ................................ sccsdiff(1)
         expression  regcmp, regex    compile and execute regular ......................................... regcmp(3G)
   /step, advance regular expression  compile and match routines ............................................. regexp(5)
   /step, advance regular expression  compile and match routines ........................................ regexpr(3G)
          regcmp regular expression   compile ....................................................................... regcmp(1)
    expression compile and/ regexp:   compile, step, advance regular ...................................... regexp(5)
    expression compile and/ regexpr:  compile, step, advance regular ..................................... regexpr(3G)
                          cc C        compiler ................................................................................ cc(1)
                  yacc yet another    compiler-compiler ................................................................ yacc(1)
        erf, erfc error function and  complementary error function .............................................. erf(3M)
     /strcadd, strecpy copy strings,  compressing or expanding escape/ ............................. strccpy(3G)
                          elf_hash    compute hash value ....................................................... elf_hash(3E)
                         div, ldiv   compute the quotient and remainder ................................. div(3C)
             calendar times difftime  computes the difference between two ........................ difftime(3C)
            fpathconf, pathconf get   configurable pathname variables ................................ fpathconf(2)
                      sysconf get    configurable system variables ....................................... sysconf(3C)
      a message on stderr or system   console  fmtmsg display ............................................... fmtmsg(3C)
      langinfo language information   constants ..................................................................... langinfo(5)
    file for implementation-specific  constants  limits header ............................................... limits(4)
          math math functions and    constants ............................................................................. math(5)
   control maximum system resource    consumption  getrlimit, setrlimit ..................................... getrlimit(2)
          retrieve uninterpreted file  contents  elf_rawfile ..................................... elf_rawfile(3E)
  setcontext get and set current user context  getcontext, ......................................... getcontext(2)
   set or get signal alternate stack   context  sigaltstack .................................................. sigaltstack(2)
                     ucontext user    context ..................................................................... ucontext(5)
         swapcontext manipulate user  contexts  makecontext, ......................................... makecontext(3C)
                         elf_cntl    control a file descriptor ..................................... elf_cntl(3E)
                           ioctl     control device ................................................................... ioctl(2)
                        fcntl file    control ........................................................................... fcntl(2)
    IEEE floating-point environment   control  /fpgetsticky, fpsetsticky .......................... fpgetround(3C)
      consumption  getrlimit, setrlimit  control maximum system resource ............................. getrlimit(2)
       memcntl memory management     control ....................................................................... memcntl(2)
                       jagent host   control of windowing terminal ........................................... jagent(5)
                    msgctl message   control operations ........................................................... msgctl(2)
                   semctl semaphore   control operations ........................................................... semctl(2)
             shmctl shared memory    control operations ........................................................... shmctl(2)
                        fcntl file    control options ................................................................... fcntl(5)
```

Permuted Index

priocntl process scheduler	control .... priocntl(2)
generalized process scheduler	control priocntlset .... priocntlset(2)
uadmin administrative	control .... uadmin(2)
vc version	control .... vc(1)
_tolower, toascii translate/	conv: toupper, tolower, _toupper, ... conv(3C)
formats convert	convert archive files to common .... convert(1)
long integers l3tol, ltol3	convert between 3-byte integers and .... l3tol(3C)
base-64 ASCII string a64l, l64a	convert between long integer and .... a64l(3C)
common formats	convert convert archive files to .... convert(1)
/localtime, gmtime, asctime, tzset	convert date and time to string .... ctime(3C)
strftime, cftime, ascftime	convert date and time to string .... strftime(3C)
string ecvt, fcvt, gcvt	convert floating-point number to .... ecvt(3C)
scanf, fscanf, sscanf	convert formatted input .... scanf(3S)
number strtod, atof,	convert string to double-precision .... strtod(3C)
strtol, strtoul, atol, atoi	convert string to integer .... strtol(3C)
getdate	convert user format date and time .... getdate(3C)
calendar time mktime	converts a tm structure to a .... mktime(3C)
versions elf_version	coordinate library and application .... elf_version(3E)
copylist	copy a file into memory .... copylist(3G)
strccpy: streadd, strcadd, strecpy	copy strings, compressing or/ .... strccpy(3G)
	copylist copy a file into memory .... copylist(3G)
rint,/ floor, floorf, ceil, ceilf,	copysign, fmod, fmodf, fabs, fabsf, ... floor(3M)
	core core image file .... core(4)
core	core image file .... core(4)
synchronization of the/ adjtime	correct the time to allow .... adjtime(2)
acos, acosf,/ trig: sin, sinf,	cos, cosf, tan, tanf, asin, asinf, ... trig(3M)
acosf, atan,/ trig: sin, sinf, cos,	cosf, tan, tanf, asin, asinf, acos, ... trig(3M)
asinh, acosh,/ sinh, sinhf,	cosh, coshf, tanh, tanhf, ... sinh(3M)
acosh,/ sinh, sinhf, cosh,	coshf, tanh, tanhf, asinh, ... sinh(3M)
display line-by-line execution	count profile data lprof .... lprof(1)
clock report	CPU time used .... clock(3C)
an existing one	creat create a new file or rewrite .... creat(2)
tmpnam, tempnam	create a name for a temporary file .... tmpnam(3S)
mkfifo	create a new FIFO .... mkfifo(3C)
existing one creat	create a new file or rewrite an .... creat(2)
fork	create a new process .... fork(2)
tmpfile	create a temporary file .... tmpfile(3S)
pipe	create an interprocess channel .... pipe(2)
admin	create and administer SCCS files .... admin(1)
path mkdirp, rmdirp	create, remove directories in a .... mkdirp(3G)
umask set and get file	creation mask .... umask(2)
cxref generate C program	cross-reference .... cxref(1)
functions	crypt password and file encryption .... crypt(3X)
encryption	crypt, setkey, encrypt generate .... crypt(3C)
program	cscope interactively examine a C .... cscope(1)
terminal	ctermid generate file name for .... ctermid(3S)
tzset convert date and time to/	ctime, localtime, gmtime, asctime, ... ctime(3C)

Programmer's Reference Manual

	ctrace C program debugger .... ctrace(1)
isupper, isalpha, isalnum,/	ctype: isdigit, isxdigit, islower, ... ctype(3C)
sact print	current SCCS file editing activity .... sact(1)
uname get name of	current UNIX system .... uname(2)
getcontext, setcontext get and set	current user context .... getcontext(2)
the slot in the utmp file of the	current user ttyslot find .... ttyslot(3C)
getcwd get pathname of	current working directory .... getcwd(3C)
the user	cuserid get character login name of .... cuserid(3S)
cross-reference	cxref generate C program .... cxref(1)
elf_rawdata get section	data elf_getdata, elf_newdata, ... elf_getdata(3E)
retrieve file identification	data elf_getident .... elf_getident(3E)
sputl, sgetl access long integer	data in a machine-independent/ .... sputl(3X)
execution count profile	data lprof display line-by-line .... lprof(1)
memory or unlock process, text, or	data plock lock into .... plock(2)
prof display profile	data .... prof(1)
stat	data returned by stat system call .... stat(5)
brk, sbrk change	data segment space allocation .... brk(2)
elf32_xlatetom class-dependent	data translation /elf32_xlatetof, ... elf_xlate(3E)
nl_types native language	data types .... nl_types(5)
types primitive system	data types .... types(5)
getdate convert user format	date and time .... getdate(3C)
settimeofday get or set the	date and time gettimeofday, ... gettimeofday(3C)
gmtime, asctime, tzset convert	date and time to string /localtime, ... ctime(3C)
strftime, cftime, ascftime convert	date and time to string .... strftime(3C)
ctrace C program	debugger .... ctrace(1)
sdb symbolic	debugger .... sdb(1)
strip strip symbol table,	debugging and line number/ .... strip(1)
timezone set	default system time zone .... timezone(4)
bgets read stream up to next	delimiter .... bgets(3G)
change the delta comment of an SCCS	delta cdc .... cdc(1)
delta make a	delta (change) to an SCCS file .... delta(1)
cdc change the	delta comment of an SCCS delta .... cdc(1)
rmdel remove a	delta from an SCCS file .... rmdel(1)
SCCS file	delta make a delta (change) to an .... delta(1)
comb combine SCCS	deltas .... comb(1)
ldd list dynamic	dependencies .... ldd(1)
close close a file	descriptor .... close(2)
dup duplicate an open file	descriptor .... dup(2)
dup2 duplicate an open file	descriptor .... dup2(3C)
elf_begin make a file	descriptor .... elf_begin(3E)
elf_cntl control a file	descriptor .... elf_cntl(3E)
elf_update update an	descriptor .... elf_update(3E)
sigaction	detailed signal management .... sigaction(2)
access	determine accessibility of a file .... access(2)
elf_kind	determine file type .... elf_kind(3E)
mincore	determine residency of memory pages .... mincore(2)
/isnanf, finite, fpclass, unordered	determine type of floating-point/ .... isnan(3C)

Permuted Index

buffer is encrypted isencrypt	determine whether a character .... isencrypt(3G)
ioctl control	device .... ioctl(2)
makedev, major, minor manage a	device number .... makedev(3C)
dlerror get	diagnostic information .... dlerror(3X)
times difftime computes the	difference between two calendar .... difftime(3C)
between two calendar times	difftime computes the difference .... difftime(3C)
mkdirp, rmdirp create, remove	directories in a path .... mkdirp(3G)
search for named file in named	directories pathfind .... pathfind(3G)
chdir, fchdir change working	directory .... chdir(2)
chroot change root	directory .... chroot(2)
system independent/ getdents read	directory entries and put in a file .... getdents(2)
unlink remove	directory entry .... unlink(2)
get pathname of current working	directory getcwd .... getcwd(3C)
mkdir make a	directory .... mkdir(2)
dirname report the parent	directory name of a file path name .... dirname(3G)
telldir, seekdir, rewinddir,/	directory: opendir, readdir, ... directory(3C)
seekdir, rewinddir, closedir	directory operations /telldir, ... directory(3C)
file mknod make a	directory, or a special or ordinary .... mknod(2)
rmdir remove a	directory .... rmdir(2)
name of a file path name	dirname report the parent directory .... dirname(3G)
	dis object code disassembler .... dis(1)
acct enable or	disable process accounting .... acct(2)
dis object code	disassembler .... dis(1)
system console fmtmsg	display a message on stderr or .... fmtmsg(3C)
count profile data lprof	display line-by-line execution .... lprof(1)
prof	display profile data .... prof(1)
hypot Euclidean	distance function .... hypot(3M)
/seed48, lcong48 generate uniformly	distributed pseudo-random numbers .... drand48(3C)
remainder	div, ldiv compute the quotient and .... div(3C)
	dlclose close a shared object .... dlclose(3X)
	dlerror get diagnostic information .... dlerror(3X)
	dlopen open a shared object .... dlopen(3X)
in shared object	dlsym get the address of a symbol .... dlsym(3X)
strtod, atof, convert string to	double-precision number .... strtod(3C)
mrand48, jrand48, srand48, seed48,/	drand48, erand48, lrand48, nrand48, ... drand48(3C)
channels protocol used by xt	driver xtproto multiplexed .... xtproto(5)
object file	dump dump selected parts of an .... dump(1)
file dump	dump selected parts of an object .... dump(1)
descriptor	dup duplicate an open file .... dup(2)
descriptor	dup2 duplicate an open file .... dup2(3C)
dup	duplicate an open file descriptor .... dup(2)
dup2	duplicate an open file descriptor .... dup2(3C)
ldd list	dynamic dependencies .... ldd(1)
floating-point number to string	ecvt, fcvt, gcvt convert .... ecvt(3C)
end, etext,	edata last locations in program .... end(3C)
sact print current SCCS file	editing activity .... sact(1)
ld link	editor for object files .... ld(1)

Programmer's Reference Manual

Permuted Index

effective user, real group, and	effective group IDs /get real user,	getuid(2)
/getgid, getegid get real user,	effective user, real group, and/	getuid(2)
new process in a virtual memory	efficient way vfork spawn	vfork(2)
insque, remque insert/remove	element from a queue	insque(3C)
basename return the last	element of a path name	basename(3G)
files a.out	ELF (Executable and Linking Format)	a.out(4)
	elf object file access library	elf(3E)
cof2elf COFF to	ELF object file translation	cof2elf(1)
object file type elf_fsize:	elf32_fsize return the size of an	elf_fsize(3E)
retrieve/ elf_getehdr:	elf32_getehdr, elf32_newehdr	elf_getehdr(3E)
retrieve/ elf_getphdr:	elf32_getphdr, elf32_newphdr	elf_getphdr(3E)
class-dependent/ elf_getshdr:	elf32_getshdr retrieve	elf_getshdr(3E)
elf_getehdr: elf32_getehdr,	elf32_newehdr retrieve/	elf_getehdr(3E)
elf_getphdr: elf32_getphdr,	elf32_newphdr retrieve/	elf_getphdr(3E)
class-dependent data/ elf_xlate:	elf32_xlatetof, elf32_xlatetom	elf_xlate(3E)
elf_xlate: elf32_xlatetof,	elf32_xlatetom class-dependent data/	elf_xlate(3E)
	elf_begin make a file descriptor	elf_begin(3E)
	elf_cntl control a file descriptor	elf_cntl(3E)
	elf_end finish using an object file	elf_end(3E)
handling	elf_errmsg, elf_errno error	elf_errmsg(3E)
elf_errmsg,	elf_errno error handling	elf_errmsg(3E)
	elf_fill set fill byte	elf_fill(3E)
elf_flagelf, elf_flagphdr,/	elf_flagdata, elf_flagehdr,	elf_flagdata(3E)
elf_flagphdr,/ elf_flagdata,	elf_flagehdr, elf_flagelf,	elf_flagdata(3E)
elf_flagdata, elf_flagehdr,	elf_flagelf, elf_flagphdr,/	elf_flagdata(3E)
/elf_flagehdr, elf_flagelf,	elf_flagphdr, elf_flagscn,/	elf_flagdata(3E)
/elf_flagelf, elf_flagphdr,	elf_flagscn, elf_flagshdr/	elf_flagdata(3E)
/elf_flagphdr, elf_flagscn,	elf_flagshdr manipulate flags	elf_flagdata(3E)
size of an object file type	elf_fsize: elf32_fsize return the	elf_fsize(3E)
member header	elf_getarhdr retrieve archive	elf_getarhdr(3E)
symbol table	elf_getarsym retrieve archive	elf_getarsym(3E)
an object file	elf_getbase get the base offset for	elf_getbase(3E)
elf_rawdata get section data	elf_getdata, elf_newdata,	elf_getdata(3E)
elf32_newehdr retrieve/	elf_getehdr: elf32_getehdr,	elf_getehdr(3E)
identification data	elf_getident retrieve file	elf_getident(3E)
elf32_newphdr retrieve/	elf_getphdr: elf32_getphdr,	elf_getphdr(3E)
elf_nextscn get section/	elf_getscn, elf_ndxscn, elf_newscn,	elf_getscn(3E)
class-dependent section header	elf_getshdr: elf32_getshdr retrieve	elf_getshdr(3E)
	elf_hash compute hash value	elf_hash(3E)
	elf_kind determine file type	elf_kind(3E)
get section/ elf_getscn,	elf_ndxscn, elf_newscn, elf_nextscn	elf_getscn(3E)
section data elf_getdata,	elf_newdata, elf_rawdata get	elf_getdata(3E)
elf_getscn, elf_ndxscn,	elf_newscn, elf_nextscn get section/	elf_getscn(3E)
access	elf_next sequential archive member	elf_next(3E)
elf_getscn, elf_ndxscn, elf_newscn,	elf_nextscn get section information	elf_getscn(3E)
access	elf_rand random archive member	elf_rand(3E)
elf_getdata, elf_newdata,	elf_rawdata get section data	elf_getdata(3E)

Permuted Index

file contents	elf_rawfile retrieve uninterpreted	elf_rawfile(3E)
	elf_strptr make a string pointer	elf_strptr(3E)
	elf_update update an descriptor	elf_update(3E)
application versions	elf_version coordinate library and	elf_version(3E)
elf32_xlatetom class-dependent/	elf_xlate: elf32_xlatetof,	elf_xlate(3E)
x286emul	emulate XENIX 80286	x286emul(1)
accounting acct	enable or disable process	acct(2)
crypt, setkey,	encrypt generate encryption	crypt(3C)
whether a character buffer is	encrypted isencrypt determine	isencrypt(3G)
crypt, setkey, encrypt generate	encryption	crypt(3C)
crypt password and file	encryption functions	crypt(3X)
program	end, etext, edata last locations in	end(3C)
/getgrgid, getgrnam, setgrent,	endgrent, fgetgrent get group file/	getgrent(3C)
/getpwuid, getpwnam, setpwent,	endpwent, fgetpwent manipulate/	getpwent(3C)
getspent, getspnam, setspent,	endspent, fgetspent, lckpwdf,/	getspent(3C)
/getutline, pututline, setutent,	endutent, utmpname access utmp file/	getut(3C)
/getutxline, pututxline, setutxent,	endutxent, utmpxname, getutmp,/	getutx(3C)
getdents read directory	entries and put in a file system/	getdents(2)
nlist get	entries from name list	nlist(3E)
utmp, wtmp utmp and wtmp	entry formats	utmp(4)
utmpx, wtmpx utmpx and wtmpx	entry formats	utmpx(4)
endgrent, fgetgrent get group file	entry /getgrnam, setgrent,	getgrent(3C)
getmntany get mnttab file	entry getmntent,	getmntent(3C)
fgetpwent manipulate password file	entry /setpwent, endpwent,	getpwent(3C)
manipulate shadow password file	entry /fgetspent, lckpwdf, ulckpwdf	getspent(3C)
endutent, utmpname access utmp file	entry /pututline, setutent,	getut(3C)
updwtmp, updwtmpx access utmpx file	entry /getutmp, getutmpx,	getutx(3C)
getvfsany get vfstab file	entry /getvfsfile, getvfsspec,	getvfsent(3C)
putpwent write password file	entry	putpwent(3C)
putspent write shadow password file	entry	putspent(3C)
unlink remove directory	entry	unlink(2)
	environ user environment	environ(5)
fpsetsticky IEEE floating-point	environment control /fpgetsticky,	fpgetround(3C)
environ user	environment	environ(5)
getenv return value for	environment name	getenv(3C)
putenv change or add value to	environment	putenv(3C)
jrand48, srand48, seed48,/ drand48,	erand48, lrand48, nrand48, mrand48,	drand48(3C)
complementary error function	erf, erfc error function and	erf(3M)
complementary error function erf,	erfc error function and	erf(3M)
error function erf, erfc	error function and complementary	erf(3M)
error function and complementary	error function erf, erfc	erf(3M)
elf_errmsg, elf_errno	error handling	elf_errmsg(3E)
strerror get	error message string	strerror(3C)
perror print system	error messages	perror(3C)
introduction to system calls and	error numbers intro	intro(2)
matherr	error-handling function	matherr(3M)
strings, compressing or expanding	escape codes /strcadd, strecpy copy	strccpy(3G)

10 Programmer's Reference Manual

Permuted Index

program end,	etext, edata last locations in	end(3C)
hypot	Euclidean distance function	hypot(3M)
cscope interactively	examine a C program	cscope(1)
sigprocmask change or	examine signal mask	sigprocmask(2)
and pending sigpending	examine signals that are blocked	sigpending(2)
execlp, execvp execute a file	exec: execl, execv, execle, execve,	exec(2)
execlp, execvp execute a/ exec:	execl, execv, execle, execve,	exec(2)
execute a file exec: execl, execv,	execle, execve, execlp, execvp	exec(2)
exec: execl, execv, execle, execve,	execlp, execvp execute a file	exec(2)
files a.out ELF	(Executable and Linking Format)	a.out(4)
execle, execve, execlp, execvp	execute a file exec: execl, execv,	exec(2)
regcmp, regex compile and	execute regular expression	regcmp(3G)
lprof display line-by-line	execution count profile data	lprof(1)
sleep suspend	execution for interval	sleep(3C)
monitor prepare	execution profile	monitor(3C)
profil	execution time profile	profil(2)
execvp execute a file exec: execl,	execv, execle, execve, execlp,	exec(2)
file exec: execl, execv, execle,	execve, execlp, execvp execute a	exec(2)
execv, execle, execve, execlp,	execvp execute a file exec: execl,	exec(2)
create a new file or rewrite an	existing one creat	creat(2)
exit,	exit, _exit terminate process	exit(2)
exit,	_exit terminate process	exit(2)
log10f, pow, powf, sqrt, sqrtf/	exp, expf, cbrt, log, logf, log10,	exp(3M)
copy strings, compressing or	expanding escape codes /strccpy	strccpy(3G)
log10f, pow, powf, sqrt,/ exp,	expf, cbrt, log, logf, log10,	exp(3M)
/log10f, pow, powf, sqrt, sqrtf	exponential, logarithm, power,/	exp(3M)
/compile, step, advance regular	expression compile and match/	regexp(5)
/compile, step, advance regular	expression compile and match/	regexpr(3G)
regcmp regular	expression compile	regcmp(1)
regex compile and execute regular	expression regcmp,	regcmp(3G)
/ceil, ceilf, copysign, fmod, fmodf,	fabs, fabsf, rint, remainder floor,/	floor(3M)
/ceilf, copysign, fmod, fmodf, fabs,	fabsf, rint, remainder floor,/	floor(3M)
data in a machine-independent	fashion /sgetl access long integer	sputl(3X)
chdir,	fchdir change working directory	chdir(2)
chmod,	fchmod change mode of file	chmod(2)
file chown, lchown,	fchown change owner and group of a	chown(2)
stream	fclose, fflush close or flush a	fclose(3S)
	fcntl file control	fcntl(2)
	fcntl file control options	fcntl(5)
number to string ecvt,	fcvt, gcvt convert floating-point	ecvt(3C)
fopen, freopen,	fdopen open a stream	fopen(3S)
status inquiries ferror,	feof, clearerr, fileno stream	ferror(3S)
stream status inquiries	ferror, feof, clearerr, fileno	ferror(3S)
fclose,	fflush close or flush a stream	fclose(3S)
	ffs find first set bit	ffs(3C)
from a stream getc, getchar,	fgetc, getw get character or word	getc(3S)
/getgrnam, setgrent, endgrent,	fgetgrent get group file entry	getgrent(3C)

Permuted Index

in a stream fsetpos,	fgetpos reposition a file pointer .... fsetpos(3C)
/getpwnam, setpwent, endpwent,	fgetpwent manipulate password file/ .... getpwent(3C)
gets,	fgets get a string from a stream .... gets(3S)
/getspnam, setspent, endspent,	fgetspent, lckpwdf, ulckpwdf/ .... getspent(3C)
bufsplit split buffer into	fields .... bufsplit(3G)
mkfifo create a new	FIFO .... mkfifo(3C)
utime set	file access and modification times .... utime(2)
elf object	file access library .... elf(3E)
access determine accessibility of a	file .... access(2)
chmod, fchmod change mode of	file .... chmod(2)
fchown change owner and group of a	file chown, lchown, ... chown(2)
elf_rawfile retrieve uninterpreted	file contents .... elf_rawfile(3E)
fcntl	file control .... fcntl(2)
fcntl	file control options .... fcntl(5)
core core image	file .... core(4)
umask set and get	file creation mask .... umask(2)
make a delta (change) to an SCCS	file delta .... delta(1)
close close a	file descriptor .... close(2)
dup duplicate an open	file descriptor .... dup(2)
dup2 duplicate an open	file descriptor .... dup2(3C)
elf_begin make a	file descriptor .... elf_begin(3E)
elf_cntl control a	file descriptor .... elf_cntl(3E)
dump selected parts of an object	file dump .... dump(1)
sact print current SCCS	file editing activity .... sact(1)
elf_end finish using an object	file .... elf_end(3E)
get the base offset for an object	file elf_getbase .... elf_getbase(3E)
crypt password and	file encryption functions .... crypt(3X)
endgrent, fgetgrent get group	file entry /getgrnam, setgrent, ... getgrent(3C)
getmntent, getmntany get mnttab	file entry .... getmntent(3C)
fgetpwent manipulate password	file entry /setpwent, endpwent, ... getpwent(3C)
ulckpwdf manipulate shadow password	file entry /fgetspent, lckpwdf, ... getspent(3C)
endutent, utmpname access utmp	file entry /pututline, setutent, ... getut(3C)
updwtmp, updwtmpx access utmpx	file entry /getutmp, getutmpx, ... getutx(3C)
getvfsspec, getvfsany get vfstab	file entry getvfsent, getvfsfile, ... getvfsent(3C)
putpwent write password	file entry .... putpwent(3C)
putspent write shadow password	file entry .... putspent(3C)
execve, execlp, execvp execute a	file exec: execl, execv, execle, ... exec(2)
constants limits header	file for implementation-specific .... limits(4)
ar archive	file format .... ar(4)
intro introduction to	file formats .... intro(4)
get get a version of an SCCS	file .... get(1)
retrieve class-dependent object	file header /elf32_newehdr .... elf_getehdr(3E)
elf_getident retrieve	file identification data .... elf_getident(3E)
pathfind search for named	file in named directories .... pathfind(3G)
copylist copy a	file into memory .... copylist(3G)
link link to a	file .... link(2)
the comment section of an object	file mcs manipulate .... mcs(1)

Programmer's Reference Manual

Permuted Index

directory, or a special or ordinary	file mknod make a	mknod(2)
ctermid generate	file name for terminal	ctermid(3S)
mktemp make a unique	file name	mktemp(3C)
realpath returns the real	file name	realpath(3C)
nm print name list of an object	file	nm(1)
ttyslot find the slot in the utmp	file of the current user	ttyslot(3C)
creat create a new	file or rewrite an existing one	creat(2)
the parent directory name of a	file path name dirname report	dirname(3G)
fseek, rewind, ftell reposition a	file pointer in a stream	fseek(3S)
fsetpos, fgetpos reposition a	file pointer in a stream	fsetpos(3C)
lseek move read/write	file pointer	lseek(2)
prs print an SCCS	file	prs(1)
read read from	file	read(2)
remove remove	file	remove(3C)
rename change the name of a	file	rename(2)
rmdel remove a delta from an SCCS	file	rmdel(1)
compare two versions of an SCCS	file sccsdiff	sccsdiff(1)
sccsfile format of SCCS	file	sccsfile(4)
stat, lstat, fstat get	file status	stat(2)
number information from an object	file /table, debugging and line	strip(1)
symlink make a symbolic link to a	file	symlink(2)
/read directory entries and put in a	file system independent format	getdents(2)
statvfs, fstatvfs get	file system information	statvfs(2)
mount mount a	file system	mount(2)
ustat get	file system statistics	ustat(2)
sysfs get	file system type information	sysfs(2)
umount unmount a	file system	umount(2)
tmpfile create a temporary	file	tmpfile(3S)
create a name for a temporary	file tmpnam, tempnam	tmpnam(3S)
truncate, ftruncate set a	file to a specified length	truncate(3C)
cof2elf COFF to ELF object	file translation	cof2elf(1)
ftw, nftw walk a	file tree	ftw(3C)
return the size of an object	file type elf_fsize: elf32_fsize	elf_fsize(3E)
elf_kind determine	file type	elf_kind(3E)
undo a previous get of an SCCS	file unget	unget(1)
val validate an SCCS	file	val(1)
write, writev write on a	file	write(2)
ferror, feof, clearerr,	fileno stream status inquiries	ferror(3S)
admin create and administer SCCS	files	admin(1)
ELF (Executable and Linking Format)	files a.out	a.out(4)
the physical/ fsync synchronize a	file's in-memory state with that on	fsync(2)
ld link editor for object	files	ld(1)
lockf record locking on	files	lockf(3C)
section sizes in bytes of object	files size print	size(1)
convert convert archive	files to common formats	convert(1)
elf_fill set	fill byte	elf_fill(3E)
ffs	find first set bit	ffs(3C)

Permuted Index

ttyname, isatty	find name of a terminal	ttyname(3C)
object library lorder	find ordering relation for an	lorder(1)
the current user ttyslot	find the slot in the utmp file of	ttyslot(3C)
elf_end	finish using an object file	elf_end(3E)
determine/ isnan, isnand, isnanf,	finite, fpclass, unordered	isnan(3C)
elf_flagshdr manipulate	flags /elf_flagphdr, elf_flagscn,	elf_flagdata(3E)
/fpgetsticky, fpsetsticky IEEE	floating-point environment control	fpgetround(3C)
unordered determine type of	floating-point number /fpclass,	isnan(3C)
ecvt, fcvt, gcvt convert	floating-point number to string	ecvt(3C)
scalb manipulate parts of	floating-point numbers /nextafter,	frexp(3C)
/fmodf, fabs, fabsf, rint, remainder	floor, ceiling, remainder, absolute/	floor(3M)
copysign, fmod, fmodf, fabs,/	floor, floorf, ceil, ceilf,	floor(3M)
fmod, fmodf, fabs, fabsf,/ floor,	floorf, ceil, ceilf, copysign,	floor(3M)
cflow generate C	flowgraph	cflow(1)
fclose, fflush close or	flush a stream	fclose(3S)
/floorf, ceil, ceilf, copysign,	fmod, fmodf, fabs, fabsf, rint,/	floor(3M)
/ceil, ceilf, copysign, fmod,	fmodf, fabs, fabsf, rint, remainder/	floor(3M)
for an application for use with	fmtmsg /a list of severity levels	addseverity(3C)
or system console	fmtmsg display a message on stderr	fmtmsg(3C)
stream	fopen, freopen, fdopen open a	fopen(3S)
tcsetpgrp set terminal	foreground process group id	tcsetpgrp(3C)
	fork create a new process	fork(2)
ar archive file	format	ar(4)
getdate convert user	format date and time	getdate(3C)
a.out ELF (Executable and Linking	Format) files	a.out(4)
put in a file system independent	format /read directory entries and	getdents(2)
sccsfile	format of SCCS file	sccsfile(4)
convert archive files to common	formats convert	convert(1)
intro introduction to file	formats	intro(4)
utmp, wtmp utmp and wtmp entry	formats	utmp(4)
utmpx, wtmpx utmpx and wtmpx entry	formats	utmpx(4)
scanf, fscanf, sscanf convert	formatted input	scanf(3S)
vprintf, vfprintf, vsprintf print	formatted output of a variable/	vprintf(3S)
printf, fprintf, sprintf print	formatted output	printf(3S)
localeconv get numeric	formatting information	localeconv(3C)
configurable pathname variables	fpathconf, pathconf get	fpathconf(2)
of/ isnan, isnand, isnanf, finite,	fpclass, unordered determine type	isnan(3C)
fpgetround, fpsetround,	fpgetmask, fpsetmask, fpgetsticky,/	fpgetround(3C)
fpsetmask, fpgetsticky,/	fpgetround, fpsetround, fpgetmask,	fpgetround(3C)
/fpsetround, fpgetmask, fpsetmask,	fpgetsticky, fpsetsticky IEEE/	fpgetround(3C)
output printf,	fprintf, sprintf print formatted	printf(3S)
fpgetround, fpsetround, fpgetmask,	fpsetmask, fpgetsticky, fpsetsticky/	fpgetround(3C)
fpgetsticky,/ fpgetround,	fpsetround, fpgetmask, fpsetmask,	fpgetround(3C)
/fpgetmask, fpsetmask, fpgetsticky,	fpsetsticky IEEE floating-point/	fpgetround(3C)
on a stream putc, putchar,	fputc, putw put character or word	putc(3S)
puts,	fputs put a string on a stream	puts(3S)
	fread, fwrite binary input/output	fread(3S)

Permuted Index

mallinfo memory allocator malloc,	free, realloc, calloc, mallopt, ... malloc(3X)
valloc, memory allocator malloc,	free, realloc, calloc, memalign, ... malloc(3C)
fopen,	freopen, fdopen open a stream .... fopen(3S)
nextafter, scalb manipulate parts/	frexp, ldexp, logb, modf, modff, ... frexp(3C)
input scanf,	fscanf, sscanf convert formatted .... scanf(3S)
file pointer in a stream	fseek, rewind, ftell reposition a .... fseek(3S)
pointer in a stream	fsetpos, fgetpos reposition a file .... fsetpos(3C)
stat, lstat,	fstat get file status .... stat(2)
information statvfs,	fstatvfs get file system .... statvfs(2)
in-memory state with that on the/	fsync synchronize a file's .... fsync(2)
a stream fseek, rewind,	ftell reposition a file pointer in .... fseek(3S)
communication package stdipc:	ftok standard interprocess .... stdipc(3C)
length truncate,	ftruncate set a file to a specified .... truncate(3C)
	ftw, nftw walk a file tree .... ftw(3C)
function erf, erfc error	function and complementary error .... erf(3M)
function and complementary error	function erf, erfc error .... erf(3M)
gamma, lgamma log gamma	function .... gamma(3M)
hypot Euclidean distance	function .... hypot(3M)
libwindows windowing terminal	function library .... libwindows(3X)
matherr error-handling	function .... matherr(3M)
prof profile within a	function .... prof(5)
math math	functions and constants .... math(5)
intro introduction to	functions and libraries .... intro(3)
j0, j1, jn, y0, y1, yn Bessel	functions bessel: .... bessel(3M)
crypt password and file encryption	functions .... crypt(3X)
logarithm, power, square root	functions /sqrt, sqrtf exponential, ... exp(3M)
ceiling, remainder, absolute value	functions /rint, remainder floor, ... floor(3M)
mbstowcs, wcstombs multibyte string	functions mbstring: .... mbstring(3C)
asinh, acosh, atanh hyperbolic	functions /coshf, tanh, tanhf, ... sinh(3M)
sysi86 machine specific	functions .... sysi86(2)
atanf, atan2, atan2f trigonometric	functions /acos, acosf, atan, ... trig(3M)
fread,	fwrite binary input/output .... fread(3S)
gamma, lgamma log	gamma function .... gamma(3M)
	gamma, lgamma log gamma function .... gamma(3M)
to string ecvt, fcvt,	gcvt convert floating-point number .... ecvt(3C)
/tcgetpgrp, tcsetpgrp, tcgetsid	general terminal interface .... termios(2)
control priocntlset	generalized process scheduler .... priocntlset(2)
signal abort	generate an abnormal termination .... abort(3C)
cflow	generate C flowgraph .... cflow(1)
cxref	generate C program cross-reference .... cxref(1)
crypt, setkey, encrypt	generate encryption .... crypt(3C)
ctermid	generate file name for terminal .... ctermid(3S)
lexical tasks lex	generate programs for simple .... lex(1)
/jrand48, srand48, seed48, lcong48	generate uniformly distributed/ .... drand48(3C)
siginfo signal	generation information .... siginfo(5)
rand, srand simple random-number	generator .... rand(3C)
character or word from a stream	getc, getchar, fgetc, getw get .... getc(3S)

Permuted Index

or word from a stream getc,	getchar, fgetc, getw get character	getc(3S)
current user context	getcontext, setcontext get and set	getcontext(2)
working directory	getcwd get pathname of current	getcwd(3C)
and time	getdate convert user format date	getdate(3C)
put in a file system independent/	getdents read directory entries and	getdents(2)
user,/ getuid, geteuid, getgid,	getegid get real user, effective	getuid(2)
name	getenv return value for environment	getenv(3C)
user, effective user, real/ getuid,	geteuid, getgid, getegid get real	getuid(2)
effective user,/ getuid, geteuid,	getgid, getegid get real user,	getuid(2)
setgrent, endgrent, fgetgrent get/	getgrent, getgrgid, getgrnam,	getgrent(3C)
endgrent, fgetgrent get/ getgrent,	getgrgid, getgrnam, setgrent,	getgrent(3C)
fgetgrent get/ getgrent, getgrgid,	getgrnam, setgrent, endgrent,	getgrent(3C)
supplementary group access list/	getgroups, setgroups get or set	getgroups(2)
of interval timer	getitimer, setitimer get/set value	getitimer(3C)
	getlogin get login name	getlogin(3C)
getmntent,	getmntany get mnttab file entry	getmntent(3C)
file entry	getmntent, getmntany get mnttab	getmntent(3C)
stream	getmsg get next message off a	getmsg(2)
argument vector	getopt get option letter from	getopt(3C)
	getpass read a password	getpass(3C)
and/ getpid, getpgrp, getppid,	getpgid get process, process group,	getpid(2)
process, process group,/ getpid,	getpgrp, getppid, getpgid get	getpid(2)
get process, process group, and/	getpid, getpgrp, getppid, getpgid	getpid(2)
process group,/ getpid, getpgrp,	getppid, getpgid get process,	getpid(2)
	getpw get name from UID	getpw(3C)
setpwent, endpwent, fgetpwent/	getpwent, getpwuid, getpwnam,	getpwent(3C)
fgetpwent/ getpwent, getpwuid,	getpwnam, setpwent, endpwent,	getpwent(3C)
endpwent, fgetpwent/ getpwent,	getpwuid, getpwnam, setpwent,	getpwent(3C)
maximum system resource/	getrlimit, setrlimit control	getrlimit(2)
stream	gets, fgets get a string from a	gets(3S)
getitimer, setitimer	get/set value of interval timer	getitimer(3C)
	getsid get session ID	getsid(2)
endspent, fgetspent, lckpwdf,/	getspent, getspnam, setspent,	getspent(3C)
fgetspent, lckpwdf,/ getspent,	getspnam, setspent, endspent,	getspent(3C)
string	getsubopt parse suboptions from a	getsubopt(3C)
set the date and time	gettimeofday, settimeofday get or	gettimeofday(3C)
	gettxt retrieve a text string	gettxt(3C)
get real user, effective user,/	getuid, geteuid, getgid, getegid	getuid(2)
getutline, pututline, setutent,/	getut: getutent, getutid,	getut(3C)
pututline, setutent,/ getut:	getutent, getutid, getutline,	getut(3C)
setutent,/ getut: getutent,	getutid, getutline, pututline,	getut(3C)
getut: getutent, getutid,	getutline, pututline, setutent,/	getut(3C)
/setutxent, endutxent, utmpxname,	getutmp, getutmpx, updwtmp,/	getutx(3C)
/endutxent, utmpxname, getutmp,	getutmpx, updwtmp, updwtmpx access/	getutx(3C)
getutxline, pututxline, setutxent,/	getutx: getutxent, getutxid,	getutx(3C)
pututxline, setutxent,/ getutx:	getutxent, getutxid, getutxline,	getutx(3C)
setutxent,/ getutx: getutxent,	getutxid, getutxline, pututxline,	getutx(3C)

Permuted Index

```
              getutx: getutxent, getutxid,    getutxline, pututxline, setutxent,/ ................................. getutx(3C)
        getvfsent, getvfsfile, getvfsspec,    getvfsany get vfstab file entry ..................................... getvfsent(3C)
         getvfsany get vfstab file entry     getvfsent, getvfsfile, getvfsspec, ................................. getvfsent(3C)
            get vfstab file entry  getvfsent,  getvfsfile, getvfsspec, getvfsany .................................. getvfsent(3C)
           file entry  getvfsent, getvfsfile,  getvfsspec, getvfsany get vfstab ................................. getvfsent(3C)
               stream  getc, getchar, fgetc,  getw get character or word from a ....................................... getc(3S)
                         gmatch shell         global pattern matching ............................................... gmatch(3G)
                              matching        gmatch shell global pattern ......................................... gmatch(3G)
              and time to/  ctime, localtime, gmtime, asctime, tzset convert date ................................. ctime(3C)
                  setjmp, longjmp non-local   goto ................................................................. setjmp(3C)
         sigsetjmp, siglongjmp a non-local    goto with signal state ............................................ sigsetjmp(3C)
          setgroups get or set supplementary  group access list IDs  getgroups, ................................ getgroups(2)
                 initialize the supplementary group access list  initgroups ......................................... initgroups(3C)
                /get real user, effective user, real group, and effective group IDs ................................. getuid(2)
                 /getpgid get process, process group, and parent process IDs ........................................ getpid(2)
            setgrent, endgrent, fgetgrent get group file entry  /getgrnam, ........................................ getgrent(3C)
                        setpgid set process   group ID ............................................................ setpgid(2)
                        setpgrp set process   group ID ............................................................ setpgrp(2)
              set terminal foreground process group id  tcsetpgrp ................................................. tcsetpgrp(3C)
              user, real group, and effective group IDs  /get real user, effective ..................................... getuid(2)
                       setuid, setgid set user and group IDs ...................................................... setuid(2)
            lchown, fchown change owner and   group of a file  chown, ............................................. chown(2)
              send a signal to a process or a group of processes  kill ........................................... kill(2)
              send a signal to a process or a group of processes  /sigsendset .................................... sigsend(2)
          maintain, update, and regenerate    groups of programs  make .............................................. make(1)
                                      ssignal, gsignal software signals .................................................. ssignal(3C)
                                      stdarg  handle variable argument list ............................................. stdarg(5)
                                     varargs  handle variable argument list ............................................ varargs(5)
            isprint, isgraph, isascii character handling  /iscntrl, ispunct, ........................................ ctype(3C)
                 elf_errmsg, elf_errno error  handling ............................................................ elf_errmsg(3E)
             mblen, wctomb multibyte character handling  mbchar: mbtowc, ............................................ mbchar(3C)
               hsearch, hcreate, hdestroy manage hash search tables ................................................ hsearch(3C)
                       elf_hash compute       hash value ........................................................ elf_hash(3E)
                     search tables  hsearch,  hcreate, hdestroy manage hash ...................................... hsearch(3C)
                          hsearch, hcreate,   hdestroy manage hash search tables ................................ hsearch(3C)
                    retrieve archive member   header  elf_getarhdr ................................................ elf_getarhdr(3E)
               class-dependent object file    header  /elf32_newehdr retrieve .......................... elf_getehdr(3E)
          retrieve class-dependent section    header  elf_getshdr: elf32_getshdr .................................... elf_getshdr(3E)
            implementation-specific/  limits  header file for ...................................................... limits(4)
          retrieve class-dependent program    header table  /elf32_newphdr ......................................... elf_getphdr(3E)
           numbers or SCCS commands           help ask for help with message ...................................... help(1)
                       commands  help ask for  help with message numbers or SCCS ................................... help(1)
              layers protocol used between    host and windowing terminal under/ ............................... layers(5)
                                       jagent host control of windowing terminal ................................. jagent(5)
                      hash search tables      hsearch, hcreate, hdestroy manage ................................... hsearch(3C)
              tanhf, asinh, acosh, atanh      hyperbolic functions  /tanh, ........................................ sinh(3M)
                                              hypot Euclidean distance function ................................... hypot(3M)
```

Permuted Index 17

Permuted Index

getsid get session	ID .... getsid(2)
setpgid set process group	ID .... setpgid(2)
setpgrp set process group	ID .... setpgrp(2)
setsid set session	ID .... setsid(2)
terminal foreground process group	id tcsetpgrp set .... tcsetpgrp(3C)
elf_getident retrieve file	identification data .... elf_getident(3E)
what print	identification strings .... what(1)
shmget get shared memory segment	identifier .... shmget(2)
set supplementary group access list	IDs getgroups, setgroups get or .... getgroups(2)
process group, and parent process	IDs /getppid, getpgid get process, ... getpid(2)
real group, and effective group	IDs /get real user, effective user, ... getuid(2)
setuid, setgid set user and group	IDs .... setuid(2)
/fpsetmask, fpgetsticky, fpsetsticky	IEEE floating-point environment/ .... fpgetround(3C)
core core	image file .... core(4)
limits header file for	implementation-specific constants .... limits(4)
entries and put in a file system	independent format /read directory .... getdents(2)
langinfo language	information constants .... langinfo(5)
dlerror get diagnostic	information .... dlerror(3X)
elf_newscn, elf_nextscn get section	information /elf_ndxscn, ... elf_getscn(3E)
/table, debugging and line number	information from an object file .... strip(1)
localeconv get numeric formatting	information .... localeconv(3C)
nl_langinfo language	information .... nl_langinfo(3C)
siginfo signal generation	information .... siginfo(5)
statvfs, fstatvfs get file system	information .... statvfs(2)
sysinfo get and set system	information strings .... sysinfo(2)
sysfs get file system type	information .... sysfs(2)
supplementary group access list	initgroups initialize the .... initgroups(3C)
access list initgroups	initialize the supplementary group .... initgroups(3C)
popen, pclose	initiate pipe to/from a process .... popen(3S)
fsync synchronize a file's	in-memory state with that on the/ .... fsync(2)
fscanf, sscanf convert formatted	input scanf, ... scanf(3S)
ungetc push character back onto	input stream .... ungetc(3S)
fread, fwrite binary	input/output .... fread(3S)
poll	input/output multiplexing .... poll(2)
stdio standard buffered	input/output package .... stdio(3S)
clearerr, fileno stream status	inquiries ferror, feof, ... ferror(3S)
insque, remque	insert/remove element from a queue .... insque(3C)
element from a queue	insque, remque insert/remove .... insque(3C)
process until signal sigsuspend	install a signal mask and suspend .... sigsuspend(2)
install	install commands .... install(1M)
	install install commands .... install(1M)
abs, labs return	integer absolute value .... abs(3C)
a64l, l64a convert between long	integer and base-64 ASCII string .... a64l(3C)
sputl, sgetl access long	integer data in a/ .... sputl(3X)
atol, atoi convert string to	integer strtol, strtoul, ... strtol(3C)
l3tol, ltol3 convert between 3-byte	integers and long integers .... l3tol(3C)
between 3-byte integers and long	integers l3tol, ltol3 convert .... l3tol(3C)

Permuted Index

cscope	interactively examine a C program	cscope(1)
tcgetsid general terminal	interface /tcgetpgrp, tcsetpgrp,	termios(2)
pipe create an	interprocess channel	pipe(2)
stdipc: ftok standard	interprocess communication package	stdipc(3C)
sleep suspend execution for	interval	sleep(3C)
setitimer get/set value of	interval timer getitimer,	getitimer(3C)
	intro introduction to file formats	intro(4)
libraries	intro introduction to functions and	intro(3)
libraries	intro introduction to math	intro(3M)
	intro introduction to miscellany	intro(5)
commands	intro introduction to programming	intro(1)
and error numbers	intro introduction to system calls	intro(2)
intro	introduction to file formats	intro(4)
libraries intro	introduction to functions and	intro(3)
intro	introduction to math libraries	intro(3M)
intro	introduction to miscellany	intro(5)
commands intro	introduction to programming	intro(1)
error numbers intro	introduction to system calls and	intro(2)
	ioctl control device	ioctl(2)
/islower, isupper, isalpha,	isalnum, isspace, iscntrl, ispunct,/	ctype(3C)
/isxdigit, islower, isupper,	isalpha, isalnum, isspace, iscntrl,/	ctype(3C)
/iscntrl, ispunct, isprint, isgraph,	isascii character handling	ctype(3C)
ttyname,	isatty find name of a terminal	ttyname(3C)
/isupper, isalpha, isalnum, isspace,	iscntrl, ispunct, isprint, isgraph,/	ctype(3C)
isupper, isalpha, isalnum,/ ctype:	isdigit, isxdigit, islower,	ctype(3C)
character buffer is encrypted	isencrypt determine whether a	isencrypt(3G)
/isspace, iscntrl, ispunct, isprint,	isgraph, isascii character handling	ctype(3C)
isspace,/ ctype: isdigit, isxdigit,	islower, isupper, isalpha, isalnum,	ctype(3C)
fpclass, unordered determine type/	isnan, isnand, isnanf, finite,	isnan(3C)
unordered determine type of/ isnan,	isnand, isnanf, finite, fpclass,	isnan(3C)
determine type of/ isnan, isnand,	isnanf, finite, fpclass, unordered	isnan(3C)
/isalnum, isspace, iscntrl, ispunct,	isprint, isgraph, isascii character/	ctype(3C)
/isalpha, isalnum, isspace, iscntrl,	ispunct, isprint, isgraph, isascii/	ctype(3C)
/islower, isupper, isalpha, isalnum,	isspace, iscntrl, ispunct, isprint,/	ctype(3C)
system	issue a shell command	system(3S)
ctype: isdigit, isxdigit, islower,	isupper, isalpha, isalnum, isspace,/	ctype(3C)
isalpha, isalnum,/ ctype: isdigit,	isxdigit, islower, isupper,	ctype(3C)
functions bessel:	j0, j1, jn, y0, y1, yn Bessel	bessel(3M)
bessel: j0,	j1, jn, y0, y1, yn Bessel functions	bessel(3M)
terminal	jagent host control of windowing	jagent(5)
bessel: j0, j1,	jn, y0, y1, yn Bessel functions	bessel(3M)
/erand48, lrand48, nrand48, mrand48,	jrand48, srand48, seed48, lcong48/	drand48(3C)
a group of processes	kill send a signal to a process or	kill(2)
integers and long integers	l3tol, ltol3 convert between 3-byte	l3tol(3C)
and base-64 ASCII string a64l,	l64a convert between long integer	a64l(3C)
abs,	labs return integer absolute value	abs(3C)
constants	langinfo language information	langinfo(5)

Permuted Index

nl_types native	language data types .... nl_types(5)
langinfo	language information constants .... langinfo(5)
nl_langinfo	language information .... nl_langinfo(3C)
strftime	language specific strings .... strftime(4)
and windowing terminal under/	layers protocol used between host .... layers(5)
host and windowing terminal under	layers(1) /protocol used between .... layers(5)
group of a file chown,	lchown, fchown change owner and .... chown(2)
/setspent, endspent, fgetspent,	lckpwdf, ulckpwdf manipulate shadow/ .... getspent(3C)
/mrand48, jrand48, srand48, seed48,	lcong48 generate uniformly/ .... drand48(3C)
	ld link editor for object files .... ld(1)
	ldd list dynamic dependencies .... ldd(1)
nextafter, scalb manipulate/ frexp,	ldexp, logb, modf, modff, ... frexp(3C)
remainder div,	ldiv compute the quotient and .... div(3C)
ftruncate set a file to a specified	length truncate, ... truncate(3C)
getopt get option	letter from argument vector .... getopt(3C)
with/ /build a list of severity	levels for an application for use .... addseverity(3C)
lexical tasks	lex generate programs for simple .... lex(1)
lex generate programs for simple	lexical tasks .... lex(1)
lsearch,	lfind linear search and update .... lsearch(3C)
gamma,	lgamma log gamma function .... gamma(3M)
intro introduction to functions and	libraries .... intro(3)
intro introduction to math	libraries .... intro(3M)
elf_version coordinate	library and application versions .... elf_version(3E)
ar maintain portable archive or	library .... ar(1)
elf object file access	library .... elf(3E)
windowing terminal function	library libwindows .... libwindows(3X)
ordering relation for an object	library lorder find .... lorder(1)
function library	libwindows windowing terminal .... libwindows(3X)
implementation-specific constants	limits header file for .... limits(4)
ulimit get and set user	limits .... ulimit(2)
/strip symbol table, debugging and	line number information from an/ .... strip(1)
lsearch, lfind	linear search and update .... lsearch(3C)
profile data lprof display	line-by-line execution count .... lprof(1)
ld	link editor for object files .... ld(1)
	link link to a file .... link(2)
read the value of a symbolic	link readlink .... readlink(2)
link	link to a file .... link(2)
symlink make a symbolic	link to a file .... symlink(2)
a.out ELF (Executable and	Linking Format) files .... a.out(4)
	lint a C program checker .... lint(1)
ldd	list dynamic dependencies .... ldd(1)
or set supplementary group access	list IDs getgroups, setgroups get .... getgroups(2)
the supplementary group access	list initgroups initialize .... initgroups(3C)
nlist get entries from name	list .... nlist(3E)
nm print name	list of an object file .... nm(1)
application/ addseverity build a	list of severity levels for an .... addseverity(3C)
stdarg handle variable argument	list .... stdarg(5)

Programmer's Reference Manual

Permuted Index

varargs handle variable argument	list .... varargs(5)
output of a variable argument	list /vsprintf print formatted .... vprintf(3S)
modify and query a program's	locale setlocale .... setlocale(3C)
information	localeconv get numeric formatting .... localeconv(3C)
convert date and time to/ ctime,	localtime, gmtime, asctime, tzset .... ctime(3C)
end, etext, edata last	locations in program .... end(3C)
text, or data plock	lock into memory or unlock process, ... plock(2)
mlockall, munlockall	lock or unlock address space .... mlockall(3C)
mlock, munlock	lock (or unlock) pages in memory .... mlock(3C)
	lockf record locking on files .... lockf(3C)
maillock manage	lockfile for user's mailbox .... maillock(3X)
lockf record	locking on files .... lockf(3C)
gamma, lgamma	log gamma function .... gamma(3M)
powf, sqrt, sqrtf/ exp, expf, cbrt,	log, logf, log10, log10f, pow, ... exp(3M)
sqrtf/ exp, expf, cbrt, log, logf,	log10, log10f, pow, powf, sqrt, ... exp(3M)
exp, expf, cbrt, log, logf, log10,	log10f, pow, powf, sqrt, sqrtf/ .... exp(3M)
/pow, powf, sqrt, sqrtf exponential,	logarithm, power, square root/ .... exp(3M)
manipulate parts of/ frexp, ldexp,	logb, modf, modff, nextafter, scalb .... frexp(3C)
sqrt, sqrtf/ exp, expf, cbrt, log,	logf, log10, log10f, pow, powf, ... exp(3M)
getlogin get	login name .... getlogin(3C)
cuserid get character	login name of the user .... cuserid(3S)
setjmp,	longjmp non-local goto .... setjmp(3C)
an object library	lorder find ordering relation for .... lorder(1)
execution count profile data	lprof display line-by-line .... lprof(1)
srand48, seed48,/ drand48, erand48,	lrand48, nrand48, mrand48, jrand48, ... drand48(3C)
update	lsearch, lfind linear search and .... lsearch(3C)
	lseek move read/write file pointer .... lseek(2)
stat,	lstat, fstat get file status .... stat(2)
integers and long integers l3tol,	ltol3 convert between 3-byte .... l3tol(3C)
	m4 macro processor .... m4(1)
sysi86	machine specific functions .... sysi86(2)
values	machine-dependent values .... values(5)
sgetl access long integer data in a	machine-independent fashion sputl, ... sputl(3X)
m4	macro processor .... m4(1)
maillock manage lockfile for user's	mailbox .... maillock(3X)
mailbox	maillock manage lockfile for user's .... maillock(3X)
library ar	maintain portable archive or .... ar(1)
groups of programs make	maintain, update, and regenerate .... make(1)
makedev,	major, minor manage a device number .... makedev(3C)
	makecontext, swapcontext manipulate .... makecontext(3C)
user contexts	makedev, major, minor manage a .... makedev(3C)
device number	mallinfo memory allocator malloc, ... malloc(3X)
free, realloc, calloc, mallopt,	malloc, free, realloc, calloc, ... malloc(3X)
mallopt, mallinfo memory allocator	malloc, free, realloc, calloc, ... malloc(3X)
memalign, valloc, memory allocator	mallopt, mallinfo memory allocator .... malloc(3X)
malloc, free, realloc, calloc,	manage a device number .... makedev(3C)
makedev, major, minor	manage binary search trees .... tsearch(3C)
tsearch, tfind, tdelete, twalk	

Permuted Index 21

Permuted Index

hsearch, hcreate, hdestroy	manage hash search tables	hsearch(3C)
maillock	manage lockfile for user's mailbox	maillock(3X)
swapctl	manage swap space	swapctl(2)
memcntl memory	management control	memcntl(2)
sigaction detailed signal	management	sigaction(2)
sigpause simplified signal	management /sigrelse, sigignore,	signal(2)
elf_flagscn, elf_flagshdr	manipulate flags /elf_flagphdr,	elf_flagdata(3E)
/logb, modf, modff, nextafter, scalb	manipulate parts of floating-point/	frexp(3C)
/setpwent, endpwent, fgetpwent	manipulate password file entry	getpwent(3C)
/sigaddset, sigdelset, sigismember	manipulate sets of signals	sigemptyset(3C)
entry /fgetspent, lckpwdf, ulckpwdf	manipulate shadow password file	getspent(3C)
an object file mcs	manipulate the comment section of	mcs(1)
makecontext, swapcontext	manipulate user contexts	makecontext(3C)
strfind, strrspn, strtrns string	manipulations str:	str(3G)
ascii	map of ASCII character set	ascii(5)
mmap	map pages of memory	mmap(2)
mprotect set protection of memory	mapping	mprotect(2)
signal sigsuspend install a signal	mask and suspend process until	sigsuspend(2)
change or examine signal	mask sigprocmask	sigprocmask(2)
umask set and get file creation	mask	umask(2)
regular expression compile and	match routines /step, advance	regexp(5)
regular expression compile and	match routines /step, advance	regexpr(3G)
gmatch shell global pattern	matching	gmatch(3G)
math	math functions and constants	math(5)
intro introduction to	math libraries	intro(3M)
math	math math functions and constants	math(5)
	matherr error-handling function	matherr(3M)
	maximum system resource consumption	getrlimit(2)
getrlimit, setrlimit control	mbchar: mbtowc, mblen, wctomb	mbchar(3C)
multibyte character handling	mblen, wctomb multibyte character	mbchar(3C)
handling mbchar: mbtowc,	mbstowcs, wcstombs multibyte string	mbstring(3C)
functions mbstring:	mbstring: mbstowcs, wcstombs	mbstring(3C)
multibyte string functions	mbtowc, mblen, wctomb multibyte	mbchar(3C)
character handling mbchar:	mcs manipulate the comment section	mcs(1)
of an object file	medium /a file's in-memory	fsync(2)
state with that on the physical	memalign, valloc, memory allocator	malloc(3C)
malloc, free, realloc, calloc,	member access	elf_next(3E)
elf_next sequential archive	member access	elf_rand(3E)
elf_rand random archive	member header	elf_getarhdr(3E)
elf_getarhdr retrieve archive	member	offsetof(3C)
offsetof offset of structure	memccpy, memchr, memcmp, memcpy,	memory(3C)
memmove, memset memory/ memory:	memchr, memcmp, memcpy, memmove,	memory(3C)
memset memory/ memory: memccpy,	memcmp, memcpy, memmove, memset	memory(3C)
memory/ memory: memccpy, memchr,	memcntl memory management control	memcntl(2)
	memcpy, memmove, memset memory/	memory(3C)
memory: memccpy, memchr, memcmp,	memmove, memset memory operations	memory(3C)
/memccpy, memchr, memcmp, memcpy,	memory allocator malloc, free,	malloc(3C)
realloc, calloc, memalign, valloc,		

Permuted Index

realloc, calloc, mallopt, mallinfo	memory allocator malloc, free,	malloc(3X)
shmctl shared	memory control operations	shmctl(2)
copylist copy a file into	memory	copylist(3G)
spawn new process in a virtual	memory efficient way vfork	vfork(2)
memcntl	memory management control	memcntl(2)
mprotect set protection of	memory mapping	mprotect(2)
memcpy, memmove, memset memory/	memory: memccpy, memchr, memcmp,	memory(3C)
munlock lock (or unlock) pages in	memory mlock,	mlock(3C)
mmap map pages of	memory	mmap(2)
munmap unmap pages of	memory	munmap(2)
memcmp, memcpy, memmove, memset	memory operations /memccpy, memchr,	memory(3C)
shmop: shmat, shmdt shared	memory operations	shmop(2)
data plock lock into	memory or unlock process, text, or	plock(2)
mincore determine residency of	memory pages	mincore(2)
shmget get shared	memory segment identifier	shmget(2)
msync synchronize	memory with physical storage	msync(3C)
memchr, memcmp, memcpy, memmove,	memset memory operations /memccpy,	memory(3C)
catopen, catclose open/close a	message catalogue	catopen(3C)
catgets read a program	message	catgets(3C)
msgctl	message control operations	msgctl(2)
help ask for help with	message numbers or SCCS commands	help(1)
getmsg get next	message off a stream	getmsg(2)
putmsg send a	message on a stream	putmsg(2)
fmtmsg display a	message on stderr or system console	fmtmsg(3C)
msgop: msgsnd, msgrcv	message operations	msgop(2)
msgget get	message queue	msgget(2)
strerror get error	message string	strerror(3C)
perror print system error	messages	perror(3C)
psignal, psiginfo system signal	messages	psignal(3C)
memory pages	mincore determine residency of	mincore(2)
makedev, major,	minor manage a device number	makedev(3C)
intro introduction to	miscellany	intro(5)
	mkdir make a directory	mkdir(2)
directories in a path	mkdirp, rmdirp create, remove	mkdirp(3G)
	mkfifo create a new FIFO	mkfifo(3C)
special or ordinary file	mknod make a directory, or a	mknod(2)
	mktemp make a unique file name	mktemp(3C)
calendar time	mktime converts a tm structure to a	mktime(3C)
pages in memory	mlock, munlock lock (or unlock)	mlock(3C)
address space	mlockall, munlockall lock or unlock	mlockall(3C)
	mmap map pages of memory	mmap(2)
getmntent, getmntany get	mnttab file entry	getmntent(3C)
chmod, fchmod change	mode of file	chmod(2)
manipulate/ frexp, ldexp, logb,	modf, modff, nextafter, scalb	frexp(3C)
parts of/ frexp, ldexp, logb, modf,	modff, nextafter, scalb manipulate	frexp(3C)
utime set file access and	modification times	utime(2)
setlocale	modify and query a program's locale	setlocale(3C)

23

Permuted Index

	monitor prepare execution profile	monitor(3C)
mount	mount a file system	mount(2)
	mount mount a file system	mount(2)
lseek	move read/write file pointer	lseek(2)
mapping	mprotect set protection of memory	mprotect(2)
drand48, erand48, lrand48, nrand48,	mrand48, jrand48, srand48, seed48,/	drand48(3C)
	msgctl message control operations	msgctl(2)
	msgget get message queue	msgget(2)
operations	msgop: msgsnd, msgrcv message	msgop(2)
msgop: msgsnd,	msgrcv message operations	msgop(2)
msgop:	msgsnd, msgrcv message operations	msgop(2)
physical storage	msync synchronize memory with	msync(3C)
mbchar: mbtowc, mblen, wctomb	multibyte character handling	mbchar(3C)
mbstring: mbstowcs, wcstombs	multibyte string functions	mbstring(3C)
by xt driver xtproto	multiplexed channels protocol used	xtproto(5)
poll input/output	multiplexing	poll(2)
memory mlock,	munlock lock (or unlock) pages in	mlock(3C)
space mlockall,	munlockall lock or unlock address	mlockall(3C)
	munmap unmap pages of memory	munmap(2)
return the last element of a path	name basename	basename(3G)
directory name of a file path	name dirname report the parent	dirname(3G)
tmpnam, tempnam create a	name for a temporary file	tmpnam(3S)
ctermid generate file	name for terminal	ctermid(3S)
getpw get	name from UID	getpw(3C)
getenv return value for environment	name	getenv(3C)
getlogin get login	name	getlogin(3C)
nlist get entries from	name list	nlist(3E)
nm print	name list of an object file	nm(1)
mktemp make a unique file	name	mktemp(3C)
dirname report the parent directory	name of a file path name	dirname(3G)
rename change the	name of a file	rename(2)
ttyname, isatty find	name of a terminal	ttyname(3C)
uname get	name of current UNIX system	uname(2)
cuserid get character login	name of the user	cuserid(3S)
realpath returns the real file	name	realpath(3C)
pathfind search for named file in	named directories	pathfind(3G)
pathfind search for	named file in named directories	pathfind(3G)
nl_types	native language data types	nl_types(5)
bgets read stream up to	next delimiter	bgets(3G)
getmsg get	next message off a stream	getmsg(2)
frexp, ldexp, logb, modf, modff,	nextafter, scalb manipulate parts/	frexp(3C)
ftw,	nftw walk a file tree	ftw(3C)
time-sharing process	nice change priority of a	nice(2)
	nlist get entries from name list	nlist(3E)
	nl_langinfo language information	nl_langinfo(3C)
	nl_types native language data types	nl_types(5)
file	nm print name list of an object	nm(1)

Permuted Index

setjmp, longjmp	non-local goto .... setjmp(3C)
sigsetjmp, siglongjmp a	non-local goto with signal state .... sigsetjmp(3C)
seed48,/ drand48, erand48, lrand48,	nrand48, mrand48, jrand48, srand48, ... drand48(3C)
/symbol table, debugging and line	number information from an object/ .... strip(1)
determine type of floating-point	number /finite, fpclass, unordered .... isnan(3C)
major, minor manage a device	number makedev, ... makedev(3C)
convert string to double-precision	number strtod, atof, ... strtod(3C)
fcvt, gcvt convert floating-point	number to string ecvt, ... ecvt(3C)
uniformly distributed pseudo-random	numbers /seed48, lcong48 generate .... drand48(3C)
manipulate parts of floating-point	numbers /modff, nextafter, scalb .... frexp(3C)
to system calls and error	numbers intro introduction .... intro(2)
help ask for help with message	numbers or SCCS commands .... help(1)
localeconv get	numeric formatting information .... localeconv(3C)
dis	object code disassembler .... dis(1)
dlclose close a shared	object .... dlclose(3X)
dlopen open a shared	object .... dlopen(3X)
the address of a symbol in shared	object dlsym get .... dlsym(3X)
elf	object file access library .... elf(3E)
dump dump selected parts of an	object file .... dump(1)
elf_end finish using an	object file .... elf_end(3E)
get the base offset for an	object file elf_getbase .... elf_getbase(3E)
retrieve class-dependent	object file header /elf32_newehdr .... elf_getehdr(3E)
the comment section of an	object file mcs manipulate .... mcs(1)
nm print name list of an	object file .... nm(1)
and line number information from an	object file /table, debugging .... strip(1)
cof2elf COFF to ELF	object file translation .... cof2elf(1)
elf32_fsize return the size of an	object file type elf_fsize: .... elf_fsize(3E)
ld link editor for	object files .... ld(1)
print section sizes in bytes of	object files size .... size(1)
find ordering relation for an	object library lorder .... lorder(1)
elf_getbase get the base	offset for an object file .... elf_getbase(3E)
offsetof	offset of structure member .... offsetof(3C)
	offsetof offset of structure member .... offsetof(3C)
ungetc push character back	onto input stream .... ungetc(3S)
dlopen	open a shared object .... dlopen(3X)
fopen, freopen, fdopen	open a stream .... fopen(3S)
command p2open, p2close	open, close pipes to and from a .... p2open(3G)
dup duplicate an	open file descriptor .... dup(2)
dup2 duplicate an	open file descriptor .... dup2(3C)
open	open for reading or writing .... open(2)
	open open for reading or writing .... open(2)
catopen, catclose	open/close a message catalogue .... catopen(3C)
rewinddir, closedir/ directory:	opendir, readdir, telldir, seekdir, ... directory(3C)
rewinddir, closedir directory	operations /telldir, seekdir, ... directory(3C)
memcpy, memmove, memset memory	operations /memchr, memcmp, ... memory(3C)
msgctl message control	operations .... msgctl(2)
msgop: msgsnd, msgrcv message	operations .... msgop(2)

Permuted Index   25

Permuted Index

semctl semaphore control	operations	semctl(2)
semop semaphore	operations	semop(2)
shmctl shared memory control	operations	shmctl(2)
shmop: shmat, shmdt shared memory	operations	shmop(2)
strcspn, strtok, strstr string	operations /strpbrk, strspn,	string(3C)
getopt get	option letter from argument vector	getopt(3C)
fcntl file control	options	fcntl(5)
mlock, munlock lock	(or unlock) pages in memory	mlock(3C)
library lorder find	ordering relation for an object	lorder(1)
make a directory, or a special or	ordinary file mknod	mknod(2)
/vfprintf, vsprintf print formatted	output of a variable argument list	vprintf(3S)
fprintf, sprintf print formatted	output printf,	printf(3S)
chown, lchown, fchown change	owner and group of a file	chown(2)
from a command p2open,	p2close open, close pipes to and	p2open(3G)
to and from a command	p2open, p2close open, close pipes	p2open(3G)
standard buffered input/output	package stdio	stdio(3S)
standard interprocess communication	package stdipc: ftok	stdipc(3C)
mlock, munlock lock (or unlock)	pages in memory	mlock(3C)
determine residency of memory	pages mincore	mincore(2)
mmap map	pages of memory	mmap(2)
munmap unmap	pages of memory	munmap(2)
path name dirname report the	parent directory name of a file	dirname(3G)
get process, process group, and	parent process IDs /getpgid	getpid(2)
getsubopt	parse suboptions from a string	getsubopt(3C)
dump dump selected	parts of an object file	dump(1)
/modff, nextafter, scalb manipulate	parts of floating-point numbers	frexp(3C)
functions crypt	password and file encryption	crypt(3X)
endpwent, fgetpwent manipulate	password file entry /setpwent,	getpwent(3C)
lckpwdf, ulckpwdf manipulate shadow	password file entry /fgetspent,	getspent(3C)
putpwent write	password file entry	putpwent(3C)
putspent write shadow	password file entry	putspent(3C)
getpass read a	password	getpass(3C)
create, remove directories in a	path mkdirp, rmdirp	mkdirp(3G)
return the last element of a	path name basename	basename(3G)
the parent directory name of a file	path name dirname report	dirname(3G)
variables fpathconf,	pathconf get configurable pathname	fpathconf(2)
named directories	pathfind search for named file in	pathfind(3G)
directory getcwd get	pathname of current working	getcwd(3C)
pathconf get configurable	pathname variables fpathconf,	fpathconf(2)
gmatch shell global	pattern matching	gmatch(3G)
	pause suspend process until signal	pause(2)
process popen,	pclose initiate pipe to/from a	popen(3S)
signals that are blocked and	pending sigpending examine	sigpending(2)
	perror print system error messages	perror(3C)
in-memory state with that on the	physical medium /a file's	fsync(3C)
msync synchronize memory with	physical storage	msync(3C)
	pipe create an interprocess channel	pipe(2)

Permuted Index

popen, pclose initiate	pipe to/from a process .... popen(3S)
p2open, p2close open, close	pipes to and from a command .... p2open(3G)
process, text, or data	plock lock into memory or unlock .... plock(2)
elf_strptr make a string	pointer .... elf_strptr(3E)
rewind, ftell reposition a file	pointer in a stream fseek, ... fseek(3S)
fsetpos, fgetpos reposition a file	pointer in a stream .... fsetpos(3C)
lseek move read/write file	pointer .... lseek(2)
	poll input/output multiplexing .... poll(2)
a process	popen, pclose initiate pipe to/from .... popen(3S)
ar maintain	portable archive or library .... ar(1)
/cbrt, log, logf, log10, log10f,	pow, powf, sqrt, sqrtf exponential,/ .... exp(3M)
sqrt, sqrtf exponential, logarithm,	power, square root functions /powf, ... exp(3M)
/log, logf, log10, log10f, pow,	powf, sqrt, sqrtf exponential,/ .... exp(3M)
monitor	prepare execution profile .... monitor(3C)
unget undo a	previous get of an SCCS file .... unget(1)
types	primitive system data types .... types(5)
prs	print an SCCS file .... prs(1)
activity sact	print current SCCS file editing .... sact(1)
vprintf, vfprintf, vsprintf	print formatted output of a/ .... vprintf(3S)
printf, fprintf, sprintf	print formatted output .... printf(3S)
what	print identification strings .... what(1)
nm	print name list of an object file .... nm(1)
object files size	print section sizes in bytes of .... size(1)
perror	print system error messages .... perror(3C)
formatted output	printf, fprintf, sprintf print .... printf(3S)
	priocntl process scheduler control .... priocntl(2)
scheduler control	priocntlset generalized process .... priocntlset(2)
nice change	priority of a time-sharing process .... nice(2)
acct enable or disable	process accounting .... acct(2)
alarm set a	process alarm clock .... alarm(2)
times get	process and child process times .... times(2)
exit, _exit terminate	process .... exit(2)
fork create a new	process .... fork(2)
IDs /getppid, getpgid get process,	process group, and parent process .... getpid(2)
setpgid set	process group ID .... setpgid(2)
setpgrp set	process group ID .... setpgrp(2)
tcsetpgrp set terminal foreground	process group id .... tcsetpgrp(3C)
process, process group, and parent	process IDs /getppid, getpgid get .... getpid(2)
efficient way vfork spawn new	process in a virtual memory .... vfork(2)
change priority of a time-sharing	process nice .... nice(2)
kill send a signal to a	process or a group of processes .... kill(2)
/sigsendset send a signal to a	process or a group of processes .... sigsend(2)
pclose initiate pipe to/from a	process popen, ... popen(3S)
/getpgrp, getppid, getpgid get	process, process group, and parent/ .... getpid(2)
priocntl	process scheduler control .... priocntl(2)
priocntlset generalized	process scheduler control .... priocntlset(2)
plock lock into memory or unlock	process, text, or data .... plock(2)

Permuted Index

times get process and child	process times	times(2)
waitid wait for child	process to change state	waitid(2)
waitpid wait for child	process to change state	waitpid(2)
wait wait for child	process to stop or terminate	wait(2)
ptrace	process trace	ptrace(2)
pause suspend	process until signal	pause(2)
install a signal mask and suspend	process until signal sigsuspend	sigsuspend(2)
a signal to a process or a group of	processes kill send	kill(2)
a signal to a process or a group of	processes sigsend, sigsendset send	sigsend(2)
m4 macro	processor	m4(1)
	prof display profile data	prof(1)
	prof profile within a function	prof(5)
	profil execution time profile	profil(2)
line-by-line execution count	profile data lprof display	lprof(1)
prof display	profile data	prof(1)
monitor prepare execution	profile	monitor(3C)
profil execution time	profile	profil(2)
prof	profile within a function	prof(5)
assert verify	program assertion	assert(3X)
cb C	program beautifier	cb(1)
lint a C	program checker	lint(1)
cxref generate C	program cross-reference	cxref(1)
cscope interactively examine a C	program	cscope(1)
ctrace C	program debugger	ctrace(1)
end, etext, edata last locations in	program	end(3C)
retrieve class-dependent	program header table /elf32_newphdr	elf_getphdr(3E)
catgets read a	program message	catgets(3C)
raise send signal to	program	raise(3C)
atexit add	program termination routine	atexit(3C)
intro introduction to	programming commands	intro(1)
lex generate	programs for simple lexical tasks	lex(1)
setlocale modify and query a	program's locale	setlocale(3C)
update, and regenerate groups of	programs make maintain,	make(1)
mprotect set	protection of memory mapping	mprotect(2)
windowing terminal under/ layers	protocol used between host and	layers(5)
xtproto multiplexed channels	protocol used by xt driver	xtproto(5)
	prs print an SCCS file	prs(1)
generate uniformly distributed	pseudo-random numbers /lcong48	drand48(3C)
psignal,	psiginfo system signal messages	psignal(3C)
messages	psignal, psiginfo system signal	psignal(3C)
	ptrace process trace	ptrace(2)
stream ungetc	push character back onto input	ungetc(3S)
puts, fputs	put a string on a stream	puts(3S)
putc, putchar, fputc, putw	put character or word on a stream	putc(3S)
getdents read directory entries and	put in a file system independent/	getdents(2)
character or word on a stream	putc, putchar, fputc, putw put	putc(3S)
or word on a stream putc,	putchar, fputc, putw put character	putc(3S)

environment	putenv change or add value to .... putenv(3C)
	putmsg send a message on a stream .... putmsg(2)
	putpwent write password file entry .... putpwent(3C)
stream	puts, fputs put a string on a .... puts(3S)
entry	putspent write shadow password file .... putspent(3C)
/getutent, getutid, getutline,	pututline, setutent, endutent,/ .... getut(3C)
/getutxent, getutxid, getutxline,	pututxline, setutxent, endutxent,/ .... getutx(3C)
stream putc, putchar, fputc,	putw put character or word on a .... putc(3S)
	qsort quicker sort .... qsort(3C)
setlocale modify and	query a program's locale .... setlocale(3C)
remque insert/remove element from a	queue insque, ... insque(3C)
msgget get message	queue .... msgget(2)
qsort	quicker sort .... qsort(3C)
div, ldiv compute the	quotient and remainder .... div(3C)
	raise send signal to program .... raise(3C)
generator	rand, srand simple random-number .... rand(3C)
elf_rand	random archive member access .... elf_rand(3E)
rand, srand simple	random-number generator .... rand(3C)
getpass	read a password .... getpass(3C)
catgets	read a program message .... catgets(3C)
file system independent/ getdents	read directory entries and put in a .... getdents(2)
read	read from file .... read(2)
	read read from file .... read(2)
bgets	read stream up to next delimiter .... bgets(3G)
readlink	read the value of a symbolic link .... readlink(2)
rewinddir,/ directory: opendir,	readdir, telldir, seekdir, ... directory(3C)
open open for	reading or writing .... open(2)
symbolic link	readlink read the value of a .... readlink(2)
lseek move	read/write file pointer .... lseek(2)
realpath returns the	real file name .... realpath(3C)
/get real user, effective user,	real group, and effective group IDs .... getuid(2)
/geteuid, getgid, getegid get	real user, effective user, real/ .... getuid(2)
memory allocator malloc, free,	realloc, calloc, mallopt, mallinfo .... malloc(3X)
memory allocator malloc, free,	realloc, calloc, memalign, valloc, ... malloc(3C)
	realpath returns the real file name .... realpath(3C)
lockf	record locking on files .... lockf(3C)
regular expression	regcmp, regex compile and execute .... regcmp(3G)
	regcmp regular expression compile .... regcmp(1)
make maintain, update, and	regenerate groups of programs .... make(1)
expression regcmp,	regex compile and execute regular .... regcmp(3G)
regular expression compile and/	regexp: compile, step, advance .... regexp(5)
regular expression compile and/	regexpr: compile, step, advance .... regexpr(3G)
regexp: compile, step, advance	regular expression compile and/ .... regexp(5)
regexpr: compile, step, advance	regular expression compile and/ .... regexpr(3G)
regcmp	regular expression compile .... regcmp(1)
regcmp, regex compile and execute	regular expression .... regcmp(3G)
lorder find ordering	relation for an object library .... lorder(1)

Permuted Index

/rint, remainder floor, ceiling,	remainder, absolute value functions .... floor(3M)
div, ldiv compute the quotient and	remainder .... div(3C)
/fmod, fmodf, fabs, fabsf, rint,	remainder floor, ceiling, / .... floor(3M)
rmdel	remove a delta from an SCCS file .... rmdel(1)
rmdir	remove a directory .... rmdir(2)
mkdirp, rmdirp create,	remove directories in a path .... mkdirp(3G)
unlink	remove directory entry .... unlink(2)
remove	remove file .... remove(3C)
	remove remove file .... remove(3C)
queue insque,	remque insert/remove element from a .... insque(3C)
	rename change the name of a file .... rename(2)
clock	report CPU time used .... clock(3C)
a file path name dirname	report the parent directory name of .... dirname(3G)
stream fseek, rewind, ftell	reposition a file pointer in a .... fseek(3S)
stream fsetpos, fgetpos	reposition a file pointer in a .... fsetpos(3C)
mincore determine	residency of memory pages .... mincore(2)
setrlimit control maximum system	resource consumption getrlimit, ... getrlimit(2)
gettxt	retrieve a text string .... gettxt(3C)
elf_getarhdr	retrieve archive member header .... elf_getarhdr(3E)
elf_getarsym	retrieve archive symbol table .... elf_getarsym(3E)
file/ /elf32_getehdr, elf32_newehdr	retrieve class-dependent object .... elf_getehdr(3E)
/elf32_getphdr, elf32_newphdr	retrieve class-dependent program/ .... elf_getphdr(3E)
header elf_getshdr: elf32_getshdr	retrieve class-dependent section .... elf_getshdr(3E)
elf_getident	retrieve file identification data .... elf_getident(3E)
contents elf_rawfile	retrieve uninterpreted file .... elf_rawfile(3E)
abs, labs	return integer absolute value .... abs(3C)
name basename	return the last element of a path .... basename(3G)
type elf_fsize: elf32_fsize	return the size of an object file .... elf_fsize(3E)
getenv	return value for environment name .... getenv(3C)
stat data	returned by stat system call .... stat(5)
realpath	returns the real file name .... realpath(3C)
pointer in a stream fseek,	rewind, ftell reposition a file .... fseek(3S)
/opendir, readdir, telldir, seekdir,	rewinddir, closedir directory/ .... directory(3C)
creat create a new file or	rewrite an existing one .... creat(2)
/copysign, fmod, fmodf, fabs, fabsf,	rint, remainder floor, ceiling, / .... floor(3M)
file	rmdel remove a delta from an SCCS .... rmdel(1)
	rmdir remove a directory .... rmdir(2)
in a path mkdirp,	rmdirp create, remove directories .... mkdirp(3G)
chroot change	root directory .... chroot(2)
logarithm, power, square	root functions /sqrtf exponential, ... exp(3M)
atexit add program termination	routine .... atexit(3C)
expression compile and match	routines /step, advance regular .... regexp(5)
expression compile and match	routines /step, advance regular .... regexpr(3G)
editing activity	sact print current SCCS file .... sact(1)
allocation brk,	sbrk change data segment space .... brk(2)
logb, modf, modff, nextafter,	scalb manipulate parts of/ /ldexp, ... frexp(3C)
formatted input	scanf, fscanf, sscanf convert .... scanf(3S)

30 Programmer's Reference Manual

Permuted Index

for help with message numbers or	SCCS commands help ask	help(1)
cdc change the delta comment of an	SCCS delta	cdc(1)
comb combine	SCCS deltas	comb(1)
delta make a delta (change) to an	SCCS file	delta(1)
sact print current	SCCS file editing activity	sact(1)
get get a version of an	SCCS file	get(1)
prs print an	SCCS file	prs(1)
rmdel remove a delta from an	SCCS file	rmdel(1)
sccsdiff compare two versions of an	SCCS file	sccsdiff(1)
sccsfile format of	SCCS file	sccsfile(4)
unget undo a previous get of an	SCCS file	unget(1)
val validate an	SCCS file	val(1)
admin create and administer SCCS file	SCCS files	admin(1)
	sccsdiff compare two versions of an	sccsdiff(1)
	sccsfile format of SCCS file	sccsfile(4)
priocntl process	scheduler control	priocntl(2)
priocntlset generalized process	scheduler control	priocntlset(2)
	sdb symbolic debugger	sdb(1)
bsearch binary	search a sorted table	bsearch(3C)
lsearch, lfind linear	search and update	lsearch(3C)
directories pathfind	search for named file in named	pathfind(3G)
hcreate, hdestroy manage hash	search tables hsearch,	hsearch(3C)
tfind, tdelete, twalk manage binary	search trees tsearch,	tsearch(3C)
elf_newdata, elf_rawdata get	section data elf_getdata,	elf_getdata(3E)
retrieve class-dependent	section header /elf32_getshdr	elf_getshdr(3E)
elf_newscn, elf_nextscn get	section information /elf_ndxscn,	elf_getscn(3E)
mcs manipulate the comment	section of an object file	mcs(1)
files size print	section sizes in bytes of object	size(1)
/nrand48, mrand48, jrand48, srand48,	seed48, lcong48 generate uniformly/	drand48(3C)
/opendir, readdir, telldir,	seekdir, rewinddir, closedir/	directory(3C)
shmget get shared memory	segment identifier	shmget(2)
brk, sbrk change data	segment space allocation	brk(2)
dump dump	selected parts of an object file	dump(1)
semctl	semaphore control operations	semctl(2)
semop	semaphore operations	semop(2)
semget get set of	semaphores	semget(2)
	semctl semaphore control operations	semctl(2)
	semget get set of semaphores	semget(2)
	semop semaphore operations	semop(2)
putmsg	send a message on a stream	putmsg(2)
group of processes kill	send a signal to a process or a	kill(2)
group of/ sigsend, sigsendset	send a signal to a process or a	sigsend(2)
raise	send signal to program	raise(3C)
elf_next	sequential archive member access	elf_next(3E)
getsid get	session ID	getsid(2)
setsid set	session ID	setsid(2)
truncate, ftruncate	set a file to a specified length	truncate(3C)

Permuted Index

alarm	set a process alarm clock .... alarm(2)
umask	set and get file creation mask .... umask(2)
ascii map of ASCII character	set .... ascii(5)
ffs find first	set bit .... ffs(3C)
getcontext, setcontext get and	set current user context .... getcontext(2)
timezone	set default system time zone .... timezone(4)
times utime	set file access and modification .... utime(2)
elf_fill	set fill byte .... elf_fill(3E)
semget get	set of semaphores .... semget(2)
context sigaltstack	set or get signal alternate stack .... sigaltstack(2)
setpgid	set process group ID .... setpgid(2)
setpgrp	set process group ID .... setpgrp(2)
mprotect	set protection of memory mapping .... mprotect(2)
setsid	set session ID .... setsid(2)
IDs getgroups, setgroups get or	set supplementary group access list .... getgroups(2)
sysinfo get and	set system information strings .... sysinfo(2)
group id tcsetpgrp	set terminal foreground process .... tcsetpgrp(3C)
gettimeofday, settimeofday get or	set the date and time .... gettimeofday(3C)
stime	set time .... stime(2)
setuid, setgid	set user and group IDs .... setuid(2)
ulimit get and	set user limits .... ulimit(2)
a stream	setbuf, setvbuf assign buffering to .... setbuf(3S)
context getcontext,	setcontext get and set current user .... getcontext(2)
setuid,	setgid set user and group IDs .... setuid(2)
getgrent, getgrgid, getgrnam,	setgrent, endgrent, fgetgrent get/ .... getgrent(3C)
group access list IDs getgroups,	setgroups get or set supplementary .... getgroups(2)
timer getitimer,	setitimer get/set value of interval .... getitimer(3C)
	setjmp, longjmp non-local goto .... setjmp(3C)
crypt,	setkey, encrypt generate encryption .... crypt(3C)
program's locale	setlocale modify and query a .... setlocale(3C)
	setpgid set process group ID .... setpgid(2)
	setpgrp set process group ID .... setpgrp(2)
getpwent, getpwuid, getpwnam,	setpwent, endpwent, fgetpwent/ .... getpwent(3C)
resource consumption getrlimit,	setrlimit control maximum system .... getrlimit(2)
sigdelset, sigismember manipulate	sets of signals /sigaddset, ... sigemptyset(3C)
	setsid set session ID .... setsid(2)
lckpwdf,/ getspent, getspnam,	setspent, endspent, fgetspent, ... getspent(3C)
and time gettimeofday,	settimeofday get or set the date .... gettimeofday(3C)
IDs	setuid, setgid set user and group .... setuid(2)
/getutid, getutline, pututline,	setutent, endutent, utmpname access/ .... getut(3C)
/getutxid, getutxline, pututxline,	setutxent, endutxent, utmpxname,/ .... getutx(3C)
stream setbuf,	setvbuf assign buffering to a .... setbuf(3S)
for/ addseverity build a list of	severity levels for an application .... addseverity(3C)
machine-independent fashion sputl,	sgetl access long integer data in a .... sputl(3X)
/lckpwdf, ulckpwdf manipulate	shadow password file entry .... getspent(3C)
putspent write	shadow password file entry .... putspent(3C)
shmctl	shared memory control operations .... shmctl(2)

32   Programmer's Reference Manual

Permuted Index

shmop: shmat, shmdt	shared memory operations .... shmop(2)
shmget get	shared memory segment identifier .... shmget(2)
dlclose close a	shared object .... dlclose(3X)
dlopen open a	shared object .... dlopen(3X)
get the address of a symbol in	shared object dlsym .... dlsym(3X)
system issue a	shell command .... system(3S)
gmatch	shell global pattern matching .... gmatch(3G)
operations shmop:	shmat, shmdt shared memory .... shmop(2)
operations	shmctl shared memory control .... shmctl(2)
shmop: shmat,	shmdt shared memory operations .... shmop(2)
identifier	shmget get shared memory segment .... shmget(2)
operations	shmop: shmat, shmdt shared memory .... shmop(2)
management	sigaction detailed signal .... sigaction(2)
sigemptyset, sigfillset,	sigaddset, sigdelset, sigismember/ .... sigemptyset(3C)
alternate stack context	sigaltstack set or get signal .... sigaltstack(2)
sigemptyset, sigfillset, sigaddset,	sigdelset, sigismember manipulate/ .... sigemptyset(3C)
sigdelset, sigismember manipulate/	sigemptyset, sigfillset, sigaddset, ... sigemptyset(3C)
sigismember/ sigemptyset,	sigfillset, sigaddset, sigdelset, ... sigemptyset(3C)
sigpause/ signal, sigset,	sighold, sigrelse, sigignore, ... signal(2)
signal, sigset, sighold, sigrelse,	sigignore, sigpause simplified/ .... signal(2)
information	siginfo signal generation .... siginfo(5)
/sigfillset, sigaddset, sigdelset,	sigismember manipulate sets of/ .... sigemptyset(3C)
signal state sigsetjmp,	siglongjmp a non-local goto with .... sigsetjmp(3C)
generate an abnormal termination	signal abort .... abort(2)
sigaltstack set or get	signal alternate stack context .... sigaltstack(2)
	signal base signals .... signal(5)
siginfo	signal generation information .... siginfo(5)
sigaction detailed	signal management .... sigaction(2)
sigignore, sigpause simplified	signal management /sigrelse, ... signal(2)
until signal sigsuspend install a	signal mask and suspend process .... sigsuspend(2)
sigprocmask change or examine	signal mask .... sigprocmask(2)
psignal, psiginfo system	signal messages .... psignal(3C)
pause suspend process until	signal .... pause(2)
sigignore, sigpause simplified/	signal, sigset, sighold, sigrelse, ... signal(2)
mask and suspend process until	signal sigsuspend install a signal .... sigsuspend(2)
siglongjmp a non-local goto with	signal state sigsetjmp, ... sigsetjmp(3C)
processes kill send a	signal to a process or a group of .... kill(2)
sigsend, sigsendset send a	signal to a process or a group of/ .... sigsend(2)
raise send	signal to program .... raise(3C)
sigismember manipulate sets of	signals /sigaddset, sigdelset, ... sigemptyset(3C)
signal base	signals .... signal(5)
ssignal, gsignal software	signals .... ssignal(3C)
pending sigpending examine	signals that are blocked and .... sigpending(2)
sighold, sigrelse, sigignore,	sigpause simplified signal/ /sigset, ... signal(2)
blocked and pending	sigpending examine signals that are .... sigpending(2)
signal mask	sigprocmask change or examine .... sigprocmask(2)
signal, sigset, sighold,	sigrelse, sigignore, sigpause/ .... signal(2)

Permuted Index 33

Permuted Index

to a process or a group of/	sigsend, sigsendset send a signal	sigsend(2)
process or a group of/ sigsend,	sigsendset send a signal to a	sigsend(2)
sigignore, sigpause/ signal,	sigset, sighold, sigrelse,	signal(2)
goto with signal state	sigsetjmp, siglongjmp a non-local	sigsetjmp(3C)
and suspend process until signal	sigsuspend install a signal mask	sigsuspend(2)
lex generate programs for	simple lexical tasks	lex(1)
rand, srand	simple random-number generator	rand(3C)
/sigrelse, sigignore, sigpause	simplified signal management	signal(2)
asin, asinf, acos, acosf,/ trig:	sin, sinf, cos, cosf, tan, tanf,	trig(3M)
asinf, acos, acosf,/ trig: sin,	sinf, cos, cosf, tan, tanf, asin,	trig(3M)
tanh, tanhf, asinh, acosh,/	sinh, sinhf, cosh, coshf,	sinh(3M)
tanhf, asinh, acosh,/ sinh,	sinhf, cosh, coshf, tanh,	sinh(3M)
elf_fsize: elf32_fsize return the	size of an object file type	elf_fsize(3E)
of object files	size print section sizes in bytes	size(1)
size print section	sizes in bytes of object files	size(1)
interval	sleep suspend execution for	sleep(3C)
current user ttyslot find the	slot in the utmp file of the	ttyslot(3C)
ssignal, gsignal	software signals	ssignal(3C)
qsort quicker	sort	qsort(3C)
tsort topological	sort	tsort(1)
bsearch binary search a	sorted table	bsearch(3C)
brk, sbrk change data segment	space allocation	brk(2)
munlockall lock or unlock address	space mlockall,	mlockall(3C)
swapctl manage swap	space	swapctl(2)
memory efficient way vfork	spawn new process in a virtual	vfork(2)
mknod make a directory, or a	special or ordinary file	mknod(2)
sysi86 machine	specific functions	sysi86(2)
strftime language	specific strings	strftime(4)
truncate, ftruncate set a file to a	specified length	truncate(3C)
bufsplit	split buffer into fields	bufsplit(3G)
printf, fprintf,	sprintf print formatted output	printf(3S)
data in a machine-independent/	sputl, sgetl access long integer	sputl(3X)
/logf, log10, log10f, pow, powf,	sqrt, sqrtf exponential, logarithm,/	exp(3M)
/log10, log10f, pow, powf, sqrt,	sqrtf exponential, logarithm,/	exp(3M)
exponential, logarithm, power,	square root functions /sqrt, sqrtf	exp(3M)
generator rand,	srand simple random-number	rand(3C)
/lrand48, nrand48, mrand48, jrand48,	srand48, seed48, lcong48 generate/	drand48(3C)
scanf, fscanf,	sscanf convert formatted input	scanf(3S)
	ssignal, gsignal software signals	ssignal(3C)
set or get signal alternate	stack context sigaltstack	sigaltstack(2)
package stdio	standard buffered input/output	stdio(3S)
package stdipc: ftok	standard interprocess communication	stdipc(3C)
call	stat data returned by stat system	stat(5)
	stat, lstat, fstat get file status	stat(2)
stat data returned by	stat system call	stat(5)
ustat get file system	statistics	ustat(2)
feof, clearerr, fileno stream	status inquiries ferror,	ferror(3S)

34   Programmer's Reference Manual

stat, lstat, fstat get file status	stat(2)
wstat wait status	wstat(5)
information statvfs, fstatvfs get file system	statvfs(2)
list stdarg handle variable argument	stdarg(5)
fmtmsg display a message on stderr or system console	fmtmsg(3C)
input/output package stdio standard buffered	stdio(3S)
communication package stdipc: ftok standard interprocess	stdipc(3C)
compile and match/ regexp: compile, step, advance regular expression	regexp(5)
compile and/ regexpr: compile, step, advance regular expression	regexpr(3G)
stime set time	stime(2)
wait wait for child process to stop or terminate	wait(2)
synchronize memory with physical storage msync	msync(3C)
string manipulations str: strfind, strrspn, strtrns	str(3G)
compressing or/ strccpy: streadd, strcadd, strecpy copy strings,	strccpy(3G)
strncmp, strcpy, strncpy,/ string: strcat, strdup, strncat, strcmp,	string(3C)
copy strings, compressing or/ strccpy: streadd, strcadd, strecpy	strccpy(3G)
/strncmp, strcpy, strncpy, strlen, strchr, strrchr, strpbrk, strspn,/	string(3C)
string: strcat, strdup, strncat, strcmp, strncmp, strcpy, strncpy,/	string(3C)
strcoll string collation	strcoll(3C)
/strdup, strncat, strcmp, strncmp, strcpy, strncpy, strlen, strchr,/	string(3C)
/strchr, strrchr, strpbrk, strspn, strcspn, strtok, strstr string/	string(3C)
strcpy, strncpy,/ string: strcat, strdup, strncat, strcmp, strncmp,	string(3C)
strings, compressing or/ strccpy: streadd, strcadd, strecpy copy	strccpy(3G)
fclose, fflush close or flush a stream	fclose(3S)
fopen, freopen, fdopen open a stream	fopen(3S)
reposition a file pointer in a stream fseek, rewind, ftell	fseek(3S)
reposition a file pointer in a stream fsetpos, fgetpos	fsetpos(3C)
getw get character or word from a stream getc, getchar, fgetc,	getc(3S)
getmsg get next message off a stream	getmsg(2)
gets, fgets get a string from a stream	gets(3S)
putw put character or word on a stream putc, putchar, fputc,	putc(3S)
putmsg send a message on a stream	putmsg(2)
puts, fputs put a string on a stream	puts(3S)
setvbuf assign buffering to a stream setbuf,	setbuf(3S)
ferror, feof, clearerr, fileno stream status inquiries	ferror(3S)
push character back onto input stream ungetc	ungetc(3S)
bgets read stream up to next delimiter	bgets(3G)
or/ strccpy: streadd, strcadd, strecpy copy strings, compressing	strccpy(3G)
strerror get error message string	strerror(3C)
manipulations str: strfind, strrspn, strtrns string	str(3G)
date and time to string strftime, cftime, ascftime convert	strftime(3C)
strftime language specific strings	strftime(4)
long integer and base-64 ASCII string a64l, l64a convert between	a64l(3C)
strcoll string collation	strcoll(3C)
tzset convert date and time to string /localtime, gmtime, asctime,	ctime(3C)
convert floating-point number to string ecvt, fcvt, gcvt	ecvt(3C)
gets, fgets get a string from a stream	gets(3S)

Permuted Index

mbstowcs, wcstombs multibyte	string functions mbstring:	mbstring(3C)
getsubopt parse suboptions from a	string	getsubopt(3C)
gettxt retrieve a text	string	gettxt(3C)
str: strfind, strrspn, strtrns	string manipulations	str(3G)
puts, fputs put a	string on a stream	puts(3S)
strspn, strcspn, strtok, strstr	string operations /strpbrk,	string(3C)
elf_strptr make a	string pointer	elf_strptr(3E)
strcmp, strncmp, strcpy, strncpy,/	string: strcat, strdup, strncat,	string(3C)
strerror get error message	string	strerror(3C)
ascftime convert date and time to	string strftime, cftime,	strftime(3C)
strtod, atof, convert	string to double-precision number	strtod(3C)
strtol, strtoul, atol, atoi convert	string to integer	strtol(3C)
strxfrm	string transformation	strxfrm(3C)
/streadd, strcadd, strecpy copy	strings, compressing or expanding/	strccpy(3G)
strftime language specific	strings	strftime(4)
get and set system information	strings sysinfo	sysinfo(2)
what print identification	strings	what(1)
and line number information from/	strip strip symbol table, debugging	strip(1)
line number information from/ strip	strip symbol table, debugging and	strip(1)
/strcmp, strncmp, strcpy, strncpy,/	strlen, strchr, strrchr, strpbrk,/	string(3C)
strncpy,/ string: strcat, strdup,	strncat, strcmp, strncmp, strcpy,	string(3C)
/strcat, strdup, strncat, strcmp,	strncmp, strcpy, strncpy, strlen,/	string(3C)
/strncat, strcmp, strncmp, strcpy,	strncpy, strlen, strchr, strrchr,/	string(3C)
/strncpy, strlen, strchr, strrchr,	strpbrk, strspn, strcspn, strtok,/	string(3C)
/strcpy, strncpy, strlen, strchr,	strrchr, strpbrk, strspn, strcspn,/	string(3C)
manipulations str: strfind,	strrspn, strtrns string	str(3G)
/strlen, strchr, strrchr, strpbrk,	strspn, strcspn, strtok, strstr /	string(3C)
strpbrk, strspn, strcspn, strtok,	strstr string operations /strrchr,	string(3C)
double-precision number	strtod, atof, convert string to	strtod(3C)
/strrchr, strpbrk, strspn, strcspn,	strtok, strstr string operations	string(3C)
string to integer	strtol, strtoul, atol, atoi convert	strtol(3C)
to integer strtol,	strtoul, atol, atoi convert string	strtol(3C)
str: strfind, strrspn,	strtrns string manipulations	str(3G)
offsetof offset of	structure member	offsetof(3C)
mktime converts a tm	structure to a calendar time	mktime(3C)
	strxfrm string transformation	strxfrm(3C)
getsubopt parse	suboptions from a string	getsubopt(3C)
sync update	super block	sync(2)
getgroups, setgroups get or set	supplementary group access list IDs	getgroups(2)
initgroups initialize the	supplementary group access list	initgroups(3C)
sleep	suspend execution for interval	sleep(3C)
pause	suspend process until signal	pause(2)
/install a signal mask and	suspend process until signal	sigsuspend(2)
	swab swap bytes	swab(3C)
swab	swap bytes	swab(3C)
swapctl manage	swap space	swapctl(2)
contexts makecontext,	swapcontext manipulate user	makecontext(3C)

36   Programmer's Reference Manual

swapctl manage swap space	swapctl(2)
dlsym get the address of a symbol in shared object	dlsym(3X)
number information/ strip strip symbol table, debugging and line	strip(1)
elf_getarsym retrieve archive symbol table	elf_getarsym(3E)
sdb symbolic debugger	sdb(1)
readlink read the value of a symbolic link	readlink(2)
symlink make a symbolic link to a file	symlink(2)
symlink make a symbolic link to a	symlink(2)
file sync update super block	sync(2)
adjtime correct the time to allow synchronization of the system clock	adjtime(2)
state with that on the/ fsync synchronize a file's in-memory	fsync(2)
storage msync synchronize memory with physical	msync(3C)
variables sysconf get configurable system	sysconf(3C)
information sysfs get file system type	sysfs(2)
sysi86 machine specific functions	sysi86(2)
information strings sysinfo get and set system	sysinfo(2)
stat data returned by stat system call	stat(5)
intro introduction to system calls and error numbers	intro(2)
to allow synchronization of the system clock /correct the time	adjtime(2)
display a message on stderr or system console fmtmsg	fmtmsg(3C)
types primitive system data types	types(5)
perror print system error messages	perror(3C)
directory entries and put in a file system independent format /read	getdents(2)
statvfs, fstatvfs get file system information	statvfs(2)
sysinfo get and set system information strings	sysinfo(2)
system issue a shell command	system(3S)
mount mount a file system	mount(2)
/setrlimit control maximum system resource consumption	getrlimit(2)
psignal, psiginfo system signal messages	psignal(3C)
ustat get file system statistics	ustat(2)
timezone set default system time zone	timezone(4)
sysfs get file system type information	sysfs(2)
umount unmount a file system	umount(2)
uname get name of current UNIX system	uname(2)
sysconf get configurable system variables	sysconf(3C)
bsearch binary search a sorted table	bsearch(3C)
information/ strip strip symbol table, debugging and line number	strip(1)
retrieve archive symbol table elf_getarsym	elf_getarsym(3E)
class-dependent program header table /elf32_newphdr retrieve	elf_getphdr(3E)
hdestroy manage hash search tables hsearch, hcreate,	hsearch(3C)
acosf,/ trig: sin, sinf, cos, cosf, tan, tanf, asin, asinf, acos,	trig(3M)
trig: sin, sinf, cos, cosf, tan, tanf, asin, asinf, acos, acosf,/	trig(3M)
sinh, sinhf, cosh, coshf, tanh, tanhf, asinh, acosh,/	sinh(3M)
/sinhf, cosh, coshf, tanh, tanhf, asinh, acosh, atanh/	sinh(3M)
programs for simple lexical tasks lex generate	lex(1)
tcgetattr, tcsetattr, tcsendbreak, tcdrain, tcflush, tcflow,/ termios:	termios(2)
/tcsendbreak, tcdrain, tcflush, tcflow, cfgetospeed, cfgetispeed,/	termios(2)

Permuted Index

/tcsetattr, tcsendbreak, tcdrain,	tcflush, tcflow, cfgetospeed,/	termios(2)
tcdrain, tcflush, tcflow,/ termios:	tcgetattr, tcsetattr, tcsendbreak,	termios(2)
general/ /cfsetispeed, cfsetospeed,	tcgetpgrp, tcsetpgrp, tcgetsid	termios(2)
/cfsetospeed, tcgetpgrp, tcsetpgrp,	tcgetsid general terminal interface	termios(2)
termios: tcgetattr, tcsetattr,	tcsendbreak, tcdrain, tcflush,/	termios(2)
tcflush,/ termios: tcgetattr,	tcsetattr, tcsendbreak, tcdrain,	termios(2)
process group id	tcsetpgrp set terminal foreground	tcsetpgrp(3C)
terminal/ /cfsetospeed, tcgetpgrp,	tcsetpgrp, tcgetsid general	termios(2)
trees tsearch, tfind,	tdelete, twalk manage binary search	tsearch(3C)
directory: opendir, readdir,	telldir, seekdir, rewinddir,/	directory(3C)
temporary file tmpnam,	tempnam create a name for a	tmpnam(3S)
tmpfile create a	temporary file	tmpfile(3S)
tmpnam, tempnam create a name for a	temporary file	tmpnam(3S)
ctermid generate file name for	terminal	ctermid(3S)
id tcsetpgrp set	terminal foreground process group	tcsetpgrp(3C)
libwindows windowing	terminal function library	libwindows(3X)
tcsetpgrp, tcgetsid general	terminal interface /tcgetpgrp,	termios(2)
jagent host control of windowing	terminal	jagent(5)
ttyname, isatty find name of a	terminal	ttyname(3C)
used between host and windowing	terminal under layers(1) /protocol	layers(5)
exit, _exit	terminate process	exit(2)
wait for child process to stop or	terminate wait	wait(2)
atexit add program	termination routine	atexit(3C)
abort generate an abnormal	termination signal	abort(3C)
tcsendbreak, tcdrain, tcflush,/	termios: tcgetattr, tcsetattr,	termios(2)
lock into memory or unlock process,	text, or data plock	plock(2)
gettxt retrieve a	text string	gettxt(3C)
search trees tsearch,	tfind, tdelete, twalk manage binary	tsearch(3C)
setitimer get/set value of interval	timer getitimer,	getitimer(3C)
the difference between two calendar	times difftime computes	difftime(3C)
times	times get process and child process	times(2)
times get process and child process	times	times(2)
set file access and modification	times utime	utime(2)
nice change priority of a	time-sharing process	nice(2)
zone	timezone set default system time	timezone(4)
mktime converts a	tm structure to a calendar time	mktime(3C)
	tmpfile create a temporary file	tmpfile(3S)
temporary file	tmpnam, tempnam create a name for a	tmpnam(3S)
/tolower, _toupper, _tolower,	toascii translate characters	conv(3C)
popen, pclose initiate pipe	to/from a process	popen(3S)
conv: toupper, tolower, _toupper,	_tolower, toascii translate/	conv(3C)
toascii translate/ conv: toupper,	tolower, _toupper, _tolower,	conv(3C)
tsort	topological sort	tsort(1)
translate/ conv: toupper, tolower,	_toupper, _tolower, toascii	conv(3C)
_tolower, toascii translate/ conv:	toupper, tolower, _toupper,	conv(3C)
ptrace process	trace	ptrace(2)
strxfrm string	transformation	strxfrm(3C)

_toupper, _tolower, toascii translate characters /tolower,	conv(3C)
cof2elf COFF to ELF object file translation	cof2elf(1)
elf32_xlatetom class-dependent data translation /elf32_xlatetof,	elf_xlate(3E)
ftw, nftw walk a file tree	ftw(3C)
tdelete, twalk manage binary search trees tsearch, tfind,	tsearch(3C)
tanf, asin, asinf, acos, acosf,/ trig: sin, sinf, cos, cosf, tan,	trig(3M)
acosf, atan, atanf, atan2, atan2f trigonometric functions /acos,	trig(3M)
specified length truncate, ftruncate set a file to a	truncate(3C)
manage binary search trees tsearch, tfind, tdelete, twalk	tsearch(3C)
tsort topological sort	tsort(1)
terminal ttyname, isatty find name of a	ttyname(3C)
file of the current user ttyslot find the slot in the utmp	ttyslot(3C)
tsearch, tfind, tdelete, twalk manage binary search trees	tsearch(3C)
return the size of an object file type elf_fsize: elf32_fsize	elf_fsize(3E)
elf_kind determine file type	elf_kind(3E)
sysfs get file system type information	sysfs(2)
/fpclass, unordered determine type of floating-point number	isnan(3C)
nl_types native language data types	nl_types(5)
types primitive system data types	types(5)
types primitive system data types	types(5)
ctime, localtime, gmtime, asctime, tzset convert date and time to/	ctime(3C)
uadmin administrative control	uadmin(2)
ucontext user context	ucontext(5)
getpw get name from UID	getpw(3C)
file/ /endspent, fgetspent, lckpwdf, ulckpwdf manipulate shadow password	getspent(3C)
ulimit get and set user limits	ulimit(2)
mask umask set and get file creation	umask(2)
umount unmount a file system	umount(2)
system uname get name of current UNIX	uname(2)
unget undo a previous get of an SCCS file	unget(1)
SCCS file unget undo a previous get of an	unget(1)
input stream ungetc push character back onto	ungetc(3S)
/srand48, seed48, lcong48 generate uniformly distributed pseudo-random/	drand48(3C)
elf_rawfile retrieve uninterpreted file contents	elf_rawfile(3E)
mktemp make a unique file name	mktemp(3C)
uname get name of current UNIX system	uname(2)
unlink remove directory entry	unlink(2)
mlockall, munlockall lock or unlock address space	mlockall(3C)
mlock, munlock lock (or unlock) pages in memory	mlock(3C)
plock lock into memory or unlock process, text, or data	plock(2)
munmap unmap pages of memory	munmap(2)
umount unmount a file system	umount(2)
isnand, isnanf, finite, fpclass, unordered determine type of/ isnan,	isnan(3C)
pause suspend process until signal	pause(2)
a signal mask and suspend process until signal sigsuspend install	sigsuspend(2)
elf_update update an descriptor	elf_update(3E)
programs make maintain, update, and regenerate groups of	make(1)

Permuted Index

lsearch, lfind linear search and	update .... lsearch(3C)
sync	update super block .... sync(2)
/utmpxname, getutmp, getutmpx,	updwtmp, updwtmpx access utmpx file/ .... getutx(3C)
/getutmp, getutmpx, updwtmp,	updwtmpx access utmpx file entry .... getutx(3C)
levels for an application for	use with fmtmsg /a list of severity .... addseverity(3C)
setuid, setgid set	user and group IDs .... setuid(2)
setcontext get and set current	user context getcontext, ... getcontext(2)
ucontext	user context .... ucontext(5)
makecontext, swapcontext manipulate	user contexts .... makecontext(3C)
get character login name of the	user cuserid .... cuserid(3S)
/geteuid, getgid, getegid get real	user, effective user, real group,/ .... getuid(2)
environ	user environment .... environ(5)
getdate convert	user format date and time .... getdate(3C)
ulimit get and set	user limits .... ulimit(2)
/getegid get real user, effective	user, real group, and effective/ .... getuid(2)
in the utmp file of the current	user ttyslot find the slot .... ttyslot(3C)
maillock manage lockfile for	user's mailbox .... maillock(3X)
elf_end finish	using an object file .... elf_end(3E)
	ustat get file system statistics .... ustat(2)
modification times	utime set file access and .... utime(2)
utmp, wtmp	utmp and wtmp entry formats .... utmp(4)
setutent, endutent, utmpname access	utmp file entry /pututline, ... getut(3C)
ttyslot find the slot in the	utmp file of the current user .... ttyslot(3C)
formats	utmp, wtmp utmp and wtmp entry .... utmp(4)
/pututline, setutent, endutent,	utmpname access utmp file entry .... getut(3C)
utmpx, wtmpx	utmpx and wtmpx entry formats .... utmpx(4)
getutmpx, updwtmp, updwtmpx access	utmpx file entry /getutmp, ... getutx(3C)
formats	utmpx, wtmpx utmpx and wtmpx entry .... utmpx(4)
/pututxline, setutxent, endutxent,	utmpxname, getutmp, getutmpx,/ .... getutx(3C)
val	val validate an SCCS file .... val(1)
	validate an SCCS file .... val(1)
free, realloc, calloc, memalign,	valloc, memory allocator malloc, ... malloc(3C)
abs, labs return integer absolute	value .... abs(3C)
elf_hash compute hash	value .... elf_hash(3E)
getenv return	value for environment name .... getenv(3C)
floor, ceiling, remainder, absolute	value functions /rint, remainder .... floor(3M)
readlink read the	value of a symbolic link .... readlink(2)
getitimer, setitimer get/set	value of interval timer .... getitimer(3C)
putenv change or add	value to environment .... putenv(3C)
	values machine-dependent values .... values(5)
values machine-dependent	values .... values(5)
list	varargs handle variable argument .... varargs(5)
stdarg handle	variable argument list .... stdarg(5)
varargs handle	variable argument list .... varargs(5)
print formatted output of a	variable argument list /vsprintf .... vprintf(3S)
pathconf get configurable pathname	variables fpathconf, ... fpathconf(2)
sysconf get configurable system	variables .... sysconf(3C)

40   Programmer's Reference Manual

Permuted Index

	vc version control .... vc(1)
get option letter from argument	vector getopt .... getopt(3C)
assert	verify program assertion .... assert(3X)
vc	version control .... vc(1)
get get a	version of an SCCS file .... get(1)
coordinate library and application	versions elf_version .... elf_version(3E)
sccsdiff compare two	versions of an SCCS file .... sccsdiff(1)
virtual memory efficient way	vfork spawn new process in a .... vfork(2)
output of a variable/ vprintf,	vfprintf, vsprintf print formatted .... vprintf(3S)
getvfsspec, getvfsany get	vfstab file entry /getvfsfile, ... getvfsent(3C)
vfork spawn new process in a	virtual memory efficient way .... vfork(2)
formatted output of a variable/	vprintf, vfprintf, vsprintf print .... vprintf(3S)
a variable/ vprintf, vfprintf,	vsprintf print formatted output of .... vprintf(3S)
state waitid	wait for child process to change .... waitid(2)
state waitpid	wait for child process to change .... waitpid(2)
terminate wait	wait for child process to stop or .... wait(2)
wstat	wait status .... wstat(5)
or terminate	wait wait for child process to stop .... wait(2)
change state	waitid wait for child process to .... waitid(2)
change state	waitpid wait for child process to .... waitpid(2)
ftw, nftw	walk a file tree .... ftw(3C)
mbstring: mbstowcs,	wcstombs multibyte string functions .... mbstring(3C)
mbchar: mbtowc, mblen,	wctomb multibyte character handling .... mbchar(3C)
encrypted isencrypt determine	whether a character buffer is .... isencrypt(3G)
libwindows	windowing terminal function library .... libwindows(3X)
jagent host control of	windowing terminal .... jagent(5)
/protocol used between host and	windowing terminal under layers(1) .... layers(5)
prof profile	within a function .... prof(5)
fgetc, getw get character or	word from a stream getc, getchar, ... getc(3S)
fputc, putw put character or	word on a stream putc, putchar, ... putc(3S)
chdir, fchdir change	working directory .... chdir(2)
getcwd get pathname of current	working directory .... getcwd(3C)
write, writev	write on a file .... write(2)
putpwent	write password file entry .... putpwent(3C)
putspent	write shadow password file entry .... putspent(3C)
	write, writev write on a file .... write(2)
	writev write on a file .... write(2)
write,	writing .... open(2)
open open for reading or	
	wstat wait status .... wstat(5)
utmp, wtmp utmp and	wtmp entry formats .... utmp(4)
utmp,	wtmp utmp and wtmp entry formats .... utmp(4)
utmpx, wtmpx utmpx and	wtmpx entry formats .... utmpx(4)
utmpx,	wtmpx utmpx and wtmpx entry formats .... utmpx(4)
	x286emul emulate XENIX 80286 .... x286emul(1)
x286emul emulate	XENIX 80286 .... x286emul(1)
channels protocol used by	xt driver xtproto multiplexed .... xtproto(5)
protocol used by xt driver	xtproto multiplexed channels .... xtproto(5)

Permuted Index 41

Permuted Index

bessel: j0, j1, jn,	y0, y1, yn Bessel functions .... bessel(3M)
bessel: j0, j1, jn, y0,	y1, yn Bessel functions .... bessel(3M)
	yacc yet another compiler-compiler .... yacc(1)
yacc	yet another compiler-compiler .... yacc(1)
bessel: j0, j1, jn, y0, y1,	yn Bessel functions .... bessel(3M)
timezone set default system time	zone .... timezone(4)

COMMANDS (1)

COMMANDS (1)

intro(1)

NAME
intro – introduction to programming commands

DESCRIPTION
This section describes the programming commands in alphabetical order. Unless otherwise noted, the commands accept options and other arguments according to the following syntax:

name [*option*(*s*)] [*cmdarg*(*s*)]

where:

name	is the name of an executable file.
option	is –*noargletter*(*s*) or –*argletter* <> *optarg*, where:
	noargletter is a single letter representing an option without an option argument;
	argletter is a single letter representing an option requiring an option argument;
	<> is optional white space;
	optarg is an option argument (character string) satisfying the preceding *argletter*.
cmdarg	is "–" by itself, which indicates the standard input, or a path name (or other command argument) *not* beginning with "–".

Throughout the manual pages there are references to *TMPDIR, BINDIR, INCDIR,* and *LIBDIR*. These represent directory names whose value is specified on each manual page as necessary. For example, *TMPDIR* might refer to /var/tmp. These are not environment variables and cannot be set. [There is an environment variable called **TMPDIR** which can be set. See tmpnam(3S).] There are also references to *LIBPATH*, the default search path of the link editor and other tools.

SEE ALSO
exit(2), wait(2), getopt(3C).
getopts(1) in the *User's Reference Manual*.

DIAGNOSTICS
Upon termination, each command returns two bytes of status, one supplied by the system and giving the cause for termination, and (in the case of "normal" termination) one supplied by the program [see **wait**(2) and **exit**(2)]. The former byte is 0 for normal termination; the latter is customarily 0 for successful execution and non-zero to indicate troubles such as erroneous parameters, or bad or inaccessible data. It is called variously "exit code," "exit status," or "return code," and is described only where special conventions are involved.

WARNINGS
Some commands produce unexpected results when processing files containing null characters. These commands often treat text input lines as strings and therefore become confused upon encountering a null character (the string terminator) within a line.

admin(1)   admin(1)

NAME
admin − create and administer SCCS files

SYNOPSIS
admin [−n] [−i[*name*]] [−r*rel*] [−t[*name*]] [−f*flag*[*flag-val*]] [−d*flag*[*flag-val*]] [−a*login*] [−e*login*] [−m[*mrlist*]] [−y[*comment*]] [−h] [−z] *files*

DESCRIPTION
admin is used to create new SCCS files and change parameters of existing ones. Arguments to admin, which may appear in any order, consist of keyletter arguments (that begin with −) and named files (note that SCCS file names must begin with the characters s.). If a named file does not exist, it is created and its parameters are initialized according to the specified keyletter arguments. Parameters not initialized by a keyletter argument are assigned a default value. If a named file does exist, parameters corresponding to specified keyletter arguments are changed, and other parameters are left unchanged.

If a directory is named, admin behaves as though each file in the directory were specified as a named file, except that non-SCCS files (last component of the path name does not begin with s.) and unreadable files are silently ignored. If a name of − is given, the standard input is read; each line of the standard input is taken to be the name of an SCCS file to be processed. Again, non-SCCS files and unreadable files are silently ignored.

The keyletter arguments are listed below. Each argument is explained as if only one named file were to be processed because the effect of each argument applies independently to each named file.

- −n   This keyletter indicates that a new SCCS file is to be created.

- −i[*name*]   The *name* of a file from which the text for a new SCCS file is to be taken. The text constitutes the first delta of the file (see −r keyletter for delta numbering scheme). If the −i keyletter is used, but the file name is omitted, the text is obtained by reading the standard input until an end-of-file is encountered. If this keyletter is omitted, then the SCCS file is created empty. Only one SCCS file may be created by an admin command on which the i keyletter is supplied. Using a single admin to create two or more SCCS files requires that they be created empty (no −i keyletter). Note that the −i keyletter implies the −n keyletter.

- −r*rel*   The *rel*ease into which the initial delta is inserted. This keyletter may be used only if the −i keyletter is also used. If the −r keyletter is not used, the initial delta is inserted into release 1. The level of the initial delta is always 1 (by default initial deltas are named 1.1).

- −t[*name*]   The *name* of a file from which descriptive text for the SCCS file is to be taken. If the −t keyletter is used and admin is creating a new SCCS file (the −n and/or −i keyletters also used), the descriptive text file name must also be supplied. In the case of existing SCCS files: (1) a −t keyletter without a file name causes removal of the descriptive text (if any) that is currently in the SCCS file, and (2) a −t keyletter with a file name causes text (if any) in the named file to replace the descriptive text (if any) that is currently in the SCCS file.

admin(1) admin(1)

−f*flag* This keyletter specifies a *flag*, and, possibly, a value for the *flag*, to be placed in the SCCS file. Several −f keyletters may be supplied on a single admin command line. The allowable *flag*s and their values are:

b Allows use of the −b keyletter on a get command to create branch deltas.

c*ceil* The highest release (i.e., ceiling): a number greater than 0 but less than or equal to 9999 that may be retrieved by a get command for editing. The default value for an unspecified c flag is 9999.

f*floor* The lowest release (i.e., floor): a number greater than 0 but less than 9999 that may be retrieved by a get command for editing. The default value for an unspecified f flag is 1.

d*SID* The default delta number (SID) to be used by a get command.

i[*str*] Causes the No id keywords (ge6) message issued by get or delta to be treated as a fatal error. In the absence of this flag, the message is only a warning. The message is issued if no SCCS identification keywords [see get(1)] are found in the text retrieved or stored in the SCCS file. If a value is supplied, the keywords must exactly match the given string. The string must contain a keyword, and no embedded newlines.

j Allows concurrent get commands for editing on the same SID of an SCCS file. This flag allows multiple concurrent updates to the same version of the SCCS file.

l*list* A *list* of releases to which deltas can no longer be made (get −e against one of these "locked" releases fails). The *list* has the following syntax:

<list> ::= <range> | <list> , <range>
<range> ::= RELEASE NUMBER | a

The character a in the *list* is equivalent to specifying all releases for the named SCCS file.

n Causes delta to create a null delta in each of those releases (if any) being skipped when a delta is made in a new release (e.g., in making delta 5.1 after delta 2.7, releases 3 and 4 are skipped). These null deltas serve as anchor points so that branch deltas may later be created from them. The absence of this flag causes skipped releases to be non-existent in the SCCS file, preventing branch deltas from being created from them in the future.

q*text* User-definable text substituted for all occurrences of the %Q% keyword in SCCS file text retrieved by get.

admin(1)   admin(1)

    m*mod* *mod*ule name of the SCCS file substituted for all
         occurrences of the %M% keyword in SCCS file text retrieved
         by **get**. If the m flag is not specified, the value assigned is
         the name of the SCCS file with the leading **s.** removed.

    t*type* *type* of module in the SCCS file substituted for all
         occurrences of %Y% keyword in SCCS file text retrieved by
         get.

    v[*pgm*] Causes **delta** to prompt for Modification Request (MR)
         numbers as the reason for creating a delta. The optional
         value specifies the name of an MR number validity check-
         ing program [see **delta**(1)]. This program will receive as
         arguments the module name, the value of the type flag
         (see t*type* above), and the *mrlist*. (If this flag is set when
         creating an SCCS file, the m keyletter must also be used
         even if its value is null).

-d*flag* Causes removal (deletion) of the specified *flag* from an SCCS file. The
    -d keyletter may be specified only when processing existing SCCS
    files. Several -d keyletters may be supplied in a single **admin** com-
    mand. See the -f keyletter for allowable *flag* names.

    (1*list* used with -d indicates a *list* of releases to be unlocked. See the
    -f keyletter for a description of the 1 flag and the syntax of a *list*.)

-a*login* A login name, or numerical UNIX System group ID, to be added to
    the list of users who may make deltas (changes) to the SCCS file. A
    group ID is equivalent to specifying all login names common to that
    group ID. Several **a** keyletters may be used on a single **admin** com-
    mand line. As many logins or numerical group IDs as desired may
    be on the list simultaneously. If the list of users is empty, then any-
    one may add deltas. If login or group ID is preceded by a ! they are
    to be denied permission to make deltas.

-e*login* A login name, or numerical group ID, to be erased from the list of
    users allowed to make deltas (changes) to the SCCS file. Specifying a
    group ID is equivalent to specifying all **login** names common to that
    group ID. Several -e keyletters may be used on a single **admin** com-
    mand line.

-m[*mrlist*] The list of Modification Requests (MR) numbers is inserted into the
    SCCS file as the reason for creating the initial delta in a manner ident-
    ical to **delta**. The **v** flag must be set and the MR numbers are vali-
    dated if the **v** flag has a value (the name of an MR number validation
    program). Diagnostics will occur if the **v** flag is not set or MR valida-
    tion fails.

-y[*comment*]
    The *comment* text is inserted into the SCCS file as a comment for the
    initial delta in a manner identical to that of **delta**. Omission of the
    -y keyletter results in a default comment line being inserted.

admin(1)   admin(1)

           The −y keyletter is valid only if the −i and/or −n keyletters are
           specified (i.e., a new SCCS file is being created).
 −h   Causes **admin** to check the structure of the SCCS file [see
           sccsfile(4)], and to compare a newly computed check-sum (the
           sum of all the characters in the SCCS file except those in the first line)
           with the check-sum that is stored in the first line of the SCCS file.
           Appropriate error diagnostics are produced. This keyletter inhibits
           writing to the file, nullifying the effect of any other keyletters sup-
           plied; therefore, it is only meaningful when processing existing files.
 −z   The SCCS file check-sum is recomputed and stored in the first line of
           the SCCS file (see −h, above). Note that use of this keyletter on a
           truly corrupted file may prevent future detection of the corruption.

The last component of all SCCS file names must be of the form **s**.*file*. New SCCS
files are given mode 444 [see **chmod**(1)]. Write permission in the pertinent directory is, of course, required to create a file. All writing done by **admin** is to a temporary x-file, called **x**.*file*, [see **get**(1)], created with mode 444 if the **admin** command is creating a new SCCS file, or with the same mode as the SCCS file if it
exists. After successful execution of **admin**, the SCCS file is removed (if it exists),
and the x-file is renamed with the name of the SCCS file. This renaming process
ensures that changes are made to the SCCS file only if no errors occurred.

It is recommended that directories containing SCCS files be mode 755 and that
SCCS files themselves be mode 444. The mode of the directories allows only the
owner to modify SCCS files contained in the directories. The mode of the SCCS
files prevents any modification at all except by SCCS commands.

admin also makes use of a transient lock file (called **z**.*file*), which is used to
prevent simultaneous updates to the SCCS file by different users. See **get**(1) for
further information.

FILES
    x-file   [see **delta**(1)]
    z-file   [see **delta**(1)]
    bdiff   Program to compute differences between the "gotten" file and
                     the g-file [see **get**(1)].

SEE ALSO
    bdiff(1), **ed**(1), **delta**(1), **get**(1), **help**(1), **prs**(1), **what**(1), **sccsfile**(4).

DIAGNOSTICS
    Use the **help** command for explanations.

NOTES
    If it is necessary to patch an SCCS file for any reason, the mode may be changed
    to 644 by the owner allowing use of a text editor. You must run **admin** −h on the
    edited file to check for corruption followed by an **admin** −z to generate a proper
    check-sum. Another **admin** −h is recommended to ensure the SCCS file is valid.

ar(1)

NAME
ar – maintain portable archive or library

SYNOPSIS
ar [−V] − *key* [*arg*] [*posname*] *afile* [*name*. . .]

DESCRIPTION
The **ar** command maintains groups of files combined into a single archive file. Its main use is to create and update library files. However, it can be used for any similar purpose. The magic string and the file headers used by **ar** consist of printable ASCII characters. If an archive is composed of printable files, the entire archive is printable.

When **ar** creates an archive, it creates headers in a format that is portable across all machines. The portable archive format and structure are described in detail in ar(4). The archive symbol table [described in **ar**(4)] is used by the link editor ld to effect multiple passes over libraries of object files in an efficient manner. An archive symbol table is only created and maintained by **ar** when there is at least one object file in the archive. The archive symbol table is in a specially named file that is always the first file in the archive. This file is never mentioned or accessible to the user. Whenever the **ar** command is used to create or update the contents of such an archive, the symbol table is rebuilt. The **s** option described below will force the symbol table to be rebuilt.

The –V option causes **ar** to print its version number on standard error.

Unlike command options, the *key* is a required part of the **ar** command line. The *key* is formed with one of the following letters: **drqtpmx**. Arguments to the *key*, alternatively, are made with one of more of the following set: **vuaibcls**. *posname* is an archive member name used as a reference point in positioning other files in the archive. *afile* is the archive file. The *name*s are constituent files in the archive file. The meanings of the *key* characters are as follows:

- **d**   Delete the named files from the archive file.

- **r**   Replace the named files in the archive file. If the optional character **u** is used with **r**, then only those files with dates of modification later than the archive files are replaced. If an optional positioning character from the set **abi** is used, then the *posname* argument must be present and specifies that new files are to be placed after (**a**) or before (**b** or **i**) *posname*. Otherwise new files are placed at the end.

- **q**   Quickly append the named files to the end of the archive file. Optional positioning characters are invalid. The command does not check whether the added members are already in the archive. This option is useful to avoid quadratic behavior when creating a large archive piece-by-piece.

- **t**   Print a table of contents of the archive file. If no names are given, all files in the archive are listed. If names are given, only those files are listed.

- **p**   Print the named files in the archive.

- **m**   Move the named files to the end of the archive. If a positioning character is present, then the *posname* argument must be present and, as in **r**, specifies where the files are to be moved.

x	Extract the named files. If no names are given, all files in the archive are extracted. In neither case does x alter the archive file.

The meanings of the other key arguments are as follows:

v	Give a verbose file-by-file description of the making of a new archive file from the old archive and the constituent files. When used with t, give a long listing of all information about the files. When used with x, print the filename preceding each extraction.
c	Suppress the message that is produced by default when *afile* is created.
l	This option is obsolete. It is recognized, but ignored, and will be removed in the next release.
s	Force the regeneration of the archive symbol table even if ar(1) is not invoked with a command which will modify the archive contents. This command is useful to restore the archive symbol table after the strip(1) command has been used on the archive.

SEE ALSO

ld(1), lorder(1), strip(1), a.out(4), ar(4).

NOTES

If the same file is mentioned twice in an argument list, it may be put in the archive twice.

Since the archiver no longer uses temporary files, the −l option is obsolete and will be removed in the next release.

By convention, archives are suffixed with the characters .a.

as(1)

NAME
as – assembler

SYNOPSIS
as [*options*] *file*

DESCRIPTION
The **as** command creates object files from assembly language source *files*. The following flags may be specified in any order:

-o *objfile* Put the output of the assembly in *objfile*. By default, the output file name is formed by removing the .s suffix, if there is one, from the input file name and appending a .o suffix.

-n Turn off long/short address optimization. By default, address optimization takes place.

-m Run the **m4** macro processor on the input to the assembler.

-R Remove (unlink) the input file after assembly is completed.

-dl Obsolete. Assembler issues a warning saying that it is ignoring the -dl option.

-T Accept obsolete assembler directives.

-V Write the version number of the assembler being run on the standard error output.

-Q{y|n} If -Qy is specified, place the version number of the assembler being run in the object file. The default is -Qn.

-Y [md],*dir* Find the m4 preprocessor (m) and/or the file of predefined macros (d) in directory *dir* instead of in the customary place.

FILES
By default, **as** creates its temporary files in /var/tmp. This location can be changed by setting the environment variable TMPDIR [see tempnam in tmpnam(3S)].

SEE ALSO
cc(1), ld(1), m4(1), nm(1), strip(1), tmpnam(3S), a.out(4).

NOTES
If the -m (m4 macro processor invocation) option is used, keywords for m4 [see m4(1)] cannot be used as symbols (variables, functions, labels) in the input file since m4 cannot determine which keywords are assembler symbols and which keywords are real m4 macros.

The .align assembler directive may not work in the .text section when long/short address optimization is performed.

Arithmetic expressions may only have one forward referenced symbol per expression.

Whenever possible, you should access the assembler through a compilation system interface program such as **cc**.

cb(1)

NAME
cb – C program beautifier

SYNOPSIS
cb [-s] [-j] [-l *leng*] [-V] [*file* ...]

DESCRIPTION
The cb comand reads syntactically correct C programs either from its arguments or from the standard input, and writes them on the standard output with spacing and indentation that display the structure of the C code. By default, cb preserves all user new-lines.

cb accepts the following options.

- -s   Write the code in the style of Kernighan and Ritchie found in *The C Programming Language*.
- -j   Put split lines back together.
- -l *leng*   Split lines that are longer than *leng*.
- -V   Print on standard error output the version of cb invoked.

NOTES
cb treats asm as a keyword.

The format of structure initializations is unchanged by cb.

Punctuation that is hidden in preprocessing directives causes indentation errors.

SEE ALSO
cc(1).

Kernighan, B. W., and Ritchie, D. M., *The C Programming Language*, Second Edition, Prentice-Hall, 1988.

cc(1)

NAME
cc – C compiler

SYNOPSIS
cc [*options*] *file* ...

DESCRIPTION
cc is the interface to the C compilation system. The compilation tools conceptually consist of a preprocessor, compiler, optimizer, basic block analyzer, assembler, and link editor. cc processes the supplied options and then executes the various tools with the proper arguments. cc accepts several types of files as arguments.

Files whose names end with .c are taken to be C source files and may be preprocessed, compiled, optimized, instrumented for profiling, assembled, and link edited. The compilation process may be stopped after the completion of any pass if the appropriate options are supplied. If the compilation process runs through the assembler, then an object file is produced whose name is that of the source with .o substituted for .c. However, the .o file is normally deleted if a single C file is compiled and then immediately link edited. In the same way, files whose names end in .s are taken to be assembly source files; they may be assembled and link edited. Files whose names end in .i are taken to be preprocessed C source files, and they may be compiled, optimized, instrumented for profiling, assembled, and link edited. Files whose names do not end in .c, .s, or .i are handed to the link editor, which produces a dynamically linked executable whose name by default is a.out.

Since cc usually creates files in the current directory during the compilation process, it is necessary to run cc in a directory in which a file can be created.

The following options are interpreted by cc:

-A *name*[(tokens)]
    Associates *name* as a predicate with the specified *tokens* as if by a #assert preprocessing directive.

    Preassertions: system(unix)
                           cpu(i386)
                           machine(i386)

-A -   Causes all predefined macros (other than those that begin with __) and predefined assertions to be forgotten.

-B *c*   *c* can be either dynamic or static. -B dynamic causes the link editor to look for files named lib*x*.so and then for files named lib*x*.a when given the -l*x* option. -B static causes the link editor to look only for files named lib*x*.a. This option may be specified multiple times on the command line as a toggle. This option and its argument are passed to ld.

-C   Cause the preprocessing phase to pass along all comments other than those on preprocessing directive lines.

-c   Suppress the link editing phase of the compilation and do not remove any produced object files.

−D *name*[=*tokens*]

Associates *name* with the specified *tokens* as if by a **#define** preprocessing directive. If no =*tokens* is specified, the token 1 is supplied.

    Predefinitions: i386
                                      unix

−d *c*   *c* can be either **y** or **n**. −**dy** specifies dynamic linking, which is the default, in the link editor. −**dn** specifies static linking in the link editor. This option and its argument are passed to **ld**.

−E   Only preprocess the named C files and send the result to the standard output. The output will contain preprocessing directives for use by the next pass of the compilation system.

−f   This option is obsolete and will be ignored.

−G   Used to direct the link editor to produce a shared object rather than a dynamically linked executable. This option is passed to **ld**. It cannot be used with the −**dn** option.

−g   Cause the compiler to generate additional information needed for the use of **sdb**. Use of **sdb** on a program compiled with both the −**g** and −**O** options is not recommended unless the user understands the behavior of optimization.

−H   Print, one per line, the path name of each file included during the current compilation on the standard error output.

−I *dir*   Alter the search for included files whose names do not begin with / to look in *dir* prior to the usual directories. The directories for multiple −**I** options are searched in the order specified.

−K [PIC, minabi]
    −**K PIC** causes position-independent code (PIC) to be generated. −**K minabi** directs the compilation system to use a version of the C library that minimizes dynamic linking, without changing the application's ABI conformance (or non-conformance, as the case may be). Applications that use the Network Services Library or the X library may not use −**K minabi**.

−L *dir*   Add *dir* to the list of directories searched for libraries by **ld**. This option and its argument are passed to **ld**.

−l *name*
    Search the library lib*name*.so or lib*name*.a. Its placement on the command line is significant as a library is searched at a point in time relative to the placement of other libraries and object files on the command line. This option and its argument are passed to **ld**.

−O   Arrange for compilation phase optimization. This option has no effect on .s files.

−o *pathname*
    Produce an output object file *pathname*, instead of the default a.out. This option and its argument are passed to **ld**.

-P   Only preprocess the named C files and leave the result in corresponding files suffixed .i. The output will not contain any preprocessing directives, unlike −E.

-p   Arrange for the compiler to produce code that counts the number of times each routine is called; also, if link editing takes place, profiled versions of libc.a and libm.a (with the −lm option) are linked if the −dn option is used. A mon.out file will then be produced at normal termination of execution of the object program. An execution profile can then be generated by use of prof.

−Q c   c can be either y or n. If c is y, identification information about each invoked compilation tool will be added to the output files (the default behavior). This can be useful for software administration. Giving n for c suppresses this information.

−q c   c can be either l or p. −ql causes the invocation of the basic block analyzer and arranges for the production of code that counts the number of times each source line is executed. A listing of these counts can be generated by use of lprof. −qp is a synonym for −p.

−S   Compile, optimize (if −O is present), and do not assemble or link edit the named C files. The assembler-language output is left in corresponding files suffixed .s.

−U *name*
          Causes any definition of *name* to be forgotten, as if by a #undef preprocessing directive. If the same *name* is specified for both −D and −U, *name* is not defined, regardless of the order of the options.

−V   Cause each invoked tool to print its version information on the standard error output.

−v   Cause the compiler to perform more and stricter semantic checks, and to enable certain lint-like checks on the named C files.

−W *tool*, arg_1[, arg_2 ...]
          Hand off the argument(s) arg_i each as a separate argument to *tool*. Each argument must be separated from the preceding by only a comma. (A comma can be part of an argument by escaping it by an immediately preceding backslash (\) character; the backslash is removed from the resulting argument.) *tool* can be one of the following:

p	A synonym for 0
0	compiler
2	optimizer
b	basic block analyzer
a	assembler
l	link editor

          For example, −Wa,−o,*objfile* passes −o and *objfile* to the assembler, in that order; also −Wl,−I,*name* causes the linking phase to override the default name of the dynamic linker, /usr/lib/libc.so.1.

The order in which the argument(s) are passed to a tool with respect to the other specified command line options may change.

−X *c* Specify the degree of conformance to the ANSI C standard. *c* can be one of the following:

    t (transition)
        The compiled language includes all new features compatible with older (pre-ANSI) C (the default behavior). The compiler warns about all language constructs that have differing behavior between the new and old versions and uses the pre-ANSI C interpretation. This includes, for example, warning about the use of trigraphs the new escape sequence \a, and the changes to the integral promotion rules.

    a (ANSI)
        The compiled language includes all new features of ANSI C and uses the new interpretation of constructs with differing behavior. The compiler continues to warn about the integral promotion rule changes, but does not warn about trigraph replacements or new escape sequences.

    c (conformance)
        The compiled language and associated header files are ANSI C conforming, but include all conforming extensions of −Xa. Warnings will be produced about some of these. Also, only ANSI defined identifiers are visible in the standard header files.

The predefined macro __STDC__ has the value 0 for −Xt and −Xa, and 1 for −Xc. All warning messages about differing behavior can be eliminated in −Xa through appropriate coding; for example, use of casts can eliminate the integral promotion change warnings.

−Y *item*, *dir*
    Specify a new directory *dir* for the location of *item*. *item* can consist of any of the characters representing tools listed under the −W option or the following characters representing directories containing special files:

    F   obsolete. Use −YP instead. For this release, −YF will be simulated using −YP. −YF will be removed in the next release.
    I   directory searched last for include files: INCDIR (see −I)
    S   directory containing the start-up object files: LIBDIR
    L   obsolete. Use −YP instead. For this release, −YL will be simulated using −YP. −YL will be removed in the next release.
    U   obsolete. Use −YP instead. For this release, −YU will be simulated using −YP. −YU will be removed in the next release.
    P   Change the default directories used for finding libraries. *dir* is a colon-separated path list.

If the location of a tool is being specified, then the new path name for the tool will be *dir/tool*. If more than one −Y option is applied to any one item, then the last occurrence holds.

cc recognizes −a, −B, −e, −h −m, −o, −r, −s, −t, −u, and −z and passes these options and their arguments to ld. cc also passes any unrecognized options to ld without any diagnostic.

When cc is put in a file *prefix*cc, the prefix will be recognized and used to prefix the names of each tool executed. For example, OLDcc will execute OLDacomp, OLDoptim, OLDbasicblk, OLDas, and OLDld, and will link the object file(s) with OLDcrt1.o. Therefore, be careful when moving cc around. The prefix applies to the compiler, optimizer, basic block analyzer, assembler, link editor, and the start-up routines.

FILES

file.c	C source file
file.i	preprocessed C source file
file.o	object file
file.s	assembly language file
a.out	link-edited output
LIBDIR/*crti.o	startup initialization code
LIBDIR/*crt1.o	startup routine
LIBDIR/*crtn.o	last startup routine
TMPDIR/*	temporary files
LIBDIR/acomp	preprocessor and compiler
LIBDIR/optim	optimizer
LIBDIR/basicblk	basic block analyzer
BINDIR/as	assembler
BINDIR/ld	link editor
LIBDIR/libc.so	shared standard C library
LIBDIR/libc.a	archive standard C library
INCDIR	usually /usr/include
LIBDIR	usually /usr/ccs/lib
BINDIR	usually /usr/ccs/bin
TMPDIR	usually /var/tmp but can be redefined by setting the environment variable TMPDIR (see tempnam in tmpnam(3S)).

SEE ALSO

as(1), ld(1), lint(1), lprof(1), prof(1), sdb(1), monitor(3C), tmpnam(3S).

The "C Compilation System" chapter in the *Programmer's Guide: ANSI C and Programming Support Tools*.

Kernighan, B. W., and Ritchie, D. M., *The C Programming Language*, Second Edition, Prentice-Hall, 1988.

American National Standard for Information Systems − Programming Language C, X3.159-1989.

NOTES

Obsolescent but still recognized cc options include −f, −F, −YF, −YL, and −YU. The −ql and −O options do not work together; −O will be ignored.

cdc(1)

NAME
cdc – change the delta comment of an SCCS delta

SYNOPSIS
cdc −r *SID* [−m[*mrlist*]] [−y[*comment*]] *file*...

DESCRIPTION
cdc changes the delta comment, for the SID (SCCS identification string) specified by the −r keyletter, of each named SCCS file.

The delta comment is the Modification Request (MR) and comment information normally specified via the −m and −y keyletters of the **delta** command.

If *file* is a directory, **cdc** behaves as though each file in the directory were specified as a named file, except that non-SCCS files (last component of the path name does not begin with **s.**) and unreadable files are silently ignored. If a name of − is given, the standard input is read (see the NOTES section) and each line of the standard input is taken to be the name of an SCCS file to be processed.

Arguments to **cdc**, which may appear in any order, consist of keyletter arguments and file names.

All the described keyletter arguments apply independently to each named file:

    −r*SID*   Used to specify the SCCS IDentification (SID) string of a delta for which the delta comment is to be changed.

    −m*mrlist*   If the SCCS file has the v flag set [see **admin**(1)] then a list of MR numbers to be added and/or deleted in the delta comment of the SID specified by the −r keyletter may be supplied. A null MR list has no effect.

    mrlist entries are added to the list of MRs in the same manner as that of **delta**. In order to delete an MR, precede the MR number with the character ! (see the EXAMPLES section). If the MR to be deleted is currently in the list of MRs, it is removed and changed into a comment line. A list of all deleted MRs is placed in the comment section of the delta comment and preceded by a comment line stating that they were deleted.

    If −m is not used and the standard input is a terminal, the prompt **MRs?** is issued on the standard output before the standard input is read; if the standard input is not a terminal, no prompt is issued. The **MRs?** prompt always precedes the **comments?** prompt (see −y keyletter).

    mrlist entries in a list are separated by blanks and/or tab characters. An unescaped new-line character terminates the MR list.

    Note that if the v flag has a value [see **admin**(1)], it is taken to be the name of a program (or shell procedure) that validates the correctness of the MR numbers. If a non-zero exit status is returned from the MR number validation program, **cdc** terminates and the delta comment remains unchanged.

−y[comment]
> Arbitrary text used to replace the *comment*(s) already existing for the delta specified by the −r keyletter. The previous comments are kept and preceded by a comment line stating that they were changed. A null *comment* has no effect.
>
> If −y is not specified and the standard input is a terminal, the prompt comments? is issued on the standard output before the standard input is read; if the standard input is not a terminal, no prompt is issued. An unescaped new-line character terminates the *comment* text.

If you made the delta and have the appropriate file permissions, you can change its delta comment. If you own the file and directory you can modify the delta comment.

EXAMPLES

    cdc -r1.6 -m"b188-12345 !b187-54321 b189-00001" -ytrouble s.file

adds b188-12345 and b189-00001 to the MR list, removes b187-54321 from the MR list, and adds the comment trouble to delta 1.6 of s.file.

Entering:

    cdc -r1.6 s.file
    MRs? !b187-54321 b188-12345 b189-00001
    comments? trouble

produces the same result.

FILES

    x-file   [see delta(1)]
    z-file   [see delta(1)]

SEE ALSO

admin(1), delta(1), get(1), help(1), prs(1), sccsfile(4).

DIAGNOSTICS

Use help for explanations.

NOTES

If SCCS file names are supplied to the cdc command via the standard input (− on the command line), then the −m and −y keyletters must also be used.

cflow(1)

NAME
cflow – generate C flowgraph

SYNOPSIS
cflow [-r] [-ix] [-i_] [-d*num*] *files*

DESCRIPTION

The `cflow` command analyzes a collection of C, `yacc`, `lex`, assembler, and object files and builds a graph charting the external function references. Files suffixed with `.y`, `.l`, and `.c` are processed by `yacc`, `lex`, and the C compiler as appropriate. The results of the preprocessed files, and files suffixed with `.i`, are then run through the first pass of `lint`. Files suffixed with `.s` are assembled. Assembled files, and files suffixed with `.o`, have information extracted from their symbol tables. The results are collected and turned into a graph of external references that is written on the standard output.

Each line of output begins with a reference number, followed by a suitable number of tabs indicating the level, then the name of the global symbol followed by a colon and its definition. Normally only function names that do not begin with an underscore are listed (see the -i options below). For information extracted from C source, the definition consists of an abstract type declaration (e.g., char *), and, delimited by angle brackets, the name of the source file and the line number where the definition was found. Definitions extracted from object files indicate the file name and location counter under which the symbol appeared (e.g., *text*). Leading underscores in C-style external names are deleted. Once a definition of a name has been printed, subsequent references to that name contain only the reference number of the line where the definition may be found. For undefined references, only < > is printed.

As an example, suppose the following code is in `file.c`:

```
int    i;

main()
{
        f();
        g();
        f();
}
f()
{
        i = h();
}
```

The command

```
cflow -ix file.c
```

produces the output

```
1       main: int(), <file.c 4>
2               f: int(), <file.c 11>
3                       h: <>
4                       i: int, <file.c 1>
5               g: <>
```

When the nesting level becomes too deep, the output of cflow can be piped to the pr command, using the −e option, to compress the tab expansion to something less than every eight spaces.

In addition to the −D, −I, and −U options [which are interpreted just as they are by cc], the following options are interpreted by cflow:

−r   Reverse the "caller:callee" relationship producing an inverted listing showing the callers of each function. The listing is also sorted in lexicographical order by callee.

−ix Include external and static data symbols. The default is to include only functions in the flowgraph.

−i_ Include names that begin with an underscore. The default is to exclude these functions (and data if −ix is used).

−dnum The *num* decimal integer indicates the depth at which the flowgraph is cut off. By default this number is very large. Attempts to set the cutoff depth to a nonpositive integer will be ignored.

SEE ALSO
as(1), cc(1), lex(1), lint(1), nm(1), yacc(1).
pr(1) in the *User's Reference Manual*.

DIAGNOSTICS
Complains about multiple definitions and only believes the first.

NOTES
Files produced by lex and yacc cause the reordering of line number declarations, which can confuse cflow. To get proper results, feed cflow the yacc or lex input.

cof2elf(1)

NAME
cof2elf – COFF to ELF object file translation

SYNOPSIS
cof2elf [-iqV] [-Q{yn}] [-s *directory*] *files*

DESCRIPTION
cof2elf converts one or more COFF object *files* to ELF. This translation occurs in place, meaning the original file contents are modified. If an input file is an archive, each member will be translated as necessary, and the archive will be rebuilt with its members in the original order. cof2elf does not change input files that are not COFF.

Options have the following meanings.

-i Normally, the files are modified only when full translation occurs. Unrecognized data, such as unknown relocation types, are treated as errors and prevent translation. Giving the -i flag ignores these partial translation conditions and modifies the file anyway.

-q Normally, cof2elf prints a message for each file it examines, telling whether the file was translated, ignored, etc. The -q flag (for quiet) suppresses these messages.

-Q*arg* If *arg* is y, identification information about cof2elf will be added to the output files. This can be useful for software administration. Giving n for *arg* explicitly asks for no such information, which is the default behavior.

-s*directory* As mentioned above, cof2elf modifies the input files. This option saves a copy of the original files in the specified *directory*, which must exist. cof2elf does not save files it does not modify.

-V This flag tells cof2elf to print a version message on standard error.

SEE ALSO
ld(1), elf(3E), a.out(4), ar(4).

NOTES
Some debugging information is discarded. Although this does not affect the behavior of a running program, it may affect the information available for symbolic debugging.

cof2elf translates only COFF relocatable files. It does not translate executable or static shared library files for two main reasons. First, the operating system supports executable files and static shared libraries, making translation unnecessary. Second, those files have specific address and alignment constraints determined by the file format. Matching the constraints with a different object file format is problematic.

When possible, programmers should recompile their source code to build new object files. cof2elf is provided for those times when source code is unavailable.

comb(1)

NAME
comb – combine SCCS deltas

SYNOPSIS
comb [-o] [-s] [-pSID] [-clist] *files*

DESCRIPTION
comb generates a shell procedure [see sh(1)] that, when run, reconstructs the given SCCS files. The reconstructed files are typically smaller than the original files. The arguments may be specified in any order, but all keyletter arguments apply to all named SCCS files. If a directory is named, comb behaves as though each file in the directory were specified as a named file, except that non-SCCS files (last component of the path name does not begin with s.) and unreadable files are silently ignored. If a name of – is given, the standard input is read; each line of the input is taken to be the name of an SCCS file to be processed; non-SCCS files and unreadable files are silently ignored. The generated shell procedure is written on the standard output.

The keyletter arguments are as follows. Each argument is explained as if only one named file is to be processed, but the effects of any keyletter argument apply independently to each named file.

-o   For each get -e, this argument causes the reconstructed file to be accessed at the release of the delta to be created, otherwise the reconstructed file would be accessed at the most recent ancestor. Use of the -o keyletter may decrease the size of the reconstructed SCCS file. It may also alter the shape of the delta tree of the original file.

-s   This argument causes comb to generate a shell procedure that, when run, produces a report that gives for each file: the file name, size (in blocks) after combining, original size (also in blocks), and percentage change computed by:

$$100 * (original - combined) / original$$

It is recommended that before any SCCS files are actually combined, one should use this option to determine exactly how much space is saved by the combining process.

-pSID   The SCCS identification string (SID) of the oldest delta to be preserved. All older deltas are discarded in the reconstructed file.

-clist   A *list* of deltas to be preserved. All other deltas are discarded. See get(1) for the syntax of a *list*.

If no keyletter arguments are specified, comb preserves only leaf deltas and the minimal number of ancestors needed to preserve the tree.

FILES
s.COMB   the reconstructed SCCS file
comb?????   temporary file

SEE ALSO
admin(1), delta(1), get(1), help(1), prs(1), sccsfile(4).
sh(1) in the *User's Reference Manual*.

DIAGNOSTICS
Use help(1) for explanations.

NOTES
comb may rearrange the shape of the tree of deltas.

comb may not save any space; in fact, it is possible for the reconstructed file to be larger than the original.

convert(1)

NAME
convert – convert archive files to common formats

SYNOPSIS
convert [-x] *infile outfile*

DESCRIPTION
The convert command transforms input *infile1 to output outfile*. *infile* must be a UNIX System V Release 1.0 archive file and *outfile* will be the equivalent UNIX System V Release 2.0 archive file. All other types of input to the convert command will be passed unmodified from the input file to the output file (along with appropriate warning messages).

The -x option is required to convert a XENIX archive. (XENIX is a registered trademark of Microsoft Corporation.) Using this option will convert the general archive but leave archive members unmodified.

infile must be different from *outfile*.

FILES
TMPDIR/conv*   temporary files

TMPDIR is usually /usr/tmp but can be redefined by setting the environment variable TMPDIR [see tempnam() in tmpnam(3S)].

SEE ALSO
ar(1), tmpnam(3S), a.out(4), ar(4).

cscope(1)

NAME
cscope – interactively examine a C program

SYNOPSIS
cscope [*options*] *files*...

DESCRIPTION
cscope is an interactive screen-oriented tool that allows the user to browse through C source files for specified elements of code.

By default, cscope examines the C (.c and .h), lex (.l), and yacc (.y) source files in the current directory. cscope may also be invoked for source files named on the command line. In either case, cscope searches the standard directories for #include files that it does not find in the current directory. cscope uses a symbol cross-reference, cscope.out by default, to locate functions, function calls, macros, variables, and preprocessor symbols in the files.

cscope builds the symbol cross-reference the first time it is used on the source files for the program being browsed. On a subsequent invocation, cscope rebuilds the cross-reference only if a source file has changed or the list of source files is different. When the cross-reference is rebuilt, the data for the unchanged files are copied from the old cross-reference, which makes rebuilding faster than the initial build.

The following options can appear in any combination:

-b   Build the cross-reference only.

-C   Ignore letter case when searching.

-c   Use only ASCII characters in the cross-reference file, that is, do not compress the data.

-d   Do not update the cross-reference.

-e   Suppress the ^e command prompt between files.

-f *reffile*   Use *reffile* as the cross-reference file name instead of the default cscope.out.

-I *incdir*   Look in *incdir* (before looking in INCDIR, the standard place for header files, normally /usr/include) for any #include files whose names do not begin with / and that are not specified on the command line or in *namefile* below. (The #include files may be specified with either double quotes or angle brackets.) The *incdir* directory is searched in addition to the current directory (which is searched first) and the standard list (which is searched last). If more than one occurrence of -I appears, the directories are searched in the order they appear on the command line.

-i *namefile*   Browse through all source files whose names are listed in *namefile* (file names separated by spaces, tabs, or new-lines) instead of the default (cscope.files). If this option is specified, cscope ignores any files appearing on the command line.

-L   Do a single search with line-oriented output when used with the
           −*num pattern* option.

-l   Line-oriented interface (see "Line-Oriented Interface" below).

-num pattern   Go to input field *num* (counting from 0) and find *pattern*.

-P *path* Prepend *path* to relative file names in a pre-built cross-reference
           file so you do not have to change to the directory where the
           cross-reference file was built. This option is only valid with the
           −d option.

-p *n*   Display the last *n* file path components instead of the default (1).
           Use 0 to not display the file name at all.

-s *dir*   Look in *dir* for additional source files. This option is ignored if
           source files are given on the command line.

-T   Use only the first eight characters to match against C symbols. A
           regular expression containing special characters other than a
           period (.) will not match any symbol if its minimum length is
           greater than eight characters.

-U   Do not check file time stamps (assume that no files have
           changed).

-u   Unconditionally build the cross-reference file (assume that all
           files have changed).

-V   Print on the first line of screen the version number of cscope.

The −I, −p, and −T options can also be in the cscope.files file.

Requesting the Initial Search

After the cross-reference is ready, cscope will display this menu:

```
Find this C symbol:
Find this function definition:
Find functions called by this function:
Find functions calling this function:
Find this text string:
Change this text string:
Find this egrep pattern:
Find this file:
Find files #including this file:
```

Press the TAB key repeatedly to move to the desired input field, type the text to search for, and then press the RETURN key.

Issuing Subsequent Requests

If the search is successful, any of these single-character commands can be used:

1-9   Edit the file referenced by the given line number.
SPACE   Display next set of matching lines.
+   Display next set of matching lines.

–	Display previous set of matching lines.
^e	Edit displayed files in order.
>	Append the displayed list of lines to a file.
|	Pipe all lines to a shell command.

At any time these single-character commands can also be used:

TAB	Move to next input field.
RETURN	Move to next input field.
^n	Move to next input field.
^p	Move to previous input field.
^y	Search with the last text typed.
^b	Move to previous input field and search pattern.
^f	Move to next input field and search pattern.
^c	Toggle ignore/use letter case when searching. (When ignoring letter case, search for FILE will match File and file.)
^r	Rebuild the cross-reference.
!	Start an interactive shell (type ^d to return to cscope).
^l	Redraw the screen.
?	Give help information about cscope commands.
^d	Exit cscope.

Note: If the first character of the text to be searched for matches one of the above commands, escape it by typing a \ (backslash) first.

Substituting New Text for Old Text

After the text to be changed has been typed, cscope will prompt for the new text, and then it will display the lines containing the old text. Select the lines to be changed with these single-character commands:

1-9	Mark or unmark the line to be changed.
*	Mark or unmark all displayed lines to be changed.
SPACE	Display next set of lines.
+	Display next set of lines.
–	Display previous set of lines.
a	Mark all lines to be changed.
^d	Change the marked lines and exit.
ESCAPE	Exit without changing the marked lines.
!	Start an interactive shell (type ^d to return to cscope).
^l	Redraw the screen.
?	Give help information about cscope commands.

Special Keys

If your terminal has arrow keys that work in vi(1), you can use them to move around the input fields. The up-arrow key is useful to move to the previous input field instead of using the TAB key repeatedly. If you have CLEAR, NEXT, or PREV keys they will act as the ^l, +, and – commands, respectively.

Line-Oriented Interface

The −l option lets you use cscope where a screen-oriented interface would not be useful, e.g., from another screen-oriented program.

cscope will prompt with >> when it is ready for an input line starting with the field number (counting from 0) immediately followed by the search pattern, e.g., 1main finds the definition of the main function.

If you just want a single search, instead of the −l option use the −L and −*num pattern* options, and you won't get the >> prompt.

For −l, cscope outputs the number of reference lines

    cscope: 2 lines

For each reference found, cscope outputs a line consisting of the file name, function name, line number, and line text, separated by spaces, e.g.,

    main.c main 161 main(argc, argv)

Note that the editor is not called to display a single reference, unlike the screen-oriented interface.

You can use the r command to rebuild the database.

cscope will quit when it detects end-of-file, or when the first character of an input line is ^d or q.

ENVIRONMENT VARIABLES

EDITOR	Preferred editor, which defaults to vi(1).
INCLUDEDIRS	Colon-separated list of directories to search for #include files.
HOME	Home directory, which is automatically set at login.
SHELL	Preferred shell, which defaults to sh(1).
SOURCEDIRS	Colon-separated list of directories to search for additional source files.
TERM	Terminal type, which must be a screen terminal.
TERMINFO	Terminal information directory full path name. If your terminal is not in the standard terminfo directory, see curses(3X) and terminfo(4) for how to make your own terminal description.
TMPDIR	Temporary file directory, which defaults to /var/tmp.
VIEWER	Preferred file display program [such as pg], which overrides EDITOR (see above).
VPATH	A colon-separated list of directories, each of which has the same directory structure below it. If VPATH is set, cscope searches for source files in the directories specified; if it is not set, cscope searches only in the current directory.

FILES

cscope.files	Default files containing −I, −p, and −T options and the list of source files (overridden by the −i option).
cscope.out	Symbol cross-reference file, which is put in the home directory if it cannot be created in the current directory.
ncscope.out	Temporary file containing new cross-reference before it replaces the old cross-reference.
INCDIR	Standard directory for #include files (usually /usr/include).

SEE ALSO

The "cscope" chapter in the *Programmer's Guide: ANSI C and Programming Support Tools.*

curses and **terminfo** in the *Programmer's Guide: Character User Interface (FMLI and ETI).*

NOTES

cscope recognizes function definitions of the form:

fname blank **(** *args* **)** *white arg_decs white* **{**

where:

fname	is the function name
blank	is zero or more spaces or tabs, not including newlines
args	is any string that does not contain a " or a newline
white	is zero or more spaces, tabs, or newlines
arg_decs	are zero or more argument declarations (*arg_decs* may include comments and white space)

It is not necessary for a function declaration to start at the beginning of a line. The return type may precede the function name; **cscope** will still recognize the declaration. Function definitions that deviate from this form will not be recognized by **cscope**.

The Function column of the search output for the menu option Find functions called by this function: input field will only display the first function called in the line, that is, for this function

```
e()
{
    return (f() + g());
}
```

the display would be

```
Functions called by this function: e

File Function Line
a.c  f    3 return(f() + g());
```

Occasionally, a function definition or call may not be recognized because of braces inside **#if** statements. Similarly, the use of a variable may be incorrectly recognized as a definition.

A **typedef** name preceding a preprocessor statement will be incorrectly recognized as a global definition, e.g.,

```
LDFILE *
#if AR16WR
```

Preprocessor statements can also prevent the recognition of a global definition, e.g.,

```
char flag
#ifdef ALLOCATE_STORAGE
    = -1
```

```
#endif
;
```
A function declaration inside a function is incorrectly recognized as a function call, e.g.,
```
f()
{
        void g();
}
```
is incorrectly recognized as a call to g().

cscope recognizes C++ classes by looking for the class keyword, but doesn't recognize that a **struct** is also a class, so it doesn't recognize inline member function definitions in a structure. It also doesn't expect the class keyword in a typedef, so it incorrectly recognizes X as a definition in
```
typedef class X * Y;
```
It also doesn't recognize operator function definitions
```
Bool Feature::operator==(const Feature & other)
{
        ...
}
```

ctrace(1)

NAME
ctrace – C program debugger

SYNOPSIS
ctrace [*options*] [*file*]

DESCRIPTION
The ctrace command allows the user to monitor the sequential execution of a C program as each program statement executes. The effect is similar to executing a shell procedure with the −x option. ctrace reads the C program in *file* (or from standard input if the user does not specify *file*), inserts statements to print the text of each executable statement and the values of all variables referenced or modified, and writes the modified program to the standard output. The output of ctrace must be placed into a temporary file because the cc(1) command does not allow the use of a pipe. This file can then be compiled and executed.

As each statement in the program executes, it will be listed at the terminal, followed by the name and value of any variables referenced or modified in the statement; these variable names and values will be followed by any output from the statement. Loops in the trace output are detected and tracing is stopped until the loop is exited or a different sequence of statements within the loop is executed. A warning message is printed after each 1000 loop cycles to help the user detect infinite loops. The trace output goes to the standard output so the user can put it into a file for examination with an editor or the bfs(1) or tail(1) commands.

The options commonly used are:

−f *functions*   Trace only these *functions*.
−v *functions*   Trace all but these *functions*.

The user may want to add to the default formats for printing variables. Long and pointer variables are always printed as signed integers. Pointers to character arrays are also printed as strings if appropriate. char, short, and int variables are also printed as signed integers and, if appropriate, as characters. double variables are printed as floating point numbers in scientific notation. The user can request that variables be printed in additional formats, if appropriate, with these options:

−o   Octal
−x   Hexadecimal
−u   Unsigned
−e   Floating point

These options are used only in special circumstances:

−l *n*   Check *n* consecutively executed statements for looping trace output, instead of the default of 20. Use 0 to get all the trace output from loops.
−s   Suppress redundant trace output from simple assignment statements and string copy function calls. This option can hide a bug caused by use of the = operator in place of the == operator.
−t *n*   Trace *n* variables per statement instead of the default of 10 (the maximum number is 20). The diagnostics section explains when to use this option.

-P   Preprocess the input before tracing it. The user can also use the –D, –I, and –U cc(1) options.

-p *string*
     Change the trace print function from the default of `printf`. For example, `fprintf(stderr,` would send the trace to the standard error output.

-r *f*   Use file *f* in place of the `runtime.c` trace function package. This replacement lets the user change the entire print function, instead of just the name and leading arguments (see the –p option).

-v   Prints version information on the standard error.

-Q*arg* If *arg* is y, identification information about `ctrace` will be added to the output files. This can be useful for software administration. Giving n for *arg* exlicitly asks for no such information, which is the default behavior.

EXAMPLE

If the file lc.c contains this C program:

```
 1 #include <stdio.h>
 2 main()  /* count lines in input */
 3 {
 4     int c, nl;
 5
 6     nl = 0;
 7     while ((c = getchar()) != EOF)
 8         if (c = '\n')
 9             ++nl;
10     printf("%d\n", nl);
11 }
```

these commands and test data are entered:

```
cc lc.c
a.out
1
(cntl-d)
```

the program will be compiled and executed. The output of the program will be the number 2, which is incorrect because there is only one line in the test data. The error in this program is common, but subtle. If the user invokes `ctrace` with these commands:

```
ctrace lc.c >temp.c
cc temp.c
a.out
```

the output will be:

```
 2 main()
 6     nl = 0;
       /* nl == 0 */
 7     while ((c = getchar()) != EOF)
```

The program is now waiting for input. If the user enters the same test data as before, the output will be:

```
              /* c == 49 or '1' */
     8        if (c = '\n')
              /* c == 10 or '\n' */
     9            ++nl;
              /* nl == 1 */
     7        while ((c = getchar()) != EOF)
              /* c == 10 or '\n' */
     8        if (c = '\n')
              /* c == 10 or '\n' */
     9            ++nl;
              /* nl == 2 */
     7        while ((c = getchar()) != EOF)
```

If an end-of-file character (cntl-d) is entered, the final output will be:

```
              /* c == -1 */
    10        printf("%d\n", nl);
              /* nl == 2 */2
                 return
```

Note the information printed out at the end of the trace line for the nl variable following line 10. Also note the **return** comment added by **ctrace** at the end of the trace output. This shows the implicit return at the terminating brace in the function.

The trace output shows that variable c is assigned the value '1' in line 7, but in line 8 it has the value '\n'. Once user attention is drawn to this **if** statement, he or she will probably realize that the assignment operator (=) was used in place of the equality operator (==). This error can easily be missed during code reading.

EXECUTION-TIME TRACE CONTROL

The default operation for **ctrace** is to trace the entire program file, unless the −f or −v options are used to trace specific functions. The default operation does not give the user statement-by-statement control of the tracing, nor does it let the user turn the tracing off and on when executing the traced program.

The user can do both of these by adding ctroff() and ctron() function calls to the program to turn the tracing off and on, respectively, at execution time. Thus, complex criteria can be arbitrarily coded for trace control with **if** statements, and this code can even be conditionally included because **ctrace** defines the CTRACE preprocessor variable. For example:

```
#ifdef CTRACE
        if (c == '!' && i > 1000)
            ctron();
#endif
```

These functions can also be called from sdb(1) if they are compiled with the −g option. For example, to trace all but lines 7 to 10 in the main function, enter:

```
sdb a.out
main:7b ctroff()
main:11b ctron()
r
```

The trace can be turned off and on by setting static variable `tr_ct_` to 0 and 1, respectively. This on/off option is useful if a user is using a debugger that can not call these functions directly.

FILES

/usr/ccs/lib/ctrace/runtime.c   run-time trace package

SEE ALSO

sdb(1), ctype(3C), fclose(3S), printf(3S), string(3C).
bfs(1), tail(1) in the *User's Reference Manual*.

DIAGNOSTICS

This section contains diagnostic messages from both `ctrace` and cc(1), since the traced code often gets some cc warning messages. The user can get cc error messages in some rare cases, all of which can be avoided.

ctrace Diagnostics

warning: some variables are not traced in this statement
Only 10 variables are traced in a statement to prevent the C compiler "out of tree space; simplify expression" error. Use the −t option to increase this number.

warning: statement too long to trace
This statement is over 400 characters long. Make sure that tabs are used to indent the code, not spaces.

cannot handle preprocessor code, use −P option
This is usually caused by #ifdef/#endif preprocessor statements in the middle of a C statement, or by a semicolon at the end of a #define preprocessor statement.

'if ... else if' sequence too long
Split the sequence by removing an `else` from the middle.

possible syntax error, try −P option
Use the −P option to preprocess the `ctrace` input, along with any appropriate −D, −I, and −U preprocessor options.

NOTES

Defining a function with the same name as a system function may cause a syntax error if the number of arguments is changed. Just use a different name.

`ctrace` assumes that BADMAG is a preprocessor macro, and that EOF and NULL are #defined constants. Declaring any of these to be variables, e.g., "int EOF;", will cause a syntax error.

Pointer values are always treated as pointers to character strings.

ctrace does not know about the components of aggregates like structures, unions, and arrays. It cannot choose a format to print all the components of an aggregate when an assignment is made to the entire aggregate. ctrace may choose to print the address of an aggregate or use the wrong format (e.g., 3.149050e-311 for a structure with two integer members) when printing the value of an aggregate.

The loop trace output elimination is done separately for each file of a multi-file program. Separate output elimination can result in functions called from a loop still being traced, or the elimination of trace output from one function in a file until another in the same file is called.

NAME

cxref – generate C program cross-reference

SYNOPSIS

cxref [*options*] *files*

DESCRIPTION

The cxref command analyzes a collection of C files and builds a cross-reference table. cxref uses a special version of cc to include #define'd information in its symbol table. It generates a list of all symbols (auto, static, and global) in each individual file, or, with the –c option, in combination. The table includes four fields: NAME, FILE, FUNCTION, and LINE. The line numbers appearing in the LINE field also show reference marks as appropriate. The reference marks include:

```
assignment  =
declaration –
definition  *
```

If no reference marks appear, you can assume a general reference.

OPTIONS

cxref interprets the –D, –I, –U options in the same manner that cc does. In addition, cxref interprets the following options:

- **–c** Combine the source files into a single report. Without the –c option, cxref generates a separate report for each file on the command line.
- **–d** Disables printing declarations, making the report easier to read.
- **–l** Does not print local variables. Prints only global and file scope statistics.
- **–o** *file* Direct output to *file*.
- **–s** Operates silently; does not print input file names.
- **–t** Format listing for 80-column width.
- **–w***num* Width option that formats output no wider than *num* (decimal) columns. This option will default to 80 if *num* is not specified or is less than 51.
- **–C** Runs only the first pass of cxref, creating a .cx file that can later be passed to cxref. This is similar to the –c option of cc or lint.
- **–F** Prints the full path of the referenced file names.
- **–L***cols* Modifies the number of columns in the LINE field. If you do not specify a number, cxref defaults to five columns.
- **–V** Prints version information on the standard error.

−Wname,file, function, line
Changes the default width of at least one field. The default widths are:

Field	Characters
NAME	15
FILE	13
FUNCTION	15
LINE	20 (4 per column)

FILES

TMPDIR/tcx.*   temporary files

TMPDIR/cx.*   temporary files

LIBDIR/xref   accessed by cxref

LIBDIR   usually /usr/ccs/lib

TMPDIR   usually /var/tmp but can be redefined by setting the environment variable TMPDIR [see tempnam in tmpnam(3S)].

EXAMPLE
```
     a.c

     1      main()
     2      {
     3              int i;
     4              extern char c;
     5
     6              i=65;
     7              c=(char)i;
     8      }
```

Resulting cross-reference table:

NAME	FILE	FUNCTION	LINE		
c	a.c	---	4−	7=	
i	a.c	main	3*	6=	7
main	a.c	---	2*		
u3b2	predefined	---	0*		
unix	predefined	---	0*		

SEE ALSO
   cc(1), lint(1).

DIAGNOSTICS
   Error messages usually mean you cannot compile the files.

delta(1)

NAME
delta – make a delta (change) to an SCCS file

SYNOPSIS
delta [-rSID] [-s] [-n] [-glist] [-m[mrlist]] [-y[comment]] [-p] *files*

DESCRIPTION
delta is used to permanently introduce into the named SCCS file changes that were made to the file retrieved by get -e (called the g-file or generated file).

delta makes a delta to each named SCCS file. If a directory is named, delta behaves as though each file in the directory were specified as a named file, except that non-SCCS files (last component of the path name does not begin with s.) and unreadable files are silently ignored. If a name of – is given, the standard input is read (see the NOTES section); each line of the standard input is taken to be the name of an SCCS file to be processed.

delta may issue prompts on the standard output depending on certain keyletters specified and flags [see admin(1)] that may be present in the SCCS file (see -m and -y keyletters below).

Keyletter arguments apply independently to each named file.

-rSID
: Uniquely identifies which delta is to be made to the SCCS file. The use of this keyletter is necessary only if two or more outstanding gets for editing (get -e) on the same SCCS file were done by the same person (login name). The SID value specified with the -r keyletter can be either the SID specified on the get command line or the SID to be made as reported by the get command [see get(1)]. A diagnostic results if the specified SID is ambiguous, or, if necessary and omitted on the command line.

-s
: Suppresses the issue, on the standard output, of the created delta's SID, as well as the number of lines inserted, deleted and unchanged in the SCCS file.

-n
: Specifies retention of the edited g-file (normally removed at completion of delta processing).

-glist
: Specify a *list* [see get(1) for the definition of *list*] of deltas that are to be ignored when the file is accessed at the change level (SID) created by this delta.

-m[mrlist]
: If the SCCS file has the v flag set [see admin(1)] then a Modification Request (MR) number must be supplied as the reason for creating the new delta. If -m is not used and the standard input is a terminal, the prompt MRs? is issued on the standard output before the standard input is read; if the standard input is not a terminal, no prompt is issued. The MRs? prompt always precedes the comments? prompt (see -y keyletter). MRs in a list are separated by blanks and/or tab characters. An unescaped new-line character terminates the MR list. Note that if the v flag has a value [see admin(1)], it is taken to be the name of a program (or shell

procedure) that will validate the correctness of the MR numbers. If a non-zero exit status is returned from the MR number validation program, **delta** terminates. (It is assumed that the MR numbers were not all valid.)

-y[comment] Arbitrary text used to describe the reason for making the delta. A null string is considered a valid *comment*. If -y is not specified and the standard input is a terminal, the prompt **comments?** is issued on the standard output before the standard input is read; if the standard input is not a terminal, no prompt is issued. An unescaped new-line character terminates the comment text.

-p Causes **delta** to print (on the standard output) the SCCS file differences before and after the delta is applied in a **diff**(1) format.

FILES

g-file Existed before the execution of **delta**; removed after completion of **delta**.

p-file Existed before the execution of **delta**; may exist after completion of **delta**.

q-file Created during the execution of **delta**; removed after completion of **delta**.

x-file Created during the execution of **delta**; renamed to SCCS file after completion of **delta**.

z-file Created during the execution of **delta**; removed during the execution of **delta**.

d-file Created during the execution of **delta**; removed after completion of **delta**.

bdiff Program to compute differences between the "gotten" file and the g-file.

SEE ALSO

admin(1), cdc(1), get(1), help(1), prs(1), rmdel(1), sccsfile(4).
bdiff(1) in the *User's Reference Manual*.

DIAGNOSTICS

Use **help**(1) for explanations.

NOTES

A **get** of many SCCS files, followed by a **delta** of those files, should be avoided when the **get** generates a large amount of data. Instead, multiple **get**/**delta** sequences should be used.

If the standard input (-) is specified on the **delta** command line, the -m (if necessary) and -y keyletters must also be present. Omission of these keyletters causes an error.

Comments are limited to text strings of at most 1024 characters. Line lengths greater than 1000 characters cause undefined results.

dis(1)

NAME
dis – object code disassembler

SYNOPSIS
dis [-o] [-V] [-L] [-s] [-d *sec*] [-D *sec*] [-F *function*] [-t *sec*] [-l *string*] *file* ...

DESCRIPTION
The dis command produces an assembly language listing of *file*, which may be an object file or an archive of object files. The listing includes assembly statements and an octal or hexadecimal representation of the binary that produced those statements.

The following *options* are interpreted by the disassembler and may be specified in any order.

-d *sec* Disassemble the named section as data, printing the offset of the data from the beginning of the section.

-D *sec* Disassemble the named section as data, printing the actual address of the data.

-F *function* Disassemble only the named function in each object file specified on the command line. The -F option may be specified multiple times on the command line.

-L Lookup source labels for subsequent printing. This option works only if the file was compiled with additional debugging information [e.g., the -g option of cc].

-l *string* Disassemble the archive file specified by *string*. For example, one would issue the command dis -l x -l z to disassemble libx.a and libz.a, which are assumed to be in *LIBDIR*.

-o Print numbers in octal. The default is hexadecimal.

-s Perform symbolic disassembly where possible. Symbolic disassembly output will appear on the line following the instruction. Symbol names will be printed using C syntax.

-t *sec* Disassemble the named section as text.

-V Print, on standard error, the version number of the disassembler being executed.

If the -d, -D or -t options are specified, only those named sections from each user-supplied file name will be disassembled. Otherwise, all sections containing text will be disassembled.

On output, a number enclosed in brackets at the beginning of a line, such as [5], indicates that the break-pointable line number starts with the following instruction. These line numbers will be printed only if the file was compiled with additional debugging information [e.g., the -g option of cc]. An expression such as <40> in the operand field or in the symbolic disassembly, following a relative displacement for control transfer instructions, is the computed address within the section to which control will be transferred. A function name will appear in the first column, followed by ( ) if the object file contains a symbol table.

FILES
    LIBDIR   usually `/usr/ccs/lib`

SEE ALSO
    as(1), cc(1), ld(1), a.out(4).

DIAGNOSTICS
    The self-explanatory diagnostics indicate errors in the command line or problems encountered with the specified files.

NOTES
    Since the −da option did not adhere to the command syntax rules, it has been replaced by −D.

    At this time, symbolic disassembly does not take advantage of additional information available if the file is compiled with the −g option.

dump(1)

NAME
dump – dump selected parts of an object file

SYNOPSIS
dump [*options*] *files*

DESCRIPTION
The dump command dumps selected parts of each of its object *file* arguments.

This command will accept both object files and archives of object files. It processes each file argument according to one or more of the following options:

-a	Dump the archive header of each member of an archive.
-C	Dump decoded C++ symbol table names.
-c	Dump the string table(s).
-D	Dump debugging information.
-f	Dump each file header.
-g	Dump the global symbols in the symbol table of an archive.
-h	Dump the section headers.
-L	Dump dynamic linking information and static shared library information, if available.
-l	Dump line number information.
-o	Dump each program execution header.
-r	Dump relocation information.
-s	Dump section contents in hexadecimal.

-T *index* or -T *index1*, *index2*
  Dump only the indexed symbol table entry defined by *index* or a range of entries defined by *index1*, *index2*.

-t	Dump symbol table entries.
-u	When reading a COFF object file, dump translates the file to ELF internally (this translation does not affect the file contents). This option controls how much translation occurs from COFF values to ELF. Normally (without -u), the COFF values are preserved as much as possible, showing the actual bytes in the file. If -u is used, dump updates the values and completes the internal translation, giving a consistent ELF view of the contents. Although the bytes displayed under this option might not match the file itself, they show how the file would look if it were converted to ELF. (See cof2elf(1) for more information.)
-V	Print version information.

The following modifiers are used in conjunction with the options listed above to modify their capabilities.

dump(1)   **dump(1)**

    −d *number* or −d *number1*, *number2*
           Dump the section number indicated by *number* or the range of sections starting at *number1* and ending at *number2*. This modifier can be used with −h, −s, and −r. When −d is used with −h or −s, the argument is treated as the number of a section or range of sections. When −d is used with −r, the argument is treated as the number of the section or range of sections to which the relocation applies. For example, to print out all relocation entries associated with the .text section, specify the number of the section as the argument to −d. If .text is section number 2 in the file, dump −r −d 2 will print all associated entries. To print out a specific relocation section use dump −s −n *name* for raw data output, or dump −sv −n *name* for interpreted output.

    −n *name*   Dump information pertaining only to the named entity. This modifier can be used with −h, −s, −r, and −t. When −n is used with −h or −s, the argument will be treated as the name of a section. When −n is used with −t or −r, the argument will be treated as the name of a symbol. For example, dump −t −n .text will dump the symbol table entry associated with the symbol whose name is .text, where dump −h −n .text will dump the section header information for the .text section.

    −p   Suppress printing of the headings.

    −v   Dump information in symbolic representation rather than numeric. This modifier can be used with −a (date, user id, group id), −f (class, data, type, machine, version, flags), −h (type, flags), −o (type, flags), −r (name, type), −s (interpret section contents wherever possible), −t (type, bind), and −L (value). When −v is used with −s, all sections that can be interpreted, such as the string table or symbol table, will be interpreted. For example, dump −sv −n .symtab *files* will produce the same formatted output as dump −tv *files*, but dump −s −n .symtab *files* will print raw data in hexadecimal. Without additional modifiers, dump −sv *files* will dump all sections in the files interpreting all those that it can and dumping the rest (such as .text or .data) as raw data.

The dump command attempts to format the information it dumps in a meaningful way, printing certain information in character, hexadecimal, octal or decimal representation as appropriate.

SEE ALSO
     a.out(4), ar(4).

get(1)

NAME
get – get a version of an SCCS file

SYNOPSIS
get [-aseq-no.] [-ccutoff] [-ilist] [-rSID] [-wstring] [-xlist] [-l[p]] [-b] [-e] [-g] [-k] [-m] [-n] [-p] [-s] [-t] file...

DESCRIPTION
get generates an ASCII text file from each named SCCS file according to the specifications given by its keyletter arguments, which begin with –. The arguments may be specified in any order, but all keyletter arguments apply to all named SCCS files. If a directory is named, get behaves as though each file in the directory were specified as a named file, except that non-SCCS files (last component of the path name does not begin with s.) and unreadable files are silently ignored. If a name of – is given, the standard input is read; each line of the standard input is taken to be the name of an SCCS file to be processed.

The generated text is normally written into a file called the g-file whose name is derived from the SCCS file name by simply removing the leading "s." (see also the FILES section below).

Each of the keyletter arguments is explained below as though only one SCCS file is to be processed, but the effects of any keyletter argument apply independently to each named file.

-rSID   The SCCS identification string (SID) of the version (delta) of an SCCS file to be retrieved. Table 1 below shows, for the most useful cases, what version of an SCCS file is retrieved (as well as the SID of the version to be eventually created by delta(1) if the –e keyletter is also used), as a function of the SID specified.

-ccutoff   Cutoff date-time, in the form:

    YY[MM[DD[HH[MM[SS]]]]]

No changes (deltas) to the SCCS file that were created after the specified *cutoff* date-time are included in the generated ASCII text file. Units omitted from the date-time default to their maximum possible values; that is, –c7502 is equivalent to –c750228235959. Any number of non-numeric characters may separate the two-digit pieces of the *cutoff* date-time. This feature allows one to specify a *cutoff* date in the form:

    -c"77/2/2 9:22:25".

-ilist   A *list* of deltas to be included (forced to be applied) in the creation of the generated file. The *list* has the following syntax:

    <list> ::= <range> | <list> , <range>
    <range> ::= SID | SID – SID

SID, the SCCS Identification of a delta, may be in any form shown in the "SID Specified" column of Table 1.

-x_list_ A _list_ of deltas to be excluded in the creation of the generated file. See the **-i** keyletter for the _list_ format.

-e Indicates that the **get** is for the purpose of editing or making a change (delta) to the SCCS file via a subsequent use of **delta**(1). The **-e** keyletter used in a **get** for a particular version (SID) of the SCCS file prevents further **get**s for editing on the same SID until **delta** is executed or the **j** (joint edit) flag is set in the SCCS file [see **admin**(1)]. Concurrent use of **get -e** for different SIDs is always allowed.

If the g-file generated by **get** with an **-e** keyletter is accidentally ruined in the process of editing it, it may be regenerated by re-executing the **get** command with the **-k** keyletter in place of the **-e** keyletter.

SCCS file protection specified via the ceiling, floor, and authorized user list stored in the SCCS file [see **admin**(1)] are enforced when the **-e** keyletter is used.

-b Used with the **-e** keyletter to indicate that the new delta should have an SID in a new branch as shown in Table 1. This keyletter is ignored if the **b** flag is not present in the file [see **admin**(1)] or if the retrieved **delta** is not a leaf **delta**. (A leaf **delta** is one that has no successors on the SCCS file tree.) A branch **delta** may always be created from a non-leaf **delta**. Partial SIDs are interpreted as shown in the "SID Retrieved" column of Table 1.

-k Suppresses replacement of identification keywords (see below) in the retrieved text by their value. The **-k** keyletter is implied by the **-e** keyletter.

-l[p] Causes a delta summary to be written into an l-file. If **-lp** is used, then an l-file is not created; the delta summary is written on the standard output instead. See IDENTIFICATION KEYWORDS for detailed information on the l-file.

-p Causes the text retrieved from the SCCS file to be written on the standard output. No g-file is created. All output that normally goes to the standard output goes to file descriptor 2 instead, unless the **-s** keyletter is used, in which case it disappears.

-s Suppresses all output normally written on the standard output. However, fatal error messages (which always go to file descriptor 2) remain unaffected.

-m Causes each text line retrieved from the SCCS file to be preceded by the SID of the delta that inserted the text line in the SCCS file. The format is: SID, followed by a horizontal tab, followed by the text line.

-n Causes each generated text line to be preceded with the %M% identification keyword value (see below). The format is: %M% value, followed by a horizontal tab, followed by the text line. When both the **-m** and **-n** keyletters are used, the format is: %M%

value, followed by a horizontal tab, followed by the –m keyletter generated format.

-g Suppresses the actual retrieval of text from the SCCS file. It is primarily used to generate an l-file, or to verify the existence of a particular SID.

-t Used to access the most recently created delta in a given release (e.g., -r1), or release and level (e.g., -r1.2).

-w *string* Substitute *string* for all occurrences of %W% when getting the file. Substitution occurs prior to keyword expansion.

-a*seq-no.* The delta sequence number of the SCCS file delta (version) to be retrieved. This keyletter is used by the comb command; it is not a generally useful keyletter. If both the -r and -a keyletters are specified, only the -a keyletter is used. Care should be taken when using the -a keyletter in conjunction with the -e keyletter, as the SID of the delta to be created may not be what one expects. The -r keyletter can be used with the -a and -e keyletters to control the naming of the SID of the delta to be created.

For each file processed, get responds (on the standard output) with the SID being accessed and with the number of lines retrieved from the SCCS file.

If the -e keyletter is used, the SID of the delta to be made appears after the SID accessed and before the number of lines generated. If there is more than one named file or if a directory or standard input is named, each file name is printed (preceded by a new-line) before it is processed. If the -i keyletter is used, included deltas are listed following the notation "Included"; if the -x keyletter is used, excluded deltas are listed following the notation "Excluded".

TABLE 1. Determination of SCCS Identification String

SID* Specified	-b Keyletter Used†	Other Conditions	SID Retrieved	SID of Delta to be Created
none‡	no	R defaults to mR	mR.mL	mR.(mL+1)
none‡	yes	R defaults to mR	mR.mL	mR.mL.(mB+1).1
R	no	R > mR	mR.mL	R.1***
R	no	R = mR	mR.mL	mR.(mL+1)
R	yes	R > mR	mR.mL	mR.mL.(mB+1).1
R	yes	R = mR	mR.mL	mR.mL.(mB+1).1
R	–	R < mR and R does *not* exist	hR.mL**	hR.mL.(mB+1).1
R	–	Trunk succ.# in release > R and R exists	R.mL	R.mL.(mB+1).1
R.L	no	No trunk succ.	R.L	R.(L+1)
R.L	yes	No trunk succ.	R.L	R.L.(mB+1).1
R.L	–	Trunk succ. in release ≥ R	R.L	R.L.(mB+1).1
R.L.B	no	No branch succ.	R.L.B.mS	R.L.B.(mS+1)
R.L.B	yes	No branch succ.	R.L.B.mS	R.L.(mB+1).1
R.L.B.S	no	No branch succ.	R.L.B.S	R.L.B.(S+1)
R.L.B.S	yes	No branch succ.	R.L.B.S	R.L.(mB+1).1
R.L.B.S	–	Branch succ.	R.L.B.S	R.L.(mB+1).1

    *   "R", "L", "B", and "S" are the "release", "level", "branch", and "sequence" components of the SID, respectively; "m" means "maximum". Thus, for example, "R.mL" means "the maximum level number within release R"; "R.L.(mB+1).1" means "the first sequence number on the new branch (i.e., maximum branch number plus one) of level L within release R". Note that if the SID specified is of the form "R.L", "R.L.B", or "R.L.B.S", each of the specified components must exist.

   **   "hR" is the highest existing release that is lower than the specified, nonexistent, release R.

 ***   This is used to force creation of the first delta in a new release.

    #   Successor.

    †   The -b keyletter is effective only if the b flag [see **admin**(1)] is present in the file. An entry of - means "irrelevant".

    ‡   This case applies if the d (default SID) flag is not present in the file. If the d flag is present in the file, then the SID obtained from the d flag is interpreted as if it had been specified on the command line. Thus, one of the other cases in this table applies.

IDENTIFICATION KEYWORDS

Identifying information is inserted into the text retrieved from the SCCS file by replacing identification keywords with their value wherever they occur. The following keywords may be used in the text stored in an SCCS file:

Keyword	Value
%M%	Module name: either the value of the m flag in the file [see admin(1)], or if absent, the name of the SCCS file with the leading s. removed.
%I%	SCCS identification (SID) (%R%.%L%.%B%.%S%) of the retrieved text.
%R%	Release.
%L%	Level.
%B%	Branch.
%S%	Sequence.
%D%	Current date (YY/MM/DD).
%H%	Current date (MM/DD/YY).
%T%	Current time (HH:MM:SS).
%E%	Date newest applied delta was created (YY/MM/DD).
%G%	Date newest applied delta was created (MM/DD/YY).
%U%	Time newest applied delta was created (HH:MM:SS).
%Y%	Module type: value of the t flag in the SCCS file [see admin(1)].
%F%	SCCS file name.
%P%	Fully qualified SCCS file name.
%Q%	The value of the q flag in the file [see admin(1)].
%C%	Current line number. This keyword is intended for identifying messages output by the program such as "this should not have happened" type errors. It is not intended to be used on every line to provide sequence numbers.
%Z%	The four-character string @(#) recognizable by the what command.
%W%	A shorthand notation for constructing what strings for UNIX System program files. %W% = %Z%%M%<tab>%I%
%A%	Another shorthand notation for constructing what strings for non-UNIX System program files: %A% = %Z%%Y% %M% %T%%Z%

Several auxiliary files may be created by get. These files are known generically as the g-file, l-file, p-file, and z-file. The letter before the hyphen is called the tag. An auxiliary file name is formed from the SCCS file name: the last component of all SCCS file names must be of the form s.*module-name*, the auxiliary files are named by replacing the leading s with the tag. The g-file is an exception to this scheme: the g-file is named by removing the s. prefix. For example, s.xyz.c, the auxiliary file names would be xyz.c, l.xyz.c, p.xyz.c, and z.xyz.c, respectively.

The g-file, which contains the generated text, is created in the current directory (unless the −p keyletter is used). A g-file is created in all cases, whether or not any lines of text were generated by the get. It is owned by the real user. If the −k keyletter is used or implied, its mode is 644; otherwise its mode is 444. Only the real user need have write permission in the current directory.

The l-file contains a table showing which deltas were applied in generating the retrieved text. The l-file is created in the current directory if the −l keyletter is used; its mode is 444 and it is owned by the real user. Only the real user need have write permission in the current directory.

Lines in the l-file have the following format:
  a. A blank character if the delta was applied; * otherwise.
  b. A blank character if the delta was applied or was not applied and ignored; * if the delta was not applied and was not ignored.
  c. A code indicating a "special" reason why the delta was or was not applied: "I" (included), "X" (excluded), or "C" (cut off by a −c keyletter).
  d. Blank.
  e. SCCS identification (SID).
  f. Tab character.
  g. Date and time (in the form YY/MM/DD HH:MM:SS) of creation.
  h. Blank.
  i. Login name of person who created delta.

The comments and MR data follow on subsequent lines, indented one horizontal tab character. A blank line terminates each entry.

The p-file is used to pass information resulting from a get with an −e keyletter along to delta. Its contents are also used to prevent a subsequent execution of get with an −e keyletter for the same SID until delta is executed or the joint edit flag, j, [see admin(1)] is set in the SCCS file. The p-file is created in the directory containing the SCCS file and the effective user must have write permission in that directory. Its mode is 644 and it is owned by the effective user. The format of the p-file is: the gotten SID, followed by a blank, followed by the SID that the new delta will have when it is made, followed by a blank, followed by the login name of the real user, followed by a blank, followed by the date-time the get was executed, followed by a blank and the −i keyletter argument if it was present, followed by a blank and the −x keyletter argument if it was present, followed by a new-line. There can be an arbitrary number of lines in the p-file at any time; no two lines can have the same new delta SID.

The z-file serves as a lock-out mechanism against simultaneous updates. Its contents are the binary (2 bytes) process ID of the command (i.e., get) that created it. The z-file is created in the directory containing the SCCS file for the duration of get. The same protection restrictions as those for the p-file apply for the z-file. The z-file is created with mode 444.

FILES

g-file	Created by the execution of get.
p-file	[see delta(1)]
q-file	[see delta(1)]
z-file	[see delta(1)]
bdiff	Program to compute differences between the "gotten" file and the g-file.

SEE ALSO
admin(1), delta(1), help(1), prs(1), what(1).
bdiff(1) in the *User's Reference Manual*.

DIAGNOSTICS
Use help(1) for explanations.

NOTES
If the effective user has write permission (either explicitly or implicitly) in the directory containing the SCCS files, but the real user does not, then only one file may be named when the −e keyletter is used.

help (1)

NAME
help – ask for help with message numbers or SCCS commands

SYNOPSIS
help [*args*]

DESCRIPTION
help finds information to explain a message from a command or explain the use of a SCCS command. Zero or more arguments may be supplied. If no arguments are given, help will prompt for one.

The arguments may be either information within the parentheses following a message or SCCS command names.

The response of the program will be the explanatory information related to the argument, if there is any.

When all else fails, try "help stuck".

FILES

LIBDIR/help	directory containing files of message text.
LIBDIR/help/helploc	file containing locations of help files not in *LIBDIR*/help.
LIBDIR	usually /usr/ccs/lib

install (1M)

NAME
install – install commands

SYNOPSIS
/usr/sbin/install [-c *dira*] [-f *dirb*] [-i] [-n *dirc*] [-m *mode*] [-u *user*] [-g *group*] [-o] [-s] *file* [*dirx* ...]

DESCRIPTION
The install command is most commonly used in "makefiles" [see make(1)] to install a *file* (updated target file) in a specific place within a file system. Each *file* is installed by copying it into the appropriate directory, thereby retaining the mode and owner of the original command. The program prints messages telling the user exactly what files it is replacing or creating and where they are going.

If no options or directories (*dirx* ...) are given, install will search a set of default directories (/bin, /usr/bin, /etc, /lib, and /usr/lib, in that order) for a file with the same name as *file*. When the first occurrence is found, install issues a message saying that it is overwriting that file with *file*, and proceeds to do so. If the file is not found, the program states this and exits without further action.

If one or more directories (*dirx* ...) are specified after *file*, those directories will be searched before the directories specified in the default list.

The meanings of the options are:

-c *dira*   Installs a new command (*file*) in the directory specified by *dira*, only if it is not found. If it is found, install issues a message saying that the file already exists, and exits without overwriting it. May be used alone or with the -s option.

-f *dirb*   Forces *file* to be installed in given directory, whether or not one already exists. If the file being installed does not already exist, the mode and owner of the new file will be set to 755 and bin, respectively. If the file already exists, the mode and owner will be that of the already existing file. May be used alone or with the -o or -s options.

-i   Ignores default directory list, searching only through the given directories (*dirx* ...). May be used alone or with any other options except -c and -f.

-n *dirc*   If *file* is not found in any of the searched directories, it is put in the directory specified in *dirc*. The mode and owner of the new file will be set to 755 and bin, respectively. May be used alone or with any other options except -c and -f.

-m *mode*   The mode of the new file is set to *mode*.

-u *user*   The owner of the new file is set to *user*.

install (1M)

-g *group*
: The group id of the new file is set to *group*. Only available to the superuser.

-o
: If *file* is found, this option saves the "found" file by copying it to OLD*file* in the directory in which it was found. This option is useful when installing a frequently used file such as /bin/sh or /lib/saf/ttymon, where the existing file cannot be removed. May be used alone or with any other options except -c.

-s
: Suppresses printing of messages other than error messages. May be used alone or with any other options.

SEE ALSO
make(1).

ld(1)

NAME
ld – link editor for object files

SYNOPSIS
ld [*options*] *files* ...

DESCRIPTION
The `ld` command combines relocatable object files, performs relocation, and resolves external symbols. `ld` operates in two modes, static or dynamic, as governed by the –d option. In static mode, –dn, relocatable object files given as arguments are combined to produce an executable object file; if the –r option is specified, relocatable object files are combined to produce one relocatable object file. In dynamic mode, –dy, the default, relocatable object files given as arguments are combined to produce an executable object file that will be linked at execution with any shared object files given as arguments; if the –G option is specified, relocatable object files are combined to produce a shared object. In all cases, the output of `ld` is left in `a.out` by default.

If any argument is a library, it is searched exactly once at the point it is encountered in the argument list. The library may be either a relocatable archive or a shared object. For an archive library, only those routines defining an unresolved external reference are loaded. The archive library symbol table [see `ar(4)`] is searched sequentially with as many passes as are necessary to resolve external references that can be satisfied by library members. Thus, the ordering of members in the library is functionally unimportant, unless there exist multiple library members defining the same external symbol. A shared object consists of a single entity all of whose references must be resolved within the executable being built or within other shared objects with which it is linked.

The following options are recognized by `ld`:

-a   In static mode only, produce an executable object file; give errors for undefined references. This is the default behavior for static mode. –a may not be used with the –r option.

-b   In dynamic mode only, when creating an executable, do not do special processing for relocations that reference symbols in shared objects. Without the –b option, the link editor will create special position-independent relocations for references to functions defined in shared objects and will arrange for data objects defined in shared objects to be copied into the memory image of the executable by the dynamic linker at run time. With the –b option, the output code may be more efficient, but it will be less sharable.

-d[y|n]
When –dy, the default, is specified, `ld` uses dynamic linking; when –dn is specified, `ld` uses static linking.

-e *epsym*
Set the entry point address for the output file to be that of the symbol *epsym*.

-h *name*
: In dynamic mode only, when building a shared object, record *name* in the object's dynamic section. *name* will be recorded in executables that are linked with this object rather than the object's UNIX System file name. Accordingly, *name* will be used by the dynamic linker as the name of the shared object to search for at run time.

-l*x*
: Search a library `lib`*x*`.so` or `lib`*x*`.a`, the conventional names for shared object and archive libraries, respectively. In dynamic mode, unless the **-Bstatic** option is in effect, `ld` searches each directory specified in the library search path for a file `lib`*x*`.so` or `lib`*x*`.a`. The directory search stops at the first directory containing either. `ld` chooses the file ending in `.so` if **-l***x* expands to two files whose names are of the form `lib`*x*`.so` and `lib`*x*`.a`. If no `lib`*x*`.so` is found, then `ld` accepts `lib`*x*`.a`. In static mode, or when the **-Bstatic** option is in effect, `ld` selects only the file ending in `.a`. A library is searched when its name is encountered, so the placement of **-l** is significant.

-m
: Produce a memory map or listing of the input/output sections on the standard output.

-o *outfile*
: Produce an output object file named *outfile*. The name of the default object file is `a.out`.

-r
: Combine relocatable object files to produce one relocatable object file. `ld` will not complain about unresolved references. This option cannot be used in dynamic mode or with **-a**.

-s
: Strip symbolic information from the output file. The debug and line sections and their associated relocation entries will be removed. Except for relocatable files or shared objects, the symbol table and string table sections will also be removed from the output object file.

-t
: Turn off the warning about multiply defined symbols that are not the same size.

-u *symname*
: Enter *symname* as an undefined symbol in the symbol table. This is useful for loading entirely from an archive library, since initially the symbol table is empty and an unresolved reference is needed to force the loading of the first routine. The placement of this option on the command line is significant; it must be placed before the library that will define the symbol.

-z defs
: Force a fatal error if any undefined symbols remain at the end of the link. This is the default when building an executable. It is also useful when building a shared object to assure that the object is self-contained, that is, that all its symbolic references are resolved internally.

-z nodefs
: Allow undefined symbols. This is the default when building a shared object. It may be used when building an executable in dynamic mode and linking with a shared object that has unresolved references in routines not used by that executable. This option should be used with caution.

-z text
　　In dynamic mode only, force a fatal error if any relocations against non-writable, allocatable sections remain.

-B [dynamic|static]
　　Options governing library inclusion. -Bdynamic is valid in dynamic mode only. These options may be specified any number of times on the command line as toggles: if the -Bstatic option is given, no shared objects will be accepted until -Bdynamic is seen. See also the -l option.

-Bsymbolic
　　In dynamic mode only, when building a shared object, bind references to global symbols to their definitions within the object, if definitions are available. Normally, references to global symbols within shared objects are not bound until run time, even if definitions are available, so that definitions of the same symbol in an executable or other shared objects can override the object's own definition. ld will issue warnings for undefined symbols unless -z defs overrides.

-G　In dynamic mode only, produce a shared object. Undefined symbols are allowed.

-I *name*
　　When building an executable, use *name* as the path name of the interpreter to be written into the program header. The default in static mode is no interpreter; in dynamic mode, the default is the name of the dynamic linker, /usr/lib/libc.so.1. Either case may be overrridden by -I. exec will load this interpreter when it loads the a.out and will pass control to the interpreter rather than to the a.out directly.

-L *path*
　　Add *path* to the library search directories. ld searches for libraries first in any directories specified with -L options, then in the standard directories. This option is effective only if it precedes the -l option on the command line.

-M *mapfile*
　　In *static* mode only, read *mapfile* as a text file of directives to ld. Because these directives change the shape of the output file created by ld, use of this option is strongly discouraged.

-Q[y|n]
　　Under -Qy, an ident string is added to the .comment section of the output file to identify the version of the link editor used to create the file. This will result in multiple ld idents when there have been multiple linking steps, such as when using ld -r. This is identical with the default action of the cc command. -Qn suppresses version.

-V　Output a message giving information about the version of ld being used.

-YP, *dirlist*
　　Change the default directories used for finding libraries. *dirlist* is a colon-separated path list.

The environment variable `LD_LIBRARY_PATH` may be used to specify library search directories. In the most general case, it will contain two directory lists separated by a semicolon:

   dirlist1 ; dirlist2

If `ld` is called with any number of occurences of `-L`, as in

   `ld` ... `-L`*path1* ...`-L`*pathn* ...

then the search path ordering is

   dirlist1 path1 ... pathn dirlist2 LIBPATH

`LD_LIBRARY_PATH` is also used to specify library search directories to the dynamic linker at run time. That is, if `LD_LIBRARY_PATH` exists in the environment, the dynamic linker will search the directories named in it, before its default directory, for shared objects to be linked with the program at execution.

The environment variable `LD_RUN_PATH`, containing a directory list, may also be used to specify library search directories to the dynamic linker. If present and not null, it is passed to the dynamic linker by `ld` via data stored in the output object file.

FILES

`lib`*x*`.so`	libraries
`lib`*x*`.a`	libraries
`a.out`	output file
LIBPATH	usually `/usr/ccs/lib:/usr/lib`

SEE ALSO

`as`(1), `cc`(1), `exec`(2), `exit`(2), `end`(3C), `a.out`(4), `ar`(4).
The "C Compilation System" chapter and the "Mapfile Option" appendix in the *Programmer's Guide: ANSI C and Programming Support Tools.*

NOTES

Through its options, the link editor gives users great flexibility; however, those who use the **–M** *mapfile* option must assume some added responsibilities. Use of this feature is *strongly* discouraged.

ldd(1)

NAME
ldd – list dynamic dependencies

SYNOPSIS
ldd [-d | -r] *file*

DESCRIPTION
The ldd command lists the path names of all shared objects that would be loaded as a result of executing *file*. If *file* is a valid executable but does not require any shared objects, ldd will succeed, producing no output.

ldd may also be used to check the compatibility of *file* with the shared objects it uses. It does this by optionally printing warnings for any unresolved symbol references that would occur if *file* were executed. Two options govern this mode of ldd:

-d   Causes ldd to check all references to data objects.

-r   Causes ldd to check references to both data objects and functions.

Only one of the above options may be given during any single invocation of ldd.

SEE ALSO
cc(1), ld(1).

The "C Compilation System" chapter in the *Programmer's Guide: ANSI C and Programming Support Tools*.

DIAGNOSTICS
ldd prints its record of shared object path names to stdout. The optional list of symbol resolution problems are printed to stderr. If *file* is not an executable file or cannot be opened for reading, a non-zero exit status is returned.

NOTES
ldd doesn't list shared objects explicitly attached via dlopen(3X).

ldd uses the same algorithm as the dynamic linker to locate shared objects.

lex(1)

NAME
lex – generate programs for simple lexical tasks

SYNOPSIS
lex [–ctvn –V –Q[y|n]] [*file*]

DESCRIPTION
The `lex` command generates programs to be used in simple lexical analysis of text.

The input *file*s (standard input default) contain strings and expressions to be searched for and C text to be executed when these strings are found.

`lex` generates a file named `lex.yy.c`. When `lex.yy.c` is compiled and linked with the lex library, it copies the input to the output except when a string specified in the file is found. When a specified string is found, then the corresponding program text is executed. The actual string matched is left in `yytext`, an external character array. Matching is done in order of the patterns in the *file*. The patterns may contain square brackets to indicate character classes, as in [abx–z] to indicate a, b, x, y, and z; and the operators *, +, and ? mean, respectively, any non-negative number of, any positive number of, and either zero or one occurrence of, the previous character or character class. Thus, [a–zA–Z]+ matches a string of letters. The character . is the class of all ASCII characters except new-line. Parentheses for grouping and vertical bar for alternation are also supported. The notation r{d,e} in a rule indicates between *d* and *e* instances of regular expression *r*. It has higher precedence than |, but lower than *, ?, +, and concatenation. The character ^ at the beginning of an expression permits a successful match only immediately after a new-line, and the character $ at the end of an expression requires a trailing new-line. The character / in an expression indicates trailing context; only the part of the expression up to the slash is returned in `yytext`, but the remainder of the expression must follow in the input stream. An operator character may be used as an ordinary symbol if it is within " symbols or preceded by \.

Three macros are expected: `input()` to read a character; `unput(c)` to replace a character read; and `output(c)` to place an output character. They are defined in terms of the standard streams, but you can override them. The program generated is named `yylex()`, and the lex library contains a `main()` that calls it. The action `REJECT` on the right side of the rule causes this match to be rejected and the next suitable match executed; the function `yymore()` accumulates additional characters into the same `yytext`; and the function `yyless(n)` pushes back `yyleng` – n characters into the input stream. (`yyleng` is an external `int` variable giving the length of `yytext`.) The macros `input` and `output` use files `yyin` and `yyout` to read from and write to, defaulted to `stdin` and `stdout`, respectively.

Any line beginning with a blank is assumed to contain only C text and is copied; if it precedes %%, it is copied into the external definition area of the `lex.yy.c` file. All rules should follow a %%, as in `yacc`. Lines preceding %% that begin with a non-blank character define the string on the left to be the remainder of the line; it can be called out later by surrounding it with { }. In this section, C code (and preprocessor statements) can also be included between %{ and %}. Note that curly brackets do not imply parentheses; only string substitution is done.

EXAMPLE

```
D       [0-9]
%{
void
skipcommnts(void)
{
        for(;;)
        {
                while(input()!='*')
                        ;
                if(input()=='/')
                        return;
                else
                        unput(yytext[yyleng-1]);
        }
}
%}
%%
if      printf("IF statement\n");
[a-z]+  printf("tag, value %s\n",yytext);
0{D}+   printf("octal number %s\n",yytext);
{D}+    printf("decimal number %s\n",yytext);
"++"    printf("unary op\n");
"+"     printf("binary op\n");
"\n"    ;/*no action */
"/*"      skipcommnts();
%%
```

The external names generated by lex all begin with the prefix yy or YY.

The flags must appear before any files.

-c   Indicates C actions and is the default.

-t   Causes the lex.yy.c program to be written instead to standard output.

-v   Provides a two-line summary of statistics.

-n   Will not print out the -v summary.

-V   Print out version information on standard error.

-Q[y|n] Print out version information to output file lex.yy.c by using -Qy. The -Qn option does not print out version information and is the default.

Multiple files are treated as a single file. If no files are specified, standard input is used.

Certain default table sizes are too small for some users. The table sizes for the resulting finite state machine can be set in the definitions section:

%p *n*	number of positions is *n* (default 2500)
%n *n*	number of states is *n* (500)
%e *n*	number of parse tree nodes is *n* (1000)
%a *n*	number of transitions is *n* (2000)
%k *n*	number of packed character classes is *n* (2500)
%o *n*	size of output array is *n* (3000)

The use of one or more of the above automatically implies the −v option, unless the −n option is used.

SEE ALSO
yacc(1).
The "`lex`" chapter in the *Programmer's Guide: ANSI C and Programming Support Tools*.

lint(1)   lint(1)

NAME
lint – a C program checker

SYNOPSIS
lint [*options*] *files*

DESCRIPTION
lint detects features of C program files which are likely to be bugs, non-portable, or wasteful. It also checks type usage more strictly than the compiler. lint issues error and warning messages. Among the things it detects are unreachable statements, loops not entered at the top, automatic variables declared and not used, and logical expressions whose value is constant. lint checks for functions that return values in some places and not in others, functions called with varying numbers or types of arguments, and functions whose values are not used or whose values are used but none returned.

Arguments whose names end with .c are taken to be C source files. Arguments whose names end with .ln are taken to be the result of an earlier invocation of lint with either the –c or the –o option used. The .ln files are analogous to .o (object) files that are produced by the cc(1) command when given a .c file as input. Files with other suffixes are warned about and ignored.

lint takes all the .c, .ln, and llib-lx.ln (specified by –lx) files and processes them in their command line order. By default, lint appends the standard C lint library (llib-lc.ln) to the end of the list of files. When the –c option is used, the .ln and the llib-lx.ln files are ignored. When the –c option is not used, the second pass of lint checks the .ln and the llib-lx.ln list of files for mutual compatibility.

Any number of lint options may be used, in any order, intermixed with file-name arguments. The following options are used to suppress certain kinds of complaints:

–a   Suppress complaints about assignments of long values to variables that are not long.

–b   Suppress complaints about **break** statements that cannot be reached.

–h   Do not apply heuristic tests that attempt to intuit bugs, improve style, and reduce waste.

–m   Suppress complaints about external symbols that could be declared static.

–u   Suppress complaints about functions and external variables used and not defined, or defined and not used. (This option is suitable for running lint on a subset of files of a larger program).

–v   Suppress complaints about unused arguments in functions.

–x   Do not report variables referred to by external declarations but never used.

The following arguments alter `lint`'s behavior:

- **-I***dir* Search for included header files in the directory *dir* before searching the current directory and/or the standard place.

- **-l***x* Include the lint library `llib-lx.ln`. For example, you can include a lint version of the math library `llib-lm.ln` by inserting **-lm** on the command line. This argument does not suppress the default use of `llib-lc.ln`. These lint libraries must be in the assumed directory. This option can be used to reference local lint libraries and is useful in the development of multi-file projects.

- **-L***dir* Search for lint libraries in *dir* before searching the standard place.

- **-n** Do not check compatibility against the standard C lint library.

- **-p** Attempt to check portability to other dialects of C. Along with stricter checking, this option causes all non-external names to be truncated to eight characters and all external names to be truncated to six characters and one case.

- **-s** Produce one-line diagnostics only. `lint` occasionally buffers messages to produce a compound report.

- **-k** Alter the behavior of /*LINTED [*message*]*/ directives. Normally, `lint` will suppress warning messages for the code following these directives. Instead of suppressing the messages, `lint` prints an additional message containing the comment inside the directive.

- **-y** Specify that the file being linted will be treated as if the /*LINTLIBRARY*/ directive had been used. A lint library is normally created by using the /*LINTLIBRARY*/ directive.

- **-F** Print pathnames of files. `lint` normally prints the filename without the path.

- **-c** Cause `lint` to produce a `.ln` file for every `.c` file on the command line. These `.ln` files are the product of `lint`'s first pass only, and are not checked for inter-function compatibility.

- **-o***x* Cause `lint` to create a lint library with the name `llib-lx.ln`. The **-c** option nullifies any use of the **-o** option. The lint library produced is the input that is given to `lint`'s second pass. The **-o** option simply causes this file to be saved in the named lint library. To produce a `llib-lx.ln` without extraneous messages, use of the **-x** option is suggested. The **-v** option is useful if the source file(s) for the lint library are just external interfaces.

  Some of the above settings are also available through the use of "lint comments" (see below).

- **-V** Write to standard error the product name and release.

- **-W***file* Write a `.ln` file to *file*, for use by `cflow`(1).

lint(1)   lint(1)

-R*file*   Write a .ln file to *file*, for use by cxref(1).

lint recognizes many cc(1) command line options, including −D, −U, −g, −O, −Xt, −Xa, and −Xc, although −g and −O are ignored. Unrecognized options are warned about and ignored. The predefined macro lint is defined to allow certain questionable code to be altered or removed for lint. Thus, the symbol lint should be thought of as a reserved word for all code that is planned to be checked by lint.

Certain conventional comments in the C source will change the behavior of lint:

/*ARGSUSED*n*/
: makes lint check only the first *n* arguments for usage; a missing *n* is taken to be 0 (this option acts like the −v option for the next function).

/*CONSTCOND*/ or /*CONSTANTCOND*/ or /*CONSTANTCONDITION*/
: suppresses complaints about constant operands for the next expression.

/*EMPTY*/
: suppresses complaints about a null statement consequent on an if statement. This directive should be placed after the test expression, and before the semicolon. This directive is supplied to support empty if statements when a valid else statement follows. It suppresses messages on an empty else consequent.

/*FALLTHRU*/ or /*FALLTHROUGH*/
: suppresses complaints about fall through to a case or default labelled statement. This directive should be placed immediately preceding the label.

/*LINTLIBRARY*/
: at the beginning of a file shuts off complaints about unused functions and function arguments in this file. This is equivalent to using the −v and −x options.

/*LINTED [*message*]*/
: suppresses any intra-file warning except those dealing with unused variables or functions. This directive should be placed on the line immediately preceding where the lint warning occurred. The −k option alters the way in which lint handles this directive. Instead of suppressing messages, lint will print an additional message, if any, contained in the comment. This directive is useful in conjunction with the −s option for post-lint filtering.

/*NOTREACHED*/
: at appropriate points stops comments about unreachable code. [This comment is typically placed just after calls to functions like exit(2)].

/*PRINTFLIKE*n*/
: makes lint check the first *(n-1)* arguments as usual. The *nth* argument is interpreted as a printf format string that is used to check the remaining arguments.

/*PROTOLIB*n**/
: causes `lint` to treat function declaration prototypes as function definitions if *n* is non-zero. This directive can only be used in conjunction with the
/* LINTLIBRARY */ directive. If *n* is zero, function prototypes will be treated normally.

/*SCANFLIKE*n**/
: makes `lint` check the first *(n-1)* arguments as usual. The *n*th argument is interpreted as a `scanf` format string that is used to check the remaining arguments.

/*VARARGS*n**/
: suppresses the usual checking for variable numbers of arguments in the following function declaration. The data types of the first *n* arguments are checked; a missing *n* is taken to be 0. The use of the ellipsis terminator (...) in the definition is suggested in new or updated code.

`lint` produces its first output on a per-source-file basis. Complaints regarding included files are collected and printed after all source files have been processed, if −s is not specified. Finally, if the −c option is not used, information gathered from all input files is collected and checked for consistency. At this point, if it is not clear whether a complaint stems from a given source file or from one of its included files, the source filename will be printed followed by a question mark.

The behavior of the −c and the −o options allows for incremental use of `lint` on a set of C source files. Generally, one invokes `lint` once for each source file with the −c option. Each of these invocations produces a `.ln` file that corresponds to the `.c` file, and prints all messages that are about just that source file. After all the source files have been separately run through `lint`, it is invoked once more (without the −c option), listing all the `.ln` files with the needed −l*x* options. This will print all the inter-file inconsistencies. This scheme works well with **make**; it allows **make** to be used to `lint` only the source files that have been modified since the last time the set of source files were `lint`ed.

FILES

LIBDIR	the directory where the lint libraries specified by the −l*x* option must exist
LIBDIR/`lint`[12]	first and second passes
LIBDIR/`llib-lc.ln`	declarations for C Library functions (binary format; source is in *LIBDIR*/`llib-lc`)
LIBPATH/`llib-lm.ln`	declarations for Math Library functions (binary format; source is in *LIBDIR*/llib-lm)
TMPDIR/*`lint`*	temporaries
TMPDIR	usually `/var/tmp` but can be redefined by setting the environment variable `TMPDIR` [see **tempnam** in **tmpnam**(3S)].

LIBDIR	usually `/ccs/lib`
LIBPATH	usually `/usr/ccs/lib:/usr/lib`

SEE ALSO

cc(1), make(1).

See the "lint" chapter in the *C Programmer's Guide: ANSI C and Programming Support Tools.*

lorder(1)

NAME
lorder – find ordering relation for an object library

SYNOPSIS
`lorder` *file* ...

DESCRIPTION
The input is one or more object or library archive *files* [see `ar`(1)]. The standard output is a list of pairs of object file or archive member names; the first file of the pair refers to external identifiers defined in the second. The output may be processed by `tsort`(1) to find an ordering of a library suitable for one-pass access by `ld`. Note that the link editor `ld` is capable of multiple passes over an archive in the portable archive format [see `ar`(4)] and does not require that `lorder` be used when building an archive. The usage of the `lorder` command may, however, allow for a more efficient access of the archive during the link edit process.

The following example builds a new library from existing .o files.

    ar -cr library ' lorder *.o | tsort'

FILES
TMPDIR/`*symref`	temporary files
TMPDIR/`*symdef`	temporary files
TMPDIR	usually `/var/tmp` but can be redefined by setting the environment variable `TMPDIR` [see `tempnam`() in `tmpnam`(3S)].

SEE ALSO
`ar`(1), `ld`(1), `tsort`(1), `tempnam`(3S), `tmpname`(3S), `ar`(4).

NOTES
`lorder` will accept as input any object or archive file, regardless of its suffix, provided there is more than one input file. If there is but a single input file, its suffix must be .o.

NAME
lprof – display line-by-line execution count profile data

SYNOPSIS
lprof [–p] [–s] [–x] [–I *incdir*] [–r *srcfile*] [–c *cntfile*] [–o *prog*] [–V]

lprof –m *file1*.cnt *file2*.cnt *filen*.cnt [–T] –d *destfile*.cnt

DESCRIPTION
lprof reports the execution characteristics of a program on a (source) line by line basis. This is useful as a means to determine which and how often portions of the code were executed.

lprof interprets a profile file (*prog*.cnt by default) produced by the profiled program *prog* (a.out by default). *prog* creates a profile file if it has been loaded with the –ql option of cc. The profile information is computed for functions in a source file if the –ql option was used when the source file was compiled.

A shared object may also be profiled by specifying –ql when the shared object is created. When a dynamically linked executable is run, one profile file is produced for each profiled shared object linked to the executable. This feature is useful in building a single report covering multiple and disparate executions of a common library. For example, if programs prog1 and prog2 both use library libx.a, running these profiled programs will produce two profile files, prog1.cnt and prog2.cnt, which cannot be combined. However, if libx is built as a profiled shared object, libx.so, and prog1 and prog2 are built as profiled dynamically linked executables, then running these programs with the merge option will produce three profile files; one of them, libx.so.cnt, will contain the libx profile information from both runs.

By default, lprof prints a listing of source files (the names of which are stored in the symbol table of the executable file), with each line preceded by its line number (in the source file) and the number of times the line was executed.

The following options may appear singly or be combined in any order:

    –p   Print listing, each line preceded by the line number and the number of times it was executed (default). This option can be used together with the –s option to print both the source listing and summary information.

    –s   Print summary information of percentage of lines of code executed per function.

    –x   Instead of printing the execution count numbers for each line, print each line preceded by its line number and a [U] if the line was not executed. If the line was executed, print only the line number.

    –I *incdir*   Look for source or header files in the directory *incdir* in addition to the current directory and the standard place for #include files (usually /usr/include). The user can specify more than one directory by using multiple –I options.

lprof(1)   **lprof(1)**

-r *srcfile*   Instead of printing all source files, print only those files named in -r options (to be used with the -p option only). The user can specify multiple files with a single -r option.

-c *cntfile*   Use the file *cntfile* instead of *prog*.cnt as the input profile file.

-o *prog*   Use the name of the program *prog* instead of the name used when creating the profile file. Because the program name stored in the profile file contains the relative path, this option is necessary if the executable file or profile file has been moved.

-V   Print, on standard error, the version number of lprof.

Merging Data Files

lprof can also be used to merge profile files. The -m option must be accompanied by the -d option:

-m *file1*.cnt *file2*.cnt *filen*.cnt -d *destfile*.cnt
        Merge the data files *file1*.cnt through *filen*.cnt by summing the execution counts per line, so that data from several runs can be accumulated. The result is written to *destfile*.cnt. The data files must contain profiling data for the same *prog* (see the -T option below).

-T   Time stamp override. Normally, the time stamps of the executable files being profiled are checked, and data files will not be merged if the time stamps do not match. If -T is specified, this check is skipped.

CONTROLLING THE RUN-TIME PROFILING ENVIRONMENT

The environment variable PROFOPTS provides run-time control over profiling. When a profiled program (or shared object) is about to terminate, it examines the value of PROFOPTS to determine how the profiling data are to be handled. A terminating shared object will honor every PROFOPTS option except file=*filename*.

The environment variable PROFOPTS is a comma-separated list of options interpreted by the program being profiled. If PROFOPTS is not defined in the environment, then the default action is taken: The profiling data are saved in a file (with the default name, *prog*.cnt) in the current directory. If PROFOPTS is set to the null string, no profiling data are saved. The following are the available options:

msg=[y|n]   If msg=y is specified, a message stating that profile data are being saved is printed to stderr. If msg=n is specified, only the profiling error messages are printed. The default is msg=y.

merge=[y|n]
        If merge=y is specified, the data files will be merged after successive runs. If merge=n is specified, the data files are not merged after successive runs, and the data file is overwritten after each execution. The merge will fail if the program has been recompiled, and the data file will be left in TMPDIR. The default is merge=n.

pid=[y|n]   If pid=y is specified, the name of the data file will include the process ID of the profiled program. Inclusion of the process ID allows for the creation of different data files for programs calling fork. If pid=n is specified, the default name is used. The default is pid=n. For lprof to generate its profiling report, the -c option must be specified with lprof otherwise the default will fail.

dir=*dirname*
: The data file is placed in the directory *dirname* if this option is specified. Otherwise, the data file is created in the directory that is current at the end of execution.

file=*filename*
: *filename* is used as the name of the data file in *dir* created by the profiled program if this option is specified. Otherwise, the default name is used. For lprof to generate its profiling report, the -c option must be specified with lprof if the file option has been used at execution time; otherwise the default will fail.

FILES

prog.cnt   profile data
TMPDIR   usually /var/tmp but can be redefined by setting the environment variable TMPDIR [see tempnam in tmpnam(3S)].

SEE ALSO

cc(1), prof(1), fork(2), tmpnam(3S).
The "lprof" chapter in the *Programmer's Guide: ANSI C and Programming Support Tools*.

NOTES

For the -m option, if *destfile*.cnt exists, its previous contents are destroyed.

Optimized code cannot be profiled; if both optimization and line profiling are requested, profiling has precedence.

Different parts of one line of a source file may be executed different numbers of times (e.g., the for loop below); the count corresponds to the first part of the line.

For example, in the following for loop

```
                    main()
        1   [2]     {
                        int j;
        1   [5]         for (j = 0; j < 5; j++)
        5   [6]             sub(j);
        1   [8]     }
                    sub(a)
                    int a;
        5   [12]    {
        5   [13]        printf("a is %d\n", a);
        5   [14]    }
```

line 5 consists of three parts. The line count listed, however, is for the initialization part, that is, j = 0.

NAME
m4 – macro processor

SYNOPSIS
m4 [*options*] [*files*]

DESCRIPTION
The **m4** command is a macro processor intended as a front end for C, assembler, and other languages. Each of the argument files is processed in order; if there are no files, or if a file name is –, the standard input is read. The processed text is written on the standard output.

The options and their effects are as follows:

- **–e**   Operate interactively. Interrupts are ignored and the output is unbuffered.
- **–s**   Enable line sync output for the C preprocessor (#line ...)
- **–B***int*   Change the size of the push-back and argument collection buffers from the default of 4,096.
- **–H***int*   Change the size of the symbol table hash array from the default of 199. The size should be prime.
- **–S***int*   Change the size of the call stack from the default of 100 slots. Macros take three slots, and non-macro arguments take one.
- **–T***int*   Change the size of the token buffer from the default of 512 bytes.

To be effective, the above flags must appear before any file names and before any –D or –U flags:

–D*name*[*=val*]
      Defines *name* to *val* or to null in *val*'s absence.

–U*name*
      undefines *name*.

Macro calls have the form:

   name(*arg1*,*arg2*, ..., *argn*)

The (must immediately follow the name of the macro. If the name of a defined macro is not followed by a (, it is deemed to be a call of that macro with no arguments. Potential macro names consist of alphanumeric characters and underscore (_), where the first character is not a digit.

Leading unquoted blanks, tabs, and new-lines are ignored while collecting arguments. Left and right single quotes are used to quote strings. The value of a quoted string is the string stripped of the quotes.

When a macro name is recognized, its arguments are collected by searching for a matching right parenthesis. If fewer arguments are supplied than are in the macro definition, the trailing arguments are taken to be null. Macro evaluation proceeds normally during the collection of the arguments, and any commas or right parentheses that happen to turn up within the value of a nested call are as effective as those in the original input text. After argument collection, the value of the macro is pushed back onto the input stream and rescanned.

m4 makes available the following built-in macros. These macros may be redefined, but once this is done the original meaning is lost. Their values are null unless otherwise stated.

define
: the second argument is installed as the value of the macro whose name is the first argument. Each occurrence of $n in the replacement text, where n is a digit, is replaced by the n-th argument. Argument 0 is the name of the macro; missing arguments are replaced by the null string; $# is replaced by the number of arguments; $* is replaced by a list of all the arguments separated by commas; $@ is like $*, but each argument is quoted (with the current quotes).

undefine
: removes the definition of the macro named in its argument.

defn
: returns the quoted definition of its argument(s). It is useful for renaming macros, especially built-ins.

pushdef
: like define, but saves any previous definition.

popdef
: removes current definition of its argument(s), exposing the previous one, if any.

ifdef
: if the first argument is defined, the value is the second argument, otherwise the third. If there is no third argument, the value is null. The word unix is predefined.

shift
: returns all but its first argument. The other arguments are quoted and pushed back with commas in between. The quoting nullifies the effect of the extra scan that will subsequently be performed.

changequote
: change quote symbols to the first and second arguments. The symbols may be up to five characters long. changequote without arguments restores the original values (i.e., ` ').

changecom
: change left and right comment markers from the default # and new-line. With no arguments, the comment mechanism is effectively disabled. With one argument, the left marker becomes the argument and the right marker becomes new-line. With two arguments, both markers are affected. Comment markers may be up to five characters long.

divert
: m4 maintains 10 output streams, numbered 0-9. The final output is the concatenation of the streams in numerical order; initially stream 0 is the current stream. The divert macro changes the current output stream to its (digit-string) argument. Output diverted to a stream other than 0 through 9 is discarded.

undivert
: causes immediate output of text from diversions named as arguments, or all diversions if no argument. Text may be undiverted into another diversion. Undiverting discards the diverted text.

`divnum`	returns the value of the current output stream.
`dnl`	reads and discards characters up to and including the next newline.
`ifelse`	has three or more arguments. If the first argument is the same string as the second, then the value is the third argument. If not, and if there are more than four arguments, the process is repeated with arguments 4, 5, 6 and 7. Otherwise, the value is either the fourth string, or, if it is not present, null.
`incr`	returns the value of its argument incremented by 1. The value of the argument is calculated by interpreting an initial digit-string as a decimal number.
`decr`	returns the value of its argument decremented by 1.
`eval`	evaluates its argument as an arithmetic expression, using 32-bit arithmetic. Operators include +, −, *, /, %, ** (exponentiation), bitwise &, |, ^, and ~; relationals; parentheses. Octal and hex numbers may be specified as in C. The second argument specifies the radix for the result; the default is 10. The third argument may be used to specify the minimum number of digits in the result.
`len`	returns the number of characters in its argument.
`index`	returns the position in its first argument where the second argument begins (zero origin), or −1 if the second argument does not occur.
`substr`	returns a substring of its first argument. The second argument is a zero origin number selecting the first character; the third argument indicates the length of the substring. A missing third argument is taken to be large enough to extend to the end of the first string.
`translit`	transliterates the characters in its first argument from the set given by the second argument to the set given by the third. No abbreviations are permitted.
`include`	returns the contents of the file named in the argument.
`sinclude`	is identical to `include`, except that it says nothing if the file is inaccessible.
`syscmd`	executes the UNIX System command given in the first argument. No value is returned.
`sysval`	is the return code from the last call to `syscmd`.
`maketemp`	fills in a string of XXXXX in its argument with the current process ID.
`m4exit`	causes immediate exit from `m4`. Argument 1, if given, is the exit code; the default is 0.
`m4wrap`	argument 1 will be pushed back at final EOF; example: `m4wrap(`cleanup()´)`

errprint   prints its argument on the diagnostic output file.

dumpdef   prints current names and definitions, for the named items, or for all if no arguments are given.

traceon   with no arguments, turns on tracing for all macros (including built-ins). Otherwise, turns on tracing for named macros.

traceoff   turns off trace globally and for any macros specified. Macros specifically traced by **traceon** can be untraced only by specific calls to **traceoff**.

SEE ALSO

as(1), cc(1).

NAME
make – maintain, update, and regenerate groups of programs

SYNOPSIS
make [-f *makefile*] [-eiknpqrst] [*names*]

DESCRIPTION
make allows the programmer to maintain, update, and regenerate groups of computer programs. make executes commands in *makefile* to update one or more target *names* (*names* are typically programs). If the -f option is not present, then makefile, Makefile, and the Source Code Control System (SCCS) files s.makefile, and s.Makefile are tried in order. If *makefile* is -, the standard input is taken. More than one -f *makefile* argument pair may appear.

make updates a target only if its dependents are newer than the target. All prerequisite files of a target are added recursively to the list of targets. Missing files are deemed to be outdated.

The following list of four directives can be included in *makefile* to extend the options provided by make. They are used in *makefile* as if they were targets:

.DEFAULT: If a file must be made but there are no explicit commands or relevant built-in rules, the commands associated with the name .DEFAULT are used if it exists.

.IGNORE: Same effect as the -i option.

.PRECIOUS: Dependents of the .PRECIOUS entry will not be removed when quit or interrupt are hit.

.SILENT: Same effect as the -s option.

The options for make are listed below:

-e Environment variables override assignments within makefiles.

-f *makefile* Description filename (*makefile* is assumed to be the name of a description file).

-i Ignore error codes returned by invoked commands.

-k Abandon work on the current entry if it fails, but continue on other branches that do not depend on that entry.

-n No execute mode. Print commands, but do not execute them. Even command lines beginning with an @ are printed.

-p Print out the complete set of macro definitions and target descriptions.

-q Question. make returns a zero or non-zero status code depending on whether or not the target file has been updated.

-r Do not use the built-in rules.

-s Silent mode. Do not print command lines before executing.

-t Touch the target files (causing them to be updated) rather than issue the usual commands.

Creating the makefile

The makefile invoked with the −f option is a carefully structured file of explicit instructions for updating and regenerating programs, and contains a sequence of entries that specify dependencies. The first line of an entry is a blank-separated, non-null list of targets, then a :, then a (possibly null) list of prerequisite files or dependencies. Text following a ; and all following lines that begin with a tab are shell commands to be executed to update the target. The first non-empty line that does not begin with a tab or # begins a new dependency or macro definition. Shell commands may be continued across lines with a backslash-new-line (\ new-line) sequence. Everything printed by make (except the initial tab) is passed directly to the shell as is. Thus,

```
echo a\
b
```

will produce

```
ab
```

exactly the same as the shell would.

Sharp (#) and new-line surround comments including contained \ new-line sequences.

The following makefile says that pgm depends on two files a.o and b.o, and that they in turn depend on their corresponding source files (a.c and b.c) and a common file incl.h:

```
pgm: a.o b.o
     cc a.o b.o -o pgm
a.o: incl.h a.c
     cc -c a.c
b.o: incl.h b.c
     cc -c b.c
```

Command lines are executed one at a time, each by its own shell. The SHELL environment variable can be used to specify which shell make should use to execute commands. The default is /usr/bin/sh. The first one or two characters in a command can be the following: @, −, @−, or −@. If @ is present, printing of the command is suppressed. If − is present, make ignores an error. A line is printed when it is executed unless the −s option is present, or the entry .SILENT: is included in *makefile*, or unless the initial character sequence contains a @. The −n option specifies printing without execution; however, if the command line has the string $(MAKE) in it, the line is always executed (see the discussion of the MAKEFLAGS macro in the "Environment" section below). The −t (touch) option updates the modified date of a file without executing any commands.

Commands returning non-zero status normally terminate make. If the −i option is present, if the entry .IGNORE: is included in *makefile*, or if the initial character sequence of the command contains −, the error is ignored. If the −k option is present, work is abandoned on the current entry, but continues on other branches that do not depend on that entry.

Interrupt and quit cause the target to be deleted unless the target is a dependent of the directive .PRECIOUS.

Environment

The environment is read by **make**. All variables are assumed to be macro definitions and are processed as such. The environment variables are processed before any makefile and after the internal rules; thus, macro assignments in a makefile override environment variables. The −e option causes the environment to override the macro assignments in a makefile. Suffixes and their associated rules in the makefile will override any identical suffixes in the built-in rules.

The **MAKEFLAGS** environment variable is processed by **make** as containing any legal input option (except −f and −p) defined for the command line. Further, upon invocation, **make** "invents" the variable if it is not in the environment, puts the current options into it, and passes it on to invocations of commands. Thus, **MAKEFLAGS** always contains the current input options. This feature proves very useful for "super-makes". In fact, as noted above, when the −n option is used, the command $(MAKE) is executed anyway; hence, one can perform a **make** −n recursively on a whole software system to see what would have been executed. This result is possible because the −n is put in **MAKEFLAGS** and passed to further invocations of $(MAKE). This usage is one way of debugging all of the makefiles for a software project without actually doing anything.

Include Files

If the string include appears as the first seven letters of a line in a *makefile*, and is followed by a blank or a tab, the rest of the line is assumed to be a filename and will be read by the current invocation, after substituting for any macros.

Macros

Entries of the form *string1* = *string2* are macro definitions. *string2* is defined as all characters up to a comment character or an unescaped new-line. Subsequent appearances of $(*string1*[:*subst1*=[*subst2*]]) are replaced by *string2*. The parentheses are optional if a single-character macro name is used and there is no substitute sequence. The optional :*subst1*=*subst2* is a substitute sequence. If it is specified, all non-overlapping occurrences of *subst1* in the named macro are replaced by *subst2*. Strings (for the purposes of this type of substitution) are delimited by blanks, tabs, new-line characters, and beginnings of lines. An example of the use of the substitute sequence is shown in the "Libraries" section below.

Internal Macros

There are five internally maintained macros that are useful for writing rules for building targets.

$*   The macro $* stands for the filename part of the current dependent with the suffix deleted. It is evaluated only for inference rules.

$@   The $@ macro stands for the full target name of the current target. It is evaluated only for explicitly named dependencies.

$<   The $< macro is only evaluated for inference rules or the .DEFAULT rule. It is the module that is outdated with respect to the target (the "manufactured" dependent file name). Thus, in the .c.o rule, the $< macro would evaluate to the .c file. An example for making optimized .o files from .c files is:

```
.c.o:
        cc -c -O $*.c
```
or:
```
.c.o:
        cc -c -O $<
```

- $? The $? macro is evaluated when explicit rules from the makefile are evaluated. It is the list of prerequisites that are outdated with respect to the target, and essentially those modules that must be rebuilt.
- $% The $% macro is only evaluated when the target is an archive library member of the form lib(file.o). In this case, $@ evaluates to lib and $% evaluates to the library member, file.o.

Four of the five macros can have alternative forms. When an upper case D or F is appended to any of the four macros, the meaning is changed to "directory part" for D and "file part" for F. Thus, $(@D) refers to the directory part of the string $@. If there is no directory part, ./ is generated. The only macro excluded from this alternative form is $?.

Suffixes

Certain names (for instance, those ending with .o) have inferable prerequisites such as .c, .s, etc. If no update commands for such a file appear in *makefile*, and if an inferable prerequisite exists, that prerequisite is compiled to make the target. In this case, **make** has inference rules that allow building files from other files by examining the suffixes and determining an appropriate inference rule to use. The current default inference rules are:

```
.c      .c~     .f      .f~     .s      .s~     .sh     .sh~    .C      .C~
.c.a    .c.o    .c~.a   .c~.c   .c~.o   .f.a    .f.o    .f~.a   .f~.f   .f~.o
.h~.h   .l.c    .l.o    .l~.c   .l~.l   .l~.o   .s.a    .s.o    .s~.a   .s~.o
.s~.s   .sh~.sh .y.c    .y.o    .y~.c   .y~.o   .y~.y   .C.a    .C.o    .C~.a
.C~.C   .C~.o   .L.C    .L.o    .L~.C   .L~.L   .L~.o   .Y.C    .Y.o    .Y~.C
.Y~.o   .Y~.Y
```

The internal rules for **make** are contained in the source file rules.c for the **make** program. These rules can be locally modified. To print out the rules compiled into the **make** on any machine in a form suitable for recompilation, the following command is used:

    make -pf - 2>/dev/null </dev/null

A tilde in the above rules refers to an SCCS file [see sccsfile(4)]. Thus, the rule .c~.o would transform an SCCS C source file into an object file (.o). Because the s. of the SCCS files is a prefix, it is incompatible with the **make** suffix point of view. Hence, the tilde is a way of changing any file reference into an SCCS file reference.

A rule with only one suffix (for example, .c:) is the definition of how to build *x* from *x*.c. In effect, the other suffix is null. This feature is useful for building targets from only one source file, for example, shell procedures and simple C programs.

Additional suffixes are given as the dependency list for .SUFFIXES. Order is significant: the first possible name for which both a file and a rule exist is inferred as a prerequisite. The default list is:

.SUFFIXES: .o .c .c~ .y .y~ .l .l~ .s .s~ .sh .sh~ .h .h~ .f .f~ .C .C~ .Y .Y~ .L .L~

Here again, the above command for printing the internal rules will display the list of suffixes implemented on the current machine. Multiple suffix lists accumulate; .SUFFIXES: with no dependencies clears the list of suffixes.

Inference Rules

The first example can be done more briefly.

```
pgm: a.o b.o
        cc a.o b.o -o pgm
a.o b.o: incl.h
```

This abbreviation is possible because **make** has a set of internal rules for building files. The user may add rules to this list by simply putting them in the *makefile*.

Certain macros are used by the default inference rules to permit the inclusion of optional matter in any resulting commands. For example, **CFLAGS**, **LFLAGS**, and **YFLAGS** are used for compiler options to cc(1), lex(1), and yacc(1), respectively. Again, the previous method for examining the current rules is recommended.

The inference of prerequisites can be controlled. The rule to create a file with suffix .o from a file with suffix .c is specified as an entry with .c.o: as the target and no dependents. Shell commands associated with the target define the rule for making a .o file from a .c file. Any target that has no slashes in it and starts with a dot is identified as a rule and not a true target.

Libraries

If a target or dependency name contains parentheses, it is assumed to be an archive library, the string within parentheses referring to a member within the library. Thus, lib(file.o) and $(LIB)(file.o) both refer to an archive library that contains file.o. (This example assumes the LIB macro has been previously defined.) The expression $(LIB)(file1.o file2.o) is not legal. Rules pertaining to archive libraries have the form .*XX*.a where the *XX* is the suffix from which the archive member is to be made. An unfortunate by-product of the current implementation requires the *XX* to be different from the suffix of the archive member. Thus, one cannot have lib(file.o) depend upon file.o explicitly. The most common use of the archive interface follows. Here, we assume the source files are all C type source:

```
lib: lib(file1.o) lib(file2.o) lib(file3.o)
        @echo lib is now up-to-date
.c.a:
        $(CC) -c $(CFLAGS) $<
        $(AR) $(ARFLAGS) $@ $*.o
        rm -f $*.o
```

In fact, the .c.a rule listed above is built into make and is unnecessary in this example. A more interesting, but more limited example of an archive library maintenance construction follows:

```
lib: lib(file1.o) lib(file2.o) lib(file3.o)
     $(CC) -c $(CFLAGS) $(?:.o=.c)
     $(AR) $(ARFLAGS) lib $?
     rm $?
     @echo lib is now up-to-date
.c.a:;
```

Here the substitution mode of the macro expansions is used. The $? list is defined to be the set of object filenames (inside lib) whose C source files are outdated. The substitution mode translates the .o to .c. (Unfortunately, one cannot as yet transform to .c~; however, this transformation may become possible in the future.) Also note the disabling of the .c.a: rule, which would have created each object file, one by one. This particular construct speeds up archive library maintenance considerably. This type of construct becomes very cumbersome if the archive library contains a mix of assembly programs and C programs.

FILES

[Mm]akefile and s.[Mm]akefile
/usr/bin/sh

SEE ALSO

cc(1), lex(1), yacc(1), printf(3S), sccsfile(4).

cd(1), sh(1) in the *User's Reference Manual*.

See the "make" chapter in the *Programmer's Guide: ANSI C and Programming Support Tools*.

NOTES

Some commands return non-zero status inappropriately; use -i or the - command line prefix to overcome the difficulty.

Filenames with the characters = : @ will not work. Commands that are directly executed by the shell, notably cd(1), are ineffectual across new-lines in make. The syntax lib(file1.o file2.o file3.o) is illegal. You cannot build lib(file.o) from file.o.

mcs(1)

NAME
mcs – manipulate the comment section of an object file.

SYNOPSIS
mcs [-a *string*] [-c] [-d] [-n *name*] [-p] [-V] *file* ...

DESCRIPTION
The mcs command is used to manipulate a section, by default the .comment section, in an ELF object file. It is used to add to, delete, print, and compress the contents of a section in an ELF object file, and only print the contents of a section in a COFF object file. mcs must be given one or more of the options described below. It applies each of the options in order to each file.

The following options are available.

-a *string*
: Append *string* to the comment section of the ELF object files. If *string* contains embedded blanks, it must be enclosed in quotation marks.

-c
: Compress the contents of the comment section of the ELF object files. All duplicate entries are removed. The ordering of the remaining entries is not disturbed.

-d
: Delete the contents of the comment section from the ELF object files. The section header for the comment section is also removed.

-n *name*
: Specify the name of the comment section to access if other than .comment. By default, mcs deals with the section named .comment. This option can be used to specify another section.

-p
: Print the contents of the comment section on the standard output. Each section printed is tagged by the name of the file from which it was extracted, using the format *filename*[*member_name*]: for archive files; and *filename*: for other files.

-V
: Print, on standard error, the version number of mcs.

If the input file is an archive [see ar(4)], the archive is treated as a set of individual files. For example, if the -a option is specified, the string is appended to the comment section of each ELF object file in the archive; if the archive member is not an ELF object file, then it is left unchanged.

If mcs is executed on an archive file the archive symbol table will be removed, unless only the -p option has been specified. The archive symbol table must be restored by executing the ar command with the -s option before the archive can be linked by the ld command. mcs will produce appropriate warning messages when this situation arises.

EXAMPLES

```
mcs -p file          # Print file's comment section

mcs -a string file   # Append string to file's comment section
```

FILES

TMPDIR/mcs* temporary files

TMPDIR usually /var/tmp but can be redefined by setting the environment variable TMPDIR [see tempnam() in tmpnam(3S)].

SEE ALSO

ar(1), as(1), cc(1), ld(1), tmpnam(3S), a.out(4), ar(4).
See the "Object Files" chapter in *Programmer's Guide: ANSI C and Programming Support Tools.*

NOTES

mcs cannot add to, delete or compress the contents of a section that is contained within a segment.

nm(1)

NAME
nm – print name list of an object file

SYNOPSIS
nm [-oxhvnefurplVT] *files*

DESCRIPTION
The nm command displays the symbol table of each ELF or COFF object file, specified by *file(s)*. The file may be a relocatable or absolute ELF or COFF object file; or it may be an archive of relocatable or absolute ELF or COFF object files. For each symbol, the following information will be printed:

Index	The index of the symbol. (The index appears in brackets.)
Value	The value of the symbol is one of the following: a section offset for defined symbols in a relocatable file; alignment constraints for symbols whose section index is SHN_COMMON; a virtual address in executable and dynamic library files.
Size	The size in bytes of the associated object.
Type	A symbol is of one of the following types: NOTYPE (no type was specified), OBJECT (a data object such as an array or variable), FUNC (a function or other executable code), SECTION (a section symbol), or FILE (name of the source file).
Bind	The symbol's binding attributes. LOCAL symbols have a scope limited to the object file containing their definition; GLOBAL symbols are visible to all object files being combined; and WEAK symbols are essentially global symbols with a lower precedence than GLOBAL.
Other	A field reserved for future use, currently containing 0.
Shndx	Except for three special values, this is the section header table index in relation to which the symbol is defined. The following special values exist: ABS indicates the symbol's value will not change through relocation; COMMON indicates an unallocated block and the value provides alignment constraints; and UNDEF indicates an undefined symbol.
Name	The name of the symbol.

The output of nm may be controlled using the following options:

-o	Print the value and size of a symbol in octal instead of decimal.
-x	Print the value and size of a symbol in hexadecimal instead of decimal.
-h	Do not display the output heading data.
-v	Sort external symbols by value before they are printed.
-n	Sort external symbols by name before they are printed.
-e	See NOTES below.
-f	See NOTES below.
-u	Print undefined symbols only.

-r   Prepend the name of the object file or archive to each output line.

-p   Produce easily parsable, terse output. Each symbol name is preceded by its value (blanks if undefined) and one of the letters U (undefined), N (symbol has no type), D (data object symbol), T (text symbol), S (section symbol), or F (file symbol). If the symbol's binding attribute is LOCAL, the key letter is lower case; if the symbol's binding attribute is WEAK, the key letter is upper case; if the -l modifier is specified, the upper case key letter is followed by a *; if the symbol's binding attribute is GLOBAL, the key letter is upper case.

-l   Distinguish between WEAK and GLOBAL symbols by appending a * to the key letter for WEAK symbols.

-V   Print the version of the nm command executing on the standard error output.

-T   See NOTES below.

Options may be used in any order, either singly or in combination, and may appear anywhere in the command line. When conflicting options are specified (such as nm -v -n) the first is taken and the second ignored with a warning message to the user.

SEE ALSO

as(1), cc(1), dump(1), ld(1), a.out(4), ar(4).

NOTES

The following options are obsolete because of changes to the object file format and will be deleted in a future release.

-e   Print only external and static symbols. The symbol table now contains only static and external symbols. Automatic symbols no longer appear in the symbol table. They do appear in the debugging information produced by cc -g, which may be examined using dump(1).

-f   Produce full output. Redundant symbols (such as .text, .data, etc). which existed previously do not exist and producing full output will be identical to the default output.

-T   By default, nm prints the entire name of the symbols listed. Since symbol names have been moved to the last column, the problem of overflow is removed and it is no longer necessary to truncate the symbol name.

prof(1)

NAME
prof – display profile data

SYNOPSIS
prof [-t | c | a | n] [-o | x] [-g | 1] [-z] [-h] [-s] [-m *mdata*] -V [*prog*]

DESCRIPTION
The `prof` command interprets a profile file produced by the `monitor` function. The symbol table in the object file *prog* (a.out by default) is read and correlated with a profile file (mon.out by default). For each external text symbol the percentage of time spent executing between the address of that symbol and the address of the next is printed, together with the number of times that function was called and the average number of milliseconds per call.

The mutually exclusive options -t, -c, -a, and -n determine the type of sorting of the output lines:

-t   Sort by decreasing percentage of total time (default).

-c   Sort by decreasing number of calls.

-a   Sort by increasing symbol address.

-n   Sort lexically by symbol name.

The mutually exclusive options -o and -x specify the printing of the address of each symbol monitored:

-o   Print each symbol address (in octal) along with the symbol name.

-x   Print each symbol address (in hexadecimal) along with the symbol name.

The mutually exclusive options -g and -1 control the type of symbols to be reported. The -1 option must be used with care; it applies the time spent in a static function to the preceding (in memory) global function, instead of giving the static function a separate entry in the report. If all static functions are properly located (see example below), this feature can be very useful. If not, the resulting report may be misleading.

Assume that A and B are global functions and only A calls static function S. If S is located immediately after A in the source code (that is, if S is properly located), then, with the -1 option, the amount of time spent in A can easily be determined, including the time spent in S. If, however, both A and B call S, then, if the -1 option is used, the report will be misleading; the time spent during B's call to S will be attributed to A, making it appear as if more time had been spent in A than really had. In this case, function S cannot be properly located.

-g   Include static (non-global) functions.

-1   Do not include static (non-global) functions (default).

The following options may be used in any combination:

-z   Include all symbols in the profile range, even if associated with zero number of calls and zero time.

-h   Suppress the heading normally printed on the report. (This is useful if the report is to be processed further.)

-s   Print a summary of several of the monitoring parameters and statistics on the standard error output.

-m *mdata*
   Use file *mdata* instead of mon.out as the input profile file.

-V   Print prof version information on the standard error output.

A program creates a profile file if it has been link edited with the -p option of cc. This option to the cc command arranges for calls to monitor at the beginning and end of execution. It is the call to monitor at the end of execution that causes the system to write a profile file. The number of calls to a function is tallied if the -p option was used when the file containing the function was compiled.

The name of the file created by a profiled program is controlled by the environmental variable PROFDIR. If PROFDIR is not set, mon.out is produced in the directory current when the program terminates. If PROFDIR=*string*, *string/pid.progname* is produced, where *progname* consists of argv[0] with any path prefix removed, and *pid* is the process ID of the program. If PROFDIR is set, but null, no profiling output are produced.

A single function may be split into subfunctions for profiling by means of the MARK macro [see prof(5)].

FILES
    mon.out   default profile file
    a.out   default namelist (object) file

SEE ALSO
    cc(1), lprof(1), exit(2), profil(2), monitor(3C), prof(5).
    The "lprof" chapter in the *Programmer's Guide: ANSI C and Programming Support Tools*.

NOTES
The times reported in successive identical runs may show variances because of varying cache-hit ratios that result from sharing the cache with other processes. Even if a program seems to be the only one using the machine, hidden background or asynchronous processes may blur the data. In rare cases, the clock ticks initiating recording of the program counter may "beat" with loops in a program, grossly distorting measurements. Call counts are always recorded precisely, however.

Only programs that call exit or return from main are guaranteed to produce a profile file, unless a final call to monitor is explicitly coded.

The times for static functions are attributed to the preceding external text symbol if the -g option is not used. However, the call counts for the preceding function are still correct; that is, the static function call counts are not added to the call counts of the external function.

If more than one of the options −t, −c, −a, and −n is specified, the last option specified is used and the user is warned.

Profiling may be used with dynamically linked executables, but care must be applied. Currently, shared objects cannot be profiled with **prof**. Thus, when a profiled, dynamically linked program is executed, only the "main" portion of the image is sampled. This means that all time spent outside of the "main" object, that is, time spent in a shared object, will not be included in the profile summary; the total time reported for the program may be less than the total time used by the program.

Because the time spent in a shared object cannot be accounted for, the use of shared objects should be minimized whenever a program is profiled with **prof**. If possible, the program should be linked statically before being profiled.

Consider an extreme case. A profiled program dynamically linked with the shared C library spends 100 units of time in some **libc** routine, say, **malloc**. Suppose **malloc** is called only from routine **B** and **B** consumes only 1 unit of time. Suppose further that routine **A** consumes 10 units of time, more than any other routine in the "main" (profiled) portion of the image. In this case, **prof** will conclude that most of the time is being spent in **A** and almost no time is being spent in **B**. From this it will be almost impossible to tell that the greatest improvement can be made by looking at routine **B** and not routine **A**. The value of the profiler in this case is severely degraded; the solution is to use archives as much as possible for profiling.

prs(1)

NAME
prs – print an SCCS file

SYNOPSIS
prs [–d[*dataspec*]] [–r[*SID*]] [–e] [–l] [–c[*date–time*]] [–a] *files*

DESCRIPTION
prs prints, on the standard output, parts or all of an SCCS file [see sccsfile(4)] in a user-supplied format. If a directory is named, prs prints the files in that directory, except the non-SCCS files (last component of the path name does not begin with s.) and unreadable files. If a name of – is given, the standard input is read; each line of the standard input is taken to be the name of an SCCS file or directory to be processed. prs silently ignores non-SCCS files and unreadable files.

Arguments to prs, which may appear in any order, consist of keyletter arguments and file names.

The keyletter arguments apply independently to each named file:

–d[*dataspec*]	Specifies the output data specification. The *dataspec* is a string consisting of SCCS file data keywords (see the DATA KEYWORDS section) interspersed with optional user-supplied text.
–r[*SID*]	Specifies the SCCS identification (SID) string of a delta for which information is desired. The default is the top delta.
–e	Requests information for all deltas created earlier than and including the delta designated via the –r keyletter or the date given by the –c option.
–l	Requests information for all deltas created later than and including the delta designated via the –r keyletter or the date given by the –c option.
–c[*date–time*]	The cutoff date–time in the form:
	YY[MM[DD[HH[MM[SS]]]]]
	Units omitted from the date–time default to their maximum possible values; for example, –c7502 is equivalent to –c750228235959. Any number of non-numeric characters may separate the fields of the cutoff date; for example, "–c77/2/2 9:22:25".
–a	Requests printing of information for both removed, i.e., delta type = R, [see rmdel(1)] and existing, i.e., delta type = D, deltas. If the –a keyletter is not specified, information for existing deltas only is provided.

DATA KEYWORDS
Data keywords specify those parts of an SCCS file that are to be retrieved and output. All parts of an SCCS file [see sccsfile(4)] have an associated data keyword. There is no limit on the number of times a data keyword may appear in a *dataspec*.

The information printed by **prs** consists of: (1) the user-supplied text; and (2) appropriate values (extracted from the SCCS file) substituted for the recognized data keywords in the order of appearance in the *dataspec*. The format of a data keyword value is either "Simple" (S), in which keyword substitution is direct, or "Multi-line" (M), in which keyword substitution is followed by a carriage return.

User-supplied text is any text other than recognized data keywords. A tab is specified by \t and carriage return/new-line is specified by \n. The default data keywords are:

```
":Dt:\t:DL:\nMRs:\n:MR:COMMENTS:\n:C:"
```

Keyword	Data Item	File Section	Value	Format
:Dt:	Delta information	Delta Table	See below*	S
:DL:	Delta line statistics	"	:Li:/:Ld:/:Lu:	S
:Li:	Lines inserted by Delta	"	nnnnn	S
:Ld:	Lines deleted by Delta	"	nnnnn	S
:Lu:	Lines unchanged by Delta	"	nnnnn	S
:DT:	Delta type	"	D *or* R	S
:I:	SCCS ID string (SID)	"	:R:.:L:.:B:.:S:	S
:R:	Release number	"	nnnn	S
:L:	Level number	"	nnnn	S
:B:	Branch number	"	nnnn	S
:S:	Sequence number	"	nnnn	S
:D:	Date Delta created	"	:Dy:/:Dm:/:Dd:	S
:Dy:	Year Delta created	"	nn	S
:Dm:	Month Delta created	"	nn	S
:Dd:	Day Delta created	"	nn	S
:T:	Time Delta created	"	:Th:::Tm:::Ts:	S
:Th:	Hour Delta created	"	nn	S
:Tm:	Minutes Delta created	"	nn	S
:Ts:	Seconds Delta created	"	nn	S
:P:	Programmer who created Delta	"	*logname*	S
:DS:	Delta sequence number	"	nnnn	S
:DP:	Predecessor Delta seq-no.	"	nnnn	S
:DI:	Seq-no. of deltas incl., excl., ignored	"	:Dn:/:Dx:/:Dg:	S
:Dn:	Deltas included (seq #)	"	:DS: :DS:...	S
:Dx:	Deltas excluded (seq #)	"	:DS: :DS:...	S
:Dg:	Deltas ignored (seq #)	"	:DS: :DS:...	S
:MR:	MR numbers for delta	"	*text*	M
:C:	Comments for delta	"	*text*	M
:UN:	User names	User Names	*text*	M
:FL:	Flag list	Flags	*text*	M

Keyword	Data Item	File Section	Value	Format
:Y:	Module type flag	"	text	S
:MF:	MR validation flag	"	yes or no	S
:MP:	MR validation pgm name	"	text	S
:KF:	Keyword error/warning flag	"	yes or no	S
:KV:	Keyword validation string	"	text	S
:BF:	Branch flag	"	yes or no	S
:J:	Joint edit flag	"	yes or no	S
:LK:	Locked releases	"	:R:...	S
:Q:	User-defined keyword	"	text	S
:M:	Module name	"	text	S
:FB:	Floor boundary	"	:R:	S
:CB:	Ceiling boundary	"	:R:	S
:Ds:	Default SID	"	:I:	S
:ND:	Null delta flag	"	yes or no	S
:FD:	File descriptive text	Comments	text	M
:BD:	Body	Body	text	M
:GB:	Gotten body	"	text	M
:W:	A form of what(1) string	N/A	:Z::M:\t:I:	S
:A:	A form of what(1) string	N/A	:Z::Y: :M: :I::Z:	S
:Z:	what(1) string delimiter	N/A	@(#)	S
:F:	SCCS file name	N/A	text	S
:PN:	SCCS file path name	N/A	text	S

* :Dt: = :DT: :I: :D: :T: :P: :DS: :DP:

EXAMPLES

The command

    prs -d"Users and/or user IDs for :F: are:\n:UN:" s.file

may produce on the standard output:

    Users and/or user IDs for s.file are:
    xyz
    131
    abc

The command

    prs -d"Newest delta for pgm :M:: :I: Created :D: By :P:" -r s.file

may produce on the standard output:

    Newest delta for pgm main.c: 3.7 Created 77/12/1 By cas

The default case:

    prs s.file

prs(1)

produces on the standard output:

```
D 1.1 77/12/1 00:00:00 cas 1 000000/00000/00000
MRs:
b178-12345
b179-54321
COMMENTS:
this is the comment line for s.file initial delta
```

for each delta table entry of the "D" type. The only keyletter argument allowed to be used with the "special case" is the −a keyletter.

FILES
/var/tmp/pr?????

SEE ALSO
admin(1), delta(1), get(1), help(1), sccsfile(4).

DIAGNOSTICS
Use help(1) for explanations.

regcmp(1)

NAME
regcmp – regular expression compile

SYNOPSIS
regcmp [-] *file* ...

DESCRIPTION
The regcmp command performs a function similar to regcmp and, in most cases, precludes the need for calling regcmp from C programs. Bypassing regcmp saves on both execution time and program size. The command regcmp compiles the regular expressions in *file* and places the output in *file*.i. If the - option is used, the output is placed in *file*.c. The format of entries in *file* is a name (C variable) followed by one or more blanks followed by one or more regular expressions enclosed in double quotes. The output of regcmp is C source code. Compiled regular expressions are represented as extern char vectors. *file*.i files may thus be #included in C programs, or *file*.c files may be compiled and later loaded. In the C program that uses the regcmp output, regex(abc, line) applies the regular expression named abc to line. Diagnostics are self-explanatory.

EXAMPLES
```
name    "([A-Za-z][A-Za-z0-9_]*)$0"
telno   "\({0,1}([2-9][01][1-9])$0\){0,1} *"
        "([2-9][0-9]{2})$1[ -]{0,1}"
        "([0-9]{4})$2"
```

The three arguments to telno shown above must all be entered on one line.

In the C program that uses the regcmp output,

    regex(telno, line, area, exch, rest)

applies the regular expression named telno to line.

SEE ALSO
regcmp(3G).

rmdel(1)

NAME
rmdel – remove a delta from an SCCS file

SYNOPSIS
rmdel −r*SID files*

DESCRIPTION
rmdel removes the delta specified by the *SID* (SCCS identification string) from each named SCCS file. The delta to be removed must be the newest (most recent) delta in its branch in the delta chain of each named SCCS file. In addition, the delta specified must not be that of a version being edited for the purpose of making a delta; that is, if a p-file exists for the named SCCS file [see get(1)], the delta specified must not appear in any entry of the p-file.

The −r option specifies the *SID* level of the delta to be removed.

If a directory is named, rmdel behaves as though each file in the directory were specified as a named file, except that non-SCCS files (last component of the path name does not begin with s.) and unreadable files are silently ignored. If a name of − is given, the standard input is read; each line of the standard input is taken to be the name of an SCCS file to be processed; non-SCCS files and unreadable files are silently ignored.

The rules governing the removal of a delta are as follows: if you make a delta and have appropriate file permissions, you can remove it; if you own the file and directory in which a new delta file resides, you can remove the delta.

FILES
x.file   [See delta(1)]
z.file   [See delta(1)]

SEE ALSO
delta(1), get(1), help(1), prs(1), sccsfile(4).

DIAGNOSTICS
Use help(1) for explanations.

NAME
sact – print current SCCS file editing activity

SYNOPSIS
sact *files*

DESCRIPTION
sact informs the user of any impending deltas to a named SCCS file. This situation occurs when get with the −e option has been previously executed without a subsequent execution of delta. If a directory is named on the command line, sact behaves as though each file in the directory were specified as a named file, except that non-SCCS files and unreadable files are silently ignored. If a name of − is given, the standard input is read with each line being taken as the name of an SCCS file to be processed.

The output for each named file consists of five fields separated by spaces.

Field 1	specifies the SID of a delta that currently exists in the SCCS file to which changes will be made to make the new delta.
Field 2	specifies the SID for the new delta to be created.
Field 3	contains the logname of the user who will make the delta (i.e., executed a get for editing).
Field 4	contains the date that get −e was executed.
Field 5	contains the time that get −e was executed.

SEE ALSO
delta(1), diff(1), get(1), help(1), unget(1).

DIAGNOSTICS
Use help(1) for explanations.

NAME
sccsdiff – compare two versions of an SCCS file

SYNOPSIS
sccsdiff -r*SID1* -r*SID2* [-p] [-s*n*] *files*

DESCRIPTION
sccsdiff compares two versions of an SCCS file and generates the differences between the two versions. Any number of SCCS files may be specified, but arguments apply to all files.

    -r*SID1* -r*SID2*   *SID1* and *SID2* specify the deltas of an SCCS file that are to be compared. Versions are passed to bdiff in the order given.

    -p   pipe output for each file through pr.

    -s*n*   *n* is the file segment size that bdiff will pass to diff. This option is useful when diff fails due to a high system load.

FILES
/var/tmp/get?????   temporary files

SEE ALSO
get(1), help(1).

diff(1), bdiff(1), pr(1) in the *User's Reference Manual*.

sdb(1)

NAME
sdb – symbolic debugger

SYNOPSIS
sdb [-e] [-s *signo*] [-V] [-W] [-w] [*objfile* [*corfile* [*directory-list*]]]

DESCRIPTION
sdb is the symbolic debugger for C and assembly programs. sdb may be used to examine executable program files and core files. It may also be used to examine live processes in a controlled execution environment.

The *objfile* argument is the name of an executable program file. To take full advantage of the symbolic capabilities of sdb, this file should be compiled with the -g (debug) option. If it has not been compiled with the -g option, the symbolic capabilities of sdb will be limited, but the file can still be examined and the program debugged. *objfile* may also be a path name in the /proc directory, in which case the currently executing process denoted by that path name is controlled by sdb.

The *corfile* argument is the name of a core image file. A core image file is produced by the abnormal termination of *objfile* or by the use of gcore. A core image file contains a copy of the segments of a program. The default for *corfile* is core. A core image file need not be present to use sdb. Using a hyphen (-) instead of *corfile* forces sdb to ignore an existing core image file.

The *directory-list* argument is a colon-separated list of directories that is used by sdb to locate source files used to build *objfile*. If no directory list is specified, sdb will look in the current directory.

The following options are recognized by sdb:

-e Ignore symbolic information and treat nonsymbolic addresses as file offsets.

-s *signo*
    Where *signo* is a decimal number that corresponds to a signal number [see signal(2)], do not stop live processes under control of sdb that receive the signal. This option may be used more than once on the sdb command line.

-V Print version information. If no *objfile* argument is specified on the command line, sdb will exit after printing the version information.

-W Suppress warnings about *corfile* being older than *objfile* or about source files that are older than *objfile*.

-w Allow user to write to *objfile* or *corfile*.

sdb recognizes a current line and a current file. When sdb is examining an executable program file without a core file, the current line and current file are initially set to the line and file containing the first line of main. If *corfile* exists, then current line and current file are initially set to the line and file containing the source statement where the process terminated. The current line and current file change automatically as a live process executes. They may also be changed with the source file examination commands.

Names of variables are written as in C. Variables local to a procedure may be accessed using the form *procedure:variable*. If no procedure name is given, the procedure containing the current line is used by default.

Structure members may be referred to as *variable.member*, pointers to structure members as *variable->member*, and array elements as *variable[number]*. Pointers may also be dereferenced by using the form *pointer[number]*. Combinations of these forms may also be used. The form *number->member* may be used where *number* is the address of a pointer, and *number.member* where *number* is interpreted as the address of a structure instance. The template of the structure type used in this case will be the last structure type referenced. When **sdb** displays the value of a structure, it does so by displaying the value of all elements of the structure. The address of a structure is displayed by displaying the address of the structure instance rather than the addresses of individual elements.

Elements of a multidimensional array may be referred to as *variable [number] [number]...*, or as *variable [number, number,...]*. In place of *number*, the form *number;number* may be used to indicate a range of values, * may be used to indicate all legitimate values for that subscript, or subscripts may be omitted entirely if they are the last subscripts and the full range of values is desired. If no subscripts are specified, **sdb** will display the value of all elements of the array.

A particular instance of a variable on the stack is referred to as *procedure:variable, number*. The *number* is the occurrence of the specified procedure on the stack, with the topmost occurrence being 1. The default procedure is the one containing the current line.

Addresses may be used in **sdb** commands as well. Addresses are specified by decimal, octal, or hexadecimal numbers.

Line numbers in the source program are specified by the form *filename:number* or *procedure:number*. In either case, the *number* is relative to the beginning of the file and corresponds to the line number used by text editors or the output of **pr**. A number used by itself implies a line in the current file.

While a live process is running under **sdb**, all addresses and identifiers refer to the live process. When **sdb** is not examining a live process, the addresses and identifiers refer to *objfile* or *corfile*.

Commands

The commands for examining data in the program are:

- t Prints a stack trace of the terminated or halted program. The function invoked most recently is at the top of the stack. For C programs, the stack ends with _start, which is the startup routine that invokes main.

- T Prints the top line of the stack trace.

variable/clm
  Print the value of *variable* according to length *l* and format *m*. The numeric count *c* indicates that a region of memory, beginning at the address implied by *variable*, is to be displayed. The length specifiers are:

b   one byte

h   two bytes (half word)

l   four bytes (long word)

Legal values for *m* are:

c   character

d   signed decimal

u   unsigned decimal

o   octal

x   hexadecimal

f   32-bit single precision floating point

g   64-bit double precision floating point

s   Assumes that *variable* is a string pointer and prints characters starting at the address pointed to by the variable.

a   Prints characters starting at the variable's address. Do not use this with register variables.

p   pointer to procedure

i   Disassembles machine-language instruction with addresses printed numerically and symbolically.

I   Disassembles machine-language instruction with addresses printed numerically only.

Length specifiers are effective with formats c, d, u, o, x. The length specifier determines the output length of the value to be displayed. This value may be truncated. The count specifier *c* displays that many units of memory, starting at the address of the *variable*. The number of bytes in the unit of memory is determined by *l* or by the size associated with the variable. If the specifiers *c*, *l*, and *m* are omitted, **sdb** uses defaults. If a count specifier is used with the **s** or **a** command, then that many characters are printed. Otherwise, successive characters are printed until either a null byte is reached or 128 characters are printed. The last variable may be redisplayed with the ./ command.

For a limited form of pattern matching, use the **sh** metacharacters * and ? within procedure and variable names. (**sdb** does not accept these metacharacters in file names, as the function name in a line number when setting a breakpoint, in the function call command, or as the argument to the **e** command.) If no procedure name is supplied, **sdb** matches both local and global variables. If the procedure name is specified, then **sdb** matches only local variables. To match global variables only, use :*pattern*. To print all variables, use *:*.

linenumber?*lm*
variable:?*lm*
> Prints the value at the address from the executable or text space given by *linenumber* or *variable* (procedure name), according to the format *lm*. The default format is i.

variable=*lm*
linenumber=*lm*
number=*lm*
> Prints the address of *variable* or *linenumber*, or the value of *number*. *l* specifies length and *m* specifies the format. If no format is specified, then sdb uses lx (four-byte hex). *m* allows you to convert between decimal, octal, and hexadecimal.

variable!*value*
> Sets *variable* to the given *value*. The value may be a number, a character constant, or a variable. The value must be well-defined; structures are allowed only if assigning to another structure variable of the same type. Character constants are denoted '*character*. Numbers are viewed as integers unless a decimal point or exponent is used. In this case, they are treated as having the type double. Registers, except the floating point registers, are viewed as integers. Register names are identical to those used by the assembler (for example, %*regname* where *regname* is the name of a register). If the address of a variable is given, it is regarded as the address of a variable of type int. C conventions are used in any type conversions necessary to perform the indicated assignment.

x   Prints the machine registers and the current machine-language instruction.

X   Prints the current machine-language instruction.

The commands for examining source files are:

e
e *procedure*
e *filename*
e *directory*/
> e, without arguments, prints the name of the current file. The second form sets the current file to the file containing the procedure. The third form sets the current file to *filename*. The current line is set to the first line in the named procedure or file. Source files are assumed to be in the directories in the directory list. The fourth form adds *directory* to the end of the directory list.

/*regular expression*/
> Searches forward from the current line for a line containing a string matching *regular expression*, as in ed. The trailing / may be omitted, except when associated with a breakpoint.

?*regular expression*?
> Searches backward from the current line for a line containing a string matching *regular expression*, as in ed. The trailing ? may be omitted, except when associated with a breakpoint.

p Prints the current line.

z Prints the current line and the following nine lines. Sets the current line to the last line printed.

w Prints the 10 lines (the window) around the current line.

number
Specifies the current line. Prints the new current line.

count+
Advances the current line by *count* lines. Prints the new current line.

count−
Resets the current line by *count* lines back. Prints the new current line.

The commands for controlling the execution of the source program are:

count r *args*
count R
Runs the program with the given arguments. The r command with no arguments reuses the previous arguments to the program. The R command runs the program with no arguments. An argument beginning with < or > redirects the standard input or output, respectively. Full **sh** syntax is accepted. If *count* is given, it specifies the number of breakpoints to be ignored.

linenumber c *count*
linenumber C *count*
Continues execution. **sdb** stops when it encounters *count* breakpoints. The signal that stopped the program is reactivated with the C command and ignored with the c command. If a line number is specified, then a temporary breakpoint is placed at the line and execution continues. The breakpoint is deleted when the command finishes.

linenumber g *count*
Continues with execution resumed at the given line. If *count* is given, it specifies the number of breakpoints to be ignored.

s *count*
S *count*
s single steps the program through *count* lines or if no *count* is given, then the program runs for one line. s will step from one function into a called function. S also steps a program, but it will not step into a called function. It steps over the function called.

i *count*
I *count*
Single steps by *count* machine-language instructions. The signal that caused the program to stop is reactivated with the I command and ignored with the i command.

variable$m *count*
address:m *count*
> Single steps (as with **s**) until the specified location is modified with a new value. If *count* is omitted, it is, in effect, infinity. *Variable* must be accessible from the current procedure. This command can be very slow.

level **v**
> Toggles verbose mode. This is for use when single stepping with S, s, or m. If *level* is omitted, then just the current source file and/or function name is printed when either changes. If *level* is 1 or greater, each C source line is printed before it executes. If *level* is 2 or greater, each assembler statement is also printed. A **v** turns verbose mode off.

k   Kills the program being debugged.

procedure (*arg1*,*arg2*,...)
procedure (*arg1*,*arg2*,...) /*m*
> Executes the named procedure with the given arguments. Arguments can be register names, integer, character, or string constants, or names of variables accessible from the current procedure. The second form causes the value returned by the procedure to be printed according to format *m*. If no format is given, it defaults to **d**.

linenumber **b** *commands*
> Sets a breakpoint at the given line. If a procedure name without a line number is given (e.g., *proc*:), a breakpoint is placed at the first line in the procedure even if it was not compiled with the −g option. If no *linenumber* is given, a breakpoint is placed at the current line. If no *commands* are given, execution stops at the breakpoint and control is returned to sdb. Otherwise the *commands* are executed when the breakpoint is encountered. Multiple commands are specified by separating them with semicolons. Nested associated commands are not permitted; setting breakpoints within the associated environments is permitted.

B   Prints a list of the currently active breakpoints.

linenumber **d**
> Deletes a breakpoint at the given line. If no *linenumber* is given, then the breakpoints are deleted interactively. Each breakpoint location is printed and a line is read from the standard input. If the line begins with a **y** or **d**, then the breakpoint is deleted.

D   Deletes all breakpoints.

l   Prints the last executed line.

linenumber **a**
> Announces a line number. If *linenumber* is of the form *proc*:*number*, the command effectively does a *linenumber*:**b** l;c. If *linenumber* is of the form *proc*:, the command effectively does a *proc*:**b** T;c.

Miscellaneous commands:

#*rest-of-line*
: The *rest-of-line* represents comments that are ignored by **sdb**.

!*command*
: The *command* is interpreted by **sh**.

new-line
: If the previous command printed a source line, then advance the current line by one line and print the new current line. If the previous command displayed a memory location, then display the next memory location. If the previous command disassembled an instruction, then disassemble the next instruction.

end-of-file character
: Scrolls the next 10 lines of instructions, source, or data depending on which was printed last. The end-of-file character is usually **control-d**.

< *filename*
: Read commands from *filename* until the end of file is reached, and then continue to accept commands from standard input. Commands are echoed, preceded by two asterisks, just before being executed. This command may not be nested; < may not appear as a command in a file.

M   Prints the address maps.

" *string* "
: Prints the given string. The C escape sequences of the form *character*, *octaldigits*, or \\x*hexdigits* are recognized, where *character* is a nonnumeric character. The trailing quote may be omitted.

q   Exits the debugger.

V   Prints version stamping information.

SEE ALSO
cc(1), signal(2), a.out(4), core(4), syms(4).
ed(1), gcore(1), sh(1) in the *User's Reference Manual*.
The "sdb" chapter in the *Programmer's Guide: ANSI C and Programming Support Tools*.

NOTES
If *objfile* is a dynamically linked executable, variables, function names, and so on that are defined in shared objects may not be referenced until the shared object in which the variable, etc., is defined is attached to the process. For shared objects attached at startup (e.g., libc.so.1, the default C library), this implies that such variables may not be accessed until main is called.

The *objfile* argument is accessed directly for debugging information while the process is created via the **PATH** variable.

size(1)

NAME
size – print section sizes in bytes of object files

SYNOPSIS
size [–F –f –n –o –V –x] *files*

DESCRIPTION
The **size** command produces segment or section size information in bytes for each loaded section in ELF or COFF object files. **size** prints out the size of the text, data, and bss (uninitialized data) segments (or sections) and their total.

size processes ELF and COFF object files entered on the command line. If an archive file is input to the **size** command, the information for each object file in the archive is displayed.

When calculating segment information, the **size** command prints out the total file size of the non-writable segments, the total file size of the writable segments, and the total memory size of the writable segments minus the total file size of the writable segments.

If it cannot calculate segment information, **size** calculates section information. When calculating section information, it prints out the total size of sections that are allocatable, non-writable, and not NOBITS, the total size of the sections that are allocatable, writable, and not NOBITS, and the total size of the writable sections of type NOBITS. (NOBITS sections do not actually take up space in the *file*.)

If **size** cannot calculate either segment or section information, it prints an error message and stops processing the file.

- –F   Prints out the size of each loadable segment, the permission flags of the segment, then the total of the loadable segment sizes. If there is no segment data, **size** prints an error message and stops processing the file.

- –f   Prints out the size of each allocatable section, the name of the section, and the total of the section sizes. If there is no section data, **size** prints out an error message and stops processing the file.

- –n   Prints out non-loadable segment or non-allocatable section sizes. If segment data exists, **size** prints out the memory size of each loadable segment or file size of each non-loadable segment, the permission flags, and the total size of the segments. If there is no segment data, **size** prints out, for each allocatable and non-allocatable section, the memory size, the section name, and the total size of the sections. If there is no segment or section data, **size** prints an error message and stops processing.

- –o   Prints numbers in octal, not decimal.

- –V   Prints the version information for the **size** command on the standard error output.

- –x   Prints numbers in hexadecimal; not decimal.

EXAMPLES

The examples below are typical **size** output.

size *file*	2724 + 88 + 0 = 2812
size –f *file*	26(.text) + 5(.init) + 5(.fini) = 36
size –F *file*	2724(r-x) + 88(rwx) + 0(rwx) = 2812

SEE ALSO

as(1), cc(1), ld(1), a.out(4), ar(4).

NOTES

Since the size of bss sections is not known until link-edit time, the **size** command will not give the true total size of pre-linked objects.

NAME

strip – strip symbol table, debugging and line number information from an object file.

SYNOPSIS

strip [-blrVx] *file ...*

DESCRIPTION

The `strip` command strips the symbol table, debugging information, and line number information from ELF object files; COFF object files can no longer be stripped. Once this stripping process has been done, no symbolic debugging access will be available for that file; therefore, this command is normally run only on production modules that have been debugged and tested.

If `strip` is executed on a common archive file [see ar(4)] in addition to processing the members, `strip` will remove the archive symbol table. The archive symbol table must be restored by executing the ar(1) command with the −s option before the archive can be linked by the ld(1) command. `strip` will produce appropriate warning messages when this situation arises.

The amount of information stripped from the ELF object file can be controlled by using any of the following options:

- -b   Same effect as the default behavior. This option is obsolete and will be removed in the next release.
- -l   Strip line number information only; do not strip the symbol table or debugging information.
- -r   Same effect as the default behavior. This option is obsolete and will be removed in the next release.
- -V   Print, on standard error, the version number of `strip`.
- -x   Do not strip the symbol table; debugging and line number information may be stripped.

`strip` is used to reduce the file storage overhead taken by the object file.

FILES

TMPDIR/strp*	temporary files
TMPDIR	usually /var/tmp but can be redefined by setting the environment variable TMPDIR [see tempnam() in tmpnam(3S)].

SEE ALSO

ar(1), as(1), cc(1), ld(1), tmpnam(3S), a.out(4), ar(4).

NOTES

The symbol table section will not be removed if it is contained within a segment, or the file is either a relocatable or dynamic shared object.

The line number and debugging sections will not be removed if they are contained within a segment, or their associated relocation section is contained within a segment.

tsort(1)   tsort(1)

NAME
    tsort – topological sort

SYNOPSIS
    tsort [*file*]

DESCRIPTION
    The tsort command produces on the standard output a totally ordered list of
    items consistent with a partial ordering of items mentioned in the input *file*. If no
    file is specified, the standard input is understood.

    The input consists of pairs of items (nonempty strings) separated by blanks. Pairs
    of different items indicate ordering. Pairs of identical items indicate presence, but
    not ordering.

SEE ALSO
    lorder(1).

DIAGNOSTICS
    Odd data: there is an odd number of fields in the input file.

NAME
unget – undo a previous get of an SCCS file

SYNOPSIS
unget [-rSID] [-s] [-n] *files*

DESCRIPTION
unget undoes the effect of a get -e done prior to creating the intended new delta. If a directory is named, unget behaves as though each file in the directory were specified as a named file, except that non-SCCS files and unreadable files are silently ignored. If a name of – is given, the standard input is read with each line being taken as the name of an SCCS file to be processed.

Keyletter arguments apply independently to each named file.

-rSID Uniquely identifies which delta is no longer intended. (This would have been specified by get as the "new delta"). The use of this keyletter is necessary only if two or more outstanding gets for editing on the same SCCS file were done by the same person (login name). A diagnostic results if the specified SID is ambiguous, or if it is necessary and omitted on the command line.

-s Suppresses the printout, on the standard output, of the intended delta's SID.

-n Causes the retention of the gotten file, which would normally be removed from the current directory.

unget must be performed by the same user who performed the original get -e.

FILES
p-file   [see delta(1)]
q-file   [see delta(1)]
z-file   [see delta(1)]

SEE ALSO
delta(1), get(1), help(1), sact(1).

DIAGNOSTICS
Use help(1) for explanations.

val(1)

NAME
val – validate an SCCS file

SYNOPSIS
val –

val [-s] [-rSID] [-mname] [-ytype] files

DESCRIPTION
val determines if the specified *file* is an SCCS file meeting the characteristics specified by the optional argument list. Arguments to val may appear in any order. The arguments consist of keyletter arguments, which begin with a –, and named files.

val has a special argument, –, which causes reading of the standard input until an end-of-file condition is detected. Each line read is independently processed as if it were a command line argument list.

val generates diagnostic messages on the standard output for each command line and file processed, and also returns a single 8-bit code on exit as described below.

The keyletter arguments are defined as follows. The effects of any keyletter argument apply independently to each named file on the command line.

-s The presence of this argument silences the diagnostic message normally generated on the standard output for any error that is detected while processing each named file on a given command line.

-rSID The argument value *SID* (SCCS identification string) is an SCCS delta number. A check is made to determine if the *SID* is ambiguous (e. g., -r1 is ambiguous because it physically does not exist but implies 1.1, 1.2, etc., which may exist) or invalid (e. g., r1.0 or r1.1.0 are invalid because neither can exist as a valid delta number). If the *SID* is valid and not ambiguous, a check is made to determine if it actually exists.

-mname The argument value *name* is compared with the SCCS %M% keyword in *file*.

-ytype The argument value *type* is compared with the SCCS %Y% keyword in *file*.

The 8-bit code returned by val is a disjunction of the possible errors; it can be interpreted as a bit string where (moving from left to right) set bits are interpreted as follows:

bit 0 = missing file argument
bit 1 = unknown or duplicate keyletter argument
bit 2 = corrupted SCCS file
bit 3 = cannot open file or file not SCCS
bit 4 = SID is invalid or ambiguous
bit 5 = SID does not exist
bit 6 = %Y%, -y mismatch
bit 7 = %M%, -m mismatch

val can process two or more files on a given command line and in turn can process multiple command lines (when reading the standard input). In these cases an aggregate code is returned: a logical OR of the codes generated for each command line and file processed.

SEE ALSO
admin(1), delta(1), get(1), help(1, prs(1).

DIAGNOSTICS
Use help(1) for explanations.

NOTES
val can process up to 50 files on a single command line.

vc(1)   vc(1)

NAME
        vc – version control
SYNOPSIS
        vc [-a] [-t] [-c*char*] [-s] [*keyword=value* ... *keyword=value*]
DESCRIPTION
        This command is obsolete and will be removed in the next release.

        The vc command copies lines from the standard input to the standard output under control of its arguments and of "control statements" encountered in the standard input. In the process of performing the copy operation, user-declared *keyword*s may be replaced by their string *value* when they appear in plain text and/or control statements.

        The copying of lines from the standard input to the standard output is conditional, based on tests (in control statements) of keyword values specified in control statements or as vc command arguments.

        A control statement is a single line beginning with a control character, except as modified by the -t keyletter (see below). The default control character is colon (:), except as modified by the -c keyletter (see below). Input lines beginning with a backslash (\) followed by a control character are not control lines and are copied to the standard output with the backslash removed. Lines beginning with a backslash followed by a non-control character are copied in their entirety.

        A keyword is composed of 9 or less alphanumerics; the first must be alphabetic. A value is any ASCII string that can be created with ed; a numeric value is an unsigned string of digits. Keyword values may not contain blanks or tabs.

        Replacement of keywords by values is done whenever a keyword surrounded by control characters is encountered on a version control statement. The -a keyletter (see below) forces replacement of keywords in all lines of text. An uninterpreted control character may be included in a value by preceding it with \. If a literal \ is desired, then it too must be preceded by \.

        The following options are valid:

        -a   Forces replacement of keywords surrounded by control characters with their assigned value in all text lines and not just in vc statements.

        -t   All characters from the beginning of a line up to and including the first tab character are ignored for the purpose of detecting a control statement. If a control statement is found, all characters up to and including the tab are discarded.

        -c*char*   Specifies a control character to be used in place of the ":" default.

        -s   Silences warning messages (not error) that are normally printed on the diagnostic output.

        vc recognizes the following version control statements:

        :dcl *keyword*[, ..., *keyword*]
                Declare keywords. All keywords must be declared.

:asg *keyword=value*
> Assign values to keywords. An **asg** statement overrides the assignment for the corresponding keyword on the **vc** command line and all previous **asg** statements for that keyword. Keywords that are declared but are not assigned values have null values.

:if *condition*
...
:end
> Skip lines of the standard input. If the condition is true, all lines between the **if** statement and the matching **end** statement are copied to the standard output. If the condition is false, all intervening lines are discarded, including control statements. Note that intervening **if** statements and matching **end** statements are recognized solely for the purpose of maintaining the proper **if-end** matching.
>
> The syntax of a condition is:
>
> ```
> <cond>    ::= [ "not" ] <or>
> <or>      ::= <and> | <and> "|" <or>
> <and>     ::= <exp> | <exp> "&" <and>
> <exp>     ::= "(" <or> ")" | <value> <op> <value>
> <op>      ::= "=" | "!=" | "<" | ">"
> <value>   ::= <arbitrary ASCII string> | <numeric string>
> ```
>
> The available operators and their meanings are:
>
> | | |
> |---|---|
> | = | equal |
> | != | not equal |
> | & | and |
> | \| | or |
> | > | greater than |
> | < | less than |
> | ( ) | used for logical groupings |
> | not | may only occur immediately after the **if**, and when present, inverts the value of the entire condition |
>
> The > and < operate only on unsigned integer values (e.g., : 012 > 12 is false). All other operators take strings as arguments (e.g., : 012 != 12 is true).
>
> The precedence of the operators (from highest to lowest) is:
>
> ```
> = != > <   all of equal precedence
> &
> |
> ```
>
> Parentheses may be used to alter the order of precedence.
>
> Values must be separated from operators or parentheses by at least one blank or tab.

::*text*
>   Replace keywords on lines that are copied to the standard output. The two leading control characters are removed, and keywords surrounded by control characters in text are replaced by their value before the line is copied to the output file. This action is independent of the −a keyletter.

:on
:off Turn on or off keyword replacement on all lines.

:ctl *char*
>   Change the control character to *char*.

:msg *message*
>   Print *message* on the diagnostic output.

:err *message*
>   Print *message* followed by:
>
>   ERROR: `err statement on line` ... (915)
>
>   on the diagnostic output. vc halts execution, and returns an exit code of 1.

SEE ALSO

help(1).
ed(1) in the *User's Reference Manual*.

what(1)

NAME
what – print identification strings

SYNOPSIS
what [–s] *files*

DESCRIPTION
what searches the given files for all occurrences of the pattern that the **get** command substitutes for %Z% (this is @(#) at this printing) and prints out what follows until the first ", >, new-line, \, or null character. For example, if the C program in file **f.c** contains

    #ident " @(#) *identification information* "

and **f.c** is compiled to yield **f.o** and **a.out**, then the command

    what f.c f.o a.out

prints

    f.c:
        identification information

    f.o:
        identification information

    a.out:
        identification information

what is intended to be used in conjunction with the **get** command, which automatically inserts identifying information, but it can also be used where the information is inserted manually. Only one option exists:

    –s   Quit after finding the first occurrence of pattern in each file.

SEE ALSO
get(1), help(1), mcs(1).

DIAGNOSTICS
Exit status is 0 if any matches are found, otherwise 1. See help(1) for explanations.

NAME
x286emul – emulate XENIX 80286

SYNOPSIS
x286emul [*arg* . . .] prog286

DESCRIPTION
x286emul is an emulator that allows programs from XENIX System V/286 Release 2.3 or SCO's XENIX System V/286 Release 2.3.2 on the Intel 80286 to run on the Intel 80386 processor under UNIX System V.

The UNIX system recognizes an attempt to exec(2) a 286 program, and automatically exec's the 286 emulator with the 286 program name as an additional argument. It is not necessary to specify the x286emul emulator on the command line. The 286 programs can be invoked using the same command format as on the XENIX System V/286.

x286emul reads the 286 program's text and data into memory and maps them through the LDT [via sysi86(2)] as 286 text and data segments. It also fills in the jam area, which is used by XENIX programs to do system calls and signal returns. x286emul starts the 286 program by jumping to its entry point.

When the 286 program attempts to do a system call, x286emul takes control. It does any conversions needed between the 286 system call and the equivalent 386 system call, and performs the 386 system call. The results are converted to the form the 286 program expects, and the 286 program is resumed.

The following are some of the differences between a program running on a 286 and a 286 program using x286emul on a 386:

> Attempts to unlink or write on the 286 program will fail on the 286 with ETXTBSY. Under x286emul, they will not fail.
>
> ptrace(2) is not supported under x286emul.
>
> The 286 program must be readable for the emulator to read it.

The emulator must have this name and be in /bin if it is to be automatically invoked when exec(2) is used on a 286 program.

yacc(1)

NAME
yacc – yet another compiler-compiler

SYNOPSIS
yacc [-vVdlt] [-Q[y|n]] *file*

DESCRIPTION
The **yacc** command converts a context-free grammar into a set of tables for a simple automaton that executes an LALR(1) parsing algorithm. The grammar may be ambiguous; specified precedence rules are used to break ambiguities.

The output file, **y.tab.c**, must be compiled by the C compiler to produce a program **yyparse**. This program must be loaded with the lexical analyzer program, **yylex**, as well as **main** and **yyerror**, an error handling routine. These routines must be supplied by the user; the **lex**(1) command is useful for creating lexical analyzers usable by **yacc**.

- **-v**   Prepares the file **y.output**, which contains a description of the parsing tables and a report on conflicts generated by ambiguities in the grammar.

- **-d**   Generates the file **y.tab.h** with the **#define** statements that associate the **yacc**-assigned "token codes" with the user-declared "token names." This association allows source files other than **y.tab.c** to access the token codes.

- **-l**   Specifies that the code produced in **y.tab.c** will not contain any **#line** constructs. This option should only be used after the grammar and the associated actions are fully debugged.

- **-Q[y|n]**   The **-Qy** option puts the version stamping information in **y.tab.c**. This allows you to know what version of **yacc** built the file. The **-Qn** option (the default) writes no version information.

- **-t**   Compiles runtime debugging code by default. Runtime debugging code is always generated in **y.tab.c** under conditional compilation control. By default, this code is not included when **y.tab.c** is compiled. Whether or not the -t option is used, the runtime debugging code is under the control of **YYDEBUG**, a preprocessor symbol. If YYDEBUG has a non-zero value, then the debugging code is included. If its value is zero, then the code will not be included. The size and execution time of a program produced without the runtime debugging code will be smaller and slightly faster.

- **-V**   Prints on the standard error output the version information for **yacc**.

FILES
y.output
y.tab.c
y.tab.h   defines for token names
yacc.tmp,
yacc.debug, yacc.acts   temporary files

LIBDIR/`yaccpar`	parser prototype for C programs
LIBDIR	usually `/usr/ccs/lib`

SEE ALSO
lex(1).

The "yacc" chapter in the *Programmer's Guide: ANSI C and Programming Support Tools*.

DIAGNOSTICS
The number of reduce-reduce and shift-reduce conflicts is reported on the standard error output; a more detailed report is found in the `y.output` file. Similarly, if some rules are not reachable from the start symbol, this instance is also reported.

NOTES
Because file names are fixed, at most one **yacc** process can be active in a given directory at a given time.

SYSTEM CALLS (2)

SYSTEM CALLS (2)

intro(2)

NAME
intro – introduction to system calls and error numbers

SYNOPSIS
#include <errno.h>

DESCRIPTION
This section describes all of the system calls. Most of these calls have one or more error returns. An error condition is indicated by an otherwise impossible returned value. This is almost always −1 or the NULL pointer; the individual descriptions specify the details. An error number is also made available in the external variable `errno`. `errno` is not cleared on successful calls, so it should be tested only after an error has been indicated.

Each system call description attempts to list all possible error numbers. The following is a complete list of the error numbers and their names as defined in <errno.h>.

1 EPERM   Not super-user
> Typically this error indicates an attempt to modify a file in some way forbidden except to its owner or the super-user. It is also returned for attempts by ordinary users to do things allowed only to the super-user.

2 ENOENT   No such file or directory
> A file name is specified and the file should exist but doesn't, or one of the directories in a path name does not exist.

3 ESRCH   No such process
> No process can be found corresponding to that specified by PID in the `kill` or `ptrace` routine.

4 EINTR   Interrupted system call
> An asynchronous signal (such as interrupt or quit), which the user has elected to catch, occurred during a system service routine. If execution is resumed after processing the signal, it will appear as if the interrupted routine call returned this error condition.

5 EIO   I/O error
> Some physical I/O error has occurred. This error may in some cases occur on a call following the one to which it actually applies.

6 ENXIO   No such device or address
> I/O on a special file refers to a subdevice which does not exist, or exists beyond the limit of the device. It may also occur when, for example, a tape drive is not on-line or no disk pack is loaded on a drive.

7 E2BIG   Arg list too long
> An argument list longer than ARG_MAX bytes is presented to a member of the `exec` family of routines. The argument list limit is the sum of the size of the argument list plus the size of the environment's exported shell variables.

8 ENOEXEC   Exec format error
    A request is made to execute a file which, although it has the appropriate permissions, does not start with a valid format [see a.out(4)].

9 EBADF   Bad file number
    Either a file descriptor refers to no open file, or a read [respectively, write] request is made to a file that is open only for writing (respectively, reading).

10 ECHILD   No child processes
    A wait routine was executed by a process that had no existing or unwaited-for child processes.

11 EAGAIN   No more processes
    For example, the fork routine failed because the system's process table is full or the user is not allowed to create any more processes, or a system call failed because of insufficient memory or swap space.

12 ENOMEM   Not enough space
    During execution of an exec, brk, or sbrk routine, a program asks for more space than the system is able to supply. This is not a temporary condition; the maximum size is a system parameter. The error may also occur if the arrangement of text, data, and stack segments requires too many segmentation registers, or if there is not enough swap space during the fork routine. If this error occurs on a resource associated with Remote File Sharing (RFS), it indicates a memory depletion which may be temporary, dependent on system activity at the time the call was invoked.

13 EACCES   Permission denied
    An attempt was made to access a file in a way forbidden by the protection system.

14 EFAULT   Bad address
    The system encountered a hardware fault in attempting to use an argument of a routine. For example, errno potentially may be set to EFAULT any time a routine that takes a pointer argument is passed an invalid address, if the system can detect the condition. Because systems will differ in their ability to reliably detect a bad address, on some implementations passing a bad address to a routine will result in undefined behavior.

15 ENOTBLK   Block device required
    A non-block file was mentioned where a block device was required (e.g., in a call to the mount routine).

16 EBUSY   Device busy
    An attempt was made to mount a device that was already mounted or an attempt was made to unmount a device on which there is an active file (open file, current directory, mounted-on file, active text segment). It will also occur if an attempt is made to enable accounting when it is already enabled. The device or resource is currently unavailable.

17 EEXIST   File exists
    An existing file was mentioned in an inappropriate context (e.g., call to the link routine).

18 EXDEV   Cross-device link
    A link to a file on another device was attempted.

19 ENODEV   No such device
    An attempt was made to apply an inappropriate operation to a device (e.g., read a write-only device).

20 ENOTDIR   Not a directory
    A non-directory was specified where a directory is required (e.g., in a path prefix or as an argument to the chdir routine).

21 EISDIR   Is a directory
    An attempt was made to write on a directory.

22 EINVAL   Invalid argument
    An invalid argument was specified (e.g., unmounting a non-mounted device), mentioning an undefined signal in a call to the signal or kill routine.

23 ENFILE   File table overflow
    The system file table is full (i.e., SYS_OPEN files are open, and temporarily no more files can be opened).

24 EMFILE   Too many open files
    No process may have more than OPEN_MAX file descriptors open at a time.

25 ENOTTY   Not a typewriter
    A call was made to the ioctl routine specifying a file that is not a special character device.

26 ETXTBSY   Text file busy
    An attempt was made to execute a pure-procedure program that is currently open for writing. Also an attempt to open for writing or to remove a pure-procedure program that is being executed.

27 EFBIG   File too large
    The size of a file exceeded the maximum file size, FCHR_MAX [see getrlimit].

28 ENOSPC   No space left on device
    While writing an ordinary file or creating a directory entry, there is no free space left on the device. In the fcntl routine, the setting or removing of record locks on a file cannot be accomplished because there are no more record entries left on the system.

29 ESPIPE   Illegal seek
    A call to the lseek routine was issued to a pipe.

30 **EROFS** Read-only file system
   An attempt to modify a file or directory was made on a device mounted read-only.

31 **EMLINK** Too many links
   An attempt to make more than the maximum number of links, LINK_MAX, to a file.

32 **EPIPE** Broken pipe
   A write on a pipe for which there is no process to read the data. This condition normally generates a signal; the error is returned if the signal is ignored.

33 **EDOM** Math argument out of domain of func
   The argument of a function in the math package (3M) is out of the domain of the function.

34 **ERANGE** Math result not representable
   The value of a function in the math package (3M) is not representable within machine precision.

35 **ENOMSG** No message of desired type
   An attempt was made to receive a message of a type that does not exist on the specified message queue [see msgop(2)].

36 **EIDRM** Identifier removed
   This error is returned to processes that resume execution due to the removal of an identifier from the file system's name space [see msgctl(2), semctl(2), and shmctl(2)].

37 **ECHRNG** Channel number out of range

38 **EL2NSYNC** Level 2 not synchronized

39 **EL3HLT** Level 3 halted

40 **EL3RST** Level 3 reset

41 **ELNRNG** Link number out of range

42 **EUNATCH** Protocol driver not attached

43 **ENOCSI** No CSI structure available

44 **EL2HLT** Level 2 halted

45 **EDEADLK** Deadlock condition
   A deadlock situation was detected and avoided. This error pertains to file and record locking.

46 **ENOLCK** No record locks available
   There are no more locks available. The system lock table is full [see fcntl(2)].

47–49   Reserved

58–59   Reserved

60   **ENOSTR**   Device not a stream
      A **putmsg** or **getmsg** system call was attempted on a file descriptor that is not a STREAMS device.

61   **ENODATA**   No data available

62   **ETIME**   Timer expired
      The timer set for a STREAMS **ioctl** call has expired. The cause of this error is device specific and could indicate either a hardware or software failure, or perhaps a timeout value that is too short for the specific operation. The status of the **ioctl** operation is indeterminate.

63   **ENOSR**   Out of stream resources
      During a STREAMS **open**, either no STREAMS queues or no STREAMS head data structures were available. This is a temporary condition; one may recover from it if other processes release resources.

64   **ENONET**   Machine is not on the network
      This error is Remote File Sharing (RFS) specific. It occurs when users try to advertise, unadvertise, mount, or unmount remote resources while the machine has not done the proper startup to connect to the network.

65   **ENOPKG**   Package not installed
      This error occurs when users attempt to use a system call from a package which has not been installed.

66   **EREMOTE**   Object is remote
      This error is RFS specific. It occurs when users try to advertise a resource which is not on the local machine, or try to mount/unmount a device (or pathname) that is on a remote machine.

67   **ENOLINK**   Link has been severed
      This error is RFS specific. It occurs when the link (virtual circuit) connecting to a remote machine is gone.

68   **EADV**   Advertise error
      This error is RFS specific. It occurs when users try to advertise a resource which has been advertised already, or try to stop RFS while there are resources still advertised, or try to force unmount a resource when it is still advertised.

69   **ESRMNT**   Srmount error
      This error is RFS specific. It occurs when an attempt is made to stop RFS while resources are still mounted by remote machines, or when a resource is readvertised with a client list that does not include a remote machine that currently has the resource mounted.

70   **ECOMM**   Communication error on send
      This error is RFS specific. It occurs when the current process is waiting for a message from a remote machine, and the virtual circuit fails.

71 EPROTO Protocol error
   Some protocol error occurred. This error is device specific, but is generally not related to a hardware failure.

74 EMULTIHOP Multihop attempted
   This error is RFS specific. It occurs when users try to access remote resources which are not directly accessible.

76 EDOTDOT Error 76
   This error is RFS specific. A way for the server to tell the client that a process has transferred back from mount point.

77 EBADMSG Not a data message
   During a **read**, **getmsg**, or **ioctl** I_RECVFD system call to a STREAMS device, something has come to the head of the queue that can't be processed. That something depends on the system call:
   read: control information or a passed file descriptor.
   getmsg: passed file descriptor.
   ioctl: control or data information.

78 ENAMETOOLONG File name too long
   The length of the path argument exceeds PATH_MAX, or the length of a path component exceeds NAME_MAX while _POSIX_NO_TRUNC is in effect; see limits(4).

79 EOVERFLOW
   Value too large for defined data type.

80 ENOTUNIQ Name not unique on network
   Given log name not unique.

81 EBADFD File descriptor in bad state
   Either a file descriptor refers to no open file or a read request was made to a file that is open only for writing.

82 EREMCHG Remote address changed

83 ELIBACC Cannot access a needed shared library
   Trying to **exec** an **a.out** that requires a static shared library and the static shared library doesn't exist or the user doesn't have permission to use it.

84 ELIBBAD Accessing a corrupted shared library
   Trying to **exec** an **a.out** that requires a static shared library (to be linked in) and **exec** could not load the static shared library. The static shared library is probably corrupted.

85 ELIBSCN .lib section in a.out corrupted
   Trying to **exec** an **a.out** that requires a static shared library (to be linked in) and there was erroneous data in the .lib section of the a.out. The .lib section tells **exec** what static shared libraries are needed. The a.out is probably corrupted.

86 ELIBMAX Attempting to link in more shared libraries than system limit
Trying to **exec** an **a.out** that requires more static shared libraries than is allowed on the current configuration of the system. See the *System Administrator's Guide*.

87 ELIBEXEC Cannot **exec** a shared library directly
Attempting to **exec** a shared library directly.

88 EILSEQ Error 88
Illegal byte sequence. Handle multiple characters as a single character.

89 ENOSYS Operation not applicable

90 ELOOP Number of symbolic links encountered during path name traversal exceeds **MAXSYMLINKS**

91 ESTART Error 91
Interrupted system call should be restarted.

92 ESTRPIPE Error 92
Streams pipe error (not externally visible).

93 ENOTEMPTY Directory not empty

94 EUSERS Too many users
Too many users.

95 ENOTSOCK Socket operation on non-socket
Self-explanatory.

96 EDESTADDRREQ Destination address required
A required address was omitted from an operation on a transport endpoint. Destination address required.

97 EMSGSIZE Message too long
A message sent on a transport provider was larger than the internal message buffer or some other network limit.

98 EPROTOTYPE Protocol wrong type for socket
A protocol was specified that does not support the semantics of the socket type requested.

99 ENOPROTOOPT Protocol not available
A bad option or level was specified when getting or setting options for a protocol.

120 EPROTONOSUPPORT Protocol not supported
The protocol has not been configured into the system or no implementation for it exists.

121 ESOCKTNOSUPPORT Socket type not supported
The support for the socket type has not been configured into the system or no implementation for it exists.

122 EOPNOTSUPP Operation not supported on transport endpoint
For example, trying to accept a connection on a datagram transport endpoint.

123 **EPFNOSUPPORT** Protocol family not supported
The protocol family has not been configured into the system or no implementation for it exists. Used for the Internet protocols.

124 **EAFNOSUPPORT** Address family not supported by protocol family
An address incompatible with the requested protocol was used.

125 **EADDRINUSE** Address already in use
User attempted to use an address already in use, and the protocol does not allow this.

126 **EADDRNOTAVAIL** Cannot assign requested address
Results from an attempt to create a transport endpoint with an address not on the current machine.

127 **ENETDOWN** Network is down
Operation encountered a dead network.

128 **ENETUNREACH** Network is unreachable
Operation was attempted to an unreachable network.

129 **ENETRESET** Network dropped connection because of reset
The host you were connected to crashed and rebooted.

130 **ECONNABORTED** Software caused connection abort
A connection abort was caused internal to your host machine.

131 **ECONNRESET** Connection reset by peer
A connection was forcibly closed by a peer. This normally results from a loss of the connection on the remote host due to a timeout or a reboot.

132 **ENOBUFS** No buffer space available
An operation on a transport endpoint or pipe was not performed because the system lacked sufficient buffer space or because a queue was full.

133 **EISCONN** Transport endpoint is already connected
A connect request was made on an already connected transport endpoint; or, a **sendto** or **sendmsg** request on a connected transport endpoint specified a destination when already connected.

134 **ENOTCONN** Transport endpoint is not connected
A request to send or receive data was disallowed because the transport endpoint is not connected and (when sending a datagram) no address was supplied.

143 **ESHUTDOWN** Cannot send after transport endpoint shutdown
A request to send data was disallowed because the transport endpoint has already been shut down.

144 **ETOOMANYREFS** Too many references: cannot splice

145 **ETIMEDOUT** Connection timed out
A connect or send request failed because the connected party did not properly respond after a period of time. (The timeout period is dependent on the communication protocol.)

intro (2)

146 ECONNREFUSED Connection refused
  No connection could be made because the target machine actively refused it. This usually results from trying to connect to a service that is inactive on the remote host.
147 EHOSTDOWN Host is down
  A transport provider operation failed because the destination host was down.
148 EHOSTUNREACH No route to host
  A transport provider operation was attempted to an unreachable host.
149 EALREADY Operation already in progress
  An operation was attempted on a non-blocking object that already had an operation in progress.
150 EINPROGRESS Operation now in progress
  An operation that takes a long time to complete (such as a connect) was attempted on a non-blocking object.
151 ESTALE Stale NFS file handle

DEFINITIONS

Background Process Group
  Any process group that is not the foreground process group of a session that has established a connection with a controlling terminal.

Controlling Process
  A session leader that established a connection to a controlling terminal.

Controlling Terminal
  A terminal that is associated with a session. Each session may have, at most, one controlling terminal associated with it and a controlling terminal may be associated with only one session. Certain input sequences from the controlling terminal cause signals to be sent to process groups in the session associated with the controlling terminal; see termio(7).

Directory
  Directories organize files into a hierarchical system where directories are the nodes in the hierarchy. A directory is a file that catalogues the list of files, including directories (sub-directories), that are directly beneath it in the hierarchy. Entries in a directory file are called links. A link associates a file identifier with a filename. By convention, a directory contains at least two links, . (dot) and .. (dot-dot). The link called dot refers to the directory itself while dot-dot refers to its parent directory. The root directory, which is the top-most node of the hierarchy, has itself as its parent directory. The pathname of the root directory is / and the parent directory of the root directory is /.

Downstream
  In a stream, the direction from stream head to driver.

Driver
  In a stream, the driver provides the interface between peripheral hardware and the stream. A driver can also be a pseudo-driver, such as a multiplexor or log driver [see log(7)], which is not associated with a hardware device.

Effective User ID and Effective Group ID
An active process has an effective user ID and an effective group ID that are used to determine file access permissions (see below). The effective user ID and effective group ID are equal to the process's real user ID and real group ID respectively, unless the process or one of its ancestors evolved from a file that had the set-user-ID bit or set-group ID bit set [see **exec**(2)].

File Access Permissions
Read, write, and execute/search permissions on a file are granted to a process if one or more of the following are true:

The effective user ID of the process is super-user.

The effective user ID of the process matches the user ID of the owner of the file and the appropriate access bit of the "owner" portion (0700) of the file mode is set.

The effective user ID of the process does not match the user ID of the owner of the file, but either the effective group ID or one of the supplementary group IDs of the process match the group ID of the file and the appropriate access bit of the "group" portion (0070) of the file mode is set.

The effective user ID of the process does not match the user ID of the owner of the file, and neither the effective group ID nor any of the supplementary group IDs of the process match the group ID of the file, but the appropriate access bit of the "other" portion (0007) of the file mode is set.

Otherwise, the corresponding permissions are denied.

File Descriptor
A file descriptor is a small integer used to do I/O on a file. The value of a file descriptor is from 0 to (NOFILES-1). A process may have no more than NOFILES file descriptors open simultaneously. A file descriptor is returned by system calls such as **open**, or **pipe**. The file descriptor is used as an argument by calls such as **read**, **write**, **ioctl**, and **close**.

File Name
Names consisting of 1 to NAME_MAX characters may be used to name an ordinary file, special file or directory.

These characters may be selected from the set of all character values excluding \0 (null) and the ASCII code for / (slash).

Note that it is generally unwise to use *, ?, [, or] as part of file names because of the special meaning attached to these characters by the shell [see **sh**(1)]. Although permitted, the use of unprintable characters in file names should be avoided.

A file name is sometimes referred to as a pathname component. The interpretation of a pathname component is dependent on the values of NAME_MAX and _POSIX_NO_TRUNC associated with the path prefix of that component. If any pathname component is longer than NAME_MAX and _POSIX_NO_TRUNC is in effect for the path prefix of that component [see **fpathconf**(2) and **limits**(4)], it shall be considered an error condition in that implementation. Otherwise, the implementation shall use the first NAME_MAX bytes of the pathname component.

intro(2) intro(2)

Foreground Process Group
Each session that has established a connection with a controlling terminal will distinguish one process group of the session as the foreground process group of the controlling terminal. This group has certain privileges when accessing its controlling terminal that are denied to background process groups.

Message
In a stream, one or more blocks of data or information, with associated STREAMS control structures. Messages can be of several defined types, which identify the message contents. Messages are the only means of transferring data and communicating within a stream.

Message Queue
In a stream, a linked list of messages awaiting processing by a module or driver.

Message Queue Identifier
A message queue identifier (msqid) is a unique positive integer created by a msgget system call. Each msqid has a message queue and a data structure associated with it. The data structure is referred to as msqid_ds and contains the following members:

```
struct   ipc_perm msg_perm;
struct   msg *msg_first;
struct   msg *msg_last;
ushort   msg_cbytes;
ushort   msg_qnum;
ushort   msg_qbytes;
pid_t    msg_lspid;
pid_t    msg_lrpid;
time_t   msg_stime;
time_t   msg_rtime;
time_t   msg_ctime;
```

Here are descriptions of the fields of the msqid_ds structure:

msg_perm is an ipc_perm structure that specifies the message operation permission (see below). This structure includes the following members:

```
uid_t    cuid;    /* creator user id */
gid_t    cgid;    /* creator group id */
uid_t    uid;     /* user id */
gid_t    gid;     /* group id */
mode_t   mode;    /* r/w permission */
ushort   seq;     /* slot usage sequence # */
key_t    key;     /* key */
```

*msg_first is a pointer to the first message on the queue.

*msg_last is a pointer to the last message on the queue.

msg_cbytes is the current number of bytes on the queue.

msg_qnum is the number of messages currently on the queue.

msg_qbytes is the maximum number of bytes allowed on the queue.

msg_lspid is the process ID of the last process that performed a msgsnd operation.

msg_lrpid is the process id of the last process that performed a msgrcv operation.

msg_stime is the time of the last msgsnd operation.

msg_rtime is the time of the last msgrcv operation

msg_ctime is the time of the last msgctl operation that changed a member of the above structure.

Message Operation Permissions

In the msgop and msgctl system call descriptions, the permission required for an operation is given as {*token*}, where *token* is the type of permission needed, interpreted as follows:

```
00400    READ by user
00200    WRITE by user
00040    READ by group
00020    WRITE by group
00004    READ by others
00002    WRITE by others
```

Read and write permissions on a msqid are granted to a process if one or more of the following are true:

The effective user ID of the process is super-user.

The effective user ID of the process matches msg_perm.cuid or msg_perm.uid in the data structure associated with msqid and the appropriate bit of the "user" portion (0600) of msg_perm.mode is set.

The effective group ID of the process matches msg_perm.cgid or msg_perm.gid and the appropriate bit of the "group" portion (060) of msg_perm.mode is set.

The appropriate bit of the "other" portion (006) of msg_perm.mode is set.

Otherwise, the corresponding permissions are denied.

Module

A module is an entity containing processing routines for input and output data. It always exists in the middle of a stream, between the stream's head and a driver. A module is the STREAMS counterpart to the commands in a shell pipeline except that a module contains a pair of functions which allow independent bidirectional (downstream and upstream) data flow and processing.

Multiplexor

A multiplexor is a driver that allows streams associated with several user processes to be connected to a single driver, or several drivers to be connected to a single user process. STREAMS does not provide a general multiplexing driver, but does provide the facilities for constructing them and for connecting multiplexed configurations of streams.

Orphaned Process Group
A process group in which the parent of every member in the group is either itself a member of the group, or is not a member of the process group's session.

Parent Process ID
A new process is created by a currently active process [see fork(2)]. The parent process ID of a process is the process ID of its creator.

Pathname
A pathname is a null-terminated character string starting with an optional slash (/), followed by zero or more directory names separated by slashes, optionally followed by a filename.

If a pathname begins with a slash, the path search begins at the root directory. Otherwise, the search begins from the current working directory.

A slash by itself names the root directory.

Unless specifically stated otherwise, the null pathname is treated as if it named a non-existent file.

Process ID
Each process in the system is uniquely identified during its lifetime by a positive integer called a process ID. A process ID may not be reused by the system until the process lifetime, process group lifetime and session lifetime ends for any process ID, process group ID and session ID equal to that process ID.

Privilege
Having appropriate privilege means having the capability to override system restrictions.

Process Group
Each process in the system is a member of a process group that is identified by a process group ID. Any process that is not a process group leader may create a new process group and become its leader. Any process that is not a process group leader may join an existing process group that shares the same session as the process. A newly created process joins the process group of its parent.

Process Group Leader
A process group leader is a process whose process ID is the same as its process group ID.

Process Group ID
Each active process is a member of a process group and is identified by a positive integer called the process group ID. This ID is the process ID of the group leader. This grouping permits the signaling of related processes [see kill(2)].

Process Lifetime
A process lifetime begins when the process is forked and ends after it exits, when its termination has been acknowledged by its parent process. See wait(2).

Process Group Lifetime
A process group lifetime begins when the process group is created by its process group leader, and ends when the lifetime of the last process in the group ends or when the last process in the group leaves the group.

Read Queue
In a stream, the message queue in a module or driver containing messages moving upstream.

Real User ID and Real Group ID
Each user allowed on the system is identified by a positive integer (0 to MAX-UID) called a real user ID.

Each user is also a member of a group. The group is identified by a positive integer called the real group ID.

An active process has a real user ID and real group ID that are set to the real user ID and real group ID, respectively, of the user responsible for the creation of the process.

Root Directory and Current Working Directory
Each process has associated with it a concept of a root directory and a current working directory for the purpose of resolving path name searches. The root directory of a process need not be the root directory of the root file system.

Saved User ID and Saved Group ID
The saved user ID and saved group ID are the values of the effective user ID and effective group ID prior to an exec of a file whose set user or set group file mode bit has been set [see exec(2)].

Semaphore Identifier
A semaphore identifier (semid) is a unique positive integer created by a semget system call. Each semid has a set of semaphores and a data structure associated with it. The data structure is referred to as semid_ds and contains the following members:

```
struct  ipc_perm sem_perm;   /* operation permission struct */
struct  sem *sem_base;       /* ptr to first semaphore in set */
ushort  sem_nsems;           /* number of sems in set */
time_t  sem_otime;           /* last operation time */
time_t  sem_ctime;           /* last change time */
                             /* Times measured in secs since */
                             /* 00:00:00 GMT, Jan. 1, 1970 */
```

Here are descriptions of the fields of the semid_ds structure:

sem_perm is an ipc_perm structure that specifies the semaphore operation permission (see below). This structure includes the following members:

```
uid_t   uid;     /* user id */
gid_t   gid;     /* group id */
uid_t   cuid;    /* creator user id */
gid_t   cgid;    /* creator group id */
mode_t  mode;    /* r/a permission */
ushort  seq;     /* slot usage sequence number */
key_t   key;     /* key */
```

sem_nsems is equal to the number of semaphores in the set. Each semaphore in the set is referenced by a nonnegative integer referred to as a **sem_num**. **sem_num** values run sequentially from 0 to the value of **sem_nsems** minus 1.

sem_otime is the time of the last **semop** operation.

sem_ctime is the time of the last **semctl** operation that changed a member of the above structure.

A semaphore is a data structure called **sem** that contains the following members:

```
ushort   semval;    /* semaphore value */
pid_t    sempid;    /* pid of last operation  */
ushort   semncnt;   /* # awaiting semval > cval */
ushort   semzcnt;   /* # awaiting semval = 0 */
```

semval is a non-negative integer that is the actual value of the semaphore.

sempid is equal to the process ID of the last process that performed a semaphore operation on this semaphore.

semncnt is a count of the number of processes that are currently suspended awaiting this semaphore's semval to become greater than its current value.

semzcnt is a count of the number of processes that are currently suspended awaiting this semaphore's semval to become 0.

Semaphore Operation Permissions

In the **semop** and **semctl** system call descriptions, the permission required for an operation is given as {*token*}, where *token* is the type of permission needed interpreted as follows:

```
00400    READ by user
00200    ALTER by user
00040    READ by group
00020    ALTER by group
00004    READ by others
00002    ALTER by others
```

Read and alter permissions on a semid are granted to a process if one or more of the following are true:

The effective user ID of the process is super-user.

The effective user ID of the process matches **sem_perm.cuid** or **sem_perm.uid** in the data structure associated with **semid** and the appropriate bit of the "user" portion (0600) of **sem_perm.mode** is set.

The effective group ID of the process matches **sem_perm.cgid** or **sem_perm.gid** and the appropriate bit of the "group" portion (060) of **sem_perm.mode** is set.

The appropriate bit of the "other" portion (06) of sem_perm.mode is set. Otherwise, the corresponding permissions are denied.

Session

A session is a group of processes identified by a common ID called a session ID, capable of establishing a connection with a controlling terminal. Any process that is not a process group leader may create a new session and process group, becoming the session leader of the session and process group leader of the process group. A newly created process joins the session of its creator.

Session ID

Each session in the system is uniquely identified during its lifetime by a positive integer called a session ID, the process ID of its session leader.

Session Leader

A session leader is a process whose session ID is the same as its process and process group ID.

Session Lifetime

A session lifetime begins when the session is created by its session leader, and ends when the lifetime of the last process that is a member of the session ends, or when the last process that is a member in the session leaves the session.

Shared Memory Identifier

A shared memory identifier (shmid) is a unique positive integer created by a shmget system call. Each shmid has a segment of memory (referred to as a shared memory segment) and a data structure associated with it. (Note that these shared memory segments must be explicitly removed by the user after the last reference to them is removed.) The data structure is referred to as shmid_ds and contains the following members:

```
struct ipc_perm  shm_perm;     /* operation permission struct */
int              shm_segsz;    /* size of segment */
struct region    *shm_reg;     /* ptr to region structure */
char             pad[4];       /* for swap compatibility */
pid_t            shm_lpid;     /* pid of last operation */
pid_t            shm_cpid;     /* creator pid */
ushort           shm_nattch;   /* number of current attaches */
ushort           shm_cnattch;  /* used only for shminfo */
time_t           shm_atime;    /* last attach time */
time_t           shm_dtime;    /* last detach time */
time_t           shm_ctime;    /* last change time */
                               /* Times measured in secs since */
                               /* 00:00:00 GMT, Jan. 1, 1970 */
```

Here are descriptions of the fields of the shmid_ds structure:

shm_perm is an ipc_perm structure that specifies the shared memory operation permission (see below). This structure includes the following members:

```
uid_t    cuid;   /* creator user id */
gid_t    cgid;   /* creator group id */
uid_t    uid;    /* user id */
gid_t    gid;    /* group id */
mode_t   mode;   /* r/w permission */
ushort   seq;    /* slot usage sequence # */
key_t    key;    /* key */
```

shm_segsz specifies the size of the shared memory segment in bytes.

shm_cpid is the process ID of the process that created the shared memory identifier.

shm_lpid is the process ID of the last process that performed a **shmop** operation.

shm_nattch is the number of processes that currently have this segment attached.

shm_atime is the time of the last **shmat** operation [see **shmop**(2)].

shm_dtime is the time of the last **shmdt** operation [see **shmop**(2)].

shm_ctime is the time of the last **shmctl** operation that changed one of the members of the above structure.

Shared Memory Operation Permissions

In the **shmop** and **shmctl** system call descriptions, the permission required for an operation is given as {*token*}, where *token* is the type of permission needed interpreted as follows:

```
00400    READ by user
00200    WRITE by user
00040    READ by group
00020    WRITE by group
00004    READ by others
00002    WRITE by others
```

Read and write permissions on a **shmid** are granted to a process if one or more of the following are true:

The effective user ID of the process is super-user.

The effective user ID of the process matches **shm_perm.cuid** or **shm_perm.uid** in the data structure associated with **shmid** and the appropriate bit of the "user" portion (0600) of **shm_perm.mode** is set.

The effective group ID of the process matches **shm_perm.cgid** or **shm_perm.gid** and the appropriate bit of the "group" portion (060) of **shm_perm.mode** is set.

The appropriate bit of the "other" portion (06) of **shm_perm.mode** is set.

Otherwise, the corresponding permissions are denied.

Special Processes
The process with ID 0 and the process with ID 1 are special processes referred to as proc0 and proc1; see kill(2). proc0 is the process scheduler. proc1 is the initialization process (init); proc1 is the ancestor of every other process in the system and is used to control the process structure.

STREAMS
A set of kernel mechanisms that support the development of network services and data communication drivers. It defines interface standards for character input/output within the kernel and between the kernel and user level processes. The STREAMS mechanism is composed of utility routines, kernel facilities and a set of data structures.

Stream
A stream is a full-duplex data path within the kernel between a user process and driver routines. The primary components are a stream head, a driver and zero or more modules between the stream head and driver. A stream is analogous to a shell pipeline except that data flow and processing are bidirectional.

Stream Head
In a stream, the stream head is the end of the stream that provides the interface between the stream and a user process. The principle functions of the stream head are processing STREAMS-related system calls, and passing data and information between a user process and the stream.

Super-user
A process is recognized as a super-user process and is granted special privileges, such as immunity from file permissions, if its effective user ID is 0.

Upstream
In a stream, the direction from driver to stream head.

Write Queue
In a stream, the message queue in a module or driver containing messages moving downstream.

access(2)

NAME
access – determine accessibility of a file

SYNOPSIS
    #include <unistd.h>

    int access(const char *path, int amode);

DESCRIPTION
path points to a path name naming a file. access checks the named file for accessibility according to the bit pattern contained in *amode*, using the real user ID in place of the effective user ID and the real group ID in place of the effective group ID. The bit pattern contained in *amode* is constructed by an OR of the following constants (defined in <unistd.h>):

    R_OK   read
    W_OK   write
    X_OK   execute (search)
    F_OK   check existence of file

Access to the file is denied if one or more of the following are true:

EACCES	Search permission is denied on a component of the path prefix.
EACCES	Permission bits of the file mode do not permit the requested access.
EFAULT	*path* points outside the allocated address space for the process.
EINTR	A signal was caught during the access system call.
ELOOP	Too many symbolic links were encountered in translating *path*.
EMULTIHOP	Components of *path* require hopping to multiple remote machines.
ENAMETOOLONG	The length of the *path* argument exceeds {PATH_MAX}, or the length of a *path* component exceeds {NAME_MAX} while _POSIX_NO_TRUNC is in effect.
ENOTDIR	A component of the path prefix is not a directory.
ENOENT	Read, write, or execute (search) permission is requested for a null path name.
ENOENT	The named file does not exist.
ENOLINK	*path* points to a remote machine and the link to that machine is no longer active.
EROFS	Write access is requested for a file on a read-only file system.

SEE ALSO
chmod(2), stat(2)
"File Access Permission" in intro(2)

DIAGNOSTICS

If the requested access is permitted, a value of 0 is returned. Otherwise, a value of −1 is returned and **errno** is set to indicate the error.

NAME
acct – enable or disable process accounting

SYNOPSIS
```
#include <unistd.h>

int acct(const char *path);
```

DESCRIPTION
acct enables or disables the system process accounting routine. If the routine is enabled, an accounting record will be written in an accounting file for each process that terminates. The termination of a process can be caused by one of two things: an exit call or a signal [see exit(2) and signal(2)]. The effective user ID of the process calling acct must be superuser.

path points to a pathname naming the accounting file. The accounting file format is given in acct(4).

The accounting routine is enabled if *path* is non-zero and no errors occur during the system call. It is disabled if *path* is (char *)NULL and no errors occur during the system call.

acct will fail if one or more of the following are true:

EACCES	The file named by *path* is not an ordinary file.
EBUSY	An attempt is being made to enable accounting using the same file that is currently being used.
EFAULT	*path* points to an illegal address.
ELOOP	Too many symbolic links were encountered in translating *path*.
ENAMETOOLONG	The length of the *path* argument exceeds {PATH_MAX}, or the length of a *path* component exceeds {NAME_MAX} while _POSIX_NO_TRUNC is in effect.
ENOTDIR	A component of the path prefix is not a directory.
ENOENT	One or more components of the accounting file pathname do not exist.
EPERM	The effective user of the calling process is not superuser.
EROFS	The named file resides on a read-only file system.

SEE ALSO
exit(2), signal(2).
acct(4) in the *System Administrator's Reference Manual*.

DIAGNOSTICS
Upon successful completion, a value of 0 is returned. Otherwise, a value of −1 is returned and errno is set to indicate the error.

NAME

adjtime – correct the time to allow synchronization of the system clock

SYNOPSIS

    #include <sys/time.h>

    int adjtime(struct timeval *delta, struct timeval *olddelta);

DESCRIPTION

adjtime adjusts the system's notion of the current time, as returned by gettimeofday(3C), advancing or retarding it by the amount of time specified in the struct timeval pointed to by *delta*.

The adjustment is effected by speeding up (if that amount of time is positive) or slowing down (if that amount of time is negative) the system's clock by some small percentage, generally a fraction of one percent. Thus, the time is always a monotonically increasing function. A time correction from an earlier call to adjtime may not be finished when adjtime is called again. If *delta* is 0, then *olddelta* returns the status of the effects of the previous adjtime call and there is no effect on the time correction as a result of this call. If *olddelta* is not a NULL pointer, then the structure it points to will contain, upon return, the number of seconds and/or microseconds still to be corrected from the earlier call. If *olddelta* is a NULL pointer, the corresponding information will not be returned.

This call may be used in time servers that synchronize the clocks of computers in a local area network. Such time servers would slow down the clocks of some machines and speed up the clocks of others to bring them to the average network time.

Only the super-user may adjust the time of day.

The adjustment value will be silently rounded to the resolution of the system clock.

RETURN

A 0 return value indicates that the call succeeded. A −1 return value indicates an error occurred, and in this case an error code is stored into the global variable errno.

ERRORS

The following error codes may be set in errno:

EFAULT	*delta* or *olddelta* points outside the process's allocated address space, or *olddelta* points to a region of the process' allocated address space that is not writable.
EPERM	The process's effective user ID is not that of the super-user.

SEE ALSO

gettimeofday(3C)
date(1) in the *User's Reference Manual*.

alarm(2)

NAME
alarm – set a process alarm clock

SYNOPSIS
#include <unistd.h>

unsigned alarm(unsigned sec);

DESCRIPTION
alarm instructs the alarm clock of the calling process to send the signal SIGALRM to the calling process after the number of real time seconds specified by *sec* have elapsed [see signal(2)].

Alarm requests are not stacked; successive calls reset the alarm clock of the calling process.

If *sec* is 0, any previously made alarm request is canceled.

fork sets the alarm clock of a new process to 0 [see fork(2)]. A process created by the exec family of routines inherits the time left on the old process's alarm clock.

SEE ALSO
fork(2), exec(2), pause(2), signal(2), sigset(2).

DIAGNOSTICS
alarm returns the amount of time previously remaining in the alarm clock of the calling process.

NAME
brk, sbrk – change data segment space allocation

SYNOPSIS
#include <unistd.h>

int brk(void *endds);

void *sbrk(int incr);

DESCRIPTION
brk and sbrk are used to change dynamically the amount of space allocated for the calling process's data segment [see exec(2)]. The change is made by resetting the process's break value and allocating the appropriate amount of space. The break value is the address of the first location beyond the end of the data segment. The amount of allocated space increases as the break value increases. Newly allocated space is set to zero. If, however, the same memory space is reallocated to the same process its contents are undefined.

brk sets the break value to *endds* and changes the allocated space accordingly.

sbrk adds *incr* bytes to the break value and changes the allocated space accordingly. *incr* can be negative, in which case the amount of allocated space is decreased.

brk and sbrk will fail without making any change in the allocated space if one or more of the following are true:

ENOMEM	Such a change would result in more space being allocated than is allowed by the system-imposed maximum process size [see ulimit(2)].
EAGAIN	Total amount of system memory available for a read during physical IO is temporarily insufficient [see shmop(2)]. This may occur even though the space requested was less than the system-imposed maximum process size [see ulimit(2)].

SEE ALSO
exec(2), shmop(2), ulimit(2), end(3C).

DIAGNOSTICS
Upon successful completion, brk returns a value of 0 and sbrk returns the old break value. Otherwise, a value of −1 is returned and errno is set to indicate the error.

chdir(2)

NAME
chdir, fchdir – change working directory

SYNOPSIS
```
#include <unistd.h>

int chdir(const char *path);

int fchdir(int fildes);
```

DESCRIPTION
chdir and fchdir cause a directory pointed to by *path* or *fildes* to become the current working directory, the starting point for path searches for path names not beginning with /. *path* points to the path name of a directory. The *fildes* argument to fchdir is an open file descriptor of a directory.

In order for a directory to become the current directory, a process must have execute (search) access to the directory.

chdir will fail and the current working directory will be unchanged if one or more of the following are true:

EACCES	Search permission is denied for any component of the path name.
EFAULT	*path* points outside the allocated address space of the process.
EINTR	A signal was caught during the execution of the chdir system call.
EIO	An I/O error occurred while reading from or writing to the file system.
ELOOP	Too many symbolic links were encountered in translating *path*.
ENAMETOOLONG	The length of the *path* argument exceeds {PATH_MAX}, or the length of a *path* component exceeds {NAME_MAX} while _POSIX_NO_TRUNC is in effect.
ENOTDIR	A component of the path name is not a directory.
ENOENT	Either a component of the path prefix or the directory named by *path* does not exist or is a null pathname.
ENOLINK	*path* points to a remote machine and the link to that machine is no longer active.
EMULTIHOP	Components of *path* require hopping to multiple remote machines and file system type does not allow it.

fchdir will fail and the current working directory will be unchanged if one or more of the following are true:

EACCES	Search permission is denied for *fildes*.
EBADF	*fildes* is not an open file descriptor.

chdir(2)

EINTR	A signal was caught during the execution of the fchdir system call.
EIO	An I/O error occurred while reading from or writing to the file system.
ENOLINK	*fildes* points to a remote machine and the link to that machine is no longer active.
ENOTDIR	The open file descriptor *fildes* does not refer to a directory.

SEE ALSO
    chroot(2).

DIAGNOSTICS
    Upon successful completion, a value of zero is returned. Otherwise, a value of −1 is returned and errno is set to indicate the error.

chmod(2)

NAME
chmod, fchmod – change mode of file

SYNOPSIS
```
#include <sys/types.h>
#include <sys/stat.h>

int chmod(const char *path, mode_t mode);

int fchmod(int fildes, mode_t mode);
```

DESCRIPTION
chmod and fchmod set the access permission portion of the mode of the file whose name is given by *path* or referenced by the descriptor *fildes* to the bit pattern contained in *mode*. Access permission bits are interpreted as follows:

S_ISUID	04000	Set user ID on execution.
S_ISGID	020#0	Set group ID on execution if # is 7, 5, 3, or 1
		Enable mandatory file/record locking if # is 6, 4, 2, or 0
S_ISVTX	01000	Save text image after execution.
S_IRWXU	00700	Read, write, execute by owner.
S_IRUSR	00400	Read by owner.
S_IWUSR	00200	Write by owner.
S_IXUSR	00100	Execute (search if a directory) by owner.
S_IRWXG	00070	Read, write, execute by group.
S_IRGRP	00040	Read by group.
S_IWGRP	00020	Write by group.
S_IXGRP	00010	Execute by group.
S_IRWXO	00007	Read, write, execute (search) by others.
S_IROTH	00004	Read by others.
S_IWOTH	00002	Write by others
S_IXOTH	00001	Execute by others.

Modes are constructed by OR' ing the access permission bits.

The effective user ID of the process must match the owner of the file or the process must have the appropriate privilege to change the mode of a file.

If the process is not a privileged process and the file is not a directory, mode bit 01000 (save text image on execution) is cleared.

If neither the process nor a member of the supplementary group list is privileged, and the effective group ID of the process does not match the group ID of the file, mode bit 02000 (set group ID on execution) is cleared.

If a 0410 executable file has the sticky bit (mode bit 01000) set, the operating system will not delete the program text from the swap area when the last user process terminates. If a 0413 or ELF executable file has the sticky bit set, the operating system will not delete the program text from memory when the last user process terminates. In either case, if the sticky bit is set the text will already be available (either in a swap area or in memory) when the next user of the file executes it, thus making execution faster.

If a directory is writable and has the sticky bit set, files within that directory can be removed or renamed only if one or more of the following is true [see unlink(2) and rename(2)]:

> the user owns the file
> the user owns the directory
> the file is writable by the user
> the user is a privileged user

If the mode bit 02000 (set group ID on execution) is set and the mode bit 00010 (execute or search by group) is not set, mandatory file/record locking will exist on a regular file. This may affect future calls to open(2), creat(2), read(2), and write(2) on this file.

Upon successful completion, chmod and fchmod mark for update the st_ctime field of the file.

chmod will fail and the file mode will be unchanged if one or more of the following are true:

EACCES	Search permission is denied on a component of the path prefix of *path*.
EFAULT	*path* points outside the allocated address space of the process.
EINTR	A signal was caught during execution of the system call.
EIO	An I/O error occurred while reading from or writing to the file system.
ELOOP	Too many symbolic links were encountered in translating *path*.
EMULTIHOP	Components of *path* require hopping to multiple remote machines and file system type does not allow it.
ENAMETOOLONG	The length of the *path* argument exceeds {PATH_MAX}, or the length of a *path* component exceeds {NAME_MAX} while _POSIX_NO_TRUNC is in effect.
ENOTDIR	A component of the prefix of *path* is not a directory.
ENOENT	Either a component of the path prefix, or the file referred to by *path* does not exist or is a null pathname.
ENOLINK	*fildes* points to a remote machine and the link to that machine is no longer active.
EPERM	The effective user ID does not match the owner of the file and the process does not have appropriate privilege.
EROFS	The file referred to by *path* resides on a read-only file system.

chmod(2)

fchmod will fail and the file mode will be unchanged if:

EBADF *fildes* is not an open file descriptor

EIO An I/O error occurred while reading from or writing to the file system.

EINTR A signal was caught during execution of the fchmod system call.

ENOLINK *path* points to a remote machine and the link to that machine is no longer active.

EPERM The effective user ID does not match the owner of the file and the process does not have appropriate privilege.

EROFS The file referred to by *fildes* resides on a read-only file system.

SEE ALSO

chown(2), creat(2), fcntl(2), mknod(2), open(2), read(2), stat(2), write(2), mkfifo(3C), stat(5).
chmod(1) in the *User's Reference Manual*.
The "File and Record Locking" chapter in the *Application Programmer's Guide*.

DIAGNOSTICS

Upon successful completion, a value of 0 is returned. Otherwise, a value of −1 is returned and errno is set to indicate the error.

NAME
chown, lchown, fchown – change owner and group of a file

SYNOPSIS
    #include <unistd.h>
    #include <sys/stat.h>

    int chown(const char *path, uid_t owner, gid_t group);

    int lchown(const char *path, uid_t owner, gid_t group);

    int fchown(int fildes, uid_t owner, gid_t group);

DESCRIPTION
The owner ID and group ID of the file specified by *path* or referenced by the descriptor *fildes*, are set to *owner* and *group* respectively. If *owner* or *group* is specified as −1, the corresponding ID of the file is not changed.

The function lchown sets the owner ID and group ID of the named file just as chown does, except in the case where the named file is a symbolic link. In this case lchown changes the ownership of the symbolic link file itself, while chown changes the ownership of the file or directory to which the symbolic link refers.

If chown, lchown, or fchown is invoked by a process other than super-user, the set-user-ID and set-group-ID bits of the file mode, S_ISUID and S_ISGID respectively, are cleared [see chmod(2)].

The operating system has a configuration option, {_POSIX_CHOWN_RESTRICTED}, to restrict ownership changes for the chown, lchown, and fchown system calls. When {_POSIX_CHOWN_RESTRICTED} is not in effect, the effective user ID of the process must match the owner of the file or the process must be the super-user to change the ownership of a file. When {_POSIX_CHOWN_RESTRICTED} is in effect, the chown, lchown, and fchown system calls, for users other than super-user, prevent the owner of the file from changing the owner ID of the file and restrict the change of the group of the file to the list of supplementary group IDs.

Upon successful completion, chown, fchown and lchown mark for update the st_ctime field of the file.

chown and lchown fail and the owner and group of the named file remain unchanged if one or more of the following are true:

EACCES	Search permission is denied on a component of the path prefix of *path*.
EFAULT	*path* points outside the allocated address space of the process.
EINTR	A signal was caught during the chown or lchown system calls.
EINVAL	*group* or *owner* is out of range.
EIO	An I/O error occurred while reading from or writing to the file system.

ELOOP		Too many symbolic links were encountered in translating *path*.
EMULTIHOP		Components of *path* require hopping to multiple remote machines and file system type does not allow it. Too many symbolic links were encountered in translating *path*.
ENAMETOOLONG		The length of the *path* argument exceeds {PATH_MAX}, or the length of a *path* component exceeds {NAME_MAX} while _POSIX_NO_TRUNC is in effect.
ENOLINK		*path* points to a remote machine and the link to that machine is no longer active.
ENOTDIR		A component of the path prefix of *path* is not a directory.
ENOENT		Either a component of the path prefix or the file referred to by *path* does not exist or is a null pathname.
EPERM		The effective user ID does not match the owner of the file or the process is not the super-user and {_POSIX_CHOWN_RESTRICTED} indicates that such privilege is required.
EROFS		The named file resides on a read-only file system.

fchown fails and the owner and group of the named file remain unchanged if one or more of the following are true:

EBADF		*fildes* is not an open file descriptor.
EINVAL		*group* or *owner* is out of range.
EPERM		The effective user ID does not match the owner of the file or the process is not the super-user and {_POSIX_CHOWN_RESTRICTED} indicates that such privilege is required.
EROFS		The named file referred to by *fildes* resides on a read-only file system.
EINTR		A signal was caught during execution of the system call.
EIO		An I/O error occurred while reading from or writing to the file system.
ENOLINK		*fildes* points to a remote machine and the link to that machine is no longer active.

SEE ALSO
chmod(2).
chown(1), chgrp(1) in the *User's Reference Manual*.

DIAGNOSTICS
Upon successful completion, a value of 0 is returned. Otherwise, a value of −1 is returned and **errno** is set to indicate the error.

NAME

chroot – change root directory

SYNOPSIS

```
#include <unistd.h>
```

```
int chroot(const char *path);
```

DESCRIPTION

path points to a path name naming a directory. chroot causes the named directory to become the root directory, the starting point for path searches for path names beginning with /. The user's working directory is unaffected by the chroot system call.

The effective user ID of the process must be super-user to change the root directory.

The .. entry in the root directory is interpreted to mean the root directory itself. Thus, .. cannot be used to access files outside the subtree rooted at the root directory.

chroot will fail and the root directory will remain unchanged if one or more of the following are true:

ELOOP	Too many symbolic links were encountered in translating *path*.
ENAMETOOLONG	The length of the *path* argument exceeds {PATH_MAX}, or the length of a *path* component exceeds {NAME_MAX} while _POSIX_NO_TRUNC is in effect.
EFAULT	*path* points outside the allocated address space of the process.
EINTR	A signal was caught during the chroot system call.
EMULTIHOP	Components of *path* require hopping to multiple remote machines and file system type does not allow it.
ENOLINK	*path* points to a remote machine and the link to that machine is no longer active.
ENOTDIR	Any component of the path name is not a directory.
ENOENT	The named directory does not exist or is a null pathname.
EPERM	The effective user ID is not super-user.

SEE ALSO

chdir(2).

DIAGNOSTICS

Upon successful completion, a value of 0 is returned. Otherwise, a value of −1 is returned and errno is set to indicate the error.

close(2)

NAME
close – close a file descriptor

SYNOPSIS
```
#include <unistd.h>
int close(int fildes);
```

DESCRIPTION
fildes is a file descriptor obtained from a `creat`, `open`, `dup`, `fcntl`, or `pipe` system call. `close` closes the file descriptor indicated by *fildes*. All outstanding record locks owned by the process (on the file indicated by *fildes*) are removed.

When all file descriptors associated with the open file description have been closed, the open file description is freed.

If the link count of the file is zero, when all file descriptors associated with the file have been closed, the space occupied by the file is freed and the file is no longer accessible.

If a STREAMS-based [see `intro`(2)] *fildes* is closed, and the calling process had previously registered to receive a SIGPOLL signal [see `signal`(2)] for events associated with that stream [see `I_SETSIG` in `streamio`(7)], the calling process will be unregistered for events associated with the stream. The last `close` for a stream causes the stream associated with *fildes* to be dismantled. If O_NDELAY and O_NONBLOCK are clear and there have been no signals posted for the stream, and if there are data on the module's write queue, `close` waits up to 15 seconds (for each module and driver) for any output to drain before dismantling the stream. The time delay can be changed via an `I_SETCLTIME` ioctl request [see `streamio`(7)]. If O_NDELAY or O_NONBLOCK is set, or if there are any pending signals, `close` does not wait for output to drain, and dismantles the stream immediately.

If *fildes* is associated with one end of a pipe, the last `close` causes a hangup to occur on the other end of the pipe. In addition, if the other end of the pipe has been named [see `fattach`(3C)], the last `close` forces the named end to be detached [see `fdetach`(3C)]. If the named end has no open processes associated with it and becomes detached, the stream associated with that end is also dismantled.

The named file is closed unless one or more of the following are true:

EBADF	*fildes* is not a valid open file descriptor.
EINTR	A signal was caught during the `close` system call.
ENOLINK	*fildes* is on a remote machine and the link to that machine is no longer active.

SEE ALSO
creat(2), dup(2), exec(2), fcntl(2), intro(2), open(2), pipe(2), signal(2), signal(5), streamio(7).

fattach(3C), fdetach(3C) in the *Programmer's Guide: Networking Interfaces*.

DIAGNOSTICS
Upon successful completion, a value of 0 is returned. Otherwise, a value of −1 is returned and **errno** is set to indicate the error.

NAME
creat – create a new file or rewrite an existing one

SYNOPSIS
    #include <sys/types.h>
    #include <sys/stat.h>
    #include <fcntl.h>

    int creat(const char *path, mode_t mode);

DESCRIPTION
creat creates a new ordinary file or prepares to rewrite an existing file named by the path name pointed to by *path*.

If the file exists, the length is truncated to 0 and the mode and owner are unchanged.

If the file does not exist the file's owner ID is set to the effective user ID of the process. The group ID of the file is set to the effective group ID of the process, or if the S_ISGID bit is set in the parent directory then the group ID of the file is inherited from the parent directory. The access permission bits of the file mode are set to the value of *mode* modified as follows:

> If the group ID of the new file does not match the effective group ID or one of the supplementary group IDs, the S_ISGID bit is cleared.

> All bits set in the process's file mode creation mask are cleared [see umask(2)].

> The "save text image after execution bit" of the mode is cleared [see chmod(2) for the values of mode].

Upon successful completion, a write-only file descriptor is returned and the file is open for writing, even if the mode does not permit writing. The file pointer is set to the beginning of the file. The file descriptor is set to remain open across **exec** system calls [see fcntl(2)]. A new file may be created with a mode that forbids writing.

The call **creat**(*path, mode*) is equivalent to:

> open(*path*, O_WRONLY | O_CREAT | O_TRUNC, *mode*)

creat fails if one or more of the following are true:

EACCES	Search permission is denied on a component of the path prefix.
EACCES	The file does not exist and the directory in which the file is to be created does not permit writing.
EACCES	The file exists and write permission is denied.
EAGAIN	The file exists, mandatory file/record locking is set, and there are outstanding record locks on the file [see chmod(2)].
EFAULT	*path* points outside the allocated address space of the process.

EISDIR	The named file is an existing directory.
EINTR	A signal was caught during the creat system call.
ELOOP	Too many symbolic links were encountered in translating *path*.
EMFILE	The process has too many open files [see getrlimit(2)].
ENAMETOOLONG	The length of the *path* argument exceeds {PATH_MAX}, or the length of a *path* component exceeds {NAME_MAX} while _POSIX_NO_TRUNC is in effect.
ENOTDIR	A component of the path prefix is not a directory.
ENOENT	A component of the path prefix does not exist.
ENOENT	The path name is null.
EROFS	The named file resides or would reside on a read-only file system.
ETXTBSY	The file is a pure procedure (shared text) file that is being executed.
ENFILE	The system file table is full.
ENOLINK	*path* points to a remote machine and the link to that machine is no longer active.
EMULTIHOP	Components of *path* require hopping to multiple remote machines.
ENOSPC	The file system is out of inodes.

SEE ALSO
chmod(2), close(2), dup(2), fcntl(2), getrlimit(2), lseek(2), open(2), read(2), umask(2), write(2), stat(5).

DIAGNOSTICS
Upon successful completion a non-negative integer, namely the lowest numbered unused file descriptor, is returned. Otherwise, a value of −1 is returned, no files are created or modified, and errno is set to indicate the error.

NAME

dup – duplicate an open file descriptor

SYNOPSIS

    #include <unistd.h>

    int dup(int fildes);

DESCRIPTION

fildes is a file descriptor obtained from a `creat`, `open`, `dup`, `fcntl`, or `pipe` system call. `dup` returns a new file descriptor having the following in common with the original:

>   Same open file (or pipe).
>
>   Same file pointer (i.e., both file descriptors share one file pointer).
>
>   Same access mode (read, write or read/write).

The new file descriptor is set to remain open across `exec` system calls [see `fcntl(2)`].

The file descriptor returned is the lowest one available.

`dup` will fail if one or more of the following are true:

EBADF	*fildes* is not a valid open file descriptor.
EINTR	A signal was caught during the `dup` system call.
EMFILE	The process has too many open files [see `getrlimit(2)`].
ENOLINK	*fildes* is on a remote machine and the link to that machine is no longer active.

SEE ALSO

`close(2)`, `creat(2)`, `exec(2)`, `fcntl(2)`, `getrlimit(2)`, `open(2)`, `pipe(2)`, `dup2(3C)`, `lockf(3C)`.

DIAGNOSTICS

Upon successful completion a non-negative integer, namely the file descriptor, is returned. Otherwise, a value of −1 is returned and `errno` is set to indicate the error.

exec(2)

NAME
exec: execl, execv, execle, execve, execlp, execvp – execute a file

SYNOPSIS
#include <unistd.h>

int execl (const char *path, const char *arg0, ..., const char *argn, (char *)0);

int execv (const char *path, char *const *argv);

int execle (const char *path, const char *arg0, ..., const char *argn, (char *0), const char *envp[]);

int execve (const char *path, char *const *argv, char *const *cnup);

int execlp (const char *file, const char *arg0, ..., const char *argn, (char *)0);

int execvp (const char *file, char *const *argv);

DESCRIPTION
exec in all its forms overlays a new process image on an old process. The new process image is constructed from an ordinary, executable file. This file is either an executable object file, or a file of data for an interpreter. There can be no return from a successful **exec** because the calling process image is overlaid by the new process image.

An interpreter file begins with a line of the form

   #! *pathname* [*arg*]

where *pathname* is the path of the interpreter, and *arg* is an optional argument. When an interpreter file is exec'd, the system execs the specified interpreter. The pathname specified in the interpreter file is passed as *arg0* to the interpreter. If *arg* was specified in the interpreter file, it is passed as *arg1* to the interpreter. The remaining arguments to the interpreter are *arg0* through *argn* of the originally exec'd file.

When a C program is executed, it is called as follows:

   int main (int argc, char *argv[], char *envp[]);

where *argc* is the argument count, *argv* is an array of character pointers to the arguments themselves, and *envp* is an array of character pointers to the environment strings. As indicated, *argc* is at least one, and the first member of the array points to a string containing the name of the file.

path points to a path name that identifies the new process file.

file points to the new process file. If *file* does not contain a slash character, the path prefix for this file is obtained by a search of the directories passed in the **PATH** environment variable [see **environ**(5)]. The environment is supplied typically by the shell [see **sh**(1)].

exec(2)

If the new process file is not an executable object file, **execlp** and **execvp** use the contents of that file as standard input to **sh**(1).

The arguments *arg0*, ..., *argn* point to null-terminated character strings. These strings constitute the argument list available to the new process image. Minimally, *arg0* must be present. It will become the name of the process, as displayed by the **ps** command. Conventionally, *arg0* points to a string that is the same as *path* (or the last component of *path*). The list of argument strings is terminated by a **(char *)0** argument.

argv is an array of character pointers to null-terminated strings. These strings constitute the argument list available to the new process image. By convention, *argv* must have at least one member, and it should point to a string that is the same as *path* (or its last component). *argv* is terminated by a null pointer.

envp is an array of character pointers to null-terminated strings. These strings constitute the environment for the new process image. *envp* is terminated by a null pointer. For **execl**, **execv**, **execvp**, and **execlp**, the C run-time start-off routine places a pointer to the environment of the calling process in the global object **extern char **environ**, and it is used to pass the environment of the calling process to the new process.

File descriptors open in the calling process remain open in the new process, except for those whose close-on-exec flag is set; [see **fcntl**(2)]. For those file descriptors that remain open, the file pointer is unchanged.

Signals that are being caught by the calling process are set to the default disposition in the new process image [see **signal**(2)]. Otherwise, the new process image inherits the signal dispositions of the calling process.

If the set-user-ID mode bit of the new process file is set [see **chmod**(2)], **exec** sets the effective user ID of the new process to the owner ID of the new process file. Similarly, if the set-group-ID mode bit of the new process file is set, the effective group ID of the new process is set to the group ID of the new process file. The real user ID and real group ID of the new process remain the same as those of the calling process.

If the effective user-ID is **root** or super-user, the set-user-ID and set-group-ID bits will be honored when the process is being controlled by **ptrace**.

The shared memory segments attached to the calling process will not be attached to the new process [see **shmop**(2)].

Profiling is disabled for the new process; see **profil**(2).

The new process also inherits the following attributes from the calling process:

> nice value [see **nice**(2)]
> scheduler class and priority [see **priocntl**(2)]
> process ID
> parent process ID
> process group ID
> supplementary group IDs

exec(2) exec(2)

       semadj values [see **semop**(2)]
       session ID [see **exit**(2) and **signal**(2)]
       trace flag [see **ptrace**(2) request 0]
       time left until an alarm clock signal [see **alarm**(2)]
       current working directory
       root directory
       file mode creation mask [see **umask**(2)]
       resource limits [see **getrlimit**(2)]
       utime, **stime**, **cutime**, and **cstime** [see **times**(2)]
       file-locks [see **fcntl**(2) and **lockf**(3C)]
       controlling terminal
       process signal mask [see **sigprocmask**(2)]
       pending signals [see **sigpending**(2)]

Upon successful completion, **exec** marks for update the **st_atime** field of the file. Should the **exec** succeed, the process image file is considered to have been **open()**-ed. The corresponding **close()** is considered to occur at a time after this open, but before process termination or successful completion of a subsequent call to **exec**.

exec will fail and return to the calling process if one or more of the following are true:

EACCES	Search permission is denied for a directory listed in the new process file's path prefix.
E2BIG	The number of bytes in the new process's argument list is greater than the system-imposed limit of 5120 bytes. The argument list limit is sum of the size of the argument list plus the size of the environment's exported shell variables.
EACCES	The new process file is not an ordinary file.
EACCES	The new process file mode denies execution permission.
EAGAIN	Total amount of system memory available when reading via raw I/O is temporarily insufficient.
EFAULT	Required hardware is not present.
EFAULT	An *a.out* that was compiled with the MAU or 32B flag is running on a machine without a MAU or 32B.
EFAULT	An argument points to an illegal address.
EINTR	A signal was caught during the **exec** system call.
ELIBACC	Required shared library does not have execute permission.
ELIBEXEC	Trying to **exec**(2) a shared library directly.
ELOOP	Too many symbolic links were encountered in translating *path* or *file*.
EMULTIHOP	Components of *path* require hopping to multiple remote machines and the file system type does not allow it.

ENAMETOOLONG	The length of the *file* or *path* argument exceeds {PATH_MAX}, or the length of a *file* or *path* component exceeds {NAME_MAX} while _POSIX_NO_TRUNC is in effect.
ENOENT	One or more components of the new process path name of the file do not exist or is a null pathname.
ENOTDIR	A component of the new process path of the file prefix is not a directory.
ENOEXEC	The **exec** is not an **execlp** or **execvp**, and the new process file has the appropriate access permission but an invalid magic number in its header.
ETXTBSY	The new process file is a pure procedure (shared text) file that is currently open for writing by some process.
ENOMEM	The new process requires more memory than is allowed by the system-imposed maximum MAXMEM.
ENOLINK	*path* points to a remote machine and the link to that machine is no longer active.

SEE ALSO

alarm(2), exit(2), fcntl(2), fork(2), getrlimit(2), nice(2), priocntl(2), ptrace(2), semop(2), signal(2), sigpending(2), sigprocmask(2), times(2), umask(2), lockf(3C), system(3S), a.out(4), environ(5).

sh(1), ps(1) in the *User's Reference Manual*.

DIAGNOSTICS

If **exec** returns to the calling process, an error has occurred; the return value is −1 and **errno** is set to indicate the error.

NAME

exit, _exit – terminate process

SYNOPSIS

#include <stdlib.h>

void exit(int status);

#include <unistd.h>

void _exit(int status);

DESCRIPTION

_exit terminates the calling process with the following consequences:

All of the file descriptors, directory streams and message catalogue descriptors open in the calling process are closed.

A SIGCHLD signal is sent to the calling process's parent process.

If the parent process of the calling process has not specified the SA_NOCLDWAIT flag [see sigaction(2)], the calling process is transformed into a "zombie process." A zombie process is a process that only occupies a slot in the process table. It has no other space allocated either in user or kernel space. The process table slot that it occupies is partially overlaid with time accounting information [see <sys/proc.h>] to be used by the times system call.

The parent process ID of all of the calling process's existing child processes and zombie processes is set to 1. This means the initialization process [see intro(2)] inherits each of these processes.

Each attached shared memory segment is detached and the value of shm_nattach in the data structure associated with its shared memory identifier is decremented by 1.

For each semaphore for which the calling process has set a semadj value [see semop(2)], that semadj value is added to the semval of the specified semaphore.

If the process has a process, text, or data lock, an *unlock* is performed [see plock(2)].

An accounting record is written on the accounting file if the system's accounting routine is enabled [see acct(2)].

If the process is a controlling process, SIGHUP is sent to the foreground process group of its controlling terminal and its controlling terminal is deallocated.

If the calling process has any stopped children whose process group will be orphaned when the calling process exits, or if the calling process is a member of a process group that will be orphaned when the calling process exits, that process group will be sent SIGHUP and SIGCONT signals.

The C function exit(3C) calls any functions registered through the atexit function in the reverse order of their registration. The function _exit circumvents all such functions and cleanup.

exit(2)

The symbols **EXIT_SUCCESS** and **EXIT_FAILURE** are defined in `stdlib.h` and may be used as the value of *status* to indicate successful or unsuccessful termination, respectively.

SEE ALSO
acct(2), intro(2), plock(2), semop(2), sigaction(2), signal(2), times(2), wait(2), atexit(3C).

NOTES
See `signal`(2) NOTES.

fcntl(2)

NAME
fcntl – file control

SYNOPSIS
```
#include <sys/types.h>
#include <fcntl.h>
#include <unistd.h>

int fcntl (int fildes, int cmd, ... /* arg */);
```

DESCRIPTION

fcntl provides for control over open files. *fildes* is an open file descriptor [see intro(2)].

fcntl may take a third argument, *arg*, whose data type, value and use depend upon the value of *cmd*. *cmd* specifies the operation to be performed by fcntl and may be one of the following:

F_DUPFD   Return a new file descriptor with the following characteristics:

    Lowest numbered available file descriptor greater than or equal to the integer value given as the third argument.

    Same open file (or pipe) as the original file.

    Same file pointer as the original file (i.e., both file descriptors share one file pointer).

    Same access mode (read, write, or read/write) as the original file.

    Shares any locks associated with the original file descriptor.

    Same file status flags (i.e., both file descriptors share the same file status flags) as the original file.

    The close-on-exec flag [see F_GETFD] associated with the new file descriptor is set to remain open across exec(2) system calls.

F_GETFD   Get the close-on-exec flag associated with *fildes*. If the low-order bit is 0, the file will remain open across **exec**. Otherwise, the file will be closed upon execution of **exec**.

F_SETFD   Set the close-on-exec flag associated with *fildes* to the low-order bit of the integer value given as the third argument (0 or 1 as above).

F_GETFL   Get *fildes* status flags.

F_SETFL   Set *fildes* status flags to the integer value given as the third argument. Only certain flags can be set [see fcntl(5)].

F_FREESP   Free storage space associated with a section of the ordinary file *fildes*. The section is specified by a variable of data type `struct flock` pointed to by the third argument *arg*. The data type `struct flock` is defined in the `<fcntl.h>` header file [see fcntl(5)] and contains the following members: l_whence is 0, 1, or 2 to indicate that the relative offset l_start will be measured from the start of the file, the current position, or the end of the file, respectively. `l_start` is the offset from the position specified in `l_whence`. `l_len` is the size of the section. An `l_len` of 0 frees up to the end of the file; in this case, the end of file (i.e., file size) is set to the beginning of the section freed. Any data previously written into this section is no longer accessible.

The following commands are used for record-locking. Locks may be placed on an entire file or on segments of a file.

F_SETLK   Set or clear a file segment lock according to the `flock` structure that *arg* points to [see fcntl(5)]. The *cmd* `F_SETLK` is used to establish read (`F_RDLCK`) and write (`F_WRLCK`) locks, as well as remove either type of lock (`F_UNLCK`). If a read or write lock cannot be set, `fcntl` will return immediately with an error value of −1.

F_SETLKW   This *cmd* is the same as `F_SETLK` except that if a read or write lock is blocked by other locks, `fcntl` will block until the segment is free to be locked.

F_GETLK   If the lock request described by the `flock` structure that *arg* points to could be created, then the structure is passed back unchanged except that the lock type is set to `F_UNLCK` and the `l_whence` field will be set to `SEEK_SET`.

If a lock is found that would prevent this lock from being created, then the structure is overwritten with a description of the first lock that is preventing such a lock from being created. The structure also contains the process ID and the system ID of the process holding the lock.

This command never creates a lock; it tests whether a particular lock could be created.

F_RSETLK   Used by the network lock daemon, lockd(3N), to communicate with the NFS server kernel to handle locks on NFS files.

F_RSETLKW   Used by the network lock daemon, lockd(3N), to communicate with the NFS server kernel to handle locks on NFS files.

F_RGETLK   Used by the network lock daemon, lockd(3N), to communicate with the NFS server kernel to handle locks on NFS files.

A read lock prevents any process from write locking the protected area. More than one read lock may exist for a given segment of a file at a given time. The file descriptor on which a read lock is being placed must have been opened with read access.

A write lock prevents any process from read locking or write locking the protected area. Only one write lock and no read locks may exist for a given segment of a file at a given time. The file descriptor on which a write lock is being placed must have been opened with write access.

The `flock` structure describes the type (l_type), starting offset (l_whence), relative offset (l_start), size (l_len), process ID (l_pid), and system ID (l_sysid) of the segment of the file to be affected. The process ID and system ID fields are used only with the F_GETLK *cmd* to return the values for a blocking lock. Locks may start and extend beyond the current end of a file, but may not be negative relative to the beginning of the file. A lock may be set to always extend to the end of file by setting l_len to 0. If such a lock also has l_whence and l_start set to 0, the whole file will be locked. Changing or unlocking a segment from the middle of a larger locked segment leaves two smaller segments at either end. Locking a segment that is already locked by the calling process causes the old lock type to be removed and the new lock type to take effect. All locks associated with a file for a given process are removed when a file descriptor for that file is closed by that process or the process holding that file descriptor terminates. Locks are not inherited by a child process in a fork(2) system call.

When mandatory file and record locking is active on a file [see chmod(2)], creat(2), open(2), read(2) and write(2) system calls issued on the file will be affected by the record locks in effect.

fcntl will fail if one or more of the following are true:

EACCES   *cmd* is F_SETLK, the type of lock (l_type) is a read lock (F_RDLCK) and the segment of a file to be locked is already write locked by another process, or the type is a write lock (F_WRLCK) and the segment of a file to be locked is already read or write locked by another process.

EAGAIN   *cmd* is F_FREESP, the file exists, mandatory file/record locking is set, and there are outstanding record locks on the file.

EAGAIN   *cmd* is F_SETLK or F_SETLKW and the file is currently being mapped to virtual memory via mmap [see mmap(2)].

EBADF   *fildes* is not a valid open file descriptor.

EBADF   *cmd* is F_SETLK or F_SETLKW, the type of lock (l_type) is a read lock (F_RDLCK), and *fildes* is not a valid file descriptor open for reading.

EBADF   *cmd* is F_SETLK or F_SETLKW, the type of lock (l_type) is a write lock (F_WRLCK), and *fildes* is not a valid file descriptor open for writing.

EBADF   *cmd* is F_FREESP, and *fildes* is not a valid file descriptor open for writing.

EDEADLK   *cmd* is F_SETLKW, the lock is blocked by some lock from another process, and if fcntl blocked the calling process waiting for that lock to become free, a deadlock would occur.

EDEADLK   *cmd* is F_FREESP, mandatory record locking is enabled, O_NDELAY and O_NONBLOCK are clear and a deadlock condition was detected.

EFAULT		*cmd* is **F_FREESP** and the value pointed to by the third argument *arg* resulted in an address outside the process's allocated address space.
EFAULT		*cmd* is **F_GETLK, F_SETLK** or **F_SETLKW** and the value pointed to by the third argument resulted in an address outside the program address space.
EINTR		A signal was caught during execution of the `fcntl` system call.
EIO		An I/O error occurred while reading from or writing to the file system.
EMFILE		*cmd* is **F_DUPFD** and the number of file descriptors currently open in the calling process is the configured value for the maximum number of open file descriptors allowed each user.
EINVAL		*cmd* is **F_DUPFD** and the third argument is either negative, or greater than or equal to the configured value for the maximum number of open file descriptors allowed each user.
EINVAL		*cmd* is not a valid value.
EINVAL		*cmd* is **F_GETLK, F_SETLK**, or **F_SETLKW** and the third argument or the data it points to is not valid, or *fildes* refers to a file that does not support locking.
ENOLCK		*cmd* is **F_SETLK** or **F_SETLKW**, the type of lock is a read or write lock, and there are no more record locks available (too many file segments locked) because the system maximum has been exceeded.
ENOLINK		*fildes* is on a remote machine and the link to that machine is no longer active.
ENOLINK		*cmd* is **F_FREESP**, the file is on a remote machine, and the link to that machine is no longer active.
EOVERFLOW		*cmd* is **F_GETLK** and the process ID of the process holding the requested lock is too large to be stored in the *l_pid* field.

SEE ALSO
close(2), creat(2), dup(2), exec(2), fork(2), open(2), pipe(2), fcntl(5).

The "File and Record Locking" chapter in the *Application Programmer's Guide*.

DIAGNOSTICS
On success, `fcntl` returns a value that depends on *cmd*:

F_DUPFD	A new file descriptor.
F_GETFD	Value of flag (only the low-order bit is defined). The return value will not be negative.
F_SETFD	Value other than −1.
F_FREESP	Value of 0.

F_GETFL	Value of file status flags. The return value will not be negative.
F_SETFL	Value other than −1.
F_GETLK	Value other than −1.
F_SETLK	Value other than −1.
F_SETLKW	Value other than −1.

On failure, `fcntl` returns −1 and sets **errno** to indicate the error.

NOTES

In the future, the variable **errno** will be set to **EAGAIN** rather than **EACCES** when a section of a file is already locked by another process. Therefore, portable application programs should expect and test for either value.

NAME

fork – create a new process

SYNOPSIS

#include <sys/types.h>
#include <unistd.h>

pid_t fork(void);

DESCRIPTION

fork causes creation of a new process. The new process (child process) is an exact copy of the calling process (parent process). This means the child process inherits the following attributes from the parent process:

> real user ID, real group ID, effective user ID, effective group ID
> environment
> close-on-exec flag [see exec(2)]
> signal handling settings (i.e., SIG_DFL, SIG_IGN, SIG_HOLD, function address)
> supplementary group IDs
> set-user-ID mode bit
> set-group-ID mode bit
> profiling on/off status
> nice value [see nice(2)]
> scheduler class [see priocntl(2)]
> all attached shared memory segments [see shmop(2)]
> process group ID
> session ID [see exit(2)]
> current working directory
> root directory
> file mode creation mask [see umask(2)]
> resource limits [see getrlimit(2)]
> controlling terminal

Scheduling priority and any per-process scheduling parameters that are specific to a given scheduling class may or may not be inherited according to the policy of that particular class [see priocntl(2)].

The child process differs from the parent process in the following ways:

> The child process has a unique process ID which does not match any active process group ID.

> The child process has a different parent process ID (i.e., the process ID of the parent process).

> The child process has its own copy of the parent's file descriptors and directory streams. Each of the child's file descriptors shares a common file pointer with the corresponding file descriptor of the parent.

> All semadj values are cleared [see semop(2)].

> Process locks, text locks and data locks are not inherited by the child [see plock(2)].

fork(2)

The child process's `tms` structure is cleared: `tms_utime`, `stime`, `cutime`, and `cstime` are set to 0 [see `times`(2)].

The time left until an alarm clock signal is reset to 0.

The set of signals pending for the child process is initialized to the empty set.

Record locks set by the parent process are not inherited by the child process [see `fcntl`(2)].

`fork` will fail and no child process will be created if one or more of the following are true:

EAGAIN	The system-imposed limit on the total number of processes under execution by a single user would be exceeded.
EAGAIN	Total amount of system memory available when reading via raw I/O is temporarily insufficient.
ENOMEM	There is not enough swap space.

SEE ALSO

alarm(2), exec(2), fcntl(2), getrlimit(2), nice(2), plock(2), priocntl(2), ptrace(2), semop(2), shmop(2), signal(2), times(2), umask(2), wait(2), system(3S).

DIAGNOSTICS

Upon successful completion, `fork` returns a value of 0 to the child process and returns the process ID of the child process to the parent process. Otherwise, a value of `(pid_t)-1` is returned to the parent process, no child process is created, and `errno` is set to indicate the error.

fpathconf(2)

NAME
fpathconf, pathconf – get configurable pathname variables

SYNOPSIS
#include <unistd.h>

long fpathconf (int fildes, int name);
long pathconf (char *path, int name);

DESCRIPTION
The functions fpathconf and pathconf return the current value of a configurable limit or option associated with a file or directory. The *path* argument points to the pathname of a file or directory; *fildes* is an open file descriptor; and *name* is the symbolic constant (defined in <unistd.h>) representing the configurable system limit or option to be returned.

The values returned by pathconf and fpathconf depend on the type of file specified by *path* or *fildes*. The following table contains the symbolic constants supported by pathconf and fpathconf along with the POSIX defined return value. The return value is based on the type of file specified by *path* or *fildes*.

Value of *name*	See Note
_PC_LINK_MAX	1
_PC_MAX_CANNON	2
_PC_MAX_INPUT	2
_PC_NAME_MAX	3,4
_PC_PATH_MAX	4,5
_PC_PIPE_BUF	6
_PC_CHOWN_RESTRICTED	7
_PC_NO_TRUNC	3,4
_PC_VDISABLE	2

Notes:

1   If *path* or *fildes* refers to a directory, the value returned applies to the directory itself.

2   The behavior is undefined if *path* or *fildes* does not refer to a terminal file.

3   If *path* or *fildes* refers to a directory, the value returned applies to the filenames within the directory.

4   The behavior is undefined if *path* or *fildes* does not refer to a directory.

5   If *path* or *fildes* refers to a directory, the value returned is the maximum length of a relative pathname when the specified directory is the working directory.

6   If *path* or *fildes* refers to a pipe or FIFO, the value returned applies to the FIFO itself. If *path* or *fildes* refers to a directory, the value returned applies to any FIFOs that exist or can be created within the directory. If *path* or *fildes* refer to any other type of file, the behavior is undefined.

7   If *path* or *fildes* refers to a directory, the value returned applies to any files, other than directories, that exist or can be created within the directory.

The value of the configurable system limit or option specified by *name* does not change during the lifetime of the calling process.

fpathconf fails if the following is true:

EBADF   *fildes* is not a valid file descriptor.

pathconf fails if one or more of the following are true:

EACCES   search permission is denied for a component of the path prefix.

ELOOP   too many symbolic links are encountered while translating *path*.

EMULTIHOP   components of *path* require hopping to multiple remote machines and file system type does not allow it.

ENAMETOOLONG
             the length of a pathname exceeds {PATH_MAX}, or pathname component is longer than {NAME_MAX} while (_POSIX_NO_TRUNC) is in effect.

ENOENT   *path* is needed for the command specified and the named file does not exist or if the *path* argument points to an empty string.

ENOLINK   *path* points to a remote machine and the link to that machine is no longer active.

ENOTDIR   a component of the path prefix is not a directory.

Both fpathconf and pathconf fail if the following is true:

EINVAL   if *name* is an invalid value.

SEE ALSO
sysconf(3C), limits(4)

DIAGNOSTICS
If fpathconf or pathconf are invoked with an invalid symbolic constant or the symbolic constant corresponds to a configurable system limit or option not supported on the system, a value of -1 is returned to the invoking process. If the function fails because the configurable system limit or option corresponding to *name* is not supported on the system the value of errno is not changed.

fsync(2)

NAME
fsync – synchronize a file's in-memory state with that on the physical medium

SYNOPSIS
```
#include <unistd.h>

int fsync(int fildes);
```

DESCRIPTION
fsync moves all modified data and attributes of *fildes* to a storage device. When **fsync** returns, all in-memory modified copies of buffers associated with *fildes* have been written to the physical medium. **fsync** is different from **sync**, which schedules disk I/O for all files but returns before the I/O completes.

fsync should be used by programs that require that a file be in a known state. For example, a program that contains a simple transaction facility might use **fsync** to ensure that all changes to a file or files caused by a given transaction were recorded on a storage medium.

fsync fails if one or more of the following are true:

EBADF	*fildes* is not a valid file descriptor open for writing.
ENOLINK	*fildes* is on a remote machine and the link on that machine is no longer active.
EINTR	A signal was caught during execution of the **fsync** system call.
EIO	An I/O error occurred while reading from or writing to the file system.

DIAGNOSTICS
Upon successful completion, a value of 0 is returned. Otherwise, a value of −1 is returned and **errno** is set to indicate the error.

NOTES
The way the data reach the physical medium depends on both implementation and hardware. **fsync** returns when the device driver tells it that the write has taken place.

SEE ALSO
sync(2)

getcontext(2)

NAME
getcontext, setcontext − get and set current user context

SYNOPSIS
#include <ucontext.h>

int getcontext(ucontext_t *ucp);

int setcontext(ucontext_t *ucp);

DESCRIPTION
These functions, along with those defined in makecontext(3C), are useful for implementing user level context switching between multiple threads of control within a process.

getcontext initializes the structure pointed to by *ucp* to the current user context of the calling process. The user context is defined by ucontext(5) and includes the contents of the calling process's machine registers, signal mask and execution stack.

setcontext restores the user context pointed to by *ucp*. The call to setcontext does not return; program execution resumes at the point specified by the context structure passed to setcontext. The context structure should have been one created either by a prior call to getcontext or makecontext or passed as the third argument to a signal handler [see sigaction(2)]. If the context structure was one created with getcontext, program execution continues as if the corresponding call of getcontext had just returned. If the context structure was one created with makecontext, program execution continues with the function specified to makecontext.

NOTES
When a signal handler is executed, the current user context is saved and a new context is created by the kernel. If the process leaves the signal handler via longjmp(3C) the original context will not be restored, and future calls to getcontext will not be reliable. Signal handlers should use siglongjmp(3C) or setcontext instead.

DIAGNOSTICS
On successful completion, setcontext does not return and getcontext returns 0. Otherwise, a value of -1 is returned and errno is set to indicate the error.

SEE ALSO
sigaction(2), sigaltstack(2), sigprocmask(2), makecontext(3C), ucontext(5).

getdents(2)

NAME
getdents – read directory entries and put in a file system independent format

SYNOPSIS
#include <sys/dirent.h>

int getdents (int fildes, struct dirent *buf, size_t nbyte);

DESCRIPTION
fildes is a file descriptor obtained from an open(2) or dup(2) system call.

getdents attempts to read *nbyte* bytes from the directory associated with *fildes* and to format them as file system independent directory entries in the buffer pointed to by *buf*. Since the file system independent directory entries are of variable length, in most cases the actual number of bytes returned will be strictly less than *nbyte*. See dirent(4) to calculate the number of bytes.

The file system independent directory entry is specified by the dirent structure. For a description of this see dirent(4).

On devices capable of seeking, getdents starts at a position in the file given by the file pointer associated with *fildes*. Upon return from *getdents*, the file pointer is incremented to point to the next directory entry.

This system call was developed in order to implement the readdir routine [for a description, see directory(3C)], and should not be used for other purposes.

getdents will fail if one or more of the following are true:

EBADF	*fildes* is not a valid file descriptor open for reading.
EFAULT	*buf* points outside the allocated address space.
EINVAL	*nbyte* is not large enough for one directory entry.
ENOENT	The current file pointer for the directory is not located at a valid entry.
ENOLINK	*fildes* points to a remote machine and the link to that machine is no longer active.
ENOTDIR	*fildes* is not a directory.
EIO	An I/O error occurred while accessing the file system.

SEE ALSO
directory(3C).
dirent(4) in the *System Administrator's Reference Manual*.

DIAGNOSTICS
Upon successful completion a non-negative integer is returned indicating the number of bytes actually read. A value of 0 indicates the end of the directory has been reached. If the system call failed, a −1 is returned and errno is set to indicate the error.

getgroups(2)

NAME
getgroups, setgroups – get or set supplementary group access list IDs

SYNOPSIS
#include <unistd.h>

int getgroups(int gidsetsize, gid_t *grouplist)

int setgroups(int ngroups, const gid_t *grouplist)

DESCRIPTION
getgroups gets the current supplemental group access list of the calling process and stores the result in the array of group IDs specified by *grouplist*. This array has *gidsetsize* entries and must be large enough to contain the entire list. This list cannot be greater than {NGOUPS_MAX}. If *gidsetsize* equals 0, getgroups will return the number of groups to which the calling process belongs without modifying the array pointed to by *grouplist*.

setgroups sets the supplementary group access list of the calling process from the array of group IDs specified by *grouplist*. The number of entries is specified by *ngroups* and can not be greater than {NGROUPS_MAX}. This function may be invoked only by the super-user.

getgroups will fail if:

EINVAL   The value of *gidsetsize* is non-zero and less than the number of supplementary group IDs set for the calling process.

setgroups will fail if:

EINVAL   The value of *ngroups* is greater than {NGROUPS_MAX}.

EPERM   The effective user ID is not super-user.

Either call will fail if:

EFAULT   A referenced part of the array pointed to by *grouplist* is outside of the allocated address space of the process.

SEE ALSO
chown(2), getuid(2), setuid(2), initgroups(3C).
groups(1) in the *User's Reference Manual*.

DIAGNOSTICS
Upon successful completion, getgroups returns the number of supplementary group IDs set for the calling process and setgroups returns the value 0. Otherwise, a value of −1 is returned and errno is set to indicate the error.

getmsg(2)

NAME
getmsg – get next message off a stream

SYNOPSIS
```
#include <stropts.h>

int getmsg(int fd, struct strbuf *ctlptr,
           struct strbuf *dataptr, int *flagsp);

int getpmsg(int fd, struct strbuf *ctlptr,
            struct strbuf *dataptr, int *bandp, int *flagsp);
```

DESCRIPTION
getmsg retrieves the contents of a message [see intro(2)] located at the stream head read queue from a STREAMS file, and places the contents into user specified buffer(s). The message must contain either a data part, a control part, or both. The data and control parts of the message are placed into separate buffers, as described below. The semantics of each part is defined by the STREAMS module that generated the message.

The function getpmsg does the same thing as getmsg, but provides finer control over the priority of the messages received. Except where noted, all information pertaining to getmsg also pertains to getpmsg.

fd specifies a file descriptor referencing an open stream. *ctlptr* and *dataptr* each point to a strbuf structure, which contains the following members:

```
int maxlen;     /* maximum buffer length */
int len;        /* length of data */
char *buf;      /* ptr to buffer */
```

buf points to a buffer in which the data or control information is to be placed, and maxlen indicates the maximum number of bytes this buffer can hold. On return, len contains the number of bytes of data or control information actually received, or 0 if there is a zero-length control or data part, or -1 if no data or control information is present in the message. *flagsp* should point to an integer that indicates the type of message the user is able to receive. This is described later.

ctlptr is used to hold the control part from the message and *dataptr* is used to hold the data part from the message. If *ctlptr* (or *dataptr*) is NULL or the maxlen field is -1, the control (or data) part of the message is not processed and is left on the stream head read queue. If *ctlptr* (or *dataptr*) is not NULL and there is no corresponding control (or data) part of the messages on the stream head read queue, len is set to -1. If the maxlen field is set to 0 and there is a zero-length control (or data) part, that zero-length part is removed from the read queue and len is set to 0. If the maxlen field is set to 0 and there are more than zero bytes of control (or data) information, that information is left on the read queue and len is set to 0. If the maxlen field in *ctlptr* or *dataptr* is less than, respectively, the control or data part of the message, maxlen bytes are retrieved. In this case, the remainder of the message is left on the stream head read queue and a non-zero return value is provided, as described below under DIAGNOSTICS.

By default, getmsg processes the first available message on the stream head read queue. However, a user may choose to retrieve only high priority messages by setting the integer pointed by *flagsp* to RS_HIPRI. In this case, getmsg processes the next message only if it is a high priority message. If the integer pointed by *flagsp* is 0, getmsg retrieves any message available on the stream head read queue. In this case, on return, the integer pointed to by *flagsp* will be set to RS_HIPRI if a high priority message was retrieved, or 0 otherwise.

For getpmsg, the flags are different. *flagsp* points to a bitmask with the following mutually-exclusive flags defined: MSG_HIPRI, MSG_BAND, and MSG_ANY. Like getmsg, getpmsg processes the first available message on the stream head read queue. A user may choose to retrieve only high-priority messages by setting the integer pointed to by *flagsp* to MSG_HIPRI and the integer pointed to by *bandp* to 0. In this case, getpmsg will only process the next message if it is a high-priority message. In a similar manner, a user may choose to retrieve a message from a particular priority band by setting the integer pointed to by *flagsp* to MSG_BAND and the integer pointed to by *bandp* to the priority band of interest. In this case, getpmsg will only process the next message if it is in a priority band equal to, or greater than, the integer pointed to by *bandp*, or if it is a high-priority message. If a user just wants to get the first message off the queue, the integer pointed to by *flagsp* should be set to MSG_ANY and the integer pointed to by *bandp* should be set to 0. On return, if the message retrieved was a high-priority message, the integer pointed to by *flagsp* will be set to MSG_HIPRI and the integer pointed to by *bandp* will be set to 0. Otherwise, the integer pointed to by *flagsp* will be set to MSG_BAND and the integer pointed to by *bandp* will be set to the priority band of the message.

If O_NDELAY and O_NONBLOCK are clear, getmsg blocks until a message of the type specified by *flagsp* is available on the stream head read queue. If O_NDELAY or O_NONBLOCK has been set and a message of the specified type is not present on the read queue, getmsg fails and sets errno to EAGAIN.

If a hangup occurs on the stream from which messages are to be retrieved, getmsg continues to operate normally, as described above, until the stream head read queue is empty. Thereafter, it returns 0 in the len fields of *ctlptr* and *dataptr*.

getmsg or getpmsg will fail if one or more of the following are true:

EAGAIN	The O_NDELAY or O_NONBLOCK flag is set, and no messages are available.
EBADF	*fd* is not a valid file descriptor open for reading.
EBADMSG	Queued message to be read is not valid for getmsg.
EFAULT	*ctlptr*, *dataptr*, *bandp*, or *flagsp* points to a location outside the allocated address space.
EINTR	A signal was caught during the getmsg system call.
EINVAL	An illegal value was specified in *flagsp*, or the stream referenced by *fd* is linked under a multiplexor.

getmsg(2)

ENOSTR   A stream is not associated with *fd*.

getmsg can also fail if a STREAMS error message had been received at the stream head before the call to getmsg. The error returned is the value contained in the STREAMS error message.

SEE ALSO
intro(2), poll(2), putmsg(2), read(2), write(2).
Programmer's Guide: STREAMS.

DIAGNOSTICS
Upon successful completion, a non-negative value is returned. A value of 0 indicates that a full message was read successfully. A return value of MORECTL indicates that more control information is waiting for retrieval. A return value of MOREDATA indicates that more data are waiting for retrieval. A return value of MORECTL | MOREDATA indicates that both types of information remain. Subsequent getmsg calls retrieve the remainder of the message. However, if a message of higher priority has come in on the stream head read queue, the next call to getmsg will retrieve that higher priority message before retrieving the remainder of the previously received partial message.

NAME

getpid, getpgrp, getppid, getpgid – get process, process group, and parent process IDs

SYNOPSIS

#include <sys/types.h>
#include <unistd.h>

pid_t getpid(void);

pid_t getpgrp(void);

pid_t getppid(void);

pid_t getpgid(pid_t pid);

DESCRIPTION

getpid returns the process ID of the calling process.

getpgrp returns the process group ID of the calling process.

getppid returns the parent process ID of the calling process.

getpgid returns the process group ID of the process whose process ID is equal to *pid*, or the process group ID of the calling process, if *pid* is equal to zero.

getpgid will fail if one or more of the following is true:

EPERM   The process whose process ID is equal to *pid* is not in the same session as the calling process, and the implementation does not allow access to the process group ID of that process from the calling process.

ESRCH   There is no process with a process ID equal to *pid*.

SEE ALSO

exec(2), fork(2), getpid(2), getsid(2), intro(2), setpgid(2), setsid(2) setpgrp(2), signal(2).

DIAGNOSTICS

Upon successful completion, getpgid returns a process group ID. Otherwise, a value of (pid_t) −1 is returned and errno is set to indicate the error.

getrlimit(2)

NAME
getrlimit, setrlimit – control maximum system resource consumption

SYNOPSIS
```
#include <sys/time.h>
#include <sys/resource.h>
```

int getrlimit(int resource, struct rlimit *rlp);

int setrlimit(int resource, const struct rlimit *rlp);

DESCRIPTION
Limits on the consumption of a variety of system resources by a process and each process it creates may be obtained with `getrlimit` and set with `setrlimit`.

Each call to either `getrlimit` or `setrlimit` identifies a specific resource to be operated upon as well as a resource limit. A resource limit is a pair of values: one specifying the current (soft) limit, the other a maximum (hard) limit. Soft limits may be changed by a process to any value that is less than or equal to the hard limit. A process may (irreversibly) lower its hard limit to any value that is greater than or equal to the soft limit. Only a process with an effective user ID or superuser can raise a hard limit. Both hard and soft limits can be changed in a single call to `setrlimit` subject to the constraints described above. Limits may have an infinite value of RLIM_INFINITY. *rlp* is a pointer to struct rlimit that includes the following members:

```
rlim_t    rlim_cur;    /* current (soft) limit */
rlim_t    rlim_max;    /* hard limit */
```

`rlim_t` is an arithmetic data type to which objects of type int, size_t, and off_t can be cast without loss of information.

The possible resources, their descriptions, and the actions taken when current limit is exceeded, are summarized in the table below:

Resources	Description	Action
RLIMIT_CORE	The maximum size of a core file in bytes that may be created by a process. A limit of 0 will prevent the creation of a core file.	The writing of a core file will terminate at this size.
RLIMIT_CPU	The maximum amount of CPU time in seconds used by a process.	SIGXCPU is sent to the process. If the process is holding or ignoring SIGXCPU, the behavior is scheduling class defined.
RLIMIT_DATA	The maximum size of a process's heap in bytes.	brk(2) will fail with errno set to ENOMEM.

Resources	Description	Action
RLIMIT_FSIZE	The maximum size of a file in bytes that may be created by a process. A limit of 0 will prevent the creation of a file.	SIGXFSZ is sent to the process. If the process is holding or ignoring SIGXFSZ, continued attempts to increase the size of a file beyond the limit will fail with errno set to EFBIG.
RLIMIT_NOFILE	The maximum number of open file descriptors that the process can have.	Functions that create new file descriptors will fail with errno set to EMFILE.
RLIMIT_STACK	The maximum size of a process's stack in bytes. The system will not automatically grow the stack beyond this limit.	SIGSEGV is sent to the process. If the process is holding or ignoring SIGSEGV, or is catching SIGSEGV and has not made arrangements to use an alternate stack [see sigaltstack(2)], the disposition of SIGSEGV will be set to SIG_DFL before it is sent.
RLIMIT_VMEM	The maximum size of a process's mapped address space in bytes.	brk(2) and mmap(2) functions will fail with errno set to ENOMEM. In addition, the automatic stack growth will fail with the effects outlined above.

Because limit information is stored in the per-process information, the shell builtin ulimit must directly execute this system call if it is to affect all future processes created by the shell.

The value of the current limit of the following resources affect these implementation defined constants:

Limit	Implementation Defined Constant
RLIMIT_FSIZE	FCHR_MAX
RLIMIT_NOFILE	OPEN_MAX

RETURN VALUE

Upon successful completion, the function getrlimit returns a value of 0; otherwise, it returns a value of −1 and sets errno to indicate an error.

ERRORS

Under the following conditions, the functions getrlimit and setrlimit fail and set errno to:

	EINVAL	if an invalid *resource* was specified; or in a **setrlimit** call, the new rlim_cur exceeds the new rlim_max.
	EPERM	if the limit specified to **setrlimit** would have raised the maximum limit value, and the caller is the superuser

SEE ALSO
    malloc(3C), open(2), sigaltstack(2), signal(5).

NAME
getsid – get session ID

SYNOPSIS
#include <sys/types.h>

pid_t getsid(pid_t *pid*);

DESCRIPTION
The function `getsid` returns the session ID of the process whose process ID is equal to *pid*. If *pid* is equal to (pid_t)0, `getsid` returns the session ID of the calling process.

RETURN VALUE
Upon successful completion, the function `getsid` returns the session ID of the specified process; otherwise, it returns a value of (pid_t)-1 and sets `errno` to indicate an error.

ERRORS
Under the following conditions, the function `getsid` fails and sets `errno` to:

EPERM   if the process whose process ID is equal to *pid* is not in the same session as the calling process, and the implementation does not allow access to the session ID of that process from the calling process.

ESRCH   if there is no process with a process ID equal to *pid*.

SEE ALSO
exec(2), fork(2), getpid(2), setpgid(2), setsid(2).

getuid(2)

NAME
getuid, geteuid, getgid, getegid – get real user, effective user, real group, and effective group IDs

SYNOPSIS
    #include <sys/types.h>
    #include <unistd.h>

    uid_t getuid (void);

    uid_t geteuid (void);

    gid_t getgid (void);

    gid_t getegid (void);

DESCRIPTION
getuid returns the real user ID of the calling process.

geteuid returns the effective user ID of the calling process.

getgid returns the real group ID of the calling process.

getegid returns the effective group ID of the calling process.

SEE ALSO
intro(2), setuid(2).

NAME
ioctl – control device

SYNOPSIS
#include <unistd.h>

int ioctl (int fildes, int request, ... /* arg */);

DESCRIPTION
ioctl performs a variety of control functions on devices and STREAMS. For non-STREAMS files, the functions performed by this call are device-specific control functions. *request* and an optional third argument with varying type are passed to the file designated by *fildes* and are interpreted by the device driver. This control is not frequently used on non-STREAMS devices, where the basic input/output functions are usually performed through the read(2) and write(2) system calls.

For STREAMS files, specific functions are performed by the ioctl call as described in streamio(7).

fildes is an open file descriptor that refers to a device. *request* selects the control function to be performed and depends on the device being addressed. *arg* represents a third argument that has additional information that is needed by this specific device to perform the requested function. The data type of *arg* depends upon the particular control request, but it is either an int or a pointer to a device-specific data structure.

In addition to device-specific and STREAMS functions, generic functions are provided by more than one device driver, for example, the general terminal interface [see termio(7)].

ioctl fails for any type of file if one or more of the following are true:

EBADF   *fildes* is not a valid open file descriptor.

ENOTTY   *fildes* is not associated with a device driver that accepts control functions.

EINTR   A signal was caught during the ioctl system call.

ioctl also fails if the device driver detects an error. In this case, the error is passed through ioctl without change to the caller. A particular driver might not have all of the following error cases. Under the following conditions, requests to device drivers may fail and set errno to:

EFAULT   *request* requires a data transfer to or from a buffer pointed to by *arg*, but some part of the buffer is outside the process's allocated space.

EINVAL   *request* or *arg* is not valid for this device.

EIO   Some physical I/O error has occurred.

ENXIO   The *request* and *arg* are valid for this device driver, but the service requested can not be performed on this particular subdevice.

ENOLINK   *fildes* is on a remote machine and the link to that machine is no longer active.

STREAMS errors are described in `streamio`(7).

SEE ALSO
`streamio`(7) in the *Programmer's Guide: STREAMS*.
`termio`(7) in the *System Administrator's Reference Manual*.

DIAGNOSTICS
Upon successful completion, the value returned depends upon the device control function, but must be a non-negative integer. Otherwise, a value of −1 is returned and `errno` is set to indicate the error.

kill(2)

NAME
kill − send a signal to a process or a group of processes

SYNOPSIS
#include <sys/types.h>
#include <signal.h>

    int kill (pid_t pid, int sig);

DESCRIPTION
kill sends a signal to a process or a group of processes. The process or group of processes to which the signal is to be sent is specified by *pid*. The signal that is to be sent is specified by *sig* and is either one from the list given in **signal** [see **signal**(5)], or 0. If *sig* is 0 (the null signal), error checking is performed but no signal is actually sent. This can be used to check the validity of *pid*.

The real or effective user ID of the sending process must match the real or saved [from exec(2)] user ID of the receiving process unless the effective user ID of the sending process is superuser, [see **intro**(2)], or *sig* is SIGCONT and the sending process has the same session ID as the receiving process.

The process with ID 0 and the process with ID 1 are special processes [see intro(2)] and will be referred to below as proc0 and proc1, respectively.

If *pid* is greater than 0, *sig* will be sent to the process whose process ID is equal to *pid*. *pid* may equal 1.

If *pid* is negative but not (pid_t)−1, *sig* will be sent to all processes whose process group ID is equal to the absolute value of *pid* and for which the process has permission to send a signal.

If *pid* is 0, *sig* will be sent to all processes excluding proc0 and proc1 whose process group ID is equal to the process group ID of the sender. Permission is needed to send a signal to process groups.

If *pid* is (pid_t)−1 and the effective user ID of the sender is not superuser, *sig* will be sent to all processes excluding proc0 and proc1 whose real user ID is equal to the effective user ID of the sender.

If *pid* is (pid_t)−1 and the effective user ID of the sender is superuser, *sig* will be sent to all processes excluding proc0 and proc1.

kill will fail and no signal will be sent if one or more of the following are true:

EINVAL	*sig* is not a valid signal number.
EINVAL	*sig* is SIGKILL and *pid* is (pid_t)1 (i.e., *pid* specifies proc1).
ESRCH	No process or process group can be found corresponding to that specified by *pid*.
EPERM	The user ID of the sending process is not privileged, and its real or effective user ID does not match the real or saved user ID of the receiving process, and the calling process is not sending SIGCONT to a process that shares the same session ID.

SEE ALSO
>   getpid(2), intro(2), setpgrp(2), signal(2), getsid(2), sigsend(2), sigaction(2).
>
>   kill(1) in the *User's Reference Manual*.

NOTES
>   sigsend is a more versatile way to send signals to processes. The user is encouraged to use sigsend instead of kill.

DIAGNOSTICS
>   Upon successful completion, a value of 0 is returned. Otherwise, a value of −1 is returned and errno is set to indicate the error.

link(2)   link(2)

NAME
link – link to a file

SYNOPSIS
#include <unistd.h>

int link(const char *path1, const char *path2);

DESCRIPTION
path1 points to a path name naming an existing file. *path2* points to a path name naming the new directory entry to be created. link creates a new link (directory entry) for the existing file and increments its link count by one.

Upon successful completion, link marks for update the st_ctime field of the file. Also, the st_ctime and st_mtime fields of the directory that contains the new entry are marked for update.

link will fail and no link will be created if one or more of the following are true:

EACCES	A component of either path prefix denies search permission.
EACCES	The requested link requires writing in a directory with a mode that denies write permission.
EEXIST	The link named by *path2* exists.
EFAULT	*path* points outside the allocated address space of the process.
EINTR	A signal was caught during the link system call.
ELOOP	Too many symbolic links were encountered in translating *path*.
EMLINK	The maximum number of links to a file would be exceeded.
EMULTIHOP	Components of *path* require hopping to multiple remote machines and file system type does not allow it.
ENAMETOOLONG	The length of the *path1* or *path2* argument exceeds {PATH_MAX}, or the length of a *path1* or *path2* component exceeds {NAME_MAX} while _POSIX_NO_TRUNC is in effect.
ENOTDIR	A component of either path prefix is not a directory.
ENOENT	*path1* or *path2* is a null path name.
ENOENT	A component of either path prefix does not exist.
ENOENT	The file named by *path1* does not exist.
ENOLINK	*path* points to a remote machine and the link to that machine is no longer active.
ENOSPC	the directory that would contain the link cannot be extended.
EPERM	The file named by *path1* is a directory and the effective user ID is not super-user.

	EROFS	The requested link requires writing in a directory on a read-only file system.
	EXDEV	The link named by *path2* and the file named by *path1* are on different logical devices (file systems).

SEE ALSO
   unlink(2).

DIAGNOSTICS
   Upon successful completion, a value of 0 is returned. Otherwise, a value of −1 is returned and errno is set to indicate the error.

lseek(2)

NAME
lseek – move read/write file pointer

SYNOPSIS
#include <sys/types.h>
#include <unistd.h>

off_t lseek (int fildes, off_t offset, int whence);

DESCRIPTION
fildes is a file descriptor returned from a `creat`, `open`, `dup`, or `fcntl` system call. `lseek` sets the file pointer associated with *fildes* as follows:

If *whence* is SEEK_SET, the pointer is set to *offset* bytes.

If *whence* is SEEK_CUR, the pointer is set to its current location plus *offset*.

If *whence* is SEEK_END, the pointer is set to the size of the file plus *offset*.

On success, `lseek` returns the resulting pointer location, as measured in bytes from the beginning of the file. Note that if *fildes* is a remote file descriptor and *offset* is negative, `lseek` returns the file pointer even if it is negative.

`lseek` allows the file pointer to be set beyond the existing data in the file. If data are later written at this point, subsequent reads in the gap between the previous end of data and the newly written data will return bytes of value 0 until data are written into the gap.

`lseek` fails and the file pointer remains unchanged if one or more of the following are true:

EBADF *fildes* is not an open file descriptor.

ESPIPE *fildes* is associated with a pipe or fifo.

EINVAL *whence* is not SEEK_SET, SEEK_CUR, or SEEK_END. The process also gets a SIGSYS signal.

EINVAL *fildes* is not a remote file descriptor, and the resulting file pointer would be negative.

Some devices are incapable of seeking. The value of the file pointer associated with such a device is undefined.

SEE ALSO
creat(2), dup(2), fcntl(2), open(2).

DIAGNOSTICS
Upon successful completion, a non-negative integer indicating the file pointer value is returned. Otherwise, a value of −1 is returned and `errno` is set to indicate the error.

memcntl(2)

NAME
memcntl – memory management control

SYNOPSIS
```
#include <sys/types.h>
#include <sys/mman.h>

int memcntl(caddr_t addr, size_t len, int cmd, caddr_t arg,
            int attr, int mask);
```

DESCRIPTION
The function memcntl allows the calling process to apply a variety of control operations over the address space identified by the mappings established for the address range [*addr, addr + len*].

addr must be a multiple of the pagesize as returned by **sysconf**(3C). The scope of the control operations can be further defined with additional selection criteria (in the form of attributes) according to the bit pattern contained in *attr*.

The following attributes specify page mapping selection criteria:

    SHARED   Page is mapped shared.
    PRIVATE   Page is mapped private.

The following attributes specify page protection selection criteria:

    PROT_READ   Page can be read.
    PROT_WRITE   Page can be written.
    PROT_EXEC   Page can be executed.

The selection criteria are constructed by an OR of the attribute bits and must match exactly.

In addition, the following criteria may be specified:

    PROC_TEXT   process text
    PROC_DATA   process data

where `PROC_TEXT` specifies all privately mapped segments with read and execute permission, and `PROC_DATA` specifies all privately mapped segments with write permission.

Selection criteria can be used to describe various abstract memory objects within the address space on which to operate. If an operation shall not be constrained by the selection criteria, *attr* must have the value 0.

The operation to be performed is identified by the argument *cmd*. The symbolic names for the operations are defined in `<sys/mman.h>` as follows:

    MC_LOCK   Lock in memory all pages in the range with attributes *attr*. A given page may be locked multiple times through different mappings; however, within a given mapping, page locks do not nest. Multiple lock operations on the same address in the same process will all be removed with a single unlock operation. A page locked in one process and mapped in another (or visible through a different mapping in the locking process) is locked in memory as long as the locking process does neither an implicit nor explicit unlock operation. If a locked mapping is removed, or a page is deleted through file removal or truncation, an unlock operation is implicitly performed. If a writable **MAP_PRIVATE** page in the address range is changed, the lock will be transferred to the private page.

At present *arg* is unused, but must be 0 to ensure compatibility with potential future enhancements.

MC_LOCKAS   Lock in memory all pages mapped by the address space with attributes *attr*. At present *addr* and *len* are unused, but must be **NULL** and 0 respectively, to ensure compatibility with potential future enhancements. *arg* is a bit pattern built from the flags:

MCL_CURRENT	Lock current mappings
MCL_FUTURE	Lock future mappings

The value of *arg* determines whether the pages to be locked are those currently mapped by the address space, those that will be mapped in the future, or both. If **MCL_FUTURE** is specified, then all mappings subsequently added to the address space will be locked, provided sufficient memory is available.

MC_SYNC   Write to their backing storage locations all modified pages in the range with attributes *attr*. Optionally, invalidate cache copies. The backing storage for a modified **MAP_SHARED** mapping is the file the page is mapped to; the backing storage for a modified **MAP_PRIVATE** mapping is its swap area. *arg* is a bit pattern built from the flags used to control the behavior of the operation:

MS_ASYNC	perform asynchronous writes
MS_SYNC	perform synchronous writes
MS_INVALIDATE	invalidate mappings

MS_ASYNC returns immediately once all write operations are scheduled; with **MS_SYNC** the system call will not return until all write operations are completed.

MS_INVALIDATE invalidates all cached copies of data in memory, so that further references to the pages will be obtained by the system from their backing storage locations. This operation should be used by applications that require a memory object to be in a known state.

MC_UNLOCK   Unlock all pages in the range with attributes *attr*. At present *arg* is unused, but must be 0 to ensure compatibility with potential future enhancements.

MC_UNLOCKAS   Remove address space memory locks, and locks on all pages in the address space with attributes *attr*. At present *addr*, *len*, and *arg* are unused, but must be **NULL**, 0 and 0 respectively, to ensure compatibility with potential future enhancements.

memcntl(2)

The *mask* argument must be zero; it is reserved for future use.

Locks established with the lock operations are not inherited by a child process after fork. memcntl fails if it attempts to lock more memory than a system-specific limit.

Due to the potential impact on system resources, all operations, with the exception of MC_SYNC, are restricted to processes with superuser effective user ID. The memcntl function subsumes the operations of plock and mctl.

RETURN VALUE

Upon successful completion, the function memcntl returns a value of 0; otherwise, it returns a value of −1 and sets errno to indicate an error.

ERRORS

Under the following conditions, the function memcntl fails and sets errno to:

- **EAGAIN**   if some or all of the memory identified by the operation could not be locked when MC_LOCK or MC_LOCKAS is specified.
- **EBUSY**   if some or all the addresses in the range [*addr, addr + len*) are locked and MC_SYNC with MS_INVALIDATE option is specified.
- **EINVAL**   if *addr* is not a multiple of the page size as returned by sysconf.
- **EINVAL**   if *addr* and/or *len* do not have the value 0 when MC_LOCKAS or MC_UNLOCKAS is specified.
- **EINVAL**   if *arg* is not valid for the function specified.
- **EINVAL**   if invalid selection criteria are specified in *attr*.
- **ENOMEM**   if some or all the addresses in the range [*addr, addr + len*) are invalid for the address space of the process or pages not mapped are specified.
- **EPERM**   if the process's effective user ID is not superuser and one of MC_LOCK, MC_LOCKAS, MC_UNLOCK, MC_UNLOCKAS was specified.

SEE ALSO

mmap(2), mprotect(2), plock(2), sysconf(2), mlock(3C), mlockall(3C), msync(3C).

NAME
mincore – determine residency of memory pages

SYNOPSIS
#include <unistd.h>
int mincore(caddr_t addr, size_t len, char *vec);

DESCRIPTION
mincore returns the primary memory residency status of pages in the address space covered by mappings in the range [addr, addr + len). The status is returned as a character-per-page in the character array referenced by *vec (which the system assumes to be large enough to encompass all the pages in the address range). The least significant bit of each character is set to 1 to indicate that the referenced page is in primary memory, 0 if it is not. The settings of other bits in each character are undefined and may contain other information in future implementations.

mincore returns residency information that is accurate at an instant in time. Because the system may frequently adjust the set of pages in memory, this information may quickly be outdated. Only locked pages are guaranteed to remain in memory; see memcntl(2).

RETURN VALUE
mincore returns 0 on success, −1 on failure.

ERRORS
mincore fails if:

EFAULT   *vec includes an out-of-range or otherwise inaccessible address.

EINVAL   addr is not a multiple of the page size as returned by sysconf(3C).

EINVAL   The argument len has a value less than or equal to 0.

ENOMEM   Addresses in the range [addr, addr + len) are invalid for the address space of a process, or specify one or more pages which are not mapped.

SEE ALSO
mlock(3C), mmap(2), sysconf(3C).

mkdir(2)

NAME
mkdir – make a directory

SYNOPSIS
```
#include <sys/types.h>
#include <sys/stat.h>

int mkdir(const char *path, mode_t mode);
```

DESCRIPTION
mkdir creates a new directory named by the path name pointed to by *path*. The mode of the new directory is initialized from *mode* [see chmod(2) for values of mode]. The protection part of the *mode* argument is modified by the process's file creation mask [see umask(2)].

The directory's owner ID is set to the process's effective user ID. The directory's group ID is set to the process's effective group ID, or if the S_ISGID bit is set in the parent directory, then the group ID of the directory is inherited from the parent. The S_ISGID bit of the new directory is inherited from the parent directory.

If *path* is a symbolic link, it is not followed.

The newly created directory is empty with the exception of entries for itself (.) and its parent directory (..).

Upon successful completion, mkdir marks for update the st_atime, st_ctime and st_mtime fields of the directory. Also, the st_ctime and st_mtime fields of the directory that contains the new entry are marked for update.

mkdir fails and creates no directory if one or more of the following are true:

EACCES	Either a component of the path prefix denies search permission or write permission is denied on the parent directory of the directory to be created.
EEXIST	The named file already exists.
EFAULT	*path* points outside the allocated address space of the process.
EIO	An I/O error has occurred while accessing the file system.
ELOOP	Too many symbolic links were encountered in translating *path*.
EMLINK	The maximum number of links to the parent directory would be exceeded.
EMULTIHOP	Components of *path* require hopping to multiple remote machines and the file system type does not allow it.
ENAMETOOLONG	The length of the *path* argument exceeds {PATH_MAX}, or the length of a *path* component exceeds {NAME_MAX} while _POSIX_NO_TRUNC is in effect.

ENOENT	A component of the path prefix does not exist or is a null pathname.
ENOLINK	*path* points to a remote machine and the link to that machine is no longer active.
ENOSPC	No free space is available on the device containing the directory.
ENOTDIR	A component of the path prefix is not a directory.
EROFS	The path prefix resides on a read-only file system.

DIAGNOSTICS

Upon successful completion, a value of 0 is returned. Otherwise, a value of −1 is returned, and **errno** is set to indicate the error.

SEE ALSO

chmod(2), mknod(2), umask(2), stat(5).

mknod(2)

NAME
mknod – make a directory, or a special or ordinary file

SYNOPSIS
```
#include <sys/types.h>
#include <sys/stat.h>

int mknod(const char *path, mode_t mode, dev_t dev);
```

DESCRIPTION
mknod creates a new file named by the path name pointed to by *path*. The file type and permissions of the new file are initialized from *mode*.

The file type is specified in *mode* by the S_IFMT bits, which must be set to one of the following values:

S_IFIFO	fifo special
S_IFCHR	character special
S_IFDIR	directory
S_IFBLK	block special
S_IFREG	ordinary file

The file access permissions are specified in *mode* by the 0007777 bits, and may be constructed by an OR of the following values:

S_ISUID	04000	Set user ID on execution.
S_ISGID	020#0	Set group ID on execution if # is 7, 5, 3, or 1
		Enable mandatory file/record locking if # is 6, 4, 2, or 0
S_ISVTX	01000	Save text image after execution.
S_IRWXU	00700	Read, write, execute by owner.
S_IRUSR	00400	Read by owner.
S_IWUSR	00200	Write by owner.
S_IXUSR	00100	Execute (search if a directory) by owner.
S_IRWXG	00070	Read, write, execute by group.
S_IRGRP	00040	Read by group.
S_IWGRP	00020	Write by group.
S_IXGRP	00010	Execute by group.
S_IRWXO	00007	Read, write, execute (search) by others.
S_IROTH	00004	Read by others.
S_IWOTH	00002	Write by others
S_IXOTH	00001	Execute by others.

The owner ID of the file is set to the effective user ID of the process. The group ID of the file is set to the effective group ID of the process. However, if the S_ISGID bit is set in the parent directory, then the group ID of the file is inherited from the parent. If the group ID of the new file does not match the effective group ID or one of the supplementary group IDs, the S_ISGID bit is cleared.

The access permission bits of *mode* are modified by the process's file mode creation mask: all bits set in the process's file mode creation mask are cleared [see umask(2)]. If *mode* indicates a block or character special file, *dev* is a configuration-dependent specification of a character or block I/O device. If *mode* does not indicate a block special or character special device, *dev* is ignored. See mkdev(3C).

mknod checks to see if the driver has been installed and whether or not it is an old-style driver. If the driver is installed and it is an old-style driver, the minor number is limited to 255. If it's not an old-style driver, then it must be a new-style driver or uninstalled, and the minor number is limited to the current value of the **MAXMINOR** tunable. Of course, this tunable is set to 255 by default. If the range check fails, mknod fails with **EINVAL**.

mknod may be invoked only by a privileged user for file types other than FIFO special.

If *path* is a symbolic link, it is not followed.

mknod fails and creates no new file if one or more of the following are true:

EEXIST	The named file exists.
EINVAL	*dev* is invalid.
EFAULT	*path* points outside the allocated address space of the process.
ELOOP	Too many symbolic links were encountered in translating *path*.
EMULTIHOP	Components of *path* require hopping to multiple remote machines and the file system type does not allow it.
ENAMETOOLONG	The length of the *path* argument exceeds {PATH_MAX}, or the length of a *path* component exceeds {NAME_MAX} while _POSIX_NO_TRUNC is in effect.
ENOTDIR	A component of the path prefix is not a directory.
ENOENT	A component of the path prefix does not exist or is a null pathname.
EPERM	The effective user ID of the process is not super-user.
EROFS	The directory in which the file is to be created is located on a read-only file system.
ENOSPC	No space is available.
EINTR	A signal was caught during the mknod system call.
ENOLINK	*path* points to a remote machine and the link to that machine is no longer active.

SEE ALSO
chmod(2), exec(2), umask(2), mkdev(3C), mkfifo(3C), fs(4), stat(5).
mkdir(1) in the *User's Reference Manual*.

DIAGNOSTICS
Upon successful completion a value of 0 is returned. Otherwise, a value of −1 is returned and errno is set to indicate the error.

NOTES
If mknod creates a device in a remote directory using Remote File Sharing, the major and minor device numbers are interpreted by the server.

mmap(2)

NAME
mmap – map pages of memory

SYNOPSIS
```
#include <sys/types.h>
#include <sys/mman.h>

caddr_t mmap(caddr_t addr, size_t len, int prot, int flags, int fd,
     off_t off);
```

DESCRIPTION
The function mmap establishes a mapping between a process's address space and a virtual memory object. The format of the call is as follows:

pa = mmap(addr, len, prot, flags, fd, off);

mmap establishes a mapping between the process's address space at an address *pa* for *len* bytes to the memory object represented by the file descriptor *fd* at offset *off* for *len* bytes. The value of *pa* is an implementation-dependent function of the parameter *addr* and values of *flags*, further described below. A successful mmap call returns *pa* as its result. The address ranges covered by [*pa*, *pa* + *len*) and [*off*, *off* + *len*) must be legitimate for the possible (not necessarily current) address space of a process and the object in question, respectively. mmap cannot grow a file.

The mapping established by mmap replaces any previous mappings for the process's pages in the range [*pa*, *pa* + *len*).

The parameter *prot* determines whether read, write, execute, or some combination of accesses are permitted to the pages being mapped. The protection options are defined in <sys/mman.h> as:

PROT_READ	Page can be read.
PROT_WRITE	Page can be written.
PROT_EXEC	Page can be executed.
PROT_NONE	Page can not be accessed.

Not all implementations literally provide all possible combinations. PROT_WRITE is often implemented as PROT_READ|PROT_WRITE and PROT_EXEC as PROT_READ|PROT_EXEC. However, no implementation will permit a write to succeed where PROT_WRITE has not been set. The behavior of PROT_WRITE can be influenced by setting MAP_PRIVATE in the *flags* parameter, described below.

The parameter *flags* provides other information about the handling of the mapped pages. The options are defined in <sys/mman.h> as:

MAP_SHARED	Share changes.
MAP_PRIVATE	Changes are private.
MAP_FIXED	Interpret addr exactly.

MAP_SHARED and MAP_PRIVATE describe the disposition of write references to the memory object. If MAP_SHARED is specified, write references will change the memory object. If MAP_PRIVATE is specified, the initial write reference will create a private copy of the memory object page and redirect the mapping to the copy. Either MAP_SHARED or MAP_PRIVATE must be specified, but not both. The mapping type is retained across a fork(2).

Note that the private copy is not created until the first write; until then, other users who have the object mapped **MAP_SHARED** can change the object.

MAP_FIXED informs the system that the value of *pa* must be *addr*, exactly. The use of **MAP_FIXED** is discouraged, as it may prevent an implementation from making the most effective use of system resources.

When **MAP_FIXED** is not set, the system uses *addr* in an implementation-defined manner to arrive at *pa*. The *pa* so chosen will be an area of the address space which the system deems suitable for a mapping of *len* bytes to the specified object. All implementations interpret an *addr* value of zero as granting the system complete freedom in selecting *pa*, subject to constraints described below. A non-zero value of *addr* is taken to be a suggestion of a process address near which the mapping should be placed. When the system selects a value for *pa*, it will never place a mapping at address 0, nor will it replace any extant mapping, nor map into areas considered part of the potential data or stack segments.

The parameter *off* is constrained to be aligned and sized according to the value returned by **sysconf**. When **MAP_FIXED** is specified, the parameter *addr* must also meet these constraints. The system performs mapping operations over whole pages. Thus, while the parameter *len* need not meet a size or alignment constraint, the system will include, in any mapping operation, any partial page specified by the range [*pa*, *pa* + *len*).

The system will always zero-fill any partial page at the end of an object. Further, the system will never write out any modified portions of the last page of an object which are beyond its end. References to whole pages following the end of an object will result in the delivery of a **SIGBUS** signal. **SIGBUS** signals may also be delivered on various file system conditions, including quota exceeded errors.

RETURN VALUE

On success, **mmap** returns the address at which the mapping was placed (*pa*). On failure it returns (**caddr_t**)−1 and sets **errno** to indicate an error.

ERRORS

Under the following conditions, **mmap** fails and sets **errno** to:

EAGAIN	The mapping could not be locked in memory.
EBADF	*fd* is not open.
EACCES	*fd* is not open for read, regardless of the protection specified, or *fd* is not open for write and **PROT_WRITE** was specified for a **MAP_SHARED** type mapping.
ENXIO	Addresses in the range [*off*, *off* + *len*) are invalid for *fd*.
EINVAL	The arguments *addr* (if **MAP_FIXED** was specified) or *off* are not multiples of the page size as returned by **sysconf**.
EINVAL	The field in *flags* is invalid (neither **MAP_PRIVATE** or **MAP_SHARED**).
EINVAL	The argument *len* has a value less than or equal to 0.
ENODEV	*fd* refers to an object for which **mmap** is meaningless, such as a terminal.

mmap(2)

ENOMEM   MAP_FIXED was specified and the range [*addr*, *addr* + *len*) exceeds that allowed for the address space of a process, or MAP_FIXED was not specified and there is insufficient room in the address space to effect the mapping.

NOTES

mmap allows access to resources via address space manipulations instead of the read/write interface. Once a file is mapped, all a process has to do to access it is use the data at the address to which the object was mapped. Consider the following pseudo-code:

```
fd = open(...)
lseek(fd, offset)
read(fd, buf, len)
/* use data in buf */
```

Here is a rewrite using mmap:

```
fd = open(...)
address = mmap((caddr_t) 0, len, (PROT_READ | PROT_WRITE),
        MAP_PRIVATE, fd, offset)
/* use data at address */
```

SEE ALSO

fcntl(2), fork(2), lockf(3C), mlockall(3C), mprotect(2), munmap(2), plock(2), sysconf(2).

NAME
mount – mount a file system

SYNOPSIS
```
#include <sys/types.h>
#include <sys/mount.h>

int mount (const char *spec, const char *dir, int mflag,
    .../* int fstyp, const char *dataptr, size_t datalen*/);
```

DESCRIPTION
mount requests that a removable file system contained on the block special file identified by *spec* be mounted on the directory identified by *dir*. *spec* and *dir* are pointers to path names. *fstyp* is the file system type number. The sysfs(2) system call can be used to determine the file system type number. If both the MS_DATA and MS_FSS flag bits of *mflag* are off, the file system type defaults to the root file system type. Only if either flag is on is *fstyp* used to indicate the file system type.

If the MS_DATA flag is set in *mflag* the system expects the *dataptr* and *datalen* arguments to be present. Together they describe a block of file-system specific data at address *dataptr* of length *datalen*. This is interpreted by file-system specific code within the operating system and its format depends on the file system type. If a particular file system type does not require this data, *dataptr* and *datalen* should both be zero. Note that MS_FSS is obsolete and is ignored if MS_DATA is also set, but if MS_FSS is set and MS_DATA is not, *dataptr* and *datalen* are both assumed to be zero.

After a successful call to mount, all references to the file *dir* refer to the root directory on the mounted file system.

The low-order bit of *mflag* is used to control write permission on the mounted file system: if 1, writing is forbidden; otherwise writing is permitted according to individual file accessibility.

mount may be invoked only by the super-user. It is intended for use only by the mount utility.

mount fails if one or more of the following are true:

EBUSY	*dir* is currently mounted on, is someone's current working directory, or is otherwise busy.
EBUSY	The device associated with *spec* is currently mounted.
EBUSY	There are no more mount table entries.
EFAULT	*spec*, *dir*, or *datalen* points outside the allocated address space of the process.
EINVAL	The super block has an invalid magic number or the *fstyp* is invalid.
ELOOP	Too many symbolic links were encountered in translating *spec* or *dir*.

ENAMETOOLONG		The length of the *path* argument exceeds {PATH_MAX}, or the length of a *path* component exceeds {NAME_MAX} while _POSIX_NO_TRUNC is in effect.
ENOENT		None of the named files exists or is a null pathname.
ENOTDIR		A component of a path prefix is not a directory.
EPERM		The effective user ID is not super-user.
EREMOTE		*spec* is remote and cannot be mounted.
ENOLINK		*path* points to a remote machine and the link to that machine is no longer active.
EMULTIHOP		Components of *path* require hopping to multiple remote machines and the file system type does not allow it.
ENOTBLK		*spec* is not a block special device.
ENXIO		The device associated with *spec* does not exist.
ENOTDIR		*dir* is not a directory.
EROFS		*spec* is write protected and *mflag* requests write permission.
ENOSPC		The file system state in the super-block is not FsOKAY and *mflag* requests write permission.

SEE ALSO

sysfs(2), umount(2).

mount(1M), fs(4) in the *System Administrator's Reference Manual*.

DIAGNOSTICS

Upon successful completion a value of 0 is returned. Otherwise, a value of −1 is returned and errno is set to indicate the error.

mprotect(2)

NAME
mprotect – set protection of memory mapping

SYNOPSIS
```
#include <sys/types.h>
#include <sys/mman.h>

int mprotect(caddr_t addr, size_t len, int prot);
```

DESCRIPTION
The function **mprotect** changes the access protections on the mappings specified by the range [*addr, addr + len*) to be that specified by *prot*. Legitimate values for *prot* are the same as those permitted for mmap and are defined in <sys/mman.h> as:

```
PROT_READ       /* page can be read */
PROT_WRITE      /* page can be written */
PROT_EXEC       /* page can be executed */
PROT_NONE       /* page can not be accessed */
```

RETURN VALUE
Upon successful completion, the function **mprotect** returns a value of 0; otherwise, it returns a value of −1 and sets **errno** to indicate an error.

ERRORS
Under the following conditions, the function **mprotect** fails and sets **errno** to:

- **EACCES** — if *prot* specifies a protection that violates the access permission the process has to the underlying memory object.
- **EAGAIN** — if *prot* specifies PROT_WRITE over a MAP_PRIVATE mapping and there are insufficient memory resources to reserve for locking the private page.
- **EINVAL** — if *addr* is not a multiple of the page size as returned by sysconf.
- **EINVAL** — The argument *len* has a value less than or equal to 0.
- **ENOMEM** — if addresses in the range [*addr, addr + len*) are invalid for the address space of a process, or specify one or more pages which are not mapped.

When **mprotect** fails for reasons other than EINVAL, the protections on some of the pages in the range [*addr, addr + len*) may have been changed. If the error occurs on some page at *addr2*, then the protections of all whole pages in the range [*addr, addr2*] will have been modified.

SEE ALSO
memcntl(2), mmap(2), plock(2), mlock(3C), mlockall(3C), sysconf(3C).

msgctl(2)

NAME
msgctl – message control operations

SYNOPSIS
```
#include <sys/types.h>
#include <sys/ipc.h>
#include <sys/msg.h>

int msgctl(int msqid, int cmd, .../* struct msqid_ds *buf */);
```

DESCRIPTION
msgctl provides a variety of message control operations as specified by *cmd*. The following *cmd*s are available:

- **IPC_STAT** Place the current value of each member of the data structure associated with *msqid* into the structure pointed to by *buf*. The contents of this structure are defined in intro(2).

- **IPC_SET** Set the value of the following members of the data structure associated with *msqid* to the corresponding value found in the structure pointed to by *buf*:

      msg_perm.uid
      msg_perm.gid
      msg_perm.mode /* only access permission bits */
      msg_qbytes

  This *cmd* can only be executed by a process that has an effective user ID equal to either that of super user, or to the value of msg_perm.cuid or msg_perm.uid in the data structure associated with *msqid*. Only super user can raise the value of msg_qbytes.

- **IPC_RMID** Remove the message queue identifier specified by *msqid* from the system and destroy the message queue and data structure associated with it. This *cmd* can only be executed by a process that has an effective user ID equal to either that of super user, or to the value of msg_perm.cuid or msg_perm.uid in the data structure associated with *msqid*.

msgctl fails if one or more of the following are true:

- **EACCES**   *cmd* is IPC_STAT and operation permission is denied to the calling process [see intro(2)].
- **EFAULT**   *buf* points to an illegal address.
- **EINVAL**   *msqid* is not a valid message queue identifier.
- **EINVAL**   *cmd* is not a valid command.
- **EINVAL**   *cmd* is IPC_SET and msg_perm.uid or msg_perm.gid is not valid.
- **EOVERFLOW**   *cmd* is IPC_STAT and *uid* or *gid* is too large to be stored in the structure pointed to by *buf*.

EPERM	*cmd* is IPC_RMID or IPC_SET. The effective user ID of the calling process is not that of super user, or the value of msg_perm.cuid or msg_perm.uid in the data structure associated with *msqid*.
EPERM	*cmd* is IPC_SET, an attempt is being made to increase to the value of msg_qbytes, and the effective user ID of the calling process is not that of super user.

SEE ALSO

intro(2), msgget(2), msgop(2).

DIAGNOSTICS

Upon successful completion, a value of 0 is returned. Otherwise, a value of −1 is returned and errno is set to indicate the error.

msgget(2)

NAME
msgget – get message queue

SYNOPSIS
#include <sys/types.h>
#include <sys/ipc.h>
#include <sys/msg.h>

int msgget(key_t key, int msgflg);

DESCRIPTION
msgget returns the message queue identifier associated with *key*.

A message queue identifier and associated message queue and data structure [see intro(2)] are created for *key* if one of the following are true:

    key is IPC_PRIVATE.

    key does not already have a message queue identifier associated with it, and (*msgflg*&IPC_CREAT) is true.

On creation, the data structure associated with the new message queue identifier is initialized as follows:

    msg_perm.cuid, **msg_perm.uid**, **msg_perm.cgid**, and **msg_perm.gid** are set to the effective user ID and effective group ID, respectively, of the calling process.

    The low-order 9 bits of **msg_perm.mode** are set to the low-order 9 bits of *msgflg*.

    msg_qnum, **msg_lspid**, **msg_lrpid**, **msg_stime**, and **msg_rtime** are set to 0.

    msg_ctime is set to the current time.

    msg_qbytes is set to the system limit.

msgget fails if one or more of the following are true:

EACCES	A message queue identifier exists for *key*, but operation permission [see intro(2)] as specified by the low-order 9 bits of *msgflg* would not be granted.
ENOENT	A message queue identifier does not exist for *key* and (*msgflg*&IPC_CREAT) is false.
ENOSPC	A message queue identifier is to be created but the system-imposed limit on the maximum number of allowed message queue identifiers system wide would be exceeded.
EEXIST	A message queue identifier exists for *key* but (*msgflg*&IPC_CREAT) and (*msgflg*&IPC_EXCL) are both true.

SEE ALSO
intro(2), msgctl(2), msgop(2), stdipc(3C).

DIAGNOSTICS
Upon successful completion, a non-negative integer, namely a message queue identifier, is returned. Otherwise, a value of −1 is returned and **errno** is set to indicate the error.

msgop(2)

NAME
msgop: msgsnd, msgrcv – message operations

SYNOPSIS
```
#include <sys/types.h>
#include <sys/ipc.h>
#include <sys/msg.h>

int msgsnd(int msqid, const void *msgp,
      size_t msgsz, int msgflg);

int msgrcv(int msqid, void *msgp,
      size_t msgsz, long msgtyp, int msgflg);
```

DESCRIPTION
msgsnd sends a message to the queue associated with the message queue identifier specified by *msqid*. *msgp* points to a user defined buffer that must contain first a field of type long integer that will specify the type of the message, and then a data portion that will hold the text of the message. The following is an example of members that might be in a user defined buffer.

```
long mtype;    /* message type */
char mtext[];  /* message text */
```

mtype is a positive integer that can be used by the receiving process for message selection. mtext is any text of length *msgsz* bytes. *msgsz* can range from 0 to a system imposed maximum.

msgflg specifies the action to be taken if one or more of the following are true:

The number of bytes already on the queue is equal to msg_qbytes [see intro(2)].

The total number of messages on all queues system-wide is equal to the system-imposed limit.

These actions are as follows:

If (*msgflg*&IPC_NOWAIT) is true, the message is not sent and the calling process returns immediately.

If (*msgflg*&IPC_NOWAIT) is false, the calling process suspends execution until one of the following occurs:

The condition responsible for the suspension no longer exists, in which case the message is sent.

msqid is removed from the system [see msgctl(2)]. When this occurs, errno is set to EIDRM, and a value of −1 is returned.

The calling process receives a signal that is to be caught. In this case the message is not sent and the calling process resumes execution in the manner prescribed in signal(2).

msgsnd fails and sends no message if one or more of the following are true:

EINVAL	*msqid* is not a valid message queue identifier.
EACCES	Operation permission is denied to the calling process [see intro(2)].
EINVAL	*mtype* is less than 1.
EAGAIN	The message cannot be sent for one of the reasons cited above and (*msgflg*&IPC_NOWAIT) is true.
EINVAL	*msgsz* is less than zero or greater than the system-imposed limit.
EFAULT	*msgp* points to an illegal address.

Upon successful completion, the following actions are taken with respect to the data structure associated with *msqid* [see intro (2)].

msg_qnum is incremented by 1.

msg_lspid is set to the process ID of the calling process.

msg_stime is set to the current time.

msgrcv reads a message from the queue associated with the message queue identifier specified by *msqid* and places it in the user defined structure pointed to by *msgp*. The structure must contain a message type field followed by the area for the message text (see the structure mymsg above). mtype is the received message's type as specified by the sending process. mtext is the text of the message. *msgsz* specifies the size in bytes of mtext. The received message is truncated to *msgsz* bytes if it is larger than *msgsz* and (*msgflg*&MSG_NOERROR) is true. The truncated part of the message is lost and no indication of the truncation is given to the calling process.

msgtyp specifies the type of message requested as follows:

If *msgtyp* is 0, the first message on the queue is received.

If *msgtyp* is greater than 0, the first message of type *msgtyp* is received.

If *msgtyp* is less than 0, the first message of the lowest type that is less than or equal to the absolute value of *msgtyp* is received.

msgflg specifies the action to be taken if a message of the desired type is not on the queue. These are as follows:

If (*msgflg*&IPC_NOWAIT) is true, the calling process returns immediately with a return value of −1 and sets **errno** to ENOMSG.

If (*msgflg*&IPC_NOWAIT) is false, the calling process suspends execution until one of the following occurs:

A message of the desired type is placed on the queue.

msqid is removed from the system. When this occurs, **errno** is set to EIDRM, and a value of −1 is returned.

The calling process receives a signal that is to be caught. In this case a message is not received and the calling process resumes execution in the manner prescribed in signal(2).

msgrcv fails and receives no message if one or more of the following are true:

EINVAL   *msqid* is not a valid message queue identifier.

EACCES   Operation permission is denied to the calling process.

EINVAL   *msgsz* is less than 0.

E2BIG   The length of *mtext* is greater than *msgsz* and (*msgflg*&MSG_NOERROR) is false.

ENOMSG   The queue does not contain a message of the desired type and (*msgtyp*&IPC_NOWAIT) is true.

EFAULT   *msgp* points to an illegal address.

Upon successful completion, the following actions are taken with respect to the data structure associated with *msqid* [see intro (2)].

> msg_qnum is decremented by 1.
>
> msg_lrpid is set to the process ID of the calling process.
>
> msg_rtime is set to the current time.

SEE ALSO
intro(2), msgctl(2), msgget(2), signal(2).

DIAGNOSTICS
If msgsnd or msgrcv return due to the receipt of a signal, a value of −1 is returned to the calling process and errno is set to EINTR. If they return due to removal of *msqid* from the system, a value of −1 is returned and errno is set to EIDRM.

Upon successful completion, the return value is as follows:

> msgsnd returns a value of 0.
>
> msgrcv returns the number of bytes actually placed into *mtext*.

Otherwise, a value of −1 is returned and errno is set to indicate the error.

NAME
munmap – unmap pages of memory.

SYNOPSIS
```
#include <sys/types.h>
#include <sys/mman.h>

int munmap(caddr_t addr, size_t len);
```

DESCRIPTION
The function **munmap** removes the mappings for pages in the range [*addr, addr + len*). Further references to these pages will result in the delivery of a SIGSEGV signal to the process.

The function **mmap** often performs an implicit **munmap**.

RETURN VALUE
Upon successful completion, the function **munmap** returns a value of 0; otherwise, it returns a value of −1 and sets `errno` to indicate an error.

ERRORS
Under the following conditions, the function **munmap** fails and sets `errno` to:

EINVAL   if *addr* is not a multiple of the page size as returned by `sysconf`.

EINVAL   if addresses in the range [*addr, addr + len*) are outside the valid range for the address space of a process.

EINVAL   The argument *len* has a value less than or equal to 0.

SEE ALSO
mmap(2), sysconf(3C).

nice(2)

NAME
nice – change priority of a time-sharing process

SYNOPSIS
    #include <unistd.h>

    int nice(int incr);

DESCRIPTION
nice allows a process in the time-sharing scheduling class to change its priority. The `priocntl` system call is a more general interface to scheduler functions.

nice adds the value of *incr* to the nice value of the calling process. A process's nice value is a non-negative number for which a more positive value results in lower CPU priority.

A maximum nice value of 39 and a minimum nice value of 0 are imposed by the system. (The default nice value is 20.) Requests for values above or below these limits result in the nice value being set to the corresponding limit.

EPERM	nice fails and does not change the nice value if *incr* is negative or greater than 39 and the effective user ID of the calling process is not super-user.
EINVAL	nice fails if called by a process in a scheduling class other than time-sharing.

SEE ALSO
exec(2), `priocntl`(2).

nice(1) in the *User's Reference Manual*.

DIAGNOSTICS
Upon successful completion, nice returns the new nice value minus 20. Otherwise, a value of −1 is returned and `errno` is set to indicate the error.

open (2)

NAME
open – open for reading or writing

SYNOPSIS
```
#include <sys/types.h>
#include <sys/stat.h>
#include <fcntl.h>

int open (const char *path, int oflag, ... /* mode_t mode */);
```

DESCRIPTION
path points to a path name naming a file. **open** opens a file descriptor for the named file and sets the file status flags according to the value of *oflag*. *oflag* values are constructed by OR-ing Flags from the following list (only one of the first three flags below may be used):

O_RDONLY	Open for reading only.
O_WRONLY	Open for writing only.
O_RDWR	Open for reading and writing.
O_NDELAY or O_NONBLOCK	

These flags may affect subsequent reads and writes [see **read**(2) and **write**(2)]. If both O_NDELAY and O_NONBLOCK are set, O_NONBLOCK will take precedence.

When opening a FIFO with O_RDONLY or O_WRONLY set:

If O_NDELAY or O_NONBLOCK is set: An **open** for reading-only will return without delay; an **open** for writing-only will return an error if no process currently has the file open for reading.

If O_NDELAY and O_NONBLOCK are clear: An **open** for reading-only will block until a process opens the file for writing; an **open** for writing-only will block until a process opens the file for reading.

When opening a file associated with a terminal line:

If O_NDELAY or O_NONBLOCK is set: The **open** will return without waiting for the device to be ready or available; subsequent behavior of the device is device specific.

If O_NDELAY and O_NONBLOCK are clear: The **open** will block until the device is ready or available.

O_APPEND	If set, the file pointer will be set to the end of the file prior to each write.
O_SYNC	When opening a regular file, this flag affects subsequent writes. If set, each **write**(2) will wait for both the file data and file status to be physically updated.
O_NOCTTY	If set and the file is a terminal, the terminal will not be allocated as the calling process's controlling terminal.

O_CREAT If the file exists, this flag has no effect, except as noted under O_EXCL below. Otherwise, the file is created and the owner ID of the file is set to the effective user ID of the process, the group ID of the file is set to the effective group ID of the process, or if the S_ISGID bit is set in the directory in which the file is being created, the file's group ID is set to the group ID of its parent directory. If the group ID of the new file does not match the effective group ID or one of the supplementary groups IDs, the S_ISGID bit is cleared. The access permission bits of the file mode are set to the value of *mode*, modified as follows [see creat(2)]:

    All bits set in the file mode creation mask of the process are cleared [see umask(2)].

    The "save text image after execution bit" of the mode is cleared [see chmod(2)].

O_TRUNC If the file exists, its length is truncated to 0 and the mode and owner are unchanged. O_TRUNC has no effect on FIFO special files or directories.

O_EXCL If O_EXCL and O_CREAT are set, open will fail if the file exists. The check for the existence of the file and the creation of the file if it does not exist is atomic with respect to other processes executing open naming the same filename in the same directory with O_EXCL and O_CREAT set.

When opening a STREAMS file, *oflag* may be constructed from O_NDELAY or O_NONBLOCK OR-ed with either O_RDONLY, O_WRONLY , or O_RDWR. Other flag values are not applicable to STREAMS devices and have no effect on them. The values of O_NDELAY and O_NONBLOCK affect the operation of STREAMS drivers and certain system calls [see read(2), getmsg(2), putmsg(2), and write(2)]. For drivers, the implementation of O_NDELAY and O_NONBLOCK is device specific. Each STREAMS device driver may treat these options differently.

When open is invoked to open a named stream, and the connld module [see connld(7)] has been pushed on the pipe, open blocks until the server process has issued an I_RECVFD ioctl [see streamio(7)] to receive the file descriptor.

If *path* is a symbolic link and O_CREAT and O_EXCL are set, the link is not followed.

The file pointer used to mark the current position within the file is set to the beginning of the file.

The new file descriptor is the lowest numbered file descriptor available and is set to remain open across exec system calls [see fcntl(2)].

Certain flag values can be set following open as described in fcntl(2).

If O_CREAT is set and the file did not previously exist, upon successful completion open marks for update the st_atime, st_ctime and st_mtime fields of the file and the st_ctime and st_mtime fields of the parent directory.

open (2)

If O_TRUNC is set and the file did previously exist, upon successful completion open marks for update the st_ctime and st_mtime fields of the file.

The named file is opened unless one or more of the following are true:

EACCES	The file does not exist and write permission is denied by the parent directory of the file to be created.
EACCES	O_TRUNC is specified and write permission is denied
EACCES	A component of the path prefix denies search permission.
EACCES	*oflag* permission is denied for an existing file.
EAGAIN	The file exists, mandatory file/record locking is set, and there are outstanding record locks on the file [see chmod(2)].
EEXIST	O_CREAT and O_EXCL are set, and the named file exists.
EFAULT	*path* points outside the allocated address space of the process.
EINTR	A signal was caught during the open system call.
EIO	A hangup or error occurred during the open of the STREAMS-based device.
EISDIR	The named file is a directory and *oflag* is write or read/write.
ELOOP	Too many symbolic links were encountered in translating *path*.
EMFILE	The process has too many open files [see getrlimit(2)].
EMULTIHOP	Components of *path* require hopping to multiple remote machines and the file system does not allow it.
ENAMETOOLONG	The length of the *path* argument exceeds {PATH_MAX}, or the length of a *path* component exceeds {NAME_MAX} while {_POSIX_NO_TRUNC} is in effect.
ENFILE	The system file table is full.
ENOENT	O_CREAT is not set and the named file does not exist.
ENOENT	O_CREAT is set and a component of the path prefix does not exist or is the null pathname.
ENOLINK	*path* points to a remote machine, and the link to that machine is no longer active.
ENOMEM	The system is unable to allocate a send descriptor.
ENOSPC	O_CREAT and O_EXCL are set, and the file system is out of inodes.
ENOSPC	O_CREAT is set and the directory that would contain the file cannot be extended.

ENOSR	Unable to allocate a stream.
ENOTDIR	A component of the path prefix is not a directory.
ENXIO	The named file is a character special or block special file, and the device associated with this special file does not exist.
ENXIO	O_NDELAY or O_NONBLOCK is set, the named file is a FIFO, O_WRONLY is set, and no process has the file open for reading.
ENXIO	A STREAMS module or driver open routine failed.
EROFS	The named file resides on a read-only file system and either O_WRONLY, O_RDWR, O_CREAT, or O_TRUNC is set in *oflag* (if the file does not exist).
ETXTBSY	The file is a pure procedure (shared text) file that is being executed and *oflag* is write or read/write.

SEE ALSO
intro(2), chmod(2), close(2), creat(2), dup(2), exec(2), fcntl(2), getrlimit(2), lseek(2), read(2), getmsg(2), putmsg(2), stat(2), umask(2), write(2), stat(5).

DIAGNOSTICS
Upon successful completion, the file descriptor is returned. Otherwise, a value of −1 is returned and errno is set to indicate the error.

pause(2)

NAME
pause – suspend process until signal

SYNOPSIS
#include <unistd.h>

int pause(void);

DESCRIPTION
pause suspends the calling process until it receives a signal. The signal must be one that is not currently set to be ignored by the calling process.

If the signal causes termination of the calling process, pause does not return.

If the signal is caught by the calling process and control is returned from the signal-catching function [see signal(2)], the calling process resumes execution from the point of suspension; with a return value of −1 from pause and errno set to EINTR.

SEE ALSO
alarm(2), kill(2), signal(2), sigpause(2), wait(2).

NAME

pipe – create an interprocess channel

SYNOPSIS

#include <unistd.h>

int pipe(int fildes[2]);

DESCRIPTION

pipe creates an I/O mechanism called a pipe and returns two file descriptors, *fildes*[0] and *fildes*[1]. The files associated with *fildes*[0] and *fildes*[1] are streams and are both opened for reading and writing. The O_NDELAY and O_NONBLOCK flags are cleared.

A read from *fildes*[0] accesses the data written to *fildes*[1] on a first-in-first-out (FIFO) basis and a read from *fildes*[1] accesses the data written to *fildes*[0] also on a FIFO basis.

The FD_CLOEXEC flag will be clear on both file descriptors.

Upon successful completion pipe marks for update the st_atime, st_ctime, and st_mtime fields of the pipe.

pipe fails if:

EMFILE   If {OPEN_MAX}-1 or more file descriptors are currently open for this process.

ENFILE   A file table entry could not be allocated.

SEE ALSO

fcntl(2), getmsg(2), poll(2), putmsg(2), read(2), write(2), streamio(7).

sh(1) in the *User's Reference Manual*.

DIAGNOSTICS

Upon successful completion, a value of 0 is returned. Otherwise, a value of −1 is returned and errno is set to indicate the error.

NOTES

Since a pipe is bi-directional, there are two separate flows of data. Therefore, the size (st_size) returned by a call to fstat(2) with argument *fildes*[0] or *fildes*[1] is the number of bytes available for reading from *fildes*[0] or *fildes*[1] respectively. Previously, the size (st_size) returned by a call to fstat() with argument *fildes*[1] (the write-end) was the number of bytes available for reading from *fildes*[0] (the read-end).

plock(2)

NAME
plock – lock into memory or unlock process, text, or data

SYNOPSIS
    #include <sys/lock.h>

    int plock(int op);

DESCRIPTION
plock allows the calling process to lock into memory or unlock its text segment (text lock), its data segment (data lock), or both its text and data segments (process lock). Locked segments are immune to all routine swapping. The effective user ID of the calling process must be super-user to use this call. plock performs the function specified by *op*:

PROCLOCK	Lock text and data segments into memory (process lock).
TXTLOCK	Lock text segment into memory (text lock).
DATLOCK	Lock data segment into memory (data lock).
UNLOCK	Remove locks.

plock fails and does not perform the requested operation if one or more of the following are true:

EPERM	The effective user ID of the calling process is not super-user.
EINVAL	*op* is equal to PROCLOCK and a process lock, a text lock, or a data lock already exists on the calling process.
EINVAL	*op* is equal to TXTLOCK and a text lock, or a process lock already exists on the calling process.
EINVAL	*op* is equal to DATLOCK and a data lock, or a process lock already exists on the calling process.
EINVAL	*op* is equal to UNLOCK and no lock exists on the calling process.
EAGAIN	Not enough memory.

SEE ALSO
exec(2), exit(2), fork(2), memcntl(2).

DIAGNOSTICS
Upon successful completion, a value of 0 is returned to the calling process. Otherwise, a value of −1 is returned and errno is set to indicate the error.

NOTES
memcntl is the preferred interface to process locking.

NAME
poll – input/output multiplexing

SYNOPSIS
```
#include <stropts.h>
#include <poll.h>

int poll(struct poll *fds, size_t nfds, int timeout);
```

DESCRIPTION
poll provides users with a mechanism for multiplexing input/output over a set of file descriptors that reference open files. poll identifies those files on which a user can send or receive messages, or on which certain events have occurred.

fds specifies the file descriptors to be examined and the events of interest for each file descriptor. It is a pointer to an array with one element for each open file descriptor of interest. The array's elements are pollfd structures, which contain the following members:

```
int fd;           /* file descriptor */
short events;     /* requested events */
short revents;    /* returned events */
```

fd specifies an open file descriptor and events and revents are bitmasks constructed by an OR of any combination of the following event flags:

POLLIN	Data other than high priority data may be read without blocking. For STREAMS, this flag is set even if the message is of zero length.
POLLRDNORM	Normal data (priority band = 0) may be read without blocking. For STREAMS, this flag is set even if the message is of zero length.
POLLRDBAND	Data from a non-zero priority band may be read without blocking For STREAMS, this flag is set even if the message is of zero length.
POLLPRI	High priority data may be received without blocking. For STREAMS, this flag is set even if the message is of zero length.
POLLOUT	Normal data may be written without blocking.
POLLWRNORM	The same as POLLOUT.
POLLWRBAND	Priority data (priority band > 0) may be written. This event only examines bands that have been written to at least once.
POLLMSG	An M_SIG or M_PCSIG message containing the SIGPOLL signal has reached the front of the stream head read queue.
POLLERR	An error has occured on the device or stream. This flag is only valid in the revents bitmask; it is not used in the events field.
POLLHUP	A hangup has occurred on the stream. This event and POLLOUT are mutually exclusive; a stream can never be writable if a hangup has occurred. However, this event and POLLIN, POLLRDNORM, POLLRDBAND, or POLLPRI are not mutually

exclusive. This flag is only valid in the **revents** bitmask; it is not used in the **events** field.

POLLNVAL The specified **fd** value does not belong to an open file. This flag is only valid in the **revents** field; it is not used in the **events** field.

For each element of the array pointed to by *fds*, **poll** examines the given file descriptor for the event(s) specified in **events**. The number of file descriptors to be examined is specified by *nfds*.

If the value **fd** is less than zero, **events** is ignored and **revents** is set to 0 in that entry on return from **poll**.

The results of the **poll** query are stored in the **revents** field in the **pollfd** structure. Bits are set in the **revents** bitmask to indicate which of the requested events are true. If none are true, none of the specified bits are set in **revents** when the **poll** call returns. The event flags **POLLHUP**, **POLLERR**, and **POLLNVAL** are always set in **revents** if the conditions they indicate are true; this occurs even though these flags were not present in **events**.

If none of the defined events have occurred on any selected file descriptor, **poll** waits at least *timeout* milliseconds for an event to occur on any of the selected file descriptors. On a computer where millisecond timing accuracy is not available, *timeout* is rounded up to the nearest legal value available on that system. If the value *timeout* is 0, **poll** returns immediately. If the value of *timeout* is **INFTIM** (or −1), **poll** blocks until a requested event occurs or until the call is interrupted. **poll** is not affected by the O_NDELAY and O_NONBLOCK flags.

poll fails if one or more of the following are true:

EAGAIN Allocation of internal data structures failed, but the request may be attempted again.

EFAULT Some argument points outside the allocated address space.

EINTR A signal was caught during the **poll** system call.

EINVAL The argument *nfds* is greater than {OPEN_MAX}.

SEE ALSO
intro(2), getmsg(2), getrlimit(2), putmsg(2), read(2), write(2)
Programmer's Guide: STREAMS

DIAGNOSTICS
Upon successful completion, a non-negative value is returned. A positive value indicates the total number of file descriptors that has been selected (i.e., file descriptors for which the **revents** field is non-zero). A value of 0 indicates that the call timed out and no file descriptors have been selected. Upon failure, a value of −1 is returned and **errno** is set to indicate the error.

priocntl(2)

NAME
priocntl – process scheduler control

SYNOPSIS
```
#include <sys/types.h>
#include <sys/priocntl.h>
#include <sys/rtpriocntl.h>
#include <sys/tspriocntl.h>
```

long priocntl(idtype_t idtype, id_t id, int cmd, ... /* arg */);

DESCRIPTION
priocntl provides for control over the scheduling of active processes.

Processes fall into distinct classes with a separate scheduling policy applied to each class. The two classes currently supported are the real-time class and the time-sharing class. The characteristics of these classes are described under the corresponding headings below. The class attribute of a process is inherited across the fork and exec(2) system calls. priocntl can be used to dynamically change the class and other scheduling parameters associated with a running process or set of processes given the appropriate permissions as explained below.

In the default configuration, a runnable real-time process runs before any other process. Therefore, inappropriate use of real-time processes can have a dramatic negative impact on system performance.

priocntl provides a interface for specifying a process or set of processes to which the system call is to apply. The priocntlset system call provides the same functions as priocntl, but allows a more general interface for specifying the set of processes to which the system call is to apply.

For priocntl, the *idtype* and *id* arguments are used together to specify the set of processes. The interpretation of *id* depends on the value of *idtype*. The possible values for *idtype* and corresponding interpretations of *id* are as follows:

P_PID   *id* is a process ID specifying a single process to which the priocntl system call is to apply.

P_PPID   *id* is a parent process ID. The priocntl system call applies to all processes with the specified parent process ID.

P_PGID   *id* is a process group ID. The priocntl system call applies to all processes in the specified process group.

P_SID   *id* is a session ID. The priocntl system call applies to all processes in the specified session.

P_CID   *id* is a class ID (returned by priocntl PC_GETCID as explained below). The priocntl system call applies to all processes in the specified class.

P_UID   *id* is a user ID. The priocntl system call applies to all processes with this effective user ID.

P_GID   *id* is a group ID. The priocntl system call applies to all processes with this effective group ID.

P_ALL   The `priocntl` system call applies to all existing processes. The value of *id* is ignored. The permission restrictions described below still apply.

An *id* value of P_MYID can be used in conjunction with the *idtype* value to specify the calling process's process ID, parent process ID, process group ID, session ID, class ID, user ID, or group ID.

In order to change the scheduling parameters of a process (using the PC_SETPARMS command as explained below) the real or effective user ID of the process calling `priocntl` must match the real or effective user ID of the receiving process or the effective user ID of the calling process must be super-user. These are the minimum permission requirements enforced for all classes. An individual class may impose additional permissions requirements when setting processes to that class and/or when setting class-specific scheduling parameters.

A special **sys** scheduling class exists for the purpose of scheduling the execution of certain special system processes (such as the swapper process). It is not possible to change the class of any process to **sys**. In addition, any processes in the **sys** class that are included in a specified set of processes are disregarded by `priocntl`. For example, an *idtype* of P_UID and an *id* value of zero would specify all processes with a user ID of zero except processes in the **sys** class and (if changing the parameters using PC_SETPARMS) the init process.

The init process is a special case. In order for a `priocntl` call to change the class or other scheduling parameters of the init process (process ID 1), it must be the only process specified by *idtype* and *id*. The init process may be assigned to any class configured on the system, but the time-sharing class is almost always the appropriate choice. (Other choices may be highly undesirable; see the *System Administrator's Guide* for more information.)

The data type and value of *arg* are specific to the type of command specified by *cmd*.

The following structure is used by the PC_GETCID and PC_GETCLINFO commands.

```
typedef struct {
        id_t    pc_cid;                         /* Class id */
        char    pc_clname[PC_CLNMSZ];           /* Class name */
        long    pc_clinfo[PC_CLINFOSZ];         /* Class information */
} pcinfo_t;
```

pc_cid is a class ID returned by priocntl PC_GETCID. pc_clname is a buffer of size PC_CLNMSZ (defined in <sys/priocntl.h>) used to hold the class name (RT for real-time or TS for time-sharing).

pc_clinfo is a buffer of size PC_CLINFOSZ (defined in <sys/priocntl.h>) used to return data describing the attributes of a specific class. The format of this data is class-specific and is described under the appropriate heading (REAL-TIME CLASS or TIME-SHARING CLASS) below.

The following structure is used by the `PC_SETPARMS` and `PC_GETPARMS` commands.

```
typedef struct {
    id_t    pc_cid;                    /* Process class */
    long    pc_clparms[PC_CLPARMSZ];   /* Class-specific params */
} pcparms_t;
```

`pc_cid` is a class ID (returned by `priocntl PC_GETCID`). The special class ID `PC_CLNULL` can also be assigned to `pc_cid` when using the `PC_GETPARMS` command as explained below.

The `pc_clparms` buffer holds class-specific scheduling parameters. The format of this parameter data for a particular class is described under the appropriate heading below. `PC_CLPARMSZ` is the length of the `pc_clparms` buffer and is defined in `<sys/priocntl.h>`.

Commands

Available `priocntl` commands are:

PC_GETCID
Get class ID and class attributes for a specific class given class name. The *idtype* and *id* arguments are ignored. If *arg* is non-null, it points to a structure of type `pcinfo_t`. The `pc_clname` buffer contains the name of the class whose attributes you are getting.

On success, the class ID is returned in `pc_cid`, the class attributes are returned in the `pc_clinfo` buffer, and the `priocntl` call returns the total number of classes configured in the system (including the `sys` class). If the class specified by `pc_clname` is invalid or is not currently configured the `priocntl` call returns −1 with errno set to EINVAL. The format of the attribute data returned for a given class is defined in the `<sys/rtpriocntl.h>` or `<sys/tspriocntl.h>` header file and described under the appropriate heading below.

If *arg* is a NULL pointer, no attribute data is returned but the `priocntl` call still returns the number of configured classes.

PC_GETCLINFO
Get class name and class attributes for a specific class given class ID. The *idtype* and *id* arguments are ignored. If *arg* is non-null, it points to a structure of type `pcinfo_t`. `pc_cid` is the class ID of the class whose attributes you are getting.

On success, the class name is returned in the `pc_clname` buffer, the class attributes are returned in the `pc_clinfo` buffer, and the `priocntl` call returns the total number of classes configured in the system (including the `sys` class). The format of the attribute data returned for a given class is defined in the `<sys/rtpriocntl.h>` or `<sys/tspriocntl.h>` header file and described under the appropriate heading below.

If *arg* is a NULL pointer, no attribute data is returned but the `priocntl` call still returns the number of configured classes.

PC_SETPARMS
Set the class and class-specific scheduling parameters of the specified process(es). *arg* points to a structure of type `pcparms_t`. `pc_cid` specifies the class you are setting and the `pc_clparms` buffer contains the class-specific parameters you are setting. The format of the class-specific parameter data is defined in the `<sys/rtpriocntl.h>` or `<sys/tspriocntl.h>` header file and described under the appropriate class heading below.

When setting parameters for a set of processes, `priocntl` acts on the processes in the set in an implementation-specific order. If `priocntl` encounters an error for one or more of the target processes, it may or may not continue through the set of processes, depending on the nature of the error. If the error is related to permissions (**EPERM**), `priocntl` continues through the process set, resetting the parameters for all target processes for which the calling process has appropriate permissions. `priocntl` then returns −1 with `errno` set to **EPERM** to indicate that the operation failed for one or more of the target processes. If `priocntl` encounters an error other than permissions, it does not continue through the set of target processes but returns the error immediately.

PC_GETPARMS
Get the class and/or class-specific scheduling parameters of a process. *arg* points the a structure of type `pcparms_t`.

If `pc_cid` specifies a configured class and a single process belonging to that class is specified by the *idtype* and *id* values or the `procset` structure, then the scheduling parameters of that process are returned in the `pc_clparms` buffer. If the process specified does not exist or does not belong to the specified class, the `priocntl` call returns −1 with `errno` set to **ESRCH**.

If `pc_cid` specifies a configured class and a set of processes is specified, the scheduling parameters of one of the specified processes belonging to the specified class are returned in the `pc_clparms` buffer and the `priocntl` call returns the process ID of the selected process. The criteria for selecting a process to return in this case is class dependent. If none of the specified processes exist or none of them belong to the specified class the `priocntl` call returns −1 with `errno` set to **ESRCH**.

If `pc_cid` is **PC_CLNULL** and a single process is specified the class of the specified process is returned in `pc_cid` and its scheduling parameters are returned in the `pc_clparms` buffer.

PC_ADMIN
This command provides functionality needed for the implementation of the dispadmin(1M) command. It is not intended for general use by other applications.

REAL-TIME CLASS
The real-time class provides a fixed priority preemptive scheduling policy for those processes requiring fast and deterministic response and absolute user/application control of scheduling priorities. If the real-time class is

configured in the system it should have exclusive control of the highest range of scheduling priorities on the system. This ensures that a runnable real-time process is given CPU service before any process belonging to any other class.

The real-time class has a range of real-time priority (rt_pri) values that may be assigned to processes within the class. Real-time priorities range from 0 to x, where the value of x is configurable and can be determined for a specific installation by using the priocntl PC_GETCID or PC_GETCLINFO command.

The real-time scheduling policy is a fixed priority policy. The scheduling priority of a real-time process is never changed except as the result of an explicit request by the user/application to change the rt_pri value of the process.

For processes in the real-time class, the rt_pri value is, for all practical purposes, equivalent to the scheduling priority of the process. The rt_pri value completely determines the scheduling priority of a real-time process relative to other processes within its class. Numerically higher rt_pri values represent higher priorities. Since the real-time class controls the highest range of scheduling priorities in the system it is guaranteed that the runnable real-time process with the highest rt_pri value is always selected to run before any other process in the system.

In addition to providing control over priority, priocntl provides for control over the length of the time quantum allotted to processes in the real-time class. The time quantum value specifies the maximum amount of time a process may run assuming that it does not complete or enter a resource or event wait state (sleep). Note that if another process becomes runnable at a higher priority the currently running process may be preempted before receiving its full time quantum.

The system's process scheduler keeps the runnable real-time processes on a set of scheduling queues. There is a separate queue for each configured real-time priority and all real-time processes with a given rt_pri value are kept together on the appropriate queue. The processes on a given queue are ordered in FIFO order (that is, the process at the front of the queue has been waiting longest for service and receives the CPU first). Real-time processes that wake up after sleeping, processes which change to the real-time class from some other class, processes which have used their full time quantum, and runnable processes whose priority is reset by priocntl are all placed at the back of the appropriate queue for their priority. A process that is preempted by a higher priority process remains at the front of the queue (with whatever time is remaining in its time quantum) and runs before any other process at this priority. Following a fork(2) system call by a real-time process, the parent process continues to run while the child process (which inherits its parent's rt_pri value) is placed at the back of the queue.

The following structure (defined in <sys/rtpriocntl.h>) defines the format used for the attribute data for the real-time class.

```
typedef struct {
    short    rt_maxpri;    /* Maximum real-time priority */
} rtinfo_t;
```

The priocntl PC_GETCID and PC_GETCLINFO commands return real-time class attributes in the pc_clinfo buffer in this format.

rt_maxpri specifies the configured maximum rt_pri value for the real-time class (if rt_maxpri is x, the valid real-time priorities range from 0 to x).

The following structure (defined in <sys/rtpriocntl.h>) defines the format used to specify the real-time class-specific scheduling parameters of a process.

```
typedef struct {
    short    rt_pri;       /* Real-Time priority */
    ulong    rt_tqsecs;    /* Seconds in time quantum */
    long     rt_tqnsecs;   /* Additional nanoseconds in quantum */
} rtparms_t;
```

When using the priocntl PC_SETPARMS or PC_GETPARMS commands, if pc_cid specifies the real-time class, the data in the pc_clparms buffer is in this format.

The above commands can be used to set the real-time priority to the specified value or get the current rt_pri value. Setting the rt_pri value of a process that is currently running or runnable (not sleeping) causes the process to be placed at the back of the scheduling queue for the specified priority. The process is placed at the back of the appropriate queue regardless of whether the priority being set is different from the previous rt_pri value of the process. Note that a running process can voluntarily release the CPU and go to the back of the scheduling queue at the same priority by resetting its rt_pri value to its current real-time priority value. In order to change the time quantum of a process without setting the priority or affecting the process's position on the queue, the rt_pri field should be set to the special value RT_NOCHANGE (defined in <sys/rtpriocntl.h>). Specifying RT_NOCHANGE when changing the class of a process to real-time from some other class results in the real-time priority being set to zero.

For the priocntl PC_GETPARMS command, if pc_cid specifies the real-time class and more than one real-time process is specified, the scheduling parameters of the real-time process with the highest rt_pri value among the specified processes are returned and the process ID of this process is returned by the priocntl call. If there is more than one process sharing the highest priority, the one returned is implementation-dependent.

The rt_tqsecs and rt_tqnsecs fields are used for getting or setting the time quantum associated with a process or group of processes. rt_tqsecs is the number of seconds in the time quantum and rt_tqnsecs is the number of additional nanoseconds in the quantum. For example setting rt_tqsecs to 2 and rt_tqnsecs to 500,000,000 (decimal) would result in a time quantum of two and one-half seconds. Specifying a value of 1,000,000,000 or greater in the rt_tqnsecs field results in an error return with errno set to EINVAL. Although the resolution of the tq_nsecs field is very fine, the specified time quantum length is rounded up by the system to the next integral multiple of the system clock's resolution. For example, the finest resolution currently available on the 3B2 is 10 milliseconds (1 "tick"). Setting rt_tqsecs to 0 and rt_tqnsecs to 34,000,000 would specify a time quantum of 34 milliseconds, which would be rounded up to 4 ticks (40 milliseconds) on the 3B2. The maximum time quantum that can be specified is implementation-specific and equal to LONG_MAX ticks (defined in <limits.h>). Requesting a quantum greater than this maximum results in an error return with errno set to ERANGE (although infinite quantums may be requested using a special value as explained below). Requesting a time quantum of zero (setting both rt_tqsecs and rt_tqnsecs to 0) results in an error return with errno set to EINVAL.

The rt_tqnsecs field can also be set to one of the following special values (defined in <sys/rtpriocntl.h>), in which case the value of rt_tqsecs is ignored.

RT_TQINF	Set an infinite time quantum.
RT_TQDEF	Set the time quantum to the default for this priority [see rt_dptbl(4)].
RT_NOCHANGE	Don't set the time quantum. This value is useful when you wish to change the real-time priority of a process without affecting the time quantum. Specifying this value when changing the class of a process to real-time from some other class is equivalent to specifying RT_TQDEF.

In order to change the class of a process to real-time (from any other class) the process invoking priocntl must have super-user privileges. In order to change the priority or time quantum setting of a real-time process the process invoking priocntl must have super-user privileges or must itself be a real-time process whose real or effective user ID matches the real of effective user ID of the target process.

The real-time priority and time quantum are inherited across the fork(2) and exec(2) system calls.

TIME-SHARING CLASS

The time-sharing scheduling policy provides for a fair and effective allocation of the CPU resource among processes with varying CPU consumption characteristics. The objectives of the time-sharing policy are to provide good response time to interactive processes and good throughput to CPU-bound jobs while providing a degree of user/application control over scheduling.

The time-sharing class has a range of time-sharing user priority (see ts_upri below) values that may be assigned to processes within the class. A ts_upri value of zero is defined as the default base priority for the time-sharing class. User priorities range from $-x$ to $+x$ where the value of x is configurable and can be determined for a specific installation by using the priocntl PC_GETCID or PC_GETCLINFO command.

The purpose of the user priority is to provide some degree of user/application control over the scheduling of processes in the time-sharing class. Raising or lowering the `ts_upri` value of a process in the time-sharing class raises or lowers the scheduling priority of the process. It is not guaranteed, however, that a process with a higher `ts_upri` value will run before one with a lower `ts_upri` value. This is because the `ts_upri` value is just one factor used to determine the scheduling priority of a time-sharing process. The system may dynamically adjust the internal scheduling priority of a time-sharing process based on other factors such as recent CPU usage.

In addition to the system-wide limits on user priority (returned by the `PC_GETCID` and `PC_GETCLINFO` commands) there is a per process user priority limit (see `ts_uprilim` below), which specifies the maximum `ts_upri` value that may be set for a given process; by default, `ts_uprilim` is zero.

The following structure (defined in `<sys/tspriocntl.h>`) defines the format used for the attribute data for the time-sharing class.

```
typedef struct {
    short    ts_maxupri;    /* Limits of user priority range */
} tsinfo_t;
```

The `priocntl PC_GETCID` and `PC_GETCLINFO` commands return time-sharing class attributes in the `pc_clinfo` buffer in this format.

`ts_maxupri` specifies the configured maximum user priority value for the time-sharing class. If `ts_maxupri` is x, the valid range for both user priorities and user priority limits is from $-x$ to $+x$.

The following structure (defined in `<sys/tspriocntl.h>`) defines the format used to specify the time-sharing class-specific scheduling parameters of a process.

```
typedef struct {
    short    ts_uprilim;    /* Time-Sharing user priority limit */
    short    ts_upri;       /* Time-Sharing user priority */
} tsparms_t;
```

When using the `priocntl PC_SETPARMS` or `PC_GETPARMS` commands, if `pc_cid` specifies the time-sharing class, the data in the `pc_clparms` buffer is in this format.

For the `priocntl PC_GETPARMS` command, if `pc_cid` specifies the time-sharing class and more than one time-sharing process is specified, the scheduling parameters of the time-sharing process with the highest `ts_upri` value among the specified processes is returned and the process ID of this process is returned by the `priocntl` call. If there is more than one process sharing the highest user priority, the one returned is implementation-dependent.

Any time-sharing process may lower its own `ts_uprilim` (or that of another process with the same user ID). Only a time-sharing process with super-user privileges may raise a `ts_uprilim`. When changing the class of a process to time-sharing from some other class, super-user privileges are required in order to set the initial `ts_uprilim` to a value greater than zero. Attempts by a non-super-user process to raise a `ts_uprilim` or set an initial `ts_uprilim` greater than zero fail with a return value of −1 and `errno` set to `EPERM`.

Any time-sharing process may set its own `ts_upri` (or that of another process with the same user ID) to any value less than or equal to the process's `ts_uprilim`. Attempts to set the `ts_upri` above the `ts_uprilim` (and/or set the `ts_uprilim` below the `ts_upri`) result in the `ts_upri` being set equal to the `ts_uprilim`.

Either of the `ts_uprilim` or `ts_upri` fields may be set to the special value `TS_NOCHANGE` (defined in `<sys/tspriocntl.h>`) in order to set one of the values without affecting the other. Specifying `TS_NOCHANGE` for the `ts_upri` when the `ts_uprilim` is being set to a value below the current `ts_upri` causes the `ts_upri` to be set equal to the `ts_uprilim` being set. Specifying `TS_NOCHANGE` for a parameter when changing the class of a process to time-sharing (from some other class) causes the parameter to be set to a default value. The default value for the `ts_uprilim` is 0 and the default for the `ts_upri` is to set it equal to the `ts_uprilim` which is being set.

The time-sharing user priority and user priority limit are inherited across the `fork` and `exec` system calls.

RETURN VALUE

Unless otherwise noted above, `priocntl` returns a value of 0 on success. `priocntl` returns −1 on failure and sets `errno` to indicate the error.

ERRORS

`priocntl` fails if one or more of the following are true :

EPERM	The calling process does not have the required permissions as explained above.
EINVAL	The argument *cmd* was invalid, an invalid or unconfigured class was specified, or one of the parameters specified was invalid.
ERANGE	The requested time quantum is out of range.
ESRCH	None of the specified processes exist.
EFAULT	All or part of the area pointed to by one of the data pointers is outside the process's address space.
ENOMEM	An attempt to change the class of a process failed because of insufficient memory.
EAGAIN	An attempt to change the class of a process failed because of insufficient resources other than memory (for example, class-specific kernel data structures).

SEE ALSO

fork(2), exec(2), nice(2), priocntlset(2)

priocntl(1) in the *User's Reference Manual*

dispadmin(1M), rt_dptbl(4), ts_dptbl(4) in the *System Administrator's Reference Manual*

priocntlset(2)

NAME
priocntlset – generalized process scheduler control

SYNOPSIS
```
#include <sys/types.h>
#include <sys/procset.h>
#include <sys/priocntl.h>
#include <sys/rtpriocntl.h>
#include <sys/tspriocntl.h>

long priocntlset(procset_t *psp, int cmd, ... /* arg */);
```

DESCRIPTION
priocntlset changes the scheduling properties of running processes. priocntlset has the same functions as the priocntl system call, but a more general way of specifying the set of processes whose scheduling properties are to be changed.

cmd specifies the function to be performed. *arg* is a pointer to a structure whose type depends on *cmd*. See priocntl(2) for the valid values of *cmd* and the corresponding *arg* structures.

psp is a pointer to a procset structure, which priocntlset uses to specify the set of processes whose scheduling properties are to be changed.

```
typedef struct procset {
    idop_t    p_op;        /* operator connecting left/right sets */
    idtype_t  p_lidtype;   /* left set ID type */
    id_t      p_lid;       /* left set ID */
    idtype_t  p_ridtype;   /* right set ID type */
    id_t      p_rid;       /* right set ID */
} procset_t;
```

p_lidtype and p_lid specify the ID type and ID of one ("left") set of processes; p_ridtype and p_rid specify the ID type and ID of a second ("right") set of processes. ID types and IDs are specified just as for the priocntl system call. p_op specifies the operation to be performed on the two sets of processes to get the set of processes the system call is to apply to. The valid values for p_op and the processes they specify are:

POP_DIFF   set difference: processes in left set and not in right set

POP_AND   set intersection: processes in both left and right sets

POP_OR   set union: processes in either left or right sets or both

POP_XOR   set exclusive-or: processes in left or right set but not in both

The following macro, which is defined in procset.h, offers a convenient way to initialize a procset structure:

```
#define   setprocset(psp, op, ltype, lid, rtype, rid) \
    (psp)->p_op        = (op), \
    (psp)->p_lidtype   = (ltype), \
    (psp)->p_lid       = (lid), \
    (psp)->p_ridtype   = (rtype), \
    (psp)->p_rid       = (rid),
```

DIAGNOSTICS

priocntlset has the same return values and errors as priocntl.

SEE ALSO

priocntl(2)

priocntl(1) in the *User's Reference Manual*

profil(2)

NAME
profil – execution time profile

SYNOPSIS
#include <unistd.h>

void profil(unsigned short *buff, size_t bufsiz, int offset, unsigned scale);

DESCRIPTION
profil provides CPU-use statistics by profiling the amount of CPU time expended by a program. profil generates the statistics by creating an execution histogram for a current process. The histogram is defined for a specific region of program code to be profiled, and the identified region is logically broken up into a set of equal size subdivisions, each of which corresponds to a count in the histogram. With each clock tick, the current subdivision is identified and its corresponding histogram count is incremented. These counts establish a relative measure of how much time is being spent in each code subdivision. The resulting histogram counts for a profiled region can be used to identify those functions that consume a disproportionately high percentage of CPU time.

buff is a buffer of *bufsiz* bytes in which the histogram counts are stored in an array of unsigned short int.

offset, *scale*, and *bufsiz* specify the region to be profiled.

offset is effectively the start address of the region to be profiled.

scale, broadly speaking, is a contraction factor that indicates how much smaller the histogram buffer is than the region to be profiled. More precisely, *scale* is interpreted as an unsigned 16-bit fixed-point fraction with the decimal point implied on the left. Its value is the reciprocal of the number of bytes in a subdivision, per byte of histogram buffer. Since there are two bytes per histogram counter, the effective ratio of subdivision bytes per counter is one half the scale.

Several observations can be made:

- the maximal value of *scale*, 0xffff (approximately 1), maps subdivisions 2 bytes long to each counter.
- the minimum value of *scale* (for which profiling is performed), 0x0002 (1/32,768), maps subdivision 65,536 bytes long to each counter.
- the default value of *scale* (currently used by cc -qp), 0x4000, maps subdivisions 8 bytes long to each counter.

The values are used within the kernel as follows: when the process is interrupted for a clock tick, the value of *offset* is subtracted from the current value of the program counter (pc), and the remainder is multiplied by *scale* to derive a result. That result is used as an index into the histogram array to locate the cell to be incremented. Therefore, the cell count represents the number of times that the process was executing code in the subdivision associated with that cell when the process was interrupted.

scale can be computed as (*RATIO* * 0200000L), where *RATIO* is the desired ratio of *bufsiz* to profiled region size, and has a value between 0 and 1. Qualitatively speaking, the closer *RATIO* is to 1, the higher the resolution of the profile information.

bufsiz can be computed as (*size_of_region_to_be_profiled* * *RATIO*).

SEE ALSO
prof(1), times(2), monitor(3C).

NOTES
Profiling is turned off by giving a *scale* of 0 or 1, and is rendered ineffective by giving a *bufsiz* of 0. Profiling is turned off when an exec(2) is executed, but remains on in both child and parent processes after a fork(2). Profiling is turned off if a *buff* update would cause a memory fault.

ptrace(2)

NAME
ptrace – process trace

SYNOPSIS
```
#include <unistd.h>
#include <sys/types.h>

int ptrace(int request, pid_t pid, int addr, int data);
```

DESCRIPTION

ptrace allows a parent process to control the execution of a child process. Its primary use is for the implementation of breakpoint debugging [see **sdb**(1)]. The child process behaves normally until it encounters a signal [see **signal**(5)], at which time it enters a stopped state and its parent is notified via the **wait**(2) system call. When the child is in the stopped state, its parent can examine and modify its "core image" using **ptrace**. Also, the parent can cause the child either to terminate or continue, with the possibility of ignoring the signal that caused it to stop.

The *request* argument determines the action to be taken by **ptrace** and is one of the following:

0   This request must be issued by the child process if it is to be traced by its parent. It turns on the child's trace flag that stipulates that the child should be left in a stopped state on receipt of a signal rather than the state specified by *func* [see **signal**(2)]. The *pid*, *addr*, and *data* arguments are ignored, and a return value is not defined for this request. Peculiar results ensue if the parent does not expect to trace the child.

The remainder of the requests can only be used by the parent process. For each, *pid* is the process ID of the child. The child must be in a stopped state before these requests are made.

1, 2   With these requests, the word at location *addr* in the address space of the child is returned to the parent process. If instruction and data space are separated, request 1 returns a word from instruction space, and request 2 returns a word from data space. If instruction and data space are not separated, either request 1 or request 2 may be used with equal results. The *data* argument is ignored. These two requests fail if *addr* is not the start address of a word, in which case a value of −1 is returned to the parent process and the parent's **errno** is set to EIO.

3   With this request, the word at location *addr* in the child's user area in the system's address space [see **<sys/user.h>**] is returned to the parent process. The *data* argument is ignored. This request fails if *addr* is not the start address of a word or is outside the user area, in which case a value of −1 is returned to the parent process and the parent's **errno** is set to EIO.

4, 5   With these requests, the value given by the *data* argument is written into the address space of the child at location *addr*. If instruction and data space are separated, request 4 writes a word into instruction space, and request 5 writes a word into data space. If instruction and data space are not separated, either request 4 or request 5 may be used with equal results. On success, the value written into the address space of the child is returned to the parent. These two requests fail if *addr* is not the start address of a word. On failure a value of −1 is returned to the parent process and the parent's **errno** is set to EIO.

6   With this request, a few entries in the child's user area can be written. *data* gives the value that is to be written and *addr* is the location of the entry. The few entries that can be written are the general registers and the condition codes of the Processor Status Word.

7   This request causes the child to resume execution. If the *data* argument is 0, all pending signals including the one that caused the child to stop are canceled before it resumes execution. If the *data* argument is a valid signal number, the child resumes execution as if it had incurred that signal, and any other pending signals are canceled. The *addr* argument must be equal to 1 for this request. On success, the value of *data* is returned to the parent. This request fails if *data* is not 0 or a valid signal number, in which case a value of −1 is returned to the parent process and the parent's **errno** is set to EIO.

8   This request causes the child to terminate with the same consequences as exit(2).

9   This request sets the trace bit in the Processor Status Word of the child and then executes the same steps as listed above for request 7. The trace bit causes an interrupt on completion of one machine instruction. This effectively allows single stepping of the child.

To forestall possible fraud, **ptrace** inhibits the set-user-ID facility on subsequent exec(2) calls. If a traced process calls **exec**(2), it stops before executing the first instruction of the new image showing signal SIGTRAP. **ptrace** in general fails if one or more of the following are true:

EIO   *request* is an illegal number.

ESRCH   *pid* identifies a child that does not exist or has not executed a **ptrace** with request 0.

EPERM   the involking subject does not have the appropriate MAC privilages.

SEE ALSO
sdb(1), exec(2), signal(2), wait(2).

putmsg(2)

NAME
putmsg – send a message on a stream

SYNOPSIS
#include <stropts.h>

    int putmsg(int fd, const struct strbuf *ctlptr,
            const struct strbuf *dataptr, int flags);

    int putpmsg(int fd, const struct strbuf *ctlptr,
            const struct strbuf *dataptr, int band, int flags);

DESCRIPTION
putmsg creates a message from user-specified buffer(s) and sends the message to a STREAMS file. The message may contain either a data part, a control part, or both. The data and control parts to be sent are distinguished by placement in separate buffers, as described below. The semantics of each part is defined by the STREAMS module that receives the message.

The function putpmsg does the same thing as putmsg, but provides the user the ability to send messages in different priority bands. Except where noted, all information pertaining to putmsg also pertains to putpmsg.

fd specifies a file descriptor referencing an open stream. *ctlptr* and *dataptr* each point to a strbuf structure, which contains the following members:

    int maxlen;   /* not used */
    int len;   /* length of data */
    void *buf;   /* ptr to buffer */

ctlptr points to the structure describing the control part, if any, to be included in the message. The buf field in the strbuf structure points to the buffer where the control information resides, and the len field indicates the number of bytes to be sent. The maxlen field is not used in putmsg [see getmsg(2)]. In a similar manner, *dataptr* specifies the data, if any, to be included in the message. *flags* indicates what type of message should be sent and is described later.

To send the data part of a message, *dataptr* must not be NULL and the len field of *dataptr* must have a value of 0 or greater. To send the control part of a message, the corresponding values must be set for *ctlptr*. No data (control) part is sent if either *dataptr* (*ctlptr*) is NULL or the len field of *dataptr* (*ctlptr*) is set to −1.

For putmsg(), if a control part is specified, and *flags* is set to RS_HIPRI, a high priority message is sent. If no control part is specified, and *flags* is set to RS_HIPRI, putmsg fails and sets errno to EINVAL. If *flags* is set to 0, a normal (non-priority) message is sent. If no control part and no data part are specified, and *flags* is set to 0, no message is sent, and 0 is returned.

The stream head guarantees that the control part of a message generated by putmsg is at least 64 bytes in length.

For putpmsg, the flags are different. *flags* is a bitmask with the following mutually-exclusive flags defined: MSG_HIPRI and MSG_BAND. If *flags* is set to 0, putpmsg fails and sets errno to EINVAL. If a control part is specified and *flags* is set to MSG_HIPRI and *band* is set to 0, a high-priority message is sent. If *flags* is set to MSG_HIPRI and either no control part is specified or *band* is set to a non-zero value, putpmsg() fails and sets errno to EINVAL. If flags is set to MSG_BAND, then a message is sent in the priority band specified by *band*. If a control part and data part are not specified and *flags* is set to MSG_BAND, no message is sent and 0 is returned.

Normally, putmsg() will block if the stream write queue is full due to internal flow control conditions. For high-priority messages, putmsg() does not block on this condition. For other messages, putmsg() does not block when the write queue is full and O_NDELAY or O_NONBLOCK is set. Instead, it fails and sets errno to EAGAIN.

putmsg or putpmsg also blocks, unless prevented by lack of internal resources, waiting for the availability of message blocks in the stream, regardless of priority or whether O_NDELAY or O_NONBLOCK has been specified. No partial message is sent.

putmsg fails if one or more of the following are true:

EAGAIN	A non-priority message was specified, the O_NDELAY or O_NONBLOCK flag is set and the stream write queue is full due to internal flow control conditions.
EBADF	*fd* is not a valid file descriptor open for writing.
EFAULT	*ctlptr* or *dataptr* points outside the allocated address space.
EINTR	A signal was caught during the putmsg system call.
EINVAL	An undefined value was specified in *flags*, or *flags* is set to RS_HIPRI and no control part was supplied.
EINVAL	The stream referenced by *fd* is linked below a multiplexor.
EINVAL	For putpmsg, if *flags* is set to MSG_HIPRI and *band* is nonzero.
ENOSR	Buffers could not be allocated for the message that was to be created due to insufficient STREAMS memory resources.
ENOSTR	A stream is not associated with *fd*.
ENXIO	A hangup condition was generated downstream for the specified stream, or the other end of the pipe is closed.
ERANGE	The size of the data part of the message does not fall within the range specified by the maximum and minimum packet sizes of the topmost stream module. This value is also returned if the control part of the message is larger than the maximum configured size of the control part of a message, or if the data part of a message is larger than the maximum configured size of the data part of a message.

putmsg also fails if a STREAMS error message had been processed by the stream head before the call to putmsg. The error returned is the value contained in the STREAMS error message.

SEE ALSO

getmsg(2), intro(2), poll(2), putmsg(2), read(2), write(2).

Programmer's Guide: STREAMS.

DIAGNOSTICS

Upon successful completion, a value of 0 is returned. Otherwise, a value of −1 is returned and `errno` is set to indicate the error.

read(2)

NAME
read – read from file

SYNOPSIS
`#include <sys/types.h>`
`#include <sys/uio.h>`
`#include <unistd.h>`

`int read(int fildes, void *buf, unsigned nbyte);`

`int readv(int fildes, struct iovec *iov, int iovcnt);`

DESCRIPTION
read attempts to read *nbyte* bytes from the file associated with *fildes* into the buffer pointed to by *buf*. If *nbyte* is zero, **read** returns zero and has no other results. *fildes* is a file descriptor obtained from a **creat**, **open**, **dup**, **fcntl**, or **pipe** system call.

On devices capable of seeking, the **read** starts at a position in the file given by the file pointer associated with *fildes*. On return from **read**, the file pointer is incremented by the number of bytes actually read.

Devices that are incapable of seeking always read from the current position. The value of a file pointer associated with such a file is undefined.

readv performs the same action as **read**, but places the input data into the *iovcnt* buffers specified by the members of the *iov* array: *iov*[0], *iov*[1], ..., *iov*[*iovcnt*−1].

For **readv**, the **iovec** structure contains the following members:

```
addr_t   iov_base;
size_t   iov_len;
```

Each **iovec** entry specifies the base address and length of an area in memory where data should be placed. **readv** always fills one buffer completely before proceeding to the next.

On success, **read** and **readv** return the number of bytes actually read and placed in the buffer; this number may be less than *nbyte* if the file is associated with a communication line [see **ioctl**(2) and **termio**(7)], or if the number of bytes left in the file is less than *nbyte*, or if the file is a pipe or a special file. A value of 0 is returned when an end-of-file has been reached.

read reads data previously written to a file. If any portion of an ordinary file prior to the end of file has not been written, **read** returns the number of bytes read as 0. For example, the **lseek** routine allows the file pointer to be set beyond the end of existing data in the file. If additional data is written at this point, subsequent reads in the gap between the previous end of data and newly written data return bytes with a value of 0 until data is written into the gap.

A **read** or **readv** from a STREAMS [see **intro**(2)] file can operate in three different modes: byte-stream mode, message-nondiscard mode, and message-discard mode. The default is byte-stream mode. This can be changed using the **I_SRDOPT** **ioctl**(2) request [see **streamio**(7)], and can be tested with the **I_GRDOPT** **ioctl**(2) request. In byte-stream mode, **read** and **readv** usually retrieve data from the stream until they have retrieved *nbyte* bytes, or until there is no more data to be retrieved. Byte-stream mode usually ignores message boundaries.

In STREAMS message-nondiscard mode, **read** and **readv** retrieve data until they have read *nbyte* bytes, or until they reach a message boundary. If **read** or **readv** does not retrieve all the data in a message, the remaining data is replaced on the stream and can be retrieved by the next **read** or **readv** call. Message-discard mode also retrieves data until it has retrieved *nbyte* bytes, or it reaches a message boundary. However, unread data remaining in a message after the **read** or **readv** returns is discarded, and is not available for a subsequent **read**, **readv**, or **getmsg** [see **getmsg**(2)].

When attempting to read from a regular file with mandatory file/record locking set [see **chmod**(2)], and there is a write lock owned by another process on the segment of the file to be read:

> If O_NDELAY or O_NONBLOCK is set, **read** returns −1 and sets **errno** to EAGAIN.

> If O_NDELAY and O_NONBLOCK are clear, **read** sleeps until the blocking record lock is removed.

When attempting to read from an empty pipe (or FIFO):

> If no process has the pipe open for writing, **read** returns 0 to indicate end-of-file.

> If some process has the pipe open for writing and O_NDELAY is set, **read** returns 0.

> If some process has the pipe open for writing and O_NONBLOCK is set, **read** returns −1 and sets **errno** to EAGAIN.

> If O_NDELAY and O_NONBLOCK are clear, **read** blocks until data is written to the pipe or the pipe is closed by all processes that had opened the pipe for writing.

When attempting to read a file associated with a terminal that has no data currently available:

> If O_NDELAY is set, **read** returns 0.

> If O_NONBLOCK is set, **read** returns −1 and sets **errno** to EAGAIN.

> If O_NDELAY and O_NONBLOCK are clear, **read** blocks until data becomes available.

When attempting to read a file associated with a stream that is not a pipe or FIFO, or terminal, and that has no data currently available:

> If O_NDELAY or O_NONBLOCK is set, **read** returns −1 and sets **errno** to EAGAIN.

> If O_NDELAY and O_NONBLOCK are clear, **read** blocks until data becomes available.

When reading from a STREAMS file, handling of zero-byte messages is determined by the current read mode setting. In byte-stream mode, **read** accepts data until it has read *nbyte* bytes, or until there is no more data to read, or until a zero-byte message block is encountered. **read** then returns the number of bytes read, and places the zero-byte message back on the stream to be retrieved by the next **read** or **getmsg** [see **getmsg**(2)]. In the two other modes, a zero-byte message returns a value of 0 and the message is removed from the stream. When a zero-byte message is read as the first message on a stream, a value of 0 is returned regardless of the **read** mode.

A **read** or **readv** from a STREAMS file returns the data in the message at the front of the stream head read queue, regardless of the priority band of the message.

Normally, a **read** from a STREAMS file can only process messages with data and without control information. The **read** fails if a message containing control information is encountered at the stream head. This default action can be changed by placing the stream in either control-data mode or control-discard mode with the I_SRDOPT **ioctl**(2). In control-data mode, control messages are converted to data messages by **read**. In control-discard mode, control messages are discarded by **read**, but any data associated with the control messages is returned to the user.

read and **readv** fail if one or more of the following are true:

EAGAIN	Mandatory file/record locking was set, O_NDELAY or O_NONBLOCK was set, and there was a blocking record lock.
EAGAIN	Total amount of system memory available when reading via raw I/O is temporarily insufficient.
EAGAIN	No data is waiting to be read on a file associated with a tty device and O_NONBLOCK was set.
EAGAIN	No message is waiting to be read on a stream and O_NDELAY or O_NONBLOCK was set.
EBADF	*fildes* is not a valid file descriptor open for reading.
EBADMSG	Message waiting to be read on a stream is not a data message.
EDEADLK	The **read** was going to go to sleep and cause a deadlock to occur.
EFAULT	*buf* points outside the allocated address space.
EINTR	A signal was caught during the **read** or **readv** system call.
EINVAL	Attempted to read from a stream linked to a multiplexor.
EIO	A physical I/O error has occurred, or the process is in a background process group and is attempting to read from its controlling terminal, and either the process is ignoring or blocking the SIGTTIN signal or the process group of the process is orphaned.
ENOLCK	The system record lock table was full, so the **read** or **readv** could not go to sleep until the blocking record lock was removed.

read(2)

ENOLINK *fildes* is on a remote machine and the link to that machine is no longer active.

ENXIO The device associated with *fildes* is a block special or character special file and the value of the file pointer is out of range.

In addition, `readv` may return one of the following errors:

EFAULT *iov* points outside the allocated address space.

EINVAL *iovcnt* was less than or equal to 0 or greater than 16.

EINVAL The sum of the `iov_len` values in the *iov* array overflowed a 32-bit integer.

A `read` from a STREAMS file also fails if an error message is received at the stream head. In this case, `errno` is set to the value returned in the error message. If a hangup occurs on the stream being read, `read` continues to operate normally until the stream head read queue is empty. Thereafter, it returns 0.

SEE ALSO

intro(2), creat(2), dup(2), fcntl(2), getmsg(2), ioctl(2), open(2), pipe(2)

streamio(7), termio(7) in the *System Administrator's Reference Manual*

DIAGNOSTICS

On success a non-negative integer is returned indicating the number of bytes actually read. Otherwise, a −1 is returned and `errno` is set to indicate the error.

readlink(2)

NAME
readlink – read the value of a symbolic link

SYNOPSIS
    #include <unistd.h>

    int readlink(const char *path, void *buf, size_t bufsiz);

DESCRIPTION
readlink places the contents of the symbolic link referred to by *path* in the buffer *buf*, which has size *bufsiz*. The contents of the link are not null-terminated when returned.

readlink fails and the buffer remains unchanged if:

EACCES	Search permission is denied for a component of the path prefix of *path*.
EFAULT	*path* or *buf* extends outside the allocated address space of the process.
EINVAL	The named file is not a symbolic link.
EIO	An I/O error occurs while reading from or writing to the file system.
ELOOP	Too many symbolic links are encountered in translating *path*.
ENAMETOOLONG	The length of the *path* argument exceeds {PATH_MAX}, or the length of a *path* component exceeds {NAME_MAX} while _POSIX_NO_TRUNC is in effect.
ENOENT	The named file does not exist.
ENOSYS	The file system does not support symbolic links.

DIAGNOSTICS
Upon successful completion **readlink** returns the number of characters placed in the buffer; otherwise, it returns −1 and places an error code in **errno**.

SEE ALSO
lstat(2), stat(2), symlink(2)

rename(2)

NAME
rename – change the name of a file

SYNOPSIS
#include <stdio.h>

int rename(const char *old, const char *new);

DESCRIPTION
rename renames a file. *old* is a pointer to the pathname of the file or directory to be renamed. *new* is a pointer to the new pathname of the file or directory. Both *old* and *new* must be of the same type (either both files, or both directories) and must reside on the same file system.

If *new* already exists, it is removed. Thus, if *new* names an existing directory, the directory must not have any entries other than, possibly, "." and "..". When renaming directories, the *new* pathname must not name a descendant of *old*. The implementation of **rename** ensures that upon successful completion a link named *new* will always exist.

If the final component of *old* is a symbolic link, the symbolic link is renamed, not the file or directory to which it points.

Write permission is required for both the directory containing *old* and the directory containing *new*.

rename fails, *old* is not changed, and no *new* file is created if one or more of the following are true:

EACCES	A component of either path prefix denies search permission; one of the directories containing *old* or *new* denies write permission; or one of the directories pointed to by *old* or *new* denies write permission.
EBUSY	*new* is a directory and the mount point for a mounted file system.
EDQUOT	The directory in which the entry for the new name is being placed cannot be extended because the user's quota of disk blocks on the file system containing the directory has been exhausted.
EEXIST	The link named by *new* is a directory containing entries other than "." and "..".
EFAULT	*old* or *new* points outside the process's allocated address space.
EINVAL	*old* is a parent directory of *new*, or an attempt is made to rename "." or "..".
EINTR	A signal was caught during execution of the **rename** system call.
EIO	An I/O error occurred while making or updating a directory entry.

EISDIR	*new* points to a directory but *old* points to a file that is not a directory.
ELOOP	Too many symbolic links were encountered in translating *old* or *new*.
EMULTIHOP	Components of pathnames require hopping to multiple remote machines and the file system type does not allow it.
ENAMETOOLONG	The length of the *old* or *new* argument exceeds {PATH_MAX}, or the length of a *old* or *new* component exceeds {NAME_MAX} while _POSIX_NO_TRUNC is in effect.
ENOENT	A component of either *old* or *new* does not exist, or the file referred to by either *old* or *new* does not exist.
ENOLINK	Pathnames point to a remote machine and the link to that machine is no longer active.
ENOSPC	The directory that would contain *new* is out of space.
ENOTDIR	A component of either path prefix is not a directory; or the *old* parameter names a directory and the *new* parameter names a file.
EROFS	The requested operation requires writing in a directory on a read-only file system.
EXDEV	The links named by *old* and *new* are on different file systems.

DIAGNOSTICS

Upon successful completion, a value of 0 is returned. Otherwise, a value of −1 is returned and `errno` is set to indicate the error.

NOTES

The system can deadlock if there is a loop in the file system graph. Such a loop takes the form of an entry in directory *a*, say *a/foo*, being a hard link to directory *b*, and an entry in directory *b*, say *b/bar*, being a hard link to directory *a*. When such a loop exists and two separate processes attempt to perform `rename` *a/foo b/bar* and `rename` *b/bar a/foo*, respectively, the system may deadlock attempting to lock both directories for modification. The system administrator should replace hard links to directories by symbolic links.

SEE ALSO

link(2), unlink(2)

rmdir(2)

NAME
rmdir – remove a directory

SYNOPSIS
#include <unistd.h>

int rmdir(const char *path);

DESCRIPTION
rmdir removes the directory named by the path name pointed to by *path*. The directory must not have any entries other than "." and "..".

If the directory's link count becomes zero and no process has the directory open, the space occupied by the directory is freed and the directory is no longer accessible. If one or more processes have the directory open when the last link is removed, the "." and ".." entries, if present, are removed before rmdir returns and no new entries may be created in the directory, but the directory is not removed until all references to the directory have been closed.

If *path* is a symbolic link, it is not followed.

Upon successful completion rmdir marks for update the st_ctime and st_mtime fields of the parent directory.

The named directory is removed unless one or more of the following are true:

EACCES	Search permission is denied for a component of the path prefix.
EACCES	Write permission is denied on the directory containing the directory to be removed.
EACCES	The parent directory has the sticky bit set and is not owned by the user; the directory is not owned by the user and is not writable by the user; the user is not a super-user.
EBUSY	The directory to be removed is the mount point for a mounted file system.
EEXIST	The directory contains entries other than those for "." and "..".
EFAULT	*path* points outside the process's allocated address space.
EINVAL	The directory to be removed is the current directory.
EINVAL	The directory to be removed is the "." entry of a directory.
EIO	An I/O error occurred while accessing the file system.
ELOOP	Too many symbolic links were encountered in translating *path*.
EMULTIHOP	Components of *path* require hopping to multiple remote machines and the file system does not allow it.
ENAMETOOLONG	The length of the *path* argument exceeds {PATH_MAX}, or the length of a *path* component exceeds {NAME_MAX} while _POSIX_NO_TRUNC is in effect.

ENOTDIR	A component of the path prefix is not a directory.
ENOENT	The named directory does not exist or is the null pathname.
EROFS	The directory entry to be removed is part of a read-only file system.
ENOLINK	*path* points to a remote machine, and the link to that machine is no longer active.

DIAGNOSTICS

Upon successful completion, a value of 0 is returned. Otherwise, a value of −1 is returned and errno is set to indicate the error.

SEE ALSO

mkdir(2).

rmdir(1), rm(1), and mkdir(1) in the *User's Reference Manual*.

semctl(2)

NAME
semctl - semaphore control operations

SYNOPSIS
```
#include <sys/types.h>
#include <sys/ipc.h>
#include <sys/sem.h>

union semun {
    int val;
    struct semid_ds *buf;
    ushort *array;
};

int semctl(int semid, int semnum, int cmd, ... /* union semun arg */);
```

DESCRIPTION
semctl provides a variety of semaphore control operations as specified by *cmd*.

The following *cmd*s are executed with respect to the semaphore specified by *semid* and *semnum*:

- **GETVAL**   Return the value of semval [see intro(2)]. {READ}
- **SETVAL**   Set the value of semval to *arg*.val. {ALTER}. When this command is successfully executed, the semadj value corresponding to the specified semaphore in all processes is cleared.
- **GETPID**   Return the value of (int) sempid. {READ}
- **GETNCNT**   Return the value of semncnt. {READ}
- **GETZCNT**   Return the value of semzcnt. {READ}

The following *cmd*s return and set, respectively, every semval in the set of semaphores.

- **GETALL**   Place semvals into array pointed to by *arg*.array. {READ}
- **SETALL**   Set semvals according to the array pointed to by *arg*.array. {ALTER}. When this cmd is successfully executed, the semadj values corresponding to each specified semaphore in all processes are cleared.

The following *cmd*s are also available:

- **IPC_STAT** Place the current value of each member of the data structure associated with *semid* into the structure pointed to by *arg*.buf. The contents of this structure are defined in intro(2). {READ}
- **IPC_SET**   Set the value of the following members of the data structure associated with *semid* to the corresponding value found in the structure pointed to by *arg*.buf:

    sem_perm.uid
    sem_perm.gid
    sem_perm.mode /* only access permission bits */

semctl(2)

This command can be executed only by a process that has an effective user ID equal to either that of super-user, or to the value of sem_perm.cuid or sem_perm.uid in the data structure associated with *semid*.

IPC_RMID   Remove the semaphore identifier specified by *semid* from the system and destroy the set of semaphores and data structure associated with it. This command only be executed only by a process that has an effective user ID equal to either that of super-user, or to the value of sem_perm.cuid or sem_perm.uid in the data structure associated with *semid*.

semctl fails if one or more of the following are true:

EACCES   Operation permission is denied to the calling process [see intro(2)].

EINVAL   *semid* is not a valid semaphore identifier.

EINVAL   *semnum* is less than 0 or greater than sem_nsems.

EINVAL   *cmd* is not a valid command.

EINVAL   *cmd* is IPC_SET and sem_perm.uid or sem_perm.gid is not valid.

EOVERFLOW   *cmd* is IPC_STAT and *uid* or *gid* is too large to be stored in the structure pointed to by *arg.buf*.

ERANGE   *cmd* is SETVAL or SETALL and the value to which semval is to be set is greater than the system imposed maximum.

EPERM   *cmd* is equal to IPC_RMID or IPC_SET and the effective user ID of the calling process is not equal to that of super-user, or to the value of sem_perm.cuid or sem_perm.uid in the data structure associated with *semid*.

EFAULT   *arg*.buf points to an illegal address.

SEE ALSO
intro(2), semget(2), semop(2).

DIAGNOSTICS
Upon successful completion, the value returned depends on *cmd* as follows:

GETVAL	the value of semval
GETPID	the value of (int) sempid
GETNCNT	the value of semncnt
GETZCNT	the value of semzcnt
all others	a value of 0

Otherwise, a value of −1 is returned and errno is set to indicate the error.

semget(2)

NAME
semget – get set of semaphores

SYNOPSIS
```
#include <sys/types.h>
#include <sys/ipc.h>
#include <sys/sem.h>

int semget(key_t key, int nsems, int semflg);
```

DESCRIPTION
semget returns the semaphore identifier associated with *key*.

A semaphore identifier and associated data structure and set containing *nsems* semaphores [see intro(2)] are created for *key* if one of the following is true:

    key is equal to IPC_PRIVATE.

    key does not already have a semaphore identifier associated with it, and (*semflg*&IPC_CREAT) is true.

On creation, the data structure associated with the new semaphore identifier is initialized as follows:

    sem_perm.cuid, sem_perm.uid, sem_perm.cgid, and sem_perm.gid are set equal to the effective user ID and effective group ID, respectively, of the calling process.

    The access permission bits of sem_perm.mode are set equal to the access permission bits of *semflg*.

    sem_nsems is set equal to the value of *nsems*.

    sem_otime is set equal to 0 and sem_ctime is set equal to the current time.

semget fails if one or more of the following are true:

EINVAL	*nsems* is either less than or equal to zero or greater than the system-imposed limit.
EACCES	A semaphore identifier exists for *key*, but operation permission [see intro(2)] as specified by the low-order 9 bits of *semflg* would not be granted.
EINVAL	A semaphore identifier exists for *key*, but the number of semaphores in the set associated with it is less than *nsems*, and *nsems* is not equal to zero.
ENOENT	A semaphore identifier does not exist for *key* and (*semflg*&IPC_CREAT) is false.
ENOSPC	A semaphore identifier is to be created but the system-imposed limit on the maximum number of allowed semaphore identifiers system wide would be exceeded.
ENOSPC	A semaphore identifier is to be created but the system-imposed limit on the maximum number of allowed semaphores system wide would be exceeded.

semget(2) semget(2)

    EEXIST   A semaphore identifier exists for *key* but both (*semflg*&IPC_CREAT) and (*semflg*&IPC_EXCL) are both true.

SEE ALSO
intro(2), semctl(2), semop(2), stdipc(3C).

DIAGNOSTICS
Upon successful completion, a non-negative integer, namely a semaphore identifier, is returned. Otherwise, a value of −1 is returned and **errno** is set to indicate the error.

NAME

semop – semaphore operations

SYNOPSIS

```
#include <sys/types.h>
#include <sys/ipc.h>
#include <sys/sem.h>

int semop(int semid, struct sembuf *sops, size_t nsops);
```

DESCRIPTION

semop is used to perform atomically an array of semaphore operations on the set of semaphores associated with the semaphore identifier specified by *semid*. *sops* is a pointer to the array of semaphore-operation structures. *nsops* is the number of such structures in the array. The contents of each structure includes the following members:

```
short   sem_num;    /* semaphore number */
short   sem_op;     /* semaphore operation */
short   sem_flg;    /* operation flags */
```

Each semaphore operation specified by *sem_op* is performed on the corresponding semaphore specified by *semid* and *sem_num*.

sem_op specifies one of three semaphore operations as follows, depending on whether its value is negative, positive, or zero:

If *sem_op* is a negative integer, one of the following occurs: {ALTER}

> If **semval** [see intro(2)] is greater than or equal to the absolute value of *sem_op*, the absolute value of *sem_op* is subtracted from **semval**. Also, if (*sem_flg*&SEM_UNDO) is true, the absolute value of *sem_op* is added to the calling process's **semadj** value [see exit(2)] for the specified semaphore.
>
> If **semval** is less than the absolute value of *sem_op* and (*sem_flg*&IPC_NOWAIT) is true, **semop** returns immediately.
>
> If **semval** is less than the absolute value of *sem_op* and (*sem_flg*&IPC_NOWAIT) is false, **semop** increments the **semncnt** associated with the specified semaphore and suspends execution of the calling process until one of the following conditions occur.
>
>> **semval** becomes greater than or equal to the absolute value of *sem_op*. When this occurs, the value of **semncnt** associated with the specified semaphore is decremented, the absolute value of *sem_op* is subtracted from **semval** and, if (*sem_flg*&SEM_UNDO) is true, the absolute value of *sem_op* is added to the calling process's **semadj** value for the specified semaphore.
>>
>> The *semid* for which the calling process is awaiting action is removed from the system [see semctl(2)]. When this occurs, **errno** is set equal to EIDRM, and a value of −1 is returned.
>>
>> The calling process receives a signal that is to be caught. When this occurs, the value of **semncnt** associated with the specified semaphore is decremented, and the calling process resumes execution in the manner prescribed in signal(2).

If *sem_op* is a positive integer, the value of *sem_op* is added to **semval** and, if (*sem_flg*&**SEM_UNDO**) is true, the value of *sem_op* is subtracted from the calling process's **semadj** value for the specified semaphore. {ALTER}

If *sem_op* is zero, one of the following occurs: {READ}

    If **semval** is zero, **semop** returns immediately.

    If **semval** is not equal to zero and (*sem_flg*&**IPC_NOWAIT**) is true, **semop** returns immediately.

    If **semval** is not equal to zero and (*sem_flg*&**IPC_NOWAIT**) is false, **semop** increments the **semzcnt** associated with the specified semaphore and suspends execution of the calling process until one of the following occurs:

        Semval becomes zero, at which time the value of **semzcnt** associated with the specified semaphore is decremented.

        The *semid* for which the calling process is awaiting action is removed from the system. When this occurs, **errno** is set equal to **EIDRM**, and a value of −1 is returned.

        The calling process receives a signal that is to be caught. When this occurs, the value of **semzcnt** associated with the specified semaphore is decremented, and the calling process resumes execution in the manner prescribed in **signal**(2).

semop fails if one or more of the following are true for any of the semaphore operations specified by *sops*:

EINVAL	*semid* is not a valid semaphore identifier.
EFBIG	*sem_num* is less than zero or greater than or equal to the number of semaphores in the set associated with *semid*.
E2BIG	*nsops* is greater than the system-imposed maximum.
EACCES	Operation permission is denied to the calling process [see intro(2)].
EAGAIN	The operation would result in suspension of the calling process but (*sem_flg*&IPC_NOWAIT) is true.
ENOSPC	The limit on the number of individual processes requesting an SEM_UNDO would be exceeded.
EINVAL	The number of individual semaphores for which the calling process requests a SEM_UNDO would exceed the limit.
ERANGE	An operation would cause a **semval** to overflow the system-imposed limit.
ERANGE	An operation would cause a **semadj** value to overflow the system-imposed limit.
EFAULT	*sops* points to an illegal address.

Upon successful completion, the value of **sempid** for each semaphore specified in the array pointed to by *sops* is set equal to the process ID of the calling process.

SEE ALSO
intro(2), exec(2), exit(2), fork(2), semctl(2), semget(2).

DIAGNOSTICS
If *semop* returns due to the receipt of a signal, a value of −1 is returned to the calling process and `errno` is set to `EINTR`. If it returns due to the removal of a *semid* from the system, a value of −1 is returned and `errno` is set to `EIDRM`.

Upon successful completion, a value of zero is returned. Otherwise, a value of −1 is returned and `errno` is set to indicate the error.

NAME
setpgid – set process group ID

SYNOPSIS
```
#include <sys/types.h>
#include <unistd.h>

int setpgid(pid_t pid, pid_t pgid);
```

DESCRIPTION
setpgid sets the process group ID of the process with ID *pid* to *pgid*. If *pgid* is equal to *pid*, the process becomes a process group leader. If *pgid* is not equal to *pid*, the process becomes a member of an existing process group.

If *pid* is equal to 0, the process ID of the calling process is used. If *pgid* is equal to 0, the process specified by *pid* becomes a process group leader.

setpgid fails and returns an error if one or more of the following are true:

EACCES   *pid* matches the process ID of a child process of the calling process and the child process has successfully executed an exec(2) function.

EINVAL   *pgid* is less than (pid_t) 0, or greater than or equal to {PID_MAX}.

EINVAL   The calling process has a controlling terminal that does not support job control.

EPERM   The process indicated by the *pid* argument is a session leader.

EPERM   *pid* matches the process ID of a child process of the calling process and the child process is not in the same session as the calling process.

EPERM   *pgid* does not match the process ID of the process indicated by the *pid* argument and there is no process with a process group ID that matches *pgid* in the same session as the calling process.

ESRCH   *pid* does not match the process ID of the calling process or of a child process of the calling process.

SEE ALSO
exec(2), exit(2), fork(2), getpid(2), getpgid(2), setsid(2).

DIAGNOSTICS
Upon successful completion, setpgid returns a value of 0. Otherwise, a value of −1 is returned and errno is set to indicate the error.

NAME

setpgrp – set process group ID

SYNOPSIS

#include <sys/types.h>
#include <unistd.h>

pid_t setpgrp (void);

DESCRIPTION

If the calling process is not already a session leader, **setpgrp** sets the process group ID and session ID of the calling process to the process ID of the calling process, and releases the calling process's controlling terminal.

SEE ALSO

intro(2), exec(2), fork(2), getpid(2), kill(2), setsid(2), signal(2).

DIAGNOSTICS

setpgrp returns the value of the new process group ID.

NOTES

setpgrp will be phased out in favor of the **setsid**(2) function.

setsid(2)

NAME
setsid – set session ID

SYNOPSIS
```
#include <sys/types.h>
#include <unistd.h>
```
pid_t setsid(void);

DESCRIPTION
If the calling process is not already a process group leader, `setsid` sets the process group ID and session ID of the calling process to the process ID of the calling process, and releases the process's controlling terminal.

`setsid` will fail and return an error if the following is true:

EPERM   The calling process is already a process group leader, or there are processes other than the calling process whose process group ID is equal to the process ID of the calling process.

SEE ALSO
intro(2), exec(2), exit(2), fork(2), getpid(2), getpgid(2), getsid(2), setpgid(2), setpgrp, signal(2), sigsend(2).

WARNING
If the calling process is the last member of a pipeline started by a job control shell, the shell may make the calling process a process group leader. The other processes of the pipeline become members of that process group. In this case, the call to `setsid` will fail. For this reason, a process that calls `setsid` and expects to be part of a pipeline should always first fork; the parent should exit and the child should call `setsid`, thereby insuring that the process will work reliably when started by both job control shells and non-job control shells.

DIAGNOSTICS
Upon successful completion, `setsid` returns the calling process's session ID. Otherwise, a value of -1 is returned and `errno` is set to indicate the error.

setuid(2)

NAME
setuid, setgid – set user and group IDs

SYNOPSIS
```
#include <sys/types.h>
#include <unistd.h>

int setuid(uid_t uid);

int setgid(gid_t gid);
```

DESCRIPTION
The **setuid** system call sets the real user ID, effective user ID, and saved user ID of the calling process. The **setgid** system call sets the real group ID, effective group ID, and saved group ID of the calling process.

At login time, the real user ID, effective user ID, and saved user ID of the login process are set to the login ID of the user responsible for the creation of the process. The same is true for the real, effective, and saved group IDs; they are set to the group ID of the user responsible for the creation of the process.

When a process calls **exec**(2) to execute a file (program), the user and/or group identifiers associated with the process can change. If the file executed is a set-user-ID file, the effective and saved user IDs of the process are set to the owner of the file executed. If the file executed is a set-group-ID file, the effective and saved group IDs of the process are set to the group of the file executed. If the file executed is not a set-user-ID or set-group-ID file, the effective user ID, saved user ID, effective group ID, and saved group ID are not changed.

The following subsections describe the behavior of **setuid** and **setgid** with respect to the three types of user and group IDs.

setuid
If the effective user ID of the process calling **setuid** is the superuser, the real, effective, and saved user IDs are set to the *uid* parameter.

If the effective user ID of the calling process is not the superuser, but *uid* is either the real user ID or the saved user ID of the calling process, the effective user ID is set to *uid*.

setgid
If the effective user ID of the process calling **setgid** is the superuser, the real, effective, and saved group IDs are set to the *gid* parameter.

If the effective user ID of the calling process is not the superuser, but *gid* is either the real group ID or the saved group ID of the calling process, the effective group ID is set to *gid*.

setuid and setgid fail if one or more of the following is true:

EPERM For **setuid**, if the effective user ID is not the superuser, and the *uid* parameter does not match either the real or saved user IDs. For **setgid**, if the effective user ID is not the superuser, and the *gid* parameter does not match either the real or saved group IDs.

EINVAL   The *uid* or *gid* is out of range.

DIAGNOSTICS

Upon successful completion, a value of 0 is returned. Otherwise, a value of −1 is returned and `errno` is set to indicate the error.

SEE ALSO

intro(2), exec(2), getgroups(2), getuid(2), stat(5).

shmctl(2)

NAME
shmctl – shared memory control operations

SYNOPSIS
#include <sys/types.h>
#include <sys/ipc.h>
#include <sys/shm.h>

int shmctl (int shmid, int cmd, struct shmid_ds *buf);

DESCRIPTION
shmctl provides a variety of shared memory control operations as specified by *cmd*. The following *cmd*s are available:

IPC_STAT   Place the current value of each member of the data structure associated with *shmid* into the structure pointed to by *buf*. The contents of this structure are defined in intro(2). {READ}

IPC_SET   Set the value of the following members of the data structure associated with *shmid* to the corresponding value found in the structure pointed to by *buf*:

    shm_perm.uid
    shm_perm.gid
    shm_perm.mode /* only access permission bits */

This command can be executed only by a process that has an effective user ID equal to that of super-user, or to the value of shm_perm.cuid or shm_perm.uid in the data structure associated with *shmid*.

IPC_RMID   Remove the shared memory identifier specified by *shmid* from the system and destroy the shared memory segment and data structure associated with it. This command can be executed only by a process that has an effective user ID equal to that of super-user, or to the value of shm_perm.cuid or shm_perm.uid in the data structure associated with *shmid*.

SHM_LOCK   Lock the shared memory segment specified by *shmid* in memory. This command can be executed only by a process that has an effective user ID equal to super-user.

SHM_UNLOCK Unlock the shared memory segment specified by *shmid*. This command can be executed only by a process that has an effective user ID equal to super-user.

shmctl fails if one or more of the following are true:

EACCES   *cmd* is equal to IPC_STAT and {READ} operation permission is denied to the calling process [see intro(2)].

EINVAL   *shmid* is not a valid shared memory identifier.

EINVAL   *cmd* is not a valid command.

EINVAL	*cmd* is IPC_SET and **shm_perm.uid** or **shm_perm.gid** is not valid.
EOVERFLOW	*cmd* is IPC_STAT and *uid* or *gid* is too large to be stored in the structure pointed to by *buf*.
EPERM	*cmd* is equal to IPC_RMID or IPC_SET and the effective user ID of the calling process is not equal to that of super-user, or to the value of **shm_perm.cuid** or **shm_perm.uid** in the data structure associated with *shmid*.
EPERM	*cmd* is equal to SHM_LOCK or SHM_UNLOCK and the effective user ID of the calling process is not equal to that of super-user.
EFAULT	*buf* points to an illegal address.
ENOMEM	*cmd* is equal to SHM_LOCK and there is not enough memory.

SEE ALSO
shmget(2), shmop(2).

DIAGNOSTICS
Upon successful completion, a value of 0 is returned. Otherwise, a value of −1 is returned and **errno** is set to indicate the error.

NOTES
The user must explicitly remove shared memory segments after the last reference to them has been removed.

shmget(2)

NAME
shmget – get shared memory segment identifier

SYNOPSIS
    #include <sys/types.h>
    #include <sys/ipc.h>
    #include <sys/shm.h>

    int shmget(key_t key, int size, int shmflg);

DESCRIPTION
shmget returns the shared memory identifier associated with *key*.

A shared memory identifier and associated data structure and shared memory segment of at least *size* bytes [see intro(2)] are created for *key* if one of the following are true:

> *key* is equal to IPC_PRIVATE.

> *key* does not already have a shared memory identifier associated with it, and (*shmflg*&IPC_CREAT) is true.

Upon creation, the data structure associated with the new shared memory identifier is initialized as follows:

> shm_perm.cuid, shm_perm.uid, shm_perm.cgid, and shm_perm.gid are set equal to the effective user ID and effective group ID, respectively, of the calling process.

> The access permission bits of shm_perm.mode are set equal to the access permission bits of *shmflg*. shm_segsz is set equal to the value of *size*.

> shm_lpid, shm_nattch shm_atime, and shm_dtime are set equal to 0.

> shm_ctime is set equal to the current time.

shmget fails if one or more of the following are true:

EINVAL   *size* is less than the system-imposed minimum or greater than the system-imposed maximum.

EACCES   A shared memory identifier exists for *key* but operation permission [see intro(2)] as specified by the low-order 9 bits of *shmflg* would not be granted.

EINVAL   A shared memory identifier exists for *key* but the size of the segment associated with it is less than *size* and *size* is not equal to zero.

ENOENT   A shared memory identifier does not exist for *key* and (*shmflg*&IPC_CREAT) is false.

ENOSPC   A shared memory identifier is to be created but the system-imposed limit on the maximum number of allowed shared memory identifiers system wide would be exceeded.

ENOMEM   A shared memory identifier and associated shared memory segment are to be created but the amount of available memory is not sufficient to fill the request.

shmget(2)

EEXIST   A shared memory identifier exists for *key* but both (*shmflg*&IPC_CREAT) and (*shmflg*&IPC_EXCL) are true.

SEE ALSO
intro(2), shmctl(2), shmop(2), stdipc(3C).

DIAGNOSTICS
Upon successful completion, a non-negative integer, namely a shared memory identifier is returned. Otherwise, a value of −1 is returned and errno is set to indicate the error.

NOTES
The user must explicitly remove shared memory segments after the last reference to them has been removed.

shmop(2)

NAME
shmop: shmat, shmdt − shared memory operations

SYNOPSIS
```
#include <sys/types.h>
#include <sys/ipc.h>
#include <sys/shm.h>
void *shmat(int shmid, void *shmaddr, int shmflg);

int shmdt (void *shmaddr);
```

DESCRIPTION
shmat attaches the shared memory segment associated with the shared memory identifier specified by *shmid* to the data segment of the calling process. The segment is attached at the address specified by one of the following criteria:

If *shmaddr* is equal to (void *) 0, the segment is attached at the first available address as selected by the system.

If *shmaddr* is not equal to (void *) 0 and (*shmflg*&SHM_RND) is true, the segment is attached at the address given by (*shmaddr* − (*shmaddr* modulus SHMLBA)).

If *shmaddr* is not equal to (void *) 0 and (*shmflg*&SHM_RND) is false, the segment is attached at the address given by *shmaddr*.

shmdt detaches from the calling process's data segment the shared memory segment located at the address specified by *shmaddr*.

The segment is attached for reading if (*shmflg*&SHM_RDONLY) is true {READ}, otherwise it is attached for reading and writing {READ/WRITE}.

shmat fails and does not attach the shared memory segment if one or more of the following are true:

EINVAL	*shmid* is not a valid shared memory identifier.
EACCES	Operation permission is denied to the calling process [see intro(2)].
ENOMEM	The available data space is not large enough to accommodate the shared memory segment.
EINVAL	*shmaddr* is not equal to zero, and the value of (*shmaddr* − (*shmaddr* modulus SHMLBA)). is an illegal address.
EINVAL	*shmaddr* is not equal to zero, (*shmflg*&SHM_RND) is false, and the value of *shmaddr* is an illegal address.
EMFILE	The number of shared memory segments attached to the calling process would exceed the system-imposed limit.
EINVAL	*shmdt* fails and does not detach the shared memory segment if *shmaddr* is not the data segment start address of a shared memory segment.

SEE ALSO
intro(2), **exec**(2), **exit**(2), **fork**(2), **shmctl**(2), **shmget**(2).

DIAGNOSTICS
Upon successful completion, the return value is as follows:

shmat returns the data segment start address of the attached shared memory segment.

shmdt returns a value of 0.

Otherwise, a value of −1 is returned and **errno** is set to indicate the error.

NOTES
The user must explicitly remove shared memory segments after the last reference to them has been removed.

sigaction(2)

NAME
sigaction – detailed signal management

SYNOPSIS
#include <signal.h>

int sigaction(int sig, const struct sigaction *act,
    struct sigaction *oact);

DESCRIPTION
sigaction allows the calling process to examine and/or specify the action to be taken on delivery of a specific signal. [See signal(5) for an explanation of general signal concepts.]

sig specifies the signal and can be assigned any of the signals specified in signal(5) except SIGKILL and SIGSTOP

If the argument *act* is not NULL, it points to a structure specifying the new action to be taken when delivering *sig*. If the argument *oact* is not NULL, it points to a structure where the action previously associated with *sig* is to be stored on return from sigaction.

The sigaction structure includes the following members:

```
void        (*sa_handler)();
sigset_t    sa_mask;
int         sa_flags;
```

sa_handler specifies the disposition of the signal and may take any of the values specified in signal(5).

sa_mask specifies a set of signals to be blocked while the signal handler is active. On entry to the signal handler, that set of signals is added to the set of signals already being blocked when the signal is delivered. In addition, the signal that caused the handler to be executed will also be blocked, unless the SA_NODEFER flag has been specified. SIGSTOP and SIGKILL cannot be blocked (the system silently enforces this restriction).

sa_flags specifies a set of flags used to modify the delivery of the signal. It is formed by a logical OR of any of the following values:

- **SA_ONSTACK**   If set and the signal is caught and an alternate signal stack has been declared with sigaltstack(2), the signal is delivered to the calling process on that stack. Otherwise, the signal is delivered on the same stack as the main program.

- **SA_RESETHAND**   If set and the signal is caught, the disposition of the signal is reset to SIG_DFL and the signal will not be blocked on entry to the signal handler (SIGILL, SIGTRAP, and SIGPWR cannot be automatically reset when delivered; the system silently enforces this restriction).

SA_NODEFER	If set and the signal is caught, the signal will not be automatically blocked by the kernel while it is being caught.
SA_RESTART	If set and the signal is caught, a system call that is interrupted by the execution of this signal's handler is transparently restarted by the system. Otherwise, that system call returns an EINTR error.
SA_SIGINFO	If cleared and the signal is caught, *sig* is passed as the only argument to the signal-catching function. If set and the signal is caught, pending signals of type *sig* are reliably queued to the calling process and two additional arguments are passed to the signal-catching function. If the second argument is not equal to NULL, it points to a siginfo_t structure containing the reason why the signal was generated [see siginfo(5)]; the third argument points to a ucontext_t structure containing the receiving process's context when the signal was delivered [see ucontext(5)].
SA_NOCLDWAIT	If set and *sig* equals SIGCHLD, the system will not create zombie processes when children of the calling process exit. If the calling process subsequently issues a **wait**(2), it blocks until all of the calling process's child processes terminate, and then returns a value of −1 with **errno** set to ECHILD.
SA_NOCLDSTOP	If set and *sig* equals SIGCHLD, *sig* will not be sent to the calling process when its child processes stop or continue.

sigaction fails if any of the following is true:

EINVAL	The value of the *sig* argument is not a valid signal number or is equal to SIGKILL or SIGSTOP.
EFAULT	*act* or *oact* points outside the process's allocated address space.

DIAGNOSTICS

On success, **sigaction** returns zero. On failure, it returns −1 and sets **errno** to indicate the error.

SEE ALSO

intro(2), exit(2), kill(2), pause(2), sigaltstack(2), signal(2), sigprocmask(2), sigsend(2), sigsuspend(2), wait(2), sigsetops(3C), siginfo(5), signal(5), ucontext(5).

kill(1) in the *User's Reference Manual*.

NOTES

If the system call is reading from or writing to a terminal and the terminal's NOFLSH bit is cleared, data may be flushed [see termio(7)].

sigaltstack(2)

NAME
sigaltstack – set or get signal alternate stack context

SYNOPSIS
#include <signal.h>

int sigaltstack(const stack_t *ss, stack_t *oss);

DESCRIPTION
sigaltstack allows users to define an alternate stack area on which signals are to be processed. If *ss* is non-zero, it specifies a pointer to, and the size of a stack area on which to deliver signals, and tells the system if the process is currently executing on that stack. When a signal's action indicates its handler should execute on the alternate signal stack [specified with a sigaction(2) call], the system checks to see if the process is currently executing on that stack. If the process is not currently executing on the signal stack, the system arranges a switch to the alternate signal stack for the duration of the signal handler's execution.

The structure sigaltstack includes the following members.

```
int     *ss_sp
long    ss_size
int     ss_flags
```

If *ss* is not NULL, it points to a structure specifying the alternate signal stack that will take effect upon return from sigaltstack. The ss_sp and ss_size fields specify the new base and size of the stack, which is automatically adjusted for direction of growth and alignment. The ss_flags field specifies the new stack state and may be set to the following:

SS_DISABLE   The stack is to be disabled and ss_sp and ss_size are ignored. If SS_DISABLE is not set, the stack will be enabled.

If *oss* is not NULL, it points to a structure specifying the alternate signal stack that was in effect prior to the call to sigaltstack. The ss_sp and ss_size fields specify the base and size of that stack. The ss_flags field specifies the stack's state, and may contain the following values:

SS_ONSTACK   The process is currently executing on the alternate signal stack. Attempts to modify the alternate signal stack while the process is executing on it will fail.

SS_DISABLE   The alternate signal stack is currently disabled.

sigaltstack fails if any of the following is true:

EFAULT   Either *ss* or *oss* points outside the process's allocated address space.

EINVAL   An attempt was made to disable an active stack or the ss_flags field specifies invalid flags.

ENOMEM   The size of the alternate stack area is less than MINSIGSTKSZ.

NOTES
The value SIGSTKSZ is defined to be the number of bytes that would be used to cover the usual case when allocating an alternate stack area. The value MINSIGSTKSZ is defined to be the minimum stack size for a signal handler. In

computing an alternate stack size, a program should add that amount to its stack requirements to allow for the operating system overhead.

The following code fragment is typically used to allocate an alternate stack.

```
if ((sigstk.ss_sp = (char *)malloc(SIGSTKSZ)) == NULL)
        /* error return */;

sigstk.ss_size = SIGSTKSZ;
sigstk.ss_flags = 0;
if (sigaltstack(&sigstk, (stack_t *)0) < 0)
        perror("sigaltstack");
```

SEE ALSO
getcontext(2), sigaction(2), sigsetjmp(3C), ucontext(5).

DIAGNOSTICS
On success, sigaltstack returns zero. On failure, it returns −1 and sets errno to indicate the error.

signal(2)

NAME
signal, sigset, sighold, sigrelse, sigignore, sigpause – simplified signal management

SYNOPSIS
```
#include <signal.h>

void (*signal(int sig, void (*disp)(int)))(int);

void (*sigset(int sig, void (*disp)(int)))(int);

int sighold(int sig);

int sigrelse(int sig);

int sigignore(int sig);

int sigpause(int sig);
```

DESCRIPTION
These functions provide simplified signal management for application processes. See **signal**(5) for an explanation of general signal concepts.

signal and **sigset** are used to modify signal dispositions. *sig* specifies the signal, which may be any signal except SIGKILL and SIGSTOP. *disp* specifies the signal's disposition, which may be SIG_DFL, SIG_IGN, or the address of a signal handler. If **signal** is used, *disp* is the address of a signal handler, and *sig* is not SIGILL, SIGTRAP, or SIGPWR, the system first sets the signal's disposition to SIG_DFL before executing the signal handler. If **sigset** is used and *disp* is the address of a signal handler, the system adds *sig* to the calling process's signal mask before executing the signal handler; when the signal handler returns, the system restores the calling process's signal mask to its state prior to the delivery of the signal. In addition, if **sigset** is used and *disp* is equal to SIG_HOLD, *sig* is added to the calling process's signal mask and the signal's disposition remains unchanged.

sighold adds *sig* to the calling process's signal mask.

sigrelse removes *sig* from the calling process's signal mask.

sigignore sets the disposition of *sig* to SIG_IGN.

sigpause removes *sig* from the calling process's signal mask and suspends the calling process until a signal is received.

These functions fail if any of the following are true.

EINVAL	The value of the *sig* argument is not a valid signal or is equal to SIGKILL or SIGSTOP.
EINTR	A signal was caught during the system call **sigpause**.

NOTES
sighold in conjunction with **sigrelse** or **sigpause** may be used to establish critical regions of code that require the delivery of a signal to be temporarily deferred.

If **signal** or **sigset** is used to set SIGCHLD's disposition to a signal handler, SIGCHLD will not be sent when the calling process's children are stopped or continued.

If any of the above functions are used to set SIGCHLD's disposition to SIG_IGN, the calling process's child processes will not create zombie processes when they terminate [see exit(2)]. If the calling process subsequently waits for its children, it blocks until all of its children terminate; it then returns a value of −1 with **errno** set to ECHILD [see **wait**(2), **waitid**(2)].

DIAGNOSTICS

On success, **signal** returns the signal's previous disposition. On failure, it returns SIG_ERR and sets **errno** to indicate the error.

On success, **sigset** returns SIG_HOLD if the signal had been blocked or the signal's previous disposition if it had not been blocked. On failure, it returns SIG_ERR and sets **errno** to indicate the error.

All other functions return zero on success. On failure, they return −1 and set **errno** to indicate the error.

SEE ALSO

kill(2), pause(2), sigaction(2), sigsend(2), wait(2), waitid(2), signal(5).

sigpending(2)

NAME
sigpending – examine signals that are blocked and pending

SYNOPSIS
```
#include <signal.h>
```
```
int sigpending(sigset_t *set);
```

DESCRIPTION
The `sigpending` function retrieves those signals that have been sent to the calling process but are being blocked from delivery by the calling process's signal mask. The signals are stored in the space pointed to by the argument *set*.

sigpending fails if the following is true:

EFAULT   The *set* argument points outside the process's allocated address space.

SEE ALSO
sigaction(2), sigprocmask(2), sigsetops(3C).

DIAGNOSTICS
On success, `sigpending` returns zero. On failure, it returns −1 and sets `errno` to indicate the error.

NAME

sigprocmask – change or examine signal mask

SYNOPSIS

#include <signal.h>

int sigprocmask(int how, const sigset_t *set, sigset_t *oset);

DESCRIPTION

The sigprocmask function is used to examine and/or change the calling process's signal mask. If the value is SIG_BLOCK, the set pointed to by the argument *set* is added to the current signal mask. If the value is SIG_UNBLOCK, the set pointed by the argument *set* is removed from the current signal mask. If the value is SIG_SETMASK, the current signal mask is replaced by the set pointed to by the argument *set*. If the argument *oset* is not NULL, the previous mask is stored in the space pointed to by *oset*. If the value of the argument *set* is NULL, the value *how* is not significant and the process's signal mask is unchanged; thus, the call can be used to enquire about currently blocked signals.

If there are any pending unblocked signals after the call to sigprocmask, at least one of those signals will be delivered before the call to sigprocmask returns.

It is not possible to block those signals that cannot be ignored [see sigaction(2)]; this restriction is silently imposed by the system.

If sigprocmask fails, the process's signal mask is not changed.

sigprocmask fails if any of the following is true:

EINVAL   The value of the *how* argument is not equal to one of the defined values.

EFAULT   The value of *set* or *oset* points outside the process's allocated address space.

SEE ALSO

sigaction(2), signal(2), sigsetopts(3C), signal(5).

DIAGNOSTICS

On success, sigprocmask returns zero. On failure, it returns −1 and sets errno to indicate the error.

sigsend(2)

NAME
sigsend, sigsendset – send a signal to a process or a group of processes

SYNOPSIS
    #include <sys/types.h>
    #include <sys/signal.h>
    #include <sys/procset.h>

    int sigsend(idtype_t idtype, id_t id, int sig);

    int sigsendset(procset_t *psp, int sig);

DESCRIPTION
sigsend sends a signal to the process or group of processes specified by *id* and *idtype*. The signal to be sent is specified by *sig* and is either zero or one of the values listed in signal(5). If *sig* is zero (the null signal), error checking is performed but no signal is actually sent. This value can be used to check the validity of *id* and *idtype*.

The real or effective user ID of the sending process must match the real or effective user ID of the receiving process, unless the effective user ID of the sending process is super-user, or *sig* is SIGCONT and the sending process has the same session ID as the receiving process.

If *idtype* is P_PID, *sig* is sent to the process with process ID *id*.

If *idtype* is P_PGID, *sig* is sent to any process with process group ID *id*.

If *idtype* is P_SID, *sig* is sent to any process with session ID *id*.

If *idtype* is P_UID, *sig* is sent to any process with effective user ID *id*.

If *idtype* is P_GID, *sig* is sent to any process with effective group ID *id*.

If *idtype* is P_CID, *sig* is sent to any process with scheduler class ID *id* [see priocntl(2)].

If *idtype* is P_ALL, *sig* is sent to all processes and *id* is ignored.

If *id* is P_MYID, the value of *id* is taken from the calling process.

The process with a process ID of 0 is always excluded. The process with a process ID of 1 is excluded unless *idtype* is equal to P_PID.

sigsendset provides an alternate interface for sending signals to sets of processes. This function sends signals to the set of processes specified by *psp*. *psp* is a pointer to a structure of type procset_t, defined in sys/procset.h>, which includes the following members:

        idop_t   p_op;
        idtype_t   p_lidtype;
        id_t   p_lid;
        idtype_t   p_ridtype;
        id_t   p_rid;

p_lidtype and p_lid specify the ID type and ID of one ("left") set of processes; p_ridtype and p_rid specify the ID type and ID of a second ("right") set of processes. ID types and IDs are specified just as for the *idtype* and *id* arguments to sigsend. p_op specifies the operation to be performed on the two sets of processes to get the set of processes the system call is to apply to. The valid values for p_op and the processes they specify are:

POP_DIFF	set difference: processes in left set and not in right set
POP_AND	set intersection: processes in both left and right sets
POP_OR	set union: processes in either left or right set or both
POP_XOR	set exclusive-or: processes in left or right set but not in both

`sigsend` and `sigsendset` fail if one or more of the following are true:

EINVAL	*sig* is not a valid signal number.
EINVAL	*idtype* is not a valid idtype field.
EINVAL	*sig* is SIGKILL, *idtype* is P_PID and *id* is 1 (proc1).
ESRCH	No process can be found corresponding to that specified by *id* and *idtype*.
EPERM	The user ID of the sending process is not super-user, and its real or effective user ID does not match the real or effective user ID of the receiving process, and the calling process is not sending SIGCONT to a process that shares the same session.

In addition, `sigsendset` fails if:

EFAULT	psp points outside the process's allocated address space.

SEE ALSO

getpid(2), getpgrp(2), kill(2), priocntl(2), setpid(2), signal(2), signal(5).

kill(1) in the *User's Reference Manual*.

DIAGNOSTICS

On success, `sigsend` returns zero. On failure, it returns −1 and sets `errno` to indicate the error.

sigsuspend(2)

NAME
sigsuspend – install a signal mask and suspend process until signal

SYNOPSIS
```
#include <signal.h>

int sigsuspend(const sigset_t *set);
```

DESCRIPTION
sigsuspend replaces the process's signal mask with the set of signals pointed to by the argument *set* and then suspends the process until delivery of a signal whose action is either to execute a signal catching function or to terminate the process.

If the action is to terminate the process, sigsuspend does not return. If the action is to execute a signal catching function, sigsuspend returns after the signal catching function returns. On return, the signal mask is restored to the set that existed before the call to sigsuspend.

It is not possible to block those signals that cannot be ignored [see signal(5)]; this restriction is silently imposed by the system.

sigsuspend fails if either of the following is true:

EINTR   A signal is caught by the calling process and control is returned from the signal catching function.

EFAULT   The *set* argument points outside the process's allocated address space.

DIAGNOSTICS
Since sigsuspend suspends process execution indefinitely, there is no successful completion return value. On failure, it returns −1 and sets errno to indicate the error.

SEE ALSO
sigaction(2), sigprocmask(2), sigpause(2), sigsetops(3C), signal(5).

stat(2)   **stat(2)**

NAME
stat, lstat, fstat – get file status

SYNOPSIS
#include <sys/types.h>
#include <sys/stat.h>

int stat(const char *path, struct stat *buf);

int lstat(const char *path, struct stat *buf);

int fstat(int fildes, struct stat *buf);

DESCRIPTION
path points to a path name naming a file. Read, write, or execute permission of the named file is not required, but all directories listed in the path name leading to the file must be searchable. **stat** obtains information about the named file.

Note that in a Remote File Sharing environment, the information returned by **stat** depends on the user/group mapping set up between the local and remote computers. [See **idload**(1M).]

lstat obtains file attributes similar to **stat**, except when the named file is a symbolic link; in that case **lstat** returns information about the link, while **stat** returns information about the file the link references.

fstat obtains information about an open file known by the file descriptor *fildes*, obtained from a successful **open**, **creat**, **dup**, **fcntl**, or **pipe** system call.

buf is a pointer to a **stat** structure into which information is placed concerning the file.

The contents of the structure pointed to by *buf* include the following members:

```
    mode_t   st_mode;    /* File mode [see mknod(2)] */
    ino_t    st_ino;     /* Inode number */
    dev_t    st_dev;     /* ID of device containing */
                         /* a directory entry for this file */
    dev_t    st_rdev;    /* ID of device */
                         /* This entry is defined only for */
                         /* char special or block special files */
    nlink_t  st_nlink;   /* Number of links */
    uid_t    st_uid;     /* User ID of the file's owner */
    gid_t    st_gid;     /* Group ID of the file's group */
    off_t    st_size;    /* File size in bytes */
    time_t   st_atime;   /* Time of last access */
    time_t   st_mtime;   /* Time of last data modification */
    time_t   st_ctime;   /* Time of last file status change */
                         /* Times measured in seconds since */
                         /* 00:00:00 UTC, Jan. 1, 1970 */
    long     st_blksize; /* Preferred I/O block size */
    long     st_blocks;  /* Number st_blksize blocks allocated */
```

stat (2)   **stat (2)**

st_mode   The mode of the file as described in mknod(2). In addition to the modes described in mknod(2), the mode of a file may also be S_IFLNK if the file is a symbolic link. (Note that S_IFLNK may only be returned by lstat.)

st_ino   This field uniquely identifies the file in a given file system. The pair st_ino and st_dev uniquely identifies regular files.

st_dev   This field uniquely identifies the file system that contains the file. Its value may be used as input to the ustat system call to determine more information about this file system. No other meaning is associated with this value.

st_rdev   This field should be used only by administrative commands. It is valid only for block special or character special files and only has meaning on the system where the file was configured.

st_nlink This field should be used only by administrative commands.

st_uid   The user ID of the file's owner.

st_gid   The group ID of the file's group.

st_size   For regular files, this is the address of the end of the file. For block special or character special, this is not defined. See also pipe(2).

st_atime Time when file data was last accessed. Changed by the following system calls: creat, mknod, pipe, utime, and read.

st_mtime Time when data was last modified. Changed by the following system calls: creat, mknod, pipe, utime, and write.

st_ctime Time when file status was last changed. Changed by the following system calls: chmod, chown, creat, link, mknod, pipe, unlink, utime, and write.

st_blksize
          A hint as to the "best" unit size for I/O operations. This field is not defined for block-special or character-special files.

st_blocks
          The total number of physical blocks of size 512 bytes actually allocated on disk. This field is not defined for block-special or character-special files.

stat and lstat fail if one or more of the following are true:

EACCES   Search permission is denied for a component of the path prefix.

EFAULT   *buf* or *path* points to an invalid address.

EINTR   A signal was caught during the stat or lstat system call.

ELOOP   Too many symbolic links were encountered in translating *path*.

stat(2)   stat(2)

EMULTIHOP	Components of *path* require hopping to multiple remote machines and the file system does not allow it.
ENAMETOOLONG	The length of the *path* argument exceeds {PATH_MAX}, or the length of a *path* component exceeds {NAME_MAX} while _POSIX_NO_TRUNC is in effect.
ENOENT	The named file does not exist or is the null pathname.
ENOTDIR	A component of the path prefix is not a directory.
ENOLINK	*path* points to a remote machine and the link to that machine is no longer active.
EOVERFLOW	A component is too large to store in the structure pointed to by *buf*.

`fstat` fails if one or more of the following are true:

EBADF	*fildes* is not a valid open file descriptor.
EFAULT	*buf* points to an invalid address.
EINTR	A signal was caught during the `fstat` system call.
ENOLINK	*fildes* points to a remote machine and the link to that machine is no longer active.
EOVERFLOW	A component is too large to store in the structure pointed to by *buf*.

SEE ALSO
chmod(2), chown(2), creat(2), link(2), mknod(2), pipe(2), read(2), time(2), unlink(2), utime(2), write(2), fattach(3C), stat(5).

DIAGNOSTICS
Upon successful completion a value of 0 is returned. Otherwise, a value of −1 is returned and `errno` is set to indicate the error.

NAME

statvfs, fstatvfs – get file system information

SYNOPSIS

#include <sys/types.h>
#include <sys/statvfs.h>

int statvfs (const char *path, struct statvfs *buf);

int fstatvfs (int fildes, struct statvfs *buf);

DESCRIPTION

statvfs returns a "generic superblock" describing a file system; it can be used to acquire information about mounted file systems. *buf* is a pointer to a structure (described below) that is filled by the system call.

path should name a file that resides on that file system. The file system type is known to the operating system. Read, write, or execute permission for the named file is not required, but all directories listed in the path name leading to the file must be searchable.

The **statvfs** structure pointed to by *buf* includes the following members:

```
ulong   f_bsize;          /* preferred file system block size */
ulong   f_frsize;         /* fundamental filesystem block size
                             (if supported) */
ulong   f_blocks;         /* total # of blocks on file system
                             in units of f_frsize */
ulong   f_bfree;          /* total # of free blocks */
ulong   f_bavail;         /* # of free blocks avail to
                             non-superuser */
ulong   f_files;          /* total # of file nodes (inodes) */
ulong   f_ffree;          /* total # of free file nodes */
ulong   f_favail;         /* # of inodes avail to
                             non-superuser*/
fsid_t  f_fsid;           /* file system id (dev for now) */
char    f_basetype[FSTYPSZ]; /* target fs type name,
                             null-terminated */
ulong   f_flag;           /* bit mask of flags */
ulong   f_namemax;        /* maximum file name length */
char    f_fstr[32];       /* file system specific string */
ulong   f_filler[16];     /* reserved for future expansion */
```

f_basetype contains a null-terminated FSType name of the mounted target (e.g. s5 mounted over rfs will contain s5).

The following flags can be returned in the **f_flag** field:

```
ST_RDONLY    0x01      /* read-only file system */
ST_NOSUID    0x02      /* does not support setuid/setgid
                          semantics */
ST_NOTRUNC   0x04      /* does not truncate file names
                          longer than {NAME_MAX}*/
```

statvfs(2)

fstatvfs is similar to statvfs, except that the file named by *path* in statvfs is instead identified by an open file descriptor *fildes* obtained from a successful open, creat, dup, fcntl, or pipe system call.

statvfs fails if one or more of the following are true:

EACCES	Search permission is denied on a component of the path prefix.
EFAULT	*path* or *buf* points outside the process's allocated address space.
EINTR	A signal was caught during statvfs execution.
EIO	An I/O error occurred while reading the file system.
ELOOP	Too many symbolic links were encountered in translating *path*.
EMULTIHOP	Components of *path* require hopping to multiple remote machines and file system type does not allow it.
ENAMETOOLONG	The length of a *path* component exceeds {NAME_MAX} characters, or the length of *path* exceeds {PATH_MAX} characters.
ENOENT	Either a component of the path prefix or the file referred to by *path* does not exist.
ENOLINK	*path* points to a remote machine and the link to that machine is no longer active.
ENOTDIR	A component of the path prefix of *path* is not a directory.

fstatvfs fails if one or more of the following are true:

EFAULT	*buf* points to an invalid address.
EBADF	*fildes* is not an open file descriptor.
EINTR	A signal was caught during fstatvfs execution.
EIO	An I/O error occurred while reading the file system.

DIAGNOSTICS

Upon successful completion a value of 0 is returned. Otherwise, a value of −1 is returned and errno is set to indicate the error.

SEE ALSO

chmod(2), chown(2), creat(2), link(2), mknod(2), pipe(2), read(2), time(2), unlink(2), utime(2), write(2).

NAME

stime – set time

SYNOPSIS

```
#include <unistd.h>
```

```
int stime(const time_t *tp);
```

DESCRIPTION

stime sets the system's idea of the time and date. *tp* points to the value of time as measured in seconds from 00:00:00 UTC January 1, 1970.

stime will fail if:

EPERM   the effective user ID of the calling process is not super-user.

SEE ALSO

time(2).

DIAGNOSTICS

Upon successful completion, a value of 0 is returned. Otherwise, a value of −1 is returned and **errno** is set to indicate the error.

swapctl(2) swapctl(2)

NAME
swapctl – manage swap space

SYNOPSIS
#include <sys/stat.h>
#include <sys/swap.h>

int swapctl(int cmd, void *arg);

DESCRIPTION
swapctl adds, deletes, or returns information about swap resources. *cmd* specifies one of the following options contained in <sys/swap.h>:

```
SC_ADD          /* add a resource for swapping */
SC_LIST         /* list the resources for swapping */
SC_REMOVE       /* remove a resource for swapping */
SC_GETNSWP      /* return number of swap resources */
```

When SC_ADD or SC_REMOVE is specified, *arg* is a pointer to a **swapres** structure containing the following members:

```
char    *sr_name;       /* pathname of resource */
off_t   sr_start;       /* offset to start of swap area */
off_t   sr_length;      /* length of swap area */
```

sr_start and sr_length are specified in 512-byte blocks. When SC_LIST is specified, *arg* is a pointer to a **swaptable** structure containing the following members:

```
int             swt_n;          /* number of swapents following */
struct swapent  swt_ent[];      /* array of swt_n swapents */
```

A **swapent** structure contains the following members:

```
char    *ste_path;      /* name of the swap file */
off_t   ste_start;      /* starting block for swapping */
off_t   ste_length;     /* length of swap area */
long    ste_pages;      /* number of pages for swapping */
long    ste_free;       /* number of ste_pages free */
long    ste_flags;      /* ST_INDEL bit set if swap file */
                        /* is now being deleted */
```

SC_LIST causes swapctl to return at most swt_n entries. The return value of swapctl is the number actually returned. The ST_INDEL bit is turned on in ste_flags if the swap file is in the process of being deleted. When SC_GETNSWP is specified, swapctl returns as its value the number of swap resources in use. *arg* is ignored for this operation. The SC_ADD and SC_REMOVE functions will fail if calling process does not have appropriate privileges.

RETURN VALUE
Upon successful completion, the function swapctl returns a value of 0 for SC_ADD or SC_REMOVE, the number of struct swapent entries actually returned for SC_LIST, or the number of swap resources in use for SC_GETNSWP. Upon failure, the function swapctl returns a value of –1 and sets errno to indicate an error.

swapctl(2)

ERRORS
Under the following conditions, the function **swapctl** fails and sets **errno** to:

EEXIST	Part of the range specified by **sr_start** and **sr_length** is already being used for swapping on the specified resource (SC_ADD).
EFAULT	*arg*, **sr_name**, or **ste_path** points outside the allocated address space.
EINVAL	The specified function value is not valid, the path specified is not a swap resource (SC_REMOVE), part of the range specified by **sr_start** and **sr_length** lies outside the resource specified (SC_ADD), or the specified swap area is less than one page (SC_ADD).
EISDIR	The path specified for SC_ADD is a directory.
ELOOP	Too many symbolic links were encountered in translating the pathname provided to SC_ADD or SC_REMOVE.
ENAMETOOLONG	The length of a component of the path specified for SC_ADD or SC_REMOVE exceeds {NAME_MAX} characters or the length of the path exceeds {PATH_MAX} characters and {_POSIX_NO_TRUNC} is in effect.
ENOENT	The pathname specified for SC_ADD or SC_REMOVE does not exist.
ENOMEM	An insufficient number of **struct swapent** structures were provided to SC_LIST, or there were insufficient system storage resources available during an SC_ADD or SC_REMOVE, or the system would not have enough swap space after an SC_REMOVE.
ENOSYS	The pathname specified for SC_ADD or SC_REMOVE is not a file or block special device.
ENOTDIR	Pathname provided to SC_ADD or SC_REMOVE contained a component in the path prefix that was not a directory.
EPERM	The process does not have appropriate privileges.
EROFS	The pathname specified for SC_ADD is a read-only file system.

symlink(2)

NAME
symlink – make a symbolic link to a file

SYNOPSIS
#include <unistd.h> int symlink(const char *name1, const char *name2);

DESCRIPTION
symlink creates a symbolic link *name2* to the file *name1*. Either name may be an arbitrary pathname, the files need not be on the same file system, and *name1* may be nonexistent.

The file to which the symbolic link points is used when an open(2) operation is performed on the link. A stat(2) on a symbolic link returns the linked-to file, while an lstat returns information about the link itself. This can lead to surprising results when a symbolic link is made to a directory. To avoid confusion in programs, the readlink(2) call can be used to read the contents of a symbolic link.

The symbolic link is made unless one or more of the following are true:

EACCES	Search permission is denied for a component of the path prefix of *name2*.
EDQUOT	The directory in which the entry for the new symbolic link is being placed cannot be extended because the user's quota of disk blocks on the file system containing the directory has been exhausted.
EDQUOT	The new symbolic link cannot be created because the user's quota of disk blocks on the file system which will contain the link has been exhausted.
EDQUOT	The user's quota of inodes on the file system on which the file is being created has been exhausted.
EEXIST	The file referred to by *name2* already exists.
EFAULT	*name1* or *name2* points outside the allocated address space for the process.
EIO	An I/O error occurs while reading from or writing to the file system.
ELOOP	Too many symbolic links are encountered in translating *name2*.
ENAMETOOLONG	The length of the *name1* or *name2* argument exceeds {PATH_MAX}, or the length of a *name1* or *name2* component exceeds {NAME_MAX} while (_POSIX_NO_TRUNC) is in effect.
ENOENT	A component of the path prefix of *name2* does not exist.
ENOSPC	The directory in which the entry for the new symbolic link is being placed cannot be extended because no space is left on the file system containing the directory.

symlink(2)

ENOSPC	The new symbolic link cannot be created because no space is left on the file system which will contain the link.
ENOSPC	There are no free inodes on the file system on which the file is being created.
ENOSYS	The file system does not support symbolic links
ENOTDIR	A component of the path prefix of *name2* is not a directory.
EROFS	The file *name2* would reside on a read-only file system.

DIAGNOSTICS

Upon successful completion `symlink` returns a value of 0; otherwise, it returns −1 and places an error code in `errno`.

SEE ALSO

link(2), readlink(2), unlink(2). cp(1) in the *User's Reference Manual*.

NAME
sync – update super block

SYNOPSIS
#include <unistd.h>

void sync(void);

DESCRIPTION
sync causes all information in memory that should be on disk to be written out. This includes modified super blocks, modified i-nodes, and delayed block I/O.

It should be used by programs that examine a file system, such as fsck(1M), df(1M), etc. It is mandatory before a re-boot.

The writing, although scheduled, is not necessarily completed before sync returns. The fsync system call completes the writing before it returns.

SEE ALSO
fsync(2)

NAME
sysi86 – machine specific functions

SYNOPSIS
#include <sys/sysi86.h>

int sysi86 (int cmd, ...);

DESCRIPTION
The **sysi86** system call implements machine specific functions. The *cmd* argument determines the function to be performed. The types of the arguments expected depend on the function.

Command RTODC
When *cmd* is RTODC, the expected argument is the address of a **struct rtc_t** (from the header file **sys/rtc.h**):

```
struct rtc_t {
        char rtc_sec, rtc_asec, rtc_min, rtc_amin,
        rtc_hr, rtc_ahr, rtc_dow, rtc_dom,
        rtc_mon, rtc_yr, rtc_statusa,
        rtc_statusb, rtc_statusc, rtc_statusd;
};
```

This function reads the hardware time-of-day clock and returns the data in the structure referenced by the argument. This command is only available to the *super-user*.

RDUBLK
This command reads the u-block (per process user information as defined by *struct user* in the **sys/user** header file) for a given process. When *cmd* is RDUBLK, **sysi86** takes three additional arguments: the process ID, the address of a buffer, and the number of bytes to read; i.e.,

```
sysi86(RDULBK, pid, buf, n)
        pid_t pid;
        char *buf;
        int n;
```

Command SI86FPHW
This command expects the address of an integer as its argument. After successful return from the system call, the integer specifies how floating-point computation is supported.

The low-order byte of the integer contains the value of "fpkind", a variable that specifies whether an 80287 or 80387 floating-point coprocessor is present, emulated in software, or not supported. The values are defined in the header file **sys/fp.h**.

FP_NO	no fp chip, no emulator (no fp support)
FP_SW	no fp chip, using software emulator
FP_HW	chip present bit
FP_287	80287 chip present
FP_387	80387 chip present

Command SETNAME
This command, which is only available to the super-user, expects an argument of type *char ** which points to a NULL terminated string of at most 7 characters. The command will change the running system's *sysname* and *nodename* [see uname(2)] to this string.

Command STIME
When *cmd* is STIME, an argument of type long is expected. This function sets the system time and date (not the hardware clock). The argument contains the time as measured in seconds from 00:00:00 GMT January 1, 1970. Note that this command is only available to the super-user.

Command SI86DSCR
This command sets a segment or gate descriptor in the kernel. The following descriptor types are accepted:
- executable and data segments in the LDT at DPL 3
- a call gate in the GDT at DPL 3 that points to a segment in the LDT

The argument is a pointer to a request structure that contains the values to be placed in the descriptor. The request structure is declared in the sys/sysi86.h header file.

Command SI86MEM
This command returns the size of available memory in bytes.

Command SI86SWPI
When *cmd* is SI86SWPI, individual swapping areas may be added, deleted or the current areas determined. The address of an appropriately primed swap buffer is passed as the only argument. (Refer to the sys/swap.h header file for details of loading the buffer.)

The format of the swap buffer is:

```
struct swapint {
    char  si_cmd;        /*command: SI_LIST, SI_ADD, SI_DEL*/
    char  *si_buf;       /*swap file path pointer*/
    int   si_swplo;      /*start block*/
    int   si_nblks;      /*swap size*/
}
```

Note that the add and delete options of the command may only be exercised by the super-user.

Typically, a swap area is added by a single call to sysi86. First, the swap buffer is primed with appropriate entries for the structure members. Then sysi86 is invoked.

```
#include <sys/sysi86.h>
#include <sys/swap.h>

struct swapint swapbuf;   /*swap into buffer ptr*/

sysi86(SI86SWPI, &swapbuf);
```

If this command succeeds, it returns 0 to the calling process. This command fails, returning -1, if one or more of the following is true:

[EFAULT]	*swapbuf* points to an invalid address
[EFAULT]	*swapbuf.si_buf* points to an invalid address
[ENOTBLK]	Swap area specified is not a block special device
[EEXIST]	Swap area specified has already been added
[ENOSPC]	Too many swap areas in use (if adding)
[ENOMEM]	Tried to delete last remaining swap area
[EINVAL]	Bad arguments
[ENOMEM]	No place to put swapped pages when deleting a swap area

SEE ALSO

uname(2).

swap(1M) in the *User's/System Administrator's Reference Manual*.

DIAGNOSTICS

Upon successful completion, zero is returned; otherwise, −1 is returned, and **errno** is set to indicate the error. When the *cmd* is invalid, **errno** is set to EINVAL.

sysfs(2) sysfs(2)

NAME
sysfs – get file system type information

SYNOPSIS
#include <sys/fstyp.h>
#include <sys/fsid.h>

int sysfs(int opcode, const char *fsname);

int sysfs(int opcode, int fs_index, char *buf);

int sysfs(int opcode);

DESCRIPTION
sysfs returns information about the file system types configured in the system. The number of arguments accepted by **sysfs** varies and depends on the *opcode*. The currently recognized *opcodes* and their functions are:

GETFSIND   Translate *fsname*, a null-terminated file-system type identifier, into a file-system type index.

GETFSTYP   Translate *fs_index*, a file-system type index, into a null-terminated file-system type identifier and write it into the buffer pointed to by *buf*; this buffer must be at least of size FSTYPSZ as defined in <sys/fstyp.h>.

GETNFSTYP   Return the total number of file system types configured in the system.

sysfs fails if one or more of the following are true:

EINVAL   *fsname* points to an invalid file-system identifier; *fs_index* is zero, or invalid; *opcode* is invalid.

EFAULT   *buf* or *fsname* points to an invalid user address.

DIAGNOSTICS
Upon successful completion, **sysfs** returns the file-system type index if the *opcode* is GETFSIND, a value of 0 if the *opcode* is GETFSTYP, or the number of file system types configured if the *opcode* is GETNFSTYP. Otherwise, a value of −1 is returned and **errno** is set to indicate the error.

sysinfo(2)

NAME
sysinfo – get and set system information strings

SYNOPSIS
#include <sys/systeminfo.h>

long sysinfo (int command, char *buf, long count);

DESCRIPTION
sysinfo copies information relating to the UNIX system on which the process is executing into the buffer pointed to by *buf*; **sysinfo** can also set certain information where appropriate *command*s are available. *count* is the size of the buffer.

The POSIX P1003.1 interface **sysconf** [see **sysconf**(2)] provides a similar class of configuration information, but returns an integer rather than a string.

The *command*s available are:

SI_SYSNAME Copy into the array pointed to by *buf* the string that would be returned by **uname** [see **uname**(2)] in the *sysname* field. This is the name of the implementation of the operating system, e.g., *System V* or *UTS*.

SI_HOSTNAME
Copy into the array pointed to by *buf* a string that names the present host machine. This is the string that would be returned by *uname* [see *uname*(2)] in the *nodename* field. This hostname or nodename is often the name the machine is known by locally.

The *hostname* is the name of this machine as a node in some network; different networks may have different names for the node, but presenting the nodename to the appropriate network Directory or name-to-address mapping service should produce a transport end point address. The name may not be fully qualified.

Internet host names may be up to 256 bytes in length (plus the terminating null).

SI_SET_HOSTNAME
Copy the null-terminated contents of the array pointed to by *buf* into the string maintained by the kernel whose value will be returned by succeeding calls to **sysinfo** with the command **SI_HOSTNAME**. This command requires that the effective-user-id be super-user.

SI_RELEASE Copy into the array pointed to by *buf* the string that would be returned by **uname** [see **uname**(2)] in the *release* field. Typical values might be *4.0* or *3.2*.

SI_VERSION Copy into the array pointed to by *buf* the string that would be returned by **uname** [see **uname**(2)] in the *version* field. The syntax and semantics of this string are defined by the system provider.

SI_MACHINE
Copy into the array pointed to by *buf* the string that would be returned by **uname** [see **uname**(2)] in the *machine* field, e.g., *3b2* or *580*.

SI_ARCHITECTURE
> Copy into the array pointed to by *buf* a string describing the instruction set architecture of the current system, e.g., *mc68030*, *m32100*, or *i80486*. These names may not match predefined names in the C language compilation system.

SI_HW_PROVIDER
> Copies the name of the hardware manufacturer into the array pointed to by *buf*.

SI_HW_SERIAL
> Copy into the array pointed to by *buf* a string which is the ASCII representation of the hardware-specific serial number of the physical machine on which the system call is executed. Note that this may be implemented in Read-Only Memory, via software constants set when building the operating system, or by other means, and may contain non-numeric characters. It is anticipated that manufacturers will not issue the same "serial number" to more than one physical machine. The pair of strings returned by SI_HW_PROVIDER and SI_HW_SERIAL is likely to be unique across all vendor's System V implementations.

SI_SRPC_DOMAIN
> Copies the Secure Remote Procedure Call domain name into the array pointed to by *buf*.

SI_SET_SRPC_DOMAIN
> Set the string to be returned by sysinfo with the SI_SRPC_DOMAIN command to the value contained in the array pointed to by *buf*. This command requires that the effective-user-id be super-user.

sysinfo will fail if one or both of the following are true:

EPERM The process does not have appropriate privelege for a SET commands.

EINVAL
> *buf* does not point to a valid address, or the data for a SET command exceeds the limits established by the implementation.

DIAGNOSTICS

Upon successful completion, the value returned indicates the buffer size in bytes required to hold the complete value and the terminating null character. If this value is no greater than the value passed in *count*, the entire string was copied; if this value is greater than *count*, the string copied into *buf* has been truncated to *count*−1 bytes plus a terminating null character.

Otherwise, a value of −1 is returned and *errno* is set to indicate the error.

USAGE

There is in many cases no corresponding programmatic interface to set these values; such strings are typically settable only by the system administrator modifying entries in the **master.d** directory or the code provided by the particular OEM reading a serial number or code out of read-only memory, or hard-coded in the version of the operating system.

A good starting guess for *count* is 257, which is likely to cover all strings returned by this interface in typical installations.

SEE ALSO
uname(2), `sysconf`(2);
BSD compatibility package interfaces gethostname(3), gethostid(3).

termios(2)

NAME
termios: tcgetattr, tcsetattr, tcsendbreak, tcdrain, tcflush, tcflow, cfgetospeed, cfgetispeed, cfsetispeed, cfsetospeed, tcgetpgrp, tcsetpgrp, tcgetsid – general terminal interface

SYNOPSIS
    #include <termios.h>

    int tcgetattr(int fildes, struct termios *termios_p);

    int tcsetattr(int fildes, int optional_actions,
        const struct termios *termios_p);

    int tcsendbreak(int fildes, int duration);

    int tcdrain(int fildes);

    int tcflush(int fildes, int queue_selector);

    int tcflow(int fildes, int action);

    speed_t cfgetospeed(struct termios *termios_p);

    int cfsetospeed(const struct termios *termios_p, speed_t speed);

    speed_t cfgetispeed(struct termios *termios_p);

    int cfsetispeed(const struct termios *termios_p, speed_t speed);

    #include <sys/types.h>
    #include <termios.h>

    pid_t tcgetpgrp(int fildes);

    int tcsetpgrp(int fildes, pid_t pgid);

    pid_t tcgetsid(int fildes);

DESCRIPTION
These functions describe a general terminal interface for controlling asynchronous communications ports. A more detailed overview of the terminal interface can be found in termio(7), which also describes an ioctl(2) interface that provides the same functionality. However, the function interface described here is the preferred user interface.

Many of the functions described here have a *termios_p* argument that is a pointer to a **termios** structure. This structure contains the following members:

    tcflag_t   c_iflag;   /* input modes */
    tcflag_t   c_oflag;   /* output modes */
    tcflag_t   c_cflag;   /* control modes */
    tcflag_t   c_lflag;   /* local modes */
    cc_t   c_cc[NCCS];   /* control chars */

These structure members are described in detail in termio(7).

Get and Set Terminal Attributes
The **tcgetattr** function gets the parameters associated with the object referred by *fildes* and stores them in the **termios** structure referenced by *termios_p*. This function may be invoked from a background process; however, the terminal

attributes may be subsequently changed by a foreground process.

The `tcsetattr` function sets the parameters associated with the terminal (unless support is required from the underlying hardware that is not available) from the `termios` structure referenced by *termios_p* as follows:

> If *optional_actions* is `TCSANOW`, the change occurs immediately.

> If *optional_actions* is `TCSADRAIN`, the change occurs after all output written to *fildes* has been transmitted. This function should be used when changing parameters that affect output.

> If *optional_actions* is `TCSAFLUSH`, the change occurs after all output written to the object referred by *fildes* has been transmitted, and all input that has been received but not read is discarded before the change is made.

The symbolic constants for the values of *optional_actions* are defined in `<termios.h>`.

Line Control

If the terminal is using asynchronous serial data transmission, the `tcsendbreak` function causes transmission of a continuous stream of zero-valued bits for a specific duration. If *duration* is zero, it causes transmission of zero-valued bits for at least 0.25 seconds, and not more than 0.5 seconds. If *duration* is not zero, it behaves in a way similar to `tcdrain`.

If the terminal is not using asynchronous serial data transmission, the `tcsendbreak` function sends data to generate a break condition or returns without taking any action.

The `tcdrain` function waits until all output written to the object referred to by *fildes* has been transmitted.

The `tcflush` function discards data written to the object referred to by *fildes* but not transmitted, or data received but not read, depending on the value of *queue_selector*:

> If *queue_selector* is `TCIFLUSH`, it flushes data received but not read.

> If *queue_selector* is `TCOFLUSH`, it flushes data written but not transmitted.

> If *queue_selector* is `TCIOFLUSH`, it flushes both data received but not read, and data written but not transmitted.

The `tcflow` function suspends transmission or reception of data on the object referred to by *fildes*, depending on the value of *action*:

> If *action* is `TCOOFF`, it suspends output.

> If *action* is `TCOON`, it restarts suspended output.

> If *action* if `TCIOFF`, the system transmits a STOP character, which causes the terminal device to stop transmitting data to the system.

> If *action* is `TCION`, the system transmits a START character, which causes the terminal device to start transmitting data to the system.

Get and Set Baud Rate

The baud rate functions get and set the values of the input and output baud rates in the **termios** structure. The effects on the terminal device described below do not become effective until the **tcsetattr** function is successfully called.

The input and output baud rates are stored in the **termios** structure. The values shown in the table are supported. The names in this table are defined in <termios.h>.

Name	Description	Name	Description
B0	Hang up	B600	600 baud
B50	50 baud	B1200	1200 baud
B75	75 baud	B1800	1800 baud
B110	110 baud	B2400	2400 baud
B134	134.5 baud	B4800	4800 baud
B150	150 baud	B9600	9600 baud
B200	200 baud	B19200	19200 baud
B300	300 baud	B38400	38400 baud

cfgetospeed gets the output baud rate and stores it in the **termios** structure pointed to by *termios_p*.

cfsetospeed sets the output baud rate stored in the **termios** structure pointed to by *termios_p* to *speed*. The zero baud rate, B0, is used to terminate the connection. If B0 is specified, the modem control lines are no longer be asserted. Normally, this disconnects the line.

cfgetispeed gets the input baud rate and stores it in the **termios** structure pointed to by *termios_p*.

cfsetispeed sets the input baud rate stored in the **termios** structure pointed to by *termios_p* to *speed*. If the input baud rate is set to zero, the input baud rate is specified by the value of the output baud rate. Both **cfsetispeed** and **cfsetospeed** return a value of zero if successful and −1 to indicate an error. Attempts to set unsupported baud rates are ignored. This refers both to changes to baud rates not supported by the hardware, and to changes setting the input and output baud rates to different values if the hardware does not support this.

Get and Set Terminal Foreground Process Group ID

tcsetpgrp sets the foreground process group ID of the terminal specified by *fildes* to *pgid*. The file associated with *fildes* must be the controlling terminal of the calling process and the controlling terminal must be currently associated with the session of the calling process. *pgid* must match a process group ID of a process in the same session as the calling process.

tcgetpgrp returns the foreground process group ID of the terminal specified by *fildes*. **tcgetpgrp** is allowed from a process that is a member of a background process group; however, the information may be subsequently changed by a process that is a member of a foreground process group.

Get Terminal Session ID

tcgetsid returns the session ID of the terminal specified by *fildes*.

DIAGNOSTICS

On success, **tcgetpgrp** returns the process group ID of the foreground process group associated with the specified terminal. Otherwise, it returns −1 and sets **errno** to indicate the error.

On success, **tcgetsid** returns the session ID associated with the specified terminal. Otherwise, it returns −1 and sets **errno** to indicate the error.

On success, all other functions return a value of 0. Otherwise, they return −1 and set **errno** to indicate the error.

All of the functions fail if one of more of the following is true:

EBADF	The *fildes* argument is not a valid file descriptor.
ENOTTY	The file associated with *fildes* is not a terminal.

tcsetattr also fails if the following is true:

EINVAL	The *optional_actions* argument is not a proper value, or an attempt was made to change an attribute represented in the termios structure to an unsupported value.

tcsendbreak also fails if the following is true:

EINVAL	The device does not support the **tcsendbreak** function.

tcdrain also fails if one or more of the following is true:

EINTR	A signal interrupted the **tcdrain** function.
EINVAL	The device does not support the **tcdrain** function.

tcflush also fails if the following is true:

EINVAL	The device does not support the **tcflush** function or the *queue_selector* argument is not a proper value.

tcflow also fails if the following is true:

EINVAL	The device does not support the **tcflow** function or the *action* argument is not a proper value.

tcgetpgrp also fails if the following is true:

ENOTTY	the calling process does not have a controlling terminal, or *fildes* does not refer to the controlling terminal.

tcsetpgrp also fails if the following is true:

EINVAL	*pgid* is not a valid process group ID.
ENOTTY	the calling process does not have a controlling terminal, or *fildes* does not refer to the controlling terminal, or the controlling terminal is no longer associated with the session of the calling process.
EPERM	*pgid* does not match the process group of an existing process in the same session as the calling process.

tcgetsid also fails if the following is true:

EACCES   *fildes* is a terminal that is not allocated to a session.

SEE ALSO
setsid(2), setpgid(2).
termio(7) in the *System Administrator's Reference Manual*.

NAME

time – get time

SYNOPSIS

```
#include <sys/types.h>
#include <time.h>
```

`time_t time(time_t *tloc);`

DESCRIPTION

time returns the value of time in seconds since 00:00:00 UTC, January 1, 1970.

If *tloc* is non-zero, the return value is also stored in the location to which *tloc* points.

SEE ALSO

stime(2), ctime(3C)

NOTES

time fails and its actions are undefined if *tloc* points to an illegal address.

DIAGNOSTICS

Upon successful completion, time returns the value of time. Otherwise, a value of (time_t)-1 is returned and errno is set to indicate the error.

times(2)

NAME
times – get process and child process times

SYNOPSIS
```
#include <sys/types.h>
#include <sys/times.h>

clock_t times(struct tms *buffer);
```

DESCRIPTION
times fills the **tms** structure pointed to by *buffer* with time-accounting information. The **tms** structure is defined in `<sys/times.h>` as follows:

```
struct tms {
        clock_t    tms_utime;
        clock_t    tms_stime;
        clock_t    tms_cutime;
        clock_t    tms_cstime;
};
```

This information comes from the calling process and each of its terminated child processes for which it has executed a wait routine. All times are reported in clock ticks per second. Clock ticks are a system-dependent parameter. The specific value for an implementation is defined by the variable CLK_TCK, found in the include file `limits.h`. (On a 3B2 Computer clock ticks occur 100 times per second.)

tms_utime is the CPU time used while executing instructions in the user space of the calling process.

tms_stime is the CPU time used by the system on behalf of the calling process.

tms_cutime is the sum of the **tms_utime** and the **tms_cutime** of the child processes.

tms_cstime is the sum of the **tms_stime** and the **tms_cstime** of the child processes.

times fails if:

EFAULT   *buffer* points to an illegal address.

SEE ALSO
exec(2), fork(2), time(2), wait(2), waitid(2), waitpid(3C).
time(1), timex(1) in the *User's Reference Manual*.

DIAGNOSTICS
Upon successful completion, **times** returns the elapsed real time, in clock ticks per second, from an arbitrary point in the past (e.g., system start-up time). This point does not change from one invocation of **times** to another. If **times** fails, a −1 is returned and **errno** is set to indicate the error.

NAME
uadmin – administrative control

SYNOPSIS
#include <sys/uadmin.h>

int uadmin(int *cmd*, int *fcn*, int *mdep*);

DESCRIPTION
uadmin provides control for basic administrative functions. This system call is tightly coupled to the system administrative procedures and is not intended for general use. The argument *mdep* is provided for machine-dependent use and is not defined here.

As specified by *cmd*, the following commands are available:

A_SHUTDOWN The system is shut down. All user processes are killed, the buffer cache is flushed, and the root file system is unmounted. The action to be taken after the system has been shut down is specified by *fcn*. The functions are generic; the hardware capabilities vary on specific machines.

    AD_HALT Halt the processor and turn off the power.

    AD_BOOT Reboot the system, using /stand/unix.

    AD_IBOOT Interactive reboot; the system goes to firmware mode and if the user strikes any key immediately after Booting UNIX is displayed, they are prompted for a bootable program name. If *fcn* is not supplied or is invalid, AD_IBOOT is used as the default.

A_REBOOT The system stops immediately without any further processing. The action to be taken next is specified by *fcn* as above.

A_REMOUNT The root file system is mounted again after having been fixed. This should be used only during the startup process.

uadmin fails if any of the following are true:

EPERM The effective user ID is not super-user.

DIAGNOSTICS
Upon successful completion, the value returned depends on *cmd* as follows:

    A_SHUTDOWN   Never returns.
    A_REBOOT   Never returns.
    A_REMOUNT   0

Otherwise, a value of −1 is returned and errno is set to indicate the error.

SEE ALSO
sysi86(2).

NAME
ulimit – get and set user limits

SYNOPSIS
#include <ulimit.h>

long ulimit(int cmd, ... /* newlimit */);

DESCRIPTION
This function provides for control over process limits. The *cmd* values available are:

UL_GETFSIZE   Get the regular file size limit of the process. The limit is in units of 512-byte blocks and is inherited by child processes. Files of any size can be read.

UL_SETFSIZE   Set the regular file size limit of the process to the value of *newlimit* , taken as a long. Any process may decrease this limit, but only a process with an effective user ID of super-user may increase the limit.

UL_GMEMLIM   Get the maximum possible break value [see brk(2)].

UL_GDESLIM   Get the current value of the maximum number of open files per process configured in the system.

The getrlimit system call provides a more general interface for controlling process limits.

ulimit fails if the following is true:

EINVAL   The *cmd* argument is not valid.

EPERM   A process with an effective user ID other than super user attempts to increase its file size limit.

SEE ALSO
brk(2), getrlimit(2), write(2)

NOTES
ulimit is effective in limiting the growth of regular files. Pipes are currently limited to {PIPE_MAX}.

DIAGNOSTICS
Upon successful completion, a non-negative value is returned. Otherwise, a value of −1 is returned and errno is set to indicate the error.

umask(2)

NAME
umask – set and get file creation mask

SYNOPSIS
    #include <sys/types.h>
    #include <sys/stat.h>

mode_t umask(mode_t cmask);

DESCRIPTION
umask sets the process's file mode creation mask to *cmask* and returns the previous value of the mask. Only the access permission bits of *cmask* and the file mode creation mask are used.

SEE ALSO
chmod(2), creat(2), mknod(2), open(2), stat(5).

mkdir(1), sh(1) in the *User's Reference Manual.*

DIAGNOSTICS
The previous value of the file mode creation mask is returned.

NAME
umount – unmount a file system

SYNOPSIS
#include <sys/mount.h>

int umount(const char *file);

DESCRIPTION
umount requests that a previously mounted file system contained on the block special device or directory identified by *file* be unmounted. *file* is a pointer to a path name. After unmounting the file system, the directory upon which the file system was mounted reverts to its ordinary interpretation.

umount may be invoked only by the super-user.

umount will fail if one or more of the following are true:

EPERM	The process's effective user ID is not super-user.
EINVAL	*file* does not exist.
ELOOP	Too many symbolic links were encountered in translating the path pointed to by *file*.
ENAMETOOLONG	The length of the *file* argument exceeds {PATH_MAX}, or the length of a *file* component exceeds {NAME_MAX} while _POSIX_NO_TRUNC is in effect.
ENOTBLK	*file* is not a block special device.
EINVAL	*file* is not mounted.
EBUSY	A file on *file* is busy.
EFAULT	*file* points to an illegal address.
EREMOTE	*file* is remote.
ENOLINK	*file* is on a remote machine, and the link to that machine is no longer active.
EMULTIHOP	Components of the path pointed to by *file* require hopping to multiple remote machines.

SEE ALSO
mount(2).

DIAGNOSTICS
Upon successful completion a value of 0 is returned. Otherwise, a value of −1 is returned and **errno** is set to indicate the error.

NAME
uname – get name of current UNIX system

SYNOPSIS
```
#include <sys/utsname.h>

int uname(struct utsname *name);
```

DESCRIPTION
uname stores information identifying the current UNIX system in the structure pointed to by *name*.

uname uses the structure utsname defined in <sys/utsname.h> whose members are:

```
char sysname[SYS_NMLN];
char nodename[SYS_NMLN];
char release[SYS_NMLN];
char version[SYS_NMLN];
char machine[SYS_NMLN];
```

uname returns a null-terminated character string naming the current UNIX system in the character array *sysname*. Similarly, *nodename* contains the name that the system is known by on a communications network. *release* and *version* further identify the operating system. *machine* contains a standard name that identifies the hardware that the UNIX system is running on.

EFAULT   uname fails if *name* points to an invalid address.

SEE ALSO
uname(1) in the *User's Reference Manual*.

DIAGNOSTICS
Upon successful completion, a non-negative value is returned. Otherwise, a value of −1 is returned and errno is set to indicate the error.

NAME
unlink — remove directory entry

SYNOPSIS
#include <unistd.h>

int unlink(const char *path);

DESCRIPTION
unlink removes the directory entry named by the path name pointed to by *path*. and decrements the link count of the file referenced by the directory entry. When all links to a file have been removed and no process has the file open, the space occupied by the file is freed and the file ceases to exist. If one or more processes have the file open when the last link is removed, space occupied by the file is not released until all references to the file have been closed. If *path* is a symbolic link, the symbolic link is removed. *path* should not name a directory unless the process has appropriate privileges. Applications should use rmdir to remove directories.

Upon successful completion unlink marks for update the st_ctime and st_mtime fields of the parent directory. Also, if the file's link count is not zero, the st_ctime field of the file is marked for update.

The named file is unlinked unless one or more of the following are true:

EACCES	Search permission is denied for a component of the *path* prefix.
EACCES	Write permission is denied on the directory containing the link to be removed.
EACCES	The parent directory has the sticky bit set and the file is not writable by the user; the user does not own the parent directory and the user does not own the file;
EBUSY	The entry to be unlinked is the mount point for a mounted file system.
EFAULT	*path* points outside the process's allocated address space.
EINTR	A signal was caught during the unlink system call.
ELOOP	Too many symbolic links were encountered in translating *path*.
EMULTIHOP	Components of *path* require hopping to multiple remote machines and the file system does not allow it.
ENAMETOOLONG	The length of the *path* argument exceeds {PATH_MAX}, or the length of a *path* component exceeds {NAME_MAX} while _POSIX_NO_TRUNC is in effect.
ENOENT	The named file does not exist or is a null pathname. The user is not a super-user.
ENOTDIR	A component of the *path* prefix is not a directory.

EPERM		The named file is a directory and the effective user ID of the process is not super-user.
ETXTBSY		The entry to be unlinked is the last link to a pure procedure (shared text) file that is being executed.
EROFS		The directory entry to be unlinked is part of a read-only file system.
ENOLINK		*path* points to a remote machine and the link to that machine is no longer active.

SEE ALSO
close(2), link(2), open(2), rmdir(2).
rm(1) in the *User's Reference Manual*.

DIAGNOSTICS
Upon successful completion, a value of 0 is returned. Otherwise, a value of −1 is returned and errno is set to indicate the error.

NAME
ustat – get file system statistics

SYNOPSIS
```
#include <sys/types.h>
#include <ustat.h>

int ustat(dev_t dev, struct ustat *buf);
```

DESCRIPTION
ustat returns information about a mounted file system. *dev* is a device number identifying a device containing a mounted file system [see makedev(3C)]. *buf* is a pointer to a ustat structure that includes the following elements:

```
daddr_t  f_tfree;      /* Total free blocks */
ino_t    f_tinode;     /* Number of free inodes */
char     f_fname[6];   /* Filsys name */
char     f_fpack[6];   /* Filsys pack name */
```

ustat fails if one or more of the following are true:

EINVAL   *dev* is not the device number of a device containing a mounted file system.

EFAULT   *buf* points outside the process's allocated address space.

EINTR   A signal was caught during a ustat system call.

ENOLINK   *dev* is on a remote machine and the link to that machine is no longer active.

ECOMM   *dev* is on a remote machine and the link to that machine is no longer active.

SEE ALSO
stat(2), statvfs(2), makedev(3C), fs(4).

NOTES
ustat will be phased out in favor of the statvfs function.

DIAGNOSTICS
Upon successful completion, a value of 0 is returned. Otherwise, a value of −1 is returned and errno is set to indicate the error.

NAME

utime – set file access and modification times

SYNOPSIS

```
#include <sys/types.h>
#include <utime.h>

int utime(const char *path, const struct utimbuf *times);
```

DESCRIPTION

path points to a path name naming a file. utime sets the access and modification times of the named file.

If *times* is NULL, the access and modification times of the file are set to the current time. A process must be the owner of the file or have write permission to use utime in this manner.

If *times* is not NULL, *times* is interpreted as a pointer to a utimbuf structure (defined in utime.h) and the access and modification times are set to the values contained in the designated structure. Only the owner of the file or the super-user may use utime this way.

The times in the following structure are measured in seconds since 00:00:00 UTC, Jan. 1, 1970.

```
struct utimbuf {
        time_t actime;     /* access time */
        time_t modtime;    /* modification time */
};
```

utime also causes the time of the last file status change (st_ctime) to be updated.

utime will fail if one or more of the following are true:

EACCES	Search permission is denied by a component of the *path* prefix.
EACCES	The effective user ID is not super-user and not the owner of the file and *times* is NULL and write access is denied.
EFAULT	*times* is not NULL and points outside the process's allocated address space.
EFAULT	*path* points outside the process's allocated address space.
EINTR	A signal was caught during the utime system call.
ELOOP	Too many symbolic links were encountered in translating *path*.
EMULTIHOP	Components of *path* require hopping to multiple remote machines and the file system does not allow it.
ENAMETOOLONG	The length of the *path* argument exceeds {PATH_MAX}, or the length of a *path* component exceeds {NAME_MAX} while _POSIX_NO_TRUNC is in effect.

ENOENT	The named file does not exist or is a null pathname.
ENOLINK	*path* points to a remote machine and the link to that machine is no longer active.
ENOTDIR	A component of the *path* prefix is not a directory.
EPERM	The effective user ID is not super-user and not the owner of the file and *times* is not NULL.
EROFS	The file system containing the file is mounted read-only.

SEE ALSO
  stat(2).

DIAGNOSTICS
  Upon successful completion, a value of 0 is returned. Otherwise, a value of −1 is returned and **errno** is set to indicate the error.

NAME

vfork – spawn new process in a virtual memory efficient way

SYNOPSIS

    #include <unistd.h>

    pid_t vfork (void);

DESCRIPTION

vfork can be used to create new processes without fully copying the address space of the old process, which is horrendously inefficient in a paged environment. It is useful when the purpose of fork would have been to create a new system context for an execve. vfork differs from fork in that the child borrows the parent's memory and thread of control until a call to execve or an exit (either by a call to exit or abnormally.) The parent process is suspended while the child is using its resources.

vfork returns 0 in the child's context and (later) the process ID (PID) of the child in the parent's context.

vfork can normally be used just like fork. It does not work, however, to return while running in the child's context from the procedure which called vfork since the eventual return from vfork would then return to a no longer existent stack frame. Be careful, also, to call _exit rather than exit if you cannot execve, since exit will flush and close standard I/O channels, and thereby mess up the parent processes standard I/O data structures. Even with fork it is wrong to call exit since buffered data would then be flushed twice.

DIAGNOSTICS

Upon successful completion, vfork returns a value of 0 to the child process and returns the process ID of the child process to the parent process. Otherwise, a value of −1 is returned to the parent process, no child process is created, and the global variable errno is set to indicate the error.

vfork will fail and no child process will be created if one or more of the following are true:

EAGAIN	The system-imposed limit on the total number of processes under execution would be exceeded. This limit is determined when the system is generated.
EAGAIN	The system-imposed limit on the total number of processes under execution by a single user would be exceeded. This limit is determined when the system is generated.
ENOMEM	There is insufficient swap space for the new process.

SEE ALSO

exec(2), exit(2), fork(2), ioctl(2), wait(2).

NOTES

This system call will be eliminated in a future release. System implementation changes are making the efficiency gain of vfork over fork smaller. The memory sharing semantics of vfork can be obtained through other mechanisms.

To avoid a possible deadlock situation, processes that are children in the middle of a **vfork** are never sent `SIGTTOU` or `SIGTTIN` signals; rather, output or *ioctl*s are allowed and input attempts result in an EOF indication.

On some systems, the implementation of **vfork** causes the parent to inherit register values from the child. This can create problems for certain optimizing compilers if `<unistd.h>` is not included in the source calling **vfork**.

NAME

wait – wait for child process to stop or terminate

SYNOPSIS

    #include <sys/types.h>
    #include <sys/wait.h>

    pid_t wait(int *stat_loc);

DESCRIPTION

wait suspends the calling process until one of its immediate children terminates or until a child that is being traced stops because it has received a signal. The **wait** system call will return prematurely if a signal is received. If all child processes stopped or terminated prior to the call on **wait**, return is immediate.

If **wait** returns because the status of a child process is available, it returns the process ID of the child process. If the calling process had specified a non-zero value for *stat_loc*, the status of the child process will be stored in the location pointed to by *stat_loc*. It may be evaluated with the macros described on **wstat**(5). In the following, *status* is the object pointed to by *stat_loc*:

> If the child process stopped, the high order 8 bits of *status* will contain the number of the signal that caused the process to stop and the low order 8 bits will be set equal to **WSTOPFLG**.
>
> If the child process terminated due to an **exit** call, the low order 8 bits of *status* will be 0 and the high order 8 bits will contain the low order 8 bits of the argument that the child process passed to **exit**; see **exit**(2).
>
> If the child process terminated due to a signal, the high order 8 bits of *status* will be 0 and the low order 8 bits will contain the number of the signal that caused the termination. In addition, if **WCOREFLG** is set, a "core image" will have been produced; see **signal**(2).

If **wait** returns because the status of a child process is available, then that status may be evaluated with the macros defined by **wstat**(5).

If a parent process terminates without waiting for its child processes to terminate, the parent process ID of each child process is set to 1. This means the initialization process inherits the child processes; see **intro**(2).

wait will fail if one or both of the following is true:

> ECHILD   The calling process has no existing unwaited-for child processes.
>
> EINTR   The function was interrupted by a signal.

SEE ALSO

exec(2), exit(2), fork(2), intro(2), pause(2), ptrace(2), signal(2), signal(5), wstat(5).

NOTES

See NOTES in **signal**(2).

If **SIGCLD** is held, then **wait** does not recognize death of children.

DIAGNOSTICS

If **wait** returns due to a stopped or terminated child process, the process ID of the child is returned to the calling process. Otherwise, a value of −1 is returned and **errno** is set to indicate the error.

NAME

waitid − wait for child process to change state

SYNOPSIS

```
#include <sys/types.h>
#include <wait.h>

int waitid(idtype_t idtype, id_t id, siginfo_t *infop, int options);
```

DESCRIPTION

waitid suspends the calling process until one of its children changes state. It records the current state of a child in the structure pointed to by *infop*. If a child process changed state prior to the call to waitid, waitid returns immediately.

The *idtype* and *id* arguments specify which children waitid is to wait for.

> If *idtype* is P_PID, waitid waits for the child with a process ID equal to (pid_t) *id*.
>
> If *idtype* is P_PGID, waitid waits for any child with a process group ID equal to (pid_t) *id*.
>
> If *idtype* is P_ALL, waitid waits for any children and *id* is ignored.

The *options* argument is used to specify which state changes waitid is to wait for. It is formed by an OR of any of the following flags:

WEXITED	Wait for process(es) to exit.
WTRAPPED	Wait for traced process(es) to become trapped or reach a breakpoint [see ptrace(2)].
WSTOPPED	Wait for and return the process status of any child that has stopped upon receipt of a signal.
WCONTINUED	Return the status for any child that was stopped and has been continued.
WNOHANG	Return immediately.
WNOWAIT	Keep the process in a waitable state.

infop must point to a siginfo_t structure, as defined in siginfo(5). siginfo_t is filled in by the system with the status of the process being waited for.

waitid fails if one or more of the following is true.

EFAULT	*infop* points to an invalid address.
EINTR	waitid was interrupted due to the receipt of a signal by the calling process.
EINVAL	An invalid value was specified for *options*.
EINVAL	*idtype* and *id* specify an invalid set of processes.
ECHILD	The set of processes specified by *idtype* and *id* does not contain any unwaited-for processes.

DIAGNOSTICS

If `waitid` returns due to a change of state of one of its children, a value of 0 is returned. Otherwise, a value of −1 is returned and `errno` is set to indicate the error.

SEE ALSO

intro(2), exec(2), exit(2), fork(2), pause(2), ptrace(2), signal(2), sigaction(2), wait(2), siginfo(5).

NAME

waitpid – wait for child process to change state

SYNOPSIS

```
#include <sys/types.h>
#include <sys/wait.h>

pid_t waitpid (pid_t pid, int *stat_loc, int options);
```

DESCRIPTION

waitpid suspends the calling process until one of its children changes state; if a child process changed state prior to the call to **waitpid**, return is immediate. *pid* specifies a set of child processes for which status is requested.

If *pid* is equal to (pid_t)−1, status is requested for any child process.

If *pid* is greater than (pid_t)0, it specifies the process ID of the child process for which status is requested.

If *pid* is equal to (pid_t)0 status is requested for any child process whose process group ID is equal to that of the calling process.

If *pid* is less than (pid_t)−1, status is requested for any child process whose process group ID is equal to the absolute value of *pid*.

If **waitpid** returns because the status of a child process is available, then that status may be evaluated with the macros defined by **wstat**(5). If the calling process had specified a non-zero value of *stat_loc*, the status of the child process will be stored in the location pointed to by *stat_loc*.

The *options* argument is constructed from the bitwise inclusive OR of zero or more of the following flags, defined in the header file **<sys/wait.h>**:

WCONTINUED   the status of any continued child process specified by *pid*, whose status has not been reported since it continued, shall also be reported to the calling process.

WNOHANG   waitpid will not suspend execution of the calling process if status is not immediately available for one of the child processes specified by *pid*.

WNOWAIT   keep the process whose status is returned in *stat_loc* in a waitable state. The process may be waited for again with identical results.

WUNTRACED   the status of any child processes specified by *pid* that are stopped, and whose status has not yet been reported since they stopped, shall also be reported to the calling process.

waitpid with *options* equal to WUNTRACED and *pid* equal to (pid_t)−1 is identical to a call to **wait**(2).

waitpid will fail if one or more of the following is true:

EINTR   waitpid was interrupted due to the receipt of a signal sent by the calling process.

EINVAL   An invalid value was specified for *options*.

ECHILD   The process or process group specified by *pid* does not exist or is not a child of the calling process or can never be in the states specified by *options*.

SEE ALSO

exec(2), exit(2), fork(2), intro(2), pause(2), ptrace(2), signal(2), sigaction(2), siginfo(5), wstat(5)

DIAGNOSTICS

If `waitpid` returns because the status of a child process is available, this function shall return a value equal to the process ID of the child process for which status is reported. If `waitpid` returns due to the delivery of a signal to the calling process, a value of −1 shall be returned and *errno* shall be set to EINTR. If this function was invoked with WNOHANG set in *options*, it has at least one child process specified by *pid* for which status is not available, and status is not available for any process specified by *pid*, a value of 0 shall be returned. Otherwise, a value of −1 shall be returned, and *errno* shall be set to indicate the error.

write(2)   write(2)

NAME
write, writev – write on a file

SYNOPSIS
#include <unistd.h>
int write(int fildes, const void *buf, unsigned nbyte);

#include <sys/types.h>
#include <sys/uio.h>

int writev(int fildes, const struct iovec *iov, int iovcnt);

DESCRIPTION
write attempts to write *nbyte* bytes from the buffer pointed to by *buf* to the file associated with *fildes*. If *nbyte* is zero and the file is a regular file, write returns zero and has no other results. *fildes* is a file descriptor obtained from a creat, open, dup, fcntl, or pipe system call.

writev performs the same action as write, but gathers the output data from the *iovcnt* buffers specified by the members of the *iov* array: *iov*[0], *iov*[1], ..., *iov*[*iovcnt* – 1]. The *iovcnt* is invalid if greater than 0 and less than or equal to {IOV_MAX}.

For writev, the iovec structure contains the following members:

         caddr_t   iov_base;
         int   iov_len;

Each iovec entry specifies the base address and length of an area in memory from which data should be written. writev always writes a complete area before proceeding to the next.

On devices capable of seeking, the actual writing of data proceeds from the position in the file indicated by the file pointer. On return from write, the file pointer is incremented by the number of bytes actually written. On a regular file, if the incremented file pointer is greater than the length of the file, the length of the file is set to the new file pointer.

On devices incapable of seeking, writing always takes place starting at the current position. The value of a file pointer associated with such a device is undefined.

If the O_APPEND flag of the file status flags is set, the file pointer is set to the end of the file prior to each write.

For regular files, if the O_SYNC flag of the file status flags is set, write does not return until both the file data and file status have been physically updated. This function is for special applications that require extra reliability at the cost of performance. For block special files, if O_SYNC is set, write does not return until the data has been physically updated.

A write to a regular file is blocked if mandatory file/record locking is set [see chmod(2)], and there is a record lock owned by another process on the segment of the file to be written:

If O_NDELAY or O_NONBLOCK is set, write returns −1 and sets errno to EAGAIN.

If O_NDELAY and O_NONBLOCK are clear, write sleeps until all blocking locks are removed or the write is terminated by a signal.

If a write requests that more bytes be written than there is room for—for example, if the write would exceed the process file size limit [see getrlimit(2) and ulimit(2)], the system file size limit, or the free space on the device—only as many bytes as there is room for will be written. For example, suppose there is space for 20 bytes more in a file before reaching a limit. A write of 512-bytes returns 20. The next write of a non-zero number of bytes gives a failure return (except as noted for pipes and FIFO below).

Write requests to a pipe or FIFO are handled the same as a regular file with the following exceptions:

There is no file offset associated with a pipe, hence each write request appends to the end of the pipe.

Write requests of {PIPE_BUF} bytes or less are guaranteed not to be interleaved with data from other processes doing writes on the same pipe. Writes of greater than {PIPE_BUF} bytes may have data interleaved, on arbitrary boundaries, with writes by other processes, whether or not the O_NONBLOCK or O_NDELAY flags are set.

If O_NONBLOCK and O_NDELAY are clear, a write request may cause the process to block, but on normal completion it returns *nbyte*.

If O_NONBLOCK is set, write requests are handled in the following way: the write does not block the process; write requests for {PIPE_BUF} or fewer bytes either succeed completely and return *nbyte*, or return −1 and set errno to EAGAIN. A write request for greater than {PIPE_BUF} bytes either transfers what it can and returns the number of bytes written, or transfers no data and returns −1 with errno set to EAGAIN. Also, if a request is greater than {PIPE_BUF} bytes and all data previously written to the pipe has been read, write transfers at least {PIPE_BUF} bytes.

If O_NDELAY is set, write requests are handled in the following way: the write does not block the process; write requests for {PIPE_BUF} or fewer bytes either succeed completely and return *nbyte*, or return 0. A write request for greater than {PIPE_BUF} bytes either transfers what it can and returns the number of bytes written, or transfers no data and returns 0. Also, if a request is greater than {PIPE_BUF} bytes and all data previously written to the pipe has been read, write transfers at least {PIPE_BUF} bytes.

When attempting to write to a file descriptor (other than a pipe or FIFO) that supports nonblocking writes and cannot accept the data immediately:

If O_NONBLOCK and O_NDELAY are clear, write blocks until the data can be accepted.

write (2)

If O_NONBLOCK or O_NDELAY is set, **write** does not block the process. If some data can be written without blocking the process, **write** writes what it can and returns the number of bytes written. Otherwise, if O_NONBLOCK is set, it returns −1 and sets **errno** to EAGAIN or if O_NDELAY is set, it returns 0.

For STREAMS files [see intro(2)], the operation of **write** is determined by the values of the minimum and maximum *nbyte* range ("packet size") accepted by the stream. These values are contained in the topmost stream module. Unless the user pushes the topmost module [see I_PUSH in streamio(7)], these values can not be set or tested from user level. If *nbyte* falls within the packet size range, *nbyte* bytes are written. If *nbyte* does not fall within the range and the minimum packet size value is zero, **write** breaks the buffer into maximum packet size segments prior to sending the data downstream (the last segment may be smaller than the maximum packet size). If *nbyte* does not fall within the range and the minimum value is non-zero, **write** fails and sets **errno** to ERANGE. Writing a zero-length buffer (*nbyte* is zero) to a STREAMS device sends a zero length message with zero returned. However, writing a zero-length buffer to a pipe or FIFO sends no message and zero is returned. The user program may issue the I_SWROPT ioctl(2) to enable zero-length messages to be sent across the pipe or FIFO [see streamio(7)].

When writing to a stream, data messages are created with a priority band of zero. When writing to a stream that is not a pipe or FIFO:

If O_NDELAY and O_NONBLOCK are not set, and the stream cannot accept data (the stream write queue is full due to internal flow control conditions), **write** blocks until data can be accepted.

If O_NDELAY or O_NONBLOCK is set and the stream cannot accept data, **write** returns −1 and sets **errno** to EAGAIN.

If O_NDELAY or O_NONBLOCK is set and part of the buffer has already been written when a condition occurs in which the stream cannot accept additional data, **write** terminates and returns the number of bytes written.

write and **writev** fail and the file pointer remains unchanged if one or more of the following are true:

EAGAIN	Mandatory file/record locking is set, O_NDELAY or O_NONBLOCK is set, and there is a blocking record lock.
EAGAIN	Total amount of system memory available when reading via raw I/O is temporarily insufficient.
EAGAIN	An attempt is made to write to a stream that can not accept data with the O_NDELAY or O_NONBLOCK flag set.
EAGAIN	If a **write** to a pipe or FIFO of {PIPE_BUF} bytes or less is requested and less than *nbytes* of free space is available.
EBADF	*fildes* is not a valid file descriptor open for writing.

EDEADLK	The **write** was going to go to sleep and cause a deadlock situation to occur.
EFAULT	*buf* points outside the process's allocated address space.
EFBIG	An attempt is made to write a file that exceeds the process's file size limit or the maximum file size [see **getrlimit**(2) and **ulimit**(2)].
EINTR	A signal was caught during the **write** system call.
EINVAL	An attempt is made to write to a stream linked below a multiplexor.
EIO	The process is in the background and is attempting to write to its controlling terminal whose TOSTOP flag is set; the process is neither ignoring nor blocking SIGTTOU signals, and the process group of the process is orphaned.
ENOLCK	The system record lock table was full, so the **write** could not go to sleep until the blocking record lock was removed.
ENOLINK	*fildes* is on a remote machine and the link to that machine is no longer active.
ENOSR	An attempt is made to write to a stream with insufficient STREAMS memory resources available in the system.
ENOSPC	During a **write** to an ordinary file, there is no free space left on the device.
ENXIO	A hangup occurred on the stream being written to.

EPIPE and SIGPIPE signal
    An attempt is made to write to a pipe that is not open for reading by any process.

EPIPE	An attempt is made to write to a FIFO that is not open for reading by any process.
EPIPE	An attempt is made to write to a pipe that has only one end open.
ERANGE	An attempt is made to write to a stream with *nbyte* outside specified minimum and maximum write range, and the minimum value is non-zero.
ENOLCK	Enforced record locking was enabled and {LOCK_MAX} regions are already locked in the system.

In addition, **writev** may return one of the following errors:

EINVAL	*iovcnt* was less than or equal to 0, or greater than 16.
EINVAL	One of the `iov_len` values in the *iov* array was negative.
EINVAL	The sum of the `iov_len` values in the *iov* array overflowed a 32-bit integer.

write(2)　　　　　　　　　　　　　　　　　　　　　　　　　　　　　　write(2)

A **write** to a STREAMS file can fail if an error message has been received at the stream head. In this case, **errno** is set to the value included in the error message.

Upon successful completion **write** and **writev** mark for update the st_ctime and st_mtime fields of the file.

SEE ALSO

intro(2), creat(2), dup(2), fcntl(2), getrlimit(2), lseek(2), open(2), pipe(2), ulimit(2).

DIAGNOSTICS

On success, **write** returns the number of bytes actually written. Otherwise, it returns −1 and sets **errno** to indicate the error.

SUBROUTINES (3)

SUBROUTINES (3)

intro (3)

NAME
intro – introduction to functions and libraries

DESCRIPTION
This section describes functions found in various libraries, other than those functions that directly invoke UNIX system primitives, which are described in Section 2 of this volume. Function declarations can be obtained from the #include files indicated on each page. Certain major collections are identified by a letter after the section number:

(3C) These functions, together with those of Section 2 and those marked (3S), constitute the standard C library, libc, which is automatically linked by the C compilation system. The standard C library is implemented as a shared object, libc.so, and an archive, libc.a. C programs are linked with the shared object version of the standard C library by default. Specify –dn on the cc command line to link with the archive version. [See cc(1) for other overrides, and the "C Compilation System" chapter of the *Programmer's Guide: ANSI C and Programming Support Tools* for a discussion.]

(3S) These functions constitute the "standard I/O package" [see stdio(3S)].

(3E) These functions constitute the ELF access library, libelf. This library is not implemented as a shared object, and is not automatically linked by the C compilation system. Specify –lelf on the cc command line to link with this library.

(3G) These functions constitute the general-purpose library, libgen. This library is not implemented as a shared object, and is not automatically linked by the C compilation system. Specify –lgen on the cc command line to link with this library.

(3M) These functions constitute the math library, libm. [See intro(3M) and math(5).] This library is not implemented as a shared object, and is not automatically linked by the C compilation system. Specify –lm on the cc command line to link with this library.

(3X) Specialized libraries. The files in which these libraries are found are given on the appropriate pages.

DEFINITIONS
A character is any bit pattern able to fit into a byte on the machine. The null character is a character with value 0, conventionally represented in the C language as \0. A character array is a sequence of characters. A null-terminated character array (a *string*) is a sequence of characters, the last of which is the null character. The null string is a character array containing only the terminating null character. A NULL pointer is the value that is obtained by casting 0 into a pointer. C guarantees that this value will not match that of any legitimate pointer, so many functions that return pointers return NULL to indicate an error. The macro NULL is defined in stdio.h. Types of the form size_t are defined in the appropriate header files.

FILES

    INCDIR   usually /usr/include
    LIBDIR   usually /usr/ccs/lib
    LIBDIR/libc.so
    LIBDIR/libc.a
    LIBDIR/libgen.a
    LIBDIR/libm.a
    LIBDIR/libsfm.sa
    /usr/lib/libc.so.1

SEE ALSO

ar(1), cc(1), ld(1), lint(1), nm(1), intro(2), intro(3M), stdio(3S), math(5).
The "C Compilation System" chapter in the *Programmer's Guide: ANSI C and Programming Support Tools*.

DIAGNOSTICS

For functions that return floating-point values, error handling varies according to compilation mode. Under the -Xt (default) option to cc, these functions return the conventional values 0, ±HUGE, or NaN when the function is undefined for the given arguments or when the value is not representable. In the -Xa and -Xc compilation modes, ±HUGE_VAL is returned instead of ±HUGE. (HUGE_VAL and HUGE are defined in math.h to be infinity and the largest-magnitude single-precision number, respectively.)

NOTES

None of the functions, external variables, or macros should be redefined in the user's programs. Any other name may be redefined without affecting the behavior of other library functions, but such redefinition may conflict with a declaration in an included header file.

The header files in *INCDIR* provide function prototypes (function declarations including the types of arguments) for most of the functions listed in this manual. Function prototypes allow the compiler to check for correct usage of these functions in the user's program. The lint program checker may also be used and will report discrepancies even if the header files are not included with #include statements. Definitions for Sections 2, 3C, and 3S are checked automatically. Other definitions can be included by using the -l option to lint. (For example, -lm includes definitions for libm.) Use of lint is highly recommended.

Users should carefully note the difference between STREAMS and *stream*. STREAMS is a set of kernel mechanisms that support the development of network services and data communication drivers. It is composed of utility routines, kernel facilities, and a set of data structures. A *stream* is a file with its associated buffering. It is declared to be a pointer to a type FILE defined in stdio.h.

In detailed definitions of components, it is sometimes necessary to refer to symbolic names that are implementation-specific, but which are not necessarily expected to be accessible to an application program. Many of these symbolic names describe boundary conditions and system limits.

In this section, for readability, these implementation-specific values are given symbolic names. These names always appear enclosed in curly brackets to distinguish them from symbolic names of other implementation-specific constants that are accessible to application programs by header files. These names are not necessarily accessible to an application program through a header file, although they may be defined in the documentation for a particular system.

In general, a portable application program should not refer to these symbolic names in its code. For example, an application program would not be expected to test the length of an argument list given to a routine to determine if it was greater than {ARG_MAX}.

3C AND 3S

3C AND 3S

NAME
a64l, l64a – convert between long integer and base-64 ASCII string

SYNOPSIS
#include <stdlib.h>

long a64l (const char *s);

char *l64a (long l);

DESCRIPTION
These functions are used to maintain numbers stored in base-64 ASCII characters. These characters define a notation by which long integers can be represented by up to six characters; each character represents a "digit" in a radix-64 notation.

The characters used to represent "digits" are . for 0, / for 1, 0 through 9 for 2–11, A through Z for 12–37, and a through z for 38–63.

a64l takes a pointer to a null-terminated base-64 representation and returns a corresponding long value. If the string pointed to by s contains more than six characters, a64l will use the first six.

a64l scans the character string from left to right with the least significant digit on the left, decoding each character as a 6-bit radix-64 number.

l64a takes a long argument and returns a pointer to the corresponding base-64 representation. If the argument is 0, l64a returns a pointer to a null string.

NOTES
The value returned by l64a is a pointer into a static buffer, the contents of which are overwritten by each call.

abort(3C) abort(3C)

NAME
abort – generate an abnormal termination signal

SYNOPSIS
#include <stdlib.h>

void abort (void);

DESCRIPTION
abort first closes all open files, stdio(3S) streams, directory streams and message catalogue descriptors, if possible, then causes the signal SIGABRT to be sent to the calling process.

SEE ALSO
sdb(1), exit(2), kill(2), signal(2), catopen(3C), stdio(3S).
sh(1) in the *User's Reference Manual*.

DIAGNOSTICS
If SIGABRT is neither caught nor ignored, and the current directory is writable, a core dump is produced and the message **abort – core dumped** is written by the shell [see sh(1)].

NAME

abs, labs – return integer absolute value

SYNOPSIS

#include <stdlib.h>

int abs (int val);

long labs (long lval);

DESCRIPTION

abs returns the absolute value of its int operand. labs returns the absolute value of its long operand.

SEE ALSO

floor(3M).

NOTES

In 2's-complement representation, the absolute value of the largest magnitude negative integral value is undefined.

NAME

addseverity – build a list of severity levels for an application for use with fmtmsg

SYNOPSIS

#include <fmtmsg.h>

int addseverity(int severity, const char *string);

DESCRIPTION

The **addseverity** function builds a list of severity levels for an application to be used with the message formatting facility, **fmtmsg**. *severity* is an integer value indicating the seriousness of the condition, and *string* is a pointer to a string describing the condition (string is not limited to a specific size).

If **addseverity** is called with an integer value that has not been previously defined, the function adds that new severity value and print string to the existing set of standard severity levels.

If **addseverity** is called with an integer value that has been previously defined, the function redefines that value with the new print string. Previously defined severity levels may be removed by supplying the NULL string. If **addseverity** is called with a negative number or an integer value of 0, 1, 2, 3, or 4, the function fails and returns −1. The values 0–4 are reserved for the standard severity levels and cannot be modified. Identifiers for the standard levels of severity are:

- **MM_HALT**   indicates that the application has encountered a severe fault and is halting. Produces the print string HALT.
- **MM_ERROR**   indicates that the application has detected a fault. Produces the print string ERROR.
- **MM_WARNING**   indicates a condition that is out of the ordinary, that might be a problem, and should be watched. Produces the print string WARNING.
- **MM_INFO**   provides information about a condition that is not in error. Produces the print string INFO.
- **MM_NOSEV**   indicates that no severity level is supplied for the message.

Severity levels may also be defined at run time using the SEV_LEVEL environment variable [see fmtmsg(3C)].

EXAMPLES

When the function **addseverity** is used as follows:

    addseverity(7,"ALERT")

the following call to **fmtmsg**:

    fmtmsg(MM_PRINT, "UX:cat", 7, "invalid syntax", "refer to manual", "UX:cat:001")

produces:

    UX:cat: ALERT: invalid syntax
    TO FIX: refer to manual   UX:cat:001

addseverity(3C)

SEE ALSO
   fmtmsg(1M), fmtmsg(3C), gettxt(3C), printf(3S).

DIAGNOSTICS
   addseverity returns **MM_OK** on success or **MM_NOTOK** on failure.

NAME
atexit – add program termination routine

SYNOPSIS
#include <stdlib.h>

int atexit (void (*func)(void));

DESCRIPTION
atexit adds the function *func* to a list of functions to be called without arguments on normal termination of the program. Normal termination occurs by either a call to the exit system call or a return from main. At most 32 functions may be registered by atexit; the functions will be called in the reverse order of their registration.

atexit returns 0 if the registration succeeds, nonzero if it fails.

SEE ALSO
exit(2).

bsearch (3C)

NAME
bsearch – binary search a sorted table

SYNOPSIS
#include <stdlib.h>

void *bsearch (const void *key, const void *base, size_t nel,
    size_t size, int (*compar)(const void *, const void *));

DESCRIPTION
bsearch is a binary search routine generalized from Knuth (6.2.1) Algorithm B. It returns a pointer into a table (an array) indicating where a datum may be found or a null pointer if the datum cannot be found. The table must be previously sorted in increasing order according to a comparison function pointed to by *compar*. *key* points to a datum instance to be sought in the table. *base* points to the element at the base of the table. *nel* is the number of elements in the table. *size* is the number of bytes in each element. The function pointed to by *compar* is called with two arguments that point to the elements being compared. The function must return an integer less than, equal to, or greater than 0 as accordingly the first argument is to be considered less than, equal to, or greater than the second.

EXAMPLE
The example below searches a table containing pointers to nodes consisting of a string and its length. The table is ordered alphabetically on the string in the node pointed to by each entry.

This program reads in strings and either finds the corresponding node and prints out the string and its length, or prints an error message.

```
#include <stdio.h>
#include <stdlib.h>
#include <string.h>

struct node {               /* these are stored in the table */
    char *string;
    int length;
};
static struct node table[] =    /* table to be searched */
{
    { "asparagus", 10 },
    { "beans", 6 },
    { "tomato", 7 },
    { "watermelon", 11 },
};

main()
{
    struct node *node_ptr, node;
    /* routine to compare 2 nodes */
    static int node_compare(const void *, const void *);
    char str_space[20];    /* space to read string into */
```

```
            node.string = str_space;
            while (scanf("%20s", node.string) != EOF) {
                node_ptr = bsearch( &node,
                        table, sizeof(table)/sizeof(struct node),
                        sizeof(struct node), node_compare);
                if (node_ptr != NULL) {
                        (void) printf("string = %20s, length = %d\n",
                            node_ptr->string, node_ptr->length);
                } else {
                        (void)printf("not found: %20s\n", node.string);
                }
            }
            return(0);
    }

    /* routine to compare two nodes based on an  */
    /* alphabetical ordering of the string field */
    static int
    node_compare(const void *node1, const void *node2)
    {
            return (strcmp(
                    ((const struct node *)node1)->string,
                    ((const struct node *)node2)->string));
    }
```

SEE ALSO
hsearch(3C), lsearch(3C), qsort(3C), tsearch(3C).

DIAGNOSTICS
A null pointer is returned if the key cannot be found in the table.

NOTES
The pointers to the key and the element at the base of the table should be of type pointer-to-*element*.

The comparison function need not compare every byte, so arbitrary data may be contained in the elements in addition to the values being compared.

If the number of elements in the table is less than the size reserved for the table, *nel* should be the lower number.

NAME
catgets – read a program message

SYNOPSIS
#include <nl_types.h>

char *catgets (nl_catd catd, int set_num, int msg_num, char *s);

DESCRIPTION
catgets attempts to read message *msg_num*, in set *set_num*, from the message catalogue identified by *catd*. *catd* is a catalogue descriptor returned from an earlier call to catopen. *s* points to a default message string which will be returned by catgets if the identified message catalogue is not currently available.

SEE ALSO
catopen(3C).

DIAGNOSTICS
If the identified message is retrieved successfully, catgets returns a pointer to an internal buffer area containing the null terminated message string. If the call is unsuccessful because the message catalogue identified by *catd* is not currently available, a pointer to *s* is returned.

catopen(3C)

NAME
catopen, catclose – open/close a message catalogue

SYNOPSIS
#include <nl_types.h>

nl_catd catopen (char *name, int oflag);

int catclose (nl_catd catd);

DESCRIPTION
catopen opens a message catalogue and returns a catalogue descriptor. *name* specifies the name of the message catalogue to be opened. If *name* contains a "/" then *name* specifies a pathname for the message catalogue. Otherwise, the environment variable NLSPATH is used. If NLSPATH does not exist in the environment, or if a message catalogue cannot be opened in any of the paths specified by NLSPATH, then the default path is used [see nl_types(5)].

The names of message catalogues, and their location in the filestore, can vary from one system to another. Individual applications can choose to name or locate message catalogues according to their own special needs. A mechanism is therefore required to specify where the catalogue resides.

The NLSPATH variable provides both the location of message catalogues, in the form of a search path, and the naming conventions associated with message catalogue files. For example:

NLSPATH=/nlslib/%L/%N.cat:/nlslib/%N/%L

The metacharacter % introduces a substitution field, where %L substitutes the current setting of the LANG environment variable (see following section), and %N substitutes the value of the *name* parameter passed to catopen. Thus, in the above example, catopen will search in /nlslib/$LANG/*name*.cat, then in /nlslib/*name*/$LANG, for the required message catalogue.

NLSPATH will normally be set up on a system wide basis (e.g., in /etc/profile) and thus makes the location and naming conventions associated with message catalogues transparent to both programs and users.

The full set of metacharacters is:

- %N   The value of the name parameter passed to catopen.
- %L   The value of LANG.
- %l   The value of the language element of LANG.
- %t   The value of the territory element of LANG.
- %c   The value of the codeset element of LANG.
- %%   A single %.

The LANG environment variable provides the ability to specify the user's requirements for native languages, local customs and character set, as an ASCII string in the form

LANG=language[_territory[.codeset]]

A user who speaks German as it is spoken in Austria and has a terminal which operates in ISO 8859/1 codeset, would want the setting of the **LANG** variable to be

> LANG=De_A.88591

With this setting it should be possible for that user to find any relevant catalogues should they exist.

Should the **LANG** variable not be set then the value of **LC_MESSAGES** as returned by **setlocale** is used. If this is **NULL** then the default path as defined in **nl_types** is used.

oflag is reserved for future use and should be set to 0. The results of setting this field to any other value are undefined.

catclose closes the message catalogue identified by *catd*.

SEE ALSO
catgets(3C), setlocale(3C), environ(5), nl_types(5).

DIAGNOSTICS
If successful, **catopen** returns a message catalogue descriptor for use on subsequent calls to **catgets** and **catclose**. Otherwise **catopen** returns (nl_catd) −1.

catclose returns 0 if successful, otherwise −1.

clock(3C)

NAME
clock – report CPU time used

SYNOPSIS
#include <time.h>

clock_t clock (void);

DESCRIPTION
clock returns the amount of CPU time (in microseconds) used since the first call to clock in the calling process. The time reported is the sum of the user and system times of the calling process and its terminated child processes for which it has executed the **wait** system call, the **pclose** function, or the **system** function.

Dividing the value returned by clock by the constant CLOCKS_PER_SEC, defined in the time.h header file, will give the time in seconds.

The resolution of the clock is 10 milliseconds on AT&T 3B computers.

SEE ALSO
times(2), wait(2), popen(3S), system(3S).

NOTES
The value returned by clock is defined in microseconds for compatibility with systems that have CPU clocks with much higher resolution. Because of this, the value returned will wrap around after accumulating only 2147 seconds of CPU time (about 36 minutes). If the process time used is not available or cannot be represented, clock returns the value (clock_t)-1.

NAME

conv: toupper, tolower, _toupper, _tolower, toascii − translate characters

SYNOPSIS

#include <ctype.h>

int toupper (int c);

int tolower (int c);

int _toupper (int c);

int _tolower (int c);

int toascii (int c);

DESCRIPTION

toupper and **tolower** have as their domain the range of the function **getc**: all values represented in an **unsigned char** and the value of the macro **EOF** as defined in **stdio.h**. If the argument of **toupper** represents a lower-case letter, the result is the corresponding upper-case letter. If the argument of **tolower** represents an upper-case letter, the result is the corresponding lower-case letter. All other arguments in the domain are returned unchanged.

The macros **_toupper** and **_tolower** accomplish the same things as **toupper** and **tolower**, respectively, but have restricted domains and are faster. **_toupper** requires a lower-case letter as its argument; its result is the corresponding upper-case letter. **_tolower** requires an upper-case letter as its argument; its result is the corresponding lower-case letter. Arguments outside the domain cause undefined results.

toascii yields its argument with all bits turned off that are not part of a standard 7-bit ASCII character; it is intended for compatibility with other systems.

toupper, tolower, _toupper, and **_tolower** are affected by **LC_CTYPE**. In the C locale, or in a locale where shift information is not defined, these functions determine the case of characters according to the rules of the ASCII-coded character set. Characters outside the ASCII range of characters are returned unchanged.

SEE ALSO

ctype(3C), getc(3S), setlocale(3C), environ(5).

crypt(3C)

NAME
crypt, setkey, encrypt – generate encryption

SYNOPSIS
#include <crypt.h>

char *crypt (const char *key, const char *salt);

void setkey (const char *key);

void encrypt (char *block, int edflag);

DESCRIPTION
crypt is the password encryption function. It is based on a one-way encryption algorithm with variations intended (among other things) to frustrate use of hardware implementations of a key search.

key is the input string to encrypt, for instance, a user's typed password. Only the first eight characters are used; the rest are ignored. *salt* is a two-character string chosen from the set a-zA-Z0-9./; this string is used to perturb the hashing algorithm in one of 4096 different ways, after which the input string is used as the key to encrypt repeatedly a constant string. The returned value points to the encrypted input string. The first two characters of the return value are the *salt* itself.

The setkey and encrypt functions provide (rather primitive) access to the actual hashing algorithm. The argument of setkey is a character array of length 64 containing only the characters with numerical value 0 and 1. This string is divided into groups of 8, the low-order bit in each group is ignored; this gives a 56-bit key that is set into the machine. This is the key that will be used with the hashing algorithm to encrypt the string *block* with the encrypt function.

The *block* argument of encrypt is a character array of length 64 containing only the characters with numerical value 0 and 1. The argument array is modified in place to a similar array representing the bits of the argument after having been subjected to the hashing algorithm using the key set by setkey. The argument *edflag*, indicating decryption rather than encryption, is ignored; use encrypt in libcrypt [see crypt(3X)] for decryption.

SEE ALSO
getpass(3C), crypt(3X), passwd(4).

login(1), passwd(1) in the *User's Reference Manual*.

DIAGNOSTICS
If *edflag* is set to anything other than zero, errno will be set to ENOSYS.

NOTES
The return value for crypt points to static data that are overwritten by each call.

NAME
ctermid – generate file name for terminal

SYNOPSIS
#include <stdio.h>

char *ctermid (char *s);

DESCRIPTION
ctermid generates the path name of the controlling terminal for the current process, and stores it in a string.

If *s* is a NULL pointer, the string is stored in an internal static area, the contents of which are overwritten at the next call to ctermid, and the address of which is returned. Otherwise, *s* is assumed to point to a character array of at least L_ctermid elements; the path name is placed in this array and the value of *s* is returned. The constant L_ctermid is defined in the stdio.h header file.

SEE ALSO
ttyname(3C).

NOTES
The difference between ctermid and ttyname(3C) is that ttyname must be handed a file descriptor and returns the actual name of the terminal associated with that file descriptor, while ctermid returns a string (/dev/tty) that will refer to the terminal if used as a file name. Thus ttyname is useful only if the process already has at least one file open to a terminal.

ctime(3C)

NAME
ctime, localtime, gmtime, asctime, tzset – convert date and time to string

SYNOPSIS
```
#include <time.h>

char *ctime (const time_t *clock);

struct tm *localtime (const time_t *clock);

struct tm *gmtime (const time_t *clock);

char *asctime (const struct tm *tm);

extern time_t timezone, altzone;

extern int daylight;

extern char *tzname[2];

void tzset (void);
```

DESCRIPTION
ctime, localtime, and gmtime accept arguments of type time_t, pointed to by clock, representing the time in seconds since 00:00:00 UTC, January 1, 1970. ctime returns a pointer to a 26-character string as shown below. Time zone and daylight savings corrections are made before the string is generated. The fields are constant in width:

```
Fri Sep 13 00:00:00 1986\n\0
```

localtime and gmtime return pointers to tm structures, described below. localtime corrects for the main time zone and possible alternate ("daylight savings") time zone; gmtime converts directly to Coordinated Universal Time (UTC), which is the time the UNIX system uses internally.

asctime converts a tm structure to a 26-character string, as shown in the above example, and returns a pointer to the string.

Declarations of all the functions and externals, and the tm structure, are in the time.h header file. The structure declaration is:

```
struct      tm {
    int     tm_sec;     /* seconds after the minute - [0, 61] */
                        /* for leap seconds */
    int     tm_min;     /* minutes after the hour - [0, 59] */
    int     tm_hour;    /* hour since midnight - [0, 23] */
    int     tm_mday;    /* day of the month - [1, 31] */
    int     tm_mon;     /* months since January - [0, 11] */
    int     tm_year;    /* years since 1900 */
    int     tm_wday;    /* days since Sunday - [0, 6] */
    int     tm_yday;    /* days since January 1 - [0, 365] */
    int     tm_isdst;   /* flag for alternate daylight */
                        /* savings time */
};
```

The value of `tm_isdst` is positive if daylight savings time is in effect, zero if daylight savings time is not in effect, and negative if the information is not available. (Previously, the value of `tm_isdst` was defined as non-zero if daylight savings time was in effect.)

The external `time_t` variable `altzone` contains the difference, in seconds, between Coordinated Universal Time and the alternate time zone. The external variable `timezone` contains the difference, in seconds, between UTC and local standard time. The external variable `daylight` indicates whether time should reflect daylight savings time. Both `timezone` and `altzone` default to 0 (UTC). The external variable `daylight` is non-zero if an alternate time zone exists. The time zone names are contained in the external variable `tzname`, which by default is set to:

```
char *tzname[2] = { "GMT", "   " };
```

These functions know about the peculiarities of this conversion for various time periods for the U.S. (specifically, the years 1974, 1975, and 1987). They will handle the new daylight savings time starting with the first Sunday in April, 1987.

`tzset` uses the contents of the environment variable `TZ` to override the value of the different external variables. The function `tzset` is called by `asctime` and may also be called by the user. See `environ`(5) for a description of the `TZ` environment variable.

`tzset` scans the contents of the environment variable and assigns the different fields to the respective variable. For example, the most complete setting for New Jersey in 1986 could be

```
EST5EDT4,116/2:00:00,298/2:00:00
```

or simply

```
EST5EDT
```

An example of a southern hemisphere setting such as the Cook Islands could be

```
KDT9:30KST10:00,63/5:00,302/20:00
```

In the longer version of the New Jersey example of `TZ`, `tzname[0]` is EST, `timezone` will be set to 5*60*60, `tzname[1]` is EDT, `altzone` will be set to 4*60*60, the starting date of the alternate time zone is the 117th day at 2 AM, the ending date of the alternate time zone is the 299th day at 2 AM (using zero-based Julian days), and `daylight` will be set positive. Starting and ending times are relative to the alternate time zone. If the alternate time zone start and end dates and the time are not provided, the days for the United States that year will be used and the time will be 2 AM. If the start and end dates are provided but the time is not provided, the time will be 2 AM. The effects of `tzset` are thus to change the values of the external variables `timezone`, `altzone`, `daylight`, and `tzname`. `ctime`, `localtime`, `mktime`, and `strftime` will also update these external variables as if they had called `tzset` at the time specified by the `time_t` or `struct tm` value that they are converting.

Note that in most installations, `TZ` is set to the correct value by default when the user logs on, via the local /etc/profile file [see `profile`(4) and `timezone`(4)].

FILES

/usr/lib/locale/*language*/LC_TIME – file containing locale specific date and time information

SEE ALSO

time(2), getenv(3C), mktime(3C), putenv(3C), printf(3S), setlocale(3C), strftime(3C), cftime(4), profile(4), timezone(4), environ(5).

NOTES

The return values for ctime, localtime, and gmtime point to static data whose content is overwritten by each call.

Setting the time during the interval of change from timezone to altzone or vice versa can produce unpredictable results. The system administrator must change the Julian start and end days annually.

ctype(3C)

NAME
ctype: isdigit, isxdigit, islower, isupper, isalpha, isalnum, isspace, iscntrl, ispunct, isprint, isgraph, isascii – character handling

SYNOPSIS
#include <ctype.h>

int isalpha(int c);

int isupper(int c);

int islower(int c);

int isdigit(int c);

int isxdigit(int c);

int isalnum(int c);

int isspace(int c);

int ispunct(int c);

int isprint(int c);

int isgraph(int c);

int iscntrl(int c);

int isascii(int c);

DESCRIPTION
These macros classify character-coded integer values. Each is a predicate returning non-zero for true, zero for false. The behavior of these macros, except isascii, is affected by the current locale [see setlocale(3C)]. To modify the behavior, change the LC_TYPE category in setlocale, that is, setlocale (LC_CTYPE, *newlocale*). In the C locale, or in a locale where character type information is not defined, characters are classified according to the rules of the US-ASCII 7-bit coded character set.

The macro isascii is defined on all integer values; the rest are defined only where the argument is an int, the value of which is representable as an unsigned char, or EOF, which is defined by the stdio.h header file and represents end-of-file.

isalpha tests for any character for which isupper or islower is true, or any character that is one of an implementation-defined set of characters for which none of iscntrl, isdigit, ispunct, or isspace is true. In the C locale, isalpha returns true only for the characters for which isupper or islower is true.

isupper tests for any character that is an upper-case letter or is one of an implementation-defined set of characters for which none of iscntrl, isdigit, ispunct, isspace, or islower is true. In the C locale, isupper returns true only for the characters defined as upper-case ASCII characters.

`islower`	tests for any character that is a lower-case letter or is one of an implementation-defined set of characters for which none of `iscntrl`, `isdigit`, `ispunct`, `isspace`, or `isupper` is true. In the C locale, `islower` returns true only for the characters defined as lower-case ASCII characters.
`isdigit`	tests for any decimal-digit character.
`isxdigit`	tests for any hexadecimal-digit character ([0-9], [A-F] or [a-f]).
`isalnum`	tests for any character for which `isalpha` or `isdigit` is true (letter or digit).
`isspace`	tests for any space, tab, carriage-return, newline, vertical-tab or form-feed (standard white-space characters) or for one of an implementation-defined set of characters for which `isalnum` is false. In the C locale, `isspace` returns true only for the standard white-space characters.
`ispunct`	tests for any printing character which is neither a space nor a character for which `isalnum` is true.
`isprint`	tests for any printing character, including space (" ").
`isgraph`	tests for any printing character, except space.
`iscntrl`	tests for any "control character" as defined by the character set.
`isascii`	tests for any ASCII character, code between 0 and 0177 inclusive.

All the character classification macros and the conversion functions and macros use a table lookup.

Functions exist for all the above-defined macros. To get the function form, the macro name must be undefined (e.g., `#undef isdigit`).

FILES
/usr/lib/locale/*locale*/LC_CTYPE

SEE ALSO
chrtbl(1M), setlocale(3C), stdio(3S), ascii(5), environ(5).

DIAGNOSTICS
If the argument to any of the character handling macros is not in the domain of the function, the result is undefined.

cuserid (3S)

NAME
cuserid – get character login name of the user

SYNOPSIS
    #include <stdio.h>

    char *cuserid (char *s);

DESCRIPTION
cuserid generates a character-string representation of the login name that the owner of the current process is logged in under. If s is a NULL pointer, this representation is generated in an internal static area, the address of which is returned. Otherwise, s is assumed to point to an array of at least L_cuserid characters; the representation is left in this array. The constant L_cuserid is defined in the stdio.h header file.

SEE ALSO
getlogin(3C), getpwent(3C).

DIAGNOSTICS
If the login name cannot be found, cuserid returns a NULL pointer; if s is not a NULL pointer, a null character `\0´ will be placed at s[0].

NAME

difftime – computes the difference between two calendar times

SYNOPSIS

    #include <time.h>

    double difftime (time_t time1, time_t time0);

DESCRIPTION

difftime computes the difference between two calendar times. difftime returns the difference *(time1-time0)* expressed in seconds as a double. This function is provided because there are no general arithmetic properties defined for type time_t.

SEE ALSO

ctime(3C).

directory(3C)

NAME
directory: opendir, readdir, telldir, seekdir, rewinddir, closedir – directory operations

SYNOPSIS
#include <dirent.h>

DIR *opendir (const char *filename);

struct dirent *readdir (DIR *dirp);

long telldir (DIR *dirp);

void seekdir (DIR *dirp, long loc);

void rewinddir (DIR *dirp);

int closedir (DIR *dirp);

DESCRIPTION
opendir opens the directory named by *filename* and associates a directory stream with it. **opendir** returns a pointer to be used to identify the directory stream in subsequent operations. The directory stream is positioned at the first entry. A null pointer is returned if *filename* cannot be accessed or is not a directory, or if it cannot malloc(3C) enough memory to hold a DIR structure or a buffer for the directory entries.

readdir returns a pointer to the next active directory entry and positions the directory stream at the next entry. No inactive entries are returned. It returns NULL upon reaching the end of the directory or upon detecting an invalid location in the directory. **readdir** buffers several directory entries per actual read operation; **readdir** marks for update the st_atime field of the directory each time the directory is actually read.

telldir returns the current location associated with the named directory stream.

seekdir sets the position of the next **readdir** operation on the directory stream. The new position reverts to the position associated with the directory stream at the time the **telldir** operation that provides *loc* was performed. Values returned by **telldir** are valid only if the directory has not changed because of compaction or expansion. This situation is not a problem with System V, but it may be a problem with some file system types.

rewinddir resets the position of the named directory stream to the beginning of the directory. It also causes the directory stream to refer to the current state of the corresponding directory, as a call to **opendir** would.

closedir closes the named directory stream and frees the DIR structure.

The following errors can occur as a result of these operations.

opendir returns NULL on failure and sets **errno** to one of the following values:

ENOTDIR	A component of *filename* is not a directory.
EACCES	A component of *filename* denies search permission.

EACCES	Read permission is denied on the specified directory.
EMFILE	The maximum number of file descriptors are currently open.
ENFILE	The system file table is full.
EFAULT	*filename* points outside the allocated address space.
ELOOP	Too many symbolic links were encountered in translating *filename*.
ENAMETOOLONG	The length of the *filename* argument exceeds {PATH_MAX}, or the length of a *filename* component exceeds {NAME_MAX} while {_POSIX_NO_TRUNC} is in effect.
ENOENT	A component of *filename* does not exist or is a null pathname.

readdir returns NULL on failure and sets errno to one of the following values:

ENOENT	The current file pointer for the directory is not located at a valid entry.
EBADF	The file descriptor determined by the DIR stream is no longer valid. This result occurs if the DIR stream has been closed.

telldir, seekdir, and closedir return −1 on failure and set errno to the following value:

EBADF	The file descriptor determined by the DIR stream is no longer valid. This results if the DIR stream has been closed.

EXAMPLE

Here is a sample program that prints the names of all the files in the current directory:

```
#include <stdio.h>
#include <dirent.h>

main()
{
    DIR *dirp;
    struct dirent *direntp;

    dirp = opendir( "." );
    while ( (direntp = readdir( dirp )) != NULL )
        (void)printf( "%s\n", direntp->d_name );
    closedir( dirp );
    return (0);
}
```

directory(3C)

SEE ALSO
getdents(2), dirent(4).

NOTES
rewinddir is implemented as a macro, so its function address cannot be taken.

NAME

div, ldiv – compute the quotient and remainder

SYNOPSIS

#include <stdlib.h>

div_t div (int numer, int denom);

ldiv_t ldiv (long int numer, long int denom);

DESCRIPTION

div computes the quotient and remainder of the division of the numerator *numer* by the denominator *denom*. This function provides a well-defined semantics for the signed integral division and remainder operations, unlike the implementation-defined semantics of the built-in operations. The sign of the resulting quotient is that of the algebraic quotient, and, if the division is inexact, the magnitude of the resulting quotient is the largest integer less than the magnitude of the algebraic quotient. If the result cannot be represented, the behavior is undefined; otherwise, *quotient* * *denom* + *remainder* will equal *numer*.

div returns a structure of type div_t, comprising both the quotient and remainder:

```
typedef struct div_t {
    int   quot; /*quotient*/
    int   rem;  /*remainder*/
} div_t;
```

ldiv is similar to div, except that the arguments and the members of the returned structure (which has type ldiv_t) all have type long int.

drand48(3C)

NAME
drand48, erand48, lrand48, nrand48, mrand48, jrand48, srand48, seed48, lcong48 – generate uniformly distributed pseudo-random numbers

SYNOPSIS
#include <stdlib.h>

double drand48 (void);

double erand48 (unsigned short xsubi[3]);

long lrand48 (void);

long nrand48 (unsigned short xsubi[3]);

long mrand48 (void);

long jrand48 (unsigned short xsubi[3]);

void srand48 (long seedval);

unsigned short *seed48 (unsigned short seed16v[3]);

void lcong48 (unsigned short param[7]);

DESCRIPTION
This family of functions generates pseudo-random numbers using the well-known linear congruential algorithm and 48-bit integer arithmetic.

Functions **drand48** and **erand48** return non-negative double-precision floating-point values uniformly distributed over the interval [0.0, 1.0).

Functions **lrand48** and **nrand48** return non-negative long integers uniformly distributed over the interval [0, 2^{31}).

Functions **mrand48** and **jrand48** return signed long integers uniformly distributed over the interval [-2^{31}, 2^{31}).

Functions **srand48**, **seed48**, and **lcong48** are initialization entry points, one of which should be invoked before either **drand48**, **lrand48**, or **mrand48** is called. (Although it is not recommended practice, constant default initializer values will be supplied automatically if **drand48**, **lrand48**, or **mrand48** is called without a prior call to an initialization entry point.) Functions **erand48**, **nrand48**, and **jrand48** do not require an initialization entry point to be called first.

All the routines work by generating a sequence of 48-bit integer values, X_i, according to the linear congruential formula

$$X_{n+1} = (aX_n + c)_{\mod m} \qquad n \geq 0.$$

The parameter $m = 2^{48}$; hence 48-bit integer arithmetic is performed. Unless **lcong48** has been invoked, the multiplier value a and the addend value c are given by

$a = \text{5DEECE66D}_{16} = 273673163155_8$
$c = \text{B}_{16} = 13_8.$

The value returned by any of the functions **drand48**, **erand48**, **lrand48**, **nrand48**, **mrand48**, or **jrand48** is computed by first generating the next 48-bit X_i in the sequence. Then the appropriate number of bits, according to the type of data item to be returned, are copied from the high-order (leftmost) bits of X_i and transformed into the returned value.

The functions **drand48**, **lrand48**, and **mrand48** store the last 48-bit X_i generated in an internal buffer. X_i must be initialized prior to being invoked. The functions **erand48**, **nrand48**, and **jrand48** require the calling program to provide storage for the successive X_i values in the array specified as an argument when the functions are invoked. These routines do not have to be initialized; the calling program must place the desired initial value of X_i into the array and pass it as an argument. By using different arguments, functions **erand48**, **nrand48**, and **jrand48** allow separate modules of a large program to generate several *independent* streams of pseudo-random numbers, i.e., the sequence of numbers in each stream will *not* depend upon how many times the routines have been called to generate numbers for the other streams.

The initializer function **srand48** sets the high-order 32 bits of X_i to the 32 bits contained in its argument. The low-order 16 bits of X_i are set to the arbitrary value $330E_{16}$.

The initializer function **seed48** sets the value of X_i to the 48-bit value specified in the argument array. In addition, the previous value of X_i is copied into a 48-bit internal buffer, used only by **seed48**, and a pointer to this buffer is the value returned by **seed48**. This returned pointer, which can just be ignored if not needed, is useful if a program is to be restarted from a given point at some future time — use the pointer to get at and store the last X_i value, and then use this value to reinitialize via **seed48** when the program is restarted.

The initialization function **lcong48** allows the user to specify the initial X_i, the multiplier value *a*, and the addend value *c*. Argument array elements *param[0-2]* specify X_i, *param[3-5]* specify the multiplier *a*, and *param[6]* specifies the 16-bit addend *c*. After **lcong48** has been called, a subsequent call to either **srand48** or **seed48** will restore the "standard" multiplier and addend values, *a* and *c*, specified on the previous page.

SEE ALSO
rand(3C).

NAME

dup2 – duplicate an open file descriptor

SYNOPSIS

#include <unistd.h>

int dup2 (int fildes, int fildes2);

DESCRIPTION

fildes is a file descriptor referring to an open file, and *fildes2* is a non-negative integer less than {OPEN_MAX} (the maximum number of open files). dup2 causes *fildes2* to refer to the same file as *fildes*. If *fildes2* already referred to an open file, not *fildes*, it is closed first. If *fildes2* refers to *fildes*, or if *fildes* is not a valid open file descriptor, *fildes2* will not be closed first.

dup2 will fail if one or more of the following are true:

EBADF	*fildes* is not a valid open file descriptor.
EBADF	*fildes2* is negative or greater than or equal to {OPEN_MAX}.
EINTR	a signal was caught during the dup2 call.
%[EMFILE	{OPEN_MAX} file descriptors are currently open.

SEE ALSO

creat(2), close(2), exec(2), fcntl(2), open(2), pipe(2), lockf(3C), limits(4).

DIAGNOSTICS

Upon successful completion a non-negative integer, namely, the file descriptor, is returned. Otherwise, a value of −1 is returned and errno is set to indicate the error.

NAME
ecvt, fcvt, gcvt - convert floating-point number to string

SYNOPSIS
#include <stdlib.h>

char *ecvt (double value, int ndigit, int *decpt, int *sign);

char *fcvt (double value, int ndigit, int *decpt, int *sign);

char *gcvt (double value, int ndigit, char *buf);

DESCRIPTION
ecvt converts *value* to a null-terminated string of *ndigit* digits and returns a pointer thereto. The high-order digit is non-zero, unless the value is zero. The low-order digit is rounded. The position of the decimal point relative to the beginning of the string is stored indirectly through *decpt* (negative means to the left of the returned digits). The decimal point is not included in the returned string. If the sign of the result is negative, the word pointed to by *sign* is non-zero, otherwise it is zero.

fcvt is identical to *ecvt*, except that the correct digit has been rounded for printf %f output of the number of digits specified by *ndigit*.

gcvt converts the *value* to a null-terminated string in the array pointed to by *buf* and returns *buf*. It attempts to produce *ndigit* significant digits in %f format if possible, otherwise %e format (scientific notation), ready for printing. A minus sign, if there is one, or a decimal point will be included as part of the returned string. Trailing zeros are suppressed.

SEE ALSO
printf(3S).

NOTES
The values returned by *ecvt* and *fcvt* point to a single static data array whose content is overwritten by each call.

end(3C)

NAME
end, etext, edata – last locations in program

SYNOPSIS
    extern etext;

    extern edata;

    extern end;

DESCRIPTION
These names refer neither to routines nor to locations with interesting contents; only their addresses are meaningful.

etext The address of **etext** is the first address above the program text.

edata The address of **edata** is the first address above the initialized data region.

end   The address of **end** is the first address above the uninitialized data region.

SEE ALSO
cc(1), brk(2), malloc(3C), stdio(3S).

NOTE
When execution begins, the program break (the first location beyond the data) coincides with **end**, but the program break may be reset by the routines brk, malloc, the standard input/output library [see stdio(3S)], by the profile (–p) option of cc, and so on. Thus, the current value of the program break should be determined by sbrk ((char *)0) [see brk(2)].

fclose(3S)

NAME
fclose, fflush – close or flush a stream

SYNOPSIS
#include <stdio.h>

int fclose (FILE *stream);

int fflush (FILE *stream);

DESCRIPTION
fclose causes any buffered data waiting to be written for the named *stream* [see intro(3)] to be written out, and the *stream* to be closed. If the underlying file pointer is not already at end of file, and the file is one capable of seeking, the file pointer is adjusted so that the next operation on the open file pointer deals with the byte after the last one read from or written to the file being closed.

fclose is performed automatically for all open files upon calling **exit**.

If *stream* points to an output stream or an update stream on which the most recent operation was not input, **fflush** causes any buffered data waiting to be written for the named *stream* to be written to that file. Any unread data buffered in *stream* is discarded. The *stream* remains open. If *stream* is open for reading, the underlying file pointer is not already at end of file, and the file is one capable of seeking, the file pointer is adjusted so that the next operation on the open file pointer deals with the byte after the last one read from or written to the stream.

When calling **fflush**, if *stream* is a null pointer, all files open for writing are flushed.

SEE ALSO
close(2), exit(2), intro(3), fopen(3S), setbuf(3S), stdio(3S).

DIAGNOSTICS
Upon successful completion these functions return a value of zero. Otherwise EOF is returned.

NAME
ferror, feof, clearerr, fileno – stream status inquiries

SYNOPSIS
#include <stdio.h>

int ferror (FILE *stream);

int feof (FILE *stream);

void clearerr (FILE *stream);

int fileno (FILE *stream);

DESCRIPTION
ferror returns non-zero when an error has previously occurred reading from or writing to the named *stream* [see intro(3)], otherwise zero.

feof returns non-zero when EOF has previously been detected reading the named input *stream*, otherwise zero.

clearerr resets the error indicator and EOF indicator to zero on the named *stream*.

fileno returns the integer file descriptor associated with the named *stream*; see open(2).

SEE ALSO
open(2), fopen(3S), stdio(3S).

NAME
ffs – find first set bit

SYNOPSIS
#include <string.h>

int ffs(const int i);

DESCRIPTION
ffs finds the first bit set in the argument passed it and returns the index of that bit. Bits are numbered starting at 1 from the low order bit. A return value of zero indicates that the value passed is zero.

fmtmsg(3C)

NAME
fmtmsg – display a message on stderr or system console

SYNOPSIS
#include <fmtmsg.h>

int fmtmsg(long classification, const char *label, int severity,
    const char *text, const char *action, const char *tag);

DESCRIPTION
Based on a message's classification component, fmtmsg writes a formatted message to stderr, to the console, or to both.

fmtmsg can be used instead of the traditional printf interface to display messages to stderr. fmtmsg, in conjunction with gettxt, provides a simple interface for producing language-independent applications.

A formatted message consists of up to five standard components as defined below. The component, *classification*, is not part of the standard message displayed to the user, but rather defines the source of the message and directs the display of the formatted message.

classification
  Contains identifiers from the following groups of major classifications and subclassifications. Any one identifier from a subclass may be used in combination by ORing the values together with a single identifier from a different subclass. Two or more identifiers from the same subclass should not be used together, with the exception of identifiers from the display subclass. (Both display subclass identifiers may be used so that messages can be displayed to both stderr and the system console).

  "Major classifications" identify the source of the condition. Identifiers are: MM_HARD (hardware), MM_SOFT (software), and MM_FIRM (firmware).

  "Message source subclassifications" identify the type of software in which the problem is spotted. Identifiers are: MM_APPL (application), MM_UTIL (utility), and MM_OPSYS (operating system).

  "Display subclassifications" indicate where the message is to be displayed. Identifiers are: MM_PRINT to display the message on the standard error stream, MM_CONSOLE to display the message on the system console. Neither, either, or both identifiers may be used.

  "Status subclassifications" indicate whether the application will recover from the condition. Identifiers are: MM_RECOVER (recoverable) and MM_NRECOV (non-recoverable).

  An additional identifier, MM_NULLMC, indicates that no classification component is supplied for the message.

label
  Identifies the source of the message. The format of this component is two fields separated by a colon. The first field is up to 10 characters long; the second is up to 14 characters. Suggested usage is that *label* identifies the package in which the application resides as well as the program or application name. For example, the *label* UX:cat indicates the UNIX System V package and the cat application.

severity
: Indicates the seriousness of the condition. Identifiers for the standard levels of *severity* are:

    MM_HALT indicates that the application has encountered a severe fault and is halting. Produces the print string HALT.

    MM_ERROR indicates that the application has detected a fault. Produces the print string ERROR.

    MM_WARNING indicates a condition out of the ordinary that might be a problem and should be watched. Produces the print string WARNING.

    MM_INFO provides information about a condition that is not in error. Produces the print string INFO.

    MM_NOSEV indicates that no severity level is supplied for the message.

    Other severity levels may be added by using the addseverity routine.

text
: Describes the condition that produced the message. The *text* string is not limited to a specific size.

action
: Describes the first step to be taken in the error recovery process. fmtmsg precedes each action string with the prefix: TO FIX:. The *action* string is not limited to a specific size.

tag
: An identifier which references on-line documentation for the message. Suggested usage is that *tag* includes the *label* and a unique identifying number. A sample *tag* is UX:cat:146.

Environment Variables

There are two environment variables that control the behavior of fmtmsg: MSGVERB and SEV_LEVEL.

MSGVERB tells fmtmsg which message components it is to select when writing messages to stderr. The value of MSGVERB is a colon-separated list of optional keywords. MSGVERB can be set as follows:

    MSGVERB=[*keyword*[:*keyword*[:...]]]
    export MSGVERB

Valid *keywords* are: label, severity, text, action, and tag. If MSGVERB contains a keyword for a component and the component's value is not the component's null value, fmtmsg includes that component in the message when writing the message to stderr. If MSGVERB does not include a keyword for a message component, that component is not included in the display of the message. The keywords may appear in any order. If MSGVERB is not defined, if its value is the null-string, if its value is not of the correct format, or if it contains keywords other than the valid ones listed above, fmtmsg selects all components.

The first time fmtmsg is called, it examines the MSGVERB environment variable to see which message components it is to select when generating a message to write to the standard error stream, stderr. The values accepted on the initial call are saved for future calls.

MSGVERB affects only which components are selected for display to the standard error stream. All message components are included in console messages.

SEV_LEVEL defines severity levels and associates print strings with them for use by **fmtmsg**. The standard severity levels shown below cannot be modified. Additional severity levels can also be defined, redefined, and removed using **addseverity** [see **addseverity**(3C)]. If the same severity level is defined by both **SEV_LEVEL** and **addseverity**, the definition by **addseverity** is controlling.

```
0    (no severity is used)
1    HALT
2    ERROR
3    WARNING
4    INFO
```

SEV_LEVEL can be set as follows:

SEV_LEVEL=[*description*[:*description*[:...]]]
export SEV_LEVEL

description is a comma-separated list containing three fields:

description=*severity_keyword*, *level*, *printstring*

severity_keyword is a character string that is used as the keyword on the −s *severity* option to the **fmtmsg** command. (This field is not used by the **fmtmsg** function.)

level is a character string that evaluates to a positive integer (other than 0, 1, 2, 3, or 4, which are reserved for the standard severity levels). If the keyword *severity_keyword* is used, *level* is the severity value passed on to the **fmtmsg** function.

printstring is the character string used by **fmtmsg** in the standard message format whenever the severity value *level* is used.

If a *description* in the colon list is not a three-field comma list, or, if the second field of a comma list does not evaluate to a positive integer, that *description* in the colon list is ignored.

The first time **fmtmsg** is called, it examines the **SEV_LEVEL** environment variable, if defined, to see whether the environment expands the levels of severity beyond the five standard levels and those defined using **addseverity**. The values accepted on the initial call are saved for future calls.

Use in Applications

One or more message components may be systematically omitted from messages generated by an application by using the null value of the argument for that component.

The table below indicates the null values and identifiers for **fmtmsg** arguments.

Argument	Type	Null-Value	Identifier
label	char*	(char*) NULL	MM_NULLLBL
severity	int	0	MM_NULLSEV
class	long	0L	MM_NULLMC
text	char*	(char*) NULL	MM_NULLTXT
action	char*	(char*) NULL	MM_NULLACT
tag	char*	(char*) NULL	MM_NULLTAG

Another means of systematically omitting a component is by omitting the component keyword(s) when defining the MSGVERB environment variable (see the "Environment Variables" section).

EXAMPLES

Example 1:

The following example of fmtmsg:

```
fmtmsg(MM_PRINT, "UX:cat", MM_ERROR, "invalid syntax", "refer
to manual", "UX:cat:001")
```

produces a complete message in the standard message format:

```
UX:cat: ERROR: invalid syntax
        TO FIX: refer to manual    UX:cat:001
```

Example 2:

When the environment variable MSGVERB is set as follows:

```
MSGVERB=severity:text:action
```

and the Example 1 is used, fmtmsg produces:

```
ERROR: invalid syntax
TO FIX: refer to manual
```

Example 3:

When the environment variable SEV_LEVEL is set as follows:

```
SEV_LEVEL=note,5,NOTE
```

the following call to fmtmsg:

```
fmtmsg(MM_UTIL | MM_PRINT, "UX:cat", 5, "invalid syntax",
"refer to manual", "UX:cat:001")
```

produces:

```
UX:cat: NOTE: invalid syntax
        TO FIX: refer to manual    UX:cat:001
```

SEE ALSO

addseverity(3C), gettxt(3C), printf(3S).
fmtmsg(1) in the *User's Reference Manual*.

fmtmsg(3C)

DIAGNOSTICS

The exit codes for **fmtmsg** are the following:

MM_OK   The function succeeded.

MM_NOTOK The function failed completely.

MM_NOMSG The function was unable to generate a message on the standard error stream, but otherwise succeeded.

MM_NOCON The function was unable to generate a console message, but otherwise succeeded.

fopen(3S)

NAME
fopen, freopen, fdopen – open a stream

SYNOPSIS
#include <stdio.h>

FILE *fopen (const char *filename, const char *type);

FILE *freopen (const char *filename, const char *type, FILE *stream);

FILE *fdopen (int fildes, const char *type);

DESCRIPTION
fopen opens the file named by *filename* and associates a *stream* with it. fopen returns a pointer to the FILE structure associated with the *stream*.

filename points to a character string that contains the name of the file to be opened.

type is a character string beginning with one of the following sequences:

"r" or "rb"   open for reading

"w" or "wb"   truncate to zero length or create for writing

"a" or "ab"   append; open for writing at end of file, or create for writing

"r+", "r+b" or "rb+"
  open for update (reading and writing)

"w+", "w+b" or "wb+"
  truncate or create for update

"a+", "a+b" or "ab+"
  append; open or create for update at end-of-file

The "b" is ignored in the above *type*s. The "b" exists to distinguish binary files from text files. However, there is no distinction between these types of files on a UNIX system.

freopen substitutes the named file in place of the open *stream*. A flush is first attempted, and then the original *stream* is closed, regardless of whether the open ultimately succeeds. Failure to flush or close *stream* successfully is ignored. freopen returns a pointer to the FILE structure associated with *stream*.

freopen is typically used to attach the preopened *streams* associated with stdin, stdout, and stderr to other files. stderr is by default unbuffered, but the use of freopen will cause it to become buffered or line-buffered.

fdopen associates a *stream* with a file descriptor. File descriptors are obtained from open, dup, creat, or pipe, which open files but do not return pointers to a FILE structure *stream*. Streams are necessary input for almost all of the Section 3S library routines. The *type* of *stream* must agree with the mode of the open file. The file position indicator associated with *stream* is set to the position indicated by the file offset associated with *fildes*.

When a file is opened for update, both input and output may be done on the resulting *stream*. However, output may not be directly followed by input without an intervening **fflush**, **fseek**, **fsetpos**, or **rewind**, and input may not be directly followed by output without an intervening **fseek**, **fsetpos**, or **rewind**, or an input operation that encounters end-of-file.

When a file is opened for append (i.e., when *type* is "a", "ab", "a+", or "ab+"), it is impossible to overwrite information already in the file. **fseek** may be used to reposition the file pointer to any position in the file, but when output is written to the file, the current file pointer is disregarded. All output is written at the end of the file and causes the file pointer to be repositioned at the end of the output. If two separate processes open the same file for append, each process may write freely to the file without fear of destroying output being written by the other. The output from the two processes will be intermixed in the file in the order in which it is written.

When opened, a *stream* is fully buffered if and only if it can be determined not to refer to an interactive device. The error and end-of-file indicators are cleared for the *stream*.

SEE ALSO

close(2), creat(2), dup(2), open(2), pipe(2), write(2), fclose(3S), fseek(3S), setbuf(3S), stdio(3S).

DIAGNOSTICS

The functions **fopen** and **freopen** return a null pointer if *path* cannot be accessed, or if *type* is invalid, or if the file cannot be opened.

The function **fdopen** returns a null pointer if *fildes* is not an open file descriptor, or if *type* is invalid, or if the file cannot be opened.

The functions **fopen** or **fdopen** may fail and not set **errno** if there are no free stdio streams.

File descriptors used by **fdopen** must be less than 255.

fpgetround(3C)

NAME
fpgetround, fpsetround, fpgetmask, fpsetmask, fpgetsticky, fpsetsticky – IEEE floating-point environment control

SYNOPSIS
#include <ieeefp.h>

fp_rnd fpgetround (void);

fp_rnd fpsetround (fp_rnd rnd_dir);

fp_except fpgetmask (void);

fp_except fpsetmask (fp_except mask);

fp_except fpgetsticky (void);

fp_except fpsetsticky (fp_except sticky);

DESCRIPTION
There are five floating-point exceptions: divide-by-zero, overflow, underflow, imprecise (inexact) result, and invalid operation. When a floating-point exception occurs, the corresponding sticky bit is set (1), and if the mask bit is enabled (1), the trap takes place. These routines let the user change the behavior on occurrence of any of these exceptions, as well as change the rounding mode for floating-point operations.

```
FP_X_INV      /* invalid operation exception */
FP_X_OFL      /* overflow exception */
FP_X_UFL      /* underflow exception */
FP_X_DZ       /* divide-by-zero exception */
FP_X_IMP      /* imprecise (loss of precision) */
FP_RN         /* round to nearest representative number */
FP_RP         /* round to plus infinity */
FP_RM         /* round to minus infinity */
FP_RZ         /* round to zero (truncate) */
```

fpgetround returns the current rounding mode.

fpsetround sets the rounding mode and returns the previous rounding mode.

fpgetmask returns the current exception masks.

fpsetmask sets the exception masks and returns the previous setting.

fpgetsticky returns the current exception sticky flags.

fpsetsticky sets (clears) the exception sticky flags and returns the previous setting.

The default environment is rounding mode set to nearest (FP_RN) and all traps disabled.

Individual bits may be examined using the constants defined in ieeefp.h.

SEE ALSO
isnan(3C).

NOTES

fpsetsticky modifies all sticky flags. **fpsetmask** changes all mask bits. **fpsetmask** clears the sticky bit corresponding to any exception being enabled.

C requires truncation (round to zero) for floating point to integral conversions. The current rounding mode has no effect on these conversions.

One must clear the sticky bit to recover from the trap and to proceed. If the sticky bit is not cleared before the next trap occurs, a wrong exception type may be signaled.

NAME
fread, fwrite − binary input/output

SYNOPSIS
#include <stdio.h>

size_t fread (void *ptr, size_t size, size_t nitems, FILE *stream);

size_t fwrite (const void *ptr, size_t size, size_t nitems, FILE *stream);

DESCRIPTION
fread reads into an array pointed to by *ptr* up to *nitems* items of data from *stream*, where an item of data is a sequence of bytes (not necessarily terminated by a null byte) of length *size*. fread stops reading bytes if an end-of-file or error condition is encountered while reading *stream*, or if *nitems* items have been read. fread increments the data pointer in *stream* to point to the byte following the last byte read if there is one. fread does not change the contents of *stream*. fread returns the number of items read.

fwrite writes to the named output *stream* at most *nitems* items of data from the array pointed to by *ptr*, where an item of data is a sequence of bytes (not necessarily terminated by a null byte) of length *size*. fwrite stops writing when it has written *nitems* items of data or if an error condition is encountered on *stream*. fwrite does not change the contents of the array pointed to by *ptr*. fwrite increments the data-pointer in *stream* by the number of bytes written. fwrite returns the number of items written.

If *size* or *nitems* is zero, then fread and fwrite return a value of 0 and do not effect the state of *stream*.

The ferror or feof routines must be used to distinguish between an error condition and end-of-file condition.

SEE ALSO
exit(2), lseek(2), read(2), write(2), abort(3C), fclose(3S), fopen(3S), getc(3S), gets(3S), printf(3S), putc(3S), puts(3S), scanf(3S), stdio(3S).

DIAGNOSTICS
If an error occurs, the error indicator for *stream* is set.

NAME

frexp, ldexp, logb, modf, modff, nextafter, scalb – manipulate parts of floating-point numbers

SYNOPSIS

#include <math.h>

double frexp (double value, int *eptr);

double ldexp (double value, int exp);

double logb (double value);

double nextafter (double value1, double value2);

double scalb (double value, double exp);

double modf (double value, double *iptr);

float modff (float value, float *iptr);

DESCRIPTION

Every non-zero number can be written uniquely as $x * 2^n$, where the "mantissa" (fraction) x is in the range $0.5 \leq |x| < 1.0$, and the "exponent" n is an integer. frexp returns the mantissa of a double *value*, and stores the exponent indirectly in the location pointed to by *eptr*. If *value* is zero, both results returned by frexp are zero.

ldexp and scalb return the quantity $value * 2^{exp}$. The only difference between the two is that scalb of a signaling NaN will result in the invalid operation exception being raised.

logb returns the unbiased exponent of its floating-point argument as a double-precision floating-point value.

modf and modff (single-precision version) return the signed fractional part of *value* and store the integral part indirectly in the location pointed to by *iptr*.

nextafter returns the next representable double-precision floating-point value following *value1* in the direction of *value2*. Thus, if *value2* is less than *value1*, nextafter returns the largest representable floating-point number less than *value1*.

SEE ALSO

cc(1), intro(3M).

DIAGNOSTICS

If ldexp would cause overflow, ±HUGE (defined in math.h) is returned (according to the sign of *value*), and errno is set to ERANGE. If ldexp would cause underflow, zero is returned and errno is set to ERANGE. If the input *value* to ldexp is NaN or infinity, that input is returned and errno is set to EDOM. The same error conditions apply to scalb except that a signaling NaN as input will result in the raising of the invalid operation exception.

logb of NaN returns that NaN, logb of infinity returns positive infinity, and logb of zero returns negative infinity and results in the raising of the divide by zero exception. In each of these conditions errno is set to EDOM.

If input *value1* to **nextafter** is positive or negative infinity, that input is returned and **errno** is set to **EDOM**. The overflow and inexact exceptions are signalled when input *value1* is finite, but **nextafter**(*value1*, *value2*) is not. The underflow and inexact exceptions are signalled when **nextafter**(*value1*, *value2*) lies strictly between $\pm 2^{-1022}$. In both cases **errno** is set to **ERANGE**.

When the program is compiled with the cc options −Xc or −Xa, HUGE_VAL is returned instead of HUGE.

fseek(3S)

NAME
fseek, rewind, ftell – reposition a file pointer in a stream

SYNOPSIS
#include <stdio.h>

int fseek (FILE *stream, long offset, int ptrname);

void rewind (FILE *stream);

long ftell (FILE *stream);

DESCRIPTION
fseek sets the position of the next input or output operation on the *stream* [see intro(3)]. The new position is at the signed distance *offset* bytes from the beginning, from the current position, or from the end of the file, according to a *ptrname* value of SEEK_SET, SEEK_CUR, or SEEK_END (defined in stdio.h) as follows:

SEEK_SET   set position equal to *offset* bytes.

SEEK_CUR   set position to current location plus *offset*.

SEEK_END   set position to EOF plus *offset*.

fseek allows the file position indicator to be set beyond the end of the existing data in the file. If data is later written at this point, subsequent reads of data in the gap will return zero until data is actually written into the gap. fseek, by itself, does not extend the size of the file.

rewind (stream) is equivalent to:

   (void) fseek (stream, 0L, SEEK_SET);

except that rewind also clears the error indicator on *stream*.

fseek and rewind clear the EOF indicator and undo any effects of ungetc on *stream*. After fseek or rewind, the next operation on a file opened for update may be either input or output.

If *stream* is writable and buffered data has not been written to the underlying file, fseek and rewind cause the unwritten data to be written to the file.

ftell returns the offset of the current byte relative to the beginning of the file associated with the named *stream*.

SEE ALSO
lseek(2), write(2), fopen(3S), popen(3S), stdio(3S), ungetc(3S).

DIAGNOSTICS
fseek returns −1 for improper seeks, otherwise zero. An improper seek can be, for example, an fseek done on a file that has not been opened via fopen; in particular, fseek may not be used on a terminal or on a file opened via popen. After a stream is closed, no further operations are defined on that stream.

NOTES
Although on the UNIX system an offset returned by ftell is measured in bytes, and it is permissible to seek to positions relative to that offset, portability to non-UNIX systems requires that an offset be used by fseek directly. Arithmetic may not meaningfully be performed on such an offset, which is not necessarily measured in bytes.

fsetpos(3C)

NAME
fsetpos, fgetpos – reposition a file pointer in a stream

SYNOPSIS
#include <stdio.h>

int fsetpos (FILE *stream, const fpos_t *pos);

int fgetpos (FILE *stream, fpos_t *pos);

DESCRIPTION
fsetpos sets the position of the next input or output operation on the *stream* according to the value of the object pointed to by *pos*. The object pointed to by *pos* must be a value returned by an earlier call to **fgetpos** on the same stream.

fsetpos clears the end-of-file indicator for the stream and undoes any effects of the **ungetc** function on the same stream. After **fsetpos**, the next operation on a file opened for update may be either input or output.

fgetpos stores the current value of the file position indicator for *stream* in the object pointed to by *pos*. The value stored contains information usable by **fsetpos** for repositioning the stream to its position at the time of the call to **fgetpos**.

If successful, both **fsetpos** and **fgetpos** return zero. Otherwise, they both return nonzero.

SEE ALSO
fseek(3S), lseek(2) ungetc(3S).

ftw(3C)

NAME
ftw, nftw – walk a file tree

SYNOPSIS
#include <ftw.h>

int ftw (const char *path, int (*fn) (const char *, const struct stat *, int), int depth);

int nftw (const char *path, int (*fn) (const char *, const struct stat *, int, struct FTW*), int depth, int flags);

DESCRIPTION
ftw recursively descends the directory hierarchy rooted in *path*. For each object in the hierarchy, ftw calls the user-defined function *fn*, passing it a pointer to a null-terminated character string containing the name of the object, a pointer to a stat structure (see stat(2)) containing information about the object, and an integer. Possible values of the integer, defined in the ftw.h header file, are:

FTW_F   The object is a file.

FTW_D   The object is a directory.

FTW_DNR   The object is a directory that cannot be read. Descendants of the directory will not be processed.

FTW_NS   stat failed on the object because of lack of appropriate permission or the object is a symbolic link that points to a non-existent file. The stat buffer passed to *fn* is undefined.

ftw visits a directory before visiting any of its descendants.

The tree traversal continues until the tree is exhausted, an invocation of *fn* returns a nonzero value, or some error is detected within ftw (such as an I/O error). If the tree is exhausted, ftw returns zero. If *fn* returns a nonzero value, ftw stops its tree traversal and returns whatever value was returned by *fn*. If ftw detects an error other than EACCES, it returns −1, and sets the error type in errno.

The function nftw is similar to ftw except that it takes an additional argument, *flags*. The *flags* field is used to specify:

FTW_PHYS   Physical walk, does not follow symbolic links. Otherwise, nftw will follow links but will not walk down any path that crosses itself.

FTW_MOUNT   The walk will not cross a mount point.

FTW_DEPTH   All subdirectories will be visited before the directory itself.

FTW_CHDIR   The walk will change to each directory before reading it.

The function nftw calls *fn* with four arguments at each file and directory. The first argument is the pathname of the object, the second is a pointer to the stat buffer, the third is an integer giving additional information, and the fourth is a struct FTW that contains the following members:

    int base;
    int level;

base is the offset into the pathname of the base name of the object. `level` indicates the depth relative to the rest of the walk, where the root level is zero.

The values of the third argument are as follows:

FTW_F   The object is a file.

FTW_D   The object is a directory.

FTW_DP The object is a directory and subdirectories have been visited.

FTW_SLN The object is a symbolic link that points to a non-existent file.

FTW_DNR The object is a directory that cannot be read. *fn* will not be called for any of its descendants.

FTW_NS `stat` failed on the object because of lack of appropriate permission. The stat buffer passed to *fn* is undefined. `stat` failure other than lack of appropriate permission (EACCES) is considered an error and `nftw` will return −1.

Both `ftw` and `nftw` use one file descriptor for each level in the tree. The *depth* argument limits the number of file descriptors so used. If *depth* is zero or negative, the effect is the same as if it were 1. *depth* must not be greater than the number of file descriptors currently available for use. `ftw` will run faster if *depth* is at least as large as the number of levels in the tree. When `ftw` and `nftw` return, they close any file descriptors they have opened; they do not close any file descriptors that may have been opened by *fn*.

SEE ALSO

stat(2), malloc(3C).

NOTES

Because `ftw` is recursive, it is possible for it to terminate with a memory fault when applied to very deep file structures.

`ftw` uses `malloc`(3C) to allocate dynamic storage during its operation. If `ftw` is forcibly terminated, such as by `longjmp` being executed by *fn* or an interrupt routine, `ftw` will not have a chance to free that storage, so it will remain permanently allocated. A safe way to handle interrupts is to store the fact that an interrupt has occurred, and arrange to have *fn* return a nonzero value at its next invocation.

getc(3S)

NAME
getc, getchar, fgetc, getw – get character or word from a stream

SYNOPSIS
#include <stdio.h>

int getc (FILE *stream);

int getchar (void);

int fgetc (FILE *stream);

int getw (FILE *stream);

DESCRIPTION
getc returns the next character (i.e., byte) from the named input *stream* [see intro(3)] as an **unsigned char** converted to an **int**. It also moves the file pointer, if defined, ahead one character in *stream*. *getchar* is defined as *getc(stdin)*. *getc* and *getchar* are macros.

fgetc behaves like *getc*, but is a function rather than a macro. *fgetc* runs more slowly than *getc*, but it takes less space per invocation and its name can be passed as an argument to a function.

getw returns the next word (i.e., integer) from the named input *stream*. *getw* increments the associated file pointer, if defined, to point to the next word. The size of a word is the size of an integer and varies from machine to machine. *getw* assumes no special alignment in the file.

SEE ALSO
fclose(3S), ferror(3S), fopen(3S), fread(3S), gets(3S), putc(3S), scanf(3S), stdio(3S), ungetc(3S).

DIAGNOSTICS
These functions return the constant EOF at end-of-file or upon an error and set the EOF or error indicator of *stream*, respectively. Because EOF is a valid integer, *ferror* should be used to detect *getw* errors.

NOTES
If the integer value returned by *getc*, *getchar*, or *fgetc* is stored into a character variable and then compared against the integer constant EOF, the comparison may never succeed, because sign-extension of a character on widening to integer is implementation dependent.

The macro version of *getc* evaluates a *stream* argument more than once and may treat side effects incorrectly. In particular, *getc(*f++)* does not work sensibly. Use *fgetc* instead.

Because of possible differences in word length and byte ordering, files written using *putw* are implementation dependent, and may not be read using *getw* on a different processor.

Functions exist for all the above-defined macros. To get the function form, the macro name must be undefined (e.g., #undef getc).

NAME
getcwd – get pathname of current working directory

SYNOPSIS
    #include <unistd.h>

    char *getcwd (char *buf, int size);

DESCRIPTION
getcwd returns a pointer to the current directory pathname. The value of *size* must be at least one greater than the length of the pathname to be returned.

If *buf* is not NULL, the pathname will be stored in the space pointed to by *buf*.

If *buf* is a NULL pointer, getcwd will obtain *size* bytes of space using malloc(3C). In this case, the pointer returned by getcwd may be used as the argument in a subsequent call to free.

getcwd will fail if one or more of the following are true:

EACCES	A parent directory cannot be read to get its name.
EINVAL	*size* is equal to 0.
ERANGE	*size* is lwss than 0 or is greater than 0 and less than the length of the pathname plus 1.

EXAMPLE
Here is a program that prints the current working directory.

    #include <unistd.h>
    #include <stdio.h>

    main()
    {
        char *cwd;
        if ((cwd = getcwd(NULL, 64)) == NULL)
        {
            perror("pwd");
            exit(2);
        }
        (void)printf("%s\n", cwd);
        return(0);
    }

SEE ALSO
malloc(3C).

DIAGNOSTICS
Returns NULL with errno set if *size* is not large enough, or if an error occurs in a lower-level function.

getdate(3C)

NAME
getdate – convert user format date and time

SYNOPSIS
    #include <time.h>

    struct tm *getdate (const char *string);

    extern int getdate_err;

DESCRIPTION
getdate converts user-definable date and/or time specifications pointed to by *string* into a tm structure. The structure declaration is in the time.h header file [see also ctime(3C)].

User-supplied templates are used to parse and interpret the input string. The templates are text files created by the user and identified via the environment variable DATEMSK. Each line in the template represents an acceptable date and/or time specification using some of the same field descriptors as the ones used by the date command. The first line in the template that matches the input specification is used for interpretation and conversion into the internal time format. If successful, the function getdate returns a pointer to a tm structure; otherwise, it returns NULL and sets the global variable getdate_err to indicate the error.

The following field descriptors are supported:

%%	same as %
%a	abbreviated weekday name
%A	full weekday name
%b	abbreviated month name
%B	full month name
%c	locale's appropriate date and time representation
%d	day of month (01-31; the leading 0 is optional)
%e	same as %d
%D	date as %m/%d/%y
%h	abbreviated month name
%H	hour (00-23)
%I	hour (01-12)
%m	month number (01-12)
%M	minute (00-59)
%n	same as \n
%p	locale's equivalent of either AM or PM
%r	time as %I:%M:%S %p
%R	time as %H:%M
%S	seconds (00-59)
%t	insert a tab
%T	time as %H:%M:%S
%w	weekday number (0-6; Sunday = 0)
%x	locale's appropriate date representation

%X   locale's appropriate time representation
%y   year with century (00-99)
%Y   year as ccyy (e.g., 1986)
%Z   time zone name or no characters if no time zone exists

The month and weekday names can consist of any combination of upper and lower case letters. The user can request that the input date or time specification be in a specific language by setting the categories LC_TIME and LC_CTYPE of setlocale.

The following example shows the possible contents of a template:

```
%m
%A %B %d %Y, %H:%M:%S
%A
%B
%m/%d/%y %I %p
%d,%m,%Y %H:%M
at %A the %dst of %B in %Y
run job at %I %p,%B %dnd
%A den %d. %B %Y %H.%M Uhr
```

The following are examples of valid input specifications for the above template:

```
getdate("10/1/87 4 PM")
getdate("Friday")
getdate("Friday September 19 1987, 10:30:30")
getdate("24,9,1986 10:30")
getdate("at monday the 1st of december in 1986")
getdate("run job at 3 PM, december %2nd")
```

If the LANG environment variable is set to german, the following is valid:

```
getdate("freitag den 10. oktober 1986 10.30 Uhr")
```

Local time and date specification are also supported. The following examples show how local date and time specification can be defined in the template.

Invocation	Line in Template
getdate("11/27/86")	%m/%d/%y
getdate("27.11.86")	%d.%m.%y
getdate("86-11-27")	%y-%m-%d
getdate("Friday 12:00:00")	%A %H:%M:%S

The following rules are applied for converting the input specification into the internal format:

If only the weekday is given, today is assumed if the given day is equal to the current day and next week if it is less.

If only the month is given, the current month is assumed if the given month is equal to the current month and next year if it is less and no year is given. (The first day of month is assumed if no day is given.)

getdate(3C)

If no hour, minute, and second are given, the current hour, minute, and second are assumed.

If no date is given, today is assumed if the given hour is greater than the current hour and tomorrow is assumed if it is less.

The following examples illustrate the above rules. Assume that the current date is Mon Sep 22 12:19:47 EDT 1986 and the LANG environment variable is not set.

Input	Line in Template	Date
Mon	%a	Mon Sep 22 12:19:48 EDT 1986
Sun	%a	Sun Sep 28 12:19:49 EDT 1986
Fri	%a	Fri Sep 26 12:19:49 EDT 1986
September	%B	Mon Sep 1 12:19:49 EDT 1986
January	%B	Thu Jan 1 12:19:49 EST 1987
December	%B	Mon Dec 1 12:19:49 EST 1986
Sep Mon	%b %a	Mon Sep 1 12:19:50 EDT 1986
Jan Fri	%b %a	Fri Jan 2 12:19:50 EST 1987
Dec Mon	%b %a	Mon Dec 1 12:19:50 EST 1986
Jan Wed 1989	%b %a %Y	Wed Jan 4 12:19:51 EST 1989
Fri 9	%a %H	Fri Sep 26 09:00:00 EDT 1986
Feb 10:30	%b %H:%S	Sun Feb 1 10:00:30 EST 1987
10:30	%H:%M	Tue Sep 23 10:30:00 EDT 1986
13:30	%H:%M	Mon Sep 22 13:30:00 EDT 1986

FILES

/usr/lib/locale/<locale>/LC_TIME   language specific printable files
/usr/lib/locale/<locale>/LC_CTYPE   code set specific printable files

SEE ALSO

setlocale(3C), ctype(3C), environ(5).

DIAGNOSTICS

On failure getdate returns NULL and sets the variable getdate_err to indicate the error.

The following is a complete list of the getdate_err settings and their meanings.

1   The DATEMSK environment variable is null or undefined.

2   The template file cannot be opened for reading.

3   Failed to get file status information.

4   The template file is not a regular file.

5   An error is encountered while reading the template file.

6   malloc failed (not enough memory is available).

7   There is no line in the template that matches the input.

8   The input specification is invalid (e.g., February 31).

NOTES

Subsequent calls to getdate alter the contents of getdate_err.

Dates before 1970 and after 2037 are illegal.

getdate makes explicit use of macros described in ctype(3C).

Previous implementations of getdate may return char *.

getenv(3C)

NAME
getenv – return value for environment name

SYNOPSIS
#include <stdlib.h>

char *getenv (const char *name);

DESCRIPTION
getenv searches the environment list [see environ(5)] for a string of the form *name=value* and, if the string is present, returns a pointer to the *value* in the current environment. Otherwise, it returns a null pointer.

SEE ALSO
exec(2), putenv(3C), environ(5).

getgrent(3C)

NAME
getgrent, getgrgid, getgrnam, setgrent, endgrent, fgetgrent – get group file entry

SYNOPSIS
#include <grp.h>

struct group *getgrent (void);

struct group *getgrgid (gid_t gid);

struct group *getgrnam (const char *name);

void setgrent (void);

void endgrent (void);

struct group *fgetgrent (FILE *f);

DESCRIPTION
getgrent, getgrgid, and getgrnam each return pointers to an object containing the broken-out fields of a line in the /etc/group file. Each line contains a "group" structure, defined in the grp.h header file with the following members:

```
char  *gr_name;    /* the name of the group */
char  *gr_passwd;  /* the encrypted group password */
gid_t gr_gid;      /* the numerical group ID */
char  **gr_mem;    /* vector of pointers to member names */
```

When first called, getgrent returns a pointer to the first group structure in the file; thereafter, it returns a pointer to the next group structure in the file; so, successive calls may be used to search the entire file. getgrgid searches from the beginning of the file until a numerical group id matching *gid* is found and returns a pointer to the particular structure in which it was found.

getgrnam searches from the beginning of the file until a group name matching *name* is found and returns a pointer to the particular structure in which it was found. If an end-of-file or an error is encountered on reading, these functions return a null pointer.

A call to setgrent has the effect of rewinding the group file to allow repeated searches. endgrent may be called to close the group file when processing is complete.

fgetgrent returns a pointer to the next group structure in the stream *f*, which matches the format of /etc/group.

FILES
/etc/group

SEE ALSO
getlogin(3C), getpwent(3C).
group(4) in the *System Administrator's Reference Manual*.

DIAGNOSTICS
getgrent, getgrgid, getgrnam, and fgetgrent return a null pointer on EOF or error.

NOTES
All information is contained in a static area, so it must be copied if it is to be saved.

getitimer(3C)

NAME
getitimer, setitimer – get/set value of interval timer

SYNOPSIS
#include <sys/time.h>

int getitimer(int which, struct itimerval *value);

int setitimer(int which, struct itimerval *value, struct itimerval *ovalue);

DESCRIPTION
The system provides each process with three interval timers, defined in sys/time.h. The getitimer call stores the current value of the timer specified by *which* into the structure pointed to by *value*. The setitimer call sets the value of the timer specified by *which* to the value specified in the structure pointed to by *value*, and if *ovalue* is not NULL, stores the previous value of the timer in the structure pointed to by *ovalue*.

A timer value is defined by the itimerval structure [see gettimeofday(3C) for the definition of timeval], which includes the following members:

    struct timeval it_interval;   /* timer interval */
    struct timeval it_value;   /* current value */

If it_value is non-zero, it indicates the time to the next timer expiration. If it_interval is non-zero, it specifies a value to be used in reloading it_value when the timer expires. Setting it_value to zero disables a timer, regardless of the value of it_interval. Setting it_interval to zero disables a timer after its next expiration (assuming it_value is non-zero).

Time values smaller than the resolution of the system clock are rounded up to this resolution.

The three timers are:

ITIMER_REAL
: Decrements in real time. A SIGALRM signal is delivered when this timer expires.

ITIMER_VIRTUAL
: Decrements in process virtual time. It runs only when the process is executing. A SIGVTALRM signal is delivered when it expires.

ITIMER_PROF
: Decrements both in process virtual time and when the system is running on behalf of the process. It is designed to be used by interpreters in statistically profiling the execution of interpreted programs. Each time the ITIMER_PROF timer expires, the SIGPROF signal is delivered. Because this signal may interrupt in-progress system calls, programs using this timer must be prepared to restart interrupted system calls.

SEE ALSO
alarm(2), gettimeofday(3C).

DIAGNOSTICS
If the calls succeed, a value of 0 is returned. If an error occurs, the value −1 is returned, and an error code is placed in the global variable errno.

Under the following conditions, the functions `getitimer` and `setitimer` fail and set **errno** to:

EINVAL The specified number of seconds is greater than 100,000,000, the number of microseconds is greater than or equal to 1,000,000, or the *which* parameter is unrecognized.

NOTES

The microseconds field should not be equal to or greater than one second.

`setitimer` is independent of the `alarm` system call.

Do not use `setitimer` with the `sleep` routine. A `sleep` following a `setitimer` wipes out knowledge of the user signal handler.

NAME
getlogin - get login name

SYNOPSIS
#include <stdlib.h>

char *getlogin (void);

DESCRIPTION
getlogin returns a pointer to the login name as found in /var/adm/utmp. It may be used in conjunction with getpwnam to locate the correct password file entry when the same user id is shared by several login names.

If getlogin is called within a process that is not attached to a terminal, it returns a null pointer. The correct procedure for determining the login name is to call cuserid, or to call getlogin and if it fails to call getpwuid.

FILES
/var/adm/utmp

SEE ALSO
cuserid(3S), getgrent(3C), getpwent(3C), utmp(4).

DIAGNOSTICS
Returns a null pointer if the login name is not found.

NOTES
The return values point to static data whose content is overwritten by each call.

getmntent (3C)

NAME
getmntent, getmntany – get mnttab file entry

SYNOPSIS
    #include <stdio.h>
    #include <sys/mnttab.h>

    int getmntent (FILE *fp, struct mnttab *mp);

    int getmntany (FILE *fp, struct mnttab *mp, struct mnttab *mpref);

DESCRIPTION
getmntent and getmntany each fill in the structure pointed to by *mp* with the broken-out fields of a line in the /etc/mnttab file. Each line in the file contains a mnttab structure, declared in the sys/mnttab.h header file:

    struct mnttab {
        char *mnt_special;
        char *mnt_mountp;
        char *mnt_fstype;
        char *mnt_mntopts;
        char *mnt_time;
    };

The fields have meanings described in mnttab(4).

getmntent returns a pointer to the next mnttab structure in the file; so successive calls can be used to search the entire file. getmntany searches the file referenced by *fp* until a match is found between a line in the file and *mpref*. *mpref* matches the line if all non-null entries in *mpref* match the corresponding fields in the file. Note that these routines do not open, close, or rewind the file.

FILES
/etc/mnttab

SEE ALSO
mnttab(4).

DIAGNOSTICS
If the next entry is successfully read by getmntent or a match is found with getmntany, 0 is returned. If an end-of-file is encountered on reading, these functions return −1. If an error is encountered, a value greater than 0 is returned. The possible error values are:

MNT_TOOLONG	A line in the file exceeded the internal buffer size of MNT_LINE_MAX.
MNT_TOOMANY	A line in the file contains too many fields.
MNT_TOOFEW	A line in the file contains too few fields.

NOTES
The members of the mnttab structure point to information contained in a static area, so it must be copied if it is to be saved.

getopt(3C)

NAME
getopt – get option letter from argument vector

SYNOPSIS
#include <stdlib.h>

int getopt (int argc, char * const *argv, const char *optstring);

extern char *optarg;

extern int optind, opterr, optopt;

DESCRIPTION
getopt returns the next option letter in *argv* that matches a letter in *optstring*. It supports all the rules of the command syntax standard [see intro(1)]. Since all new commands are intended to adhere to the command syntax standard, they should use getopts(1), getopt(3C), or getsubopts(3C) to parse positional parameters and check for options that are legal for that command.

optstring must contain the option letters the command using getopt will recognize; if a letter is followed by a colon, the option is expected to have an argument, or group of arguments, which may be separated from it by white space. *optarg* is set to point to the start of the option argument on return from getopt.

getopt places in *optind* the *argv* index of the next argument to be processed. *optind* is external and is initialized to 1 before the first call to getopt. When all options have been processed (i.e., up to the first non-option argument), getopt returns EOF. The special option "--" (two hyphens) may be used to delimit the end of the options; when it is encountered, EOF is returned and "--" is skipped. This is useful in delimiting non-option arguments that begin with "-" (hyphen).

EXAMPLE
The following code fragment shows how one might process the arguments for a command that can take the mutually exclusive options a and b, and the option o, which requires an argument:

```
#include <stdlib.h>
#include <stdio.h>

main (int argc, char **argv)
{
    int c;
    extern char *optarg;
    extern int optind;
    int aflg = 0;
    int bflg = 0;
    int errflg = 0;
    char *ofile = NULL;

    while ((c = getopt(argc, argv, "abo:")) != EOF)
        switch (c) {
        case 'a':
            if (bflg)
                errflg++;
```

```
                else
                        aflg++;
                break;
            case 'b':
                if (aflg)
                        errflg++;
                else
                        bflg++;
                break;
            case 'o':
                ofile = optarg;
                (void)printf("ofile = %s\n", ofile);
                break;
            case '?':
                errflg++;
            }
        if (errflg) {
            (void)fprintf(stderr,
                "usage: cmd [-a|-b] [-o<file>] files...\n");
            exit(2);
        }
        for ( ; optind < argc; optind++)
            (void)printf("%s\n", argv[optind]);
        return 0;
    }
```

SEE ALSO

getsubopt(3C).
getopts(1), intro(1) in the *User's Reference Manual*.

DIAGNOSTICS

getopt prints an error message on the standard error and returns a "?" (question mark) when it encounters an option letter not included in *optstring* or no argument after an option that expects one. This error message may be disabled by setting opterr to 0. The value of the character that caused the error is in optopt.

NOTES

The library routine getopt does not fully check for mandatory arguments. That is, given an option string a:b and the input −a −b, getopt assumes that −b is the mandatory argument to the option −a and not that −a is missing a mandatory argument.

It is a violation of the command syntax standard [see intro(1)] for options with arguments to be grouped with other options, as in cmd −aboxxx file, where a and b are options, o is an option that requires an argument, and xxx is the argument to o. Although this syntax is permitted in the current implementation, it should not be used because it may not be supported in future releases. The correct syntax is cmd −ab −oxxx file.

getpass(3C)

NAME
getpass – read a password

SYNOPSIS
#include <stdlib.h>

char *getpass (const char *prompt);

DESCRIPTION
getpass reads up to a newline or EOF from the file /dev/tty, after prompting on the standard error output with the null-terminated string *prompt* and disabling echoing. A pointer is returned to a null-terminated string of at most 8 characters. If /dev/tty cannot be opened, a null pointer is returned. An interrupt will terminate input and send an interrupt signal to the calling program before returning.

FILES
/dev/tty

NOTE
The return value points to static data whose content is overwritten by each call.

NAME

getpw – get name from UID

SYNOPSIS

#include <stdlib.h>

int getpw (uid_t uid, char *buf);

DESCRIPTION

getpw searches the password file for a user id number that equals *uid*, copies the line of the password file in which *uid* was found into the array pointed to by *buf*, and returns 0. getpw returns non-zero if *uid* cannot be found.

This routine is included only for compatibility with prior systems and should not be used; see getpwent(3C) for routines to use instead.

FILES

/etc/passwd

SEE ALSO

getpwent(3C).
passwd(4) in the *System Administrator's Reference Manual*.

DIAGNOSTICS

getpw returns non-zero on error.

getpwent (3C)

NAME
getpwent, getpwuid, getpwnam, setpwent, endpwent, fgetpwent – manipulate password file entry

SYNOPSIS
#include <pwd.h>

struct passwd *getpwent (void);

struct passwd *getpwuid (uid_t uid);

struct passwd *getpwnam (const char *name);

void setpwent (void);

void endpwent (void);

struct passwd *fgetpwent (FILE *f);

DESCRIPTION
getpwent, getpwuid, and getpwnam each returns a pointer to an object with the following structure containing the broken-out fields of a line in the /etc/passwd file. Each line in the file contains a passwd structure, declared in the pwd.h header file:

```
struct passwd {
    char *pw_name;
    char *pw_passwd;
    uid_t pw_uid;
    gid_t pw_gid;
    char *pw_age;
    char *pw_comment;
    char *pw_gecos;
    char *pw_dir;
    char *pw_shell;
};
```

getpwent when first called returns a pointer to the first passwd structure in the file; thereafter, it returns a pointer to the next passwd structure in the file; so successive calls can be used to search the entire file. getpwuid searches from the beginning of the file until a numerical user id matching *uid* is found and returns a pointer to the particular structure in which it was found. getpwnam searches from the beginning of the file until a login name matching *name* is found, and returns a pointer to the particular structure in which it was found. If an end-of-file or an error is encountered on reading, these functions return a null pointer.

A call to setpwent has the effect of rewinding the password file to allow repeated searches. endpwent may be called to close the password file when processing is complete.

fgetpwent returns a pointer to the next passwd structure in the stream *f*, which matches the format of /etc/passwd.

FILES
/etc/passwd

getpwent (3C) getpwent (3C)

SEE ALSO
getlogin(3C), getgrent(3C).
passwd(4) in the *System Administrator's Reference Manual*.

DIAGNOSTICS
getpwent, getpwnid, getpwnam, and fgetpwent return a null pointer on EOF or error.

NOTES
All information is contained in a static area, so it must be copied if it is to be saved.

NAME
gets, fgets – get a string from a stream

SYNOPSIS
#include <stdio.h>

char *gets (char *s);

char *fgets (char *s, int n, FILE *stream);

DESCRIPTION
gets reads characters from the standard input stream [see intro(3)], stdin, into the array pointed to by s, until a newline character is read or an end-of-file condition is encountered. The newline character is discarded and the string is terminated with a null character.

fgets reads characters from the *stream* into the array pointed to by s, until $n-1$ characters are read, or a newline character is read and transferred to s, or an end-of-file condition is encountered. The string is then terminated with a null character.

When using gets, if the length of an input line exceeds the size of s, indeterminate behavior may result. For this reason, it is strongly recommended that gets be avoided in favor of fgets.

SEE ALSO
lseek(2), read(2), ferror(3S), fopen(3S), fread(3S), getc(3S), scanf(3S), stdio(3S), ungetc(3S).

DIAGNOSTICS
If end-of-file is encountered and no characters have been read, no characters are transferred to s and a null pointer is returned. If a read error occurs, such as trying to use these functions on a file that has not been opened for reading, a null pointer is returned and the error indicator for the stream is set. If end-of-file is encountered, the EOF indicator for the stream is set. Otherwise s is returned.

getspent(3C)

NAME
getspent, getspnam, setspent, endspent, fgetspent, lckpwdf, ulckpwdf – manipulate shadow password file entry

SYNOPSIS
```
#include <shadow.h>
```
struct spwd *getspent (void);

struct spwd *getspnam (const char *name);

int lckpwdf (void);

int ulckpwdf (void);

void setspent (void);

void endspent (void);

struct spwd *fgetspent (FILE *fp);

DESCRIPTION
The **getspent** and **getspnam** routines each return a pointer to an object with the following structure containing the broken-out fields of a line in the /etc/shadow file. Each line in the file contains a "shadow password" structure, declared in the shadow.h header file:

```
struct spwd{
      char   *sp_namp;
      char   *sp_pwdp;
      long   sp_lstchg;
      long   sp_min;
      long   sp_max;
      long   sp_warn;
      long   sp_inact;
      long   sp_expire;
      unsigned long   sp_flag;
};
```

The **getspent** routine when first called returns a pointer to the first **spwd** structure in the file; thereafter, it returns a pointer to the next **spwd** structure in the file; so successive calls can be used to search the entire file. The **getspnam** routine searches from the beginning of the file until a login name matching *name* is found, and returns a pointer to the particular structure in which it was found. The getspent and getspnam routines populate the sp_min, sp_max, sp_lstchg, sp_warn, sp_inact, sp_expire, or sp_flag field with −1 if the corresponding field in /etc/shadow is empty. If an end-of-file or an error is encountered on reading, or there is a format error in the file, these functions return a null pointer and set **errno** to EINVAL.

/etc/.pwd.lock is the lock file. It is used to coordinate modification access to the password files /etc/passwd and /etc/shadow. lckpwdf and ulckpwdf are routines that are used to gain modification access to the password files, through the lock file. A process first uses lckpwdf to lock the lock file, thereby gaining exclusive rights to modify the /etc/passwd or /etc/shadow password file. Upon completing modifications, a process should release the lock on the lock file via `ulckpwdf`. This mechanism prevents simultaneous modification of the password files.

`lckpwdf` attempts to lock the file `/etc/.pwd.lock` within 15 seconds. If unsuccessful, e.g., `/etc/.pwd.lock` is already locked, it returns -1. If successful, a return code other than -1 is returned.

`ulckpwdf` attempts to unlock the file `/etc/.pwd.lock`. If unsuccessful, e.g., `/etc/.pwd.lock` is already unlocked, it returns -1. If successful, it returns 0.

A call to the `setspent` routine has the effect of rewinding the shadow password file to allow repeated searches. The `endspent` routine may be called to close the shadow password file when processing is complete.

The `fgetspent` routine returns a pointer to the next `spwd` structure in the stream *fp*, which matches the format of `/etc/shadow`.

FILES
/etc/shadow
/etc/passwd
/etc/.pwd.lock

SEE ALSO
getpwent(3C), putpwent(3C), putspent(3C).

DIAGNOSTICS
`getspent`, `getspnam`, `lckpwdf`, `ulckpwdf`, and `fgetspent` return a null pointer on EOF or error.

NOTES
This routine is for internal use only; compatibility is not guaranteed.

All information is contained in a static area, so it must be copied if it is to be saved.

getsubopt(3C)

NAME
getsubopt – parse suboptions from a string

SYNOPSIS
#include <stdlib.h>

int getsubopt (char **optionp, char * const *tokens, char **valuep);

DESCRIPTION
getsubopt parses suboptions in a flag argument that was initially parsed by getopt. These suboptions are separated by commas and may consist of either a single token or a token-value pair separated by an equal sign. Since commas delimit suboptions in the option string, they are not allowed to be part of the suboption or the value of a suboption. A command that uses this syntax is mount(1M), which allows the user to specify mount parameters with the −o option as follows:

            mount −o rw,hard,bg,wsize=1024 speed:/usr /usr

In this example there are four suboptions: rw, hard, bg, and wsize, the last of which has an associated value of 1024.

getsubopt takes the address of a pointer to the option string, a vector of possible tokens, and the address of a value string pointer. It returns the index of the token that matched the suboption in the input string or −1 if there was no match. If the option string at *optionp* contains only one subobtion, getsubopt updates *optionp* to point to the null character at the end of the string; otherwise it isolates the suboption by replacing the comma separator with a null character, and updates *optionp* to point to the start of the next suboption. If the suboption has an associated value, getsubopt updates *valuep* to point to the value's first character. Otherwise it sets *valuep* to NULL.

The token vector is organized as a series of pointers to null strings. The end of the token vector is identified by a null pointer.

When getsubopt returns, if *valuep* is not NULL, then the suboption processed included a value. The calling program may use this information to determine if the presence or lack of a value for this subobtion is an error.

Additionally, when getsubopt fails to match the suboption with the tokens in the *tokens* array, the calling program should decide if this is an error, or if the unrecognized option should be passed to another program.

EXAMPLE
The following code fragment shows how to process options to the mount command using getsubopt.

```
#include <stdlib.h>

char *myopts[] = {
#define READONLY        0
                "ro",
#define READWRITE       1
                "rw",
```

getsubopt(3C)

```
      #define WRITESIZE    2
                  "wsize",
      #define READSIZE    3
                  "rsize",
                  NULL};

      main(argc, argv)
          int   argc;
          char **argv;
      {
          int sc, c, errflag;
          char *options, *value;
          extern char *optarg;
          extern int optind;
          .
          .
          .
          while((c = getopt(argc, argv, "abf:o:")) != -1) {
              switch (c) {
              case 'a': /* process a option */
                  break;
              case 'b': /* process b option */
                  break;
              case 'f':
                  ofile = optarg;
                  break;
              case '?':
                  errflag++;
                  break;
              case 'o':
                  options = optarg;
                  while (*options != '\0') {
                      switch(getsubopt(&options,myopts,&value) {
                      case READONLY : /* process ro option */
                          break;
                      case READWRITE : /* process rw option */
                          break;
                      case WRITESIZE : /* process wsize option */
                          if (value == NULL) {
                              error_no_arg();
                              errflag++;
                          } else
                              write_size = atoi(value);
                          break;
                      case READSIZE : /* process rsize option */
                          if (value == NULL) {
                              error_no_arg();
                              errflag++;
                          } else
```

```
                                read_size = atoi(value);
                            break;
                        default :
                            /* process unknown token */
                            error_bad_token(value);
                            errflag++;
                            break;
                        }
                    }
                    break;
                }
            }
            if (errflag) {
                /* print usage instructions etc. */
            }
            for (; optind<argc; optind++) {
                /* process remaining arguments */
            }
            .
            .
            .
        }
```

SEE ALSO
getopt(3C).

DIAGNOSTICS
getsubopt returns −1 when the token it is scanning is not in the token vector. The variable addressed by *valuep* contains a pointer to the first character of the token that was not recognized rather than a pointer to a value for that token.

The variable addressed by *optionp* points to the next option to be parsed, or a null character if there are no more options.

NOTES
During parsing, commas in the option input string are changed to null characters. White space in tokens or token-value pairs must be protected from the shell by quotes.

gettimeofday(3C)

NAME
gettimeofday, settimeofday - get or set the date and time

SYNOPSIS
#include <sys/time.h>

int gettimeofday (struct timeval *tp);

int settimeofday (struct timeval *tp);

DESCRIPTION
gettimeofday gets and **settimeofday** sets the system's notion of the current time. The current time is expressed in elapsed seconds and microseconds since 00:00 Universal Coordinated Time, January 1, 1970. The resolution of the system clock is hardware dependent; the time may be updated continuously or in clock ticks.

tp points to a **timeval** structure, which includes the following members:

```
long    tv_sec;     /* seconds since Jan. 1, 1970 */
long    tv_usec;    /* and microseconds */
```

If *tp* is a null pointer, the current time information is not returned or set.

The **TZ** environment variable holds time zone information. See **timezone**(4).

Only the privileged user may set the time of day.

SEE ALSO
adjtime(2), ctime(3C), timezone(4).

DIAGNOSTICS
A −1 return value indicates that an error occurred and **errno** has been set. The following error codes may be set in **errno**:

EINVAL   *tp* specifies an invalid time.

EPERM   A user other than the privileged user attempted to set the time or time zone.

NOTES
The implementation of **settimeofday** ignores the **tv_usec** field of **tp**. If the time needs to be set with better than one second accuracy, call **settimeofday** for the seconds and then **adjtime** for finer accuracy.

gettxt(3C)

NAME
gettxt – retrieve a text string

SYNOPSIS
#include <unistd.h>

char *gettxt (const char *msgid, const char *dflt_str);

DESCRIPTION
gettxt retrieves a text string from a message file. The arguments to the function are a message identification *msgid* and a default string *dflt_str* to be used if the retrieval fails.

The text strings are in files created by the mkmsgs utility [see mkmsgs(1)] and installed in directories in /usr/lib/locale/<*locale*>/LC_MESSAGES.

The directory <*locale*> can be viewed as the language in which the text strings are written. The user can request that messages be displayed in a specific language by setting the environment variable LC_MESSAGES. If LC_MESSAGES is not set, the environment variable LANG will be used. If LANG is not set, the files containing the strings are in /usr/lib/locale/C/LC_MESSAGES/*.

The user can also change the language in which the messages are displayed by invoking the setlocale function with the appropriate arguments.

If gettxt fails to retrieve a message in a specific language it will try to retrieve the same message in U.S. English. On failure, the processing depends on what the second argument *dflt_str* points to. A pointer to the second argument is returned if the second argument is not the null string. If *dflt_str* points to the null string, a pointer to the U.S. English text string "Message not found!!\n" is returned.

The following depicts the acceptable syntax of *msgid* for a call to gettxt.

<*msgid*> = <*msgfilename*>:<*msgnumber*>

The first field is used to indicate the file that contains the text strings and must be limited to 14 characters. These characters must be selected from the set of all character values excluding \0 (null) and the ASCII code for / (slash) and : (colon). The names of message files must be the same as the names of files created by mkmsgs and installed in /usr/lib/locale/<*locale*>/LC_MESSAGES/*. The numeric field indicates the sequence number of the string in the file. The strings are numbered from *1* to *n* where *n* is the number of strings in the file.

On failure to pass the correct msgid or a valid message number to gettxt a pointer to the text string "Message not found!!\n" is returned.

EXAMPLE
gettxt("UX:10", "hello world\n")
gettxt("UX:10", "")

UX is the name of the file that contains the messages. 10 is the message number.

FILES
/usr/lib/locale/C/LC_MESSAGES/*   contains default message files created by mkmsgs

gettxt(3C)

/usr/lib/locale/*locale*/LC_MESSAGES/*   contains message files for different languages created by **mkmsgs**

SEE ALSO
fmtmsg(3C), setlocale(3C), environ(5).
exstr(1), mkmsgs(1), srchtxt(1) in the *User's Reference Manual*.

getut(3C)

NAME
getut: getutent, getutid, getutline, pututline, setutent, endutent, utmpname − access utmp file entry

SYNOPSIS
#include <utmp.h>

struct utmp *getutent (void);

struct utmp *getutid (const struct utmp *id);

struct utmp *getutline (const struct utmp *line);

struct utmp *pututline (const struct utmp *utmp);

void setutent (void);

void endutent (void);

int utmpname (const char *file);

DESCRIPTION
getutent, getutid, getutline, and pututline each return a pointer to a structure with the following members:

```
char    ut_user[8];     /* user login name */
char    ut_id[4];       /* /sbin/inittab id (usually line #) */
char    ut_line[12];    /* device name (console, lnxx) */
short   ut_pid;         /* process id    */
short   ut_type;        /* type of entry */
struct  exit_status {
} ut_exit;              /* exit status of a process */
                        /* marked as DEAD_PROCESS */
time_t  ut_time;        /* time entry was made */
```

The structure exit status includes the following members:

```
short   e_termination;  /* termination status */
short   e_exit;         /* exit status */
```

getutent reads in the next entry from a utmp-like file. If the file is not already open, it opens it. If it reaches the end of the file, it fails.

getutid searches forward from the current point in the utmp file until it finds an entry with a *ut_type* matching id->ut_type if the type specified is RUN_LVL, BOOT_TIME, OLD_TIME, or NEW_TIME. If the type specified in id is INIT_PROCESS, LOGIN_PROCESS, USER_PROCESS, or DEAD_PROCESS, then getutid will return a pointer to the first entry whose type is one of these four and whose ut_id field matches id->ut_id . If the end of file is reached without a match, it fails.

getutline searches forward from the current point in the utmp file until it finds an entry of the type LOGIN_PROCESS or USER_PROCESS that also has a *ut_line* string matching the line->ut_line string. If the end of file is reached without a match, it fails.

pututline writes out the supplied utmp structure into the utmp file. It uses getutid to search forward for the proper place if it finds that it is not already at the proper place. It is expected that normally the user of pututline will have searched for the proper entry using one of the getut routines. If so, pututline will not search. If pututline does not find a matching slot for the new entry, it will add a new entry to the end of the file. It returns a pointer to the utmp structure.

setutent resets the input stream to the beginning of the file. This reset should be done before each search for a new entry if it is desired that the entire file be examined.

endutent closes the currently open file.

utmpname allows the user to change the name of the file examined, from /var/adm/utmp to any other file. It is most often expected that this other file will be /var/adm/wtmp. If the file does not exist, this will not be apparent until the first attempt to reference the file is made. utmpname does not open the file. It just closes the old file if it is currently open and saves the new file name. If the file name given is longer than 79 characters, utmpname returns 0. Otherwise, it will return 1.

FILES

/var/adm/utmp
/var/adm/wtmp

SEE ALSO

ttyslot(3C), utmp(4).

DIAGNOSTICS

A null pointer is returned upon failure to read, whether for permissions or having reached the end of file, or upon failure to write.

NOTES

The most current entry is saved in a static structure. Multiple accesses require that it be copied before further accesses are made. On each call to either getutid or getutline, the routine examines the static structure before performing more I/O. If the contents of the static structure match what it is searching for, it looks no further. For this reason, to use getutline to search for multiple occurrences, it would be necessary to zero out the static area after each success, or getutline would just return the same structure over and over again. There is one exception to the rule about emptying the structure before further reads are done. The implicit read done by pututline (if it finds that it is not already at the correct place in the file) will not hurt the contents of the static structure returned by the getutent, getutid or getutline routines, if the user has just modified those contents and passed the pointer back to pututline.

These routines use buffered standard I/O for input, but pututline uses an unbuffered non-standard write to avoid race conditions between processes trying to modify the utmp and wtmp files.

getutx(3C)

NAME
getutx: getutxent, getutxid, getutxline, pututxline, setutxent, endutxent, utmpxname, getutmp, getutmpx, updwtmp, updwtmpx – access utmpx file entry

SYNOPSIS
#include <utmpx.h>

struct utmpx *getutxent (void);

struct utmpx *getutxid (const struct utmpx *id);

struct utmpx *getutxline (const struct utmpx *line);

struct utmpx *pututxline (const struct utmpx *utmpx);

void setutxent (void);

void endutxent (void);

int utmpxname (const char *file);

void getutmp (struct utmpx *utmpx, struct utmp *utmp);

void getutmpx (struct utmp *utmp, struct utmpx *utmpx);

void updwtmp (char *wfile, struct utmp *utmp);

void updwtmpx (char *wfilex, struct utmpx *utmpx);

DESCRIPTION
getutxent, getutxid, and getutxline each return a pointer to a structure of the following type:

```
struct      utmpx {
    char       ut_user[32];    /* user login name */
    char       ut_id[4];       /* /sbin/inittab id (usually */
                               /* line #) */
    char       ut_line[32];    /* device name (console, lnxx) */
    pid_t      ut_pid;         /* process id */
    short      ut_type;        /* type of entry */
    struct     exit_status {
        short      e_termination; /* termination status */
        short      e_exit;        /* exit status */
    } ut_exit;    /* exit status of a process
                   /* marked as DEAD_PROCESS */
    struct timeval    ut_tv;     /* time entry was made */
    short ut_syslen;             /* significant length of ut_host */
                                 /* including terminating null */
    char       ut_host[257];     /* host name, if remote */
};
```

getutxent reads in the next entry from a utmpx-like file. If the file is not already open, it opens it. If it reaches the end of the file, it fails.

getutxid searches forward from the current point in the utmpx file until it finds an entry with a ut_type matching *id*->ut_type if the type specified is RUN_LVL, BOOT_TIME, OLD_TIME, or NEW_TIME. If the type specified in *id* is INIT_PROCESS, LOGIN_PROCESS, USER_PROCESS, or DEAD_PROCESS, then getutxid will return a pointer to the first entry whose type is one of these four and whose *ut_id* field matches *id->ut_id*. If the end of file is reached without a match, it fails.

getutxline searches forward from the current point in the utmpx file until it finds an entry of the type LOGIN_PROCESS or USER_PROCESS which also has a *ut_line* string matching the *line->ut_line* string. If the end of file is reached without a match, it fails.

pututxline writes out the supplied utmpx structure into the utmpx file. It uses getutxid to search forward for the proper place if it finds that it is not already at the proper place. It is expected that normally the user of pututxline will have searched for the proper entry using one of the getutx routines. If so, pututxline will not search. If pututxline does not find a matching slot for the new entry, it will add a new entry to the end of the file. It returns a pointer to the utmpx structure.

setutxent resets the input stream to the beginning of the file. This should be done before each search for a new entry if it is desired that the entire file be examined.

endutxent closes the currently open file.

utmpxname allows the user to change the name of the file examined, from /var/adm/utmpx to any other file. It is most often expected that this other file will be /var/adm/wtmpx. If the file does not exist, this will not be apparent until the first attempt to reference the file is made. utmpxname does not open the file. It just closes the old file if it is currently open and saves the new file name. The new file name must end with the "x" character to allow the name of the corresponding utmp file to be easily obtainable (otherwise an error code of 1 is returned).

getutmp copies the information stored in the fields of the utmpx structure to the corresponding fields of the utmp structure. If the information in any field of utmpx does not fit in the corresponding utmp field, the data is truncated.

getutmpx copies the information stored in the fields of the utmp structure to the corresponding fields of the utmpx structure.

updwtmp checks the existence of *wfile* and its parallel file, whose name is obtained by appending an "x" to *wfile*. If only one of them exists, the second one is created and initialized to reflect the state of the existing file. *utmp* is written to *wfile* and the corresponding utmpx structure is written to the parallel file.

updwtmpx checks the existence of *wfilex* and its parallel file, whose name is obtained by truncating the final "x" from *wfilex*. If only one of them exists, the second one is created and initialized to reflect the state of the existing file. *utmpx* is written to *wfilex*, and the corresponding utmp structure is written to the parallel file.

FILES

/var/adm/utmp, /var/adm/utmpx
/var/adm/wtmp, /var/adm/wtmpx

SEE ALSO
ttyslot(3C), utmp(4), utmpx(4).

DIAGNOSTICS
A null pointer is returned upon failure to read, whether for permissions or having reached the end of file, or upon failure to write.

NOTES
The most current entry is saved in a static structure. Multiple accesses require that it be copied before further accesses are made. On each call to either getutxid or getutxline, the routine examines the static structure before performing more I/O. If the contents of the static structure match what it is searching for, it looks no further. For this reason, to use getutxline to search for multiple occurrences it would be necessary to zero out the static after each success, or getutxline would just return the same structure over and over again. There is one exception to the rule about emptying the structure before further reads are done. The implicit read done by pututxline (if it finds that it is not already at the correct place in the file) will not hurt the contents of the static structure returned by the getutxent, getutxid, or getutxline routines, if the user has just modified those contents and passed the pointer back to pututxline.

These routines use buffered standard I/O for input, but pututxline uses an unbuffered write to avoid race conditions between processes trying to modify the utmpx and wtmpx files.

getvfsent(3C)

NAME
getvfsent, getvfsfile, getvfsspec, getvfsany – get vfstab file entry

SYNOPSIS
```
#include <stdio.h>
#include <sys/vfstab.h>

int getvfsent (FILE *fp, struct vfstab *vp);

int getvfsfile (FILE *fp, struct vfstab *vp, char *file);

int getvfsspec (FILE *, struct vfstab *vp, char *spec);

int getvfsany (FILE *, struct vfstab *vp, vfstab *vref);
```

DESCRIPTION
getvfsent, getvfsfile, getvfsspec, and getvfsany each fill in the structure pointed to by *vp* with the broken-out fields of a line in the /etc/vfstab file. Each line in the file contains a vfstab structure, declared in the sys/vfstab.h header file:

```
char    *vfs_special;
char    *vfs_fsckdev;
char    *vfs_mountp;
char    *vfs_fstype;
char    *vfs_fsckpass;
char    *vfs_automnt;
char    *vfs_mntopts;
```

The fields have meanings described in vfstab(4).

getvfsent returns a pointer to the next vfstab structure in the file; so successive calls can be used to search the entire file. getvfsfile searches the file referenced by *fp* until a mount point matching *file* is found and fills *vp* with the fields from the line in the file. getvfsspec searches the file referenced by *fp* until a special device matching *spec* is found and fills *vp* with the fields from the line in the file. *spec* will try to match on device type (block or character special) and major and minor device numbers. If it cannot match in this manner, then it compares the strings. getvfsany searches the file referenced by *fp* until a match is found between a line in the file and *vref*. *vref* matches the line if all non-null entries in *vref* match the corresponding fields in the file.

Note that these routines do not open, close, or rewind the file.

FILES
/etc/vfstab

DIAGNOSTICS
If the next entry is successfully read by getvfsent or a match is found with getvfsfile, getvfsspec, or getvfsany, 0 is returned. If an end-of-file is encountered on reading, these functions return −1. If an error is encountered, a value greater than 0 is returned. The possible error values are:

VFS_TOOLONG		A line in the file exceeded the internal buffer size of **VFS_LINE_MAX**.
VFS_TOOMANY		A line in the file contains too many fields.
VFS_TOOFEW		A line in the file contains too few fields.

NOTES

The members of the **vfstab** structure point to information contained in a static area, so it must be copied if it is to be saved.

hsearch(3C)

NAME
hsearch, hcreate, hdestroy – manage hash search tables

SYNOPSIS
#include <search.h>

ENTRY *hsearch (ENTRY item, ACTION action);

int hcreate (size_t nel);

void hdestroy (void);

DESCRIPTION
hsearch is a hash-table search routine generalized from Knuth (6.4) Algorithm D. It returns a pointer into a hash table indicating the location at which an entry can be found. The comparison function used by hsearch is strcmp [see string(3C)]. *item* is a structure of type ENTRY (defined in the search.h header file) containing two pointers: *item.key* points to the comparison key, and *item.data* points to any other data to be associated with that key. (Pointers to types other than void should be cast to pointer-to-void.) *action* is a member of an enumeration type ACTION (defined in search.h) indicating the disposition of the entry if it cannot be found in the table. ENTER indicates that the item should be inserted in the table at an appropriate point. Given a duplicate of an existing item, the new item is not entered and hsearch returns a pointer to the existing item. FIND indicates that no entry should be made. Unsuccessful resolution is indicated by the return of a null pointer.

hcreate allocates sufficient space for the table, and must be called before hsearch is used. *nel* is an estimate of the maximum number of entries that the table will contain. This number may be adjusted upward by the algorithm in order to obtain certain mathematically favorable circumstances.

hdestroy destroys the search table, and may be followed by another call to hcreate.

EXAMPLE
The following example will read in strings followed by two numbers and store them in a hash table, discarding duplicates. It will then read in strings and find the matching entry in the hash table and print it out.

```
#include <stdio.h>
#include <search.h>
#include <string.h>
#include <stdlib.h>

struct info {         /* this is the info stored in table */
    int age, room;    /* other than the key */
};

#define NUM_EMPL   5000    /* # of elements in search table */

main( )
{
    /* space to store strings */
```

```
            char string_space[NUM_EMPL*20];
            /* space to store employee info */
            struct info info_space[NUM_EMPL];
            /* next avail space in string_space */
            char *str_ptr = string_space;
            /* next avail space in info_space */
            struct info *info_ptr = info_space;
            ENTRY item, *found_item;
            /* name to look for in table */
            char name_to_find[30];
            int i = 0;

            /* create table */
            (void) hcreate(NUM_EMPL);
            while (scanf("%s%d%d", str_ptr, &info_ptr->age,
                    &info_ptr->room) != EOF && i++ < NUM_EMPL) {
                /* put info in structure, and structure in item */
                item.key = str_ptr;
                item.data = (void *)info_ptr;
                str_ptr += strlen(str_ptr) + 1;
                info_ptr++;
                /* put item into table */
                (void) hsearch(item, ENTER);
            }

            /* access table */
            item.key = name_to_find;
            while (scanf("%s", item.key) != EOF) {
                if ((found_item = hsearch(item, FIND)) != NULL) {
                /* if item is in the table */
                (void)printf("found %s, age = %d, room = %d\n",
                    found_item->key,
                    ((struct info *)found_item->data)->age,
                    ((struct info *)found_item->data)->room);
                } else {
                (void)printf("no such employee %s\n",
                    name_to_find)
                }
            }
            return 0;
        }
```

SEE ALSO
bsearch(3C), lsearch(3C), malloc(3C), malloc(3X), string(3C), tsearch(3C).

DIAGNOSTICS
hsearch returns a null pointer if either the action is **FIND** and the item could not be found or the action is **ENTER** and the table is full.

hcreate returns zero if it cannot allocate sufficient space for the table.

NOTES
hsearch and hcreate use malloc(3C) to allocate space.

Only one hash search table may be active at any given time.

initgroups(3C)

NAME
initgroups – initialize the supplementary group access list

SYNOPSIS
    #include <grp.h>
    #include <sys/types.h>

int initgroups (const char *name, gid_t basegid)

DESCRIPTION
initgroups reads the group file, using **getgrent**, to get the group membership for the user specified by *name* and then initializes the supplementary group access list of the calling process using **setgroups**. The *basegid* group id is also included in the supplementary group access list. This is typically the real group id from the password file.

While scanning the group file, if the number of groups, including the *basegid* entry, exceeds {NGROUPS_MAX}, subsequent group entries are ignored.

initgroups will fail and not change the supplementary group access list if:

EPERM   The effective user id is not superuser.

SEE ALSO
setgroups(2), getgrent(3C).

DIAGNOSTICS
Upon successful completion, a value of 0 is returned. Otherwise, a value of −1 is returned and **errno** is set to indicate the error.

insque(3C)

NAME
insque, remque – insert/remove element from a queue

SYNOPSIS
include <search.h>

void insque(struct qelem *elem, struct qelem *pred);

void remque(struct qelem *elem);

DESCRIPTION
insque and remque manipulate queues built from doubly linked lists. Each element in the queue must be in the following form:

```
struct qelem {
    struct    qelem *q_forw;
    struct    qelem *q_back;
    char  q_data[];
};
```

insque inserts *elem* in a queue immediately after *pred*. remque removes an entry *elem* from a queue.

isnan(3C)

NAME
isnan, isnand, isnanf, finite, fpclass, unordered – determine type of floating-point number

SYNOPSIS
#include <ieeefp.h>

int isnand (double dsrc);

int isnanf (float fsrc);

int finite (double dsrc);

fpclass_t fpclass (double dsrc);

int unordered (double dsrc1, double dsrc2);

#include <math.h>

int isnan (double dsrc);

DESCRIPTION
isnan, isnand, and isnanf return true (1) if the argument *dsrc* or *fsrc* is a NaN; otherwise they return false (0). The functionalty of isnan is identical to that of isnand.

isnanf is implemented as a macro included in the ieeefp.h header file.

fpclass returns the class the *dsrc* belongs to. The 10 possible classes are as follows:

FP_SNAN	signaling NaN
FP_QNAN	quiet NaN
FP_NINF	negative infinity
FP_PINF	positive infinity
FP_NDENORM	negative denormalized non-zero
FP_PDENORM	positive denormalized non-zero
FP_NZERO	negative zero
FP_PZERO	positive zero
FP_NNORM	negative normalized non-zero
FP_PNORM	positive normalized non-zero

finite returns true (1) if the argument *dsrc* is neither infinity nor NaN; otherwise it returns false (0).

unordered returns true (1) if one of its two arguments is unordered with respect to the other argument. This is equivalent to reporting whether either argument is NaN. If neither of the arguments is NaN, false (0) is returned.

None of these routines generate any exception, even for signaling NaNs.

SEE ALSO
fpgetround(3C), intro(3M).

l3tol(3C)   l3tol(3C)

NAME
l3tol, ltol3 – convert between 3-byte integers and long integers

SYNOPSIS
#include <stdlib.h>

void l3tol (long *lp, const char *cp, int n);

void ltol3 (char *cp, const long *lp, int n);

DESCRIPTION
l3tol converts a list of *n* three-byte integers packed into a character string pointed to by *cp* into a list of long integers pointed to by *lp*.

ltol3 performs the reverse conversion from long integers (*lp*) to three-byte integers (*cp*).

These functions are useful for file-system maintenance where the block numbers are three bytes long.

SEE ALSO
fs(4).

NOTES
Because of possible differences in byte ordering, the numerical values of the long integers are machine-dependent.

localeconv(3C)

NAME
localeconv – get numeric formatting information

SYNOPSIS
```
#include <locale.h>

struct lconv *localeconv (void);
```

DESCRIPTION
localeconv sets the components of an object with type **struct lconv** (defined in **locale.h**) with the values appropriate for the formatting of numeric quantities (monetary and otherwise) according to the rules of the current locale [see setlocale(3C)]. The definition of **struct lconv** is given below (the values for the fields in the C locale are given in comments):

```
char *decimal_point;          /* "." */
char *thousands_sep;          /* "" (zero length string) */
char *grouping;               /* "" */
char *int_curr_symbol;        /* "" */
char *currency_symbol;        /* "" */
char *mon_decimal_point;      /* "" */
char *mon_thousands_sep;      /* "" */
char *mon_grouping;           /* "" */
char *positive_sign;          /* "" */
char *negative_sign;          /* "" */
char int_frac_digits;         /* CHAR_MAX */
char frac_digits;             /* CHAR_MAX */
char p_cs_precedes;           /* CHAR_MAX */
char p_sep_by_space;          /* CHAR_MAX */
char n_cs_precedes;           /* CHAR_MAX */
char n_sep_by_space;          /* CHAR_MAX */
char p_sign_posn;             /* CHAR_MAX */
char n_sign_posn;             /* CHAR_MAX */
```

The members of the structure with type **char *** are strings, any of which (except decimal_point) can point to "", to indicate that the value is not available in the current locale or is of zero length. The members with type **char** are nonnegative numbers, any of which can be **CHAR_MAX** (defined in the **limits.h** header file) to indicate that the value is not available in the current locale. The members are the following:

char *decimal_point
The decimal-point character used to format non-monetary quantities.

char *thousands_sep
The character used to separate groups of digits to the left of the decimal-point character in formatted non-monetary quantities.

char *grouping
A string in which each element is taken as an integer that indicates the number of digits that comprise the current group in a formatted non-monetary quantity. The elements of grouping are interpreted according to the following:

CHAR-MAX No further grouping is to be performed.

0 The previous element is to be repeatedly used for the remainder of the digits.

other The value is the number of digits that comprise the current group. The next element is examined to determine the size of the next group of digits to the left of the current group.

char *int_curr_symbol
  The international currency symbol applicable to the current locale, left-justified within a four-character space-padded field. The character sequences should match with those specified in: *ISO 4217 Codes for the Representation of Currency and Funds*.

char *currency_symbol
  The local currency symbol applicable to the current locale.

char *mon_decimal_point
  The decimal point used to format monetary quantities.

char *mon_thousands_sep
  The separator for groups of digits to the left of the decimal point in formatted monetary quantities.

char *mon_grouping
  A string in which each element is taken as an integer that indicates the number of digits that comprise the current group in a formatted monetary quantity. The elements of mon_grouping are interpreted according to the rules described under grouping.

char *positive_sign
  The string used to indicate a nonnegative-valued formatted monetary quantity.

char *negative_sign
  The string used to indicate a negative-valued formatted monetary quantity.

char int_frac_digits
  The number of fractional digits (those to the right of the decimal point) to be displayed in an internationally formatted monetary quantity.

char frac_digits
  The number of fractional digits (those to the right of the decimal point) to be displayed in a formatted monetary quantity.

char p_cs_precedes
  Set to 1 or 0 if the currency_symbol respectively precedes or succeeds the value for a nonnegative formatted monetary quantity.

char p_sep_by_space
  Set to 1 or 0 if the currency_symbol respectively is or is not separated by a space from the value for a nonnegative formatted monetary quantity.

localeconv (3C)

char n_cs_precedes
Set to 1 or 0 if the currency_symbol respectively precedes or succeeds the value for a negative formatted monetary quantity.

char n_sep_by_space
Set to 1 or 0 if the currency_symbol respectively is or is not separated by a space from the value for a negative formatted monetary quantity.

char p_sign_posn
Set to a value indicating the positioning of the positive_sign for a non-negative formatted monetary quantity. The value of p_sign_posn is interpreted according to the following:

- 0 Parentheses surround the quantity and currency_symbol.
- 1 The sign string precedes the quantity and currency_symbol.
- 2 The sign string succeeds the quantity and currency_symbol.
- 3 The sign string immediately precedes the currency_symbol.
- 4 The sign string immediately succeeds the currency_symbol.

char n_sign_posn
Set to a value indicating the positioning of the negative_sign for a negative formatted monetary quantity. The value of n_sign_posn is interpreted according to the rules described under p_sign_posn.

RETURNS

localeconv returns a pointer to the filled-in object. The structure pointed to by the return value may be overwritten by a subsequent call to localeconv.

EXAMPLES

The following table illustrates the rules used by four countries to format monetary quantities.

Country	Positive format	Negative format	International format
Italy	L.1.234	-L.1.234	ITL.1.234
Netherlands	F 1.234,56	F -1.234,56	NLG 1.234,56
Norway	kr1.234,56	kr1.234,56-	NOK 1.234,56
Switzerland	SFrs.1,234.56	SFrs.1,234.56C	CHF 1,234.56

For these four countries, the respective values for the monetary members of the structure returned by localeconv are as follows:

	Italy	Netherlands	Norway	Switzerland
int_curr_symbol	"ITL."	"NLG "	"NOK "	"CHF "
currency_symbol	"L."	"F"	"kr"	"SFrs."
mon_decimal_point	""	","	","	"."
mon_thousands_sep	"."	"."	"."	","
mon_grouping	"\3"	"\3"	"\3"	"\3"
positive_sign	""	""	""	""
negative_sign	"-"	"-"	"-"	"C"
int_frac_digits	0	2	2	2
frac_digits	0	2	2	2

p_cs_precedes	1	1	1	1
p_sep_by_space	0	1	0	0
n_cs_precedes	1	1	1	1
n_sep_by_space	0	1	0	0
p_sign_posn	1	1	1	1
n_sign_posn	1	4	2	2

FILES

/usr/lib/locale/*locale*/LC_MONETARY   LC_MONETARY database for *locale*
/usr/lib/locale/*locale*/LC_NUMERIC   LC_NUMERIC database for *locale*

SEE ALSO

setlocale(3C).
chrtbl(1M), montbl(1M) in the *System Administrator's Reference Manual*.

NAME
lockf – record locking on files

SYNOPSIS
#include <unistd.h>

int lockf (int fildes, int function, long size);

DESCRIPTION
lockf allows sections of a file to be locked; advisory or mandatory write locks depending on the mode bits of the file [see chmod(2)]. Locking calls from other processes that attempt to lock the locked file section will either return an error value or be put to sleep until the resource becomes unlocked. All the locks for a process are removed when the process terminates. [See fcntl(2) for more information about record locking.]

fildes is an open file descriptor. The file descriptor must have O_WRONLY or O_RDWR permission in order to establish locks with this function call.

function is a control value that specifies the action to be taken. The permissible values for *function* are defined in unistd.h as follows:

```
#define   F_ULOCK    0    /* unlock previously locked section */
#define   F_LOCK     1    /* lock section for exclusive use */
#define   F_TLOCK    2    /* test & lock section for exclusive use */
#define   F_TEST     3    /* test section for other locks */
```

All other values of *function* are reserved for future extensions and will result in an error return if not implemented.

F_TEST is used to detect if a lock by another process is present on the specified section. F_LOCK and F_TLOCK both lock a section of a file if the section is available. F_ULOCK removes locks from a section of the file.

size is the number of contiguous bytes to be locked or unlocked. The resource to be locked or unlocked starts at the current offset in the file and extends forward for a positive size and backward for a negative size (the preceding bytes up to but not including the current offset). If *size* is zero, the section from the current offset through the largest file offset is locked (i.e., from the current offset through the present or any future end-of-file). An area need not be allocated to the file in order to be locked as such locks may exist past the end-of-file.

The sections locked with F_LOCK or F_TLOCK may, in whole or in part, contain or be contained by a previously locked section for the same process. Locked sections will be unlocked starting at the the point of the offset through *size* bytes or to the end of file if *size* is (off_t) 0. When this situation occurs, or if this situation occurs in adjacent sections, the sections are combined into a single section. If the request requires that a new element be added to the table of active locks and this table is already full, an error is returned, and the new section is not locked.

F_LOCK and F_TLOCK requests differ only by the action taken if the resource is not available. F_LOCK will cause the calling process to sleep until the resource is available. F_TLOCK will cause the function to return a −1 and set errno to EACCES if the section is already locked by another process.

F_ULOCK requests may, in whole or in part, release one or more locked sections controlled by the process. When sections are not fully released, the remaining sections are still locked by the process. Releasing the center section of a locked section requires an additional element in the table of active locks. If this table is full, an `errno` is set to `ENOLK` and the requested section is not released.

A potential for deadlock occurs if a process controlling a locked resource is put to sleep by requesting another process's locked resource. Thus calls to `lockf` or `fcntl` scan for a deadlock prior to sleeping on a locked resource. An error return is made if sleeping on the locked resource would cause a deadlock.

Sleeping on a resource is interrupted with any signal. The `alarm` system call may be used to provide a timeout facility in applications that require this facility.

`lockf` will fail if one or more of the following are true:

EBADF   *fildes* is not a valid open descriptor.

EAGAIN   *cmd* is F_TLOCK or F_TEST and the section is already locked by another process.

EDEADLK   *cmd* is F_LOCK and a deadlock would occur.

ENOLK   *cmd* is F_LOCK, F_TLOCK, or F_ULOCK and the number of entries in the lock table would exceed the number allocated on the system.

ECOMM   *fildes* is on a remote machine and the link to that machine is no longer active.

SEE ALSO
intro(2), alarm(2), chmod(2), close(2), creat(2), fcntl(2), open(2), read(2), write(2).

DIAGNOSTICS
Upon successful completion, a value of 0 is returned. Otherwise, a value of −1 is returned and `errno` is set to indicate the error.

NOTES
Unexpected results may occur in processes that do buffering in the user address space. The process may later read/write data that is/was locked. The standard I/O package is the most common source of unexpected buffering.

Because in the future the variable `errno` will be set to EAGAIN rather than EACCES when a section of a file is already locked by another process, portable application programs should expect and test for either value.

lsearch(3C)

NAME
lsearch, lfind – linear search and update

SYNOPSIS
#include <search.h>

void *lsearch (const void *key, void * base, size_t *nelp,
    size_t width, int (*compar) (const void *, const void *));

void *lfind (const void *key, const void *base, size_t *nelp,
    size_t width, int (*compar)(const void *, const void *));

DESCRIPTION
lsearch is a linear search routine generalized from Knuth (6.1) Algorithm S. It returns a pointer into a table indicating where a datum may be found. If the datum does not occur, it is added at the end of the table. *key* points to the datum to be sought in the table. *base* points to the first element in the table. *nelp* points to an integer containing the current number of elements in the table. The integer is incremented if the datum is added to the table. *width* is the size of an element in bytes. *compar* is a pointer to the comparison function that the user must supply (strcmp, for example). It is called with two arguments that point to the elements being compared. The function must return zero if the elements are equal and non-zero otherwise.

lfind is the same as lsearch except that if the datum is not found, it is not added to the table. Instead, a null pointer is returned.

NOTES
The pointers to the key and the element at the base of the table may be pointers to any type.

The comparison function need not compare every byte, so arbitrary data may be contained in the elements in addition to the values being compared.

The value returned should be cast into type pointer-to-element.

EXAMPLE
This program will read in less than TABSIZE strings of length less than ELSIZE and store them in a table, eliminating duplicates, and then will print each entry.

```
#include <search.h>
#include <string.h>
#include <stdlib.h>
#include <stdio.h>

#define TABSIZE 50
#define ELSIZE 120

main()
{
        char line[ELSIZE];    /* buffer to hold input string */
        char tab[TABSIZE][ELSIZE]; /* table of strings */
        size_t nel = 0;       /* number of entries in tab */
        int i;
```

```
            while (fgets(line, ELSIZE, stdin) != NULL &&
                nel < TABSIZE)
                (void) lsearch(line, tab, &nel, ELSIZE, mycmp);
            for( i = 0; i < nel; i++ )
                (void)fputs(tab[i], stdout);
            return 0;
        }
```

SEE ALSO

bsearch(3C), hsearch(3C), string(3C), tsearch(3C).

NOTES

If the searched-for datum is found, both lsearch and lfind return a pointer to it. Otherwise, lfind returns NULL and lsearch returns a pointer to the newly added element.

Undefined results can occur if there is not enough room in the table to add a new item.

makecontext(3C)

NAME
makecontext, swapcontext – manipulate user contexts

SYNOPSIS
#include <ucontext.h>

void makecontext (ucontext_t *ucp, (void(*)()) func, int argc,...);

int swapcontext (ucontext_t *oucp, ucontext_t *ucp);

DESCRIPTION
These functions are useful for implementing user-level context switching between multiple threads of control within a process.

makecontext modifies the context specified by *ucp*, which has been initialized using getcontext; when this context is resumed using swapcontext or setcontext [see getcontext(2)], program execution continues by calling the function *func*, passing it the arguments that follow *argc* in the makecontext call. The integer value of *argc* must match the number of arguments that follow *argc*. Otherwise the behavior is undefined.

swapcontext saves the current context in the context structure pointed to by *oucp* and sets the context to the context structure pointed to by *ucp*.

These functions will fail if either of the following is true:

ENOMEM   *ucp* does not have enough stack left to complete the operation.

EFAULT   *ucp* or *oucp* points to an invalid address.

SEE ALSO
exit(2), getcontext(2), sigaction(2), sigprocmask(2), ucontext(5).

DIAGNOSTICS
On successful completion, swapcontext return a value of zero. Otherwise, a value of −1 is returned and errno is set to indicate the error.

NOTES
The size of the ucontext_t structure may change in future releases. To remain binary compatible, users of these features must always use makecontext or getcontext to create new instances of them.

makedev(3C)

NAME
makedev, major, minor – manage a device number

SYNOPSIS
    #include <sys/types.h>
    #include <sys/mkdev.h>

dev_t makedev(major_t maj, minor_t min);

major_t major(dev_t device);

minor_t minor(dev_t device);

DESCRIPTION
The makedev routine returns a formatted device number on success and NODEV on failure. *maj* is the major number. *min* is the minor number. makedev can be used to create a device number for input to mknod(2).

The major routine returns the major number component from *device*.

The minor routine returns the minor number component from *device*.

makedev will fail if one or more of the following are true:

EINVAL	One or both of the arguments *maj* and *min* is too large.
EINVAL	The *device* number created from *maj* and *min* is NODEV.

major will fail if one or more of the following are true:

EINVAL	The *device* argument is NODEV.
EINVAL	The major number component of *device* is too large.

minor will fail if the following is true:

EINVAL	The *device* argument is NODEV.

SEE ALSO
stat(2), mknod(2).

DIAGNOSTICS
On failure, NODEV is returned and errno is set to indicate the error.

malloc(3C)

NAME
malloc, free, realloc, calloc, memalign, valloc, – memory allocator

SYNOPSIS
#include <stdlib.h>

void *malloc (size_t size);

void free (void *ptr);

void *realloc (void *ptr, size_t size);

void *calloc (size_t nelem, size_t elsize);

void *memalign(size_t alignment, size_t size);

void *valloc(size_t size);

DESCRIPTION
malloc and free provide a simple general-purpose memory allocation package. malloc returns a pointer to a block of at least *size* bytes suitably aligned for any use.

The argument to free is a pointer to a block previously allocated by malloc, calloc or realloc. After free is performed this space is made available for further allocation. If *ptr* is a NULL pointer, no action occurs.

Undefined results will occur if the space assigned by malloc is overrun or if some random number is handed to free.

realloc changes the size of the block pointed to by *ptr* to *size* bytes and returns a pointer to the (possibly moved) block. The contents will be unchanged up to the lesser of the new and old sizes. If *ptr* is NULL, realloc behaves like malloc for the specified size. If *size* is zero and *ptr* is not a null pointer, the object pointed to is freed.

calloc allocates space for an array of *nelem* elements of size *elsize*. The space is initialized to zeros.

memalign allocates *size* bytes on a specified alignment boundary, and returns a pointer to the allocated block. The value of the returned address is guaranteed to be an even multiple of *alignment*. Note: the value of *alignment* must be a power of two, and must be greater than or equal to the size of a word.

valloc(size) is equivalent to memalign(sysconf(_SC_PAGESIZE),size).

Each of the allocation routines returns a pointer to space suitably aligned (after possible pointer coercion) for storage of any type of object.

malloc, realloc, calloc, memalign, and valloc will fail if there is not enough available memory.

SEE ALSO
malloc(3X).

DIAGNOSTICS
If there is no available memory, malloc, realloc, memalign, valloc, and calloc return a null pointer. When realloc returns NULL, the block pointed to by *ptr* is left intact. If *size*, *nelem*, or *elsize* is 0, a unique pointer to the arena is returned.

NAME

mbchar: mbtowc, mblen, wctomb – multibyte character handling

SYNOPSIS

    #include <stdlib.h>

    int mbtowc (wchar_t *pwc, const char *s, size_t n);

    int mblen (const char *s, size_t n);

    int wctomb (char *s, wchar_t wchar);

DESCRIPTION

Multibyte characters are used to represent characters in an extended character set. This is needed for locales where 8 bits are not enough to represent all the characters in the character set.

The multibyte character handling functions provide the means of translating multibyte characters into wide characters and back again. Wide characters have type wchar_t (defined in stdlib.h), which is an integral type whose range of values can represent distinct codes for all members of the largest extended character set specified among the supported locales.

A maximum of 3 extended character sets are supported for each locale. The number of bytes in an extended character set is defined by the LC_CTYPE category of the locale [see setlocale(3C)]. However, the maximum number of bytes in any multibyte character will never be greater than MB_LEN_MAX. which is defined in stdlib.h. The maximum number of bytes in a character in an extended character set in the current locale is given by the macro, MB_CUR_MAX, also defined in stdlib.h.

mbtowc determines the number of bytes that comprise the multibyte character pointed to by s. Also, if *pwc* is not a null pointer, mbtowc converts the multibyte character to a wide character and places the result in the object pointed to by *pwc*. (The value of the wide character corresponding to the null character is zero.) At most *n* characters will be examined, starting at the character pointed to by s.

If s is a null pointer, mbtowc simply returns 0. If s is not a null pointer, then, if *s* points to the null character, mbtowc returns 0; if the next *n* or fewer bytes form a valid multibyte character, mbtowc returns the number of bytes that comprise the converted multibyte character; otherwise, s does not point to a valid multibyte character and mbtowc returns −1.

mblen determines the number of bytes comprising the multibyte character pointed to by *s*. It is equivalent to

    mbtowc ((wchar_t *)0, s, n);

wctomb determines the number of bytes needed to represent the multibyte character corresponding to the code whose value is *wchar*, and, if s is not a null pointer, stores the multibyte character representation in the array pointed to by *s*. At most MB_CUR_MAX characters are stored.

If s is a null pointer, wctomb simply returns 0. If s is not a null pointer, wctomb returns −1 if the value of *wchar* does not correspond to a valid multibyte character; otherwise it returns the number of bytes that comprise the multibyte character corresponding to the value of *wchar*.

SEE ALSO
    mbstring(3C), setlocale(3C), environ(5).
    chrtbl(1M) in the *System Administrator's Reference Manual*.

NAME
mbstring: mbstowcs, wcstombs – multibyte string functions

SYNOPSIS
```
#include <stdlib.h>

size_t mbstowcs (wchar_t *pwcs, const char *s, size_t n);

size_t wcstombs (char *s, const wchar_t *pwcs, size_t n);
```

DESCRIPTION
mbstowcs converts a sequence of multibyte characters from the array pointed to by *s* into a sequence of corresponding wide character codes and stores these codes into the array pointed to by *pwcs*, stopping after *n* codes are stored or a code with value zero (a converted null character) is stored. If an invalid multibyte character is encountered, mbstowcs returns (size_t)–1. Otherwise, mbstowcs returns the number of array elements modified, not including the terminating zero code, if any.

wcstombs converts a sequence of wide character codes from the array pointed to by *pwcs* into a sequence of multibyte characters and stores these multibyte characters into the array pointed to by *s*, stopping if a multibyte character would exceed the limit of *n* total bytes or if a null character is stored. If a wide character code is encountered that does not correspond to a valid multibyte character, wcstombs returns (size_t)–1. Otherwise, wcstombs returns the number of bytes modified, not including a terminating null character, if any.

SEE ALSO
mbchar(3C), setlocale(3C), environ(5).
chrtbl(1M) in the *System Administrator's Reference Manual*.

memory(3C)

NAME
memory: memccpy, memchr, memcmp, memcpy, memmove, memset – memory operations

SYNOPSIS
#include <string.h>

void *memccpy (void *s1, const void *s2, int c, size_t n);

void *memchr (const void *s, int c, size_t n);

int memcmp (const void *s1, const void *s2, size_t n);

void *memcpy (void *s1, const void *s2, size_t n);

void *memmove (void *s1, const void *s2, size_t n);

void *memset (void *s, int c, size_t n);

DESCRIPTION
These functions operate as efficiently as possible on memory areas (arrays of bytes bounded by a count, not terminated by a null character). They do not check for the overflow of any receiving memory area.

memccpy copies bytes from memory area *s2* into *s1*, stopping after the first occurrence of *c* (converted to an unsigned char) has been copied, or after *n* bytes have been copied, whichever comes first. It returns a pointer to the byte after the copy of *c* in *s1*, or a null pointer if *c* was not found in the first *n* bytes of *s2*.

memchr returns a pointer to the first occurrence of *c* (converted to an unsigned char) in the first *n* bytes (each interpreted as an unsigned char) of memory area *s*, or a null pointer if *c* does not occur.

memcmp compares its arguments, looking at the first *n* bytes (each interpreted as an unsigned char), and returns an integer less than, equal to, or greater than 0, according as *s1* is lexicographically less than, equal to, or greater than *s2* when taken to be unsigned characters.

memcpy copies *n* bytes from memory area *s2* to *s1*. It returns *s1*.

memmove copies *n* bytes from memory areas *s2* to *s1*. Copying between objects that overlap will take place correctly. It returns *s1*.

memset sets the first *n* bytes in memory area *s* to the value of *c* (converted to an unsigned char). It returns *s*.

SEE ALSO
string(3C).

NAME
mkfifo – create a new FIFO

SYNOPSIS
```
#include <sys/types.h>
#include <sys/stat.h>
int mkfifo (const char *path, mode_t mode);
```

DESCRIPTION
The **mkfifo** routine creates a new FIFO special file named by the pathname pointed to by *path*. The mode of the new FIFO is initialized from *mode*. The file permission bits of the *mode* argument are modified by the process's file creation mask [see umask(2)].

The FIFO's owner id is set to the process's effective user id. The FIFO's group id is set to the process's effective group id, or if the S_ISGID bit is set in the parent directory then the group id of the FIFO is inherited from the parent.

mkfifo calls the system call **mknod** to make the file.

SEE ALSO
chmod(2), exec(2), mknod(2), umask(2), fs(4), stat(5).
mkdir(1) in the *User's Reference Manual*.

DIAGNOSTICS
Upon successful completion a value of 0 is returned. Otherwise, a value of −1 is returned and **errno** is set to indicate the error.

NOTES
Bits other than the file permission bits in *mode* are ignored.

mktemp(3C)

NAME
mktemp – make a unique file name

SYNOPSIS
#include <stdlib.h>

char *mktemp(char *template);

DESCRIPTION
mktemp replaces the contents of the string pointed to by *template* with a unique file name, and returns *template*. The string in *template* should look like a file name with six trailing Xs; mktemp will replace the Xs with a character string that can be used to create a unique file name.

SEE ALSO
tmpfile(3S), tmpnam(3S).

DIAGNOSTIC
mktemp will assign to *template* the empty string if it cannot create a unique name.

NOTES
mktemp can create only 26 unique file names per process for each unique *template*.

NAME
mktime – converts a tm structure to a calendar time

SYNOPSIS
#include <time.h>

time_t mktime (struct tm *timeptr);

DESCRIPTION
mktime converts the time represented by the tm structure pointed to by *timeptr* into a calendar time (the number of seconds since 00:00:00 UTC, January 1, 1970).

The tm structure has the following format.

```
struct     tm {
    int    tm_sec;      /* seconds after the minute [0, 61]  */
    int    tm_min;      /* minutes after the hour [0, 59] */
    int    tm_hour;     /* hour since midnight [0, 23] */
    int    tm_mday;     /* day of the month [1, 31] */
    int    tm_mon;      /* months since January [0, 11] */
    int    tm_year;     /* years since 1900 */
    int    tm_wday;     /* days since Sunday [0, 6] */
    int    tm_yday;     /* days since January 1 [0, 365] */
    int    tm_isdst;    /* flag for daylight savings time */
};
```

In addition to computing the calendar time, mktime normalizes the supplied tm structure. The original values of the tm_wday and tm_yday components of the structure are ignored, and the original values of the other components are not restricted to the ranges indicated in the definition of the structure. On successful completion, the values of the tm_wday and tm_yday components are set appropriately, and the other components are set to represent the specified calendar time, but with their values forced to be within the appropriate ranges. The final value of tm_mday is not set until tm_mon and tm_year are determined.

The original values of the components may be either greater than or less than the specified range. For example, a tm_hour of −1 means 1 hour before midnight, tm_mday of 0 means the day preceding the current month, and tm_mon of −2 means 2 months before January of tm_year.

If tm_isdst is positive, the original values are assumed to be in the alternate timezone. If it turns out that the alternate timezone is not valid for the computed calendar time, then the components are adjusted to the main timezone. Likewise, if tm_isdst is zero, the original values are assumed to be in the main timezone and are converted to the alternate timezone if the main timezone is not valid. If tm_isdst is negative, the correct timezone is determined and the components are not adjusted.

Local timezone information is used as if mktime had called tzset.

mktime returns the specified calendar time. If the calendar time cannot be represented, the function returns the value (time_t)−1.

EXAMPLE
What day of the week is July 4, 2001?

```
#include <stdio.h>
#include <time.h>

static char *const wday[] = {
    "Sunday", "Monday", "Tuesday", "Wednesday",
    "Thursday", "Friday", "Saturday", "-unknown-"
};
struct tm time_str;
/*...*/
time_str.tm_year= 2001 - 1900;
time_str.tm_mon = 7 - 1;
time_str.tm_mday= 4;
time_str.tm_hour= 0;
time_str.tm_min = 0;
time_str.tm_sec     = 1;
time_str.tm_isdst   = -1;
if (mktime(&time_str)== -1)
    time_str.tm_wday=7;
printf("%s\n", wday[time_str.tm_wday]);
```

SEE ALSO
ctime(3C), getenv(3C), timezone(4).

NOTES
tm_year of the tm structure must be for year 1970 or later. Calendar times before 00:00:00 UTC, January 1, 1970 or after 03:14:07 UTC, January 19, 2038 cannot be represented.

mlock(3C)

NAME
mlock, munlock – lock (or unlock) pages in memory

SYNOPSIS
    #include <sys/types.h>

    int mlock(caddr_t addr, size_t len);

    int munlock(caddr_t addr, size_t len);

DESCRIPTION
The function mlock uses the mappings established for the address range [addr, addr + len) to identify pages to be locked in memory. The effect of mlock(addr, len) is equivalent to memcntl(addr, len, MC_LOCK, 0, 0, 0).

munlock removes locks established with mlock. The effect of munlock(addr, len) is equivalent to memcntl(addr, len, MC_UNLOCK, 0, 0, 0).

Locks established with mlock are not inherited by a child process after a fork and are not nested.

SEE ALSO
fork(2), memcntl(2), mmap(2), mlockall(3C), plock(2), sysconf(3C).

DIAGNOSTICS
Upon successful completion, the functions mlock and munlock return 0; otherwise, they return −1 and set errno to indicate the error.

NOTES
Use of mlock and munlock requires that the user have appropriate privileges.

mlockall(3C)

NAME
mlockall, munlockall – lock or unlock address space

SYNOPSIS
#include <sys/mman.h>

int mlockall(int flags);

int munlockall(void);

DESCRIPTION
The function mlockall causes all pages mapped by an address space to be locked in memory. The effect of mlockall (*flags*) is equivalent to:

memcntl(0, 0, MC_LOCKAS, *flags*, 0, 0)

The value of *flags* determines whether the pages to be locked are those currently mapped by the address space, those that will be mapped in the future, or both:

MCL_CURRENT	Lock current mappings
MCL_FUTURE	Lock future mappings

The function munlockall removes address space locks and locks on mappings in the address space. The effect of munlockall is equivalent to:

memcntl(0, 0, MC_UNLOCKAS, 0, 0, 0)

Locks established with mlockall are not inherited by a child process after a fork and are not nested.

SEE ALSO
fork(2), memcntl(2), mlock(3C), mmap(2), plock(2), sysconf(3C).

DIAGNOSTICS
Upon successful completion, the functions mlockall and munlockall return 0; otherwise, they return −1 and set errno to indicate the error.

NOTES
Use of mlockall and munlockall requires that the user have appropriate privileges.

monitor(3C)

NAME
monitor – prepare execution profile

SYNOPSIS
```
#include <mon.h>

void monitor (int (*lowpc)(), int (*highpc)(), WORD *buffer,
    size_t bufsize, size_t nfunc);
```

DESCRIPTION
monitor is an interface to profil, and is called automatically with default parameters by any program created by cc –p. Except to establish further control over profiling activity, it is not necessary to explicitly call monitor.

When used, monitor is called at least at the beginning and the end of a program. The first call to monitor initiates the recording of two different kinds of execution-profile information: execution-time distribution and function call count. Execution-time distribution data is generated by profil and the function call counts are generated by code supplied to the object file (or files) by cc –p. Both types of information are collected as a program executes. The last call to monitor writes this collected data to the output file mon.out.

lowpc and *highpc* are the beginning and ending addresses of the region to be profiled.

buffer is the address of a user-supplied array of WORD (WORD is defined in the header file mon.h). *buffer* is used by monitor to store the histogram generated by profil and the call counts.

bufsize identifies the number of array elements in *buffer*.

nfunc is the number of call count cells that have been reserved in *buffer*. Additional call count cells will be allocated automatically as they are needed.

bufsize should be computed using the following formula:

```
size_of_buffer =
    sizeof(struct hdr) +
    nfunc * sizeof(struct cnt) +
    ((highpc-lowpc)/BARSIZE) * sizeof(WORD) +
    sizeof(WORD) - 1 ;

bufsize = (size_of_buffer / sizeof(WORD)) ;
```

where:

lowpc, highpc, nfunc are the same as the arguments to monitor;

BARSIZE is the number of program bytes that correspond to each histogram bar, or cell, of the profil buffer;

the hdr and cnt structures and the type WORD are defined in the header file mon.h.

The default call to monitor is shown below:

    monitor (&eprol, &etext, wbuf, wbufsz, 600);
where:

> eprol is the beginning of the user's program when linked with cc -p [see end(3C)];
>
> etext is the end of the user's program [see end(3C)];
>
> wbuf is an array of WORD with wbufsz elements;
>
> wbufsz is computed using the bufsize formula shown above with BARSIZE of 8;
>
> 600 is the number of call count cells that have been reserved in buffer.

These parameter settings establish the computation of an execution-time distribution histogram that uses profil for the entire program, initially reserves room for 600 call count cells in buffer, and provides for enough histogram cells to generate significant distribution-measurement results. [For more information on the effects of bufsize on execution-distribution measurements, see profil(2).]

To stop execution monitoring and write the results to a file, use the following:

    monitor((int (*)( ))0, (int (*)( ))0, (WORD *)0, 0, 0);

Use prof to examine the results.

FILES
mon.out

SEE ALSO
cc(1), prof(1), profil(2), end(3C).

NOTE
Additional calls to monitor after main has been called and before exit has been called will add to the function-call count capacity, but such calls will also replace and restart the profil histogram computation.

The name of the file written by monitor is controlled by the environment variable PROFDIR. If PROFDIR does not exist, the file mon.out is created in the current directory. If PROFDIR exists but has no value, monitor does no profiling and creates no output file. If PROFDIR is *dirname*, and monitor is called automatically by compilation with cc -p, the file created is *dirname/pid.progname* where *progname* is the name of the program.

NAME

msync – synchronize memory with physical storage

SYNOPSIS

```
#include <sys/types.h>
#include <sys/mman.h>

int msync(caddr_t addr, size_t len, int flags);
```

DESCRIPTION

The function msync writes all modified copies of pages over the range [*addr*, *addr* + *len*) to their backing storage locations. msync optionally invalidates any copies so that further references to the pages will be obtained by the system from their backing storage locations. The backing storage for a modified **MAP_SHARED** mapping is the file the page is mapped to; the backing storage for a modified **MAP_PRIVATE** mapping is its swap area.

flags is a bit pattern built from the following values:

MS_ASYNC	perform asynchronous writes
MS_SYNC	perform synchronous writes
MS_INVALIDATE	invalidate mappings

If MS_ASYNC is set, msync returns immediately once all write operations are scheduled; if MS_SYNC is set, msync does not return until all write operations are completed.

MS_INVALIDATE invalidates all cached copies of data in memory, so that further references to the pages will be obtained by the system from their backing storage locations.

The effect of msync(*addr*, *len*, *flags*) is equivalent to:

memcntl(*addr*, *len*, MC_SYNC, *flags*, 0, 0)

SEE ALSO

memcntl(2), mmap(2), sysconf(3C).

DIAGNOSTICS

Upon successful completion, the function msync returns 0; otherwise, it returns −1 and sets **errno** to indicate the error.

NOTES

msync should be used by programs that require a memory object to be in a known state, for example, in building transaction facilities.

nl_langinfo(3C)

NAME
nl_langinfo – language information

SYNOPSIS
```
#include <nl_types.h>
#include <langinfo.h>

char *nl_langinfo (nl_item item);
```

DESCRIPTION
nl_langinfo returns a pointer to a null-terminated string containing information relevant to a particular language or cultural area defined in the programs locale. The manifest constant names and values of *item* are defined by `langinfo.h`.

For example:

    nl_langinfo (ABDAY_1);

would return a pointer to the string "Dim" if the identified language was French and a French locale was correctly installed; or "Sun" if the identified language was English.

SEE ALSO
gettxt(3C), localeconv(3C), setlocale(3C), strftime(3C), langinfo(5), nl_types(5).

DIAGNOSTICS
If `setlocale` has not been called successfully, or if langinfo data for a supported language is either not available or *item* is not defined therein, then nl_langinfo returns a pointer to the corresponding string in the C locale. In all locales, nl_langinfo returns a pointer to an empty string if *item* contains an invalid setting.

WARNING
The array pointed to by the return value should not be modified by the program. Subsequent calls to nl_langinfo may overwrite the array.

The nl_langinfo function is built upon the functions `localeconv`, `strftime`, and `gettxt` [see langinfo(5)]. Where possible users are advised to use these interfaces to the required data instead of using calls to nl_langinfo.

offsetof(3C)

NAME
offsetof – offset of structure member

SYNOPSIS
    #include <stddef.h>

    size_t offsetof (type, member-designator);

DESCRIPTION
offsetof is a macro defined in stddef.h which expands to an integral constant expression that has type size_t, the value of which is the offset in bytes, to the structure member (designated by *member-designator*), from the beginning of its structure (designated by *type*).

NAME

perror – print system error messages

SYNOPSIS

#include <stdio.h>

void perror (const char *s);

DESCRIPTION

perror produces a message on the standard error output (file descriptor 2), describing the last error encountered during a call to a system or library function. The argument string s is printed first, then a colon and a blank, then the message and a newline. (However, if s is a null pointer or points to a null string, the colon is not printed.) To be of most use, the argument string should include the name of the program that incurred the error. The error number is taken from the external variable **errno**, which is set when errors occur but not cleared when non-erroneous calls are made.

SEE ALSO

intro(2), fmtmsg(3C), strerror(3C).

popen(3S)

NAME
popen, pclose – initiate pipe to/from a process

SYNOPSIS
#include <stdio.h>

FILE *popen (const char *command, const char *type);

int pclose (FILE *stream);

DESCRIPTION
popen creates a pipe between the calling program and the command to be executed. The arguments to popen are pointers to null-terminated strings. *command* consists of a shell command line. *type* is an I/O mode, either r for reading or w for writing. The value returned is a stream pointer such that one can write to the standard input of the command, if the I/O mode is w, by writing to the file *stream* [see intro(3)]; and one can read from the standard output of the command, if the I/O mode is r, by reading from the file *stream*.

A stream opened by popen should be closed by pclose, which waits for the associated process to terminate and returns the exit status of the command.

Because open files are shared, a type r command may be used as an input filter and a type w as an output filter.

EXAMPLE
Here is an example of a typical call:

```
#include <stdio.h>
#include <stdlib.h>

main()
{
        char *cmd = "/usr/bin/ls *.c";
        char buf[BUFSIZ];
        FILE *ptr;

        if ((ptr = popen(cmd, "r")) != NULL)
            while (fgets(buf, BUFSIZ, ptr) != NULL)
                (void) printf("%s", buf);
        return 0;
}
```

This program will print on the standard output [see stdio(3S)] all the file names in the current directory that have a .c suffix.

SEE ALSO
pipe(2), wait(2), fclose(3S), fopen(3S), stdio(3S), system(3S).

DIAGNOSTICS
popen returns a null pointer if files or processes cannot be created.

pclose returns −1 if *stream* is not associated with a popened command.

NOTES

If the original and **popened** processes concurrently read or write a common file, neither should use buffered I/O. Problems with an output filter may be forestalled by careful buffer flushing, e.g., with `fflush` [see `fclose`(3S)].

A security hole exists through the `IFS` and `PATH` environment variables. Full pathnames should be used (or `PATH` reset) and `IFS` should be set to space and tab (" `\t`").

printf(3S)

NAME
printf, fprintf, sprintf – print formatted output

SYNOPSIS
#include <stdio.h>

int printf(const char *format, .../* args */);

int fprintf(FILE *strm, const char *format, .../* args */);

int sprintf(char *s, const char *format, .../* args */);

DESCRIPTION
printf places output on the standard output stream stdout.

fprintf places output on *strm*.

sprintf places output, followed by the null character (\0), in consecutive bytes starting at *s*. It is the user's responsibility to ensure that enough storage is available. Each function returns the number of characters transmitted (not including the \0 in the case of sprintf) or a negative value if an output error was encountered.

Each of these functions converts, formats, and prints its *args* under control of the *format*. The *format* is a character string that contains three types of objects defined below:

1. plain characters that are simply copied to the output stream;
2. escape sequences that represent non-graphic characters;
3. conversion specifications.

The following escape sequences produce the associated action on display devices capable of the action:

\a Alert. Ring the bell.

\b Backspace. Move the printing position to one character before the current position, unless the current position is the start of a line.

\f Form feed. Move the printing position to the initial printing position of the next logical page.

\n Newline. Move the printing position to the start of the next line.

\r Carriage return. Move the printing position to the start of the current line.

\t Horizontal tab. Move the printing position to the next implementation-defined horizontal tab position on the current line.

\v Vertical tab. Move the printing position to the start of the next implementation-defined vertical tab position.

All forms of the printf functions allow for the insertion of a language-dependent decimal-point character. The decimal-point character is defined by the program's locale (category LC_NUMERIC). In the C locale, or in a locale where the decimal-point character is not defined, the decimal-point character defaults to a period (.).

Each conversion specification is introduced by the character %. After the character %, the following appear in sequence:

> An optional field, consisting of a decimal digit string followed by a $, specifying the next *args* to be converted. If this field is not provided, the *args* following the last *args* converted will be used.
>
> Zero or more *flags*, which modify the meaning of the conversion specification.
>
> An optional string of decimal digits to specify a minimum *field width*. If the converted value has fewer characters than the field width, it will be padded on the left (or right, if the left-adjustment flag (-), described below, has been given) to the field width.
>
> An optional precision that gives the minimum number of digits to appear for the d, i, o, u, x, or X conversions (the field is padded with leading zeros), the number of digits to appear after the decimal-point character for the e, E, and f conversions, the maximum number of significant digits for the g and G conversions, or the maximum number of characters to be printed from a string in s conversion. The precision takes the form of a period (.) followed by a decimal digit string; a null digit string is treated as zero. Padding specified by the precision overrides the padding specified by the field width.
>
> An optional h specifies that a following d, i, o, u, x, or X conversion specifier applies to a short int or unsigned short int argument (the argument will be promoted according to the integral promotions and its value converted to short int or unsigned short int before printing); an optional h specifies that a following n conversion specifier applies to a pointer to a short int argument. An optional l (ell) specifies that a following d, i, o, u, x, or X conversion specifier applies to a long int or unsigned long int argument; an optional l (ell) specifies that a following n conversion specifier applies to a pointer to long int argument. An optional L specifies that a following e, E, f, g, or G conversion specifier applies to a long double argument. If an h, l, or L appears before any other conversion specifier, the behavior is undefined.
>
> A conversion character (see below) that indicates the type of conversion to be applied.

A field width or precision may be indicated by an asterisk (*) instead of a digit string. In this case, an integer *args* supplies the field width or precision. The *args* that is actually converted is not fetched until the conversion letter is seen, so the *args* specifying field width or precision must appear before the *args* (if any) to be converted. If the *precision* argument is negative, it will be changed to zero. A negative field width argument is taken as a - flag, followed by a positive field width.

In format strings containing the *digits$ form of a conversion specification, a field width or precision may also be indicated by the sequence *digits$, giving the position in the argument list of an integer *args* containing the field width or precision.

When numbered argument specifications are used, specifying the Nth argument requires that all the leading arguments, from the first to the (N−1)th, be specified in the format string.

The *flag* characters and their meanings are:

- The result of the conversion will be left-justified within the field. (It will be right-justified if this flag is not specified.)

+ The result of a signed conversion will always begin with a sign (+ or −). (It will begin with a sign only when a negative value is converted if this flag is not specified.)

space If the first character of a signed conversion is not a sign, a space will be placed before the result. This means that if the space and + flags both appear, the space flag will be ignored.

The value is to be converted to an alternate form. For c, d, i, s, and u conversions, the flag has no effect. For an o conversion, it increases the precision to force the first digit of the result to be a zero. For x (or X) conversion, a non-zero result will have 0x (or 0X) prepended to it. For e, E, f, g, and G conversions, the result will always contain a decimal-point character, even if no digits follow the point (normally, a decimal point appears in the result of these conversions only if a digit follows it). For g and G conversions, trailing zeros will not be removed from the result as they normally are.

0 For d, i, o, u, x, X, e, E, f, g, and G conversions, leading zeros (following any indication of sign or base) are used to pad to the field width; no space padding is performed. If the 0 and − flags both appear, the 0 flag will be ignored. For d, i, o, u, x, and X conversions, if a precision is specified, the 0 flag will be ignored. For other conversions, the behavior is undefined.

Each conversion character results in fetching zero or more *args*. The results are undefined if there are insufficient *args* for the format. If the format is exhausted while *args* remain, the excess *args* are ignored.

The conversion characters and their meanings are:

d,i,o,u,x,X The integer *arg* is converted to signed decimal (d or i), (unsigned octal (o), unsigned decimal (u), or unsigned hexadecimal notation (x and X). The x conversion uses the letters abcdef and the X conversion uses the letters ABCDEF. The precision specifies the minimum number of digits to appear. If the value being converted can be represented in fewer digits than the specified minimum, it will be expanded with leading zeros. The default precision is 1. The result of converting a zero value with a precision of zero is no characters.

f The double *arg* is converted to decimal notation in the style [−]*ddd*.*ddd*, where the number of digits after the decimal-point character [see setlocale(3C)] is equal to the precision specification. If the precision is omitted from *arg*, six digits are output; if the precision is explicitly zero and the # flag is not specified, no decimal-point character appears. If a decimal-point

	character appears, at least 1 digit appears before it. The value is rounded to the appropriate number of digits.
e,E	The double *args* is converted to the style [−]*d.ddd*e±*dd*, where there is one digit before the decimal-point character (which is non-zero if the argument is non-zero) and the number of digits after it is equal to the precision. When the precision is missing, six digits are produced; if the precision is zero and the # flag is not specified, no decimal-point character appears. The E conversion character will produce a number with E instead of e introducing the exponent. The exponent always contains at least two digits. The value is rounded to the appropriate number of digits.
g,G	The double *args* is printed in style f or e (or in style E in the case of a G conversion character), with the precision specifying the number of significant digits. If the precision is zero, it is taken as one. The style used depends on the value converted: style e (or E) will be used only if the exponent resulting from the conversion is less than −4 or greater than or equal to the precision. Trailing zeros are removed from the fractional part of the result. A decimal-point character appears only if it is followed by a digit.
c	The int *args* is converted to an unsigned char, and the resulting character is printed.
s	The *args* is taken to be a string (character pointer) and characters from the string are written up to (but not including) a terminating null character; if the precision is specified, no more than that many characters are written. If the precision is not specified, it is taken to be infinite, so all characters up to the first null character are printed. A NULL value for *args* will yield undefined results.
p	The *args* should be a pointer to void. The value of the pointer is converted to an implementation-defined set of sequences of printable characters, which should be the same as the set of sequences that are matched by the %p conversion of the scanf function.
n	The argument should be a pointer to an integer into which is written the number of characters written to the output standard I/O stream so far by this call to printf, fprintf, or sprintf. No argument is converted.
%	Print a %; no argument is converted.

If the character after the % or %*digits*$ sequence is not a valid conversion character, the results of the conversion are undefined.

If a floating-point value is the internal representation for infinity, the output is [±]*inf*, where *inf* is either inf or INF, depending on the conversion character. Printing of the sign follows the rules described above.

If a floating-point value is the internal representation for "not-a-number," the output is [±]*nan*0*xm*. Depending on the conversion character, *nan* is either nan or NAN. Additionally, 0*xm* represents the most significant part of the mantissa. Again depending on the conversion character, *x* will be x or X, and *m* will use the letters abcdef or ABCDEF. Printing of the sign follows the rules described above.

In no case does a non-existent or small field width cause truncation of a field; if the result of a conversion is wider than the field width, the field is simply expanded to contain the conversion result. Characters generated by printf and fprintf are printed as if the putc routine had been called.

EXAMPLE

To print a date and time in the form Sunday, July 3, 10:02, where weekday and month are pointers to null-terminated strings:

```
printf("%s, %s %i, %d:%.2d",
       weekday, month, day, hour, min);
```

To print π to 5 decimal places:

```
printf("pi = %.5f", 4 * atan(1.0));
```

SEE ALSO

exit(2), lseek(2), write(2), abort(3C), ecvt(3C), putc(3S), scanf(3S), setlocale(3C), stdio(3S).

DIAGNOSTICS

printf, fprintf, and sprintf return the number of characters transmitted, or return a negative value if an error was encountered.

NAME

psignal, psiginfo – system signal messages

SYNOPSIS

#include <siginfo.h>

void psignal (int sig, const char *s);

void psiginfo (siginfo_t *pinfo, char *s);

DESCRIPTION

psignal and psiginfo produce messages on the standard error output describing a signal. *sig* is a signal that may have been passed as the first argument to a signal handler. *pinfo* is a pointer to a siginfo structure that may have been passed as the second argument to an enhanced signal handler [see sigaction(2)]. The argument string *s* is printed first, then a colon and a blank, then the message and a newline.

SEE ALSO

sigaction(2), perror(3), siginfo(5), signal(5).

NAME

putc, putchar, fputc, putw – put character or word on a stream

SYNOPSIS

#include <stdio.h>

int putc (int c, FILE *stream);

int putchar (int c);

int fputc (int c, FILE *stream);

int putw (int w, FILE *stream);

DESCRIPTION

putc writes c (converted to an unsigned char) onto the output *stream* [see intro(3)] at the position where the file pointer (if defined) is pointing, and advances the file pointer appropriately. If the file cannot support positioning requests, or *stream* was opened with append mode, the character is appended to the output *stream*. putchar(c) is defined as putc(c, stdout). putc and putchar are macros.

fputc behaves like putc, but is a function rather than a macro. fputc runs more slowly than putc, but it takes less space per invocation and its name can be passed as an argument to a function.

putw writes the word (i.e., integer) *w* to the output *stream* (where the file pointer, if defined, is pointing). The size of a word is the size of an integer and varies from machine to machine. putw neither assumes nor causes special alignment in the file.

SEE ALSO

exit(2), lseek(2), write(2), abort(3C), fclose(3S), ferror(3S), fopen(3S), fread(3S), printf(3S), puts(3S), setbuf(3S), stdio(3S).

DIAGNOSTICS

On success, these functions (with the exception of putw) each return the value they have written. putw returns ferror (*stream*). On failure, they return the constant EOF. This result will occur, for example, if the file *stream* is not open for writing or if the output file cannot grow.

NOTES

Because it is implemented as a macro, putc evaluates a *stream* argument more than once. In particular, putc(c, *f++); doesn't work sensibly. fputc should be used instead.

Because of possible differences in word length and byte ordering, files written using putw are machine-dependent, and may not be read using getw on a different processor.

Functions exist for all the above defined macros. To get the function form, the macro name must be undefined (e.g., #undef putc).

NAME

puts, fputs – put a string on a stream

SYNOPSIS

#include <stdio.h>

int puts (const char *s);

int fputs (const char *s, FILE *stream);

DESCRIPTION

puts writes the string pointed to by s, followed by a new-line character, to the standard output stream stdout [see intro(3)].

fputs writes the null-terminated string pointed to by s to the named output *stream*.

Neither function writes the terminating null character.

SEE ALSO

exit(2), lseek(2), write(2), abort(3C), fclose(3S), ferror(3S), fopen(3S), fread(3S), printf(3S), putc(3S), stdio(3S).

DIAGNOSTICS

On success both routines return the number of characters written; otherwise they return EOF.

NOTES

puts appends a new-line character while fputs does not.

NAME
putenv – change or add value to environment

SYNOPSIS
#include <stdlib.h>

int putenv (char *string);

DESCRIPTION
string points to a string of the form *"name=value."* putenv makes the value of the environment variable *name* equal to *value* by altering an existing variable or creating a new one. In either case, the string pointed to by *string* becomes part of the environment, so altering the string will change the environment. The space used by *string* is no longer used once a new string-defining *name* is passed to putenv. Because of this limitation, *string* should be declared static if it is declared within a function.

SEE ALSO
exec(2), getenv(3C), malloc(3C), environ(5).

DIAGNOSTICS
putenv returns non-zero if it was unable to obtain enough space via malloc for an expanded environment, otherwise zero.

NOTES
putenv manipulates the environment pointed to by *environ*, and can be used in conjunction with getenv. However, *envp* (the third argument to *main*) is not changed.

This routine uses malloc(3C) to enlarge the environment.

After putenv is called, environmental variables are not in alphabetical order. A potential error is to call the function putenv with a pointer to an automatic variable as the argument and to then exit the calling function while *string* is still part of the environment.

NAME

putpwent – write password file entry

SYNOPSIS

#include <pwd.h>

int putpwent (const struct passwd *p, FILE *f);

DESCRIPTION

putpwent is the inverse of getpwent(3C). Given a pointer to a `passwd` structure created by getpwent (or getpwuid or getpwnam), putpwent writes a line on the stream f, which matches the format of /etc/passwd.

SEE ALSO

getpwent(3C).

DIAGNOSTICS

putpwent returns non-zero if an error was detected during its operation, otherwise zero.

putspent(3C)

NAME
putspent – write shadow password file entry

SYNOPSIS
#include <shadow.h>

int putspent (const struct spwd *p, FILE *fp);

DESCRIPTION
The putspent routine is the inverse of getspent. Given a pointer to a spwd structure created by the getspent routine (or the getspnam routine), the putspent routine writes a line on the stream *fp*, which matches the format of /etc/shadow.

If the sp_min, sp_max, sp_lstchg, sp_warn, sp_inact, or sp_expire field of the spwd structure is −1, or if sp_flag is 0, the corresponding /etc/shadow field is cleared.

SEE ALSO
getspent(3C), getpwent(3C), putpwent(3C).

DIAGNOSTICS
The putspent routine returns non-zero if an error was detected during its operation, otherwise zero.

NOTES
This routine is for internal use only, compatibility is not guaranteed.

NAME
qsort – quicker sort

SYNOPSIS
#include <stdlib.h>

void qsort (void* base, size_t nel, size_t width), int (*compar)
    (const void *, const void *));

DESCRIPTION
qsort is an implementation of the quicker-sort algorithm. It sorts a table of data in place. The contents of the table are sorted in ascending order according to the user-supplied comparison function.

base points to the element at the base of the table. *nel* is the number of elements in the table. *width* specifies the size of each element in bytes. *compar* is the name of the comparison function, which is called with two arguments that point to the elements being compared. The function must return an integer less than, equal to, or greater than zero to indicate if the first argument is to be considered less than, equal to, or greater than the second.

The contents of the table are sorted in ascending order according to the user supplied comparison function.

SEE ALSO
bsearch(3C), lsearch(3C), string(3C).
sort(1) in the *User's Reference Manual*.

NOTES
The comparison function need not compare every byte, so arbitrary data may be contained in the elements in addition to the values being compared.

The relative order in the output of two items that compare as equal is unpredictable.

NAME
raise – send signal to program

SYNOPSIS
#include <signal.h>

int raise (int sig);

DESCRIPTION
raise sends the signal *sig* to the executing program.

raise returns zero if the operation succeeds. Otherwise, **raise** returns −1 and *errno* is set to indicate the error. **raise** uses **kill** to send the signal to the executing program:

kill(getpid(), sig);

See kill(2) for a detailed list of failure conditions. See signal(2) for a list of signals.

SEE ALSO
getpid(2), kill(2), signal(2).

NAME
rand, srand – simple random-number generator

SYNOPSIS
#include <stdlib.h>

int rand (void);

void srand (unsigned int seed);

DESCRIPTION
rand uses a multiplicative congruential random-number generator with period 2^{32} that returns successive pseudo-random numbers in the range from 0 to RAND_MAX (defined in stdlib.h).

The function srand uses the argument *seed* as a seed for a new sequence of pseudo-random numbers to be returned by subsequent calls to the function rand. If the function srand is then called with the same *seed* value, the sequence of pseudo-random numbers will be repeated. If the function rand is called before any calls to srand have been made, the same sequence will be generated as when srand is first called with a *seed* value of 1.

NOTES
The spectral properties of rand are limited. drand48(3C) provides a much better, though more elaborate, random-number generator.

SEE ALSO
drand48(3C).

realpath(3C)   realpath(3C)

NAME
realpath – returns the real file name

SYNOPSIS
#include <stdlib.h>
#include <sys/param.h>

char *realpath (char * file_name, char * resolved_name);

DESCRIPTION
realpath resolves all links and references to "." and ".." in *file_name* and stores it in *resolved_name*.

It can handle both relative and absolute path names. For absolute path names and the relative names whose resolved name cannot be expressed relatively (e.g., ../../reldir), it returns the *resolved absolute* name. For the other relative path names, it returns the *resolved relative* name.

resolved_name must be big enough (**MAXPATHLEN**) to contain the fully resolved path name.

SEE ALSO
getcwd(3C).

DIAGNOSTICS
If there is no error, realpath returns a pointer to the *resolved_name*. Otherwise it returns a null pointer and places the name of the offending file in *resolved_name*. The global variable **errno** is set to indicate the error.

NOTES
realpath operates on null-terminated strings.

One should have execute permission on all the directories in the given and the resolved path.

realpath may fail to return to the current directory if an error occurs.

NAME
remove – remove file

SYNOPSIS
#include <stdio.h>

int remove(const char *path);

DESCRIPTION
remove causes the file or empty directory whose name is the string pointed to by *path* to be no longer accessible by that name. A subsequent attempt to open that file using that name will fail, unless the file is created anew.

For files, remove is identical to unlink. For directories, remove is identical to rmdir.

See rmdir(2) and unlink(2) for a detailed list of failure conditions.

SEE ALSO
rmdir(2), unlink(2).

RETURN VALUE
Upon successful completion, remove returns a value of 0; otherwise, it returns a value of −1 and sets errno to indicate an error.

scanf(3S)

NAME
scanf, fscanf, sscanf – convert formatted input

SYNOPSIS
#include <stdio.h>

int scanf(const char *format, ...);

int fscanf(FILE *strm, const char *format, ...);

int sscanf(const char *s, const char *format, ...);

DESCRIPTION
scanf reads from the standard input stream, stdin.

fscanf reads from the stream *strm*.

sscanf reads from the character string *s*.

Each function reads characters, interprets them according to a format, and stores the results in its arguments. Each expects, as arguments, a control string, *format*, described below and a set of pointer arguments indicating where the converted input should be stored. If there are insufficient arguments for the format, the behavior is undefined. If the format is exhausted while arguments remain, the excess arguments are simply ignored.

The control string usually contains conversion specifications, which are used to direct interpretation of input sequences. The control string may contain:

1. White-space characters (blanks, tabs, new-lines, or form-feeds) that, except in two cases described below, cause input to be read up to the next non-white-space character.

2. An ordinary character (not %) that must match the next character of the input stream.

3. Conversion specifications consisting of the character % or the character sequence %*digits*$, an optional assignment suppression character *, a decimal digit string that specifies an optional numerical maximum field width, an optional letter l (ell), L, or h indicating the size of the receiving object, and a conversion code. The conversion specifiers d, i, and n should be preceded by h if the corresponding argument is a pointer to short int rather than a pointer to int, or by l if it is a pointer to long int. Similarly, the conversion specifiers o, u, and x should be preceded by h if the corresponding argument is a pointer to unsigned short int rather than a pointer to unsigned int, or by l if it is a pointer to unsigned long int. Finally, the conversion specifiers e, f, and g should be preceded by l if the corresponding argument is a pointer to double rather than a pointer to float, or by L if it is a pointer to long double. The h, l, or L modifier is ignored with any other conversion specifier.

A conversion specification directs the conversion of the next input field; the result is placed in the variable pointed to by the corresponding argument unless assignment suppression was indicated by the character *. The suppression of assignment provides a way of describing an input field that is to be skipped. An input field is defined as a string of non-space characters; it extends to the next inappropriate character or until the maximum field width, if one is specified, is exhausted. For all descriptors except the character [and the character c, white space leading an input field is ignored.

Conversions can be applied to the *nth* argument in the argument list, rather than to the next unused argument. In this case, the conversion character % (see above) is replaced by the sequence %*digits*$ where *digits* is a decimal integer *n*, giving the position of the argument in the argument list. The first such argument, %1$, immediately follows *format*. The control string can contain either form of a conversion specification, i.e., % or %*digits*$, although the two forms cannot be mixed within a single control string.

The conversion code indicates the interpretation of the input field; the corresponding pointer argument must usually be of a restricted type. For a suppressed field, no pointer argument is given. The following conversion codes are valid:

%   A single % is expected in the input at this point; no assignment is done.

d   Matches an optionally signed decimal integer, whose format is the same as expected for the subject sequence of the **strtol** function with the value 10 for the *base* argument. The corresponding argument should be a pointer to integer.

u   Matches an optionally signed decimal integer, whose format is the same as expected for the subject sequence of the **strtoul** function with the value 10 for the *base* argument. The corresponding argument should be a pointer to unsigned integer.

o   Matches an optionally signed octal integer, whose format is the same as expected for the subject sequence of the **strtoul** function with the value 8 for the *base* argument. The corresponding argument should be a pointer to unsigned integer.

x   Matches an optionally signed hexadecimal integer, whose format is the same as expected for the subject sequence of the **strtoul** function with the value 16 for the *base* argument. The corresponding argument should be a pointer to unsigned integer.

i   Matches an optionally signed integer, whose format is the same as expected for the subject sequence of the **strtol** function with the value 0 for the *base* argument. The corresponding argument should be a pointer to integer.

n   No input is consumed. The corresponding argument should be a pointer to integer into which is to be written the number of characters read from the input stream so far by the call to the function. Execution of a %n directive does not increment the assignment count returned at the completion of execution of the function.

e,f,g   Matches an optionally signed floating point number, whose format is the same as expected for the subject string of the **strtod** function. The corresponding argument should be a pointer to floating.

s A character string is expected; the corresponding argument should be a character pointer pointing to an array of characters large enough to accept the string and a terminating \0, which will be added automatically. The input field is terminated by a white-space character.

c Matches a sequence of characters of the number specified by the field width (1 if no field width is present in the directive). The corresponding argument should be a pointer to the initial character of an array large enough to accept the sequence. No null character is added. The normal skip over white space is suppressed.

[Matches a nonempty sequence of characters from a set of expected characters (the *scanset*). The corresponding argument should be a pointer to the initial character of an array large enough to accept the sequence and a terminating null character, which will be added automatically. The conversion specifier includes all subsequent characters in the *format* string, up to and including the matching right bracket (]). The characters between the brackets (the *scanlist*) comprise the scanset, unless the character after the left bracket is a circumflex (^), in which case the scanset contains all characters that do not appear in the scanlist between the circumflex and the right bracket. If the conversion specifier begins with [] or [^], the right bracket character is in the scanlist and the next right bracket character is the matching right bracket that ends the specification; otherwise the first right bracket character is the one that ends the specification.

A range of characters in the scanset may be represented by the construct *first* − *last*; thus [0123456789] may be expressed [0−9]. Using this convention, *first* must be lexically less than or equal to *last*, or else the dash will stand for itself. The character − will also stand for itself whenever it is the first or the last character in the scanlist. To include the right bracket as an element of the scanset, it must appear as the first character (possibly preceded by a circumflex) of the scanlist and in this case it will not be syntactically interpreted as the closing bracket. At least one character must match for this conversion to be considered successful.

p Matches an implementation-defined set of sequences, which should be the same as the set of sequences that may be produced by the %p conversion of the printf function. The corresponding argument should be a pointer to void. The interpretation of the input item is implementation-defined. If the input item is a value converted earlier during the same program execution, the pointer that results shall compare equal to that value; otherwise, the behavior of the %p conversion is undefined.

If an invalid conversion character follows the %, the results of the operation may not be predictable.

The conversion specifiers E, G, and X are also valid and, under the −Xa and −Xc compilation modes [see cc(1)], behave the same as e, g, and x, respectively. Under the −Xt compilation mode, E, G, and X behave the same as le, lg, and lx, respectively.

Each function allows for detection of a language-dependent decimal point character in the input string. The decimal point character is defined by the program's locale (category LC_NUMERIC). In the "C" locale, or in a locale where the decimal point character is not defined, the decimal point character defaults to a period (.).

The scanf conversion terminates at end of file, at the end of the control string, or when an input character conflicts with the control string.

If end-of-file is encountered during input, conversion is terminated. If end-of-file occurs before any characters matching the current directive have been read (other than leading white space, where permitted), execution of the current directive terminates with an input failure; otherwise, unless execution of the current directive is terminated with a matching failure, execution of the following directive (if any) is terminated with an input failure.

If conversion terminates on a conflicting input character, the offending input character is left unread in the input stream. Trailing white space (including new-line characters) is left unread unless matched by a directive. The success of literal matches and suppressed assignments is not directly determinable other than via the %n directive.

EXAMPLES

The call to the function scanf:

```
int i, n; float x; char name[50];
n = scanf ("%d%f%s", &i, &x, name);
```

with the input line:

```
25 54.32E-1 thompson
```

will assign to n the value 3, to i the value 25, to x the value 5.432, and name will contain thompson\0.

The call to the function scanf:

```
int i; float x; char name[50];
(void) scanf ("%2d%f%*d %[0-9]", &i, &x, name);
```

with the input line:

```
56789 0123 56a72
```

will assign 56 to i, 789.0 to x, skip 0123, and place the characters 56\0 in name. The next character read from stdin will be a.

SEE ALSO

cc(1), printf(3S), strtod(3C), strtol(3C), strtoul(3C).

DIAGNOSTICS

These routines return the number of successfully matched and assigned input items; this number can be zero in the event of an early matching failure between an input character and the control string. If the input ends before the first matching failure or conversion, EOF is returned.

setbuf(3S)

NAME
setbuf, setvbuf – assign buffering to a stream

SYNOPSIS
#include <stdio.h>

void setbuf (FILE *stream, char *buf);

int setvbuf (FILE *stream, char *buf, int type, size_t size);

DESCRIPTION
setbuf may be used after a *stream* [see intro(3)] has been opened but before it is read or written. It causes the array pointed to by *buf* to be used instead of an automatically allocated buffer. If *buf* is the NULL pointer input/output will be completely unbuffered.

While there is no limititation on the size of the buffer, the constant BUFSIZ, defined in the <stdio.h> header file, is typically a good buffer size:

>   char buf[BUFSIZ];

setvbuf may be used after a stream has been opened but before it is read or written. *type* determines how *stream* will be buffered. Legal values for *type* (defined in stdio.h) are:

_IOFBF   causes input/output to be fully buffered.

_IOLBF   causes output to be line buffered; the buffer will be flushed when a newline is written, the buffer is full, or input is requested.

_IONBF   causes input/output to be completely unbuffered.

If *buf* is not the NULL pointer, the array it points to will be used for buffering, instead of an automatically allocated buffer. *size* specifies the size of the buffer to be used. If input/output is unbuffered, *buf* and *size* are ignored.

For a further discussion of buffering, see stdio(3S).

SEE ALSO
fopen(3S), getc(3S), malloc(3C), putc(3S), stdio(3S).

DIAGNOSTICS
If an illegal value for *type* is provided, setvbuf returns a non-zero value. Otherwise, it returns zero.

NOTES
A common source of error is allocating buffer space as an "automatic" variable in a code block, and then failing to close the stream in the same block.

Parts of buf will be used for internal bookkeeping of the stream and, therefore, buf will contain less than *size* bytes when full. It is recommended that the automatically allocated buffer is used when using setvbuf.

NAME

setjmp, longjmp – non-local goto

SYNOPSIS

#include <setjmp.h>

int setjmp (jmp_buf env);

void longjmp (jmp_buf env, int val);

DESCRIPTION

These functions are useful for dealing with errors and interrupts encountered in a low-level subroutine of a program.

setjmp saves its stack environment in **env** (whose type, *jmp_buf*, is defined in the <setjmp.h> header file) for later use by longjmp. It returns the value 0.

longjmp restores the environment saved by the last call of **setjmp** with the corresponding **env** argument. After longjmp is completed, program execution continues as if the corresponding call of **setjmp** had just returned the value **val**. (The caller of **setjmp** must not have returned in the interim.) longjmp cannot cause **setjmp** to return the value 0. If longjmp is invoked with a second argument of 0, **setjmp** will return 1. At the time of the second return from **setjmp**, all external and static variables have values as of the time longjmp is called (see example). The values of register and automatic variables are undefined.

Register or automatic variables whose value must be relied upon must be declared as volatile.

EXAMPLE

```
#include <stdio.h>
#include <stdlib.h>
#include <setjmp.h>

jmp_buf env;
int i = 0;
main ()
{
    void exit();

    if(setjmp(env) != 0) {
        (void) printf("value of i on 2nd return from setjmp: %d\n", i);
        exit(0);
    }
    (void) printf("value of i on 1st return from setjmp: %d\n", i);
    i = 1;
    g();
    /* NOTREACHED */
}
g()
{
    longjmp(env, 1);
    /* NOTREACHED */
}
```

If the a.out resulting from this C language code is run, the output will be:

    value of i on 1st return from setjmp: 0

    value of i on 2nd return from setjmp: 1

SEE ALSO
signal(2), sigsetjmp(3C).

NOTES
If longjmp is called even though env was never primed by a call to setjmp, or when the last such call was in a function that has since returned, absolute chaos is guaranteed.

setlocale (3C)

NAME
setlocale – modify and query a program's locale

SYNOPSIS
#include <locale.h>

char *setlocale (int category, const char *locale);

DESCRIPTION
setlocale selects the appropriate piece of the program's locale as specified by the *category* and *locale* arguments. The *category* argument may have the following values: LC_CTYPE, LC_NUMERIC, LC_TIME, LC_COLLATE, LC_MONETARY, LC_MESSAGES and LC_ALL. These names are defined in the locale.h header file. LC_CTYPE affects the behavior of the character handling functions (isdigit, tolower, etc.) and the multibyte character functions (such as mbtowc and wctomb). LC_NUMERIC affects the decimal-point character for the formatted input/output functions and the string conversion functions as well as the non-monetary formatting information returned by localeconv. [See localeconv(3C).]. LC_TIME affects the behavior of ascftime, cftime, getdate and strftime. LC_COLLATE affects the behavior of strcoll and strxfrm. LC_MONETARY affects the monetary formatted information returned by localeconv. LC_MESSAGES affects the behavior of gettxt, catopen, catclose, and catgets. [See catopen(3C) and catgets(3C).] LC_ALL names the program's entire locale.

Each category corresponds to a set of databases which contain the relevant information for each defined locale. The location of a database is given by the following path, /usr/lib/locale/*locale*/*category*, where *locale* and *category* are the names of locale and category, respectively. For example, the database for the LC_CTYPE category for the "german" locale would be found in /usr/lib/locale/german/LC_CTYPE.

A value of "C" for *locale* specifies the default environment.

A value of "" for *locale* specifies that the locale should be taken from environment variables. The order in which the environment variables are checked for the various categories is given below:

Category	1st Env. Var.	2nd Env. Var
LC_CTYPE:	LC_CTYPE	LANG
LC_COLLATE:	LC_COLLATE	LANG
LC_TIME:	LC_TIME	LANG
LC_NUMERIC:	LC_NUMERIC	LANG
LC_MONETARY:	LC_MONETARY	LANG
LC_MESSAGES:	LC_MESSAGES	LANG

At program startup, the equivalent of

setlocale(LC_ALL, "C")

is executed. This has the effect of initializing each category to the locale described by the environment "C".

setlocale(3C)

If a pointer to a string is given for *locale*, `setlocale` attempts to set the locale for the given category to *locale*. If `setlocale` succeeds, *locale* is returned. If `setlocale` fails, a null pointer is returned and the program's locale is not changed.

For category LC_ALL, the behavior is slightly different. If a pointer to a string is given for *locale* and LC_ALL is given for *category*, `setlocale` attempts to set the locale for all the categories to *locale*. The *locale* may be a simple locale, consisting of a single locale, or a composite locale. A composite locale is a string beginning with a "/" followed by the locale of each category separated by a "/". If `setlocale` fails to set the locale for any category, a null pointer is returned and the program's locale for all categories is not changed. Otherwise, locale is returned.

A null pointer for *locale* causes `setlocale` to return the current locale associated with the *category*. The program's locale is not changed.

FILES

/usr/lib/locale/C/LC_CTYPE − LC_CTYPE database for the C locale.
/usr/lib/locale/C/LC_NUMERIC − LC_NUMERIC database for the C locale.
/usr/lib/locale/C/LC_TIME − LC_TIME database for the C locale.
/usr/lib/locale/C/LC_COLLATE − LC_COLLATE database for the C locale.
/usr/lib/locale/C/LC_MESSAGES − LC_MESSAGES database for the C locale.
/usr/lib/locale/*locale*/*category* − files containing the locale specific information for each locale and category.

SEE ALSO

ctime(3C), ctype(3C), getdate(3C), gettxt(3G), localeconv(3C), mbtowc(3C), printf(3S), strcoll(3C), strftime(3C), strtod(3C), strxfrm(3C), wctomb(3C), environ(5).

NAME

sigsetjmp, siglongjmp – a non-local goto with signal state

SYNOPSIS

#include <setjmp.h>

int sigsetjmp (sigjmp_buf env, int savemask);

void siglongjmp (sigjmp_buf env, int val);

DESCRIPTION

These functions are useful for dealing with errors and interrupts encountered in a low-level subroutine of a program.

sigsetjmp saves the calling process's registers and stack environment [see sigaltstack(2)] in *env* (whose type, sigjmp_buf, is defined in the <setjmp.h> header file) for later use by siglongjmp. If *savemask* is non-zero, the calling process's signal mask [see sigprocmask(2)] and scheduling parameters [see priocntl(2)] are also saved. sigsetjmp returns the value 0.

siglongjmp restores the environment saved by the last call of sigsetjmp with the corresponding *env* argument. After siglongjmp is completed, program execution continues as if the corresponding call of sigsetjmp had just returned the value *val*. siglongjmp cannot cause sigsetjmp to return the value zero. If siglongjmp is invoked with a second argument of zero, sigsetjmp will return 1. At the time of the second return from sigsetjmp, all external and static variables have values as of the time siglongjmp is called. The values of register and automatic variables are undefined. Register or automatic variables whose value must be relied upon must be declared as volatile.

If a signal-catching function interrupts sleep and calls siglongjmp to restore an environment saved prior to the sleep call, the action associated with SIGALRM and time it is scheduled to be generated are unspecified. It is also unspecified whether the SIGALRM signal is blocked, unless the process's signal mask is restored as part of the environment.

The function siglongjmp restores the saved signal mask if and only if the *env* argument was initialized by a call to the sigsetjmp function with a non-zero *savemask* argument.

SEE ALSO

getcontext(2), priocntl(2), sigaction(2), sigaltstack(2), sigprocmask(2), setjmp(3C).

NOTES

If siglongjmp is called even though *env* was never primed by a call to sigsetjmp, or when the last such call was in a function that has since returned, absolute chaos is guaranteed.

sigsetops(3C)

NAME
sigemptyset, sigfillset, sigaddset, sigdelset, sigismember – manipulate sets of signals.

SYNOPSIS
#include <signal.h>

int sigemptyset (sigset_t *set);

int sigfillset (sigset_t *set);

int sigaddset (sigset_t *set, int signo);

int sigdelset (sigset_t *set, int signo);

int sigismember (sigset_t *set, int signo);

DESCRIPTION
These functions manipulate *sigset_t* data types, representing the set of signals supported by the implementation.

sigemptyset initializes the set pointed to by *set* to exclude all signals defined by the system.

sigfillset initializes the set pointed to by *set* to include all signals defined by the system.

sigaddset adds the individual signal specified by the value of *signo* to the set pointed to by *set*.

sigdelset deletes the individual signal specified by the value of *signo* from the set pointed to by *set*.

sigismember checks whether the signal specified by the value of *signo* is a member of the set pointed to by *set*.

Any object of type *sigset_t* must be initialized by applying either **sigemptyset** or **sigfillset** before applying any other operation.

sigaddset, **sigdelset** and **sigismember** will fail if the following is true:

EINVAL   The value of the *signo* argument is not a valid signal number.

sigfillset will fail if the following is true:

EFAULT   The *set* argument specifies an invalid address.

SEE ALSO
sigaction(2), sigprocmask(2), sigpending(2), sigsuspend(2), signal(5).

DIAGNOSTICS
Upon successful completion, the **sigismember** function returns a value of one if the specified signal is a member of the specified set, or a value of zero if it is not. Upon successful completion, the other functions return a value of zero. Otherwise a value of -1 is returned and *errno* is set to indicate the error.

NAME

sleep – suspend execution for interval

SYNOPSIS

#include <unistd.h>

unsigned sleep (unsigned seconds);

DESCRIPTION

The current process is suspended from execution for the number of *seconds* specified by the argument. The actual suspension time may be less than that requested because any caught signal will terminate the sleep following execution of that signal's catching routine. Also, the suspension time may be longer than requested by an arbitrary amount because of the scheduling of other activity in the system. The value returned by sleep will be the "unslept" amount (the requested time minus the time actually slept) in case the caller had an alarm set to go off earlier than the end of the requested sleep time, or premature arousal because of another caught signal.

The routine is implemented by setting an alarm signal and pausing until it (or some other signal) occurs. The previous state of the alarm signal is saved and restored. The calling program may have set up an alarm signal before calling sleep. If the sleep time exceeds the time until such alarm signal, the process sleeps only until the alarm signal would have occurred. The caller's alarm catch routine is executed just before the sleep routine returns. But if the sleep time is less than the time till such alarm, the prior alarm time is reset to go off at the same time it would have without the intervening sleep.

SEE ALSO

alarm(2), pause(2), signal(2), wait(2).

NAME
ssignal, gsignal – software signals

SYNOPSIS
#include <signal.h>

int (*ssignal (int sig, int (*action) (int))) (int);

int gsignal (int sig);

DESCRIPTION
ssignal and gsignal implement a software facility similar to signal(2). This facility is made available to users for their own purposes.

Software signals made available to users are associated with integers in the inclusive range 1 through 17. A call to ssignal associates a procedure, *action*, with the software signal *sig*; the software signal, *sig*, is raised by a call to gsignal. Raising a software signal causes the action established for that signal to be *taken*.

The first argument to ssignal is a number identifying the type of signal for which an action is to be established. The second argument defines the action; it is either the name of a (user-defined) *action function* or one of the manifest constants SIG_DFL (default) or SIG_IGN (ignore). ssignal returns the action previously established for that signal type; if no action has been established or the signal number is illegal, ssignal returns SIG_DFL.

gsignal raises the signal identified by its argument, *sig*:

If an action function has been established for *sig*, then that action is reset to SIG_DFL and the action function is entered with argument *sig*. gsignal returns the value returned to it by the action function.

If the action for *sig* is SIG_IGN, gsignal returns the value 1 and takes no other action.

If the action for *sig* is SIG_DFL, gsignal returns the value 0 and takes no other action.

If *sig* has an illegal value or no action was ever specified for *sig*, gsignal returns the value 0 and takes no other action.

SEE ALSO
signal(2), sigset(2), raise(3C).

stdipc(3C)

NAME
stdipc: ftok – standard interprocess communication package

SYNOPSIS
    #include <sys/types.h>
    #include <sys/ipc.h>

    key_t ftok(const char *path, int id);

DESCRIPTION
All interprocess communication facilities require the user to supply a key to be used by the msgget(2), semget(2), and shmget(2) system calls to obtain interprocess communication identifiers. One suggested method for forming a key is to use the ftok subroutine described below. Another way to compose keys is to include the project ID in the most significant byte and to use the remaining portion as a sequence number. There are many other ways to form keys, but it is necessary for each system to define standards for forming them. If some standard is not adhered to, it will be possible for unrelated processes to unintentionally interfere with each other's operation. It is still possible to interface intentionally. Therefore, it is strongly suggested that the most significant byte of a key in some sense refer to a project so that keys do not conflict across a given system.

ftok returns a key based on *path* and *id* that is usable in subsequent msgget, semget, and shmget system calls. *path* must be the path name of an existing file that is accessible to the process. *id* is a character that uniquely identifies a project. Note that ftok will return the same key for linked files when called with the same *id* and that it will return different keys when called with the same file name but different *ids*.

SEE ALSO
intro(2), msgget(2), semget(2), shmget(2).

DIAGNOSTICS
ftok returns (key_t) −1 if *path* does not exist or if it is not accessible to the process.

NOTES
If the file whose *path* is passed to ftok is removed when keys still refer to the file, future calls to ftok with the same *path* and *id* will return an error. If the same file is recreated, then ftok is likely to return a different key than it did the original time it was called.

stdio(3S)

NAME
stdio – standard buffered input/output package

SYNOPSIS
#include <stdio.h>

FILE *stdin, *stdout, *stderr;

DESCRIPTION
The functions described in the entries of sub-class 3S of this manual constitute an efficient, user-level I/O buffering scheme. The in-line macros getc and putc handle characters quickly. The macros getchar and putchar, and the higher-level routines fgetc, fgets, fprintf, fputc, fputs, fread, fscanf, fwrite, gets, getw, printf, puts, putw, and scanf all use or act as if they use getc and putc; they can be freely intermixed.

A file with associated buffering is called a *stream* [see intro(3)] and is declared to be a pointer to a defined type FILE. fopen creates certain descriptive data for a stream and returns a pointer to designate the stream in all further transactions. Normally, there are three open streams with constant pointers declared in the <stdio.h> header file and associated with the standard open files:

stdin   standard input file
stdout standard output file
stderr standard error file

The following symbolic values in <unistd.h> define the file descriptors that will be associated with the C-language *stdin*, *stdout* and *stderr* when the application is started:

STDIN_FILENO   Standard input value, stdin. It has the value of 0.
STDOUT_FILENO Standard output value, stdout. It has the value of 1.
STDERR_FILENO Standard error value, stderr. It has the value of 2.

A constant null designates a null pointer.

An integer-constant EOF (−1) is returned upon end-of-file or error by most integer functions that deal with streams (see the individual descriptions for details).

An integer constant BUFSIZ specifies the size of the buffers used by the particular implementation.

An integer constant FILENAME_MAX specifies the size needed for an array of char large enough to hold the longest file name string that the implementation guarantees can be opened.

An integer constant FOPEN_MAX specifies the minimum number of files that the implementation guarantees can be open simultaneously. Note that no more than 255 files may be opened via fopen, and only file descriptors 0 through 255 are valid.

Any program that uses this package must include the header file of pertinent macro definitions, as follows:

#include <stdio.h>

The functions and constants mentioned in the entries of sub-class 3S of this manual are declared in that header file and need no further declaration. The constants and the following "functions" are implemented as macros (redeclaration of these names is perilous): **getc, getchar, putc, putchar, ferror, feof, clearerr,** and **fileno**. There are also function versions of **getc, getchar, putc, putchar, ferror, feof, clearerr,** and **fileno**.

Output streams, with the exception of the standard error stream **stderr**, are by default buffered if the output refers to a file and line-buffered if the output refers to a terminal. The standard error output stream **stderr** is by default unbuffered, but use of **freopen** [see **fopen**(3S)] will cause it to become buffered or line-buffered. When an output stream is unbuffered, information is queued for writing on the destination file or terminal as soon as written; when it is buffered, many characters are saved up and written as a block. When it is line-buffered, each line of output is queued for writing on the destination terminal as soon as the line is completed (that is, as soon as a new-line character is written or terminal input is requested). **setbuf** or **setvbuf** [both described in setbuf(3S)] may be used to change the stream's buffering strategy.

SEE ALSO

open(2), close(2), lseek(2), pipe(2), read(2), write(2), ctermid(3S), cuserid(3S), fclose(3S), ferror(3S), fopen(3S), fread(3S), fseek(3S), getc(3S), gets(3S), popen(3S), printf(3S), putc(3S), puts(3S), scanf(3S), setbuf(3S), system(3S), tmpfile(3S), tmpnam(3S), ungetc(3S).

DIAGNOSTICS

Invalid *stream* pointers usually cause grave disorder, possibly including program termination. Individual function descriptions describe the possible error conditions.

NAME
strcoll – string collation

SYNOPSIS
#include <string.h>

int strcoll (const char *s1, const char *s2);

DESCRIPTION
strcoll returns an integer greater than, equal to, or less than zero in direct correlation to whether string *s1* is greater than, equal to, or less than the string *s2*. The comparison is based on strings interpreted as appropriate to the program's locale for category LC_COLLATE [see setlocale(3C)].

Both strcoll and strxfrm provide for locale-specific string sorting. strcoll is intended for applications in which the number of comparisons per string is small. When strings are to be compared a number of times, strxfrm is a more appropriate utility because the transformation process occurs only once.

FILES
/usr/lib/locale/*locale*/LC_COLLATE   LC_COLLATE database for *locale*.

SEE ALSO
setlocale(3C), string(3C), strxfrm(3C), environ(5).
colltbl(1M) in the *System Administrator's Reference Manual*.

NAME
strerror – get error message string

SYNOPSIS
#include <string.h>

char *strerror (int errnum);

DESCRIPTION
strerror maps the error number in *errnum* to an error message string, and returns a pointer to that string. **strerror** uses the same set of error messages as **perror**. The returned string should not be overwritten.

SEE ALSO
perror(3C).

strftime(3C)

NAME
strftime, cftime, ascftime - convert date and time to string

SYNOPSIS
#include <time.h>

size_t *strftime (char *s, size_t maxsize, const char *format, const struct tm *timeptr);

int cftime (char *s, char *format, const time_t *clock);

int ascftime (char *s, const char *format, const struct tm *timeptr);

DESCRIPTION
strftime, ascftime, and cftime place characters into the array pointed to by s as controlled by the string pointed to by *format*. The *format* string consists of zero or more directives and ordinary characters. All ordinary characters (including the terminating null character) are copied unchanged into the array. For strftime, no more than *maxsize* characters are placed into the array.

If *format* is (char *)0, then the locale's default format is used. For strftime the default format is the same as "%c", for cftime and ascftime the default format is the same as "%C". cftime and ascftime first try to use the value of the environment variable CFTIME, and if that is undefined or empty, the default format is used.

Each directive is replaced by appropriate characters as described in the following list. The appropriate characters are determined by the LC_TIME category of the program's locale and by the values contained in the structure pointed to by *timeptr* for strftime and ascftime, and by the time represented by *clock* for cftime.

%%	same as %
%a	locale's abbreviated weekday name
%A	locale's full weekday name
%b	locale's abbreviated month name
%B	locale's full month name
%c	locale's appropriate date and time representation
%C	locale's date and time representation as produced by date(1)
%d	day of month (01 - 31)
%D	date as %m/%d/%y
%e	day of month (1-31; single digits are preceded by a blank)
%h	locale's abbreviated month name.
%H	hour (00 - 23)
%I	hour (01 - 12)
%j	day number of year (001 - 366)
%m	month number (01 - 12)
%M	minute (00 - 59)
%n	same as \n
%p	locale's equivalent of either AM or PM

%r	time as %I:%M:%S [AM|PM]
%R	time as %H:%M
%S	seconds (00 - 61), allows for leap seconds
%t	insert a tab
%T	time as %H:%M:%S
%U	week number of year (00 - 53), Sunday is the first day of week 1
%w	weekday number (0 - 6), Sunday = 0
%W	week number of year (00 - 53), Monday is the first day of week 1
%x	locale's appropriate date representation
%X	locale's appropriate time representation
%y	year within century (00 - 99)
%Y	year as ccyy (e.g. 1986)
%Z	time zone name or no characters if no time zone exists

The difference between %U and %W lies in which day is counted as the first of the week. Week number 01 is the first week in January starting with a Sunday for %U or a Monday for %W. Week number 00 contains those days before the first Sunday or Monday in January for %U and %W, respectively.

If the total number of resulting characters including the terminating null character is not more than *maxsize*, strftime, cftime and ascftime return the number of characters placed into the array pointed to by s not including the terminating null character. Otherwise, zero is returned and the contents of the array are indeterminate. cftime and ascftime return the number of characters placed into the array pointed to by s not including the terminating null character.

Selecting the Output's Language
By default, the output of strftime, cftime, and ascftime appear in US English. The user can request that the output of strftime, cftime or ascftime be in a specific language by setting the *locale* for *category* LC_TIME in setlocale.

Timezone
The timezone is taken from the environment variable TZ [see ctime(3C) for a description of TZ].

EXAMPLES
The example illustrates the use of strftime. It shows what the string in str would look like if the structure pointed to by *tmptr* contains the values corresponding to Thursday, August 28, 1986 at 12:44:36 in New Jersey.

    strftime (str, strsize, "%A %b %d %j", tmptr)

This results in str containing "Thursday Aug 28 240".

FILES
/usr/lib/locale/*locale*/LC_TIME − file containing locale specific date and time information

SEE ALSO
ctime(3C), getenv(3C), setlocale(3C), strftime(4), timezone(4), environ(5).

NOTE
cftime and ascftime are obsolete. strftime should be used instead.

string (3C)

NAME
string: strcat, strdup, strncat, strcmp, strncmp, strcpy, strncpy, strlen, strchr, strrchr, strpbrk, strspn, strcspn, strtok, strstr – string operations

SYNOPSIS
#include <string.h>

char *strcat (char *s1, const char *s2);

char *strdup (const char *s1);

char *strncat (char *s1, const char *s2, size_t n);

int strcmp (const char *s1, const char *s2);

int strncmp (const char *s1, const char *s2, size_t n);

char *strcpy (char *s1, const char *s2);

char *strncpy (char *s1, const char *s2, size_t n);

size_t strlen (const char *s);

char *strchr (const char *s, int c);

char *strrchr (const char *s, int c);

char *strpbrk (const char *s1, const char *s2);

size_t strspn (const char *s1, const char *s2);

size_t strcspn (const char *s1, const char *s2);

char *strtok (char *s1, const char *s2);

char *strstr (const char *s1, const char *s2);

DESCRIPTION
The arguments *s*, *s1*, and *s2* point to strings (arrays of characters terminated by a null character). The functions strcat, strncat, strcpy, strncpy, and strtok. all alter *s1*. These functions do not check for overflow of the array pointed to by *s1*.

strcat appends a copy of string *s2*, including the terminating null character, to the end of string *s1*. strncat appends at most *n* characters. Each returns a pointer to the null-terminated result. The initial character of *s2* overrides the null character at the end of *s1*.

strcmp compares its arguments and returns an integer less than, equal to, or greater than 0, based upon whether *s1* is lexicographically less than, equal to, or greater than *s2*. strncmp makes the same comparison but looks at at most *n* characters. Characters following a null character are not compared.

strcpy copies string *s2* to *s1* including the terminating null character, stopping after the null character has been copied. strncpy copies exactly *n* characters, truncating *s2* or adding null characters to *s1* if necessary. The result will not be null-terminated if the length of *s2* is *n* or more. Each function returns *s1*.

string (3C)

strdup returns a pointer to a new string which is a duplicate of the string pointed to by *s1*. The space for the new string is obtained using `malloc`(3C). If the new string can not be created, a NULL pointer is returned.

strlen returns the number of characters in *s*, not including the terminating null character.

strchr (or **strrchr**) returns a pointer to the first (last) occurrence of *c* (converted to a `char`) in string *s*, or a NULL pointer if *c* does not occur in the string. The null character terminating a string is considered to be part of the string.

strpbrk returns a pointer to the first occurrence in string *s1* of any character from string *s2*, or a NULL pointer if no character from *s2* exists in *s1*.

strspn (or **strcspn**) returns the length of the initial segment of string *s1* which consists entirely of characters from (not from) string *s2*.

strtok considers the string *s1* to consist of a sequence of zero or more text tokens separated by spans of one or more characters from the separator string *s2*. The first call (with pointer *s1* specified) returns a pointer to the first character of the first token, and will have written a null character into *s1* immediately following the returned token. The function keeps track of its position in the string between separate calls, so that subsequent calls (which must be made with the first argument a NULL pointer) will work through the string *s1* immediately following that token. In this way subsequent calls will work through the string *s1* until no tokens remain. The separator string *s2* may be different from call to call. When no token remains in *s1*, a NULL pointer is returned.

strstr locates the first occurrence in string *s1* of the sequence of characters (excluding the terminating null character) in string *s2*. **strstr** returns a pointer to the located string, or a null pointer if the string is not found. If *s2* points to a string with zero length (i.e., the string ""), the function returns *s1*.

SEE ALSO

malloc(3C), setlocale(3C), strxfrm(3C).

NOTES

All of these functions assume the default locale "C." For some locales, **strxfrm** should be applied to the strings before they are passed to the functions.

strtod(3C)   strtod(3C)

NAME
strtod, atof, – convert string to double-precision number

SYNOPSIS
#include <stdlib.h>

double strtod (const char *nptr, char **endptr);

double atof (const char *nptr);

DESCRIPTION
strtod returns as a double-precision floating-point number the value represented by the character string pointed to by *nptr*. The string is scanned up to the first unrecognized character.

strtod recognizes an optional string of "white-space" characters [as defined by isspace in ctype(3C)], then an optional sign, then a string of digits optionally containing a decimal point character, then an optional exponent part including an e or E followed by an optional sign, followed by an integer.

If the value of *endptr* is not (char **)NULL, a pointer to the character terminating the scan is returned in the location pointed to by *endptr*. If no number can be formed, *endptr* is set to *nptr*, and zero is returned.

atof(nptr) is equivalent to:
    strtod(nptr, (char **)NULL).

SEE ALSO
ctype(3C), scanf(3S), strtol(3C).

DIAGNOSTICS
If the correct value would cause overflow, ±HUGE is returned (according to the sign of the value), and *errno* is set to ERANGE.

If the correct value would cause underflow, zero is returned and *errno* is set to ERANGE.

When the –Xc or –Xa compilation options are used, HUGE_VAL is returned instead of HUGE.

NAME
strtol, strtoul, atol, atoi – convert string to integer

SYNOPSIS
#include <stdlib.h>

long strtol (const char *str, char **ptr, int base);

unsigned long strtoul (const char *str, char **ptr, int base);

long atol (const char *str);

int atoi (const char *str);

DESCRIPTION
strtol returns as a long integer the value represented by the character string pointed to by str. The string is scanned up to the first character inconsistent with the base. Leading "white-space" characters [as defined by isspace in ctype(3C)] are ignored.

If the value of *ptr* is not (char **)NULL, a pointer to the character terminating the scan is returned in the location pointed to by *ptr*. If no integer can be formed, that location is set to str, and zero is returned.

If *base* is positive (and not greater than 36), it is used as the base for conversion. After an optional leading sign, leading zeros are ignored, and "0x" or "0X" is ignored if *base* is 16.

If *base* is zero, the string itself determines the base as follows: After an optional leading sign a leading zero indicates octal conversion, and a leading "0x" or "0X" hexadecimal conversion. Otherwise, decimal conversion is used.

Truncation from long to int can, of course, take place upon assignment or by an explicit cast.

If the value represented by *str* would cause overflow, LONG_MAX or LONG_MIN is returned (according to the sign of the value), and errno is set to the value, ERANGE.

strtoul is similar to strtol except that strtoul returns as an unsigned long integer the value represented by *str*. If the value represented by *str* would cause overflow, ULONG_MAX is returned, and errno is set to the value, ERANGE.

Except for behavior on error, atol(str) is equivalent to: strtol(str, (char **)NULL, 10).

Except for behavior on error, atoi(str) is equivalent to: (int) strtol(str, (char **)NULL, 10).

DIAGNOSTICS
If strtol is given a *base* greater than 36, it returns 0 and sets errno to EINVAL.

SEE ALSO
ctype(3C), scanf(3S), strtod(3C).

NOTES
strtol no longer accepts values greater than LONG_MAX as valid input. Use strtoul instead.

strxfrm(3C)

NAME
strxfrm – string transformation

SYNOPSIS
#include <string.h>

size_t strxfrm (char *s1, const char *s2, size_t n);

DESCRIPTION
strxfrm transforms the string *s2* and places the resulting string into the array *s1*. The transformation is such that if strcmp is applied to two transformed strings, it will return the same result as strcoll applied to the same two original strings. The transformation is based on the program's locale for category LC_COLLATE [see setlocale(3C)].

No more than *n* characters will be placed into the resulting array pointed to by *s1*, including the terminating null character. If *n* is 0, then *s1* is permitted to be a null pointer. If copying takes place between objects that overlap, the behavior is undefined.

strxfrm returns the length of the transformed string (not including the terminating null character). If the value returned is *n* or more, the contents of the array *s1* are indeterminate.

EXAMPLE
The value of the following expression is the size of the array needed to hold the transformation of the string pointed to by *s*.

    1 + strxfrm(NULL, s, 0);

FILES
/usr/lib/locale/*locale*/LC_COLLATE   LC_COLLATE database for *locale*.

SEE ALSO
colltbl(1M) in the *System Administrator's Reference Manual*.
setlocale(3C), strcoll(3C), string(3C), environ(5).

DIAGNOSTICS
On failure, strxfrm returns (size_t) −1.

NAME
swab – swap bytes

SYNOPSIS
#include <stdlib.h>

void **swab** (const char *from, char *to, int nbytes);

DESCRIPTION
swab copies *nbytes* bytes pointed to by *from* to the array pointed to by *to*, exchanging adjacent even and odd bytes. *nbytes* should be even and non-negative. If *nbytes* is odd and positive, **swab** uses *nbytes*−1 instead. If *nbytes* is negative, **swab** does nothing.

sysconf(3C)

NAME
sysconf – get configurable system variables

SYNOPSIS
    #include <unistd.h>

    long sysconf(int name);

DESCRIPTION
The sysconf function provides a method for the application to determine the current value of a configurable system limit or option (variable).

The *name* argument represents the system variable to be queried. The following table lists the minimal set of system variables from <limits.h> and <unistd.h> that can be returned by sysconf, and the symbolic constants, defined in <unistd.h> that are the corresponding values used for *name*.

NAME	RETURN VALUE
_SC_ARG_MAX	ARG_MAX
_SC_CHILD_MAX	CHILD_MAX
_SC_CLK_TCK	CLK_TCK
_SC_NGROUPS_MAX	NGROUPS_MAX
_SC_OPEN_MAX	OPEN_MAX
_SC_PASS_MAX	PASS_MAX
_SC_PAGESIZE	PAGESIZE
_SC_JOB_CONTROL	_POSIX_JOB_CONTROL
_SC_SAVED_IDS	_POSIX_SAVED_IDS
_SC_VERSION	_POSIX_VERSION
_SC_XOPEN_VERSION	_XOPEN_VERSION
_SC_LOGNAME_MAX	LOGNAME_MAX

The value of CLK_TCK may be variable and it should not be assumed that CLK_TCK is a compile-time constant. The value of CLK_TCK is the same as the value of sysconf(_SC_CLK_TCK).

SEE ALSO
fpathconf(3C).

DIAGNOSTICS
If *name* is an invalid value, sysconf will return −1 and set errno to indicate the error. If sysconf fails due to a value of *name* that is not defined on the system, the function will return a value of −1 without changing the value of errno.

NOTES
A call to setrlimit may cause the value of OPEN_MAX to change.

system (3S)   system (3S)

NAME
system – issue a shell command

SYNOPSIS
#include <stdlib.h>

int system (const char *string);

DESCRIPTION
system causes the *string* to be given to the shell [see sh(1)] as input, as if the string had been typed as a command at a terminal. The current process waits until the shell has completed, then returns the exit status of the shell in the format specified by **waitpid**.

If *string* is a NULL pointer, system checks if /sbin/sh exists and is executable. If /sbin/sh is available, system returns non-zero; otherwise it returns zero.

system fails if one or more of the following are true:

EAGAIN	The system-imposed limit on the total number of processes under execution by a single user would be exceeded.
EINTR	system was interupted by a signal.
ENOMEM	The new process requires more memory than is allowed by the system-imposed maximum MAXMEM.

SEE ALSO
exec(2), wait(3C).

sh(1) in the *User's Reference Manual*.

DIAGNOSTICS
system forks to create a child process that in turn execs /sbin/sh in order to execute *string*. If the fork or exec fails, system returns a value of -1 and sets errno.

tcsetpgrp(3C)

NAME
tcsetpgrp – set terminal foreground process group id

SYNOPSIS
#include <unistd.h>

int tcsetpgrp (int fildes, pid_t pgid)

DESCRIPTION
tcsetpgrp sets the foreground process group ID of the terminal specified by *fildes* to *pgid*. The file associated with *fildes* must be the controlling terminal of the calling process and the controlling terminal must be currently associated with the session of the calling process. The value of *pgid* must match a process group ID of a process in the same session as the calling process.

tcsetpgrp fails if one or more of the following is true:

EBADF	The *fildes* argument is not a valid file descriptor.
EINVAL	The *fildes* argument is a terminal that does not support tcsetpgrp, or *pgid* is not a valid process group ID.
ENOTTY	The calling process does not have a controlling terminal, or the file is not the controlling terminal, or the controlling terminal is no longer associated with the session of the calling process.
EPERM	*pgid* does not match the process group ID of an existing process in the same session as the calling process.

SEE ALSO
tcsetpgrp(3C), tcsetsid(3C).
termio(7) in the *System Administrator's Reference Manual*.

DIAGNOSTICS
Upon successful completion, tcsetpgrp returns a value of 0. Otherwise, a value of −1 is returned and **errno** is set to indicate the error.

NAME

tmpfile – create a temporary file

SYNOPSIS

#include <stdio.h>

FILE *tmpfile (void);

DESCRIPTION

tmpfile creates a temporary file using a name generated by the tmpnam routine and returns a corresponding FILE pointer. If the file cannot be opened, a NULL pointer is returned. The file is automatically deleted when the process using it terminates or when the file is closed. The file is opened for update ("w+").

SEE ALSO

creat(2), open(2), unlink(2), fopen(3S), mktemp(3C), perror(3C), stdio(3S), tmpnam(3S).

NAME
tmpnam, tempnam – create a name for a temporary file

SYNOPSIS
    #include <stdio.h>

    char *tmpnam (char *s);

    char *tempnam (const char *dir, const char *pfx);

DESCRIPTION
These functions generate file names that can safely be used for a temporary file.

tmpnam always generates a file name using the path-prefix defined as P_tmpdir in the <stdio.h> header file. If s is NULL, tmpnam leaves its result in an internal static area and returns a pointer to that area. The next call to tmpnam will destroy the contents of the area. If s is not NULL, it is assumed to be the address of an array of at least L_tmpnam bytes, where L_tmpnam is a constant defined in <stdio.h>; tmpnam places its result in that array and returns s.

tempnam allows the user to control the choice of a directory. The argument *dir* points to the name of the directory in which the file is to be created. If *dir* is NULL or points to a string that is not a name for an appropriate directory, the path-prefix defined as P_tmpdir in the <stdio.h> header file is used. If that directory is not accessible, /tmp will be used as a last resort. This entire sequence can be up-staged by providing an environment variable TMPDIR in the user's environment, whose value is the name of the desired temporary-file directory.

Many applications prefer their temporary files to have certain favorite initial letter sequences in their names. Use the *pfx* argument for this. This argument may be NULL or point to a string of up to five characters to be used as the first few characters of the temporary-file name.

tempnam uses malloc to get space for the constructed file name, and returns a pointer to this area. Thus, any pointer value returned from tempnam may serve as an argument to free [see malloc(3C)]. If tempnam cannot return the expected result for any reason—e.g., malloc failed—or none of the above mentioned attempts to find an appropriate directory was successful, a NULL pointer will be returned.

tempnam fails if there is not enough space.

FILES
    p_tmpdir /var/tmp

SEE ALSO
creat(2), unlink(2), fopen(3S), malloc(3C), mktemp(3C), tmpfile(3S).

NOTES
These functions generate a different file name each time they are called.

Files created using these functions and either fopen or creat are temporary only in the sense that they reside in a directory intended for temporary use, and their names are unique. It is the user's responsibility to remove the file when its use is ended.

If called more than **TMP_MAX** (defined in `stdio.h`) times in a single process, these functions start recycling previously used names.

Between the time a file name is created and the file is opened, it is possible for some other process to create a file with the same name. This can never happen if that other process is using these functions or **mktemp** and the file names are chosen to render duplication by other means unlikely.

truncate (3C)

NAME
truncate, ftruncate – set a file to a specified length

SYNOPSIS
#include <unistd.h>

int truncate (const char *path, off_t length);

int ftruncate (int fildes, off_t length);

DESCRIPTION
The file whose name is given by *path* or referenced by the descriptor *fildes* has its size set to *length* bytes.

If the file was previously longer than *length*, bytes past *length* will no longer be accessible. If it was shorter, bytes from the EOF before the call to the EOF after the call will be read in as zeros. The effective user ID of the process must have write permission for the file, and for ftruncate the file must be open for writing.

truncate fails if one or more of the following are true:

EACCES	Search permission is denied on a component of the path prefix.
EACCES	Write permission is denied for the file referred to by *path*.
EFAULT	*path* points outside the process's allocated address space.
EINTR	A signal was caught during execution of the truncate routine.
EINVAL	*path* is not an ordinary file.
EIO	An I/O error occurred while reading from or writing to the file system.
EISDIR	The file referred to by *path* is a directory.
ELOOP	Too many symbolic links were encountered in translating *path*.
EMFILE	The maximum number of file descriptors available to the process has been reached.
EMULTIHOP	Components of *path* require hopping to multiple remote machines and file system type does not allow it.
ENAMETOOLONG	The length of a *path* component exceeds {NAME_MAX} characters, or the length of *path* exceeds {PATH_MAX} characters.
ENFILE	Could not allocate any more space for the system file table.
ENOENT	Either a component of the path prefix or the file referred to by *path* does not exist.
ENOLINK	*path* points to a remote machine and the link to that machine is no longer active.
ENOTDIR	A component of the path prefix of *path* is not a directory.

EROFS	The file referred to by *path* resides on a read-only file system.
ETXTBSY	The file referred to by *path* is a pure procedure (shared text) file that is being executed.

`ftruncate` fails if one or more of the following are true:

EAGAIN	The file exists, mandatory file/record locking is set, and there are outstanding record locks on the file [see chmod(2)].
EBADF	*fildes* is not a file descriptor open for writing.
EINTR	A signal was caught during execution of the `ftruncate` routine.
EIO	An I/O error occurred while reading from or writing to the file system.
ENOLINK	*fildes* points to a remote machine and the link to that machine is no longer active.
EINVAL	*fildes* does not correspond to an ordinary file.

SEE ALSO
fcntl(2), open(2)

DIAGNOSTICS
Upon successful completion, a value of 0 is returned. Otherwise, a value of −1 is returned and `errno` is set to indicate the error.

tsearch(3C)

NAME
tsearch, tfind, tdelete, twalk – manage binary search trees

SYNOPSIS
#include <search.h>

void *tsearch (const void *key, void **rootp, int (*compar)
    (const void *, const void *));

void *tfind (const void *key, void * const *rootp, int (*compar)
    (const void *, const void *));

void *tdelete (const void *key, void **rootp, int (*compar)
    (const void *, const void *));

void twalk (void *root, void(*action) (void *, VISIT, int));

DESCRIPTION
tsearch, tfind, tdelete, and twalk are routines for manipulating binary search trees. They are generalized from Knuth (6.2.2) Algorithms T and D. All comparisons are done with a user-supplied routine. This routine is called with two arguments, the pointers to the elements being compared. It returns an integer less than, equal to, or greater than 0, according to whether the first argument is to be considered less than, equal to or greater than the second argument. The comparison function need not compare every byte, so arbitrary data may be contained in the elements in addition to the values being compared.

tsearch is used to build and access the tree. *key* is a pointer to a datum to be accessed or stored. If there is a datum in the tree equal to *key (the value pointed to by *key*), a pointer to this found datum is returned. Otherwise, *key is inserted, and a pointer to it returned. Only pointers are copied, so the calling routine must store the data. *rootp* points to a variable that points to the root of the tree. A NULL value for the variable pointed to by *rootp* denotes an empty tree; in this case, the variable will be set to point to the datum which will be at the root of the new tree.

Like tsearch, tfind will search for a datum in the tree, returning a pointer to it if found. However, if it is not found, tfind will return a NULL pointer. The arguments for tfind are the same as for tsearch.

tdelete deletes a node from a binary search tree. The arguments are the same as for tsearch. The variable pointed to by *rootp* will be changed if the deleted node was the root of the tree. tdelete returns a pointer to the parent of the deleted node, or a NULL pointer if the node is not found.

twalk traverses a binary search tree. *root* is the root of the tree to be traversed. (Any node in a tree may be used as the root for a walk below that node.) *action* is the name of a routine to be invoked at each node. This routine is, in turn, called with three arguments. The first argument is the address of the node being visited. The second argument is a value from an enumeration data type *typedef enum { preorder, postorder, endorder, leaf } VISIT;* (defined in the search.h header file), depending on whether this is the first, second or third time that the node has been visited (during a depth-first, left-to-right traversal of the tree), or whether the node is a leaf. The third argument is the level of the node in the tree, with the root being level zero.

The pointers to the key and the root of the tree should be of type pointer-to-element, and cast to type pointer-to-character. Similarly, although declared as type pointer-to-character, the value returned should be cast into type pointer-to-element.

EXAMPLE

The following code reads in strings and stores structures containing a pointer to each string and a count of its length. It then walks the tree, printing out the stored strings and their lengths in alphabetical order.

```
#include <string.h>
#include <stdio.h>
#include <search.h>

struct node {
      char *string;
      int length;
};
char string_space[10000];
struct node nodes[500];
void *root = NULL;

int node_compare(const void *node1, const void *node2) {
      return strcmp(((const struct node *) node1)->string,
                    ((const struct node *) node2)->string);
}

void print_node(void **node, VISIT order, int level) {
      if (order == preorder || order == leaf) {
            printf("length=%d, string=%20s\n",
                  (*(struct node **)node)->length,
                  (*(struct node **)node)->string);
      }
}

main() {
      char *strptr = string_space;
      struct node *nodeptr = nodes;
      int i = 0;

      while (gets(strptr) != NULL && i++ < 500) {
            nodeptr->string = strptr;
            nodeptr->length = strlen(strptr);
            (void) tsearch((void *)nodeptr,
                        &root, node_compare);
            strptr += nodeptr->length + 1;
            nodeptr++;
      }
      twalk(root, print_node);
}
```

SEE ALSO
bsearch(3C), hsearch(3C), lsearch(3C).

DIAGNOSTICS
A NULL pointer is returned by **tsearch** if there is not enough space available to create a new node.

A NULL pointer is returned by **tfind** and **tdelete** if *rootp* is NULL on entry.

If the datum is found, both **tsearch** and **tfind** return a pointer to it. If not, **tfind** returns NULL, and **tsearch** returns a pointer to the inserted item.

NOTES
The *root* argument to **twalk** is one level of indirection less than the *rootp* arguments to **tsearch** and **tdelete**.

There are two nomenclatures used to refer to the order in which tree nodes are visited. **tsearch** uses preorder, postorder and endorder to refer respectively to visiting a node before any of its children, after its left child and before its right, and after both its children. The alternate nomenclature uses preorder, inorder and postorder to refer to the same visits, which could result in some confusion over the meaning of postorder.

If the calling function alters the pointer to the root, results are unpredictable.

NAME

ttyname, isatty – find name of a terminal

SYNOPSIS

#include <stdlib.h>

char *ttyname (int fildes);

int isatty (int fildes);

DESCRIPTION

ttyname returns a pointer to a string containing the null-terminated path name of the terminal device associated with file descriptor *fildes*.

isatty returns 1 if *fildes* is associated with a terminal device, 0 otherwise.

FILES

/dev/*

DIAGNOSTICS

ttyname returns a NULL pointer if *fildes* does not describe a terminal device in directory /dev.

NOTES

The return value points to static data whose content is overwritten by each call.

NAME
ttyslot – find the slot in the utmp file of the current user

SYNOPSIS
#include <stdlib.h>

int ttyslot (void);

DESCRIPTION
ttyslot returns the index of the current user's entry in the /var/adm/utmp file. The returned index is accomplished by scanning files in /dev for the name of the terminal associated with the standard input, the standard output, or the standard error output (0, 1, or 2).

FILES
/var/adm/utmp

SEE ALSO
getut(3C), ttyname(3C).

DIAGNOSTICS
A value of −1 is returned if an error was encountered while searching for the terminal name or if none of the above file descriptors are associated with a terminal device.

ungetc(3S)

NAME
ungetc – push character back onto input stream

SYNOPSIS
#include <stdio.h>

int ungetc (int c, FILE *stream);

DESCRIPTION
ungetc inserts the character specified by *c* (converted to an **unsigned char**) into the buffer associated with an input *stream* [see intro(3)]. That character, *c*, will be returned by the next getc(3S) call on that *stream*. ungetc returns *c*, and leaves the file corresponding to *stream* unchanged. A successful call to ungetc clears the EOF indicator for stream.

Four bytes of pushback are guaranteed.

The value of the file position indicator for *stream* after reading or discarding all pushed-back characters will be the same as it was before the characters were pushed back.

If *c* equals EOF, ungetc does nothing to the buffer and returns EOF.

fseek, rewind [both described on fseek(3S)], and fsetpos erase the memory of inserted characters for the stream on which they are applied.

SEE ALSO
fseek(3S), fsetpos(3C), getc(3S), setbuf(3S), stdio(3S).

DIAGNOSTICS
ungetc returns EOF if it cannot insert the character.

vprintf(3S)

NAME
vprintf, vfprintf, vsprintf – print formatted output of a variable argument list

SYNOPSIS
#include <stdio.h>
#include <stdarg.h>

int vprintf(const char *format, va_list ap);

int vfprintf(FILE *stream, const char *format, va_list ap);

int vsprintf(char *s, const char *format, va_list ap);

DESCRIPTION
vprintf, vfprintf and vsprintf are the same as printf, fprintf, and sprintf respectively, except that instead of being called with a variable number of arguments, they are called with an argument list as defined by the <stdarg.h> header file.

The <stdarg.h> header file defines the type va_list and a set of macros for advancing through a list of arguments whose number and types may vary. The argument *ap* to the vprint family of routines is of type va_list. This argument is used with the <stdarg.h> header file macros va_start, va_arg and va_end [see va_start, va_arg, and va_end in stdarg(5)]. The EXAMPLE section below shows their use with vprintf.

EXAMPLE
The following demonstrates how vfprintf could be used to write an error routine:

```
#include <stdio.h>
#include <stdarg.h>
/*
 *   error should be called like
 *           error(function_name, format, arg1, ...);
 */
void error(char *function_name, char *format, ...)
{
    va_list ap;

    va_start(ap, format);
    /* print out name of function causing error */
    (void) fprintf(stderr, "ERR in %s: ", function_name);
    va_arg(ap, char*);
    /* print out remainder of message */
    (void) vfprintf(stderr, format, ap);
    va_end(ap);
    (void) abort;
}
```

SEE ALSO
      `printf`(3S), **`stdarg`**(5).

DIAGNOSTICS
      `vprintf` and **`vfprintf`** return the number of characters transmitted, or return −1 if an error was encountered.

3E

elf(3E)

NAME
elf – object file access library

SYNOPSIS
cc [*flag* ...] *file* ... -lelf [*library* ...]
#include <libelf.h>

DESCRIPTION
Functions in the ELF access library let a program manipulate ELF (Executable and Linking Format) object files, archive files, and archive members. The header file provides type and function declarations for all library services.

Programs communicate with many of the higher-level routines using an *ELF descriptor*. That is, when the program starts working with a file, elf_begin creates an ELF descriptor through which the program manipulates the structures and information in the file. These ELF descriptors can be used both to read and to write files. After the program establishes an ELF descriptor for a file, it may then obtain *section descriptors* to manipulate the sections of the file [see elf_getscn(3E)]. Sections hold the bulk of an object file's real information, such as text, data, the symbol table, and so on. A section descriptor "belongs" to a particular ELF descriptor, just as a section belongs to a file. Finally, *data descriptors* are available through section descriptors, allowing the program to manipulate the information associated with a section. A data descriptor "belongs" to a section descriptor.

Descriptors provide private handles to a file and its pieces. In other words, a data descriptor is associated with one section descriptor, which is associated with one ELF descriptor, which is associated with one file. Although descriptors are private, they give access to data that may be shared. Consider programs that combine input files, using incoming data to create or update another file. Such a program might get data descriptors for an input and an output section. It then could update the output descriptor to reuse the input descriptor's data. That is, the descriptors are distinct, but they could share the associated data bytes. This sharing avoids the space overhead for duplicate buffers and the performance overhead for copying data unnecessarily.

FILE CLASSES
ELF provides a framework in which to define a family of object files, supporting multiple processors and architectures. An important distinction among object files is the *class*, or capacity, of the file. The 32-bit class supports architectures in which a 32-bit object can represent addresses, file sizes, etc., as in the following.

Name	Purpose
Elf32_Addr	Unsigned address
Elf32_Half	Unsigned medium integer
Elf32_Off	Unsigned file offset
Elf32_Sword	Signed large integer
Elf32_Word	Unsigned large integer
unsigned char	Unsigned small integer

Other classes will be defined as necessary, to support larger (or smaller) machines. Some library services deal only with data objects for a specific class, while others are class-independent. To make this distinction clear, library function names reflect their status, as described below.

DATA REPRESENTATIONS

Conceptually, two parallel sets of objects support cross compilation environments. One set corresponds to file contents, while the other set corresponds to the native memory image of the program manipulating the file. Type definitions supplied by the header files work on the native machine, which may have different data encodings (size, byte order, etc.) than the target machine. Although native memory objects should be at least as big as the file objects (to avoid information loss), they may be bigger if that is more natural for the host machine.

Translation facilities exist to convert between file and memory representations. Some library routines convert data automatically, while others leave conversion as the program's responsibility. Either way, programs that create object files must write file-typed objects to those files; programs that read object files must take a similar view. See **elf_xlate**(3E) and **elf_fsize**(3E) for more information.

Programs may translate data explicitly, taking full control over the object file layout and semantics. If the program prefers not to have and exercise complete control, the library provides a higher-level interface that hides many object file details. **elf_begin** and related functions let a program deal with the native memory types, converting between memory objects and their file equivalents automatically when reading or writing an object file.

ELF VERSIONS

Object file versions allow ELF to adapt to new requirements. Three—independent—versions can be important to a program. First, an application program knows about a particular version by virtue of being compiled with certain header files. Second, the access library similarly is compiled with header files that control what versions it understands. Third, an ELF object file holds a value identifying its version, determined by the ELF version known by the file's creator. Ideally, all three versions would be the same, but they may differ.

> If a program's version is newer than the access library, the program might use information unknown to the library. Translation routines might not work properly, leading to undefined behavior. This condition merits installing a new library.
>
> The library's version might be newer than the program's and the file's. The library understands old versions, thus avoiding compatibility problems in this case.
>
> Finally, a file's version might be newer than either the program or the library understands. The program might or might not be able to process the file properly, depending on whether the file has extra information and whether that information can be safely ignored. Again, the safe alternative is to install a new library that understands the file's version.

elf(3E)

To accommodate these differences, a program must use elf_version to pass its version to the library, thus establishing the *working version* for the process. Using this, the library accepts data from and presents data to the program in the proper representations. When the library reads object files, it uses each file's version to interpret the data. When writing files or converting memory types to the file equivalents, the library uses the program's working version for the file data.

SYSTEM SERVICES

As mentioned above, elf_begin and related routines provide a higher-level interface to ELF files, performing input and output on behalf of the application program. These routines assume a program can hold entire files in memory, without explicitly using temporary files. When reading a file, the library routines bring the data into memory and perform subsequent operations on the memory copy. Programs that wish to read or write large object files with this model must execute on a machine with a large process virtual address space. If the underlying operating system limits the number of open files, a program can use elf_cntl to retrieve all necessary data from the file, allowing the program to close the file descriptor and reuse it.

Although the elf_begin interfaces are convenient and efficient for many programs, they might be inappropriate for some. In those cases, an application may invoke the elf_xlate data translation routines directly. These routines perform no input or output, leaving that as the application's responsibility. By assuming a larger share of the job, an application controls its input and output model.

LIBRARY NAMES

Names associated with the library take several forms.

elf_*name*	These class-independent names perform some service, *name*, for the program.
elf32_*name*	Service names with an embedded class, 32 here, indicate they work only for the designated class of files.
Elf_*Type*	Data types can be class-independent as well, distinguished by *Type*.
Elf32_*Type*	Class-dependent data types have an embedded class name, 32 here.
ELF_C_*CMD*	Several functions take commands that control their actions. These values are members of the Elf_Cmd enumeration; they range from zero through ELF_C_NUM−1.
ELF_F_*FLAG*	Several functions take flags that control library status and/or actions. Flags are bits that may be combined.
ELF32_FSZ_*TYPE*	These constants give the file sizes in bytes of the basic ELF types for the 32-bit class of files. See elf_fsize for more information.
ELF_K_*KIND*	The function elf_kind identifies the *KIND* of file associated with an ELF descriptor. These values are members of the Elf_Kind enumeration; they range from zero through ELF_K_NUM−1.

ELF_T_TYPE   When a service function, such as `elf_xlate`, deals with multiple types, names of this form specify the desired *TYPE*. Thus, for example, `ELF_T_EHDR` is directly related to `Elf32_Ehdr`. These values are members of the `Elf_Type` enumeration; they range from zero through `ELF_T_NUM-1`.

SEE ALSO

cof2elf(1), `elf_begin`(3E), `elf_cntl`(3E), `elf_end`(3E), `elf_error`(3E), `elf_fill`(3E), `elf_flag`(3E), `elf_fsize`(3E), `elf_getarhdr`(3E), `elf_getarsym`(3E), `elf_getbase`(3E), `elf_getdata`(3E), `elf_getehdr`(3E), `elf_getident`(3E), `elf_getphdr`(3E), `elf_getscn`(3E), `elf_getshdr`(3E), `elf_hash`(3E), `elf_kind`(3E), `elf_next`(3E), `elf_rand`(3E), `elf_rawfile`(3E), `elf_strptr`(3E), `elf_update`(3E), `elf_version`(3E), `elf_xlate`(3E), a.out(4) ar(4)

The "Object Files" in the chapter *Programmer's Guide: ANSI C and Programming Support Tools*.

NOTES

Information in the ELF header files is separated into common parts and processor-specific parts. A program can make a processor's information available by including the appropriate header file: `<sys/elf_NAME.h>` where *NAME* matches the processor name as used in the ELF file header.

Symbol	Processor
M32	AT&T WE 32100
SPARC	SPARC
386	Intel 80386
486	Intel 80486
860	Intel 80860
68K	Motorola 68000
88K	Motorola 88000

Other processors will be added to the table as necessary. To illustrate, a program could use the following code to "see" the processor-specific information for the WE 32100.

```
#include <libelf.h>
#include <sys/elf_M32.h>
```

Without the `<sys/elf_M32.h>` definition, only the common ELF information would be visible.

elf_begin(3E)

NAME
elf_begin – make a file descriptor

SYNOPSIS
cc [*flag* ...] *file* ... -lelf [*library* ...]

#include <libelf.h>

Elf *elf_begin(int fildes, Elf_Cmd cmd, Elf *ref);

DESCRIPTION
elf_begin, elf_next, elf_rand, and elf_end work together to process ELF object files, either individually or as members of archives. After obtaining an ELF descriptor from elf_begin, the program may read an existing file, update an existing file, or create a new file. *fildes* is an open file descriptor that elf_begin uses for reading or writing. The initial file offset [see lseek(2)] is unconstrained, and the resulting file offset is undefined.

cmd may have the following values.

ELF_C_NULL   When a program sets *cmd* to this value, elf_begin returns a null pointer, without opening a new descriptor. *ref* is ignored for this command. See elf_next(3E) and the examples below for more information.

ELF_C_READ   When a program wishes to examine the contents of an existing file, it should set *cmd* to this value. Depending on the value of *ref*, this command examines archive members or entire files. Three cases can occur.

First, if *ref* is a null pointer, elf_begin allocates a new ELF descriptor and prepares to process the entire file. If the file being read is an archive, elf_begin also prepares the resulting descriptor to examine the initial archive member on the next call to elf_begin, as if the program had used elf_next or elf_rand to "move" to the initial member.

Second, if *ref* is a non-null descriptor associated with an archive file, elf_begin lets a program obtain a separate ELF descriptor associated with an individual member. The program should have used elf_next or elf_rand to position *ref* appropriately (except for the initial member, which elf_begin prepares; see the example below). In this case, *fildes* should be the same file descriptor used for the parent archive.

Finally, if *ref* is a non-null ELF descriptor that is not an archive, elf_begin increments the number of activations for the descriptor and returns *ref*, without allocating a new descriptor and without changing the descriptor's read/write permissions. To terminate the descriptor for *ref*, the program must call elf_end once for each activation. See elf_next(3E) and the examples below for more information.

ELF_C_RDWR   This command duplicates the actions of `ELF_C_READ` and additionally allows the program to update the file image [see `elf_update`(3E)]. That is, using `ELF_C_READ` gives a read-only view of the file, while `ELF_C_RDWR` lets the program read *and* write the file. `ELF_C_RDWR` is not valid for archive members. If *ref* is non-null, it must have been created with the `ELF_C_RDWR` command.

ELF_C_WRITE   If the program wishes to ignore previous file contents, presumably to create a new file, it should set *cmd* to this value. *ref* is ignored for this command.

`elf_begin` "works" on all files (including files with zero bytes), providing it can allocate memory for its internal structures and read any necessary information from the file. Programs reading object files thus may call `elf_kind` or `elf_getehdr` to determine the file type (only object files have an ELF header). If the file is an archive with no more members to process, or an error occurs, `elf_begin` returns a null pointer. Otherwise, the return value is a non-null ELF descriptor.

Before the first call to `elf_begin`, a program must call `elf_version` to coordinate versions.

SYSTEM SERVICES

When processing a file, the library decides when to read or write the file, depending on the program's requests. Normally, the library assumes the file descriptor remains usable for the life of the ELF descriptor. If, however, a program must process many files simultaneously and the underlying operating system limits the number of open files, the program can use `elf_cntl` to let it reuse file descriptors. After calling `elf_cntl` with appropriate arguments, the program may close the file descriptor without interfering with the library.

All data associated with an ELF descriptor remain allocated until `elf_end` terminates the descriptor's last activation. After the descriptors have been terminated, the storage is released; attempting to reference such data gives undefined behavior. Consequently, a program that deals with multiple input (or output) files must keep the ELF descriptors active until it finishes with them.

EXAMPLES

A prototype for reading a file appears below. If the file is a simple object file, the program executes the loop one time, receiving a null descriptor in the second iteration. In this case, both `elf` and `arf` will have the same value, the activation count will be two, and the program calls `elf_end` twice to terminate the descriptor. If the file is an archive, the loop processes each archive member in turn, ignoring those that are not object files.

```
        if (elf_version(EV_CURRENT) == EV_NONE)
        {
                /* library out of date */
                /* recover from error */
        }
        cmd = ELF_C_READ;
        arf = elf_begin(fildes, cmd, (Elf *)0);
        while ((elf = elf_begin(fildes, cmd, arf)) != 0)
        {
                if ((ehdr = elf32_getehdr(elf)) != 0)
                {
                        /* process the file ... */
                }
                cmd = elf_next(elf);
                elf_end(elf);
        }
        elf_end(arf);
```

Alternatively, the next example illustrates random archive processing. After identifying the file as an archive, the program repeatedly processes archive members of interest. For clarity, this example omits error checking and ignores simple object files. Additionally, this fragment preserves the ELF descriptors for all archive members, because it does not call `elf_end` to terminate them.

```
        elf_version(EV_CURRENT);
        arf = elf_begin(fildes, ELF_C_READ, (Elf *)0);
        if (elf_kind(arf) != ELF_K_AR)
        {
                /* not an archive */
        }
        /* initial processing */
        /* set offset = ... for desired member header */
        while (elf_rand(arf, offset) == offset)
        {
                if ((elf = elf_begin(fildes, ELF_C_READ, arf)) == 0)
                        break;
                if ((ehdr = elf32_getehdr(elf)) != 0)
                {
                        /* process archive member ... */
                }
                /* set offset = ... for desired member header */
        }
```

The following outline shows how one might create a new ELF file. This example is simplified to show the overall flow.

```
        elf_version(EV_CURRENT);
        fildes = open("path/name", O_RDWR|O_TRUNC|O_CREAT, 0666);
        if ((elf = elf_begin(fildes, ELF_C_WRITE, (Elf *)0)) == 0)
                return;
        ehdr = elf32_newehdr(elf);
        phdr = elf32_newphdr(elf, count);
        scn = elf_newscn(elf);
        shdr = elf32_getshdr(scn);
        data = elf_newdata(scn);
        elf_update(elf, ELF_C_WRITE);
        elf_end(elf);
```

Finally, the following outline shows how one might update an existing ELF file. Again, this example is simplified to show the overall flow.

```
        elf_version(EV_CURRENT);
        fildes = open("path/name", O_RDWR);
        elf = elf_begin(fildes, ELF_C_RDWR, (Elf *)0);

        /* add new or delete old information ... */

        close(creat("path/name", 0666));
        elf_update(elf, ELF_C_WRITE);
        elf_end(elf);
```

In the example above, the call to **creat** truncates the file, thus ensuring the resulting file will have the "right" size. Without truncation, the updated file might be as big as the original, even if information were deleted. The library truncates the file, if it can, with **ftruncate** [see **truncate**(2)]. Some systems, however, do not support **ftruncate**, and the call to **creat** protects against this.

Notice that both file creation examples open the file with write *and* read permissions. On systems that support **mmap**, the library uses it to enhance performance, and **mmap** requires a readable file descriptor. Although the library can use a write-only file descriptor, the application will not obtain the performance advantages of **mmap**.

SEE ALSO

cof2elf(1), creat(2), lseek(2), mmap(2), open(2), truncate(2), elf(3E), elf_cntl(3E), elf_end(3E), elf_getarhdr(3E), elf_getbase(3E), elf_getdata(3E), elf_getehdr(3E), elf_getphdr(3E), elf_getscn(3E), elf_kind(3E), elf_next(3E), elf_rand(3E), elf_rawfile(3E), elf_update(3E), elf_version(3E), ar(4).

NOTES

COFF is an object file format that preceded ELF. When a program calls `elf_begin` on a COFF file, the library translates COFF structures to their ELF equivalents, allowing programs to read (but not to write) a COFF file as if it were ELF. This conversion happens only to the memory image and *not* to the file itself. After the initial `elf_begin`, file offsets and addresses in the ELF header, the program headers, and the section headers retain the original COFF values [see elf_getehdr, elf_getphdr, and elf_getshdr]. A program may call elf_update to adjust these values (without writing the file), and the library will then present a consistent, ELF view of the file. Data obtained through **elf_getdata** are translated (the COFF symbol table is presented as ELF , etc.). Data viewed through **elf_rawdata** undergo no conversion, allowing the program to view the bytes from the file itself.

Some COFF debugging information is not translated, though this does not affect the semantics of a running program.

Although the ELF library supports COFF , programmers are strongly encouraged to recompile their programs, obtaining ELF object files.

NAME
`elf_cntl` – control a file descriptor

SYNOPSIS
cc [*flag* ...] *file* ... -lelf [*library* ...]

#include <libelf.h>

int elf_cntl(Elf *elf, Elf_Cmd cmd);

DESCRIPTION
`elf_cntl` instructs the library to modify its behavior with respect to an ELF descriptor, *elf*. As `elf_begin`(3E) describes, an ELF descriptor can have multiple activations, and multiple ELF descriptors may share a single file descriptor. Generally, `elf_cntl` commands apply to all activations of *elf*. Moreover, if the ELF descriptor is associated with an archive file, descriptors for members within the archive will also be affected as described below. Unless stated otherwise, operations on archive members do not affect the descriptor for the containing archive.

The *cmd* argument tells what actions to take and may have the following values.

ELF_C_FDDONE
> This value tells the library not to use the file descriptor associated with *elf*. A program should use this command when it has requested all the information it cares to use and wishes to avoid the overhead of reading the rest of the file. The memory for all completed operations remains valid, but later file operations, such as the initial `elf_getdata` for a section, will fail if the data are not in memory already.

ELF_C_FDREAD
> This command is similar to ELF_C_FDDONE, except it forces the library to read the rest of the file. A program should use this command when it must close the file descriptor but has not yet read everything it needs from the file. After `elf_cntl` completes the ELF_C_FDREAD command, future operations, such as `elf_getdata`, will use the memory version of the file without needing to use the file descriptor.

If `elf_cntl` succeeds, it returns zero. Otherwise *elf* was null or an error occurred, and the function returns −1.

SEE ALSO
elf(3E), elf_begin(3E), elf_getdata(3E), elf_rawfile(3E).

NOTE
If the program wishes to use the "raw" operations [see `elf_rawdata`, which `elf_getdata`(3E) describes, and `elf_rawfile`(3E)] after disabling the file descriptor with ELF_C_FDDONE or ELF_C_FDREAD, it must execute the raw operations explicitly beforehand. Otherwise, the raw file operations will fail. Calling `elf_rawfile` makes the entire image available, thus supporting subsequent `elf_rawdata` calls.

elf_end(3E)

NAME
elf_end – finish using an object file

SYNOPSIS
cc [*flag* ...] *file* ... −lelf [*library* ...]

#include <libelf.h>

int elf_end(Elf *elf);

DESCRIPTION
A program uses **elf_end** to terminate an ELF descriptor, *elf*, and to deallocate data associated with the descriptor. Until the program terminates a descriptor, the data remain allocated. *elf* should be a value previously returned by **elf_begin**; a null pointer is allowed as an argument, to simplify error handling. If the program wishes to write data associated with the ELF descriptor to the file, it must use **elf_update** before calling **elf_end**.

As **elf_begin**(3E) explains, a descriptor can have more than one activation. Calling **elf_end** removes one activation and returns the remaining activation count. The library does not terminate the descriptor until the activation count reaches zero. Consequently, a zero return value indicates the ELF descriptor is no longer valid.

SEE ALSO
elf(3E), elf_begin(3E), elf_update(3E).

NAME
elf_errmsg, elf_errno – error handling

SYNOPSIS
cc [flag ...] file ... -lelf [library ...]

#include <libelf.h>

const char *elf_errmsg(int err);
int elf_errno(void);

DESCRIPTION
If an ELF library function fails, a program may call elf_errno to retrieve the library's internal error number. As a side effect, this function resets the internal error number to zero, which indicates no error.

elf_errmsg takes an error number, *err*, and returns a null-terminated error message (with no trailing new-line) that describes the problem. A zero *err* retrieves a message for the most recent error. If no error has occurred, the return value is a null pointer (not a pointer to the null string). Using *err* of −1 also retrieves the most recent error, except it guarantees a non-null return value, even when no error has occurred. If no message is available for the given number, elf_errmsg returns a pointer to an appropriate message. This function does not have the side effect of clearing the internal error number.

EXAMPLE
The following fragment clears the internal error number and checks it later for errors. Unless an error occurs after the first call to elf_errno, the next call will return zero.

```
(void)elf_errno();
while (more_to_do)
{
        /* processing ... */
        if ((err = elf_errno()) != 0)
        {
                msg = elf_errmsg(err);
                /* print msg */
        }
}
```

SEE ALSO
elf(3E), elf_version(3E).

elf_fill(3E)

NAME
elf_fill – set fill byte

SYNOPSIS
cc [*flag* ...] *file* ... −lelf [*library* ...]

#include <libelf.h>

void elf_fill(int fill);

DESCRIPTION
Alignment constraints for ELF files sometimes require the presence of "holes." For example, if the data for one section are required to begin on an eight-byte boundary, but the preceding section is too "short," the library must fill the intervening bytes. These bytes are set to the *fill* character. The library uses zero bytes unless the application supplies a value. See elf_getdata(3E) for more information about these holes.

SEE ALSO
elf(3E), elf_getdata(3E), elf_flag(3E), elf_update(3E).

NOTE
An application can assume control of the object file organization by setting the ELF_F_LAYOUT bit [see elf_flag(3E)]. When this is done, the library does *not* fill holes.

elf_flag(3E)

NAME
elf_flagdata, elf_flagehdr, elf_flagelf, elf_flagphdr, elf_flagscn, elf_flagshdr – manipulate flags

SYNOPSIS
cc [*flag* ...] *file* ... -lelf [*library* ...]

#include <libelf.h>

unsigned elf_flagdata(Elf_Data *data, Elf_Cmd cmd, unsigned flags);

unsigned elf_flagehdr(Elf *elf, Elf_Cmd cmd, unsigned flags);

unsigned elf_flagelf(Elf *elf, Elf_Cmd cmd, unsigned flags);

unsigned elf_flagphdr(Elf *elf, Elf_Cmd cmd, unsigned flags);

unsigned elf_flagscn(Elf_Scn *scn, Elf_Cmd cmd, unsigned flags);

unsigned elf_flagshdr(Elf_Scn *scn, Elf_Cmd cmd, unsigned flags);

DESCRIPTION
These functions manipulate the flags associated with various structures of an ELF file. Given an ELF descriptor (*elf*), a data descriptor (*data*), or a section descriptor (*scn*), the functions may set or clear the associated status bits, returning the updated bits. A null descriptor is allowed, to simplify error handling; all functions return zero for this degenerate case.

cmd may have the following values.

- **ELF_C_CLR** The functions clear the bits that are asserted in *flags*. Only the non-zero bits in *flags* are cleared; zero bits do not change the status of the descriptor.

- **ELF_C_SET** The functions set the bits that are asserted in *flags*. Only the non-zero bits in *flags* are set; zero bits do not change the status of the descriptor.

Descriptions of the defined *flags* bits appear below.

- **ELF_F_DIRTY** When the program intends to write an ELF file, this flag asserts the associated information needs to be written to the file. Thus, for example, a program that wished to update the ELF header of an existing file would call elf_flagehdr with this bit set in *flags* and *cmd* equal to ELF_C_SET. A later call to elf_update would write the marked header to the file.

- **ELF_F_LAYOUT** Normally, the library decides how to arrange an output file. That is, it automatically decides where to place sections, how to align them in the file, etc. If this bit is set for an ELF descriptor, the program assumes responsibility for determining all file positions. This bit is meaningful only for elf_flagelf and applies to the entire file associated with the descriptor.

When a flag bit is set for an item, it affects all the subitems as well. Thus, for example, if the program sets the `ELF_F_DIRTY` bit with `elf_flagelf`, the entire logical file is "dirty."

EXAMPLE

The following fragment shows how one might mark the ELF header to be written to the output file.

```
ehdr = elf32_getehdr(elf);
/* dirty ehdr ... */
elf_flagehdr(elf, ELF_C_SET, ELF_F_DIRTY);
```

SEE ALSO

`elf`(3E), `elf_end`(3E), `elf_getdata`(3E), `elf_getehdr`(3E), `elf_update`(3E).

elf_fsize(3E)

NAME
elf_fsize: elf32_fsize − return the size of an object file type

SYNOPSIS
cc [*flag* ...] *file* ... −lelf [*library* ...]

#include <libelf.h>

size_t elf32_fsize(Elf_Type type, size_t count, unsigned ver);

DESCRIPTION
elf32_fsize gives the size in bytes of the 32-bit file representation of *count* data objects with the given *type*. The library uses version *ver* to calculate the size [see elf(3E) and elf_version(3E)].

Constant values are available for the sizes of fundamental types.

Elf_Type	File Size	Memory Size
ELF_T_ADDR	ELF32_FSZ_ADDR	sizeof(Elf32_Addr)
ELF_T_BYTE	1	sizeof(unsigned char)
ELF_T_HALF	ELF32_FSZ_HALF	sizeof(Elf32_Half)
ELT_T_OFF	ELF32_FSZ_OFF	sizeof(Elf32_Off)
ELF_T_SWORD	ELF32_FSZ_SWORD	sizeof(Elf32_Sword)
ELF_T_WORD	ELF32_FSZ_WORD	sizeof(Elf32_Word)

elf32_fsize returns zero if the value of *type* or *ver* is unknown. See elf_xlate(3E) for a list of the *type* values.

SEE ALSO
elf(3E), elf_version(3E), elf_xlate(3E).

elf_getarhdr(3E)

NAME
elf_getarhdr – retrieve archive member header

SYNOPSIS
cc [flag ...] file ... -lelf [library ...]

#include <libelf.h>

Elf_Arhdr *elf_getarhdr(Elf *elf);

DESCRIPTION
elf_getarhdr returns a pointer to an archive member header, if one is available for the ELF descriptor *elf*. Otherwise, no archive member header exists, an error occurred, or *elf* was null; elf_getarhdr then returns a null value. The header includes the following members:

```
char          *ar_name;
time_t        ar_date;
long          ar_uid;
long          ar_gid;
unsigned long ar_mode;
off_t         ar_size;
char          *ar_rawname;
```

An archive member name, available through ar_name, is a null-terminated string, with the ar format control characters removed. The ar_rawname member holds a null-terminated string that represents the original name bytes in the file, including the terminating slash and trailing blanks as specified in the archive format.

In addition to "regular" archive members, the archive format defines some special members. All special member names begin with a slash (/), distinguishing them from regular members (whose names may not contain a slash). These special members have the names (ar_name) defined below.

/   This is the archive symbol table. If present, it will be the first archive member. A program may access the archive symbol table through elf_getarsym. The information in the symbol table is useful for random archive processing [see elf_rand(3E)].

//   This member, if present, holds a string table for long archive member names. An archive member's header contains a 16-byte area for the name, which may be exceeded in some file systems. The library automatically retrieves long member names from the string table, setting ar_name to the appropriate value.

Under some error conditions, a member's name might not be available. Although this causes the library to set ar_name to a null pointer, the ar_rawname member will be set as usual.

SEE ALSO
elf(3E), elf_begin(3E), elf_getarsym(3E), elf_rand(3E), ar(4).

elf_getarsym(3E)

NAME
elf_getarsym – retrieve archive symbol table

SYNOPSIS
cc [*flag* ...] *file* ... -lelf [*library* ...]

#include <libelf.h>

Elf_Arsym *elf_getarsym(Elf *elf, size_t *ptr);

DESCRIPTION
elf_getarsym returns a pointer to the archive symbol table, if one is available for the ELF descriptor *elf*. Otherwise, the archive doesn't have a symbol table, an error occurred, or *elf* was null; elf_getarsym then returns a null value. The symbol table is an array of structures that include the following members.

```
          char           *as_name;
          size_t         as_off;
          unsigned long  as_hash;
```

These members have the following semantics.

as_name   A pointer to a null-terminated symbol name resides here.

as_off   This value is a byte offset from the beginning of the archive to the member's header. The archive member residing at the given offset defines the associated symbol. Values in **as_off** may be passed as arguments to elf_rand to access the desired archive member.

as_hash   This is a hash value for the name, as computed by elf_hash.

If *ptr* is non-null, the library stores the number of table entries in the location to which *ptr* points. This value is set to zero when the return value is null. The table's last entry, which is included in the count, has a null **as_name**, a zero value for **as_off**, and ~0UL for **as_hash**.

SEE ALSO
elf(3E), elf_getarhdr(3E), elf_hash(3E), elf_rand(3E), ar(4).

elf_getbase(3E)

NAME
elf_getbase – get the base offset for an object file

SYNOPSIS
cc [*flag* ...] *file* ... -lelf [*library* ...]

#include <libelf.h>

off_t elf_getbase(Elf *elf);

DESCRIPTION
elf_getbase returns the file offset of the first byte of the file or archive member associated with *elf*, if it is known or obtainable, and −1 otherwise. A null *elf* is allowed, to simplify error handling; the return value in this case is −1. The base offset of an archive member is the beginning of the member's information, *not* the beginning of the archive member header.

SEE ALSO
elf(3E), elf_begin(3E), ar(4).

NAME
elf_getdata, elf_newdata, elf_rawdata – get section data

SYNOPSIS
cc [*flag* ...] *file* ... -lelf [*library* ...]

#include <libelf.h>

Elf_Data *elf_getdata(Elf_Scn *scn, Elf_Data *data);

Elf_Data *elf_newdata(Elf_Scn *scn);

Elf_Data *elf_rawdata(Elf_Scn *scn, Elf_Data *data);

DESCRIPTION
These functions access and manipulate the data associated with a section descriptor, *scn*. When reading an existing file, a section will have a single data buffer associated with it. A program may build a new section in pieces, however, composing the new data from multiple data buffers. For this reason, "the" data for a section should be viewed as a list of buffers, each of which is available through a data descriptor.

elf_getdata lets a program step through a section's data list. If the incoming data descriptor, *data*, is null, the function returns the first buffer associated with the section. Otherwise, *data* should be a data descriptor associated with *scn*, and the function gives the program access to the next data element for the section. If *scn* is null or an error occurs, elf_getdata returns a null pointer.

elf_getdata translates the data from file representations into memory representations [see elf_xlate(3E)] and presents objects with memory data types to the program, based on the file's *class* [see elf(3E)]. The working library version [see elf_version(3E)] specifies what version of the memory structures the program wishes elf_getdata to present.

elf_newdata creates a new data descriptor for a section, appending it to any data elements already associated with the section. As described below, the new data descriptor appears empty, indicating the element holds no data. For convenience, the descriptor's type (d_type below) is set to ELF_T_BYTE, and the version (d_version below) is set to the working version. The program is responsible for setting (or changing) the descriptor members as needed. This function implicitly sets the ELF_F_DIRTY bit for the section's data [see elf_flag(3E)]. If *scn* is null or an error occurs, elf_newdata returns a null pointer.

elf_rawdata differs from elf_getdata by returning only uninterpreted bytes, regardless of the section type. This function typically should be used only to retrieve a section image from a file being read, and then only when a program must avoid the automatic data translation described below. Moreover, a program may not close or disable [see elf_cntl(3E)] the file descriptor associated with *elf* before the initial raw operation, because elf_rawdata might read the data from the file to ensure it doesn't interfere with elf_getdata. See elf_rawfile(3E) for a related facility that applies to the entire file. When elf_getdata provides the right translation, its use is recommended over elf_rawdata. If *scn* is null or an error occurs, elf_rawdata returns a null pointer.

The `Elf_Data` structure includes the following members.

```
void         *d_buf;
Elf_Type      d_type;
size_t        d_size;
off_t         d_off;
size_t        d_align;
unsigned      d_version;
```

These members are available for direct manipulation by the program. Descriptions appear below.

d_buf   A pointer to the data buffer resides here. A data element with no data has a null pointer.

d_type This member's value specifies the type of the data to which `d_buf` points. A section's type determines how to interpret the section contents, as summarized below.

d_size This member holds the total size, in bytes, of the memory occupied by the data. This may differ from the size as represented in the file. The size will be zero if no data exist. [See the discussion of `SHT_NOBITS` below for more information.]

d_off   This member gives the offset, within the section, at which the buffer resides. This offset is relative to the file's section, not the memory object's.

d_align This member holds the buffer's required alignment, from the beginning of the section. That is, `d_off` will be a multiple of this member's value. For example, if this member's value is four, the beginning of the buffer will be four-byte aligned within the section. Moreover, the entire section will be aligned to the maximum of its constituents, thus ensuring appropriate alignment for a buffer within the section and within the file.

d_version This member holds the version number of the objects in the buffer. When the library originally read the data from the object file, it used the working version to control the translation to memory objects.

DATA ALIGNMENT

As mentioned above, data buffers within a section have explicit alignment constraints. Consequently, adjacent buffers sometimes will not abut, causing "holes" within a section. Programs that create output files have two ways of dealing with these holes.

First, the program can use `elf_fill` to tell the library how to set the intervening bytes. When the library must generate gaps in the file, it uses the fill byte to initialize the data there. The library's initial fill value is zero, and `elf_fill` lets the application change that.

Second, the application can generate its own data buffers to occupy the gaps, filling the gaps with values appropriate for the section being created. A program might even use different fill values for different sections. For example, it could set text sections' bytes to no-operation instructions, while filling data section holes with zero. Using this technique, the library finds no holes to fill, because the application eliminated them.

SECTION AND MEMORY TYPES

`elf_getdata` interprets sections' data according to the section type, as noted in the section header available through `elf_getshdr`. The following table shows the section types and how the library represents them with memory data types for the 32-bit file class. Other classes would have similar tables. By implication, the memory data types control translation by `elf_xlate`.

Section Type	Elf_Type	32-Bit Type
SHT_DYNAMIC	ELF_T_DYN	Elf32_Dyn
SHT_DYNSYM	ELF_T_SYM	Elf32_Sym
SHT_HASH	ELF_T_WORD	Elf32_Word
SHT_NOBITS	ELF_T_BYTE	unsigned char
SHT_NOTE	ELF_T_BYTE	unsigned char
SHT_NULL	*none*	*none*
SHT_PROGBITS	ELF_T_BYTE	unsigned char
SHT_REL	ELF_T_REL	Elf32_Rel
SHT_RELA	ELF_T_RELA	Elf32_Rela
SHT_STRTAB	ELF_T_BYTE	unsigned char
SHT_SYMTAB	ELF_T_SYM	Elf32_Sym
other	ELF_T_BYTE	unsigned char

`elf_rawdata` creates a buffer with type `ELF_T_BYTE`.

As mentioned above, the program's working version controls what structures the library creates for the application. The library similarly interprets section types according to the versions. If a section type "belongs" to a version newer than the application's working version, the library does not translate the section data. Because the application cannot know the data format in this case, the library presents an untranslated buffer of type `ELF_T_BYTE`, just as it would for an unrecognized section type.

A section with a special type, `SHT_NOBITS`, occupies no space in an object file, even when the section header indicates a non-zero size. `elf_getdata` and `elf_rawdata` "work" on such a section, setting the *data* structure to have a null buffer pointer and the type indicated above. Although no data are present, the *d_size* value is set to the size from the section header. When a program is creating a new section of type `SHT_NOBITS`, it should use `elf_newdata` to add data buffers to the section. These "empty" data buffers should have the *d_size* members set to the desired size and the *d_buf* members set to null.

EXAMPLE

The following fragment obtains the string table that holds section names (ignoring error checking). See `elf_strptr`(3E) for a variation of string table handling.

```
        ehdr = elf32_getehdr(elf);
        scn = elf_getscn(elf, (size_t)ehdr->e_shstrndx);
        shdr = elf32_getshdr(scn);
        if (shdr->sh_type != SHT_STRTAB)
        {
                /* not a string table */
        }
        data = 0;
        if ((data = elf_getdata(scn, data)) == 0 || data->d_size == 0)
        {
                /* error or no data */
        }
```

The **e_shstrndx** member in an ELF header holds the section table index of the string table. The program gets a section descriptor for that section, verifies it is a string table, and then retrieves the data. When this fragment finishes, **data->d_buf** points at the first byte of the string table, and **data->d_size** holds the string table's size in bytes.

SEE ALSO

elf(3E), elf_cntl(3E), elf_fill(3E), elf_flag(3E), elf_getehdr(3E), elf_getscn(3E), elf_getshdr(3E), elf_rawfile(3E), elf_version(3E), elf_xlate(3E).

elf_getehdr(3E)

NAME
elf_getehdr: elf32_getehdr, elf32_newehdr – retrieve class-dependent object file header

SYNOPSIS
cc [*flag* ...] *file* ... -lelf [*library* ...]

#include <libelf.h>

Elf32_Ehdr *elf32_getehdr(Elf *elf);

Elf32_Ehdr *elf32_newehdr(Elf *elf);

DESCRIPTION
For a 32-bit class file, `elf32_getehdr` returns a pointer to an ELF header, if one is available for the ELF descriptor *elf*. If no header exists for the descriptor, `elf32_newehdr` allocates a "clean" one, but it otherwise behaves the same as `elf32_getehdr`. It does not allocate a new header if one exists already. If no header exists (for `elf_getehdr`), one cannot be created (for `elf_newehdr`), a system error occurs, the file is not a 32-bit class file, or *elf* is null, both functions return a null pointer.

The header includes the following members.

```
unsigned char  e_ident[EI_NIDENT];
Elf32_Half     e_type;
Elf32_Half     e_machine;
Elf32_Word     e_version;
Elf32_Addr     e_entry;
Elf32_Off      e_phoff;
Elf32_Off      e_shoff;
Elf32_Word     e_flags;
Elf32_Half     e_ehsize;
Elf32_Half     e_phentsize;
Elf32_Half     e_phnum;
Elf32_Half     e_shentsize;
Elf32_Half     e_shnum;
Elf32_Half     e_shstrndx;
```

`elf32_newehdr` automatically sets the `ELF_F_DIRTY` bit [see `elf_flag`(3E)]. A program may use `elf_getident` to inspect the identification bytes from a file.

SEE ALSO
elf(3E), elf_begin(3E), elf_flag(3E), elf_getident(3E).

NAME
elf_getident − retrieve file identification data

SYNOPSIS
cc [*flag* ...] *file* ... −lelf [*library* ...]

#include <libelf.h>

char *elf_getident(Elf *elf, size_t *ptr);

DESCRIPTION
As elf(3E) explains, ELF provides a framework for various classes of files, where basic objects may have 32 bits, 64 bits, etc. To accommodate these differences, without forcing the larger sizes on smaller machines, the initial bytes in an ELF file hold identification information common to all file classes. Every ELF header's e_ident has EI_NIDENT bytes with the following interpretation.

e_ident Index	Value	Purpose
EI_MAG0	ELFMAG0	File identification
EI_MAG1	ELFMAG1	
EI_MAG2	ELFMAG2	
EI_MAG3	ELFMAG3	
EI_CLASS	ELFCLASSNONE	File class
	ELFCLASS32	
	ELFCLASS64	
EI_DATA	ELFDATANONE	Data encoding
	ELFDATA2LSB	
	ELFDATA2MSB	
EI_VERSION	EV_CURRENT	File version
7−15	0	Unused, set to zero

Other kinds of files [see elf_kind(3E)] also may have identification data, though they would not conform to e_ident.

elf_getident returns a pointer to the file's "initial bytes." If the library recognizes the file, a conversion from the file image to the memory image may occur. In any case, the identification bytes are guaranteed not to have been modified, though the size of the unmodified area depends on the file type. If *ptr* is non-null, the library stores the number of identification bytes in the location to which *ptr* points. If no data are present, *elf* is null, or an error occurs, the return value is a null pointer, with zero optionally stored through *ptr*.

SEE ALSO
elf(3E), elf_begin(3E), elf_getehdr(3E), elf_kind(3E), elf_rawfile(3E).

NAME
elf_getphdr: elf32_getphdr, elf32_newphdr − retrieve class-dependent program header table

SYNOPSIS
cc [flag ...] file ... -lelf [library ...]

#include <libelf.h>

Elf32_Phdr *elf32_getphdr(Elf *elf);

Elf32_Phdr *elf32_newphdr(Elf *elf, size_t count);

DESCRIPTION
For a 32-bit class file, **elf32_getphdr** returns a pointer to the program execution header table, if one is available for the ELF descriptor *elf*.

elf32_newphdr allocates a new table with *count* entries, regardless of whether one existed previously, and sets the ELF_F_DIRTY bit for the table [see **elf_flag**(3E)]. Specifying a zero *count* deletes an existing table. Note this behavior differs from that of **elf32_newehdr** [see **elf32_getehdr**(3E)], allowing a program to replace or delete the program header table, changing its size if necessary.

If no program header table exists, the file is not a 32-bit class file, an error occurs, or *elf* is null, both functions return a null pointer. Additionally, **elf32_newphdr** returns a null pointer if *count* is zero.

The table is an array of Elf32_Phdr structures, each of which includes the following members.

             Elf32_Word   p_type;
             Elf32_Off   p_offset;
             Elf32_Addr   p_vaddr;
             Elf32_Addr   p_paddr;
             Elf32_Word   p_filesz;
             Elf32_Word   p_memsz;
             Elf32_Word   p_flags;
             Elf32_Word   p_align;

The ELF header's **e_phnum** member tells how many entries the program header table has [see **elf_getehdr**(3E)]. A program may inspect this value to determine the size of an existing table; **elf32_newphdr** automatically sets the member's value to *count*. If the program is building a new file, it is responsible for creating the file's ELF header before creating the program header table.

SEE ALSO
elf(3E), elf_begin(3E), elf_flag(3E), elf_getehdr(3E).

elf_getscn(3E)

NAME
elf_getscn, elf_ndxscn, elf_newscn, elf_nextscn – get section information

SYNOPSIS
cc [*flag* ...] *file* ... -lelf [*library* ...]

#include <libelf.h>

Elf_Scn *elf_getscn(Elf *elf, size_t index);

size_t elf_ndxscn(Elf_Scn *scn);

Elf_Scn *elf_newscn(Elf *elf);

Elf_Scn *elf_nextscn(Elf *elf, Elf_Scn *scn);

DESCRIPTION
These functions provide indexed and sequential access to the sections associated with the ELF descriptor *elf*. If the program is building a new file, it is responsible for creating the file's ELF header before creating sections; see `elf_getehdr`(3E).

`elf_getscn` returns a section descriptor, given an *index* into the file's section header table. Note the first "real" section has index 1. Although a program can get a section descriptor for the section whose *index* is 0 (SHN_UNDEF, the undefined section), the section has no data and the section header is "empty" (though present). If the specified section does not exist, an error occurs, or *elf* is null, `elf_getscn` returns a null pointer.

`elf_newscn` creates a new section and appends it to the list for *elf*. Because the SHN_UNDEF section is required and not "interesting" to applications, the library creates it automatically. Thus the first call to `elf_newscn` for an ELF descriptor with no existing sections returns a descriptor for section 1. If an error occurs or *elf* is null, `elf_newscn` returns a null pointer.

After creating a new section descriptor, the program can use `elf_getshdr` to retrieve the newly created, "clean" section header. The new section descriptor will have no associated data [see `elf_getdata`(3E)]. When creating a new section in this way, the library updates the e_shnum member of the ELF header and sets the ELF_F_DIRTY bit for the section [see `elf_flag`(3E)]. If the program is building a new file, it is responsible for creating the file's ELF header [see `elf_getehdr`(3E)] before creating new sections.

`elf_nextscn` takes an existing section descriptor, *scn*, and returns a section descriptor for the next higher section. One may use a null *scn* to obtain a section descriptor for the section whose index is 1 (skipping the section whose index is SHN_UNDEF). If no further sections are present or an error occurs, `elf_nextscn` returns a null pointer.

`elf_ndxscn` takes an existing section descriptor, *scn*, and returns its section table index. If *scn* is null or an error occurs, `elf_ndxscn` returns SHN_UNDEF.

EXAMPLE
An example of sequential access appears below. Each pass through the loop processes the next section in the file; the loop terminates when all sections have been processed.

```
        scn = 0;
        while ((scn = elf_nextscn(elf, scn)) != 0)
        {
                /* process section */
        }
```

SEE ALSO

elf(3E), elf_begin(3E), elf_flag(3E), elf_getdata(3E), elf_getehdr(3E), elf_getshdr(3E).

NAME
elf_getshdr: elf32_getshdr – retrieve class-dependent section header

SYNOPSIS
cc [*flag* ...] *file* ... −lelf [*library* ...]

#include <libelf.h>

Elf32_Shdr *elf32_getshdr(Elf_Scn *scn);

DESCRIPTION
For a 32-bit class file, **elf32_getshdr** returns a pointer to a section header for the section descriptor *scn*. Otherwise, the file is not a 32-bit class file, *scn* was null, or an error occurred; **elf32_getshdr** then returns null.

The header includes the following members.

Elf32_Word	sh_name;
Elf32_Word	sh_type;
Elf32_Word	sh_flags;
Elf32_Addr	sh_addr;
Elf32_Off	sh_offset;
Elf32_Word	sh_size;
Elf32_Word	sh_link;
Elf32_Word	sh_info;
Elf32_Word	sh_addralign;
Elf32_Word	sh_entsize;

If the program is building a new file, it is responsible for creating the file's ELF header before creating sections.

SEE ALSO
elf(3E), elf_flag(3E), elf_getscn(3E), elf_strptr(3E).

elf_hash(3E)

NAME
elf_hash – compute hash value

SYNOPSIS
cc [*flag* ...] *file* ... -lelf [*library* ...]

#include <libelf.h>

unsigned long elf_hash(const char *name);

DESCRIPTION
elf_hash computes a hash value, given a null terminated string, *name*. The returned hash value, *h*, can be used as a bucket index, typically after computing *h* mod *x* to ensure appropriate bounds.

Hash tables may be built on one machine and used on another because elf_hash uses unsigned arithmetic to avoid possible differences in various machines' signed arithmetic. Although *name* is shown as char* above, elf_hash treats it as unsigned char* to avoid sign extension differences. Using char* eliminates type conflicts with expressions such as elf_hash("name").

ELF files' symbol hash tables are computed using this function [see elf_getdata(3E) and elf_xlate(3E)]. The hash value returned is guaranteed not to be the bit pattern of all ones (~0UL).

SEE ALSO
elf(3E), elf_getdata(3E), elf_xlate(3E).

elf_kind(3E)

NAME
elf_kind – determine file type

SYNOPSIS
cc [*flag* ...] *file* ... -lelf [*library* ...]

#include <libelf.h>

Elf_Kind elf_kind(Elf *elf);

DESCRIPTION
This function returns a value identifying the kind of file associated with an ELF descriptor (*elf*). Currently defined values appear below.

ELF_K_AR The file is an archive [see ar(4)]. An ELF descriptor may also be associated with an archive *member*, not the archive itself, and then elf_kind identifies the member's type.

ELF_K_COFF The file is a COFF object file. elf_begin(3E) describes the library's handling for COFF files.

ELF_K_ELF The file is an ELF file. The program may use elf_getident to determine the class. Other functions, such as elf_getehdr, are available to retrieve other file information.

ELF_K_NONE This indicates a kind of file unknown to the library.

Other values are reserved, to be assigned as needed to new kinds of files. *elf* should be a value previously returned by elf_begin. A null pointer is allowed, to simplify error handling, and causes elf_kind to return ELF_K_NONE.

SEE ALSO
elf(3E), elf_begin(3E), elf_getehdr(3E), elf_getident(3E), ar(4).

NAME
elf_next – sequential archive member access

SYNOPSIS
cc [*flag* ...] *file* ... -lelf [*library* ...]

#include <libelf.h>

Elf_Cmd elf_next(Elf *elf);

DESCRIPTION
`elf_next`, `elf_rand`, and `elf_begin` manipulate simple object files and archives. *elf* is an ELF descriptor previously returned from `elf_begin`.

`elf_next` provides sequential access to the next archive member. That is, having an ELF descriptor, *elf*, associated with an archive member, `elf_next` prepares the containing archive to access the following member when the program calls `elf_begin`. After successfully positioning an archive for the next member, `elf_next` returns the value `ELF_C_READ`. Otherwise, the open file was not an archive, *elf* was null, or an error occurred, and the return value is `ELF_C_NULL`. In either case, the return value may be passed as an argument to `elf_begin`, specifying the appropriate action.

SEE ALSO
elf(3E), elf_begin(3E), elf_getarsym(3E), elf_rand(3E), ar(4).

elf_rand(3E)   elf_rand(3E)

NAME
elf_rand – random archive member access

SYNOPSIS
cc [*flag* ...] *file* ... −lelf [*library* ...]

#include <libelf.h>

size_t elf_rand(Elf *elf, size_t offset);

DESCRIPTION
elf_rand, elf_next, and elf_begin manipulate simple object files and archives. *elf* is an ELF descriptor previously returned from elf_begin.

elf_rand provides random archive processing, preparing *elf* to access an arbitrary archive member. *elf* must be a descriptor for the archive itself, not a member within the archive. *offset* gives the byte offset from the beginning of the archive to the archive header of the desired member. See elf_getarsym(3E) for more information about archive member offsets. When elf_rand works, it returns *offset*. Otherwise it returns 0, because an error occurred, *elf* was null, or the file was not an archive (no archive member can have a zero offset). A program may mix random and sequential archive processing.

EXAMPLE
An archive starts with a "magic string" that has SARMAG bytes; the initial archive member follows immediately. An application could thus provide the following function to rewind an archive (the function returns −1 for errors and 0 otherwise).

```
#include <ar.h>
#include <libelf.h>

int
rewindelf(Elf *elf)
{
        if (elf_rand(elf, (size_t)SARMAG) == SARMAG)
                return 0;
        return -1;
}
```

SEE ALSO
elf(3E), elf_begin(3E), elf_getarsym(3E), elf_next(3E), ar(4).

elf_rawfile(3E)

NAME
`elf_rawfile` – retrieve uninterpreted file contents

SYNOPSIS
cc [*flag* ...] *file* ... -lelf [*library* ...]

#include <libelf.h>

char *elf_rawfile(Elf *elf, size_t *ptr);

DESCRIPTION
`elf_rawfile` returns a pointer to an uninterpreted byte image of the file. This function should be used only to retrieve a file being read. For example, a program might use `elf_rawfile` to retrieve the bytes for an archive member.

A program may not close or disable [see `elf_cntl`(3E)] the file descriptor associated with *elf* before the initial call to `elf_rawfile`, because `elf_rawfile` might have to read the data from the file if it does not already have the original bytes in memory. Generally, this function is more efficient for unknown file types than for object files. The library implicitly translates object files in memory, while it leaves unknown files unmodified. Thus asking for the uninterpreted image of an object file may create a duplicate copy in memory.

`elf_rawdata` [see `elf_getdata`(3E)] is a related function, providing access to sections within a file.

If *ptr* is non-null, the library also stores the file's size, in bytes, in the location to which *ptr* points. If no data are present, *elf* is null, or an error occurs, the return value is a null pointer, with zero optionally stored through *ptr*.

SEE ALSO
`elf`(3E), `elf_begin`(3E), `elf_cntl`(3E), `elf_getdata`(3E), `elf_getehdr`(3E), `elf_getident`(3E), `elf_kind`(3E).

NOTE
A program that uses `elf_rawfile` and that also interprets the same file as an object file potentially has two copies of the bytes in memory. If such a program requests the raw image first, before it asks for translated information (through such functions as `elf_getehdr`, `elf_getdata`, and so on), the library "freezes" its original memory copy for the raw image. It then uses this frozen copy as the source for creating translated objects, without reading the file again. Consequently, the application should view the raw file image returned by `elf_rawfile` as a read-only buffer, unless it wants to alter its own view of data subsequently translated. In any case, the application may alter the translated objects without changing bytes visible in the raw image.

Multiple calls to `elf_rawfile` with the same ELF descriptor return the same value; the library does not create duplicate copies of the file.

NAME
elf_strptr – make a string pointer

SYNOPSIS
cc [*flag* ...] *file* ... -lelf [*library* ...]

#include <libelf.h>

char *elf_strptr(Elf *elf, size_t section, size_t offset);

DESCRIPTION
This function converts a string section *offset* to a string pointer. *elf* identifies the file in which the string section resides, and *section* gives the section table index for the strings. elf_strptr normally returns a pointer to a string, but it returns a null pointer when *elf* is null, *section* is invalid or is not a section of type SHT_STRTAB, the section data cannot be obtained, *offset* is invalid, or an error occurs.

EXAMPLE
A prototype for retrieving section names appears below. The file header specifies the section name string table in the e_shstrndx member. The following code loops through the sections, printing their names.

```
            if ((ehdr = elf32_getehdr(elf)) == 0)
            {
                    /* handle the error */
                    return;
            }
            ndx = ehdr->e_shstrndx;
            scn = 0;
            while ((scn = elf_nextscn(elf, scn)) != 0)
            {
                    char    *name = 0;
                    if ((shdr = elf32_getshdr(scn)) != 0)
                      name = elf_strptr(elf, ndx, (size_t)shdr->sh_name);
                    printf("'%s'\n", name? name: "(null)");
            }
```

SEE ALSO
elf(3E), elf_getdata(3E), elf_getshdr(3E), elf_xlate(3E).

NOTE
A program may call elf_getdata to retrieve an entire string table section. For some applications, that would be both more efficient and more convenient than using elf_strptr.

NAME

elf_update – update an ELF descriptor

SYNOPSIS

cc [flag ...] file ... -lelf [library ...]

#include <libelf.h>

off_t elf_update(Elf *elf, Elf_Cmd cmd);

DESCRIPTION

elf_update causes the library to examine the information associated with an ELF descriptor, *elf*, and to recalculate the structural data needed to generate the file's image.

cmd may have the following values.

ELF_C_NULL   This value tells elf_update to recalculate various values, updating only the ELF descriptor's memory structures. Any modified structures are flagged with the ELF_F_DIRTY bit. A program thus can update the structural information and then reexamine them without changing the file associated with the ELF descriptor. Because this does not change the file, the ELF descriptor may allow reading, writing, or both reading and writing [see elf_begin(3E)].

ELF_C_WRITE   If *cmd* has this value, elf_update duplicates its ELF_C_NULL actions and also writes any "dirty" information associated with the ELF descriptor to the file. That is, when a program has used elf_getdata or the elf_flag facilities to supply new (or update existing) information for an ELF descriptor, those data will be examined, coordinated, translated if necessary [see elf_xlate(3E)], and written to the file. When portions of the file are written, any ELF_F_DIRTY bits are reset, indicating those items no longer need to be written to the file [see elf_flag(3E)]. The sections' data are written in the order of their section header entries, and the section header table is written to the end of the file.

When the ELF descriptor was created with elf_begin, it must have allowed writing the file. That is, the elf_begin command must have been either ELF_C_RDWR or ELF_C_WRITE.

If elf_update succeeds, it returns the total size of the file image (not the memory image), in bytes. Otherwise an error occurred, and the function returns −1.

When updating the internal structures, elf_update sets some members itself. Members listed below are the application's responsibility and retain the values given by the program.

	Member	Notes
ELF Header	`e_ident[EI_DATA]`	Library controls other `e_ident` values
	`e_type`	
	`e_machine`	
	`e_version`	
	`e_entry`	
	`e_phoff`	Only when `ELF_F_LAYOUT` asserted
	`e_shoff`	Only when `ELF_F_LAYOUT` asserted
	`e_flags`	
	`e_shstrndx`	

	Member	Notes
Program Header	`p_type`	The application controls all program header entries
	`p_offset`	
	`p_vaddr`	
	`p_paddr`	
	`p_filesz`	
	`p_memsz`	
	`p_flags`	
	`p_align`	

	Member	Notes
Section Header	`sh_name`	
	`sh_type`	
	`sh_flags`	
	`sh_addr`	
	`sh_offset`	Only when `ELF_F_LAYOUT` asserted
	`sh_size`	Only when `ELF_F_LAYOUT` asserted
	`sh_link`	
	`sh_info`	
	`sh_addralign`	Only when `ELF_F_LAYOUT` asserted
	`sh_entsize`	

	Member	Notes
Data Descriptor	d_buf d_type d_size d_off d_align d_version	Only when `ELF_F_LAYOUT` asserted

Note the program is responsible for two particularly important members (among others) in the ELF header. The `e_version` member controls the version of data structures written to the file. If the version is `EV_NONE`, the library uses its own internal version. The `e_ident[EI_DATA]` entry controls the data encoding used in the file. As a special case, the value may be `ELFDATANONE` to request the native data encoding for the host machine. An error occurs in this case if the native encoding doesn't match a file encoding known by the library.

Further note that the program is responsible for the `sh_entsize` section header member. Although the library sets it for sections with known types, it cannot reliably know the correct value for all sections. Consequently, the library relies on the program to provide the values for unknown section type. If the entry size is unknown or not applicable, the value should be set to zero.

When deciding how to build the output file, `elf_update` obeys the alignments of individual data buffers to create output sections. A section's most strictly aligned data buffer controls the section's alignment. The library also inserts padding between buffers, as necessary, to ensure the proper alignment of each buffer.

SEE ALSO

elf(3E), elf_begin(3E), elf_flag(3E), elf_fsize(3E), elf_getdata(3E), elf_getehdr(3E), elf_getshdr(3E), elf_xlate(3E).

NOTE

As mentioned above, the `ELF_C_WRITE` command translates data as necessary, before writing them to the file. This translation is *not* always transparent to the application program. If a program has obtained pointers to data associated with a file [for example, see elf_getehdr(3E) and elf_getdata(3E)], the program should reestablish the pointers after calling `elf_update`.

As elf_begin(3E) describes, a program may "update" a COFF file to make the image consistent for ELF. The `ELF_C_NULL` command updates only the memory image; one can use the `ELF_C_WRITE` command to modify the file as well. Absolute executable files (a.out files) require special alignment, which cannot normally be preserved between COFF and ELF. Consequently, one may not update an executable COFF file with the `ELF_C_WRITE` command (though `ELF_C_NULL` is allowed).

NAME
elf_version – coordinate ELF library and application versions

SYNOPSIS
cc [*flag* ...] *file* ... -lelf [*library* ...]

#include <libelf.h>

unsigned elf_version(unsigned ver);

DESCRIPTION
As elf(3E) explains, the program, the library, and an object file have independent notions of the "latest" ELF version. elf_version lets a program determine the ELF library's *internal version*. It further lets the program specify what memory types it uses by giving its own *working version*, *ver*, to the library. Every program that uses the ELF library must coordinate versions as described below.

The header file <libelf.h> supplies the version to the program with the macro EV_CURRENT. If the library's internal version (the highest version known to the library) is lower than that known by the program itself, the library may lack semantic knowledge assumed by the program. Accordingly, elf_version will not accept a working version unknown to the library.

Passing *ver* equal to EV_NONE causes elf_version to return the library's internal version, without altering the working version. If *ver* is a version known to the library, elf_version returns the previous (or initial) working version number. Otherwise, the working version remains unchanged and elf_version returns EV_NONE.

EXAMPLE
The following excerpt from an application program protects itself from using an older library.

```
if (elf_version(EV_CURRENT) == EV_NONE)
{
        /* library out of date */
        /* recover from error */
}
```

NOTES
The working version should be the same for all operations on a particular elf descriptor. Changing the version between operations on a descriptor will probably not give the expected results.

SEE ALSO
elf(3E), elf_begin(3E), elf_xlate(3E).

elf_xlate(3E)

NAME
elf_xlate: elf32_xlatetof, elf32_xlatetom – class-dependent data translation

SYNOPSIS
cc [*flag* ...] *file* ... -lelf [*library* ...]

#include <libelf.h>

Elf_Data *elf32_xlatetof(Elf_Data *dst, const Elf_Data *src,
    unsigned encode);

Elf_Data *elf32_xlatetom(Elf_Data *dst, const Elf_Data *src,
    unsigned encode);

DESCRIPTION
elf32_xlatetom translates various data structures from their 32-bit class file representations to their memory representations; elf32_xlatetof provides the inverse. This conversion is particularly important for cross development environments. *src* is a pointer to the source buffer that holds the original data; *dst* is a pointer to a destination buffer that will hold the translated copy. *encode* gives the byte encoding in which the file objects are (to be) represented and must have one of the encoding values defined for the ELF header's e_ident[EI_DATA] entry [see elf_getident(3E)]. If the data can be translated, the functions return *dst*. Otherwise, they return null because an error occurred, such as incompatible types, destination buffer overflow, etc.

elf_getdata(3E) describes the Elf_Data descriptor, which the translation routines use as follows.

d_buf   Both the source and destination must have valid buffer pointers.

d_type   This member's value specifies the type of the data to which d_buf points and the type of data to be created in the destination. The program supplies a d_type value in the source; the library sets the destination's d_type to the same value. These values are summarized below.

d_size   This member holds the total size, in bytes, of the memory occupied by the source data and the size allocated for the destination data. If the destination buffer is not large enough, the routines do not change its original contents. The translation routines reset the destination's d_size member to the actual size required, after the translation occurs. The source and destination sizes may differ.

d_version   This member holds version number of the objects (desired) in the buffer. The source and destination versions are independent.

Translation routines allow the source and destination buffers to coincide. That is, dst->d_buf may equal src->d_buf. Other cases where the source and destination buffers overlap give undefined behavior.

Elf_Type	32-Bit Memory Type
ELF_T_ADDR	Elf32_Addr
ELF_T_BYTE	unsigned char
ELF_T_DYN	Elf32_Dyn
ELF_T_EHDR	Elf32_Ehdr
ELF_T_HALF	Elf32_Half
ELT_T_OFF	Elf32_Off
ELF_T_PHDR	Elf32_Phdr
ELF_T_REL	Elf32_Rel
ELF_T_RELA	Elf32_Rela
ELF_T_SHDR	Elf32_Shdr
ELF_T_SWORD	Elf32_Sword
ELF_T_SYM	Elf32_Sym
ELF_T_WORD	Elf32_Word

"Translating" buffers of type ELF_T_BYTE does not change the byte order.

SEE ALSO

elf(3E), elf_fsize(3E), elf_getdata(3E), elf_getident(3E).

nlist(3E)

NAME
nlist – get entries from name list

SYNOPSIS
cc [*flag* ...] *file* ... -lelf [*library* ...]

#include <nlist.h>

int nlist (const char *filename, struct nlist *nl);

DESCRIPTION
nlist examines the name list in the executable file whose name is pointed to by *filename*, and selectively extracts a list of values and puts them in the array of nlist structures pointed to by *nl*. The name list *nl* consists of an array of structures containing names of variables, types, and values. The list is terminated with a null name, that is, a null string is in the name position of the structure. Each variable name is looked up in the name list of the file. If the name is found, the type, value, storage class, and section number of the name are inserted in the other fields. The type field may be set to 0 if the file was not compiled with the –g option to cc(1). nlist will always return the information for an external symbol of a given name if the name exists in the file. If an external symbol does not exist, and there is more than one symbol with the specified name in the file (such as static symbols defined in separate files), the values returned will be for the last occurrence of that name in the file. If the name is not found, all fields in the structure except n_name are set to 0.

This function is useful for examining the system name list kept in the file /stand/unix. In this way programs can obtain system addresses that are up to date.

SEE ALSO
a.out(4).

DIAGNOSTICS
All value entries are set to 0 if the file cannot be read or if it does not contain a valid name list.

nlist returns 0 on success, –1 on error.

3G

3G

basename(3G)

NAME
basename – return the last element of a path name

SYNOPSIS
cc [*flag* ...] *file* ... −lgen [*library* ...]

#include <libgen.h>

char *basename (char *path);

DESCRIPTION
Given a pointer to a null-terminated character string that contains a path name, basename returns a pointer to the last element of *path*. Trailing "/" characters are deleted.

If *path* or *path* is zero, pointer to a static constant "." is returned.

EXAMPLES

Input string	Output pointer
/usr/lib	lib
/usr/	usr
/	/

SEE ALSO
dirname(3G).
basename(1) in the *User's Reference Manual*.

bgets(3G)

NAME
bgets – read stream up to next delimiter

SYNOPSIS
cc [*flag* ...] *file* ... –lgen [*library* ...]

#include <libgen.h>

char *bgets (char *buffer, size_t *count, FILE *stream,
    const char *breakstring);

DESCRIPTION
bgets reads characters from *stream* into *buffer* until either *count* is exhausted or one of the characters in *breakstring* is encountered in the stream. The read data is terminated with a null byte ('\0') and a pointer to the trailing null is returned. If a *breakstring* character is encountered, the last non-null is the delimiter character that terminated the scan.

Note that, except for the fact that the returned value points to the end of the read string rather than to the beginning, the call

    bgets (buffer, sizeof buffer, stream, "\n");

is identical to

    fgets (buffer, sizeof buffer, stream);

There is always enough room reserved in the buffer for the trailing null.

If *breakstring* is a null pointer, the value of *breakstring* from the previous call is used. If *breakstring* is null at the first call, no characters will be used to delimit the string.

EXAMPLES
#include   <libgen.h>

char buffer[8];
/* read in first user name from /etc/passwd */
fp = fopen("/etc/passwd","r");
bgets(buffer, 8, fp, ":");

DIAGNOSTICS
NULL is returned on error or end-of-file. Reporting the condition is delayed to the next call if any characters were read but not yet returned.

SEE ALSO
gets(3S).

NAME

bufsplit – split buffer into fields

SYNOPSIS

cc [*flag* ...] *file* ... -lgen [*library* ...]

#include <libgen.h>

size_t bufsplit (char *buf, size_t n, char **a);

DESCRIPTION

bufsplit examines the buffer, *buf*, and assigns values to the pointer array, *a*, so that the pointers point to the first *n* fields in *buf* that are delimited by tabs or new-lines.

To change the characters used to separate fields, call bufsplit with *buf* pointing to the string of characters, and *n* and *a* set to zero. For example, to use ':', '.', and ',' as separators along with tab and new-line:

bufsplit (":.,\t\n", 0, (char**)0);

RETURN VALUE

The number of fields assigned in the array *a*. If *buf* is zero, the return value is zero and the array is unchanged. Otherwise the value is at least one. The remainder of the elements in the array are assigned the address of the null byte at the end of the buffer.

EXAMPLES

```
/*
 * set a[0] = "This", a[1] = "is", a[2] = "a",
 * a[3] = "test"
 */
bufsplit("This\tis\ta\ttest\n", 4, a);
```

NOTES

bufsplit changes the delimiters to null bytes in *buf*.

copylist(3G)

NAME
copylist – copy a file into memory

SYNOPSIS
cc [*flag* ...] *file* ... −lgen [*library* ...]

#include <libgen.h>

char *copylist (const char *filenm, off_t *szptr);

DESCRIPTION
copylist copies a list of items from a file into freshly allocated memory, replacing new-lines with null characters. It expects two arguments: a pointer *filenm* to the name of the file to be copied, and a pointer *szptr* to a variable where the size of the file will be stored.

Upon success, copylist returns a pointer to the memory allocated. Otherwise it returns NULL if it has trouble finding the file, calling malloc, or opening the file.

EXAMPLES
```
/* read "file" into buf */
off_t size;
char *buf;
buf = copylist("file", &size);
for (i = 0; i < size; i++)
    if(buf[i])
        putchar(buf[i]);
    else
        putchar('\n');
```

SEE ALSO
malloc(3C).

dirname(3G) dirname(3G)

NAME
dirname – report the parent directory name of a file path name

SYNOPSIS
cc [flag ...] file ... -lgen [library ...]

#include <libgen.h>

char *dirname (char *path);

DESCRIPTION
Given a pointer to a null-terminated character string that contains a file system path name, dirname returns a pointer to a static constant string that is the parent directory of that file. In doing this, it sometimes places a null byte in the path name after the next to last element, so the content of *path* must be disposable. Trailing "/" characters in the path are not counted as part of the path.

If *path* or *path is zero, a pointer to a static constant "." is returned.

dirname and basename together yield a complete path name. dirname (*path*) is the directory where basename (*path*) is found.

EXAMPLES
A simple file name and the strings "." and ".." all have "." as their return value.

Input string	Output pointer
/usr/lib	/usr
/usr/	/
usr	.
/	/
.	.
..	.

The following code reads a path name, changes directory to the appropriate directory [see chdir(2)], and opens the file.

```
char path[100], *pathcopy;
int fd;
gets (path);
pathcopy = strdup (path);
chdir (dirname (pathcopy) );
fd = open (basename (path), O_RDONLY);
```

SEE ALSO
chdir(2), basename(3G).

basename(1) in the *User's Reference Manual*.

NAME
gmatch – shell global pattern matching

SYNOPSIS
cc [*flag* ...] *file* ... −lgen [*library* ...]

#include <libgen.h>

int gmatch (const char *str, const char *pattern);

DESCRIPTION
gmatch checks whether the null-terminated string *str* matches the null-terminated pattern string *pattern*. See the sh(1) section "File Name Generation" for a discussion of pattern matching. gmatch returns non-zero if the pattern matches the string, zero if the pattern doesn't. A backslash ('\') is used as an escape character in pattern strings.

EXAMPLE
    char *s;

    gmatch (s, "*[a\-]")

gmatch returns non-zero (true) for all strings with 'a' or '−' as their last character.

SEE ALSO
sh(1) in the *User's Reference Manual*

isencrypt(3G)													isencrypt(3G)

NAME
isencrypt – determine whether a character buffer is encrypted

SYNOPSIS
cc [*flag* ...] *file* ... −lgen [*library* ...]

#include <libgen.h>

int isencrypt (const char *fbuf, size_t ninbuf);

DESCRIPTION
isencrypt uses heuristics to determine whether a buffer of characters is encrypted. It requires two arguments: a pointer to an array of characters and the number of characters in the buffer.

isencrypt assumes that the file is not encrypted if all the characters in the first block are ASCII characters. If there are non-ASCII characters in the first *ninbuf* characters, isencrypt assumes that the buffer is encrypted if the setlocale LC_CTYPE category is set to C or ascii.

If the LC_CTYPE category is set to a value other than C or ascii, then isencrypt uses a combination of heuristics to determine if the buffer is encrypted. If *ninbuf* has at least 64 characters, a chi-square test is used to determine if the bytes in the buffer have a uniform distribution; and isencrypt assumes the buffer is encrypted if it does. If the buffer has less than 64 characters, a check is made for null characters and a terminating new-line to determine whether the buffer is encrypted.

DIAGNOSTICS
If the buffer is encrypted, 1 is returned; otherwise zero is returned.

SEE ALSO
setlocale(3C).

mkdirp(3G)

NAME
mkdirp, rmdirp – create, remove directories in a path

SYNOPSIS
cc [*flag* ...] *file* ... −lgen [*library* ...]

#include <libgen.h>

int mkdirp (const char *path, mode_t mode);

int rmdirp (char *d, char *d1);

DESCRIPTION
mkdirp creates all the missing directories in the given *path* with the given *mode*. [See chmod(2) for the values of *mode*.]

rmdirp removes directories in path *d*. This removal starts at the end of the path and moves back toward the root as far as possible. If an error occurs, the remaining path is stored in *d1*. rmdirp returns a 0 only if it is able to remove every directory in the path.

EXAMPLES
```
/* create scratch directories */
if(mkdirp("/tmp/sub1/sub2/sub3", 0755) == -1) {
    fprintf(stderr, "cannot create directory");
    exit(1);
}
chdir("/tmp/sub1/sub2/sub3");
.
.
.
/* cleanup */
chdir("/tmp");
rmdirp("sub1/sub2/sub3");
```

SEE ALSO
mkdir(2), rmdir(2).

DIAGNOSTICS
If a needed directory cannot be created, mkdirp returns −1 and sets errno to one of the mkdir error numbers. If all the directories are created, or existed to begin with, it returns zero.

NOTES
mkdirp uses malloc to allocate temporary space for the string.

rmdirp returns −2 if a "." or ".." is in the path and −3 if an attempt is made to remove the current directory. If an error occurs other than one of the above, −1 is returned.

p2open(3G)

NAME
p2open, p2close – open, close pipes to and from a command

SYNOPSIS
cc [*flag* ...] *file* ... −lgen [*library* ...]

```
#include <libgen.h>

int p2open (const char *cmd, FILE *fp[2]);

int p2close (FILE *fp[2]);
```

DESCRIPTION
p2open forks and execs a shell running the command line pointed to by *cmd*. On return, fp[0] points to a FILE pointer to write the command's standard input and fp[1] points to a FILE pointer to read from the command's standard output. In this way the program has control over the input and output of the command.

The function returns 0 if successful; otherwise it returns −1.

p2close is used to close the file pointers that p2open opened. It waits for the process to terminate and returns the process status. It returns 0 if successful; otherwise it returns −1.

EXAMPLES
```
#include <stdio.h>
#include <libgen.h>

main(argc,argv)
int argc;
char **argv;
{
        FILE *fp[2];
        pid_t pid;
        char buf[16];

        pid=p2open("/usr/bin/cat", fp);
        if ( pid == 0 ) {
                fprintf(stderr, "p2open failed\n");
                exit(1);
        }
        write(fileno(fp[0]),"This is a test\n", 16);
        if(read(fileno(fp[1]), buf, 16) <=0)
                fprintf(stderr, "p2open failed\n");
        else
                write(1, buf, 16);
        (void)p2close(fp);
}
```

SEE ALSO
fclose(3S), popen(3S), setbuf(3S).

DIAGNOSTICS
A common problem is having too few file descriptors. p2close returns −1 if the two file pointers are not from the same p2open.

NOTES

Buffered writes on `fp[0]` can make it appear that the command is not listening. Judiciously placed `fflush` calls or unbuffering `fp[0]` can be a big help; see `fclose`(3S).

Many commands use buffered output when connected to a pipe. That, too, can make it appear as if things are not working.

Usage is not the same as for **popen**, although it is closely related.

NAME
pathfind – search for named file in named directories

SYNOPSIS
cc [*flag* ...] *file* ... −lgen [*library* ...]

#include <libgen.h>

char *pathfind (const char *path, const char *name, const char *mode);

DESCRIPTION
pathfind searches the directories named in *path* for the file *name*. The directories named in *path* are separated by semicolons. *mode* is a string of option letters chosen from the set **rwxfbcdpugks**:

Letter	Meaning
r	readable
w	writable
x	executable
f	normal file
b	block special
c	character special
d	directory
p	FIFO (pipe)
u	set user ID bit
g	set group ID bit
k	sticky bit
s	size nonzero

Options read, write, and execute are checked relative to the real (not the effective) user ID and group ID of the current process.

If the file *name*, with all the characteristics specified by *mode*, is found in any of the directories specified by *path*, then pathfind returns a pointer to a string containing the member of *path*, followed by a slash character (/), followed by *name*.

If *name* begins with a slash, it is treated as an absolute path name, and *path* is ignored.

An empty *path* member is treated as the current directory. ./ is not prepended at the occurrence of the first match; rather, the unadorned *name* is returned.

EXAMPLES
To find the **ls** command using the PATH environment variable:

pathfind (getenv ("PATH"), "ls", "rx")

SEE ALSO
access(2), mknod(2), stat(2), getenv(3C).
sh(1), test(1) in the *User's Reference Manual*.

DIAGNOSTICS
If no match is found, pathname returns a null pointer, ((char *) 0).

NOTES

The string pointed to by the returned pointer is stored in a static area that is reused on subsequent calls to `pathfind`.

regcmp(3G)

NAME
regcmp, regex – compile and execute regular expression

SYNOPSIS
#include <libgen.h>

cc [*flag* ...] *file* ... -lgen [*library* ...]

char *regcmp (const char *string1 [, char *string2, ...],
    (char *)0);

char *regex (const char *re, const char *subject
    [, char *ret0, ...]);

extern char *__loc1;

DESCRIPTION
regcmp compiles a regular expression (consisting of the concatenated arguments) and returns a pointer to the compiled form. malloc(3C) is used to create space for the compiled form. It is the user's responsibility to free unneeded space so allocated. A NULL return from regcmp indicates an incorrect argument. regcmp(1) has been written to generally preclude the need for this routine at execution time. regcmp is located in library libform.

regex executes a compiled pattern against the subject string. Additional arguments are passed to receive values back. regex returns NULL on failure or a pointer to the next unmatched character on success. A global character pointer __loc1 points to where the match began. regcmp and regex were mostly borrowed from the editor, ed(1); however, the syntax and semantics have been changed slightly. The following are the valid symbols and associated meanings.

[ ] * . ^   These symbols retain their meaning in ed(1).

$ Matches the end of the string; \n matches a newline.

-    Within brackets the minus means *through*. For example, [a-z] is equivalent to [abcd...xyz]. The – can appear as itself only if used as the first or last character. For example, the character class expression []-] matches the characters] and –.

+   A regular expression followed by + means *one or more times*. For example, [0-9]+ is equivalent to [0-9][0-9]*.

{*m*} {*m*,} {*m,u*}
    Integer values enclosed in { } indicate the number of times the preceding regular expression is to be applied. The value *m* is the minimum number and *u* is a number, less than 256, which is the maximum. If only *m* is present (i.e., {*m*}), it indicates the exact number of times the regular expression is to be applied. The value {*m*, } is analogous to {*m,infinity*}. The plus (+) and star (*) operations are equivalent to {1, } and {0, } respectively.

(...)$*n*
    The value of the enclosed regular expression is to be returned. The value will be stored in the (*n*+1)th argument following the subject argument. At most, ten enclosed regular expressions are allowed. regex makes its assignments unconditionally.

(...)   Parentheses are used for grouping. An operator, e.g., *, +, { }, can work on a single character or a regular expression enclosed in parentheses. For example, (a*(cb+)*)$0.

By necessity, all the above defined symbols are special. They must, therefore, be escaped with a \ (backslash) to be used as themselves.

EXAMPLES

The following example matches a leading newline in the subject string pointed at by cursor.

```
char *cursor, *newcursor, *ptr;
   ...
newcursor = regex((ptr = regcmp("^\n", (char *)0)), cursor);
free(ptr);
```

The following example matches through the string Testing3 and returns the address of the character after the last matched character (the "4"). The string Testing3 is copied to the character array ret0.

```
char ret0[9];
char *newcursor, *name;
   ...
name = regcmp("([A-Za-z][A-za-z0-9]{0,7})$0", (char *)0);
newcursor = regex(name, "012Testing345", ret0);
```

The following example applies a precompiled regular expression in file.i [see regcmp(1)] against *string*.

```
#include "file.i"
char *string, *newcursor;
   ...
newcursor = regex(name, string);
```

SEE ALSO

regcmp(1), malloc(3C).

ed(1) in the *User's Reference Manual*.

NOTES

The user program may run out of memory if regcmp is called iteratively without freeing the vectors no longer required.

regexpr(3G)

NAME
regexpr: compile, step, advance – regular expression compile and match routines

SYNOPSIS
cc [*flag* ...] *file* ... −lgen [*library* ...]

#include <regexpr.h>

char *compile (const char *instring, char *expbuf, char *endbuf);

int step (const char *string, char *expbuf);

int advance (const char *string, char *expbuf);

extern char *loc1, *loc2, *locs;

extern int nbra, regerrno, reglength;

extern char *braslist[], *braelist[];

DESCRIPTION
These routines are used to compile regular expressions and match the compiled expressions against lines. The regular expressions compiled are in the form used by ed.

The syntax of the compile routine is as follows:

compile (instring, expbuf, endbuf)

The parameter *instring* is a null-terminated string representing the regular expression.

The parameter *expbuf* points to the place where the compiled regular expression is to be placed. If *expbuf* is NULL, compile uses malloc to allocate the space for the compiled regular expression. If an error occurs, this space is freed. It is the user's responsibility to free unneeded space after the compiled regular expression is no longer needed.

The parameter *endbuf* is one more than the highest address where the compiled regular expression may be placed. This argument is ignored if *expbuf* is NULL. If the compiled expression cannot fit in (*endbuf*−*expbuf*) bytes, compile returns NULL and regerrno (see below) is set to 50.

If compile succeeds, it returns a non-NULL pointer whose value depends on *expbuf*. If *expbuf* is non-NULL, compile returns a pointer to the byte after the last byte in the compiled regular expression. The length of the compiled regular expression is stored in reglength. Otherwise, compile returns a pointer to the space allocated by malloc.

If an error is detected when compiling the regular expression, a NULL pointer is returned from compile and regerrno is set to one of the non-zero error numbers indicated below:

ERROR	MEANING
11	Range endpoint too large.
16	Bad number.
25	"\digit" out of range.
36	Illegal or missing delimiter.
41	No remembered search string.
42	\(~\) imbalance.
43	Too many \(.
44	More than 2 numbers given in \{ ~\}.
45	} expected after \.
46	First number exceeds second in \{ ~\}.
49	[ ] imbalance.
50	Regular expression overflow.

The call to **step** is as follows:

    step (string, expbuf)

The first parameter to **step** is a pointer to a string of characters to be checked for a match. This string should be null-terminated.

The parameter *expbuf* is the compiled regular expression obtained by a call of the function **compile**.

The function **step** returns non-zero if the given string matches the regular expression, and zero if the expressions do not match. If there is a match, two external character pointers are set as a side effect to the call to **step**. The variable set in **step** is loc1. loc1 is a pointer to the first character that matched the regular expression. The variable loc2 points to the character after the last character that matches the regular expression. Thus if the regular expression matches the entire line, loc1 points to the first character of *string* and loc2 points to the null at the end of *string*.

The purpose of **step** is to step through the *string* argument until a match is found or until the end of *string* is reached. If the regular expression begins with ^, **step** tries to match the regular expression at the beginning of the string only.

The function **advance** has the same arguments and side effects as **step**, but it always restricts matches to the beginning of the string.

If one is looking for successive matches in the same string of characters, locs should be set equal to loc2, and **step** should be called with *string* equal to loc2. locs is used by commands like **ed** and **sed** so that global substitutions like s/y*//g do not loop forever, and is NULL by default.

The external variable nbra is used to determine the number of subexpressions in the compiled regular expression. braslist and braelist are arrays of character pointers that point to the start and end of the nbra subexpressions in the matched string. For example, after calling **step** or **advance** with string sabcdefg and regular expression \(abcdef\), braslist[0] will point at a and braelist[0] will point at g. These arrays are used by commands like **ed** and **sed** for substitute replacement patterns that contain the \n notation for subexpressions.

regexpr (3G) regexpr (3G)

Note that it isn't necessary to use the external variables `regerrno`, `nbra`, `loc1`, `loc2` `locs`, `braelist`, and `braslist` if one is only checking whether or not a string matches a regular expression.

EXAMPLES

The following is similar to the regular expression code from `grep`:

```
#include <regexpr.h>
 . . .
if(compile(*argv, (char *)0, (char *)0) == (char *)0)
    regerr(regerrno);
 . . .
if (step(linebuf, expbuf))
    succeed();
```

SEE ALSO

regexp(5).
ed(1), grep(1), sed(1) in the *User's Reference Manual*.

str(3G)

NAME
str: strfind, strrspn, strtrns – string manipulations

SYNOPSIS
cc [*flag* ...] *file* ... -lgen [*library* ...]

#include <libgen.h>

int strfind (const char *as1, const char *as2);

char *strrspn (const char *string, const char *tc);

char * strtrns (const char *str, const char *old, const char *new,
    char *result);

DESCRIPTION
strfind returns the offset of the second string, *as2*, if it is a substring of string *as1*.

strrspn returns a pointer to the first character in the string to be trimmed (all characters from the first character to the end of *string* are in *tc*).

strtrns transforms str and copies it into *result*. Any character that appears in *old* is replaced with the character in the same position in *new*. The *new* result is returned.

EXAMPLES
```
/* find pointer to substring "hello" in as1 */
i = strfind(as1, "hello");

/* trim junk from end of string */
s2 = strrspn(s1, "*?#$%");
*s2 = '\0';

/* transform lower case to upper case */
a1[] = "abcdefghijklmnopqrstuvwxyz";
a2[] = "ABCDEFGHIJKLMNOPQRSTUVWXYZ";
s2 = strtrns(s1, a1, a2, s2);
```

SEE ALSO
string(3C).

DIAGNOSTICS
If the second string is not a substring of the first string strfind returns −1.

strccpy(3G)

NAME
strccpy: streadd, strcadd, strecpy – copy strings, compressing or expanding escape codes

SYNOPSIS
cc [*flag* ...] *file* ... −lgen [*library* ...]

#include <libgen.h>

char *strccpy (char *output, const char *input);

char *strcadd (char *output, const char *input);

char *strecpy (char *output, const char *input, const char *exceptions);

char *streadd (char *output, const char *input, const char *exceptions);

DESCRIPTION
strccpy copies the *input* string, up to a null byte, to the *output* string, compressing the C-language escape sequences (for example, \n, \001) to the equivalent character. A null byte is appended to the output. The *output* argument must point to a space big enough to accommodate the result. If it is as big as the space pointed to by *input* it is guaranteed to be big enough. strccpy returns the *output* argument.

strcadd is identical to strccpy, except that it returns the pointer to the null byte that terminates the output.

strecpy copies the *input* string, up to a null byte, to the *output* string, expanding non-graphic characters to their equivalent C-language escape sequences (for example, \n, \001). The *output* argument must point to a space big enough to accommodate the result; four times the space pointed to by *input* is guaranteed to be big enough (each character could become \ and 3 digits). Characters in the *exceptions* string are not expanded. The *exceptions* argument may be zero, meaning all non-graphic characters are expanded. strecpy returns the *output* argument

streadd is identical to strecpy, except that it returns the pointer to the null byte that terminates the output.

EXAMPLES
    /* expand all but newline and tab */
    strecpy(output, input, "\n\t");

    /* concatenate and compress several strings */
    cp = strcadd(output, input1);
    cp = strcadd(cp, input2);
    cp = strcadd(cp, input3);

SEE ALSO
string(3C), str(3G).

3M

NAME
intro – introduction to math libraries

SYNOPSIS
cc [*flag* ...] *file* ... -lm [*library* ...]

#include <math.h>

DESCRIPTION
This section describes the functions in the math library, libm. Declarations for these functions may be obtained from the #include file math.h. Several generally useful mathematical constants are also defined there [see intro(3) and math(5)].

The math library is not automatically loaded by the C compilation system; use the -l option to cc to access the libraries as shown above.

libm Contains the full set of double-precision routines plus some single-precision routines (designated by the suffix f) that give better performance with less precision. Selected routines are hand-optimized for performance. The optimized routines include sin, cos, tan, atan, atan2, exp, log, log10, pow, and sqrt and their single-precision equivalents.

DEFINITIONS
See intro(3) for C language definitions.

FILES
LIBDIR   usually /usr/ccs/lib
LIBDIR/libm.a

SEE ALSO
cc(1), intro(2), intro(3), math(5).

The "Floating Point Operations" chapter in the *Programmer's Guide: ANSI C and Programming Support Tools*.

DIAGNOSTICS
Error handling varies according to compilation mode. Under the -Xt (default) option to cc, these functions return the conventional values 0, ±HUGE, or NaN when the function is undefined for the given arguments or when the value is not representable. In the -Xa and -Xc compilation modes, ±HUGE_VAL is returned instead of ±HUGE. (HUGE_VAL and HUGE are defined in math.h to be infinity and the largest-magnitude single-precision number, respectively.) In every case, the external variable errno [see intro(2)] is set to the value EDOM or ERANGE, although the value may vary for a given error depending on compilation mode. See the table under matherr(3M) below.

NAME
bessel: j0, j1, jn, y0, y1, yn – Bessel functions

SYNOPSIS
cc [*flag* ...] *file* ... -lm [*library* ...]

#include <math.h>

double j0 (double x);

double j1 (double x);

double jn (int n, double x);

double y0 (double x);

double y1 (double x);

double yn (int n, double x);

DESCRIPTION
j0 and j1 return Bessel functions of x of the first kind of orders 0 and 1, respectively. jn returns the Bessel function of x of the first kind of order n.

y0 and y1 return Bessel functions of x of the second kind of orders 0 and 1, respectively. yn returns the Bessel function of x of the second kind of order n. The value of x must be positive.

SEE ALSO
matherr(3M).

DIAGNOSTICS
Non-positive arguments cause y0, y1, and yn to return the value –HUGE and to set errno to EDOM. In addition, a message indicating DOMAIN error is printed on the standard error output.

Arguments too large in magnitude cause j0, j1, y0, and y1 to return 0 and to set errno to ERANGE. In addition, a message indicating TLOSS error is printed on the standard error output.

Except when the –Xc compilation option is used, these error-handling procedures may be changed with the function matherr. When the –Xa or –Xc compilation options are used, HUGE_VAL is returned instead of HUGE and no error messages are printed.

erf(3M)

NAME
erf, erfc − error function and complementary error function

SYNOPSIS
cc [*flag* ...] *file* ... −lm [*library* ...]

#include <math.h>

double erf (double x);

double erfc (double x);

DESCRIPTION
erf returns the error function of x, defined as

$$\frac{2}{\sqrt{\pi}} \int_0^x e^{-t^2} dt$$

erfc, which returns 1.0 − erf(x), is provided because of the extreme loss of relative accuracy if erf(x) is called for large x and the result subtracted from 1.0 (e.g., for $x = 5$, 12 places are lost).

SEE ALSO
exp(3M).

exp(3M)

NAME
exp, expf, cbrt, log, logf, log10, log10f, pow, powf, sqrt, sqrtf – exponential, logarithm, power, square root functions

SYNOPSIS
cc [flag ...] file ... -lm [library ...]

cc -O -Ksd [flag ...] file ... -J sfm [library ...]

#include <math.h>

double exp (double x);

float expf (float x);

double cbrt (double x);

double log (double x);

float logf (float x);

double log10 (double x);

float log10f (float x);

double pow (double x, double y);

float powf (float x, float y);

double sqrt (double x);

float sqrtf (float x);

DESCRIPTION
exp and expf return e^x.

cbrt returns the cube root of x.

log and logf return the natural logarithm of x. The value of x must be positive.

log10 and log10f return the base ten logarithm of x. The value of x must be positive.

pow and powf return x^y. If x is 0, y must be positive. If x is negative, y must be an integer.

sqrt and sqrtf return the non-negative square root of x. The value of x may not be negative.

SEE ALSO
hypot(3M), matherr(3M), sinh(3M).

DIAGNOSTICS
exp and expf return HUGE when the correct value would overflow, or 0 when the correct value would underflow, and set errno to ERANGE.

log, logf, log10, and log10f return -HUGE and set errno to EDOM when x is non-positive. A message indicating DOMAIN error is printed on standard error.

pow and powf return 0 and set errno to EDOM when x is 0 and y is non-positive, or when x is negative and y is not an integer. In these cases, a message indicating DOMAIN error is printed on standard error. When the correct value for pow or powf would overflow or underflow, these functions return ±HUGE or 0, respectively, and set errno to ERANGE.

exp(3M)　　　　　　　　　　　　　　　　　　　　　　　　　　　　　　　　　　　　　**exp(3M)**

sqrt and sqrtf return 0 and set errno to EDOM when x is negative. A message indicating DOMAIN error is printed on standard error.

Except when the −Xc compilation option is used, these error-handling procedures may be changed with the function matherr. When the −Xa or −Xc compilation options are used, HUGE_VAL is returned instead of HUGE and no error messages are printed. In these compilation modes, pow and powf return 1, with no error, when both x and y are 0; when x is 0 and y is negative, they return −HUGE_VAL and set errno to EDOM. Under −Xc, log and logf return −HUGE_VAL and set errno to ERANGE when x is 0. Under −Xc, sqrt and sqrtf return NaN when x is negative.

NAME

floor, floorf, ceil, ceilf, copysign, fmod, fmodf, fabs, fabsf, rint, remainder − floor, ceiling, remainder, absolute value functions

SYNOPSIS

cc [*flag* ...] *file* ... −lm [*library* ...]

```
#include <math.h>

double floor (double x);

float floorf (float x);

double ceil (double x);

float ceilf (float x);

double copysign (double x, double y);

double fmod (double x, double y);

float fmodf (float x, float y);

double fabs (double x);

float fabsf (float x);

double rint (double x);

double remainder (double x, double y);
```

DESCRIPTION

`floor` and `floorf` return the largest integer not greater than x. `ceil` and `ceilf` return the smallest integer not less than x.

`copysign` returns x but with the sign of y.

`fmod` and `fmodf` return the floating point remainder of the division of x by y. More precisely, they return the number f with the same sign as x, such that $x = iy + f$ for some integer i, and $|f| < |y|$.

`fabs` and `fabsf` return the absolute value of x, $|x|$.

`rint` returns the nearest integer value to its floating point argument x as a double-precision floating point number. The returned value is rounded according to the currently set machine rounding mode. If round-to-nearest (the default mode) is set and the difference between the function argument and the rounded result is exactly 0.5, then the result will be rounded to the nearest even integer.

`remainder` returns the floating point remainder of the division of x by y. More precisely, it returns the value $r = x - yn$, where n is the integer nearest the exact value x/y. Whenever $|n - x/y| = \frac{1}{2}$, then n is even.

SEE ALSO

abs(3C), matherr(3M).

DIAGNOSTICS

`fmod` and `fmodf` return x when y is 0 and set `errno` to EDOM. `remainder` returns NaN when y is 0 and sets `errno` to EDOM. In both cases, except in compilation modes −Xa or −Xc, a message indicating DOMAIN error is printed on standard error. Except under −Xc, these error-handling procedures may be changed with the function `matherr`.

gamma(3M)

NAME
gamma, lgamma – log gamma function

SYNOPSIS
cc [*flag* ...] *file* ... -lm [*library* ...]

#include <math.h>

double gamma (double x);

double lgamma (double x);

extern int signgam;

DESCRIPTION
gamma and lgamma return

$$\ln(|\Gamma(x)|)$$

where $\Gamma(x)$ is defined as

$$\int_0^\infty e^{-t} t^{x-1} dt$$

The sign of $\Gamma(x)$ is returned in the external integer signgam. The argument x may not be a non-positive integer.

The following C program fragment might be used to calculate Γ:

```
if ((y = gamma(x)) > LN_MAXDOUBLE)
        error();
y = signgam * exp(y);
```

where LN_MAXDOUBLE is the least value that causes exp to return a range error, and is defined in the values.h header file.

SEE ALSO
exp(3M), matherr(3M), values(5).

DIAGNOSTICS
For non-positive integer arguments HUGE is returned and errno is set to EDOM. A message indicating SING error is printed on the standard error output.

If the correct value would overflow, gamma and lgamma return HUGE and set errno to ERANGE.

Except when the -Xc compilation option is used, these error-handling procedures may be changed with the function matherr. When the -Xa or -Xc compilation options are used, HUGE_VAL is returned instead of HUGE and no error messages are printed.

hypot(3M)

NAME
hypot – Euclidean distance function

SYNOPSIS
cc [*flag* ...] *file* ... -lm [*library* ...]

#include <math.h>

double hypot (double x, double y);

DESCRIPTION
hypot returns

sqrt(x * x + y * y)

taking precautions against unwarranted overflows.

SEE ALSO
matherr(3M).

DIAGNOSTICS
When the correct value would overflow, hypot returns HUGE and sets errno to ERANGE.

Except when the -Xc compilation option is used, these error-handling procedures may be changed with the function matherr. When the -Xa or -Xc compilation options are used, HUGE_VAL is returned instead of HUGE.

NAME

matherr – error-handling function

SYNOPSIS

cc [*flag* ...] *file* ... −lm [*library* ...]

#include <math.h>

int matherr (struct exception *x);

DESCRIPTION

matherr is invoked by functions in the math libraries when errors are detected. Note that matherr is not invoked when the −Xc compilation option is used. Users may define their own procedures for handling errors, by including a function named matherr in their programs. matherr must be of the form described above. When an error occurs, a pointer to the exception structure x will be passed to the user-supplied matherr function. This structure, which is defined in the math.h header file, is as follows:

```
struct exception {
    int type;
    char *name;
    double arg1, arg2, retval;
};
```

The element type is an integer describing the type of error that has occurred, from the following list of constants (defined in the header file):

DOMAIN	argument domain error
SING	argument singularity
OVERFLOW	overflow range error
UNDERFLOW	underflow range error
TLOSS	total loss of significance
PLOSS	partial loss of significance

The element name points to a string containing the name of the function that incurred the error. The variables arg1 and arg2 are the arguments with which the function was invoked. retval is set to the default value that will be returned by the function unless the user's matherr sets it to a different value.

If the user's matherr function returns non-zero, no error message will be printed, and errno will not be set.

If matherr is not supplied by the user, the default error-handling procedures, described with the math functions involved, will be invoked upon error. These procedures are also summarized in the table below. In every case, errno is set to EDOM or ERANGE and the program continues.

Default Error Handling Procedures						
	Types of Errors					
type	DOMAIN	SING	OVERFLOW	UNDERFLOW	TLOSS	PLOSS
errno	EDOM	EDOM	ERANGE	ERANGE	ERANGE	ERANGE
BESSEL: y0, y1, yn (arg ≤ 0)	– M, –H	– –	– –	– –	M, 0 –	– –
EXP, EXPF:	–	–	H	0	–	–
LOG, LOG10: LOGF, LOG10F: (arg < 0) (arg = 0)	M, –H M, –H	– –	– –	– –	– –	– –
POW, POWF: neg ** non-int 0 ** non-pos	– M, 0 M, 0	– – –	±H – –	0 – –	– – –	– – –
SQRT, SQRTF:	M, 0	–	–	–	–	–
FMOD, FMODF: (arg2 = 0)	M, X	–	–	–	–	–
REMAINDER: (arg2 = 0)	M, N	–	–	–	–	–
GAMMA, LGAMMA:	–	M, H	H	–	–	–
HYPOT:	–	–	H	–	–	–
SINH, SINHF:	–	–	±H	–	–	–
COSH, COSHF:	–	–	H	–	–	–
ASIN, ACOS, ATAN2: ASINF, ACOSF, ATAN2F:	M, 0	–	–	–	–	–
ACOSH:	M, N	–	–	–	–	–
ATANH: (| arg| > 1) (| arg| = 1)	M, N –	– M, N	– –	– –	– –	– –

	Abbreviations
M	Message is printed (not with the −Xa or −Xc options).
H	HUGE is returned (HUGE_VAL with the −Xa or −Xc options).
−H	−HUGE is returned (−HUGE_VAL with the −Xa or −Xc options).
±H	HUGE or −HUGE is returned. (HUGE_VAL or −HUGE_VAL with the −Xa or −Xc options).
0	0 is returned.
X	*arg1* is returned.
N	NaN is returned.

EXAMPLE

```
#include <math.h>
#include <stdio.h>
#include <stdlib.h>
#include <string.h>

int
matherr(register struct exception *x);
{
        switch (x->type) {
        case DOMAIN:
                /* change sqrt to return sqrt(-arg1), not 0 */
                if (!strcmp(x->name, "sqrt")) {
                        x->retval = sqrt(-x->arg1);
                        return (0); /* print message and set errno */
                }
        case SING:
                /* all other domain or sing errors, print message */
                /* and abort */
                fprintf(stderr, "domain error in %s\n", x->name);
                abort( );
        case PLOSS:
                /* print detailed error message */
                fprintf(stderr, "loss of significance in %s(%g)=%g\n",
                        x->name, x->arg1, x->retval);
                return (1); /* take no other action */
        }
        return (0); /* all other errors, execute default procedure */
}
```

NOTES

Error handling in −Xa and −Xt modes [see cc(1)] is described more completely on individual math library pages.

NAME
sinh, sinhf, cosh, coshf, tanh, tanhf, asinh, acosh, atanh – hyperbolic functions

SYNOPSIS
cc [*flag* ...] *file* ... -lm [*library* ...]

#include <math.h>

double sinh (double x);

float sinhf (float x);

double cosh (double x);

float coshf (float x);

double tanh (double x);

float tanhf (float x);

double asinh (double x);

double acosh (double x);

double atanh (double x);

DESCRIPTION
sinh, cosh, and tanh and the single-precision versions sinhf, coshf, and tanhf return, respectively, the hyberbolic sine, cosine, and tangent of their argument.

asinh, acosh, and atanh return, respectively, the inverse hyperolic sine, cosine, and tangent of their argument.

SEE ALSO
matherr(3M).

DIAGNOSTICS
sinh, sinhf, cosh, and coshf return HUGE (and sinh and sinhf may return −HUGE for negative x) when the correct value would overflow and set errno to ERANGE.

acosh returns NaN and sets errno to EDOM when the argument x is less than 1. A message indicating DOMAIN error is printed on the standard error output.

atanh returns NaN and sets errno to EDOM if $|x| \geq 1$. If $|x| = 1$, a message indicating SING error is printed on the standard error output; if $|x| > 1$ the message will indicate DOMAIN error.

Except when the −Xc compilation option is used, these error-handling procedures may be changed with the function matherr. When the −Xa or −Xc compilation options are used, HUGE_VAL is returned instead of HUGE and no error messages are printed.

trig (3M)

NAME
trig: sin, sinf, cos, cosf, tan, tanf, asin, asinf, acos, acosf, atan, atanf, atan2, atan2f – trigonometric functions

SYNOPSIS
cc [*flag* ...] *file* ... −lm [*library* ...]

cc −O −Ksd [*flag* ...] *file* ... −J sfm [*library* ...]

#include <math.h>

double sin (double x);

float sinf (float x);

double cos (double x);

float cosf (float x);

double tan (double x);

float tanf (float x);

double asin (double x);

float asinf (float x);

double acos (double x);

float acosf (float x);

double atan (double x);

float atanf (float x);

double atan2 (double y, double x);

float atan2f (float y, float x);

DESCRIPTION
sin, cos, and tan and the single-precision versions sinf, cosf, and tanf return, respectively, the sine, cosine, and tangent of their argument, x, measured in radians.

asin and asinf return the arcsine of x, in the range $[-\pi/2, +\pi/2]$.

acos and acosf return the arccosine of x, in the range $[0, +\pi]$.

atan and atanf return the arctangent of x, in the range $(-\pi/2, +\pi/2)$.

atan2 and atan2f return the arctangent of y/x, in the range $(-\pi, +\pi]$, using the signs of both arguments to determine the quadrant of the return value.

SEE ALSO
matherr(3M).

DIAGNOSTICS
If the magnitude of the argument of asin, asinf, acos, or acosf is greater than 1, or if both arguments of atan2 or atan2f are 0, 0 is returned and errno is set to EDOM. In addition, a message indicating DOMAIN error is printed on the standard error output.

Except when the −Xc compilation option is used, these error-handling procedures may be changed with the function matherr. When the −Xa or −Xc compilation options are used, no error messages are printed.

3X

3X

NAME

assert – verify program assertion

SYNOPSIS

#include <assert.h>

void assert (int expression);

DESCRIPTION

This macro is useful for putting diagnostics into programs. When it is executed, if *expression* is false (zero), assert prints

> Assertion failed: *expression*, file *xyz*, line *nnn*

on the standard error output and aborts. In the error message, *xyz* is the name of the source file and *nnn* the source line number of the assert statement. The latter are respectively the values of the preprocessor macros __FILE__ and __LINE__.

Compiling with the preprocessor option –DNDEBUG [see cc(1)], or with the preprocessor control statement #define NDEBUG ahead of the #include <assert.h> statement, will stop assertions from being compiled into the program.

SEE ALSO

cc(1), abort(3C).

NOTES

Since assert is implemented as a macro, the *expression* may not contain any string literals.

crypt(3X)

NAME
crypt – password and file encryption functions

SYNOPSIS
cc [*flag* ...] *file* ... -lcrypt [*library* ...]

#include <crypt.h>

char *crypt (const char *key, const char *salt);

void setkey (const char *key);

void encrypt (char *block, int flag);

char *des_crypt (const char *key, const char *salt);

void des_setkey (const char *key);

void des_encrypt (char *block, int flag);

int run_setkey (int *p, const char *key);

int run_crypt (long offset, char *buffer, unsigned int count, int *p);

int crypt_close(int *p);

DESCRIPTION
des_crypt is the password encryption function. It is based on a one-way hashing encryption algorithm with variations intended (among other things) to frustrate use of hardware implementations of a key search.

key is a user's typed password. *salt* is a two-character string chosen from the set [a-zA-Z0-9./]; this string is used to perturb the hashing algorithm in one of 4096 different ways, after which the password is used as the key to encrypt repeatedly a constant string. The returned value points to the encrypted password. The first two characters are the salt itself.

The des_setkey and des_encrypt entries provide (rather primitive) access to the actual hashing algorithm. The argument of des_setkey is a character array of length 64 containing only the characters with numerical value 0 and 1. If this string is divided into groups of 8, the low-order bit in each group is ignored, thereby creating a 56-bit key that is set into the machine. This key is the key that will be used with the hashing algorithm to encrypt the string *block* with the function des_encrypt.

The argument to the des_encrypt entry is a character array of length 64 containing only the characters with numerical value 0 and 1. The argument array is modified in place to a similar array representing the bits of the argument after having been subjected to the hashing algorithm using the key set by des_setkey. If *flag* is zero, the argument is encrypted; if non-zero, it is decrypted.

Note that decryption is not provided in the international version of crypt. The international version is part of the C Development Set, and the domestic version is part of the Security Administration Utilities. If decryption is attempted with the international version of des_encrypt, an error message is printed.

crypt(3X)

crypt, setkey, and **encrypt** are front-end routines that invoke *des_crypt*, *des_setkey*, and *des_encrypt* respectively.

The routines **run_setkey** and **run_crypt** are designed for use by applications that need cryptographic capabilities [such as **ed**(1) and **vi**(1)] that must be compatible with the **crypt**(1) user-level utility. **run_setkey** establishes a two-way pipe connection with the **crypt** utility, using *key* as the password argument. **run_crypt** takes a block of characters and transforms the cleartext or ciphertext into their ciphertext or cleartext using the **crypt** utility. *offset* is the relative byte position from the beginning of the file that the block of text provided in *block* is coming from. *count* is the number of characters in *block*, and *connection* is an array containing indices to a table of input and output file streams. When encryption is finished, **crypt_close** is used to terminate the connection with the **crypt** utility.

run_setkey returns −1 if a connection with the **crypt** utility cannot be established. This result will occur in international versions of the UNIX system in which the **crypt** utility is not available. If a null key is passed to **run_setkey**, 0 is returned. Otherwise, 1 is returned. **run_crypt** returns −1 if it cannot write output or read input from the pipe attached to **crypt**. Otherwise it returns 0.

The program must be linked with the object file access routine library **libcrypt.a**.

SEE ALSO
getpass(3C), passwd(4).
crypt(1), login(1), passwd(1) in the *User's Reference Manual*.

DIAGNOSTICS
In the international version of crypt(3X), a flag argument of 1 to **encrypt** or **des_encrypt** is not accepted, and **errno** is set to **ENOSYS** to indicate that the functionality is not available.

NOTES
The return value in **crypt** points to static data that are overwritten by each call.

dlclose(3X)

NAME
dlclose - close a shared object

SYNOPSIS
cc [*flag* ...] *file* ... -ldl [*library* ...]

#include <dlfcn.h>

int dlclose(void *handle);

DESCRIPTION
dlclose disassociates a shared object previously opened by dlopen from the current process. Once an object has been closed using dlclose, its symbols are no longer available to dlsym. All objects loaded automatically as a result of invoking dlopen on the referenced object [see dlopen(3X)] are also closed. *handle* is the value returned by a previous invocation of dlopen.

SEE ALSO
dlerror(3X), dlopen(3X), dlsym(3X).

DIAGNOSTICS
If the referenced object was successfully closed, dlclose returns 0. If the object could not be closed, or if *handle* does not refer to an open object, dlclose returns a non-0 value. More detailed diagnostic information will be available through dlerror.

NOTES
A successful invocation of dlclose does not guarantee that the objects associated with *handle* will actually be removed from the address space of the process. Objects loaded by one invocation of dlopen may also be loaded by another invocation of dlopen. The same object may also be opened multiple times. An object will not be removed from the address space until all references to that object through an explicit dlopen invocation have been closed and all other objects implicitly referencing that object have also been closed.

Once an object has been closed by dlclose, referencing symbols contained in that object can cause undefined behavior.

dlerror(3X)   dlerror(3X)

NAME
dlerror - get diagnostic information

SYNOPSIS
cc [flag ...] file ... -ldl [library ...]

#include <dlfcn.h>

char *dlerror(void);

DESCRIPTION
dlerror returns a null-terminated character string (with no trailing newline) that describes the last error that occurred during dynamic linking processing. If no dynamic linking errors have occurred since the last invocation of dlerror, dlerror returns NULL. Thus, invoking dlerror a second time, immediately following a prior invocation, will result in NULL being returned.

SEE ALSO
dlerror(3X), dlopen(3X), dlsym(3X).

NOTES
The messages returned by dlerror may reside in a static buffer that is overwritten on each call to dlerror. Application code should not write to this buffer. Programs wishing to preserve an error message should make their own copies of that message.

NAME
dlopen – open a shared object

SYNOPSIS
cc [flag ...] file ... -ldl [library ...]

#include <dlfcn.h>

void *dlopen(char *pathname, int mode);

DESCRIPTION
dlopen is one of a family of routines that give the user direct access to the dynamic linking facilities. (See "C Compilation System" in the *Programmer's Guide: ANSI C and Programming Support Tools*). These routines are available in a library which is loaded if the option -ldl is used with cc or ld.

dlopen makes a shared object available to a running process. dlopen returns to the process a *handle* which the process may use on subsequent calls to dlsym and dlclose. This value should not be interpreted in any way by the process. *pathname* is the path name of the object to be opened; it may be an absolute path or relative to the current directory. If the value of *pathname* is 0, dlopen will make the symbols contained in the original a.out, and all of the objects that were loaded at program startup with the a.out, available through dlsym.

When a shared object is brought into the address space of a process, it may contain references to symbols whose addresses are not known until the object is loaded. These references must be relocated before the symbols can be accessed. The *mode* parameter governs when these relocations take place and may have the following values:

RTLD_LAZY
Under this *mode*, only references to data symbols are relocated when the object is loaded. References to functions are not relocated until a given function is invoked for the first time. This *mode* should result in better performance, since a process may not reference all of the functions in any given shared object.

RTLD_NOW
Under this *mode*, all necessary relocations are performed when the object is first loaded. This may result in some wasted effort, if relocations are performed for functions that are never referenced, but is useful for applications that need to know as soon as an object is loaded that all symbols referenced during execution will be available.

SEE ALSO
cc(1), ld(1), sh(1), exec(2), dlclose(3X), dlerror(3X), dlsym(3X).

The "C Compilation System" chapter in the *Programmer's Guide: ANSI C and Programming Support Tools*.

DIAGNOSTICS
If *pathname* cannot be found, cannot be opened for reading, is not a shared object, or if an error occurs during the process of loading *pathname* or relocating its symbolic references, dlopen will return NULL. More detailed diagnostic information will be available through dlerror.

NOTES

If other shared objects were link edited with *pathname* when *pathname* was built, those objects will automatically be loaded by `dlopen`. The directory search path that will be used to find both *pathname* and the other *needed* objects may be specified by setting the environment variable `LD_LIBRARY_PATH`. This environment variable should contain a colon-separated list of directories, in the same format as the `PATH` variable [see `sh`(1)]. `LD_LIBRARY_PATH` will be ignored if the process is running `setuid` or `setgid` [see `exec`(2)] or if the name specified is not a simple file name (*i.e.* contains a / character). Objects whose names resolve to the same absolute or relative path name may be opened any number of times using `dlopen`, however, the object referenced will only be loaded once into the address space of the current process. The same object referenced by two different path names, however, may be loaded multiple times. For example, given the object `/usr/home/me/mylibs/mylib.so`, and assuming the current working directory is `/usr/home/me/workdir`,

```
...
void *handle1;
void *handle2;

handle1 = dlopen("../mylibs/mylib.so", RTLD_LAZY);
handle2 = dlopen("/usr/home/me/mylibs/mylib.so", RTLD_LAZY);
...
```

will result in `mylibs.so` being loaded twice for the current process. On the other hand, given the same object and current working directory, if `LD_LIBRARY_PATH=/usr/home/me/mylibs`, then

```
...
void *handle1;
void *handle2;

handle1 = dlopen("mylib.so", RTLD_LAZY);
handle2 = dlopen("/usr/home/me/mylibs/mylib.so", RTLD_LAZY);
...
```

will result in `mylibs.so` being loaded only once.

Objects loaded by a single invocation of `dlopen` may import symbols from one another or from any object loaded automatically during program startup, but objects loaded by one `dlopen` invocation may not directly reference symbols from objects loaded by a different `dlopen` invocation. Those symbols may, however, be referenced indirectly using `dlsym`.

Users who wish to gain access to the symbol table of the `a.out` itself using `dlsym(0, mode)` should be aware that some symbols defined in the `a.out` may not be available to the dynamic linker. The symbol table created by `ld` for use by the dynamic linker might contain only a subset of the symbols defined in the `a.out`: specifically those referenced by the shared objects with which the `a.out` is linked.

dlsym(3X)

NAME
dlsym - get the address of a symbol in shared object

SYNOPSIS
cc [*flag* ...] *file* ... -ldl [*library* ...]

#include <dlfcn.h>

void *dlsym(void *handle, char *name);

DESCRIPTION
dlsym allows a process to obtain the address of a symbol defined within a shared object previously opened by dlopen. *handle* is a value returned by a call to dlopen; the corresponding shared object must not have been closed using dlclose. *name* is the symbol's name as a character string. dlsym will search for the named symbol in all shared objects loaded automatically as a result of loading the object referenced by *handle* [see dlopen(3X)].

EXAMPLES
The following example shows how one can use dlopen and dlsym to access either function or data objects. For simplicity, error checking has been omitted.

```
void *handle;
  int i, *iptr;
  int (*fptr)(int);

  /* open the needed object */
  handle = dlopen("/usr/mydir/libx.so", RTLD_LAZY);

  /* find address of function and data objects */
  fptr = (int (*)(int))dlsym(handle, "some_function");

  iptr = (int *)dlsym(handle, "int_object");

  /* invoke function, passing value of integer as a parameter */
  i = (*fptr)(*iptr);
```

SEE ALSO
dlerror(3X), dlopen(3X), dlsym(3X).

DIAGNOSTICS
If *handle* does not refer to a valid object opened by dlopen, or if the named symbol cannot be found within any of the objects associated with *handle*, dlsym will return NULL. More detailed diagnostic information will be available through dlerror.

libwindows(3X)

NAME
libwindows – windowing terminal function library

SYNOPSIS
cc [flag ...] file ... –lwindows [library ...]

    int openagent (void);

    int New (int cntlfd, int origin_x, int origin_y,
        int corner_x, int corner_y);

    int Newlayer (int cntlfd, int origin_x, int origin_y,
        int corner_x, int corner_y);

    int openchan (int chan);

    int Runlayer (int chan, char *command);

    int Current (int cntlfd, int chan);

    int Delete (int cntlfd, int chan);

    int Top (int cntlfd, int chan);

    int Bottom (int cntlfd, int chan);

    int Move (int cntlfd, int chan, int origin_x, int origin_y);

    int Reshape (int cntlfd, int chan, int origin_x, int origin_y,
        int corner_x, int corner_y);

    int Exit (int cntlfd);

DESCRIPTION
This library of routines enables a program running on a host UNIX system to perform windowing terminal functions [see layers(1)].

The openagent routine opens the control channel of the xt(7) channel group to which the calling process belongs. Upon successful completion, openagent returns a file descriptor that can be passed to any of the other libwindows routines except openchan and Runlayer. (The file descriptor can also be passed to the close system call.) Otherwise, the value –1 is returned.

The New routine creates a new layer with a separate shell. The *origin_x, origin_y, corner_x,* and *corner_y* arguments are the coordinates of the layer rectangle. If all the coordinate arguments are 0, the user must define the layer's rectangle interactively. The layer appears on top of any overlapping layers. The layer is not made current (i.e., the keyboard is not attached to the new layer). Upon successful completion, New returns the xt(7) channel number associated with the layer. Otherwise, the value –1 is returned.

The Newlayer routine creates a new layer without executing a separate shell. Otherwise it is identical to New, described above.

The openchan routine opens the channel argument *chan* which is obtained from the New or Newlayer routine. Upon successful completion, openchan returns a file descriptor that can be used as input to write(2) or close(2). Otherwise, the value –1 is returned.

The Runlayer routine runs the specified *command* in the layer associated with the channel argument *chan*. This layer is usually a layer previously created with Newlayer. Any processes currently attached to this layer will be killed, and the new process will have the environment of the layers process.

The Current routine makes the layer associated with the channel argument *chan* current (i.e., attached to the keyboard).

The Delete routine deletes the layer associated with the channel argument *chan* and kills all host processes associated with the layer.

The Top routine makes the layer associated with the channel argument *chan* appear on top of all overlapping layers.

The Bottom routine puts the layer associated with the channel argument *chan* under all overlapping layers.

The Move routine moves the layer associated with the channel argument *chan* from its current screen location to a new screen location at the origin point (*origin_x, origin_y*). The size and contents of the layer are maintained.

The Reshape routine reshapes the layer associated with the channel argument *chan*. The arguments *origin_x, origin_y, corner_x,* and *corner_y* are the new coordinates of the layer rectangle. If all the coordinate arguments are 0, the user is allowed to define the layer's rectangle interactively.

The Exit routine causes the layers program to exit, killing all processes associated with it.

FILES

ULIBDIR/libwindows.a   windowing terminal function library
ULIBDIR   usually /usr/lib

SEE ALSO

close(2), write(2), jagent(5).
layers(1) in the *User's Reference Manual*.

DIAGNOSTICS

Upon successful completion, Runlayer, Current, Delete, Top, Bottom, Move, Reshape, and Exit return 0, while openagent, New, Newlayer, and openchan return values as described above under each routine. If an error occurs, −1 is returned.

NOTES

The values of layer rectangle coordinates are dependent on the type of terminal. This dependency affects the routines that pass layer rectangle coordinates: Move, New, Newlayer, and Reshape. Some terminals will expect these numbers to be passed as character positions (bytes); others will expect the information to be in pixels (bits).

For example, for the AT&T 5620 DMD terminal, `New`, `Newlayer`, and `Reshape` take minimum values of 8 (pixels) for *origin_x* and *origin_y* and maximum values of 792 (pixels) for *corner_x* and 1016 (pixels) for *corner_y*. The minimum layer size is 28 by 28 pixels and the maximum layer size is 784 by 1008 pixels.

It is recommended that applications use `/dev/xt/??[0-7]` instead of `/dev/xt??[0-7]` when accessing the `xt` driver.

maillock(3X)

NAME
maillock – manage lockfile for user's mailbox

SYNOPSIS
cc [*flag* ...] *file* ... -lmail [*library* ...]

#include <maillock.h>

int maillock (const char *user, int retrycnt);

int mailunlock (void);

DESCRIPTION
The maillock function attempts to create a lockfile for the user's mailfile. If a lockfile already exists, maillock assumes the contents of the file is the process ID (as a null-terminated ASCII string) of the process that created the lockfile (presumably with a call to maillock). If the process that created the lockfile is still alive, maillock will sleep and try again *retrycnt* times before returning with an error indication. The sleep algorithm is to sleep for 5 seconds times the attempt number. That is, the first sleep will be for 5 seconds, the next sleep will be for 10 seconds, etc. until the number of attempts reaches *retrycnt*. When the lockfile is no longer needed, it should be removed by calling mailunlock.

user is the login name of the user for whose mailbox the lockfile will be created. maillock assumes that users' mailfiles are in the "standard" place as defined in maillock.h.

RETURN VALUE
The following return code definitions are contained in maillock.h.

```
#define   L_SUCCESS    0   /* Lockfile created or removed */
#define   L_NAMELEN    1   /* Recipient name > 13 chars */
#define   L_TMPLOCK    2   /* Can't create tmp file */
#define   L_TMPWRITE   3   /* Can't write pid into lockfile */
#define   L_MAXTRYS    4   /* Failed after retrycnt attempts */
#define   L_ERROR      5   /* Check errno for reason */
```

FILES
LIBDIR/llib-mail.ln
LIBDIR/mail.a
/var/mail/*
/var/mail/*.lock

NOTES
mailunlock will only remove the lockfile created from the most previous call to maillock. Calling maillock for different users without intervening calls to mailunlock will cause the initially created lockfile(s) to remain, potentially blocking subsequent message delivery until the current process finally terminates.

malloc(3X)

NAME
malloc, free, realloc, calloc, mallopt, mallinfo – memory allocator

SYNOPSIS
cc [*flag* ...] *file* ... -lmalloc [*library* ...]

#include <stdlib.h>

void *malloc (size_t size)

void free (void *ptr)

void *realloc (void *ptr, size_t size)

void *calloc (size_t nelem, size_t elsize)

#include <malloc.h>

int mallopt (int cmd, int value)

struct mallinfo mallinfo (void)

DESCRIPTION
malloc and free provide a simple general-purpose memory allocation package.

malloc returns a pointer to a block of at least *size* bytes suitably aligned for any use.

The argument to free is a pointer to a block previously allocated by malloc; after free is performed this space is made available for further allocation, and its contents have been destroyed (but see mallopt below for a way to change this behavior). If *ptr* is a null pointer, no action occurs.

Undefined results occur if the space assigned by malloc is overrun or if some random number is handed to free.

realloc changes the size of the block pointed to by *ptr* to *size* bytes and returns a pointer to the (possibly moved) block. The contents are unchanged up to the lesser of the new and old sizes. If *ptr* is a null pointer, realloc behaves like malloc for the specified size. If *size* is zero and *ptr* is not a null pointer, the object it points to is freed.

calloc allocates space for an array of *nelem* elements of size *elsize*. The space is initialized to zeros.

mallopt provides for control over the allocation algorithm. The available values for *cmd* are:

- **M_MXFAST** Set *maxfast* to *value*. The algorithm allocates all blocks below the size of *maxfast* in large groups and then doles them out very quickly. The default value for *maxfast* is 24.

- **M_NLBLKS** Set *numlblks* to *value*. The above mentioned "large groups" each contain *numlblks* blocks. *numlblks* must be greater than 0. The default value for *numlblks* is 100.

- **M_GRAIN** Set *grain* to *value*. The sizes of all blocks smaller than *maxfast* are considered to be rounded up to the nearest multiple of *grain*. *grain* must be greater than 0. The default value of *grain* is the smallest number of bytes that will allow alignment of any data type. Value will be rounded up to a multiple of the default when *grain* is set.

M_KEEP   Preserve data in a freed block until the next malloc, realloc, or calloc. This option is provided only for compatibility with the old version of malloc and is not recommended.

These values are defined in the malloc.h header file.

mallopt may be called repeatedly, but may not be called after the first small block is allocated.

mallinfo provides instrumentation describing space usage. It returns the structure:

```
struct mallinfo {
    int arena;      /* total space in arena */
    int ordblks;    /* number of ordinary blocks */
    int smblks;     /* number of small blocks */
    int hblkhd;     /* space in holding block headers */
    int hblks;      /* number of holding blocks */
    int usmblks;    /* space in small blocks in use */
    int fsmblks;    /* space in free small blocks */
    int uordblks;   /* space in ordinary blocks in use */
    int fordblks;   /* space in free ordinary blocks */
    int keepcost;   /* space penalty if keep option */
                    /* is used */
}
```

This structure is defined in the malloc.h header file.

Each of the allocation routines returns a pointer to space suitably aligned (after possible pointer coercion) for storage of any type of object.

SEE ALSO
brk(2), malloc(3C).

DIAGNOSTICS
malloc, realloc, and calloc return a NULL pointer if there is not enough available memory. When realloc returns NULL, the block pointed to by *ptr* is left intact. If mallopt is called after any allocation or if *cmd* or *value* are invalid, non-zero is returned. Otherwise, it returns zero.

NOTES
Note that unlike malloc(3C), this package does not preserve the contents of a block when it is freed, unless the M_KEEP option of mallopt is used.

Undocumented features of malloc(3C) have not been duplicated.

Function prototypes for malloc, realloc, calloc and free are also defined in the <malloc.h> header file for compatibility with old applications. New applications should include <stdlib.h> to access the prototypes for these functions.

sputl(3X)

NAME
sputl, sgetl – access long integer data in a machine-independent fashion

SYNOPSIS
cc [*flag* ...] *file* ... −lld [*library* ...]

#include <ldfcn.h>

void sputl (long value, char *buffer);

long sgetl (const char *buffer);

DESCRIPTION
sputl takes the four bytes of the long integer *value* and places them in memory starting at the address pointed to by *buffer*. The ordering of the bytes is the same across all machines.

sgetl retrieves the four bytes in memory starting at the address pointed to by *buffer* and returns the long integer value in the byte ordering of the host machine.

The combination of `sputl` and `sgetl` provides a machine-independent way of storing long numeric data in a file in binary form without conversion to characters.

FILE FORMATS (4)

FILE FORMATS (4)

intro(4)

NAME
intro – introduction to file formats

DESCRIPTION
This section outlines the formats of various files. The C structure declarations for the file formats are given where applicable. Usually, the header files containing these structure declarations can be found in the directories **/usr/include** or **/usr/include/sys**. For inclusion in C language programs, however, the syntax #include <*filename.h*> or #include <*sys/filename.h*> should be used.

a.out(4)

NAME
a.out – ELF (Executable and Linking Format) files

SYNOPSIS
#include <elf.h>

DESCRIPTION
The file name **a.out** is the default output file name from the link editor, ld(1). The link editor will make an **a.out** executable if there were no errors in linking. The output file of the assembler, as(1), also follows the format of the **a.out** file although its default file name is different.

Programs that manipulate ELF files may use the library that elf(3E) describes. An overview of the file format follows. For more complete information, see the references given below.

Linking View
ELF header
Program header table *optional*
Section 1
...
Section *n*
...
Section header table

Execution View
ELF header
Program header table
Segment 1
Segment 2
...
Section header table *optional*

An ELF header resides at the beginning and holds a "road map" describing the file's organization. Sections hold the bulk of object file information for the linking view: instructions, data, symbol table, relocation information, and so on. Segments hold the object file information for the program execution view. As shown, a segment may contain one or more sections.

A program header table, if present, tells the system how to create a process image. Files used to build a process image (execute a program) must have a program header table; relocatable files do not need one. A section header table contains information describing the file's sections. Every section has an entry in the table; each entry gives information such as the section name, the section size, etc. Files used during linking must have a section header table; other object files may or may not have one.

Although the figure shows the program header table immediately after the ELF header, and the section header table following the sections, actual files may differ. Moreover, sections and segments have no specified order. Only the ELF header has a fixed position in the file.

When an **a.out** file is loaded into memory for execution, three logical segments are set up: the text segment, the data segment (initialized data followed by uninitialized, the latter actually being initialized to all 0's), and a stack. The text segment is not writable by the program; if other processes are executing the same **a.out** file, the processes will share a single text segment.

The data segment starts at the next maximal page boundary past the last text address. (If the system supports more than one page size, the "maximal page" is the largest supported size.) When the process image is created, the part of the file holding the end of text and the beginning of data may appear twice. The duplicated chunk of text that appears at the beginning of data is never executed; it is duplicated so that the operating system may bring in pieces of the file in multiples of the actual page size without having to realign the beginning of the data section to a page boundary. Therefore, the first data address is the sum of the next maximal page boundary past the end of text plus the remainder of the last text address divided by the maximal page size. If the last text address is a multiple of the maximal page size, no duplication is necessary. The stack is automatically extended as required. The data segment is extended as requested by the brk(2) system call.

SEE ALSO

as(1), cc(1), ld(1), brk(2), elf(3E).

The "Object Files" chapter in the *Programmer's Guide: ANSI C and Programming Support Tools*.

NAME
ar – archive file format

SYNOPSIS
#include <ar.h>

DESCRIPTION
The archive command `ar` is used to combine several files into one. Archives are used mainly as libraries to be searched by the link editor `ld`.

Each archive begins with the archive magic string.

```
#define  ARMAG   "!<arch>\n"   /* magic string */
#define  SARMAG  8             /* length of magic string */
```

Following the archive magic string are the archive file members. Each file member is preceded by a file member header which is of the following format:

```
#define  ARFMAG   "`\n"   /* header trailer string */

struct  ar_hdr              /* file member header */
{
    char    ar_name[16];   /* '/' terminated file member name */
    char    ar_date[12];   /* file member date */
    char    ar_uid[6];     /* file member user identification */
    char    ar_gid[6];     /* file member group identification */
    char    ar_mode[8];    /* file member mode (octal) */
    char    ar_size[10];   /* file member size */
    char    ar_fmag[2];    /* header trailer string */
};
```

All information in the file member headers is in printable ASCII. The numeric information contained in the headers is stored as decimal numbers (except for *ar_mode* which is in octal). Thus, if the archive contains printable files, the archive itself is printable.

If the file member name fits, the *ar_name* field contains the name directly, and is terminated by a slash (/) and padded with blanks on the right. If the member's name does not fit, *ar_name* contains a slash (/) followed by a decimal representation of the name's offset in the archive string table described below.

The *ar_date* field is the modification date of the file at the time of its insertion into the archive. Common format archives can be moved from system to system as long as the portable archive command `ar` is used.

Each archive file member begins on an even byte boundary; a newline is inserted between files if necessary. Nevertheless, the size given reflects the actual size of the file exclusive of padding.

Notice there is no provision for empty areas in an archive file.

Each archive that contains object files [see a.out(4)] includes an archive symbol table. This symbol table is used by the link editor ld to determine which archive members must be loaded during the link edit process. The archive symbol table (if it exists) is always the first file in the archive (but is never listed) and is automatically created and/or updated by ar.

The archive symbol table has a zero length name (i.e., ar_name[0] is '/'), ar_name[1]==' ', etc.). All "words" in this symbol table have four bytes, using the machine-independent encoding shown below. (All machines use the encoding described here for the symbol table, even if the machine's "natural" byte order is different.)

	0	1	2	3
0x01020304	01	02	03	04

The contents of this file are as follows:

1. The number of symbols. Length: 4 bytes.
2. The array of offsets into the archive file. Length: 4 bytes * "the number of symbols".
3. The name string table. Length: ar_size − 4 bytes * ("the number of symbols" + 1).

As an example, the following symbol table defines 4 symbols. The archive member at file offset 114 defines name and object. The archive member at file offset 426 defines function and a second version of name.

Offset	+0	+1	+2	+3	
0	4				4 offset entries
4	114				name
8	114				object
12	426				function
16	426				name
20	n	a	m	e	
24	\0	o	b	j	
28	e	c	t	\0	
32	f	u	n	c	
36	t	i	o	n	
40	\0	n	a	m	
44	e	\0			

The number of symbols and the array of offsets are managed with sgetl and sputl. The string table contains exactly as many null terminated strings as there are elements in the offsets array. Each offset from the array is associated with the corresponding name from the string table (in order). The names in the string table are all the defined global symbols found in the common object files in the archive. Each offset is the location of the archive header for the associated symbol.

If some archive member's name is more than 15 bytes long, a special archive member contains a table of file names, each followed by a slash and a new-line. This string table member, if present, will precede all "normal" archive members. The special archive symbol table is not a "normal" member, and must be first if it exists. The *ar_name* entry of the string table's member header holds a zero length name ar_name[0]=='/', followed by one trailing slash (ar_name[1]=='/'), followed by blanks (ar_name[2]==' ', etc.). Offsets into the string table begin at zero. Example *ar_name* values for short and long file names appear below.

Offset	+0	+1	+2	+3	+4	+5	+6	+7	+8	+9
0	f	i	l	e	_	n	a	m	e	_
10	s	a	m	p	l	e	/	\n	l	o
20	n	g	e	r	f	i	l	e	n	a
30	m	e	x	a	m	p	l	e	/	\n

Member Name	ar_name	Note
short-name	short-name/	Not in string table
file_name_sample	/0	Offset 0 in string table
longerfilenamexample	/18	Offset 18 in string table

SEE ALSO
ar(1), ld(1), strip(1), sputl(3X), a.out(4).

NOTES
`strip` will remove all archive symbol entries from the header. The archive symbol entries must be restored via the −ts options of the `ar` command before the archive can be used with the link editor `ld`.

core (4)

NAME
core – core image file

DESCRIPTION
The UNIX system writes out a core image of a process when it is terminated due to the receipt of some signals. The core image is called **core** and is written in the process's working directory (provided it can be; normal access controls apply). A process with an effective user ID different from the real user ID will not produce a core image.

The core file contains all the process information pertinent to debugging: contents of hardware registers, process status and process data. The format of a core file is object file specific.

For ELF executable programs [see **a.out**(4)], the core file generated is also an ELF file, containing ELF program and file headers. The **e_type** field in the file header has type **ET_CORE**. The program header contains an entry for every loadable and writeable segment that was part of the process address space, including shared library segments. The contents of the segments themselves are also part of the core image.

The program header of an ELF core file also contains a NOTE segment. This segment may contain the following entries. Each has entry name "CORE" and presents the contents of a system structure:

prstatus_t
> The entry containing this structure has a NOTE type of 1. This structure contains things of interest to a debugger from the operating system's u-area, such as the general registers, signal dispositions, state, reason for stopping, process ID and so forth. The structure is defined in <sys/procfs.h>.

fpregset_t
> This entry is present only if the process used the floating-point hardware. It has a NOTE type of 2 and contains the floating-point registers. The fpregset_t structure is defined in <sys/regset.h>.

prpsinfo_t
> The entry containing this structure has a NOTE type of 3. It contains information of interest to the **ps**(1) command, such as process status, cpu usage, "nice" value, controlling terminal, user ID, process ID, the name of the executable and so forth. The structure is defined in <sys/procfs.h>.

COFF executable programs produce core files consisting of two parts: the first section is a copy of the system's per-user data for the process, including the general registers. The format of this section is defined in the header files <sys/user.h> and <sys/reg.h>. The remainder of a COFF core image represents the actual contents of the process data space.

The size of the core file created by a process may be controlled by the user [see **getrlimit**(2)].

SEE ALSO

sdb(1), getrlimit(2), setuid(2), elf(3E), a.out(4), signal(5).
crash(1M) in the *System Administrator's Reference Manual*.
The "Object Files" chapter in the *Programmer's Guide: ANSI C and Programming Support Tools*.

limits(4)

NAME
limits – header file for implementation-specific constants

SYNOPSIS
#include <limits.h>

DESCRIPTION
The header file `limits.h` is a list of minimal magnitude limitations imposed by a specific implementation of the operating system.

ARG_MAX	5120	/* max length of arguments to exec */
CHAR_BIT	8	/* max # of bits in a "char" */
CHAR_MAX	127	/* max value of a "char" */
CHAR_MIN	-128	/* min value of a "char" */
CHILD_MAX	25	/* max # of processes per user id */
CLK_TCK	_sysconf(3)	/* clock ticks per second */
DBL_DIG	15	/* digits of precision of a "double" */
DBL_MAX	1.7976931348623157E+308	/* max decimal value of a "double"*/
DBL_MIN	2.2250738585072014E-308	/* min decimal value of a "double"*/
FCHR_MAX	1048576	/* max size of a file in bytes */
FLT_DIG	6	/* digits of precision of a "float" */
FLT_MAX	3.40282347e+38F	/* max decimal value of a "float" */
FLT_MIN	1.17549435E-38F	/* min decimal value of a "float" */
INT_MAX	2147483647	/* max value of an "int" */
INT_MIN	(-2147483647-1)	/* min value of an "int" */
LINK_MAX	1000	/* max # of links to a single file */
LOGNAME_MAX	8	/* max # of characters in a login name */
LONG_BIT	32	/* # of bits in a "long" */
LONG_MAX	2147483647	/* max value of a "long int" */
LONG_MIN	(-2147483647-1)	/* min value of a "long int" */
MAX_CANON	256	/* max bytes in a line for canonical processing */
MAX_INPUT	512	/* max size of a char input buffer */
MB_LEN_MAX	5	/* max # of bytes in a multibyte character */
NAME_MAX	14	/* max # of characters in a file name */
NGROUPS_MAX	16	/* max # of groups for a user */
NL_ARGMAX	9	/* max value of "digit" in calls to the NLS printf() and scanf() */
NL_LANGMAX	14	/* max # of bytes in a LANG name */
NL_MSGMAX	32767	/* max message number */
NL_NMAX	1	/* max # of bytes in N-to-1 mapping characters */
NL_SETMAX	255	/* max set number */
NL_TEXTMAX	255	/* max # of bytes in a message string */
NZERO	20	/* default process priority */
OPEN_MAX	60	/* max # of files a process can have open */
PASS_MAX	8	/* max # of characters in a password */

```
PATH_MAX         1024              /* max # of characters in a path name */
PID_MAX          30000             /* max value for a process ID */
PIPE_BUF         5120              /* max # bytes atomic in write to a pipe */
PIPE_MAX         5120              /* max # bytes written to a pipe
                                     in a write */
SCHAR_MAX        127               /* max value of a "signed char" */
SCHAR_MIN        (-128)            /* min value of a "signed char" */
SHRT_MAX         32767             /* max value of a "short int" */
SHRT_MIN         (-32768)          /* min value of a "short int" */
STD_BLK          1024              /* # bytes in a physical I/O block */
SYS_NMLN         257               /* 4.0 size of utsname elements */
                                   /* also defined in sys/utsname.h */
SYSPID_MAX       1                 /* max pid of system processes */
TMP_MAX          17576             /* max # of unique names generated
                                     by tmpnam */
UCHAR_MAX        255               /* max value of an "unsigned char" */
UID_MAX          60000             /* max value for a user or group ID */
UINT_MAX         4294967295        /* max value of an "unsigned int" */
ULONG_MAX        4294967295        /* max value of an "unsigned long int" */
USHRT_MAX        65535             /* max value of an "unsigned short int" */
USI_MAX          4294967295        /* max decimal value of an "unsigned" */
WORD_BIT         32                /* # of bits in a "word" or "int" */
```

The following POSIX definitions are the most restrictive values to be used by a POSIX conformant application. Conforming implementations shall provide values at least this large.

```
_POSIX_ARG_MAX          4096       /* max length of arguments to exec */
_POSIX_CHILD_MAX        6          /* max # of processes per user ID */
_POSIX_LINK_MAX         8          /* max # of links to a single file */
_POSIX_MAX_CANON        255        /* max # of bytes in a line of input */
_POSIX_MAX_INPUT        255        /* max # of bytes in terminal
                                     input queue */
_POSIX_NAME_MAX         14         /* # of bytes in a filename */
_POSIX_NGROUPS_MAX      0          /* max # of groups in a process */
_POSIX_OPEN_MAX         16         /* max # of files a process can have open */
_POSIX_PATH_MAX         255        /* max # of characters in a pathname */
_POSIX_PIPE_BUF         512        /* max # of bytes atomic in write
                                     to a pipe */
```

sccsfile(4)

NAME
sccsfile – format of SCCS file

DESCRIPTION
An SCCS (Source Code Control System) file is an ASCII file. It consists of six logical parts: the checksum, the delta table (contains information about each delta), user names (contains login names and/or numerical group IDs of users who may add deltas), flags (contains definitions of internal keywords), comments (contains arbitrary descriptive information about the file), and the body (contains the actual text lines intermixed with control lines).

Throughout an SCCS file there are lines which begin with the ASCII SOH (start of heading) character (octal 001). This character is hereafter referred to as the control character and will be represented graphically as @. Any line described below that is not depicted as beginning with the control character is prevented from beginning with the control character.

Entries of the form *DDDDD* represent a five-digit string (a number between 00000 and 99999).

Each logical part of an SCCS file is described in detail below.

Checksum
The checksum is the first line of an SCCS file. The form of the line is:

> @h*DDDDD*

The value of the checksum is the sum of all characters, except those of the first line. The @h provides a magic number of (octal) 064001, depending on byte order.

Delta table
The delta table consists of a variable number of entries of one of the following forms:

> @s *DDDDD/DDDDD/DDDDD*
> @d *<type> <SCCS ID> yr/mo/da hr:mi:se <pgmr> DDDDD DDDDD*
> @i *DDDDD* ...
> @x *DDDDD* ...
> @g *DDDDD* ...
> @m *<MR number>*
>   . . .
> @c *<comments>* . . .
>   . . .
> @e

The first line (@s) contains the number of lines inserted/deleted/unchanged, respectively. The second line (@d) contains the type of the delta (normal: D or removed: R), the SCCS ID of the delta, the date and time of creation of the delta, the login name corresponding to the real user ID at the time the delta was created, and the serial numbers of the delta and its predecessor, respectively.

The @i, @x, and @g lines contain the serial numbers of deltas included, excluded, and ignored, respectively. These lines are optional.

The @m lines (optional) each contain one MR number associated with the delta; the @c lines contain comments associated with the delta. The @e line ends the delta table entry.

User names

The list of login names and/or numerical group IDs of users who may add deltas to the file, separated by new-lines. The lines containing these login names and/or numerical group IDs are surrounded by the bracketing lines @u and @U. An empty list allows anyone to make a delta. Any line starting with a ! prohibits the succeeding group or user from making deltas.

Flags

Keywords used internally. See admin(1) for more information on their use. Each flag line takes the form:

 @f <flag> <optional text>

The following flags are defined:

 @f t <type of program>
 @f v <program name>
 @f i <keyword string>
 @f b
 @f m <module name>
 @f f <floor>
 @f c <ceiling>
 @f d <default-sid>
 @f n
 @f j
 @f l <lock-releases>
 @f q <user defined>
 @f z <reserved for use in interfaces>

The t flag defines the replacement for the %Y% identification keyword. The v flag controls prompting for MR numbers in addition to comments; if the optional text is present it defines an MR number validity checking program. The i flag controls the warning/error aspect of the "No id keywords" message. When the i flag is not present, this message is only a warning; when the i flag is present, this message causes a fatal error (the file will not be "gotten", or the delta will not be made). When the b flag is present the –b keyletter may be used on the get command to cause a branch in the delta tree. The m flag defines the first choice for the replacement text of the %M% identification keyword. The f flag defines the floor release; the release below which no deltas may be added. The c flag defines the ceiling release; the release above which no deltas may be added. The d flag defines the default SID to be used when none is specified on a get command. The n flag causes delta to insert a null delta (a delta that applies no changes) in those releases that are skipped when a delta is made in a new release (e.g., when delta 5.1 is made after delta 2.7, releases 3 and 4 are skipped). The absence of the n flag causes skipped releases to be completely empty. The j flag causes get to allow concurrent edits of the same base SID. The l flag defines a *list* of releases that are locked against editing. The q flag defines the replacement for the %Q% identification keyword. The z flag is used in specialized interface programs.

Comments
Arbitrary text is surrounded by the bracketing lines @t and @T. The comments section typically will contain a description of the file's purpose.

Body
The body consists of text lines and control lines. Text lines do not begin with the control character, control lines do. There are three kinds of control lines: insert, delete, and end, represented by:

>@I *DDDDD*
>@D *DDDDD*
>@E *DDDDD*

respectively. The digit string is the serial number corresponding to the delta for the control line.

SEE ALSO
admin(1), delta(1), get(1), prs(1).

strftime(4)

NAME
strftime – language specific strings

DESCRIPTION
There can exist one printable file per locale to specify its date and time formatting information. These files must be kept in the directory /usr/lib/locale/<*locale*>/LC_TIME. The contents of these files are:

1. abbreviated month names (in order)

2. month names (in order)

3. abbreviated weekday names (in order)

4. weekday names (in order)

5. default strings that specify formats for locale time (%X) and locale date (%x).

6. default format for cftime, if the argument for cftime is zero or null.

7. AM (ante meridian) string

8. PM (post meridian) string

Each string is on a line by itself. All white space is significant. The order of the strings in the above list is the same order in which they must appear in the file.

EXAMPLE
/usr/lib/locale/C/LC_TIME

```
Jan
Feb
...
January
February
...
Sun
Mon
...
Sunday
Monday
...
%H:%M:%S
%m/%d/%y
%a %b %d %T %Z %Y
AM
PM
```

FILES
/usr/lib/locale/<*locale*>/LC_TIME

SEE ALSO
ctime(3C), setlocale(3C), strftime(3C).

timezone(4)

NAME
timezone – set default system time zone

SYNOPSIS
/etc/TIMEZONE

DESCRIPTION
This file sets and exports the time zone environmental variable TZ.

This file is "dotted" into other files that must know the time zone.

EXAMPLES
/etc/TIMEZONE for the east coast:

```
#     Time Zone
TZ=EST5EDT
export TZ
```

SEE ALSO
ctime(3C), environ(5).
rc2(1M), profile(4) in the *System Administrator's Reference Manual*.

NAME

utmp, wtmp − utmp and wtmp entry formats

SYNOPSIS

#include <utmp.h>

DESCRIPTION

These files, which hold user and accounting information for such commands as who, write, and login, have the following structure, defined in <utmp.h>:

```
#define   UTMP_FILE    "/var/adm/utmp"
#define   WTMP_FILE    "/var/adm/wtmp"
#define   ut_name      ut_user

struct    utmp {
   char      ut_user[8];        /* user login name */
   char      ut_id[4];          /* /sbin/inittab id (created by */
                                /* process that puts entry in utmp) */
   char      ut_line[12];       /* device name (console, lnxx) */
   short     ut_pid;            /* process id */
   short     ut_type;           /* type of entry */
   struct    exit_status {
      short     e_termination;  /* process termination status */
      short     e_exit;         /* process exit status */
   } ut_exit;                   /* exit status of a process
                                 * marked as DEAD_PROCESS */
   time_t    ut_time;           /* time entry was made */
};

/*  Definitions for ut_type  */

#define EMPTY           0
#define RUN_LVL         1
#define BOOT_TIME       2
#define OLD_TIME        3
#define NEW_TIME        4
#define INIT_PROCESS    5   /* process spawned by "init" */
#define LOGIN_PROCESS   6   /* a "getty" process waiting for login */
#define USER_PROCESS    7   /* a user process */
#define DEAD_PROCESS    8
#define ACCOUNTING      9
#define UTMAXTYPE       ACCOUNTING /* max legal value of ut_type */

/*  Below are special strings or formats used in the "ut_line" */
/*  field when  accounting for something other than a process.  */
/*  No string for the ut_line field can be more than 11 chars + */
/*  a null character in length.  */
```

```
#define RUNLVL_MSG    "run-level %c"
#define BOOT_MSG      "system boot"
#define OTIME_MSG     "old time"
#define NTIME_MSG     "new time"
```

FILES
/var/adm/utmp
/var/adm/wtmp

SEE ALSO
getut(3C).
login(1), who(1), write(1) in the *User's Reference Manual*.

utmpx(4)

NAME
utmpx, wtmpx – utmpx and wtmpx entry formats

SYNOPSIS
#include <utmpx.h>

DESCRIPTION
utmpx(4) is an extended version of utmp(4).

These files, which hold user and accounting information for such commands as who, write, and login, have the following structure as defined by <utmpx.h>:

```
#define    UTMPX_FILE    "/var/adm/utmpx"
#define    WTMPX_FILE    "/var/adm/wtmpx"
#define    ut_name       ut_user
#define    ut_xtime      ut_tv.tv_sec

struct utmpx  {
   char   ut_user[32];              /* user login name */
   char   ut_id[4];                 /* inittab id */
   char   ut_line[32];              /* device name (console, lnxx) */
   pid_t  ut_pid;                   /* process id */
   short  ut_type;                  /* type of entry */
   struct exit_status ut_exit;      /* process termination/exit status */
   struct timeval ut_tv;            /* time entry was made */
   long   ut_session;               /* session ID, used for windowing */
   long   pad[5];                   /* reserved for future use */
   short  ut_syslen;                /* significant length of ut_host */
                                    /* including terminating null */
   char   ut_host[257];             /* remote host name */
} ;

                                    /* Definitions for ut_type */

#define    EMPTY          0
#define    RUN_LVL        1
#define    BOOT_TIME      2
#define    OLD_TIME       3
#define    NEW_TIME       4
#define    INIT_PROCESS   5   /* Process spawned by "init" */
#define    LOGIN_PROCESS  6   /* A "getty" process waiting for login */
#define    USER_PROCESS   7   /* A user process */
#define    DEAD_PROCESS   8
#define    ACCOUNTING     9

#define    UTMAXTYPE      ACCOUNTING  /* Largest legal value of ut_type */

/*    Below are special strings or formats used in the "ut_line"   */
/*    field when accounting for something other than a process.    */
/*    No string for the ut_line field can be more than 11 chars +  */
/*    a null character in length.                                  */
```

```
#define   RUNLVL_MSG    "run-level %c"
#define   BOOT_MSG      "system boot"
#define   OTIME_MSG     "old time"
#define   NTIME_MSG     "new time"
#define   MOD_WIN       10
```

FILES
/var/adm/utmpx
/var/adm/wtmpx

SEE ALSO
getutx(3C).
login(1), who(1), write(1) in the *User's Reference Manual*.

MISCELLANEOUS (5)

MISCELLANEOUS (5)

NAME
intro – introduction to miscellany

DESCRIPTION
This section describes miscellaneous facilities such as macro packages, character set tables, etc.

ascii(5)

NAME
ascii – map of ASCII character set

DESCRIPTION
ascii is a map of the ASCII character set, giving both octal and hexadecimal equivalents of each character, to be printed as needed. It contains:

OCTAL ASCII

```
|000 nul |001 soh |002 stx |003 etx |004 eot |005 enq |006 ack |007 bel |
|010 bs  |011 ht  |012 nl  |013 vt  |014 np  |015 cr  |016 so  |017 si  |
|020 dle |021 dc1 |022 dc2 |023 dc3 |024 dc4 |025 nak |026 syn |027 etb |
|030 can |031 em  |032 sub |033 esc |034 fs  |035 gs  |036 rs  |037 us  |
|040 sp  |041 !   |042 "   |043 #   |044 $   |045 %   |046 &   |047 '   |
|050 (   |051 )   |052 *   |053 +   |054 ,   |055 -   |056 .   |057 /   |
|060 0   |061 1   |062 2   |063 3   |064 4   |065 5   |066 6   |067 7   |
|070 8   |071 9   |072 :   |073 ;   |074 <   |075 =   |076 >   |077 ?   |
|100 @   |101 A   |102 B   |103 C   |104 D   |105 E   |106 F   |107 G   |
|110 H   |111 I   |112 J   |113 K   |114 L   |115 M   |116 N   |117 O   |
|120 P   |121 Q   |122 R   |123 S   |124 T   |125 U   |126 V   |127 W   |
|130 X   |131 Y   |132 Z   |133 [   |134 \   |135 ]   |136 ^   |137 _   |
|140 `   |141 a   |142 b   |143 c   |144 d   |145 e   |146 f   |147 g   |
|150 h   |151 i   |152 j   |153 k   |154 l   |155 m   |156 n   |157 o   |
|160 p   |161 q   |162 r   |163 s   |164 t   |165 u   |166 v   |167 w   |
|170 x   |171 y   |172 z   |173 {   |174 |   |175 }   |176 ~   |177 del |
```

HEXADECIMAL ASCII

```
| 00 nul | 01 soh | 02 stx | 03 etx | 04 eot | 05 enq | 06 ack | 07 bel |
| 08 bs  | 09 ht  | 0a nl  | 0b vt  | 0c np  | 0d cr  | 0e so  | 0f si  |
| 10 dle | 11 dc1 | 12 dc2 | 13 dc3 | 14 dc4 | 15 nak | 16 syn | 17 etb |
| 18 can | 19 em  | 1a sub | 1b esc | 1c fs  | 1d gs  | 1e rs  | 1f us  |
| 20 sp  | 21 !   | 22 "   | 23 #   | 24 $   | 25 %   | 26 &   | 27 '   |
| 28 (   | 29 )   | 2a *   | 2b +   | 2c ,   | 2d -   | 2e .   | 2f /   |
| 30 0   | 31 1   | 32 2   | 33 3   | 34 4   | 35 5   | 36 6   | 37 7   |
| 38 8   | 39 9   | 3a :   | 3b ;   | 3c <   | 3d =   | 3e >   | 3f ?   |
| 40 @   | 41 A   | 42 B   | 43 C   | 44 D   | 45 E   | 46 F   | 47 G   |
| 48 H   | 49 I   | 4a J   | 4b K   | 4c L   | 4d M   | 4e N   | 4f O   |
| 50 P   | 51 Q   | 52 R   | 53 S   | 54 T   | 55 U   | 56 V   | 57 W   |
| 58 X   | 59 Y   | 5a Z   | 5b [   | 5c \   | 5d ]   | 5e ^   | 5f _   |
| 60 `   | 61 a   | 62 b   | 63 c   | 64 d   | 65 e   | 66 f   | 67 g   |
| 68 h   | 69 i   | 6a j   | 6b k   | 6c l   | 6d m   | 6e n   | 6f o   |
| 70 p   | 71 q   | 72 r   | 73 s   | 74 t   | 75 u   | 76 v   | 77 w   |
| 78 x   | 79 y   | 7a z   | 7b {   | 7c |   | 7d }   | 7e ~   | 7f del |
```

FILES
/usr/pub/ascii

NAME
environ – user environment

DESCRIPTION
When a process begins execution, exec routines make available an array of strings called the environment [see **exec**(2)]. By convention, these strings have the form *variable=value*, for example, `PATH=/sbin:/usr/sbin`. These environmental variables provide a way to make information about a program's environment available to programs. The following environmental variables can be used by applications and are expected to be set in the target run-time environment.

HOME
: The name of the user's login directory, set by **login**(1) from the password file (see **passwd**(4)).

LANG
: The string used to specify localization information that allows users to work with different national conventions. The **setlocale**(3C) function looks for the **LANG** environment variable when it is called with "" as the *locale* argument. **LANG** is used as the default locale if the corresponding environment variable for a particular category is unset.

For example, when **setlocale**() is invoked as

setlocale(LC_CTYPE, ""),

setlocale() will query the LC_CTYPE environment variable first to see if it is set and non-null. If LC_CTYPE is not set or null, then setlocale() will check the LANG environment variable to see if it is set and non-null. If both LANG and LC_CTYPE are unset or null, the default C locale will be used to set the LC_CTYPE category.

Most commands will invoke

setlocale(LC_ALL, "")

prior to any other processing. This allows the command to be used with different national conventions by setting the appropriate environment variables.

The following environment variables are supported to correspond with each category of **setlocale**(3C):

LC_COLLATE
: This category specifies the collation sequence being used. The information corresponding to this category is stored in a database created by the **colltbl**(1M) command. This environment variable affects **strcoll**(3C) and **strxfrm**(3C).

LC_CTYPE
: This category specifies character classification, character conversion, and widths of multibyte characters. The information corresponding to this category is stored in a database created by the **chrtbl**(1M) command. The default C locale corresponds to the 7-bit ASCII character set. This environment variable is used by **ctype**(3C),

	mbchar(3C), and many commands; for example: cat(1), ed(1), ls(1), and vi(1).
LC_MESSAGES	This category specifies the language of the message database being used. For example, an application may have one message database with French messages, and another database with German messages. Message databases are created by the mkmsgs(1M) command. This environment variable is used by exstr(1), gettxt(1), gettxt(3C), and srchtxt(1).
LC_MONETARY	This category specifies the monetary symbols and delimiters used for a particular locale. The information corresponding to this category is stored in a database created by the montbl(1M) command. This environment variable is used by localeconv(3C).
LC_NUMERIC	This category specifies the decimal and thousands delimiters. The information corresponding to this category is stored in a database created by the chrtbl(1M) command. The default C locale corresponds to "." as the decimal delimiter and no thousands delimiter. This environment variable is used by localeconv(3C), printf(3C), and strtod(3C).
LC_TIME	This category specifies date and time formats. The information corresponding to this category is stored in a database specified in strftime(4). The default C locale corresponds to U.S. date and time formats. This environment variable is used by many commands and functions; for example: at(1), calendar(1), date(1), strftime(3C), and getdate(3C).
MSGVERB	Controls which standard format message components fmtmsg selects when messages are displayed to stderr [see fmtmsg(1) and fmtmsg(3C)].
SEV_LEVEL	Define severity levels and associate and print strings with them in standard format error messages [see addseverity(3C), fmtmsg(1), and fmtmsg(3C)].
NETPATH	A colon-separated list of network identifiers. A network identifier is a character string used by the Network Selection component of the system to provide application-specific default network search paths. A network identifier must consist of non-NULL characters and must have a length of at least 1. No maximum length is specified. Network identifiers are normally chosen by the system administrator. A network identifier is also the first field in any /etc/netconfig file entry. NETPATH thus provides a link into the /etc/netconfig file and the information about a network contained in that network's entry. /etc/netconfig is maintained by the system administrator.

The library routines described in getnetpath(3N) access the NET-
PATH environment variable.

NLSPATH Contains a sequence of templates which catopen(3C) uses when
attempting to locate message catalogs. Each template consists of an
optional prefix, one or more substitution fields, a filename and an
optional suffix.

For example:

  NLSPATH="/system/nlslib/%N.cat"

defines that catopen() should look for all message catalogs in the
directory /system/nlslib, where the catalog name should be constructed from the *name* parameter passed to catopen(), %N, with
the suffix .cat.

Substitution fields consist of a % symbol, followed by a single-letter
keyword. The following keywords are currently defined:

%N	The value of the *name* parameter passed to catopen().
%L	The value of LANG.
%l	The language element from LANG.
%t	The territory element from LANG.
%c	The codeset element from LANG.
%%	A single % character.

An empty string is substituted if the specified value is not currently
defined. The separators "_" and "." are not included in %t and %c
substitutions.

Templates defined in NLSPATH are separated by colons (:). A leading colon or two adjacent colons (::) is equivalent to specifying %N.

For example:

  NLSPATH=":%N.cat:/nlslib/%L/%N.cat"

indicates to catopen() that it should look for the requested message
catalog in *name*, *name*.cat and /nlslib/$LANG/*name*.cat.

PATH The sequence of directory prefixes that sh(1), time(1), nice(1),
nohup(1), etc., apply in searching for a file known by an incomplete
path name. The prefixes are separated by colons (:). login(1) sets
PATH=/usr/bin. (For more detail, see sh(1).)

TERM The kind of terminal for which output is to be prepared. This information is used by commands, such as mm(1) or vi(1), which may
exploit special capabilities of that terminal.

TZ Time zone information. The contents of the environment variable
named TZ are used by the functions ctime(3C), localtime() (see
ctime(3C)), strftime(3C) and mktime(3C) to override the default
timezone. If the first character of TZ is a colon (:), the behavior is

implementation defined, otherwise TZ has the form:

std offset [*dst* [*offset*] , [*start* [/*time*] , *end* [/*time*]]]

std and *dst*
: Three or more bytes that are the designation for the standard (*std*) and daylight savings time (*dst*) timezones. Only *std* is required, if *dst* is missing, then daylight savings time does not apply in this locale. Upper- and lower-case letters are allowed. Any characters except a leading colon (:), digits, a comma (,), a minus (−) or a plus (+) are allowed.

offset
: Indicates the value one must add to the local time to arrive at Coordinated Universal Time. The offset has the form:

  hh [: mm [: ss]]

  The minutes (mm) and seconds (ss) are optional. The hour (hh) is required and may be a single digit. The *offset* following *std* is required. If no *offset* follows *dst* , daylight savings time is assumed to be one hour ahead of standard time. One or more digits may be used; the value is always interpreted as a decimal number. The hour must be between 0 and 24, and the minutes (and seconds) if present between 0 and 59. Out of range values may cause unpredictable behavior. If preceded by a "−", the timezone is east of the Prime Meridian; otherwise it is west (which may be indicated by an optional preceding "+" sign).

start/*time*, *end*/*time*
: Indicates when to change to and back from daylight savings time, where *start*/*time* describes when the change from standard time to daylight savings time occurs, and *end*/*time* describes when the change back happens. Each *time* field describes when, in current local time, the change is made.

  The formats of *start* and *end* are one of the following:

  Jn
  : The Julian day n (1 ≤ n ≤ 365). Leap days are not counted. That is, in all years, February 28 is day 59 and March 1 is day 60. It is impossible to refer to the occasional February 29.

  n
  : The zero-based Julian day (0 ≤ n ≤ 365). Leap days are counted, and it is possible to refer to February 29.

  M$m.n.d$
  : The dth day, (0 ≤ d ≤ 6) of week n of month m of the year (1 ≤ n ≤ 5, 1 ≤ m ≤ 12), where week 5 means "the last d-day in month m" which may occur in either the fourth or the fifth week). Week 1 is the first week in which the dth day occurs. Day zero is Sunday.

Implementation specific defaults are used for *start* and *end* if these optional fields are not given.

The *time* has the same format as *offset* except that no leading sign ("−" or "+") is allowed. The default, if *time* is not given is 02:00:00.

Further names may be placed in the environment by the **export** command and *name*=*value* arguments in **sh**(1), or by **exec**(2). It is unwise to conflict with certain shell variables that are frequently exported by .profile files: MAIL, PS1, PS2, IFS (see profile(4)).

SEE ALSO

chrtbl(1M), colltbl(1M), mkmsgs(1M), montbl(1M), netconfig(4), strftime(4), passwd(4), profile(4) in the *System Administrator's Reference Manual*.

exec(2), addseverity(3C), catopen(3C), ctime(3C), ctype(3C), fmtmsg(3C), getdate(3C), gettxt(3C), localeconv(3C), mbchar(3C), mktime(3C), printf(3C), strcoll(3C), strftime(3C), strtod(3C), strxfrm(3C), strftime(4), timezone(4).

cat(1), date(1), ed(1), fmtmsg(1), ls(1), login(1), nice(1), nohup(1), sh(1), sort(1), time(1), vi(1) in the *User's Reference Manual*.

getnetpath(3N), in the *Programmer's Guide: Networking Interfaces*.

mm(1) in the *DOCUMENTER'S WORKBENCH Software Technical Discussion and Reference Manual*.

fcntl(5)

NAME
fcntl – file control options

SYNOPSIS
#include <fcntl.h>

DESCRIPTION
The <fcntl.h> header defines the following requests and arguments for use by the functions fcntl [see fcntl(2)] and open [see open(2)].

Values for *cmd* used by fcntl (the following values are unique):

F_DUPFD	Duplicate file descriptor
F_GETFD	Get file descriptor flags
F_SETFD	Set file descriptor flags
F_GETFL	Get file status flags
F_SETFL	Set file status flags
F_GETLK	Get record locking information
F_SETLK	Set record locking information
F_SETLKW	Set record locking information; wait if blocked

File descriptor flags used for fcntl:

FD_CLOEXEC	Close the file descriptor upon execution of an exec function [see exec(2)]

Values for l_type used for record locking with fcntl (the following values are unique):

F_RDLCK	Shared or read lock
F_UNLCK	Unlock
F_WRLCK	Exclusive or write lock

The following three sets of values are bitwise distinct:
Values for oflag used by open:

O_CREAT	Create file if it does not exist
O_EXCL	Exclusive use flag
O_NOCTTY	Do not assign controlling tty
O_TRUNC	Truncate flag

File status flags used for open and fcntl:

O_APPEND	Set append mode
O_NDELAY	Non-blocking mode
O_NONBLOCK	Non-blocking mode (POSIX)
O_SYNC	Synchronous writes

Mask for use with file access modes:

O_ACCMODE	Mask for file access modes

File access modes used for **open** and **fcntl**:
    O_RDONLY   Open for reading only
    O_RDWR   Open for reading and writing
    O_WRONLY   Open for writing only

The structure `flock` describes a file lock. It includes the following members:

```
short   l_type;     /* Type of lock */
short   l_whence;   /* Flag for starting offset */
off_t   l_start;    /* Relative offset in bytes */
off_t   l_len;      /* Size; if 0 then until EOF */
long    l_sysid;    /* Returned with F_GETLK */
pid_t   l_pid;      /* Returned with F_GETLK */
```

SEE ALSO
creat(2), exec(2), fcntl(2), open(2).

NAME
jagent – host control of windowing terminal

SYNOPSIS
#include <sys/jioctl.h>

int ioctl (int cntlfd, JAGENT, &arg);

DESCRIPTION
The ioctl system call, when performed on an xt(7) device with the JAGENT request, allows a host program to send information to a windowing terminal.

ioctl has three arguments:

cntlfd the xt(7) control channel file descriptor

JAGENT the xt ioctl request to invoke a windowing terminal agent routine.

&arg the address of a bagent structure, defined in <sys/jioctl.h> as follows:

```
struct  bagent {
  long  size;   /* size of src in & dest out */
  char  *src;   /* the source byte string */
  char  *dest;  /* the destination byte string */
};
```

The src pointer must be initialized to point to a byte string that is sent to the windowing terminal. See layers(5) for a list of JAGENT strings recognized by windowing terminals. Likewise, the dest pointer must be initialized to the address of a buffer to receive a byte string returned by the terminal. When ioctl is called, the size argument must be set to the length of the src string. Upon return, size is set by ioctl to the length of the destination byte string, dest.

SEE ALSO
ioctl(2), libwindows(3X), layers(5).

xt(7) in the *Programmer's Guide: STREAMS*.

DIAGNOSTICS
Upon successful completion, a non-negative value, the size of the destination byte string, is returned. If an error occurs, −1 is returned.

langinfo(5)

NAME
langinfo – language information constants

SYNOPSIS
#include <langinfo.h>

DESCRIPTION
This header file contains the constants used to identify items of langinfo data. The mode of *items* is given in **nl_types**.

DAY_1	Locale's equivalent of 'sunday'
DAY_2	Locale's equivalent of 'monday'
DAY_3	Locale's equivalent of 'tuesday'
DAY_4	Locale's equivalent of 'wednesday'
DAY_5	Locale's equivalent of 'thursday'
DAY_6	Locale's equivalent of 'friday'
DAY_7	Locale's equivalent of 'saturday'
ABDAY_1	Locale's equivalent of 'sun'
ABDAY_2	Locale's equivalent of 'mon'
ABDAY_3	Locale's equivalent of 'tue'
ABDAY_4	Locale's equivalent of 'wed'
ABDAY_5	Locale's equivalent of 'thur'
ABDAY_6	Locale's equivalent of 'fri'
ABDAY_7	Locale's equivalent of 'sat'
MON_1	Locale's equivalent of 'january'
MON_2	Locale's equivalent of 'febuary'
MON_3	Locale's equivalent of 'march'
MON_4	Locale's equivalent of 'april'
MON_5	Locale's equivalent of 'may'
MON_6	Locale's equivalent of 'june'
MON_7	Locale's equivalent of 'july'
MON_8	Locale's equivalent of 'august'
MON_9	Locale's equivalent of 'september'
MON_10	Locale's equivalent of 'october'
MON_11	Locale's equivalent of 'november'
MON_12	Locale's equivalent of 'december'
ABMON_1	Locale's equivalent of 'jan'

ABMON_2	Locale's equivalent of 'feb'
ABMON_3	Locale's equivalent of 'mar'
ABMON_4	Locale's equivalent of 'apr'
ABMON_5	Locale's equivalent of 'may'
ABMON_6	Locale's equivalent of 'jun'
ABMON_7	Locale's equivalent of 'jul'
ABMON_8	Locale's equivalent of 'aug'
ABMON_9	Locale's equivalent of 'sep'
ABMON_10	Locale's equivalent of 'oct'
ABMON_11	Locale's equivalent of 'nov'
ABMON_12	Locale's equivalent of 'dec'
RADIXCHAR	Locale's equivalent of '.'
THOUSEP	Locale's equivalent of ','
YESSTR	Locale's equivalent of 'yes'
NOSTR	Locale's equivalent of 'no'
CRNCYSTR	Locale's currency symbol
D_T_FMT	Locale's default format for date and time
D_FMT	Locale's default format for the date
T_FMT	Locale's default format for the time
AM_STR	Locale's equivalent of 'AM'
PM_STR	Locale's equivalent of 'PM'

This information is retrived by nl_langinfo.

The items CRNCYSTR, RADIXCHAR and THOUSEP are extracted from the fields currency_symbol, decimal_point and thousands_sep in the structure returned by localeconv.

The items T_FMT, D_FMT, D_T_FMT, YESSTR and NOSTR are retrived from a special message catalog named Xopen_info which should be generated for each locale supported and installed in the appropriate directory [see gettxt(3C) and mkmsgs(1M)]. This catalog should have the messages in the order T_FMT, D_FMT, D_T_FMT, YESSTR and NOSTR.

All other items are as returned by strftime.

SEE ALSO

gettxt(3C), localeconv(3C), nl_langinfo(3C), strftime(3C), cftime(4), nl_types(5).
chrtbl(1), mkmsgs(1M) in the *System Administrator's Reference Manual*.

layers(5)

NAME
layers – protocol used between host and windowing terminal under **layers**(1)

DESCRIPTION
Layers are asynchronous windows supported by the operating system in a windowing terminal. Communication between the UNIX System processes and terminal processes under the **layers** command [see **layers**(1)] occurs via multiplexed channels managed by the respective operating systems using a protocol as specified in **xtproto**(5).

The contents of packets transferring data between a UNIX System process and a layer are asymmetric. Data sent from the UNIX System to a particular terminal process are undifferentiated and it is up to the terminal process to interpret the contents of packets.

Control information for terminal processes is sent via channel 0. Process 0 in the windowing terminal performs the designated functions on behalf of the process connected to the designated channel. These packets take the form:

> *command, channel*

except for **JTIMOM** and **JAGENT** information, which takes the form

> *command, data ...*

The commands are the bottom eight bits extracted from the following **ioctl**(2) codes:

JBOOT Prepare to load a new terminal program into the designated layer.

JTERM Kill the downloaded layer program, and restore the default window program.

JTIMOM Set the timeout parameters for the protocol. The data consist of four bytes in two groups: the value of the receive timeout in milliseconds (the low eight bits followed by the high eight bits) and the value of the transmit timeout (in the same format).

JZOMBOOT Like **JBOOT**, but do not execute the program after loading.

JAGENT Send a source byte string to the terminal agent routine and wait for a reply byte string to be returned.

> The data are from a **bagent** structure [see **jagent**(5)] and consist of a one-byte size field followed by a two-byte agent command code and parameters. Two-byte integers transmitted as part of an agent command are sent with the high-order byte first. The response from the terminal is generally identical to the command packet, with the two command bytes replaced by the return code: 0 for success, −1 for failure. Note that the routines in the **libwindows**(3X) library all send parameters in an **agentrect** structure. The agent command codes and their parameters are as follows:
>
> **A_NEWLAYER** followed by a two-byte channel number and a rectangle structure (four two-byte coordinates).

A_CURRENT	followed by a two-byte channel number.
A_DELETE	followed by a two-byte channel number.
A_TOP	followed by a two-byte channel number.
A_BOTTOM	followed by a two-byte channel number.
A_MOVE	followed by a two-byte channel number and a point to move to (two two-byte coordinates).
A_RESHAPE	followed by a two-byte channel number and the new rectangle (four two-byte coordinates).
A_NEW	followed by a two-byte channel number and a rectangle structure (four two-byte coordinates).
A_EXIT	no parameters needed.
A_ROMVERSION	no parameters needed. The response packet contains the size byte, two-byte return code, two unused bytes, and the parameter part of the terminal ID string (e.g., 8;7;3).

JXTPROTO   Set xt protocol type [see xtproto(5)]. The data consist of one byte specifying maximum size for the data part of regular xt packets sent from the host to the terminal. This number may be lower than the number returned by A_XTPROTO at lower baud rates or if the −m option was specified upon invocation of layers(1). A size of 1 specifies network xt protocol.

Packets from the windowing terminal to the UNIX System all take the following form:

command, data ...

The single-byte commands are as follows:

C_SENDCHAR	Send the next byte to the UNIX System process.
C_NEW	Create a new UNIX System process group for this layer. Remember the window size parameters for this layer. The data for this command is in the form described by the jwinsize structure. The size of the window is specified by two 2-byte integers, sent low byte first.
C_UNBLK	Unblock transmission to this layer. There are no data for this command.
C_DELETE	Delete the UNIX System process group attached to this layer. There are no data for this command.
C_EXIT	Exit. Kill all UNIX System process groups associated with this terminal and terminate the session. There are no data for this command.
C_DEFUNCT	Layer program has died, send a terminate signal to the UNIX System process groups associated with this terminal. There are no data for this command.

	C_SENDNCHARS	The rest of the data are characters to be passed to the UNIX System process.
	C_RESHAPE	The layer has been reshaped. Change the window size parameters for this layer. The data take the same form as for the C_NEW command. A SIGWINCH signal is also sent to the process in the window, so that the process knows that the window has been reshaped and it can get the new window parameters.
	C_NOFLOW	Disable network xt flow control [see xtproto(5)].
	C_YESFLOW	Enable network xt flow control [see xtproto(5)].

FILES
/usr/include/windows.h
/usr/include/sys/jioctl.h

SEE ALSO
layers(1), libwindows(3X), jagent(5), xtproto(5).
xt(7) in the *Programmer's Guide: STREAMS*.

math(5) math(5)

NAME
math – math functions and constants

SYNOPSIS
#include <math.h>

DESCRIPTION
This file contains declarations of all the functions in the Math Library (described in Section 3M), as well as various functions in the C Library (Section 3C) that return floating-point values.

It defines the structure and constants used by the matherr(3M) error-handling mechanisms, including the following constant used as a error-return value:

HUGE   The maximum value of a single-precision floating-point number.

The following mathematical constants are defined for user convenience:

M_E   The base of natural logarithms (e).
M_LOG2E   The base-2 logarithm of e.
M_LOG10E   The base-10 logarithm of e.
M_LN2   The natural logarithm of 2.
M_LN10   The natural logarithm of 10.
M_PI π, the ratio of the circumference of a circle to its diameter.
M_PI_2 $\pi/2$.
M_PI_4 $\pi/4$.
M_1_PI $1/\pi$.
M_2_PI $2/\pi$.
M_2_SQRTPI $2/\sqrt{\pi}$.
M_SQRT2   The positive square root of 2.
M_SQRT1_2   The positive square root of 1/2.

The following mathematical constants are also defined in this header file:

MAXFLOAT   The maximum value of a non-infinite single-precision floating point number.
HUGE_VAL   positive infinity.

For the definitions of various machine-dependent constants, see values(5).

SEE ALSO
intro(3), matherr(3M), values(5).

nl_types(5)

NAME
nl_types – native language data types

SYNOPSIS
#include <nl_types.h>

DESCRIPTION
This header file contains the following definitions:

nl_catd	used by the message catalog functions **catopen**, **catgets** and **catclose** to identify a catalogue
nl_item	used by **nl_langinfo** to identify items of langinfo data. Values for objects of type **nl_item** are defined in **langinfo.h**.
NL_SETD	used by **gencat** when no **$set** directive is specified in a message text source file. This constant can be used in subsequent calls to **catgets** as the value of the set identifier parameter.
NL_MGSMAX	maximum number of messages per set
NL_SETMAX	maximum number of sets per catalogue.
NL_TEXTMAX	maximum size of a message.
DEF_NLSPATH	the default search path for locating catalogues.

SEE ALSO
catgets(3C), catopen(3C), nl_langinfo(3C), langinfo(5).
gencat(1M) in the *System Administrator's Reference Manual*.

NAME
prof – profile within a function

SYNOPSIS
#define MARK
#include <prof.h>

void MARK (name);

DESCRIPTION
MARK introduces a mark called *name* that is treated the same as a function entry point. Execution of the mark adds to a counter for that mark, and program-counter time spent is accounted to the immediately preceding mark or to the function if there are no preceding marks within the active function.

name may be any combination of letters, numbers, or underscores. Each *name* in a single compilation must be unique, but may be the same as any ordinary program symbol.

For marks to be effective, the symbol MARK must be defined before the header file prof.h is included, either by a preprocessor directive as in the synopsis, or by a command line argument:

cc -p -DMARK foo.c

If MARK is not defined, the MARK(*name*) statements may be left in the source files containing them and are ignored. prof -g must be used to get information on all labels.

EXAMPLE
In this example, marks can be used to determine how much time is spent in each loop. Unless this example is compiled with MARK defined on the command line, the marks are ignored.

```
#include <prof.h>
foo( )
{
    int i, j;
    . . .
    MARK(loop1);
    for (i = 0; i < 2000; i++) {
        . . .
    }
    MARK(loop2);
    for (j = 0; j < 2000; j++) {
        . . .
    }
}
```

SEE ALSO
prof(1), profil(2), monitor(3C).

regexp(5)

NAME
regexp: compile, step, advance − regular expression compile and match routines

SYNOPSIS
#define INIT *declarations*
#define GETC(void) *getc code*
#define PEEKC(void) *peekc code*
#define UNGETC(void) *ungetc code*
#define RETURN(*ptr*) *return code*
#define ERROR(*val*) *error code*

#include <regexp.h>

char *compile(char *instring, char *expbuf, char *endbuf, int eof);

int step(char *string, char *expbuf);

int advance(char *string, char *expbuf);

extern char *loc1, *loc2, *locs;

DESCRIPTION
These functions are general purpose regular expression matching routines to be used in programs that perform regular expression matching. These functions are defined by the <regexp.h> header file.

The functions **step** and **advance** do pattern matching given a character string and a compiled regular expression as input.

The function **compile** takes as input a regular expression as defined below and produces a compiled expression that can be used with **step** or **advance**.

A regular expression specifies a set of character strings. A member of this set of strings is said to be matched by the regular expression. Some characters have special meaning when used in a regular expression; other characters stand for themselves.

The regular expressions available for use with the regexp functions are constructed as follows:

Expression	*Meaning*
c	the character c where c is not a special character.
\c	the character c where c is any character, except a digit in the range 1−9.
^	the beginning of the line being compared.
$	the end of the line being compared.
.	any character in the input.
[s]	any character in the set s, where s is a sequence of characters and/or a range of characters, e.g., [c−c].

[^s]	any character not in the set s, where s is defined as above.
r*	zero or more successive occurrences of the regular expression r. The longest leftmost match is chosen.
rx	the occurrence of regular expression r followed by the occurrence of regular expression x. (Concatenation)
r\{m,n\}	any number of m through n successive occurrences of the regular expression r. The regular expression r\{m\} matches exactly m occurrences; r\{m,\} matches at least m occurrences.
\(r\)	the regular expression r. When \n (where n is a number greater than zero) appears in a constructed regular expression, it stands for the regular expression x where x is the nth regular expression enclosed in \(and \) that appeared earlier in the constructed regular expression. For example, \(r\)x\(y\)z\2 is the concatenation of regular expressions rxyzy.

Characters that have special meaning except when they appear within square brackets ([ ]) or are preceded by \ are: ., *, [, \. Other special characters, such as $ have special meaning in more restricted contexts.

The character ^ at the beginning of an expression permits a successful match only immediately after a newline, and the character $ at the end of an expression requires a trailing newline.

Two characters have special meaning only when used within square brackets. The character – denotes a range, [c–c], unless it is just after the open bracket or before the closing bracket, [–c] or [c–] in which case it has no special meaning. When used within brackets, the character ^ has the meaning *complement of* if it immediately follows the open bracket (example: [^c]); elsewhere between brackets (example: [c^]) it stands for the ordinary character ^.

The special meaning of the \ operator can be escaped only by preceding it with another \, e.g. \\.

Programs must have the following five macros declared before the #include <regexp.h> statement. These macros are used by the compile routine. The macros GETC, PEEKC, and UNGETC operate on the regular expression given as input to compile.

GETC	This macro returns the value of the next character (byte) in the regular expression pattern. Successive calls to GETC should return successive characters of the regular expression.
PEEKC	This macro returns the next character (byte) in the regular expression. Immediately successive calls to PEEKC should return the same character, which should also be the next character returned by GETC.
UNGETC	This macro causes the argument c to be returned by the next call to GETC and PEEKC. No more than one character of pushback is ever needed and this character is guaranteed to be the last character read by GETC. The return value of the macro UNGETC(c) is always ignored.

RETURN (*ptr*)   This macro is used on normal exit of the **compile** routine. The value of the argument *ptr* is a pointer to the character after the last character of the compiled regular expression. This is useful to programs which have memory allocation to manage.

ERROR (*val*)   This macro is the abnormal return from the **compile** routine. The argument *val* is an error number [see ERRORS below for meanings]. This call should never return.

The syntax of the **compile** routine is as follows:

> **compile** (*instring, expbuf, endbuf, eof*)

The first parameter, *instring*, is never used explicitly by the **compile** routine but is useful for programs that pass down different pointers to input characters. It is sometimes used in the INIT declaration (see below). Programs which call functions to input characters or have characters in an external array can pass down a value of (char *)0 for this parameter.

The next parameter, *expbuf*, is a character pointer. It points to the place where the compiled regular expression will be placed.

The parameter *endbuf* is one more than the highest address where the compiled regular expression may be placed. If the compiled expression cannot fit in (endbuf−expbuf) bytes, a call to ERROR(50) is made.

The parameter *eof* is the character which marks the end of the regular expression. This character is usually a /.

Each program that includes the <regexp.h> header file must have a #define statement for INIT. It is used for dependent declarations and initializations. Most often it is used to set a register variable to point to the beginning of the regular expression so that this register variable can be used in the declarations for GETC, PEEKC, and UNGETC. Otherwise it can be used to declare external variables that might be used by GETC, PEEKC and UNGETC. [See EXAMPLE below.]

The first parameter to the **step** and **advance** functions is a pointer to a string of characters to be checked for a match. This string should be null terminated.

The second parameter, *expbuf*, is the compiled regular expression which was obtained by a call to the function **compile**.

The function **step** returns non-zero if some substring of *string* matches the regular expression in *expbuf* and zero if there is no match. If there is a match, two external character pointers are set as a side effect to the call to **step**. The variable loc1 points to the first character that matched the regular expression; the variable loc2 points to the character after the last character that matches the regular expression. Thus if the regular expression matches the entire input string, loc1 will point to the first character of *string* and loc2 will point to the null at the end of *string*.

The function **advance** returns non-zero if the initial substring of *string* matches the regular expression in *expbuf*. If there is a match, an external character pointer, loc2, is set as a side effect. The variable loc2 points to the next character in *string* after the last character that matched.

When advance encounters a * or \{ \} sequence in the regular expression, it will advance its pointer to the string to be matched as far as possible and will recursively call itself trying to match the rest of the string to the rest of the regular expression. As long as there is no match, advance will back up along the string until it finds a match or reaches the point in the string that initially matched the * or \{ \}. It is sometimes desirable to stop this backing up before the initial point in the string is reached. If the external character pointer locs is equal to the point in the string at sometime during the backing up process, advance will break out of the loop that backs up and will return zero.

The external variables circf, sed, and nbra are reserved.

DIAGNOSTICS

The function compile uses the macro RETURN on success and the macro ERROR on failure (see above). The functions step and advance return non-zero on a successful match and zero if there is no match. Errors are:

11	range endpoint too large.
16	bad number.
25	\ *digit* out of range.
36	illegal or missing delimiter.
41	no remembered search string.
42	\ (\ ) imbalance.
43	too many \ (.
44	more than 2 numbers given in \{ \}.
45	} expected after \.
46	first number exceeds second in \{ \}.
49	[ ] imbalance.
50	regular expression overflow.

EXAMPLE

The following is an example of how the regular expression macros and calls might be defined by an application program:

```
#define INIT        register char *sp = instring;
#define GETC        (*sp++)
#define PEEKC       (*sp)
#define UNGETC(c)   (--sp)
#define RETURN(*c)  return;
#define ERROR(c)    regerr

#include <regexp.h>

. . .
    (void) compile(*argv, expbuf, &expbuf[ESIZE],'\0');
. . .
    if (step(linebuf, expbuf))
            succeed;
```

siginfo(5)

NAME
siginfo – signal generation information

SYNOPSIS
#include <siginfo.h>

DESCRIPTION
If a process is catching a signal, it may request information that tells why the system generated that signal [see sigaction(2)]. If a process is monitoring its children, it may receive information that tells why a child changed state [see waitid(2)]. In either case, the system returns the information in a structure of type siginfo_t, which includes the following information:

```
int si_signo      /* signal number */
int si_errno      /* error number */
int si_code       /* signal code */
```

si_signo contains the system-generated signal number. (For the waitid(2) function, si_signo is always SIGCHLD.)

If si_errno is non-zero, it contains an error number associated with this signal, as defined in errno.h.

si_code contains a code identifying the cause of the signal. If the value of si_code is less than or equal to 0, then the signal was generated by a user process [see kill(2) and sigsend(2)] and the siginfo structure contains the following additional information:

```
pid_t si_pid      /* sending process ID */
uid_t si_uid      /* sending user ID */
```

Otherwise, si_code contains a signal-specific reason why the signal was generated, as follows:

Signal	Code	Reason
SIGILL	ILL_ILLOPC	illegal opcode
	ILL_ILLOPN	illegal operand
	ILL_ILLADR	illegal addressing mode
	ILL_ILLTRP	illegal trap
	ILL_PRVOPC	privileged opcode
	ILL_PRVREG	privileged register
	ILL_COPROC	coprocessor error
	ILL_BADSTK	internal stack error
SIGFPE	FPE_INTDIV	integer divide by zero
	FPE_INTOVF	integer overflow
	FPE_FLTDIV	floating point divide by zero
	FPE_FLTOVF	floating point overflow
	FPE_FLTUND	floating point underflow
	FPE_FLTRES	floating point inexact result
	FPE_FLTINV	invalid floating point operation
	FPE_FLTSUB	subscript out of range

Signal	Code	Reason
SIGSEGV	SEGV_MAPERR	address not mapped to object
	SEGV_ACCERR	invalid permissions for mapped object
SIGBUS	BUS_ADRALN	invalid address alignment
	BUS_ADRERR	non-existent physical address
	BUS_OBJERR	object specific hardware error
SIGTRAP	TRAP_BRKPT	process breakpoint
	TRAP_TRACE	process trace trap
SIGCHLD	CLD_EXITED	child has exited
	CLD_KILLED	child was killed
	CLD_DUMPED	child terminated abnormally
	CLD_TRAPPED	traced child has trapped
	CLD_STOPPED	child has stopped
	CLD_CONTINUED	stopped child had continued
SIGPOLL	POLL_IN	data input available
	POLL_OUT	output buffers available
	POLL_MSG	input message available
	POLL_ERR	I/O error
	POLL_PRI	high priority input available
	POLL_HUP	device disconnected

In addition, the following signal-dependent information is available for kernel-generated signals:

Signal	Field	Value
SIGILL SIGFPE	caddr_t si_addr	address of faulting instruction
SIGSEGV SIGBUS	caddr_t si_addr	address of faulting memory reference
SIGCHLD	pid_t si_pid	child process ID
	int si_status	exit value or signal
SIGPOLL	long si_band	band event for POLL_IN, POLL_OUT, or POLL_MSG

SEE ALSO

sigaction(2), waitid(2), signal(5).

NOTES

For SIGCHLD signals, if si_code is equal to CLD_EXITED, then si_status is equal to the exit value of the process; otherwise, it is equal to the signal that caused the process to change state. For some implementations, the exact value of si_addr may not be available; in that case, si_addr is guaranteed to be on the same page as the faulting instruction or memory reference.

signal(5)

NAME
signal – base signals

SYNOPSIS
#include <signal.h>

DESCRIPTION
A signal is an asynchronous notification of an event. A signal is said to be generated for (or sent to) a process when the event associated with that signal first occurs. Examples of such events include hardware faults, timer expiration and terminal activity, as well as the invocation of the `kill` or `sigsend` system calls. In some circumstances, the same event generates signals for multiple processes. A process may request a detailed notification of the source of the signal and the reason why it was generated [see `siginfo`(5)].

Each process may specify a system action to be taken in response to each signal sent to it, called the signal's disposition. The set of system signal actions for a process is initialized from that of its parent. Once an action is installed for a specific signal, it usually remains installed until another disposition is explicitly requested by a call to either `sigaction`, `signal` or `sigset`, or until the process execs [see `sigaction`(2) and `signal`(2)]. When a process execs, all signals whose disposition has been set to catch the signal will be set to SIG_DFL. Alternatively, a process may request that the system automatically reset the disposition of a signal to SIG_DFL after it has been caught [see `sigaction`(2) and `signal`(2)].

A signal is said to be delivered to a process when the appropriate action for the process and signal is taken. During the time between the generation of a signal and its delivery, the signal is said to be pending [see `sigpending`(2)]. Ordinarily, this interval cannot be detected by an application. However, a signal can be blocked from delivery to a process [see `signal`(2) and `sigprocmask`(2)]. If the action associated with a blocked signal is anything other than to ignore the signal, and if that signal is generated for the process, the signal remains pending until either it is unblocked or the signal's disposition requests that the signal be ignored. If the signal disposition of a blocked signal requests that the signal be ignored, and if that signal is generated for the process, the signal is discarded immediately upon generation.

Each process has a signal mask that defines the set of signals currently blocked from delivery to it [see `sigprocmask`(2)]. The signal mask for a process is initialized from that of its parent.

The determination of which action is taken in response to a signal is made at the time the signal is delivered, allowing for any changes since the time of generation. This determination is independent of the means by which the signal was originally generated.

The signals currently defined in <signal.h> are as follows:

Name	Value	Default	Event
SIGHUP	1	Exit	Hangup [see termio(7)]
SIGINT	2	Exit	Interrupt [see termio(7)]
SIGQUIT	3	Core	Quit [see termio(7)]
SIGILL	4	Core	Illegal Instruction
SIGTRAP	5	Core	Trace/Breakpoint Trap
SIGIOT	6	Core	Abort
SIGEMT	7	Core	Emulation Trap
SIGFPE	8	Core	Arithmetic Exception
SIGKILL	9	Exit	Killed
SIGBUS	10	Core	Bus Error
SIGSEGV	11	Core	Segmentation Fault
SIGSYS	12	Core	Bad System Call
SIGPIPE	13	Exit	Broken Pipe
SIGALRM	14	Exit	Alarm Clock
SIGTERM	15	Exit	Terminated
SIGUSR1	16	Exit	User Signal 1
SIGUSR2	17	Exit	User Signal 2
SIGCHLD	18	Ignore	Child Status (change alias POSIX)
SIGPWR	19	Ignore	Power Fail/Restart
SIGWINCH	20	Ignore	Window Size Change
SIGURG	21	Ignore	Urgent Socket Condition
SIGIO	22	Ignore	Socket I/O Possible (SIGPOLL alias)
SIGSTOP	23	Stop	Stopped (signal)
SIGTSTP	24	Stop	Stopped (user) [see termio(7)]
SIGCONT	25	Ignore	Continued
SIGTTIN	26	Stop	Stopped (tty input) [see termio(7)]
SIGTTOU	27	Stop	Stopped (tty output) [see termio(7)]
SIGVTALRM	28	Exit	Virtual Timer Expired
SIGPROF	29	Exit	Profiling Timer Expired
SIGXCPU	30	Core	CPU time limit exceeded [see getrlimit(2)]
SIGXFSZ	31	Core	File size limit exceeded [see getrlimit(2)]

Using the signal, sigset or sigaction system call, a process may specify one of three dispositions for a signal: take the default action for the signal, ignore the signal, or catch the signal.

Default Action: SIG_DFL

A disposition of SIG_DFL specifies the default action. The default action for each signal is listed in the table above and is selected from the following:

Exit   When it gets the signal, the receiving process is to be terminated with all the consequences outlined in exit(2).

Core   When it gets the signal, the receiving process is to be terminated with all the consequences outlined in exit(2). In addition, a "core image" of the process is constructed in the current working directory.

Stop   When it gets the signal, the receiving process is to stop.

signal(5)

Ignore   When it gets the signal, the receiving process is to ignore it. This is identical to setting the disposition to SIG_IGN.

Ignore Signal: SIG_IGN
A disposition of SIG_IGN specifies that the signal is to be ignored.

Catch Signal: *function address*
A disposition that is a function address specifies that, when it gets the signal, the receiving process is to execute the signal handler at the specified address. Normally, the signal handler is passed the signal number as its only argument; if the disposition was set with the sigaction function however, additional arguments may be requested [see sigaction(2)]. When the signal handler returns, the receiving process resumes execution at the point it was interrupted, unless the signal handler makes other arrangements. If an invalid function address is specified, results are undefined.

If the disposition has been set with the sigset or sigaction function, the signal is automatically blocked by the system while the signal catcher is executing. If a longjmp [see setjmp(3C)] is used to leave the signal catcher, then the signal must be explicitly unblocked by the user [see signal(2) and sigprocmask(2)].

If execution of the signal handler interrupts a blocked system call, the handler is executed and the interrupted system call returns a −1 to the calling process with errno set to EINTR. However, if the SA_RESTART flag is set the system call will be transparently restarted.

NOTES

The dispositions of the SIGKILL and SIGSTOP signals cannot be altered from their default values. The system generates an error if this is attempted.

The SIGKILL and SIGSTOP signals cannot be blocked. The system silently enforces this restriction.

Whenever a process receives a SIGSTOP, SIGTSTP, SIGTTIN, or SIGTTOU signal, regardless of its disposition, any pending SIGCONT signal are discarded.

Whenever a process receives a SIGCONT signal, regardless of its disposition, any pending SIGSTOP, SIGTSTP, SIGTTIN, and SIGTTOU signals is discarded. In addition, if the process was stopped, it is continued.

SIGPOLL is issued when a file descriptor corresponding to a STREAMS [see intro(2)] file has a "selectable" event pending. A process must specifically request that this signal be sent using the I_SETSIG ioctl call. Otherwise, the process will never receive SIGPOLL.

If the disposition of the SIGCHLD signal has been set with signal or sigset, or with sigaction and the SA_NOCLDSTOP flag has been specified, it will only be sent to the calling process when its children exit; otherwise, it will also be sent when the calling process's children are stopped or continued due to job control.

The name SIGCLD is also defined in this header file and identifies the same signal as SIGCHLD. SIGCLD is provided for backward compatibility, new applications should use SIGCHLD.

signal(5)

The disposition of signals that are inherited as SIG_IGN should not be changed.

SEE ALSO

exit(2), getrlimit(2), intro(2), kill(2), pause(2), sigaction(2), sigaltstack(2), signal(2), sigprocmask(2), sigsend(2), sigsuspend(2), wait(2), sigsetops(3C), siginfo(5), ucontext(5)

stat(5)

NAME
stat – data returned by stat system call

SYNOPSIS
#include <sys/types.h>
#include <sys/stat.h>

DESCRIPTION
The system calls **stat**, **lstat** and **fstat** return data in a **stat** structure, which is defined in **stat.h**.

The constants used in the st_mode field are also defined in this file:

```
#define   S_IFMT      /* type of file */
#define   S_IAMB      /* access mode bits */
#define   S_IFIFO     /* fifo */
#define   S_IFCHR     /* character special */
#define   S_IFDIR     /* directory */
#define   S_IFNAM     /* XENIX special named file */
#define   S_INSEM     /* XENIX semaphore subtype of IFNAM */
#define   S_INSHD     /* XENIX shared data subtype of IFNAM */
#define   S_IFBLK     /* block special */
#define   S_IFREG     /* regular */
#define   S_IFLNK     /* symbolic link */
#define   S_ISUID     /* set user id on execution */
#define   S_ISGID     /* set group id on execution */
#define   S_ISVTX     /* save swapped text even after use */
#define   S_IREAD     /* read permission, owner */
#define   S_IWRITE    /* write permission, owner */
#define   S_IEXEC     /* execute/search permission, owner */
#define   S_ENFMT     /* record locking enforcement flag */
#define   S_IRWXU     /* read, write, execute: owner */
#define   S_IRUSR     /* read permission: owner */
#define   S_IWUSR     /* write permission: owner */
#define   S_IXUSR     /* execute permission: owner */
#define   S_IRWXG     /* read, write, execute: group */
#define   S_IRGRP     /* read permission: group */
#define   S_IWGRP     /* write permission: group */
#define   S_IXGRP     /* execute permission: group */
#define   S_IRWXO     /* read, write, execute: other */
#define   S_IROTH     /* read permission: other */
#define   S_IWOTH     /* write permission: other */
#define   S_IXOTH     /* execute permission: other */
```

stat(5)

The following macros are for POSIX conformance:

```
#define    S_ISBLK(mode)      block special file
#define    S_ISCHR(mode)      character special file
#define    S_ISDIR(mode)      directory file
#define    S_ISFIFO(mode)     pipe or fifo file
#define    S_ISREG(mode)      regular file
```

SEE ALSO

stat(2), types(5).

stdarg(5)

NAME
stdarg – handle variable argument list

SYNOPSIS
#include <stdarg.h>

va_list pvar;

void va_start(va_list pvar, parmN);

type va_arg(va_list pvar, type);

void va_end(va_list pvar);

DESCRIPTION
This set of macros allows portable procedures that accept variable numbers of arguments of variable types to be written. Routines that have variable argument lists [such as **printf**] but do not use *stdarg* are inherently non-portable, as different machines use different argument-passing conventions.

va_list is a type defined for the variable used to traverse the list.

The **va_start()** macro is invoked before any access to the unnamed arguments and initializes pvar for subsequent use by **va_arg()** and **va_end()**. The parameter *parmN* is the identifier of the rightmost parameter in the variable parameter list in the function definition (the one just before the , ...). If this parameter is declared with the **register** storage class or with a function or array type, or with a type that is not compatible with the type that results after application of the default argument promotions, the behavior is undefined.

The parameter *parmN* is required under strict ANSI C compilation. In other compilation modes, *parmN* need not be supplied and the second parameter to the **va_start()** macro can be left empty [e.g., **va_start(pvar,);**]. This allows for routines that contain no parameters before the ... in the variable parameter list.

The **va_arg()** macro expands to an expression that has the type and value of the next argument in the call. The parameter **pvar** should have been previously initialized by **va_start()**. Each invocation of **va_arg()** modifies **pvar** so that the values of successive arguments are returned in turn. The parameter *type* is the type name of the next argument to be returned. The type name must be specified in such a way so that the type of a pointer to an object that has the specified type can be obtained simply by postfixing a ***** to *type*. If there is no actual next argument, or if *type* is not compatible with the type of the actual next argument (as promoted according to the default argument promotions), the behavior is undefined.

The **va_end()** macro is used to clean up.

Multiple traversals, each bracketed by **va_start** and **va_end**, are possible.

EXAMPLE
This example gathers into an array a list of arguments that are pointers to strings (but not more than **MAXARGS** arguments) with function **f1**, then passes the array as a single argument to function **f2**. The number of pointers is specified by the first argument to **f1**.

```
#include <stdarg.h>
#define MAXARGS 31

void f1(int n_ptrs, ...)
{
    va_list ap;
    char *array[MAXARGS];
    int ptr_no = 0;

    if (n_ptrs > MAXARGS)
        n_ptrs = MAXARGS;
    va_start(ap, n_ptrs);
    while (ptr_no < n_ptrs)
        array[ptr_no++] = va_arg(ap, char*);
    va_end(ap);
    f2(n_ptrs, array);
}
```

Each call to f1 shall have visible the definition of the function or a declaration such as

```
void f1(int, ...)
```

SEE ALSO
vprintf(3S).

NOTES
It is up to the calling routine to specify in some manner how many arguments there are, since it is not always possible to determine the number of arguments from the stack frame. For example, execl is passed a zero pointer to signal the end of the list. printf can tell how many arguments there are by the format. It is non-portable to specify a second argument of char, short, or float to va_arg, because arguments seen by the called function are not char, short, or float. C converts char and short arguments to int and converts float arguments to double before passing them to a function.

NAME

types – primitive system data types

SYNOPSIS

    #include <sys/types.h>

DESCRIPTION

The data types defined in `types.h` are used in UNIX System code. Some data of these types are accessible to user code:

```
typedef  struct { int r[1]; } *physadr;
typedef  long             clock_t;
typedef  long             daddr_t;
typedef  char *           caddr_t;
typedef  unsigned char    unchar;
typedef  unsigned short   ushort;
typedef  unsigned int     uint;
typedef  unsigned long    ulong;
typedef  unsigned long    ino_t;
typedef  long             uid_t;
typedef  long             gid_t;
typedef  ulong            nlink_t;
typedef  ulong            mode_t;
typedef  short            cnt_t;
typedef  long             time_t;
typedef  int              label_t[10];
typedef  ulong            dev_t;
typedef  long             off_t;
typedef  long             pid_t;
typedef  long             paddr_t;
typedef  int              key_t;
typedef  unsigned char    use_t;
typedef  short            sysid_t;
typedef  short            index_t;
typedef  short            lock_t;
typedef  unsigned int     size_t;
typedef  long             clock_t;
typedef  long             pid_t;
```

The form `daddr_t` is used for disk addresses except in an i-node on disk, see fs(4). Times are encoded in seconds since 00:00:00 UTC, January 1, 1970. The major and minor parts of a device code specify kind and unit number of a device and are installation-dependent. Offsets are measured in bytes from the beginning of a file. The `label_t` variables are used to save the processor state while another process is running.

NAME
ucontext – user context

SYNOPSIS
#include <ucontext.h>

DESCRIPTION
The ucontext structure defines the context of a thread of control within an executing process.

This structure includes at least the following members:

```
ucontext_t    uc_link
sigset_t      uc_sigmask
stack_t       uc_stack
mcontext_t    uc_mcontext
```

uc_link is a pointer to the context that to be resumed when this context returns. If uc_link is equal to 0, then this context is the main context, and the process exits when this context returns.

uc_sigmask defines the set of signals that are blocked when this context is active [see sigprocmask(2)].

uc_stack defines the stack used by this context [see sigaltstack(2)].

uc_mcontext contains the saved set of machine registers and any implementation specific context data. Portable applications should not modify or access uc_mcontext.

SEE ALSO
getcontext(2), sigaction(2), sigprocmask(2), sigaltstack(2), makecontext(3C).

values(5)

NAME
values – machine-dependent values

SYNOPSIS
#include <values.h>

DESCRIPTION
This file contains a set of manifest constants, conditionally defined for particular processor architectures.

The model assumed for integers is binary representation (one's or two's complement), where the sign is represented by the value of the high-order bit.

BITS (*type*)   The number of bits in a specified type (e.g., int).

HIBITS   The value of a short integer with only the high-order bit set.

HIBITL   The value of a long integer with only the high-order bit set.

HIBITI   The value of a regular integer with only the high-order bit set.

MAXSHORT   The maximum value of a signed short integer.

MAXLONG   The maximum value of a signed long integer.

MAXINT   The maximum value of a signed regular integer.

MAXFLOAT, LN_MAXFLOAT
   The maximum value of a single-precision floating-point number, and its natural logarithm.

MAXDOUBLE, LN_MAXDOUBLE
   The maximum value of a double-precision floating-point number, and its natural logarithm.

MINFLOAT, LN_MINFLOAT
   The minimum positive value of a single-precision floating-point number, and its natural logarithm.

MINDOUBLE, LN_MINDOUBLE
   The minimum positive value of a double-precision floating-point number, and its natural logarithm.

FSIGNIF   The number of significant bits in the mantissa of a single-precision floating-point number.

DSIGNIF   The number of significant bits in the mantissa of a double-precision floating-point number.

SEE ALSO
intro(3), math(5).

varargs(5)   varargs(5)

NAME
varargs – handle variable argument list

SYNOPSIS
#include <varargs.h>

va_alist

va_dcl

va_list pvar;

void va_start(va_list pvar);

type va_arg(va_list pvar, *type*);

void va_end(va_list pvar);

DESCRIPTION
This set of macros allows portable procedures that accept variable argument lists to be written. Routines that have variable argument lists [such as printf(3S)] but do not use **varargs** are inherently non-portable, as different machines use different argument-passing conventions.

va_alist is used as the parameter list in a function header.

va_dcl is a declaration for va_alist. No semicolon should follow va_dcl.

va_list is a type defined for the variable used to traverse the list.

va_start is called to initialize pvar to the beginning of the list.

va_arg will return the next argument in the list pointed to by pvar. *type* is the type the argument is expected to be. Different types can be mixed, but it is up to the routine to know what type of argument is expected, as it cannot be determined at runtime.

va_end is used to clean up.

Multiple traversals, each bracketed by **va_start** and **va_end**, are possible.

EXAMPLE
This example is a possible implementation of **execl** [see exec(2)].

```
#include <unistd.h>
#include <varargs.h>
#define MAXARGS 100

/*   execl is called by
         execl(file, arg1, arg2, ..., (char *)0);
*/
execl(va_alist)
va_dcl
{
    va_list ap;
    char *file;
    char *args[MAXARGS];        /* assumed big enough*/
    int argno = 0;
```

```
            va_start(ap);
            file = va_arg(ap, char *);
            while ((args[argno++] = va_arg(ap, char *)) != 0)
                ;
            va_end(ap);
            return execv(file, args);
    }
```

SEE ALSO

exec(2), printf(3S), vprintf(3S), stdarg(5).

NOTES

It is up to the calling routine to specify in some manner how many arguments there are, since it is not always possible to determine the number of arguments from the stack frame. For example, **execl** is passed a zero pointer to signal the end of the list. **printf** can tell how many arguments are there by the format.

It is non-portable to specify a second argument of **char**, **short**, or **float** to **va_arg**, since arguments seen by the called function are not **char**, **short**, or **float**. C converts **char** and **short** arguments to **int** and converts **float** arguments to **double** before passing them to a function.

stdarg is the preferred interface.

NAME
wstat – wait status

SYNOPSIS
#include <sys/wait.h>

DESCRIPTION
When a process waits for status from its children via either the **wait** or **waitpid** function, the status returned may be evaluated with the following macros, defined in **sys/wait.h**. These macros evaluate to integral expressions. The *stat* argument to these macros is the integer value returned from **wait** or **waitpid**.

WIFEXITED (*stat*)	Evaluates to a non-zero value if status was returned for a child process that terminated normally.
WEXITSTATUS (*stat*)	If the value of **WIFEXITED** (*stat*) is non-zero, this macro evaluates to the exit code that the child process passed to **_exit** or **exit**, or the value that the child process returned from **main**.
WIFSIGNALED (*stat*)	Evaluates to a non-zero value if status was returned for a child process that terminated due to the receipt of a signal.
WTERMSIG (*stat*)	If the value of **WIFSIGNALED** (*stat*) is non-zero, this macro evaluates to the number of the signal that caused the termination of the child process.
WIFSTOPPED (*stat*)	Evaluates to a non-zero value if status was returned for a child process that is currently stopped.
WSTOPSIG (*stat*)	If the value of **WIFSTOPPED** (*stat*) is non-zero, this macro evaluates to the number of the signal that caused the child process to stop.
WIFCONTINUED(*stat*)	Evaluates to a non-zero value if status was returned for a child process that has continued.
WCOREDUMP(*stat*)	If the value of **WIFSIGNALED** (*stat*) is non-zero, this macro evaluates to a non-zero value if a core image of the terminated child was created.

SEE ALSO
exit(2), wait(2), waitpid(3C).

NAME

xtproto – multiplexed channels protocol used by xt driver

DESCRIPTION

This xt protocol is used for communication between multiple UNIX System host processes and an AT&T windowing terminal operating under the **layers** command; see xt(7). It is a multiplexed protocol that directs traffic between host processes and terminal windows, thereby allowing multiple virtual terminal sessions over a single connection. The protocol is implemented by the xt host driver and corresponding firmware in a windowing terminal.

The xt driver implements two distinct low level protocols. Which protocol is used depends on the media used for communication with the terminal. The regular xt protocol is used when communicating over unreliable media such as RS-232. The regular xt protocol provides flow control and error correction, thereby guaranteeing error-free delivery of data. The network xt protocol is used when communicating over reliable media such as a local area network. In order to achieve maximum possible throughput, the network xt protocol relies on the underlying network to provide flow control and error correction.

The **layers** command queries the windowing terminal whether to use regular or network xt protocol through an A_XTPROTO JAGENT ioctl system call [see layers(5)]. The **layers** command then decides what protocol to use based on the return value of A_XTPROTO, baud rate, and the −m option of **layers**.

The regular xt protocol uses packets with a 2-byte header containing a 3-bit sequence number, 3-bit channel number, control flag, and one byte for data size. The data part of packets sent from the host to the terminal may not be larger than 252 bytes. The maximum data part size can be less than 252 at lower baud rates, or if the −m option of **layers** was specified. Also, when communicating with some earlier windowing terminals, maximum data part size is fixed at 32 bytes. The maximum data part size of packets sent from the terminal to the host is always fixed at 32 bytes. The trailer contains a CRC-16 code in 2 bytes. Each channel is double-buffered.

Correctly received regular xt packets in sequence are acknowledged with a control packet containing an ACK; however, out of sequence packets generate a control packet containing a NAK, which causes the retransmission in sequence of all unacknowledged packets.

Unacknowledged regular xt packets are retransmitted after a timeout interval that is dependent on baud rate. Another timeout parameter specifies the interval after which incomplete receive packets are discarded.

Network xt protocol uses a 3-byte header containing a 3-bit channel number, various control flags, and 2-bytes for data size. The data part of packets sent from the host to the terminal has no size limit. The data part of packets sent from the terminal to the host is restricted to 1025 bytes.

Since network xt protocol relies on the underlying media to guarantee error-free delivery of data, no CRC codes or timeouts are needed.

Network **xt** protocol provides a simple flow control mechanism to limit the amount of data sent to a window in the terminal before a **NETWORK XT ACK** acknowledgement is received by the host. The intent of this flow control is to limit the amount of data sent to a window in the terminal not reading its input because, for example, the user has pressed the scroll lock key. This is necessary to prevent data from backing up and blocking other data directed to other windows. To improve overall throughput, network **xt** flow control can be disabled by processes in the terminal that always read their input quickly.

FILES
/usr/include/sys/xtproto.h channel multiplexing protocol definitions

SEE ALSO
jagent(5), **layers**(5).
layers(1) in the *User's Reference Manual.*
xt(7) in the *Programmer's Guide: STREAMS.*

Prentice Hall, the leading publisher of C and UNIX® System V reference books and documentation, is continuously expanding its channels of distribution in order to make book buying as easy as possible for professionals for whom access to timely information is crucial. Won't you help us to serve you more efficiently by completing this brief survey? Individuals completing this survey will be added to our C and UNIX® System bookbuyer list and will receive our new C and UNIX® System Catalog and other announcements on a regular basis.

Title Purchased: _____
Author: _____

I. How did you purchase the book?
___ by mail ___ by phone ___ by fax
___ in a bookstore ___ in a software store
___ through a corporate book distribution service
___ at a professional meeting or seminar

II. Was this purchase charged to your business?
___ Yes ___ No

III. Are you involved in developing and/or instructing training courses? ___ Yes ___ No
If so, please provide the following information:

Course Title: _____
Number of Students Per Year: _____
Books in Use: _____

IV. Are you interested in packaging UNIX System V documentation with your product?
___ Yes ___ No

V. Would you like to receive information about our custom documentation program?
___ Yes ___ No

VI. Please list topics of importance to you and your colleagues on which you would like to see books published: _____
_____

VII. Are you interested in submitting a manuscript to Prentice Hall for possible publication? ___ Yes ___ No Area of Research _____

Name _____
Title _____
Name of Firm _____
Address _____

NO POSTAGE
NECESSARY
IF MAILED IN THE
UNITED STATES

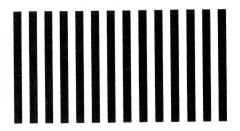

BUSINESS REPLY MAIL

FIRST CLASS   PERMIT NO. 365, ENGLEWOOD CLIFFS, NJ

POSTAGE WILL BE PAID BY ADDRESSEE

PRENTICE HALL
Attn: PTR Marketing Manager
College Marketing Department
Route 9W
Englewood Cliffs, NJ 07632-9940

What do YOU think?

AT&T values your opinion. Please indicate your opinions in each of the following areas. We'd like to know how well this document meets your needs.

Book Title: _____

	Excellent	Good	Fair	Poor
Accuracy - Is the information correct?	❏	❏	❏	❏
Completeness - Is information missing?	❏	❏	❏	❏
Organization - Is information easy to find?	❏	❏	❏	❏
Clarity - Do you understand the information?	❏	❏	❏	❏
Examples - Are there enough?	❏	❏	❏	❏
Illustrations - Are there enough?	❏	❏	❏	❏
Appearance - Do you like the page format?	❏	❏	❏	❏
Physical binding - Do you like the cover and binding?	❏	❏	❏	❏

Does the document meet your needs? Why or why not?

_____
_____
_____

What is the single most important improvement that we could make to this document?

_____
_____
_____

Please complete the following information.

Name (Optional): _____

Job Title or Function: _____

Organization: _____

Address: _____

_____

Phone: ( ) _____

If we need more information may we contact you? Yes ❏ No ❏   **Thank you.**

NO POSTAGE NECESSARY IF MAILED IN THE UNITED STATES

BUSINESS REPLY MAIL
FIRST CLASS MAIL   PERMIT NO. 199   SUMMIT, NJ

POSTAGE WILL BE PAID BY ADDRESSEE

USL
Department Head
Languages & UNIX Technologies Dept.
Room F-316
190 River Road
Summit, NJ 07901-9907